THIRD EDITION

PSYCHOLOGICAL TESTING

PRINCIPLES AND APPLICATIONS

KEVIN R. MURPHY

Colorado State University

CHARLES O. DAVIDSHOFER

Colorado State University

PRENTICE HALL, Englewood Cliffs, New Jersey 07632

Library of Congress Cataloging-in-Publication Data

Murphy, Kevin R.
    Psychological testing: principles and applications/Kevin R.
Murphy, Charles O. Davidshofer.—3rd ed.
        p.   cm.
    Includes bibliographical references and indexes.
    ISBN 0–13–226994–5
    1. Psychological tests.   2. Psychometrics.   I. Davidshofer,
Charles O.   II. Title.
BF176.M87   1994
150′.28′7—dc20   92-41594
                                                       CIP

Acquisitions editor: Peter Janzow
Editorial/production supervision, page layout,
    and interior design: Jenny Moss
Cover design: Design Solutions
Prepress buyer: Herb Klein
Manufacturing buyer: Robert Anderson
Managing editor: Heidi Freund
Editorial assistant: Tony Faber

© 1994 by Prentice-Hall, Inc.
A Simon & Schuster Company
Englewood Cliffs, New Jersey 07632

Printed in the United States of America

10   9   8   7   6   5

ISBN 0-13-226994-5

Prentice-Hall International (UK) Limited, *London*
Prentice-Hall of Australia Pty. Limited, *Sydney*
Prentice-Hall Canada Inc., *Toronto*
Prentice-Hall Hispanoamericana, S.A., *Mexico*
Prentice-Hall of India Private Limited, *New Delhi*
Prentice-Hall of Japan, Inc., *Tokyo*
Simon & Schuster Asia Pte. Ltd., *Singapore*
Editora Prentice-Hall do Brasil, Ltda., *Rio de Janeiro*

CONTENTS

PREFACE   ix

CHAPTER ONE: TESTS AND MEASUREMENTS   1

   Psychological Tests—A Definition   3
   Types of Tests   6
   Tests and Decisions—Uses of Psychological Tests   8
   Testing Activities of Psychologists   11
   Information about Tests   12
   Standards for Testing   14
   Critical Discussion: Alternatives to Psychological Tests   15
   Summary   16

CHAPTER TWO: TESTING AND SOCIETY   18

   Types of Decisions   19
   Societal Concerns   21
   Analyzing the Societal Consequences of Tests   29
   *Critical Discussion: Are There Technical Solutions to Societal
      Problems?   31*
   Summary   32

--- PART I: ---
PRINCIPLES OF PSYCHOLOGICAL MEASUREMENT

*CHAPTER THREE: BASIC CONCEPTS
   IN MEASUREMENT AND STATISTICS   33*

   Psychological Measurement   33
   Evaluating Psychological Tests   38

Statistical Concepts 40
Critical Discussion: Measurement Scales and Statistics *48*
Summary 49

CHAPTER FOUR: SCALES, TRANSFORMATIONS, AND NORMS 51

Transformations 52
Equating Scale Scores 56
Norms 59
Expectancy Tables 67
Critical Discussions: Should Black IQ Scores Be Based on White Norms? *70*
Summary 71

CHAPTER FIVE: RELIABILITY: THE CONSISTENCY OF TEST SCORES 73

Sources of Consistency and Inconsistency in Test Scores 74
General Model of Reliability 76
Simple Methods of Estimating Reliability 78
Reliability Estimates and Error 84
The Generalizability of Test Scores 85
Critical Discussion: Generalizability and Reliability Theory *87*
Summary 88

CHAPTER SIX: USING AND INTERPRETING INFORMATION ABOUT TEST RELIABILITY 90

Using the Reliability Coefficient 90
Factors Affecting Reliability 95
Special Issues in Reliability 99
How Reliable Should Tests Be? 103
Critical Discussion: Precise but Narrow—The Bandwidth-Fidelity Dilemma *104*
Summary 105

CHAPTER SEVEN: VALIDITY OF MEASUREMENT: CONTENT AND CONSTRUCT-ORIENTED VALIDATION STRATEGIES 106

Validation Strategies 106
Assessing the Validity of Measurement 108
Content-Oriented Validation Strategies 108
Construct-Oriented Validation Strategies 114
Content and Construct Validity 124
Critical Discussion: Do Intelligence Tests Really Measure Intelligence? *126*
Summary 127

CHAPTER EIGHT: VALIDITY FOR DECISIONS: CRITERION-RELATED VALIDATION STRATEGIES 129

Decisions and Prediction 130
Criteria 131
Criterion-Related Validation Strategies 132
Construct Validity and Criterion-Related Validity 137
Interpreting Validity Coefficients 140
Critical Discussion: Values and Validation 148
Summary 149

CHAPTER NINE: ITEM ANALYSIS 151

Purpose of Item Analysis 152
Distractor Analysis 152
Item Difficulty 154
Item Discrimination 156
Interactions among Item Characteristics 160
The Item Characteristic Curve 162
Critical Discussion: Using Item Response Theory to Detect Test Bias 170
Summary 171

PART II:
APPLYING THE PRINCIPLES OF PSYCHOLOGICAL MEASUREMENT

CHAPTER TEN: THE PROCESS OF TEST DEVELOPMENT 172

Constructing the Test 172
Norming and Standardizing Tests 181
Test Publication and Revision 183
Critical Discussion: Should Tests Be Normed Nationally, Regionally, or Locally? 185
Summary 186

CHAPTER ELEVEN: COMPUTERIZED TEST ADMINISTRATION AND INTERPRETATION 188

Use of Computers in Testing: A Taxonomy 189
Computerized Test Administration 190
Computerized Adaptive Testing 192
Computer-based Test Interpretation 195
Detecting Invalid or Unusual Response Patterns 199
Critical Discussion: The Barnum Effect and Computerized Test Interpretation 200
Summary 200

CHAPTER TWELVE: MEASURING PSYCHOLOGICAL ATTRIBUTES 202

Psychological Attributes and Decisions 202
Intelligence—General Mental Ability 203
Interests 216
Personality 220
*Critical Discussion: Do Different Test Formats Give Unique
  Interpretive Information? 226*
Summary 227

CHAPTER THIRTEEN: ABILITY TESTING: INDIVIDUAL TESTS 229

The Role of the Examiner 230
Individual Tests of General Mental Ability 231
Individual Tests of Specific Abilities 248
Critical Discussion: Testing Minorities 249
Summary 250

CHAPTER FOURTEEN: ABILITY TESTING: GROUP TESTS 252

Advantages and Disadvantages of Group Tests 253
Measures of General Intelligence 254
Scholastic Tests 258
Multiple Aptitude Batteries 264
Critical Discussion: The Case against Large-Scale Testing 270
Summary 271

CHAPTER FIFTEEN: ISSUES IN ABILITY TESTING 273

Bias and Fairness in Mental Testing 274
Critical Discussion: Are Judgments of Item Bias Useful? 285
Culture-Reduced Testing 285
Critical Discussion: Intelligence and Adaptive Behavior 293
Heritability, Consistency, and Modifiability of IQ 293
Critical Discussion: Project Head Start 300
Summary 301

PART III:
APPLICATION OF PSYCHOLOGICAL MEASUREMENT

CHAPTER SIXTEEN: TESTS AND EDUCATIONAL DECISIONS 302

Applications in Institutional Decision Making 303
*Critical Discussion: The National Assessment of Educational
  Progress 308*

Applications in Individual Decision Making   309
Critical Discussion: What Is Criterion-referenced Testing?   313
Summary   314

CHAPTER SEVENTEEN: INTEREST ASSESSMENT   315

The Strong Vocational Interest Inventory   316
The Kuder Occupational Interest Survey   329
Career Assessment Inventory   337
Jackson Vocational Interest Survey   342
*Critical Discussion: Should Interest Tests Be Used in Personnel
   Selection?   346*
Summary   348

CHAPTER EIGHTEEN: PSYCHOLOGICAL MEASUREMENT IN INDUSTRY: ISSUES IN PREDICTION   349

Extent and Impact of Personnel Testing   349
Predicting Performance   351
Comparative Assessment of Personnel Tests   366
*Critical Discussion: Can Graphology Predict Occupational
   Success?   368*
Assessing Integrity   369
The Validity of Personnel Tests   373
The Social and Legal Context of Employment Testing   376
*Critical Discussion: Personnel Selection from the Applicant's Point
   of View   379*
Summary   380

CHAPTER NINETEEN: PSYCHOLOGICAL MEASUREMENT IN INDUSTRY: CRITERION MEASUREMENT   382

Criterion Measures   382
Judgmental Measures   386
Can We Measure the Value of Performance?   399
*Critical Discussion: The Ethics of Evaluation–Telling More Than
   You Know   402*
Summary   402

CHAPTER TWENTY: PERSONALITY TESTING IN CLINICAL SETTINGS   404

Development of Personality Testing   405
Objective Measures of Personality   406
Projective Tests of Personality   417
*Critical Discussion: Reliability and Validity of Projective Tests,
   Personality Inventories, and Intelligence Tests   420*

*Critical Discussion: Are Scales on Personality Tests Interpreted
    Independently?* 424
Summary 425

CHAPTER TWENTY-ONE: DIAGNOSTIC TESTING: CLINICAL APPLICATIONS 426

The Minnesota Multiphasic Personality Inventory 427
MMPI-2 433
The Bender-Gestalt 434
Scatter Analysis 438
Diagnostic Classification System 441
Critical Discussion: Politics, Economics, and Diagnosis 446
Summary 446

CHAPTER TWENTY-TWO: CLINICAL ASSESSMENT 448

The Nature of Clinical Assessment 449
Studying Clinical Judgment 453
Structured Assessment Programs 461
*Critical Discussion: Psychological Assessment
    in the Courtroom* 471
Summary 473

APPENDIX A: FORTY REPRESENTATIVE TESTS 474

APPENDIX B: ETHICAL PRINCIPLES OF PSYCHOLOGISTS AND CODE OF CONDUCT 476

APPENDIX C: CODE OF FAIR TESTING PRACTICES IN EDUCATION 493

APPENDIX D: REVIEW OF BASIC STATISTICS 498

REFERENCES 505

AUTHOR INDEX 539

SUBJECT INDEX 545

PREFACE

Tests are used to make decisions. This simple sentence describes both the theme and the rationale of this book. Too often, psychological testing is presented as a dry, technical, abstract subject. It is not. Psychological tests have a substantial impact on a variety of important decisions. In some settings, such as the armed services, tests represent the *only* feasible method of making selection and classification decisions. The point is that tests affect peoples' lives, for good or for ill, and a firm understanding of psychological testing is necessary in many of the settings where important decisions (e.g., college admissions, job placement, clinical assessments) must be made about individuals.

Most students in a testing course have taken many tests and will probably take many more in the future. These students have a real, practical interest in testing. They are also likely to be skeptical about the accuracy and the value of psychological tests. A good part of your job when teaching a testing course is to present a full and fair evaluation of the advantages and drawbacks of psychological testing. We believe that this can best be done by focusing on the impact of tests on decisions. Students generally show little interest in learning a "laundry list" of test names, but they are very interested in knowing how tests are used and whether the use of tests leads to better or worse decisions than would be reached without tests.

Our text is divided into three sections. In the first, we discuss the principles of psychological measurement. Our focus here is on evaluating tests by first stating what we are trying to accomplish with a test (e.g., measure a trait or characteristic, predict a future outcome) and then determining whether the test accomplishes that goal. Our second section applies those principles to the domain of ability testing. This section illustrates the use of the testing principles covered in Chapters 3–9 in designing and evaluating measures of both broadly and narrowly defined abilities. Our third section discusses the application of psychological tests in the three contexts where tests are most often used to make decisions: in education, in industry, and in clinical settings. This section covers the major types of tests as well as their most important uses.

This book does *not* have several features found in other testing books. First, we do not cover dozens of obscure tests. Rather, we have focused on widely used or technically superior examplars of the major classes of tests. You will probably not encounter in this book many tests that are never heard of outside of a psychological measurement class, and, frankly, we see no good reason why you should. Second, we do not cover several topics that, while important, have little relevance for decision making. Thus, we do not discuss at length topics such as attitude measurement or the assessment of values.

Each chapter (except our introductory Chapter 1) contains one or more brief sections entitled *Critical Discussion*. The critical discussion sections present a variety of issues that are controversial (e.g., "Should Black IQ Scores Be Based on White Norms?" [Chapter 4]), that illustrate the applications of concepts discussed in the chapters (e.g., "Using Item Response Theory to Detect Test Bias" [Chapter 9]), or that provide a different perspective on familiar material (e.g., "Personnel Selection from the Applicant's Point of View" [Chapter 18]). These critical discussions may provide ideas for classroom discussions, term papers, or projects and are designed to help your students integrate material from this course with their other interests and knowledge bases.

As you'll note when reading through the text, we are, on the whole, optimistic about psychological testing. There are areas where the technology has failed to keep up with the theory, where the basic theories are flawed, or where the applications of testing have done more harm than good. On the whole, however, psychological tests often provide the fairest and most accurate method of making important decisions. In part this reflects the strength of tests, and in part it reflects the weakness of the competition (e.g., interviews, letters of recommendation, clinical intuition). In any case, we think that psychological tests do make a contribution and are likely to be with us for a long time to come. We hope that this text will contribute to your students' understanding of the advantages and drawbacks of psychological testing.

In preparing the current edition, we attempted to deal with topics that were not given sufficient attention in our earlier editions. The most substantial revisions include the addition of a chapter on computerized testing (Chapter 11, "Computerized Test Administration and Interpretation") and extended coverage of integrity testing (see Chapter 18) and neuropsychological testing (see Chapter 21). In addition, given that many of the tests covered in the previous editions have been revised or upgraded in recent years, our text provides up-to-date information about test revisions.

We have also attempted to make the text more user-friendly by simplifying the presentation of material that seemed especially difficult in earlier editions (e.g., "The Item Characteristic Curves" [Chapter 9]) and by adding summaries at the end of each chapter. Many individuals provided feedback about students' reactions to the first and second edition, and we have tried to incorporate a number of excellent suggestions from our colleagues.

ACKNOWLEDGMENTS

This book could not have been produced without the help and encouragement of many of our colleagues. We would like to particularly thank Frank Landy, who encouraged us to write the first edition and who suggested the overall structure for the book. We also thank Dennis Roberts, who collaborated in the early development of the book and who contributed substantially to the overall structure and focus of the book. Finally, we would like to thank colleagues who have helped us in formulating our ideas and presentations or alerted us to errors and omissions in our first two editions. These include Jeanette Cleveland, George Thornton, Kurt Geisinger, Barbara Dritschel, James Clevenger, Charmine Hartel, and Dirk Steiner. We also appreciate feedback from several of our colleagues who have suggested ways of improving our previous editions.

Kevin R. Murphy
Charles O. Davidshofer

CHAPTER 1

TESTS
AND
MEASUREMENTS

The term "psychological test" brings to mind a number of conflicting images. On the one hand, the term might make one think of the type of test so often described in television, movies, and the popular literature, wherein a patient answers questions like, "How long have you hated your mother?" and in doing so reveals hidden facets of his or her personality to the clinician. On the other hand, the term "psychological test" might refer to a long series of multiple-choice questions such as those answered by hundreds of high-school students taking college entrance examinations. Another type of "psychological test" is the self-scored type published in the *Reader's Digest,* which purport to tell you whether your marriage is on the rocks, whether you are as anxious as the next fellow, or whether you should change your job or your lifestyle.

In general, psychological tests are neither mysterious, as our first example might suggest, nor frivolous, as our last example might suggest. Rather, psychological tests represent systematic applications of a few relatively simple principles in an attempt to measure personal attributes thought to be important in describing or understanding individual behavior. The aim of this book is to describe the basic principles of psychological measurement and to describe the major types of tests and their applications. We will not present test theory in all of its technical detail, nor will we describe (or even mention) all of the different psychological tests currently available. Rather, our goal is to provide the information needed to make sensible evaluations of psychological tests and their uses within education, industry, and clinical practice.

The first question that should be addressed in a psychological testing text is, "Why is psychological testing important?" There are several possible answers to this question, but we believe that the best answer lies in the simple statement that forms the central theme of this book: *Tests are used to make important decisions about individuals.* College admissions officers consult test scores before deciding whether to admit or reject applicants. Clinical psychologists use a variety of objective and projective tests in the process of choosing a course of treatment for individual clients. The military uses test scores as aids in deciding which jobs an individual soldier might be qualified to fill. Tests are used in the world of work, both in personnel selection and in professional certification and licensure. Almost everyone reading this book has taken at least one standardized psychological test. Scores on such a test may have had some impact on an important decision that has affected your life. The area of psychological testing is therefore one of considerable practical importance.

Psychological tests are used to measure a wide variety of attributes—intelligence, motivation, mastery of seventh-grade mathematics, vocational preferences, spatial ability, anxiety, form perception, and countless others. Unfortunately, one feature that all psychological tests share in common is their limited precision. They rarely, if ever, provide exact, definitive measures of variables that are believed to have important effects on human behavior. Thus, psychological tests do not provide a basis for making *completely* accurate decisions about individuals. In reality, there is no method that guarantees complete accuracy. Thus, although psychological tests are known to be imperfect measures, a special panel of the National Academy of Sciences concluded that psychological tests generally represent the best, fairest, and most economical method of obtaining the information necessary to make sensible decisions about individuals (Wigdor & Garner, 1982a, 1982b). The conclusions reached by the National Academy panel form another important theme that runs through this book. Although psychological tests are far from perfect, *they represent the best, fairest, and most accurate technology available for making many important decisions about individuals.*

Psychological testing is highly controversial. Public debate over the use of tests, particularly standardized tests of intelligence, has raged since at least the 1920s (Cronbach, 1975; Haney, 1981; Scarr, 1989).[1] There is presently extensive literature, both popular and technical, dealing with issues such as test bias and test fairness. Federal and state laws have been passed calling for minimum competency testing and for truth in testing, a term that refers to a variety of efforts to regulate testing and to increase public access to information on test development and use. Tests and testing programs have been challenged in the courts, often successfully.

Psychological testing is not only important and controversial, it is a highly specialized and somewhat technical enterprise. In many of the natural sciences, measurement is a relatively straightforward process that involves assessing the physical properties of objects, such as height, weight, or velocity.[2] However, for the most part, psychological attributes, such as intelligence and creativity, cannot be measured by the same sorts of methods as those used to measure physical attributes. Psychological attributes are not

---

[1]Special issues of *American Psychologist* in November 1965 and October 1981 provide excellent summaries of many of the issues in this debate.

[2]Note, however, that physical measurement is neither static nor simple. Proposals to redefine the basic unit of length, the meter, in terms of the time light takes to travel from point to point (Robinson, 1983) provide an example of continuing progress in redefining the bases of physical measurement.

manifest in any simple, physical way; they are manifest only in the *behavior* of individuals. Furthermore, behavior rarely reflects any one psychological attribute, but rather a variety of physical, psychological, and social forces. Hence, psychological measurement is rarely as simple or direct as physical measurement. In order to sensibly evaluate psychological tests, therefore, it is necessary to become familiar with the specialized methods of psychological measurement.

This chapter provides a general introduction to psychological measurement. First, we define the term "test" and discuss several of the implications of that definition. We then briefly describe the types of tests available and discuss the ways in which tests are used to make decisions in educational, industrial, and clinical settings. We also discuss sources of information about tests and the standards, ethics, and laws that govern testing.

PSYCHOLOGICAL TESTS—A DEFINITION

The diversity of psychological tests is staggering. There are well over 1,000 different psychological tests that are available commercially in English-speaking countries, and doubtlessly hundreds of others are published in other parts of the world. These tests range from personality inventories to self-scored IQ tests, from scholastic examinations to perceptual tests. Yet despite this diversity, there are several features that are common to all psychological tests and that, taken together, serve to define the term "test."

A psychological test is a measurement instrument that has three defining characteristics:

1. A psychological test is a sample of behavior.
2. The sample is obtained under standardized conditions.
3. There are established rules for scoring, or for obtaining quantitative (numeric) information from the behavior sample.

Behavior Sampling

Every psychological test requires the respondent to *do* something. The subject's behavior is used to measure some specific attribute (e.g., introversion) or to predict some specific outcome (e.g., success in a job training program). Therefore, a variety of measures that do not require the respondent to engage in any overt behavior (e.g., an x-ray) or that require behavior on the part of the subject that is clearly incidental to whatever is being measured (e.g., a stress EKG) fall outside the domain of psychological tests.

The use of behavior samples in psychological measurement has several implications. First, a psychological test is not an exhaustive measurement of all possible behaviors that could be used in measuring or defining a particular attribute. Suppose, for example, that you wished to develop a test to measure a person's writing ability. One strategy would be to collect and evaluate everything that person had ever written, from term papers to laundry lists. Such a procedure would be highly accurate, but impractical. A psychological test attempts to approximate this exhaustive procedure by collecting a systematic sample of behavior. In this case, a writing test might include a series of short essays, sample letters, memos, and the like.

The second implication of using behavior samples to measure psychological variables is that the quality of a test is largely determined by the representativeness of this sample. For example, one could construct a driving test in which each examinee was required to drive the circuit of a race track. This test would certainly sample some aspects of driving but would omit others, such as parking, following signals, or negotiating in traffic. It would therefore not represent a very good driving test. The behavior elicited by the test also must somehow be representative of behaviors that would be observed outside of the testing situation. For example, if a scholastic aptitude test were administered in a burning building, it is unlikely that students' responses to that test would tell us much about their scholastic aptitude. Similarly, a test that required highly unusual or novel types of responses might not be as useful as a test that required responses to questions or situations that were similar in some way to those observed in everyday life.

Standardization

A psychological test is a sample of behavior collected under standardized conditions. The Scholastic Aptitude Test (SAT), which is administered to thousands of high school juniors and seniors, provides a good example of standardization. The test supervisor reads detailed instructions to all examinees before starting, and each portion of the test is carefully timed. In addition, the test manual includes exhaustive instructions dealing with the appropriate seating patterns, lighting, provisions for interruptions and emergencies, and answers to common procedural questions. The test manual is written in sufficient detail to ensure that the conditions under which the SAT is given are substantially the same at all test locations.

The conditions under which a test is administered are certain to affect the behavior of the person or persons taking the test. You would probably give different answers to questions on an intelligence test or a personality inventory administered in a quiet, well-lit room than you would if the same test were administered at a baseball stadium during extra innings of a play-off game. A student is likely to do better on a test that is given in a regular classroom environment than he or she would if the same test were given in a hot, noisy auditorium. Standardization of the conditions under which a test is given is therefore an important feature of psychological testing.

It is not possible to achieve the same degree of standardization with all psychological tests. A high degree of standardization might be possible with many written tests, although even within this class of tests the conditions of testing might be difficult to control precisely. For example, tests that are given relatively few times a year in a limited number of locations by a single testing agency (e.g., the Graduate Record Examinations) probably are administered under more standard conditions than are written employment tests, which are administered in hundreds of personnel offices by a variety of psychologists, personnel managers, and clerks. The greatest difficulty in standardization, however, probably lies in the broad class of tests that are administered verbally on an individual basis. For example, the Wechsler Adult Intelligence Scale (WAIS), which represents one of the best individual tests of intelligence, is administered verbally by a psychologist. It is likely that an examinee will respond differently to a friendly, calm examiner than to one who is threatening or surly.

Individually administered tests are difficult to standardize because the examiner is an integral part of the test. The same test given to the same subject by two different examiners is certain to elicit a somewhat different set of behaviors. Nevertheless, through specialized training, a good deal of standardization in the essential features of testing can be achieved. Strict adherence to standard procedures for administering various psychological tests helps to minimize the effects of extraneous variables, such as the physical conditions of testing, the characteristics of the examiner, or the subject's confusion regarding the demands of the test.

Scoring Rules

The immediate aim of testing is to measure or to describe in a quantitative way some attribute or set of attributes of the person taking the test. The final, defining characteristic of a psychological test is that there must be some set of rules or procedures for describing in quantitative or numeric terms the subject's behavior in response to the test. These rules must be sufficiently comprehensive and well-defined that different examiners will assign scores that are at least similar, if not identical, when scoring the same set of responses. For a classroom test, these rules may be simple and well-defined—the student earns a certain number of points for each item answered correctly, and the total score is determined by adding up the points. For other types of tests, the scoring rules may not be so simple or definite.

Most mass-produced standardized tests are characterized by *objective* scoring rules. In this case, the term objective should be taken to indicate that two people, each applying the same set of scoring rules to an individual's responses, will always arrive at the same score for that individual. Thus, two teachers who score the same multiple-choice test will always arrive at the same total score. On the other hand, many psychological tests are characterized by *subjective* scoring rules. Subjective scoring rules typically rely upon the judgment of the examiner and thus cannot be described with sufficient precision to allow for their automatic application. The procedures a teacher follows in grading an essay exam provide an example of subjective scoring rules. It is important to note that the term "subjective" does not necessarily imply inaccurate or unreliable methods of scoring responses to tests, but simply that human judgment is an integral part of the scoring of a test.

Tests vary considerably in the precision and detail of their scoring rules. For multiple-choice tests, it is possible to state beforehand the exact score that will be assigned to every possible combination of answers. For an unstructured test, such as the Rorschach inkblot test, in which the subject describes his or her interpretation of an ambiguous abstract figure, general principles for scoring can be described, but it may be impossible to arrive at exact, objective scoring rules. The same is true of essay tests in the classroom—although general scoring guidelines can be established, in most cases it is difficult to describe the exact rules that are used in scoring each essay. Thus, two similarly trained psychologists reading the same Rorschach protocol, or two teachers reading the same essay, generally will not score it in identical ways. However, most psychological tests are designed so that two examiners confronted with the same set of responses will give similar scores. A measure that does not meet this criterion cannot be considered a satisfactory example of a psychological test.

The existence of a set of rules and procedures, which may be general or implicit, for scoring responses to a test is of vital importance in psychological testing. Imagine a personality test in which the method of scoring is left totally to the whim of the person who administers the test. If someone were to take this test and ask three different psychologists to score it, he or she would probably receive three totally different scores. It is likely that the test scores would tell you more about the psychologist who scored the test than they would about the person who took it. Since, in this case, test scores would bear no valid relation to the behavior of the person taking the test, it is impossible to regard such a test as an accurate or useful measure of some stable characteristic or attribute of the person taking the test.

TYPES OF TESTS

Most psychological tests can be sorted into three general categories:

1. Tests in which the subject performs some specific task, such as writing an essay, answering multiple-choice items, or mentally rotating images presented on a computer screen.
2. Tests that involve observations of the subject's behavior within a particular context.
3. Self-report measures, in which the subject describes his or her feelings, attitudes, beliefs, interests, and the like.

Tests of Performance

The first and most familiar category of tests is one in which subjects are given some well-defined task they try their best to perform successfully and in which the test score is determined by the subject's success in completing each task. Cronbach (1970) refers to this type of test as a "test of maximal performance."[3] The defining feature of a performance test relates to the intent or the state of mind of the person taking the test. It is assumed in performance testing that the examinee knows what he or she should do in response to the questions or tasks that make up the performance test, and that the person being tested exerts maximum effort to succeed. Thus, performance tests are designed to assess what a person *can* do under the conditions represented by the testing situation.

Standardized tests of general mental ability, referred to as intelligence tests, are among the best exemplars of this type of test. Here, subjects may respond to hundreds of multiple-choice items, and the test score is determined by the number of items answered correctly. Tests of specific abilities, such as spatial ability or mechanical comprehension, are also examples of this type of test. Tests of more specific skills or proficiency, such as a biology test or a music test, also fall into this category.

A number of tests ask the respondent to perform some physical or psychomotor activity. Four of the computer systems used by the armed services in testing recruits are shown in Figure 1-1; two of these include special keyboards and joysticks that are used to assess a variety of psychomotor skills. In a typical computerized psychomotor ability test,

---

[3]The American Psychological Association's *Standards for Educational and Psychological Tests and Manuals* recommends that the term "test" should not appear in the formal title of a measure (e.g., Bennett Test of Mechanical Comprehension) unless it is a measure of maximal performance.

Figure 1-1   Computerized testing apparatus used by U.S. armed services

the examinee might have to use the joysticks to keep a cursor in contact with a specific spot that moves randomly on a screen; performance on this type of task can be assessed in terms of total contact time, number of times contact was broken, or some combination of these factors. Other examples of complex physical performance tests include flight simulators and even the road test you had to take before getting your driver's license. Even video games could be thought of as psychomotor performance tests.

Behavior Observations

Many psychological tests involve observing the subject's behavior and responses in a particular context. In order to assess salespeople's competence in dealing with problem customers, many stores recruit observers to come into their stores at random intervals and observe and record each salesperson's behavior. They may even play the role of a troublesome customer and record the salesperson's technique (or lack of it) for handling different sorts of problems. This type of test is different from a performance test in that the subject does not have a single, well-defined task that he or she is trying to perform. In fact, in this type of test, the subject may not even know his or her behavior is being measured. Thus, rather than assessing maximal performance on some well-defined and well-understood task, behavioral observation tests assess typical behavior or performance within a specific context (Cronbach, 1970).

Observations of typical performance or behavior are used in measuring a variety of attributes, ranging from social skills and friendship formation to job performance. Interviews, including both clinical interviews and employment interviews, can be thought of as behavior observation methods. Although an applicant may indeed try to "do his best" in an employment interview, the task confronting that applicant is relatively unstructured, and useful data may be obtained by observing the applicant's behavior in this potentially stressful dyadic interaction.

Systematic observations of behavior in naturalistic situations are particularly useful in assessing attributes such as social skills or adjustment. For example, a school psychologist who wishes to assess a child's ability to relate well with his or her peers might observe, perhaps indirectly, that child's interaction with other children in a variety of structured and unstructured situations (e.g., in the classroom, in a playground) and systematically record the frequency, intensity, or direction of several types of critical behaviors. Similarly, the behavior of a patient of a mental ward might be systematically observed and recorded in an effort to assess his or her responses to specific treatments.

Self-Reports

The final class of test includes a variety of measures that ask the subject to report or describe his or her feelings, attitudes, beliefs, values, opinions, or physical or mental state. Many personality inventories can be regarded as self-report tests. This category also includes a variety of surveys, questionnaires, and polls.

Self-reports are not necessarily taken at face value. A hypothetical personality test might include an item like, "Artichokes are out to get me." The fact that a person endorses (or fails to endorse) such an item may have little to do with his or her true feelings regarding artichokes but may provide valuable information about the respondent's state of mind. Likewise, the subject's indication that he or she prefers going to museums to reading magazines may, by itself, provide little information. However, if we knew that all successful opticians preferred magazines, whereas successful stockbrokers always preferred museums, we would be in a position to predict that in certain respects that person's interests more closely matched those of stockbrokers than those of opticians.

A number of measurement techniques contain features of both behavior observations and self-reports. For example, interviews may include questions dealing with the respondent's thoughts, opinions, or feelings; this is particularly true for clinical interviews. The two methods may not always yield comparable conclusions—a person who describes himself or herself as timid and withdrawn may nevertheless exhibit aggressive behaviors in a variety of settings. However, the two techniques will often yield comparable and complementary information about an individual.

TESTS AND DECISIONS—USES OF PSYCHOLOGICAL TESTS

Origins of Testing

The roots of psychological testing can be traced back to ancient times. Over 3,000 years ago, the Chinese used written tests in filling "civil service" posts, and systematic testing of both physical and mental prowess was employed by the ancient Greeks. At the turn of the century, experimental psychologists such as Cattell and biologists such as Galton and Pearson contributed to the development, construction, and evaluation of psychological tests (Hilgard, 1989). Developments in the theory of intelligence, together with refinements of statistical techniques such as factor analysis, also contributed to the growth of testing. The strongest impetus for the development of psychological tests, however, has been practical rather than theoretical. Consistently throughout the history of testing, major test types have been developed to meet specific practical needs.

The history of intelligence testing provides the clearest example of the influence of practical considerations on the development of psychological tests. The first successful systematic tests of general intelligence, developed by Binet and Simon, were designed to assist the French Ministry of Public Instruction in assessing and classifying mentally retarded students. Binet's tests require a highly trained examiner and are administered on a one-to-one basis. Although these tests provided a reliable method of assessing mental ability, they were not suitable for large-scale testing programs. America's sudden entry into World War I, which brought about a large influx of recruits who needed to be classified according to mental ability, pointed to the need for tests that could be administered to large groups of people. The U.S. Army's attempts to classify recruits led directly to the development of group tests of general mental ability, most notably Army Alpha and Army Beta. Today, the Armed Services Vocational Aptitude Battery, a standardized group-administered test of several abilities, represents the most widely administered test of its kind.

A combination of practical and theoretical concerns has led to several developments in intelligence testing. First is the development of the Multidimensional Aptitude Battery, which combines several of the best features of individually administered tests with a machine-scoreable multiple-choice format. Second is the development of computerized adaptive testing, in which the test is tailored to the individual respondent. Computerized tests take advantage of advances in technology to adapt tests to the responses and capabilities of the individuals examined.

The history of personality testing provides a similar example of how the practical need to make decisions about individuals has fostered test development. The major impetus for the development of a structured measure of psychopathology was, again, the need to screen large numbers of recruits during World War I (Dubois, 1970). Although developed too late to serve this function, the Woodward Personal Data Sheet became a prototype of other self-report measures. The development of objective tests such as the Minnesota Multiphasic Personality Inventory and projective tests such as the Rorschach inkblot test though not tied to such large-scale decision problems nevertheless stemmed from the need to make systematic decisions about individuals.

Yet another similar example can be drawn from the field of scholastic testing. Prior to the advent of standardized tests, college admissions procedures were typically subjective, cumbersome, and highly variable from one school to another. As the number of students applying to college increased, the need for selection procedures that were fair, accurate, and economical became apparent. Programs initiated by the College Entrance Examination Board led to the development of large-scale scholastic tests such as the Scholastic Aptitude Test and the Graduate Record Examinations (GRE). These tests are extensions of the group-testing techniques developed by the U.S. Army and represent the most extensive civilian applications of psychological testing.

Educational testing.   Educational institutions must make admissions and advancement decisions about millions of students every year. Standardized mass-produced tests, such as the SAT, are widely used in admissions, whereas decisions to advance or hold back students, particularly at the elementary and junior high school levels, are likely to be made largely on the basis of locally constructed classroom tests.

Although admissions and advancement are the most obvious applications of tests in educational settings, they are not the only applications. For example, intelligence tests are likely to be included in the assessment of students for placement in a variety of special education programs. School psychologists might use a number of performance tests and behavior observation tests in diagnosing learning difficulties. Guidance counselors might use vocational interest measures in advising students.

Tests are used by schools and localities in needs assessment and in evaluating the effectiveness of different curricula. Test results may be used in allocating funds to different schools for remedial education. Finally, the publication of average test results for each school in a district is often part of a general drive for accountability in education.

At one time, certification of a student as a bona fide high-school graduate was largely the responsibility of the individual school. Today, minimum competency tests are used in many states and communities for the purpose of certifying graduates. A student who successfully completes four years of high school but who fails such a test may now receive a certificate of attendance rather than a diploma.

Personnel testing.   Ability tests and tests of specific skills are widely used in personnel selection in both the public and private sectors. A high score on a written test is necessary in order to qualify for many jobs in the local, state, and federal governments. Ability tests are also used widely in the military, both for screening new volunteers and for the optimal placement of individual soldiers according to their skills or abilities.

A variety of formal and informal training programs are carried out at the workplace. Tests are used to assess training needs, to assess an individual worker's performance in training, and to assess the success of training programs. Tests might also be used as part of a management development and career counseling program. At regular intervals, supervisors are called upon to assess the job performance of their subordinates; such supervisory performance appraisals can be thought of as behavior observation measures. Similarly, interviews and managerial assessment tests can be thought of as applications of behavior observation testing to personnel evaluation.

Clinical testing.   Clinical psychologists employ a wide variety of tests in assessing individual clients. The most common stereotype of a clinical psychologist suggests an extensive use of diagnostic tests. Indeed, there are a number of objective and projective personality tests and diagnostic tests that are widely used by clinical psychologists. However, clinical testing is by no means limited to personality tests. Clinical psychologists also employ neuropsychological test batteries. For example, perceptual tests are quite useful in detecting and diagnosing many types of brain damage.

Many clinical psychologists receive specialized training in administering individual intelligence tests. These tests not only provide data regarding the intellectual performance of individuals; they also represent a valuable opportunity to observe the subject's behavior in response to a challenging situation. Thus, an intelligence test represents a specialized version of the most common type of clinical measurement, the clinical interview. In some respects, clinical testing is somewhat unique in that the clinician is often an integral part of the testing experience. Thus, in clinical testing, the clinician must be regarded as a measurement instrument.

TESTING ACTIVITIES OF PSYCHOLOGISTS

The consumers of tests represent a large and varied group, ranging from individual counselors to school principals and personnel administrators. Although there is considerable overlap in the ways in which psychologists and other consumers use these tests, there are some ways in which the psychologists' uses of the tests are specialized. The testing activities of psychologists are of considerable interest to psychology students, and it is useful to describe briefly some of the uses of tests by different types of psychologists.

Psychological assessment is common in several of the fields of applied psychology, although the types of assessment devices and techniques vary widely across different fields (Wise, 1989). Table 1-1 lists typical assessment activities for several fields of applied psychology. It is important to note two things. First, the table is not comprehensive. Practicing psychologists in each field may carry out a variety of assessment activities not listed here. Second, there is considerable overlap among the assessment activities of the different fields. For example, psychologists in any of the five fields listed in Table 1-1 might use tests of general intelligence in their assessments; the tests themselves may, however, vary across fields.

There are two differences in the ways in which individuals with training and those without training in psychology typically use these tests. First, psychologists who use tests in their work are more likely than other consumers of tests to have some training in measurement theory. Psychologists are, therefore, often more sophisticated consumers, who recognize the limitations of the tests they use. They are better able to effectively use the results of test research. Second, many of the tests used by psychologists require a

TABLE 1-1 TYPICAL ASSESSMENT ACTIVITIES FOR SEVERAL FIELDS OF APPLIED PSYCHOLOGY

Field	Typical assessment activities
Clinical Psychology	Assessment of intelligence Assessment of psychopathology
Counseling Psychology	Assessment of career interests Assessment of skills Assessment of social adjustment
Industrial/Organizational Psychology	Assessment of managerial potential Assessment of training needs Assessment of cognitive and psychomotor ability
School Psychology	Assessment of ability and academic progress Assessment of maturity and readiness for school Assessment of handicapped children
Neuropsychology	Assessment of brain damage

greater degree of professional judgment in their interpretation than is required for tests used by a wider audience. We should emphasize that these differences represent trends rather than blanket statements. Some psychologists are very unsophisticated in their use of tests, and some individuals with little training in psychology are very sophisticated in their use. Nevertheless, these trends are useful to consider when deciding upon the appropriateness of releasing various types of tests and test results to wide audiences.

INFORMATION ABOUT TESTS

The great diversity of psychological tests is both a help and a hindrance to the potential test user. On the positive side, tests are available to meet a wide variety of practical needs, from personnel selection to neurological diagnosis. Unfortunately, there are often many tests that might be used in any specific setting, and they vary considerably in cost and quality. Furthermore, new tests are always being developed, and research that points to unsuspected flaws or novel applications of established tests is constantly coming out. In order to make sensible choices regarding specific tests, the user must know what types of tests are available for specific purposes and must have access to current research involving those tests, as well as to critical evaluations of each test. Fortunately, the *Mental Measurements Yearbooks,* originally edited by O.K. Buros, fulfill these functions.

The *Mental Measurements Yearbooks* have been issued at somewhat irregular intervals over a period of more than 50 years. The most recent, the *Eleventh Mental Measurements Yearbook,* was issued in 1992 and deals comprehensively with tests issued or revised between 1989 and 1992, together with tests published earlier but still widely used during the period covered by the Yearbook. Together, the *Mental Measurements Yearbooks* provide detailed information regarding most of the tests currently available in English. The Yearbook entry for each test indicates the publisher, available forms, and the price of the test, together with a comprehensive bibliography of published research involving that test. Most important, more tests are critically reviewed by a number of experts. These reviews point out the technical strengths and weaknesses of each test, thereby representing an invaluable evaluation of each test. In the event that a test is judged technically deficient, reviewers are encouraged to indicate whether there exists another commercially available test that does a better job of measuring the specific attributes targeted by the test under review. A similar multivolume reference work, entitled *Test Critiques,* contains reviews of a large number of tests. The first volume of this series was released in 1984 (Keyser & Sweetland, 1984), and several additional volumes have been released since then.

Since Buros's death, the task of compiling the Yearbooks has been taken over by the Buros Institute, which is affiliated with the University of Nebraska. Figure 1-2 shows a typical *Mental Measurements Yearbook* entry, which describes a popular personality inventory. This entry is quite short because no evaluative review is attached. Other entries, especially those for widely used tests, might run several pages and might include the comments of several reviewers. In addition to the *Mental Measurements Yearbooks,* Buros compiled a comprehensive bibliography of all commercially available tests published in English-speaking countries, *Tests in Print II; Tests in Print III* (Mitchell, 1983) is an update of Buros's earlier volume. Buros also compiled *Intelligence Tests and Reviews,*

[943]

Personal Orientation Inventory. Grades 9–16 and adults; 1962–74; POI; 12 scores: time competence, inner directed, self-actualizing value, existentiality, feeling reactivity, spontaneity, self-regard, self-acceptance, nature of man, synergy, acceptance of aggression, capacity for intimate contact; I form ('63, 8 pages); manual with 1980 supplementation ('74, 56 pages); profile ('65, 2 pages); separate answer sheets (Digitek, IBM 1230, NCS, hand scored) must be used; 1983 price data: $10.50 per 25 tests; $5.50 per 50 Digitek, IBM 1230, or NCS answer sheets; $5.75 per 50 hand scored answer sheets; $10 per set of IBM or hand scoring stencils; $4 per 50 profiles; $2.75 per manual; $3.75 per specimen set; Digitek or NCS scoring service, $.95 or less per test; (30–40) minutes; Everett L. Shostrum; EdITS/Educational and Industrial Testing Service. ★

See T3:1789 (98 references); for an excerpted review by Donald J. Tosi and Cathy A. Lindamood, see 8:641 (433 references); see also T2:1315 (80 refrences); for reviews by Bruce Bloxom and Richard W. Coan, see 7:121 (97 references); see also P:193 (26 references).

TEST REFERENCES

1. Abernathy, R. W., Abramowitz, S. I., Roback, H.B., Weitz, L. J., Abramowitz, C. V., & Tittler, B. The impact of an intensive consciousness-raising curriculum on adolescent women. PSYCHOLOGY OF WOMEN QUARTERLY, 1977, 2, 138–148.
2. Reddy, W. B., & Beers, T. Sensitivity training . . . and the healthy become self-actualized. SMALL GROUP BEHAVIOR, 1977, 8, 525–532.
3. Ware, J. R., & Barr, J. E. Effects of a nine-week structured and unstructured group experience on measures of self-concept and self-actualization. SMALL GROUP BEHAVIOR, 1977, 8, 93–100.
4. MacVane, J. R., Lange, J. D., Brown, W. A., & Zayat, M. Psychological functioning of bipolar manic-depressives in remission. ARCHIVES OF GENERAL PSYCHIATRY, 1978, 35, 1351–1354.
5. Paxton, A. I., & Turner, E. J. Self-actualization and sexual permissiveness, satisfaction, prudishness, and drive among female undergraduates. THE JOURNAL OF SEX RESEARCH, 1978, 14, 65–80.
6. DeJulio, S., Bentley, J., & Cockayne, T. Pregroup norm setting: Effects on encounter group interaction. SMALL GROUP BEHAVIOR, 1979, 10, 368–388.
7. Fretz, B. R. College students as paraprofessionals with children and the aged. AMERICAN JOURNAL OF COMMUNITY PSYCHOLOGY, 1979, 7, 357–360.
8. Richards, W. A., Rhead, J. C., Grof, S., Goodman, L. E., DiLeo, F., & Rush, L. DPT as an adjunct in brief psychotherapy with cancer patients. OMEGA, 1979, 10, 9–26.
9. Shadish, W. R., Jr., & Zarle, T. The validation of an encounter group outcome measure. SMALL GROUP BEHAVIOR, 1979, 10, 101–112.
10. Waterman, C. K., Chiauzzi, E., & Gruenbaum, M. The relationship between sexual enjoyment and actualization of self and sexual partner. THE JOURNAL OF SEX RESEARCH, 1979, 15, 253–263.
11. Butterfield, G., & Woods, R. Self actualization and improvement in tennis skills at summer camps for adolescents. ADOLESCENCE, 1980, 15, 429–434.
12. Goldman, J. A., & Olczak, P. V. Effect of an innovative educational program upon self-actualization and psychosocial maturity: A replication and follow up. SOCIAL BEHAVIOR AND PERSONALITY, 1980, 8, 41–47.
13. Wise, G. W., & Strong, L. D. Self-actualization and willingness

to participate in alternative marital and family forms. ADOLESCENCE, 1980, 15, 543–554.
14. Mozdzierz, G. J., & Semyck, R. W. Further validation of the social interest index with male alcoholics. JOURNAL OF PERSONALITY ASSESSMENT, 1981, 45, 79–84.
15. Sulzbacher, S., Wong, B., McKeen, J., Glock, J., & MacDonald, B. Long term therapeutic effects of a three month intensive growth group. THE JOURNAL OF CLINICAL PSYCHIATRY, 1981, 42, 148–153.
16. Berndt, D. J., Kaiser, C. F., & Van Aalst, F. Depression and self-actualization in gifted adolescents. JOURNAL OF CLINICAL PSYCHOLOGY, 1982, 38, 142–150.
17. Brown, C. E., Franco, J. N., & DeBlassie, R. R. A computer program for scoring the Personal Orientation Inventory. EDUCATIONAL AND PSYCHOLOGICAL MEASUREMENT, 1982, 42, 843–844.
18. Byrd, J.W., Coble, C. R., & Adler, C. G. A study of personality characteristics of science teachers. SCHOOL SCIENCE AND MATHEMATICS, 1982, 82, 321–331.
19. Dodez, O., Zelhart, P. F., & Markley, R. P. Compatibility of self-actualization and anxiety. JOURNAL OF CLINICAL PSYCHOLOGY, 1982, 38, 696–702.
20. Goldberg, D., Steele, J. J., Johnson, A., & Smith, C. Ability of primary care physicians to make accurate ratings of psychiatric symptoms. ARCHIVES OF GENERAL PSYCHIATRY, 1982, 39, 829–833.
21. O'Brien, M. H., Samonds, K. W., Beal, V. A., Hosmer, D. W., & O'Donnell, J. Incorporating transactional analysis into a weight loss program. JOURNAL OF THE AMERICAN DIETETIC ASSOCIATION, 1982, 81, 450–453.
22. Ware, R., Barr, J. E., & Boone, M. Subjective changes in small group processes: An experimental investigation. SMALL GROUP BEHAVIOR, 1982, 13, 395–401.
23. Perkins, R. J., & Kemmerling, R. G. Effect of paraprofessional-led assertiveness training on levels of assertiveness and self-actualization. JOURNAL OF COLLEGE STUDENT PERSONNEL, 1983, 24, 61–66.
24. Malanowski, J. R., & Wood, P. H. Burnout and self-actualization in public school teachers. THE JOURNAL OF PSYCHOLOGY, 1984, 117, 23–26.

Figure 1-2 Ninth mental measurements yearbook entry describing personal orientation inventory

Source: Copyright © 1985 by Buros Institute of Mental Measurements. Reprinted by permission.

Personality Tests and Reviews, and *Vocational Tests and Reviews,* which contain additional material that had not appeared in any *Mental Measurements Yearbooks.* Although by no means as comprehensive as the Yearbooks, a list of representative tests, grouped according to their major application (e.g., occupational tests, clerical), is presented in Appendix A.

Research on psychological testing is published regularly in several professional journals. Several journals deal primarily with test theory, or *psychometrics,* whereas other journals deal primarily with testing applications. A list of some of the professional journals that represent primary outlets for research on psychological testing is presented in Table 1-2. It is important to note that the classification of each journal as primarily psychometric or applications-oriented is by no means ironclad; both applied and theoretical articles appear in all these journals.

TABLE 1-2   JOURNALS REPORTING RESEARCH ON TEST THEORY AND APPLICATIONS

	Journal	Orientation
General	*Psychometrika*	Psychometric
	Educational and Psychological Measurement	Psychometric/Applied
	Applied Psychological Measurement	Psychometric/Applied
Educational Testing	*Journal of Educational Measurement*	Psychometric/Applied
	Journal of Educational Psychology	Applied
Personnel Testing	*Journal of Applied Psychology*	Applied/Psychometric
	Personnel Psychology	Applied
Clinical Testing	*Journal of Consulting and Clinical Psychology*	Applied

STANDARDS FOR TESTING

Given the widespread use of tests, there is considerable potential for abuse of psychological testing. A good deal of attention has therefore been devoted to the development and enforcement of professional and legal standards and guidelines for psychological testing.

The American Psychological Association (APA) has taken a leading role in developing professional standards for testing. The most general document dealing with psychological testing is the *Ethical Principles of Psychologists and Code of Conduct;* this document is presented in Appendix B.

The preamble of the *Principles* states that "psychologists respect and protect human and civil rights, and do not knowingly participate in or condone discriminatory practices." The body of this document outlines the psychologist's responsibility with regard to issues such as competence, confidentiality, and the welfare of consumers of psychological services. The APA has issued a more specific document, the *Standards for Educational and Psychological Testing* (1985), which discusses in detail the appropriate technical and professional standards to be followed in construction, evaluation, interpretation, and application of psychological tests.[4] These standards represent

---

[4]The 1985 *Standards* represent a revision of the 1974 and 1966 *Standards for Educational and Psychological Tests and Manuals,* which in turn are a lineal descendant of the 1954 *Technical Recommendations for Psychological Tests and Diagnostic Techniques.*

the most recent revisions of testing standards followed by psychologists for over 30 years.

The use of tests in personnel selection has been an area of special concern. The Society for Industrial and Organizational Psychology has issued the *Principles for the Validation and Use of Personnel Selection Procedures* (1987) to cover issues in personnel testing that may not be adequately covered by the standards. As a result of the Civil Rights Act of 1964, and the Civil Rights Act of 1991, the area of employment testing has been the focus of legal as well as professional standards and regulations. A number of federal agencies are charged with enforcing laws that forbid discrimination in employment. The *Uniform Guidelines on Employee Selection Procedures* (1978) have been adopted by the Equal Employment Opportunity Commission, the Departments of Justice and Labor, and other federal agencies; these guidelines describe the technical standards used by the government in evaluating personnel testing programs. Although these guidelines do not have the force of law, they generally are given great deference by the courts when tests are challenged on the basis of possible discrimination.

Taken as a group, the different standards and guidelines deal with two interrelated issues: technical standards and standards for professional behavior. The technical standards are used to evaluate the psychometric characteristics of a test. Chapters 3 through 9, which deal with the principles of psychological measurement, outline the issues that form the core of these technical standards. The standards for professional behavior described in these documents make it clear that psychologists are personally and professionally responsible for safeguarding the welfare of all consumers of psychological tests. The Committee on Professional Standards of APA has issued *Speciality Guidelines* for clinical, counseling, industrial-organization, and school psychologists (APA, 1981). These, together with the *Casebook for Providers of Psychological Services,* which is regularly published in the *American Psychologist,* define in a concrete way the ethical and professional standards that regulate the uses of psychological tests in a variety of contexts.

The general goal of the ethical standards that guide the development and application of psychological tests is to safeguard the rights and the dignity of the individual who is tested. The actual ethical problems that arise in psychological testing depend in part on the context in which the test is given and used. In Chapters 16 through 22, we discuss the application of psychological testing in educational, industrial, and clinical settings. Each of these chapters includes examples to help illustrate the potential problems encountered in psychological testing and the ethical principles that are applied to safeguard the individuals tested.

CRITICAL DISCUSSION:
Alternatives to Psychological Tests

A critical issue in the debate over psychological tests is whether or not there are alternatives that would be better, fairer, or more economical. The answer may depend on the testing context; it may be easier to develop alternatives for some clinical tests than for some employment tests. In general, however, the search for alternatives has been disappointing. One reason for this is that many of the alternatives proposed *are* themselves psychological tests, albeit poorly structured or badly designed ones.

Consider the debate over the use of tests in academic admissions. Critics have suggested that grade point average (GPA), together with interviews and letters of recommendation, would lead to better decisions than those reached using psychological tests such as the Scholastic Aptitude Test. The GPA clearly reflects an assessment device that meets our definition of a "test." That is, it is based on somewhat systematic observations (typically, a large number of observations from several different courses) under reasonably standard conditions, employing systematic (if not always objective) scoring rules. Viewed in this light, the fact that the GPA is such a good predictor of success in college is evidence of the utility of testing rather than the uselessness of tests. Both letters of recommendation and interviews fall within the category of behavioral observations. Considered in this light, it should be clear that these methods are unlikely to be better than well-designed tests in predicting future behavior. These methods are not based on systematic samples of behavior; they lack standardization and are characterized by highly subjective scoring rules. As we will show in later chapters, a substantial body of research evidence shows that methods such as the interview are inferior predictors of a wide range of relevant criteria. One reason for this is that they fail to incorporate the very features that make for a good psychological test: the systematic sampling of behavior, the standardization of the conditions of measurement, and the application of well-defined scoring rules.

In our opinion, much of the opposition to testing can be traced to the perception that psychological tests involve seemingly small samples of behavior, as compared with alternatives such as recommendations from knowledgeable others and interviews. The fear that a single short testing session can undo years of hard work is not altogether unreasonable and should be taken into account. One way to defuse fears of this sort is to preserve flexibility in your testing program by allowing people to retake tests or by allowing for specfific handicaps and distractions that may impair test performance. The search for alternatives to testing is not always a reflection of problems with testing per se but, rather, may reflect legitimate concerns over inflexible and seemingly arbitrary testing and decision-making procedures.

SUMMARY

A psychological test is not simply a set of questions compiled by a psychologist. It is, rather, or it should be, a carefully developed procedure for obtaining meaningful samples of behavior and for attaching numerical scores to those samples that reflect characteristics of the individuals being assessed. Standardized conditions of measurement and well-articulated rules for assigning scores to responses are as much a part of the test as the test items themselves.

Tests might involve performance of mental or psychomotor tasks, observations of behavior, or descriptions of one's own attitudes, beliefs, and values (i.e., self-reports). They are used by psychologists in a variety of specialists to make decisions about individuals. In this book, we will concentrate on three areas—educational testing, personnel testing, and clinical testing—where the use of tests is especially widespread and important.

The sheer number of tests makes it difficult, even for professional psychologists, to stay fully informed about all the options in psychological testing. Fortunately, a number of resources are available for obtaining information about and professional reviews of psychological tests. Also available are a number of documents describing the standards and principles that govern the testing activities of psychologists. Taken together, these books and documents provide a valuable introduction to the complex technical and professional issues involved in psychological testing.

CHAPTER 2

TESTING AND SOCIETY

As we noted in Chapter 1, the widespread interest in psychological testing is not because of the intrinsic appeal of the tests themselves but, rather, because tests are used to help make decisions that have important consequences for individuals and for society. In this chapter, we will describe how a variety of societal concerns have affected the development, assessment, and use of a variety of psychological tests. The issues raised here will illustrate many of the questions examined in more detail in subsequent chapters. In subsequent chapters, we will describe how test developers and test users have studied, answered, or dealt with specific questions that arise when one considers the societal consequences of psychological testing.

In educational settings, tests are used to select, place, assess, and counsel students. A variety of questions that are of clear interest to society arise in this context, including whether the right individuals are selected, whether the correct placements or treatments are chosen, and whether the progress and achievement of different individuals is fairly and accurately assessed. In work settings, psychological tests and measurement procedures are used to make hiring and placement decisions, to guide and assess training and development, and to evaluate the performance of workers. The societal issues that arise in this context are quite similar to those encountered in education—whether the right individuals are hired for a job, whether they are assessed fairly and accurately, and whether the best methods of training and development are applied to them. In clinical settings, tests are used for a somewhat wider range of purposes, including diagnosis, the selection of treatments, and the assessment of treatment outcomes. Although there have been issues of broad societal concern that arise in the context of clinical testing and assessment (e.g., the issue of the invasion of privacy), most of the controversy over the relationship between testing and society has arisen in educational and industrial settings. Therefore, many of the examples we will use in this chapter will concentrate more on these two settings, and less on clinical testing.

TYPES OF DECISIONS

The most basic assumption of this book is that the results of psychological tests are relevant to a wide range of decisions that must be made about individuals. It is useful to draw distinctions between several types of decisions that might be made on the basis of, or with the assistance of, psychological tests. Different types of decisions may require different types of tests, or different information from a given test, and may give rise to different types of social concerns. There are two distinctions that are very useful for classifying decisions: The decision may be (a) individual or institutional and (b) comparative or absolute. These are not the only ways of classifying the types of decisions of concern to society, but these two distinctions are quite useful in understanding the relationship between tests and decisions.

Individual versus institutional decisions. The first distinction that must be made is between the decisions made by the person who takes the test as compared with those made by the institution that administers the test or uses the results of tests. In individual decisions, tests can be used to counsel or advise the examinee; presumably the results of these tests have some influence on the actions or decisions of the examinee. There are two societal concerns that are often raised in the context of individual decisions. First, there is concern that psychological tests might have an undue impact on the individual. That is, psychological tests, which appear to be objective and scientific, may be given a great deal of weight, whereas other sources of advice and counsel, such as that of parents or friends, may be ignored. Although we have already noted that psychological tests are often the best *single* method for making important decisions, this does not mean that other sources of information can be safely ignored, or that the results of a brief test are more valuable than the results of *all* other sources of advice and counsel. Second, tests might change the decisions or actions of individuals, and these changes are not always beneficial. For example, there is considerable evidence that college admissions tests, such as the Scholastic Aptitude Test (SAT), have an important bearing on the *applicant's* decisions to apply to or to avoid specific schools (Gottfredson & Crouse, 1986; Skager, 1982). A student who does not do well on a test such as the SAT may decide not to apply to academically demanding schools, even though he or she might have had a good chance of being accepted and of performing well at these schools. A person who takes a vocational interest test might avoid some careers and gravitate toward others because of test results, and these choices may adversely affect future income, career mobility, satisfaction, and so forth.

The debate over the societal consequences of psychological tests has focused for the most part on institutional decisions. In educational settings, these decisions include those concerning admission, placement in either advanced or remedial programs, and the advancement or retention of students. In industry, these decisions include those concerning personnel selection, identification of "fast track" employees who receive special attention and opportunities, placement in training programs, and evaluations of job performance and promotability. Two related issues dominate the controversy over the impact of psychological tests on institutional decisions: (a) the accuracy of the decisions and (b) the fairness of the decisions. For example, the use of tests of general mental ability often results in different decisions for whites than for minorities. Tests of specific abilities and skills, especially spatial abilities, can result in different decisions for males than for females. There is substantial research literature devoted to the question of whether differences of this sort in test scores are real or the result of bad tests or ineffective test-taking strategies on the part of some examinees. There is also much literature dealing with whether the outcomes of tests of this sort are related to success on the job, in school, or in life in general. We will review some of this literature later in this chapter, and we will return to several of the questions about institutional decisions raised here in several subsequent chapters (especially in Chapters 15, 16, and 18).

Comparative versus absolute decisions.   Both individuals and institutions are faced with a variety of decisions and choices, some of which involve comparisons of two or more people, actions, objects, options, and so forth. Other decisions and choices involve assessing a single person, option, action, or object. Personnel selection is a good example of a comparative decision on the part of an organization. If ten people apply for four jobs, the institution must decide the *relative* merits of different applicants. That is, the organization must try to identify the four best people and hire them.[1] One important feature of comparative decisions is that they often require less information than would be required for an absolute decision.

Absolute decisions do not involve an explicit choice between two well-defined options; rather, they involve a decision about a single person, option, or object. For example, if an employee who is suspected of theft fails a paper-and-pencil honesty test, the employer must decide whether or not to fire the employee. A student with very low SAT scores must decide whether or not to apply to college. Note that in both cases, two possibilities are being compared, either to do something (i.e., fire the person; attend the school) or not. However, absolute decisions do not depend so much on a comparison of those two options as they do on an evaluation of whether the information available will lead you to pursue the option being considered.

Absolute decisions often require more precise measurement than is required for comparative decisions. For example, suppose you were deciding whether or not a person's visual acuity was sharp enough to qualify as a pilot. This would require (a) fairly exact knowledge of the level of acuity actually needed to fly safely and (b) knowledge of whether the individual's acuity met that standard. In contrast, a comparative decision could be reached by simply devising a task that requires visual acuity and selecting the people who perform best, regardless of their actual acuity levels or the precise visual demands of the job.

Most of the controversy over the societal impact of psychological testing centers around comparative decisions made by institutions, especially decisions involving educa-

---

[1]Comparative decisions might, however, involve some type of absolute assessment. In personnel selection, for example, there is usually some screening to assure minimal qualifications.

tional admissions, personnel selection, and promotions. One troubling issue in this controversy is the frequent failure to distinguish between comparative and absolute decisions. For example, in research on honesty testing in personnel selection, Murphy (1987b) showed that most tests of honesty are not sufficiently accurate to tell with any real assurance who is being honest or dishonest. Some critics suggested that this means that honesty tests should not be used in employment. Sackett, Burris, and Callahan (1989) and Martin and Terris (1991) noted that this conclusion was not warranted, however, and that people who do poorly on honesty tests do indeed often turn out to be poorer employees. Thus, although the tests cannot be used to brand any individual as dishonest, they can be used to make valid and accurate comparisons among individuals.

SOCIETAL CONCERNS

Research, discussion, and debate over the societal effects of psychological tests deal with a wide range of topics and issues. Three issues, however, have dominated this literature: (a) the impact of ability testing on society, (b) the extent to which tests invade privacy, and (c) the fair use of tests. Two of these issues, ability testing and fair use of tests, overlap to some extent in that questions of the fair use of tests are often motivated by the outcomes of ability testing. Nevertheless, we feel it is useful to present these three issues separately.

Ability Testing

Controversies over tests of general mental ability, or intelligence, go back to the early years of this century (Cronbach, 1975; Hartigan & Wigdor, 1989; Hilgard, 1989; Sokal, 1987). In fact, it is fair to say that ability tests have been the focus of public debate throughout virtually the entire history of psychological testing. Over the last 25 to 35 years, the driving issue in this debate has been the existence and meaning of racial-based, ethnic-based, and gender-based differences in test scores (Gottfredson, 1988; Lerner, 1989; Scarr, 1989; Sheppard, 1982). For example, blacks and Hispanics receive lower average scores on many ability tests used for academic admissions and personnel selection than do whites. The use of these tests as the sole basis for making selection decisions will therefore result in the racial segregation of schools and the workforce (Goldstein & Patterson, 1988). Males and females also differ in the scores they receive on some tests of academic aptitude. The use of SAT scores, particularly scores from the mathematical section of the test, as the sole criterion for awarding scholarships will result in fewer scholarships for women (Burton, Lewis & Robertson, 1988). Older individuals receive lower scores on tests that require speedy responses. The use of highly speeded tests in personnel selection and placement could therefore result in discrimination against older workers.

As the examples cited above suggest, the debate over ability testing is not purely scientific; rather, it is driven by social and political concerns (Gordon, 1988). Several researchers have noted that the virtual explosion of research on issues such as the nature of ability and test bias can be explained almost entirely in terms of social concerns related to ability testing (Scarr, 1988; Sheppard, 1982). Four specific issues seem especially important: (a) whether score differences reflect real ability differences, (b) whether differences in ability are large enough to matter, (c) whether tests help or hurt minorities, and (d) whether we should emphasize equity or efficiency.

Are the differences real?   Two plausible explanations exist for group differences in ability test scores. First, these differences may be due to bias in the tests. If this is true, the tests themselves would be the cause of unfair outcomes, such as the loss of jobs, scholarships, and other opportunities (Gottfredson, 1988). This explanation is intuitively very appealing, especially because test critics can point to items that certainly appear to be biased (e.g., a test item that asks you to define *regatta* seems as if it may be biased against disadvantaged, inner-city respondents). The possibility that test bias explains differences in test scores has been the focus of literally hundreds of studies (Gottfredson, 1986; Jensen, 1980; Reynolds & Brown, 1984). The consensus among researchers is that test bias does not by itself explain differences in test scores. Further discussion of research on test bias is included in Chapter 15.

A second possibility is that differences in test scores reflect real differences in ability. Virtually all serious researchers in this area accept the finding that there are *some* real differences in the cognitive abilities of different groups and that the differences observed in test scores are not solely the result of test bias.[2] The causes of these differences, however, are the subject of acrimonious debate. In particular, arguments rage over the extent to which genetic factors or environmental factors explain differences in ability. Further, arguments continue over the implications of high or low levels of genetic influence (Jensen, 1969; Lerner, 1989; Scarr, 1989). In later chapters (especially Chapter 15), we will review research on the heritability of cognitive ability and its implications. In our opinion, however, this research shows that differences in cognitive ability are neither fixed nor permanent, and that the most effective means of reducing these differences will be through changes in the learning environment.

Are the differences large?   If differences in test scores reflect, at least in part, real differences in ability, the question still remains whether or not those differences are large enough to be at all important. For example, some researchers suggest that there are gender differences in verbal ability, but that these are so small as to be of little consequence (Hyde & Linn, 1988). A variation on this same theme is the debate over whether cognitive ability is really that important in the "real world." It is widely accepted that cognitive ability is important in school, but some critics suggest that it has little relevance in other settings. [Gottfredson (1986) reviewed evidence suggesting that cognitive ability *is* important outside of school.] If cognitive ability were unimportant outside of the classroom, differences in test scores would not be very meaningful.

Another question about the size of the differences in test scores concerns a comparison of the between-group variability (i.e., the differences between groups) to the within-group variability (i.e., the differences in test scores within a single group). A typical finding is that the differences between groups (e.g., the difference in the mean scores for whites as compared with minority examinees) are considerably smaller than the differences within groups, and that different groups in the population overlap considerably in

---

[2]Snyderman and Rothman's survey (1987) suggested that most testing experts believe that differences in test scores reflect *both* bias and real differences.

test scores.[3] Therefore, although group means may differ, many members of the lower-scoring group will have scores higher than scores of members of the higher-scoring group. Thus, there is controversy over whether findings concerning the means of different groups can be usefully applied to individual members of the group.

Do tests help or hurt? Legitimate questions concern whether cognitive ability tests help or hurt minorities, females, and other specific subgroups. Critics of testing suggest that these tests create artificial barriers to equal employment, equal access to schools, and other opportunities (Goldstein & Patterson, 1988). For example, Gordon (1988) notes that if ability tests were used as the sole criterion for admission to medical school, there would be even fewer black physicians than we presently have. On the other hand, proponents of testing suggest that tests create unique opportunities for individuals who would otherwise not be considered for jobs, for college, and for other situations (Humphreys, 1988; Jencks, 1972). These researchers argue that tests provide opportunities for talented members of underrepresented groups to demonstrate their abilities and that without tests it would be very difficult for any member of a disadvantaged group to ever get ahead.

It is instructive to consider what would happen if there were no tests. In that case, decisions about college admissions, scholarships, jobs, and other desirable opportunities would be made in the same way as they were prior to the advent of testing—on the basis of highly subjective criteria such as interviews, references, or personal contacts. Psychological tests may help to control some of the subjectivity in these methods.

Efficiency versus equity. As we have already noted, research evidence from thousands of studies establishes beyond a doubt that the use of psychological tests to help make decisions about people generally improves the quality of those decisions. For example, the use of ability tests in personnel selection will lead to the selection of more productive workers than would be selected without tests (Hunter & Hunter, 1984). Thus, tests generally contribute to the efficiency of the workforce. On the other hand, the use of ability tests in making decisions may exclude many minority applicants from a particular job. Tests may reduce equity in the assignment of jobs in the sense that they may lead to the hiring of fewer minorities than would be hired without tests.

The trade-off between equity and efficiency has been one of the most difficult and divisive issues in the debate over ability testing (Gordon, 1988; Gottfredson, 1988; Hunter & Schmidt, 1976; Jensen, 1980). One thing that complicates the debate is that efficiency and equity are measured on very different scales, and so different people might have very different ideas as to how these two concepts should be balanced. Consider a decision about whether to use each of the four tests depicted in Table 2-1 to select job applicants. Many people would agree that Test A is probably justified. Even though it has a small negative effect on minority and female hiring, its dramatic effect on profits would, in the minds of many, outweigh its effects on equity in hiring. Most people would agree that Test B is probably not justified. It leads to a small increase in profits, but it means a disastrous decline in the hiring of minorities and females. In this case, most reasonable

---

[3]Scarr (1989) suggests that individual experiences have a greater influence on intelligence than variables such as race, family, or socioeconomic status. See also Plomin and Rende (1991).

TABLE 2-1   FOUR TESTS THAT ILLUSTRATE THE TRADE-OFF BETWEEN EFFICIENCY AND EQUITY

Effects of test	Test A	Test B	Test C	Test D
Number of females and minorities hired	1% decrease	20% decrease	10% decrease	10% increase
Profits	20% increase	1% increase	10% increase	10% decrease

people would agree that the small increase in profits is not worth the human cost of the test. Tests C and D are a much tougher case. If you value efficiency more than equity, you might think Test C would be worthwhile. That is, a person might be willing to live with some decrease in representation for women and minorities in exchange for this increase in profits. On the other hand, perfectly reasonable people whose values were slightly different might conclude that this test was not justified and that Test D would be better. It is impossible to choose sensibly between Tests C and D without defining the value you place on efficiency versus equity.

Debates over ability testing often boil down to differences in the value people place on efficiency versus equity. As long as different groups in the population receive systematically different scores on ability tests, the question of efficiency versus equity will be with us. As we will see in Chapter 15, psychological research can help clarify the question, but it cannot provide the ultimate answer to how we should balance concerns of efficiency versus equity in the debate over the use of ability tests in making important decisions about individuals.

Finally, we should note that the debate over efficiency versus equity has been complicated by the often confusing nature of the data. A very good example comes from analyses of the effects of affirmative action programs in the workplace. Affirmative action refers to a wide variety of efforts to attract, recruit, and hire members of underrepresented groups. Some researchers suggest that programs of this kind can result in sizable reductions in productivity, particularly when they involve lowering employment standards (Hunter & Hunter, 1984). Others note that there is little evidence that existing affirmative action programs have, in fact, had any adverse effect on productivity and that employers strongly support these programs (Goldstein & Patterson, 1988). One reason why different researchers in this area reach such different conclusions is that they typically examine very different types of data and often use the same terms (e.g., the term "productivity") in very different ways.

Another reason for disagreements in the debate over efficiency versus equity is that the question has become political. Individuals who hold a conservative political philosophy are likely to emphasize efficiency, whereas individuals who hold a liberal political philosophy are likely to emphasize equity. Like all political questions, valid arguments can be made for either point of view, and the choice of one over the other ultimately boils down to the values the individual chooses to uphold.

Invasion of Privacy

Attitude surveys, personality inventories, integrity tests, and interest inventories all share one thing in common—they often inquire about topics that many people regard as sensitive and private. These topics range from attitudes toward public controversies (e.g., the controversy over abortion) to the most intimate details of one's personal life. Psychological tests and inventories of this kind are widely regarded as unwarranted invasions of privacy.

An outstanding example of a test that might invade one's privacy is the Minnesota Multiphasic Personality Inventory (MMPI; see Chapter 21), which contains items dealing with sex, religion, bladder control, family relations, unusual thinking, and other potentially sensitive topics. Responding to the test itself could be embarrassing for many people, and the possibility that test responses might fall into the hands of some unscrupulous person could lead an individual to be very concerned about this seeming invasion of privacy. Interestingly, Gallucci (1986) showed that students objected more to the length and repetitive nature of the MMPI than to the supposedly sensitive items. Nevertheless, it is very reasonable to assume that some people will regard tests like this as an invasion of their privacy.

Psychological tests that explore the respondent's personality, attitudes, beliefs, and so forth, pose a greater threat of the invasion of privacy than ability or achievement tests. In part, this is because most people accept the notion that decision makers have some legitimate interest in knowing your abilities, skills, achievements, and such. The same is not necessarily true for personality traits, attitudes, or beliefs. That is, individuals may not see the relevance of tests that measure these things, and they may not wish to reveal the facets of their character that these tests measure.

Invasion of privacy is a growing concern in employment testing. Until a recent law banned the practice, polygraphs (so-called lie detectors) were widely used in preemployment screening. These tests are now being replaced by paper-and-pencil tests that purport to measure honesty and integrity (Murphy, 1993; Sackett, Burris & Callahan, 1989; Sackett & Harris, 1984). Tests of urine and blood samples to determine drug and alcohol use are also becoming more common. In all these tests, behaviors and experiences away from the workplace may affect test outcomes (e.g., integrity tests may ask whether you have ever stolen anything; weekend drug use may cause you to fail an on-the-job drug test), and many individuals regard these as their personal business, not the business of a potential employer.

Confidentiality. One potential concern is that the results of psychological tests might become available to people who have no legitimate use for these results. The standards that regulate testing professionals (e.g., *Standards for Educational and Psychological Testing*) are very strict with regard to protecting the confidentiality of test results. It is important to realize that virtually all testing professionals accept the idea that the results of a psychological test should *never* be broadcast indiscriminately; this is especially true of tests whose content or results are sensitive. Nevertheless, the enforcement of these standards can be very difficult. More important, psychological tests and the results of these tests are often available to persons who are in no way regulated by any professional standards and who may be less careful about the confidentiality of test results. The possibility that test results will fall into the hands of individuals who have no business receiving the results is taken very seriously by test publishers and test users, and elaborate methods of maintaining test security are often undertaken. Nevertheless, violations of confidentiality can lead to both serious invasions of privacy and the misuse of test results.

Informed consent.   Some psychological tests and assessment procedures involve deception. For example, some honesty and integrity tests appear to be nothing more than surveys of beliefs or experiences. One widely used test is labeled the "Personal Outlook Inventory"; persons taking this test may never know that they are taking an honesty test. This sort of disguised testing is especially likely to be perceived as an invasion of privacy. To understand why this is so, consider the concept of informed consent.

In psychological research, researchers are usually required to obtain informed consent from subjects before carrying out the research. That is, subjects must be informed of the general purpose and nature of the research, as well as of the possible dangers and threats involved, and they must generally know what they are getting into before participating in a research project. Several testing guidelines also require informed consent for some testing applications (e.g., *Standards for Educational and Psychological Testing, Code of Fair Testing Practices in Education,* and *Guidelines and Ethical Considerations for Assessment Center Operations*). A person who does not know what a test or assessment procedure is designed to measure cannot give fully informed consent to testing. The lack of informed consent in some testing situations probably contributes to feelings that psychological tests invade one's privacy.

Requirements for informed consent can present a real dilemma for test developers and test users. Some kinds of tests simply will not work if test takers are fully informed about the purpose of testing. For example, it is possible to distort responses on many personality tests to either fake mental disturbances or to create specific impressions of your personality (research on test faking is reviewed in Chapter 10). If examinees know the specific purpose of a test, they may distort their responses in such a way that test scores are no longer valid or useful. Sometimes, it is necessary to balance the test takers' rights to be informed against the test users' rights to obtain valid information about the individuals who take the test. In general, the balance probably favors test users when the invasions of privacy are minor in nature and when care is taken to preserve the confidentiality of test responses. However, in situations where tests represent wholesale intrusions on the privacy of test takers, the use of tests will be difficult to justify.

Fair Use of Tests

One of the most significant concerns in the debate over the societal impact of psychological tests is whether tests are used in a fair way. As we have noted in our section on ability testing, the precise definition of fairness is difficult because the concept of fairness involves value decisions; people with different values will disagree over the fairness of some testing practices. Nevertheless, we can clarify the debate over test fairness by making a distinction between the fairness of the testing process and the fairness of the testing outcomes (Greenberg, 1987).

Several factors affect the apparent fairness of the testing process. First, there might be obstacles that prevent some persons from performing well; and unless these are removed or adequately taken into account, the test administration will probably be viewed as unfair. For example, administering a highly speeded test that requires the respondent to fill in small spaces on an answer sheet to a person with a motor impairment is probably unfair. Similarly, having an adult from one culture administer an individual intelligence test to a child from another culture is thought by many to be unfair; the differences between the examiner and examinee might make it difficult to establish rapport or may cause the examinee to be overly anxious. Second, the tests themselves must not provide unfair advantages to some examinees. One of the most frequent criticisms of intelligence tests is that they ask questions about things that would be familiar to white, middle-class children, but not to others (Jensen, 1980). Other critics cite more subtle biases, such as the use of response formats that are more familiar to some examinees than to others (Berk, 1982).

The outcomes of tests are of even more concern than the process of testing. The most widely cited outcome that is of societal concern is the differences seen in the ability test scores of whites and minorities, males and females, and other groups. We will discuss research dealing with these differences and its implications for determining the bias and fairness of ability testing in Chapter 15. A variety of other concerns, however, also fall under the heading of the fair use of tests. First, many test experts and critics believe that tests are often used for purposes for which they have little or no validity (Seymour & Rothman, 1987). In education, ability tests may be used inappropriately for the placement of students in advanced or remedial programs. In industry, tests that have no clear relationship with job performance may be used to select job applicants. Even if the tests do not systematically discriminate against particular groups in the population, the invalid use of a test can cause harm to individuals. Second, tests may be used for purposes that are inherently objectionable. Several reviewers (e.g., Friedman & Williams, 1982; Murphy, 1988) have suggested that occupational and professional licensing examinations often serve no legitimate purpose and are used merely to restrict the number of persons in a job or occupation (insuring more profits for those who hold licenses). In the early part of this century, some test researchers used intelligence tests to "prove" theories of racial or ethnic superiority (Wigdor & Garner, 1982); prior to the Civil Rights Act of 1964, some employers used the same tests as a mere pretext to deny jobs to minorities. Height, weight, and physical ability requirements have also been used to restrict the entry of women into some occupations (Hogan & Quigley, 1986). The use of psychological tests to help achieve illegitimate ends is potentially a serious concern of society.

The fair use of test results is a concern of the test developer as well as the test taker and the test user (Messick, 1988). In part, this is a simple matter of survival; tests that appear to cause blatantly unfair outcomes are very likely to be the subject of scrutiny, lawsuits, and legislation, and they are unlikely to be appealing to future test users. There is also an ethical issue involved here. Test developers cannot simply wash their hands after the test is released and ignore the outcomes of testing. Most test developers do indeed consider the likely outcomes of the tests they release, and devote considerable efforts to minimize the potentially unfair outcomes of testing.

Testing disabled examinees. There are a number of physical or mental disabilities that might affect responses to psychological tests without necessarily affecting the characteristic the test was designed to measure. For example, an individual with any of several types of motor impairment (e.g., as the result of an injury or long-term disability) might find it very difficult to respond to a speeded, multiple-choice test of scholastic ability but might nevertheless be extremely bright and capable of high levels of academic performance. How to test individuals with disabilities fairly (i.e., the development of testing methods that validly assess their abilities) and how to fairly use test information in making decisions about disabled individuals are questions that have received considerable attention in the professional and legal literature.

The recent Americans with Disabilities Act (ADA) was designed to remove artificial barriers that have prevented disabled individuals from gaining access to the workplace and to a variety of public accommodations. Although the precise requirements of ADA are still not defined, it is likely that this law will profoundly affect the assessment of disabled individuals. The law requires that otherwise qualified individuals cannot be discriminated against *solely* on the basis of their physical or mental disabilities. It does not require employers or schools to give preference to disabled individuals, but it does require reasonable accommodation to allow disabled individuals a chance to compete for and perform in jobs and assignments. Many standardized tests are potential targets for litigation under ADA because the tests may require responses that may not be job related (e.g., filling in small bubbles on an answer sheet, responding to speeded tests, making fine visual discriminations of motor responses). The task of developing assessment procedures that are fair to disabled examinees *and* that are comparable to those given to nondisabled examinees is a formidable one, and it is likely to occupy test developers for some time to come.

Test use and test fairness.   Although the process of testing and the outcomes of testing are separate issues, both of which contribute to perceptions of fairness or unfairness, they are not completely independent. Rather, the process of testing (ranging from test administration practices to decisions about test use) interacts with the outcomes of testing in ways that can substantially affect perceptions of fairness. In general, a test is most likely to be attacked as unfair when (a) it leads to adverse decisions for some groups in the population, (b) it is the sole basis for decisions, and (c) the consequences of doing poorly on the test are harsh (Seymour, 1988). For example, if minority group members fail to get jobs because of their test scores, the test is likely to be viewed as unfair and may be the subject of legal action.

The use of multiple assessment procedures is one key to reducing concerns over test fairness. When multiple methods of assessment, which consider many relevant characteristics of the individual, all lead to the same conclusion, the hypothesis that the test itself is the cause of the negative outcome can no longer be supported. When different assessment methods lead to different conclusions, this should lead to a more detailed evaluation of the individual, which should in turn reduce the impact of a single test score. Another key to reducing concerns over test fairness is to employ multiple-stage decision models. Rather than making irreversible decisions about everyone at the point of testing, you might sort individuals into several categories that lead to different outcomes. For example, in educational admissions, you might (a) accept the top candidates, who do well on all tests and assessments, (b) reject the lowest-scoring candidates, who do poorly on all tests and assessments, and (c) hold the rest for more detailed examination and consideration (Cronbach & Gleser, 1965).

Another model for reducing the possibility of test unfairness is to use more intensive screening procedures for persons who are most likely to be treated unfairly by a given test. For example, in graduate admissions, it is not uncommon for admission committees to closely examine the files of *all* minority applicants, even those who may have done poorly on one or more tests. This separate examination does not necessarily (or even usually) increase the chances that a given minority applicant with low scores will be admitted, but it does reduce the possibility that unfairly low scores on one test will completely screen out a minority applicant.

ANALYZING THE SOCIETAL CONSEQUENCES OF TESTS

Although test developers and professionals involved in testing agree that the societal impact of testing and the concerns of various groups involved in testing should be taken into account, it is not always easy to identify valid societal concerns. In particular, it is not always clear whose concerns should be given the most weight and whose should be treated as peripheral. This same problem is frequently faced by decision researchers, and the methods they use to address this problem may be usefully adapted to psychological testing.

Edwards and Newman (1983) suggest that the first step in applying decision research to real-world problems is often to identify the *stakeholders,* or those people who have some real stake in how decisions turn out. (Balzer & Sulsky, 1990, have applied a similar analysis to performance appraisals in organizations.) The *Standards for Educational and Psychological Testing* identify several participants in the testing process; their roles are described in Table 2-2. Of these participants, the test developer, the test user, and the test taker are most likely to be identified as stakeholders in decisions concerning test fairness.[4]

TABLE 2-2   PARTICIPANTS IN THE TESTING PROCESS

Participant	Role
Test Developer	Develop, publish, and market the test
Test User	Use test results to make decisions
Test Taker	Respond to test items
Test Sponsor*	Contract with test developer for a specific test or service
Test Administrator	Supervise and carry out actual testing
Test Reviewer	Conduct scholarly review of technical and practical merits of test

*Note: The same organization might serve as test sponsor, test developer, *and* test administrator, or it may serve any two of these three roles.

The test developer and the test user are likely to consider fairness primarily from the perspective of the institution, whereas the test taker is likely to consider the test's impact on the individual. Furthermore, test users often focus on comparative decisions (e.g., the selection of the best out of a group of applicants), whereas test takers, and possibly test developers, are likely to focus on absolute decisions (e.g., whether a person with a given score is likely to succeed). To help make this more concrete, consider the sometimes competing interests of the three main stakeholders in a debate over the fairness of an aptitude test that is used for academic admissions. Some of the legitimate interests of these three stakeholders are shown in Table 2-3.

[4]When an entire category of tests (e.g., the Scholastic Aptitude Tests) is under review, the test sponsor would also have a stake in the assessment.

TABLE 2-3   SOME OF THE INTERESTS OF VARIOUS STAKEHOLDERS
IN ACADEMIC ADMISSIONS TESTING

	Interests
Test Developer	Widespread use of the test
	Avoidance of costly controversies (e.g., lawsuits)
Test User	Selection of best applicants
	Economical, efficient admissions process
Test Taker	Fair chance to compete for admission
	Accurate prediction of likelihood of success

Test developers are, in the long run, concerned with the success of the test. Success is defined here in terms of both the extent to which the test is used and the expenses involved in developing and maintaining the test. Thus, a test that is so controversial that users avoid it, or is so fraught with problems that the test developers devote all their time to defending the test, will not be very successful. Test users are in the long run, concerned with the cost-effectiveness of the test. That is, the user must consider the extent to which the test helps to improve decisions, and balance that assessment against the various costs involved in testing. Costs can range from the dollar cost of test administration to the costs associated with bad publicity that might accompany a controversy over test fairness. Test takers are more concerned with the short-term results of the test than with its long-term success. That is, test takers will naturally be more concerned with how they (and others like them) do on the test, and less concerned with the long-term cost-effectiveness of the test. One of the reasons that debates over test fairness are often confusing is that different stakeholders have different perspectives on what is important (e.g., long-term versus short-term perspectives, individual versus institutional outcomes). All these perspectives are legitimate, and a complete examination of test fairness must consider all of them.

The place of advocacy groups, such as the National Association for the Advancement of Colored People (NAACP) or various consumer groups, in the debate over test fairness has not always been well defined. The interests of these groups typically relate more strongly to those of the test takers than to those of test developers and test users (other advocacy groups, however, such as the U.S. Chamber of Commerce, usually take the institutional perspective). Typically these groups also have political agendas, and these do not always work in favor of individual examinees. Nevertheless, groups concerned with the effects of tests on individuals and society clearly also have a legitimate interest in the debate over test fairness.

The federal guidelines that govern the application of equal employment laws are an example of a system that explicitly considers the perspective of at least two stakeholders, the test taker and the test user. Test takers who believe they have been discriminated against by a test or assessment procedure can initiate legal proceedings to reverse the test outcome. It is their responsibility to present evidence that the test does, in fact, have discriminatory impact.[5] The test user must then present evidence that the test serves

---

[5]A variety of federal and state laws define groups who are specifically protected by antidiscrimination laws. However, anyone who believes that he or she is being discriminated against (including white males) can bring suits under many of these laws.

some legitimate business purpose and that the test contributes to the accuracy of important, job-related decisions. These guidelines, laws, and legal procedures are by no means perfect for balancing the legitimate societal concerns of test takers and test users, but they do give both groups input into the final decision of whether or not a test that appears to discriminate against some group should be used or abandoned.

In the final analysis, it is in the best interest of all participants in the testing process to develop tests and ways of using tests that satisfy most of the legitimate concerns of all of the stakeholders. As we will show in several subsequent chapters, this can best be accomplished by developing tests that are highly reliable and valid, and in which the influence of variables that are not relevant to the decisions the test is designed for are reduced or eliminated.

CRITICAL DISCUSSION:
Are There Technical Solutions to Societal Problems?

Ability testing has a variety of consequences that are of great concern for society. It is important to identify things psychologists can and should do to help solve societal problems that arise as a result of testing. First, psychologists and other test developers and users have a responsibility to minimize the adverse effects of testing, while at the same time preserving the features of tests that make them useful. This might entail a variety of activities, ranging from efforts to minimize bias in test items to the development of decision-making strategies that reduce the undesirable outcomes of testing. Second, they can help clarify and structure the debate over topics such as test bias and test fairness. For example, by developing precise methods of defining and measuring test item bias, researchers have been able to focus the debate over bias on precise characteristics of tests and test items, rather than on abstract arguments over terms defined differently by different participants in the debate. By carrying out research on bias and fairness, psychologists can determine whether various testing problems are real or exist primarily in the minds of test critics. One example of this is in research on the effects of using test items that require knowledge that seems more relevant to upper-class and middle-class persons than to others (e.g., questions about symphonies or polo matches). Most critics of testing have cited this as a serious problem in standardized tests of intelligence (Jensen, 1980), but research has shown that questions of this sort show no more bias than questions about things that are familiar to all classes, races, or sexes.

It is also important to describe the limitations that psychologists face. The most basic limitation is that many societal problems do not have a scientific solution, because they are based on differences in values (e.g., the value of efficiency versus equity). Psychologists can determine what values underly different positions, and they can describe peoples' values with some precision, but science cannot dictate what values should or should not be followed.

The word *should* is the key to describing when technological solutions do or do not exist for societal problems. As long as the issue is one of fact (i.e., what *is* happening), scientific and technical solutions are possible. When the issue is one of value (i.e., what *should* happen), scientists have no special skill or role in solving the problem. Because many of the societal problems that arise from testing do involve values, there will be no technological "quick-fix"; in a democratic society everyone must participate in the solution of these problems.

SUMMARY

Because tests are used to make important decisions about individuals, or to help them make decisions for themselves, the potential impact of testing on society is substantial. Proponents of testing believe that psychological tests are preferable to other methods of making these same decisions; but even if they are correct, that does not relieve test developers and test users from the responsibility of considering the societal consequences of their actions.

Cognitive ability tests have been the focus of a great deal of discussion and debate. Questions of whether testing helps or hurts different sectors of society, of whether tests lead us to a better understanding of individuals and groups or to an inflated assessment of our differences, still rage. Personality inventories, interest measures, and attitude surveys have not been the focus of as much attention, but issued such as invasions of privacy, confidentiality, and informed consent are of significant concern in our society, and testing of this sort can raise any or all of these issues.

Debates of the fair use of tests involve the process of testing (e.g., how tests might be adapted to validly assess individuals with disabilities) as well as the outcomes of tests. Concerns regarding test fairness seem most pressing when the test is used to screen out individuals or to make irrevocable decisions. Some researchers have suggested that other strategies for using test scores might reduce concerns over unfairness.

Analyses of societal concerns in psychological testing are complicated by the fact that different participants in the process of test development and test use have very different interests. The valid concerns of test developers are likely to be quite different from those of test takers, and a thorough analysis of societal issues in testing must consider the perspectives of multiple stakeholders.

CHAPTER 3

BASIC CONCEPTS IN MEASUREMENT AND STATISTICS

We are all familiar with measurement, or at least with the type of measurement that involves rules, meters, gauges, mileposts, and graduated flasks. Our everyday experience with measurement, which involves assigning numbers to the physical properties of objects, may even suggest that it is impossible to measure most psychological variables. In a sense, it *is* impossible to measure psychological variables, but this is true only if one adopts a highly restrictive definition of the term "measure." In fact, measurement is an extremely broad term, and the everyday physical measurement with which we are most familiar is a highly specialized case. A psychologist who claims to have successfully measured intelligence, or need for achievement, or knowledge of biology, means something different than an engineer who has measured the span of a bridge. A proper understanding of the term "measurement" is therefore critical for the interpretation and evaluation of psychological tests.

PSYCHOLOGICAL MEASUREMENT

Defining Measurement

In the most general sense, measurement is the process of assigning numbers to objects in such a way that specific properties of objects are faithfully represented by properties of numbers (Krantz, Luce, Suppes & Tversky, 1971). This definition can be refined slightly when applied to psychological measurement, which is concerned with attributes of persons rather than attributes of objects. *Psychological measurement is the process of assigning numbers (e.g., test scores) to persons in such a way that some attributes of the persons being measured are faithfully reflected by some properties of the numbers.*

It is important to keep in mind that psychological measurement attempts to represent *some* attributes of persons in terms of *some* properties of numbers. In other words, psychological tests do not attempt to measure the total person, but only some specific set of attributes of that person. Even more important, there are many properties of individuals that may be represented in terms of specific properties of numbers. Table 3-1 illustrates how several properties of a set of numbers (2, 4, 16) can be used to represent properties of three individuals (A, B, C).

As shown by the table, the term "measurement" might include a wide variety of operations. As long as specific properties of people are faithfully represented by specific properties of numbers, a psychological test provides a valid measure of a person that can be extremely useful, especially when decisions must be made regarding that person.

Individual Differences

The cornerstone of psychological measurement is the assumption that individuals differ. In particular, there are real, relatively stable differences between individuals in behavior, interests, preferences, perceptions, and beliefs. The task of a psychologist interested in measurement is to devise systematic procedures for translating these differences into quantitative (numeric) terms. In other words, psychological measurement specialists are interested in assigning individuals numbers that will reflect their differences.

It is important to keep in mind what the assumption of stable individual differences means, as well as what it doesn't mean. It means that people differ in discernible, and potentially measurable, ways in their behavior, and that those differences persist over a sufficiently long time to make their measurement useful. If you do not believe that

TABLE 3-1   PROPERTIES OF NUMBERS THAT COULD BE USED TO REPRESENT PROPERTIES OF PERSONS

Properties of the numbers 2, 4, and 16	Properties of persons A, B, and C	Examples
1. 2 is different from 4; 4 is different from 16	A is different from B; B is different from C	A is wearing number 2; B is wearing number 4 on his uniform
2. 16 is greater than 4; 4 is greater than 2	C exhibits more of attribute X than B; B exhibits more than A	C came in second and B came in fourth in a race
3. The difference between 16 and 4 is much greater than the difference between 4 and 2	The difference between the amount of attribute X exhibited by persons C and B is much greater than the difference between the amount exhibited by persons B and A	A, B, and C received scores of 98 (2 wrong), 96 (4 wrong), and 84 (16 wrong) on a vocabulary test
4. 16 is four times as great as 4, and eight times as great as 2	Person C exhibits four times as much of attribute X as does person B, and eight times as much as does person A	C can lift 16 boxes, B can lift 4 boxes, and A can lift only 2 boxes of fruit

individuals differ at all in their psychological attributes (this belief is unlikely to be true) or that people show no stability in their behavior (the topic of behavioral stability is addressed in Chapter 12), there is not sense in trying to attach numerical values to nonexistent or ephemeral differences. We believe that there is enough evidence of stable individual differences in a wide range of psychological characteristics to make the assumption that people really differ a reasonable one. This assumption does *not* mean that differences are necessarily large or permanent, or that differences in psychological attributes indicate differences in people's inherent worth. Rather, it means that there is something out there to measure.

A second point that must be kept in mind is that psychological tests are designed to measure specific attributes of persons, not the whole person. There is not, nor should there be, a test that purports to measure whether one is a good person or a worthy human being. Psychological tests only tell us *ways* in which individuals are similar or different. Some differences are so small or so specialized that they have little impact on people's lives (e.g., Peter collects stamps from Western Africa; Joseph collects stamps from Eastern Africa). Other individual differences in psychological attributes affect one's success in school and in business, one's adjustment, and one's well-being. Systematic measurement of these differences is a key goal of applied psychology.

Scales of Measurement

As Table 3-1 suggests, there are a number of different types, or scales, of measurement that correspond to the different properties of numbers. Stevens (1946, 1951, 1961) has described four scales of measurement that are of particular importance for psychological testing and research: nominal scales, ordinal scales, interval scales, and ratio scales.[1] A *nominal scale* of measurement is one in which numbers are used to classify and identify persons; in nominal measurement, numbers are substituted for names or verbal labels. For example, in a football game each individual is given a specific uniform number, and these numbers are used to identify players throughout the game. Each player receives a different number and retains the same number for the duration of the game. Although the assignment of football numbers may not sound like "measurement," it is, in fact, a very useful level of measurement. Some of the properties of the numbers on those uniforms do indeed reflect some properties of the players; each individual player is a different person, and each receives a different number. Furthermore, the numbers serve the useful function of identifying each player during the game.

Many types of classification result in a nominal level of measurement. For example, a school psychologist may label children as either "normal" or "learning disabled." These labels could easily be replaced by numbers, so that normal children are referred to as "group 1," while learning-disabled children are referred to as "group 2." It is important to note that the actual numbers chosen are completely arbitrary. The two groups could just as easily be labelled "group 407" and "group 136"; any set of numbers will do, as long as children who are members of different groups receive unique numbers. The size of the numbers tells nothing about the persons being measured. Thus, a person wearing the

---

[1]Coombs, Dawes, and Tversky (1970) note that there are many variations on these four basic scales. See also Narens and Luce (1986).

football number of 82 is not necessary bigger, faster, or better than someone wearing number 68—he or she is merely different from the person wearing number 68.

People are very often ranked. For example, a class may agree that their psychology professor is more interesting than their accounting professor, but that both of these professors are less interesting than their biology professor. An *ordinal scale* of measurement is one that assigns numbers to individuals so that the rank order of the numbers corresponds with the rank order of the individuals in terms of the attribute(s) being measured. Consider, for example, the order of finish in a footrace—the person who completes the course in the shortest period of time comes in first, the next person comes in second, and so on. Thus, a runner who finished seventeenth needed more time to finish the course than the runner who finished sixteenth, but less time than a runner who finished eighteenth or twentieth. Note that the order of finish does not indicate, in any absolute sense, how close the runners were at the end of the race.

The outcome of a mile race at a recent track meet is shown in Table 3-2. This table illustrates the central difference between ordinal measurement and measurement on an absolute scale. In this race, O'Brien and Taylor finished in what was nearly a dead heat, and both finished well ahead of the pack. Caldwell barely made it around the track, finishing nearly a minute after everyone else. The order of finish reported in the table, however, merely indicates that O'Brien won, that Taylor came in second, and so on.

Ordinal measurement is extremely common in psychology and education. We can often state with some confidence that a person who receives a high score on an appropriate test is more outgoing or more knowledgeable in the area of mechanics or more likely to exhibit neurotic behavior patterns than someone who received a low score on the same test. However, a comparison of test scores may not tell us how much more outgoing a person with a test score of 40 is than someone with a test score of 22. Nevertheless, a test that yields ordinal information certainly fits our definition of "measurement." In addition, ordinal information is often sufficient for decision-making purposes. For example, if ten people apply for six jobs, the decision makers' task is to pick the top six, something which can be done using strictly ordinal information.

Often we are interested in measuring the differences, or intervals, between objects or people. For example, if you wanted to compare the average temperature in a city in June, July, and December, it would be useful to devise a scale with two essential properties: First, the scale should indicate which month is the warmest and which the coldest (that is, the rank order); second, the scale should indicate whether the difference between the July and December temperatures is bigger than, smaller than, or the same as the difference between the June and July temperatures. Assuming that the difference between July and December is bigger than the difference between June and July, this

TABLE 3-2 ORDER OF FINISH IN A ONE-MILE RACE

Runner	Order of finish	Actual time for the mile
O'Brien	1	3:59.35
Taylor	2	3:59.45
Dill	3	4:08
Catton	4	4:16
Caldwell	5	5:10

scale should indicate the relative sizes of these differences. The Fahrenheit and Celsius scales, which are commonly used in measuring temperature, have these properties.

The scale described above is referred to as an *interval scale*. The defining characteristic of an interval scale is that the size of the difference between the numbers assigned to two persons or objects corresponds to the degree to which those persons or objects differ on the attribute being measured. Assume, for example, that we had an interval scale measure of physical attractiveness and that Sue, Megan, and Kathleen received scores of 2, 4, and 8, respectively. These scores would tell us that (a) Kathleen is more attractive than Megan, who is more attractive than Sue, and (b) the difference in attractiveness between Kathleen and Megan is twice as great as the difference between Megan and Sue. Since individual differences are of considerable concern in psychology, interval scales of measurement can be very useful, and many test developers go to great lengths in attempting to construct interval scales. Unfortunately, such scales are somewhat difficult to construct, and, as a result, many psychological tests yield scores with ordinal properties, but without the defining characteristics of an interval scale.

In many types of measurement we are concerned with the relative size, weight, speed, or density of two objects. For example, if I measure two boards and find that one is 12 inches long and the other is 36 inches long, I can say that the second board is three times as long as the first. Similarly, a car travelling at 60 miles per hour is going twice as fast as one travelling at 30 miles per hour, and 2.4 times as fast as one that is travelling at 25 miles per hour. This type of physical measurement is accomplished using *ratio scales*. A ratio scale of measurement is one in which ratios between the numbers assigned to persons or objects correspond to ratios between the attributes measured in those persons or objects. For example, if we measure height with a ratio scale and determine that person A is 14 units tall and that person B is 7 units tall, this indicates that A is twice as tall as B. The difference between interval and ratio scales can be illustrated by returning to our example in which Megan received an (interval level) attractiveness score of 4, and Sue received an attractiveness score of 2. Even though 4 is twice as large as 2, we would not take these scores to indicate that Megan was twice as attractive as Sue. Indeed, unless attractiveness could be measured using a ratio scale, the phrase "twice as attractive" would be meaningless.

There is a simple but critical difference between interval and ratio scales. In an interval scale the unit of measurement is arbitrary; interval-level attractiveness ratings of 9, 11, and 15 could be used in place of 2, 4, and 8 without in any way affecting the measurement properties of the scale. In particular, the zero point of an interval scale is completely arbitrary. For example, the centigrade and Fahrenheit scales have different zero points, neither of which would be interpreted in any absolute sense. Hence, an attractiveness rating of zero does not indicate that a person has no attractiveness whatsoever, just as a score of zero on a French test does not indicate that the student knows no French. On a ratio scale, however, the zero point is not arbitrary. Regardless of what is being measured, the zero point on a ratio scale always has the same meaning. An object with a true height of zero inches has no height; an object with a true weight of zero grams is weightless. Thus, although the units of measurement are arbitrary (feet, meters, furlongs), ratio scales are always anchored in terms of a fixed, real zero point. As a result, values on a ratio scale can always be interpreted in terms of their distance from this real zero. Thus, a scale value of 40 (inches, pounds, miles per hour) is twice as far from zero as a scale value of 20. In an interval scale, zero has no intrinsic meaning, so that the statement that an interval-level attractiveness rating of 4 is twice as far from a rating of 0 as is a rating of 2 is literally true, but completely uninformative.

There is a clear hierarchy among the four scales of measurement. Nominal scales are the most primitive and least informative scales. Although each person or class of persons receives a unique number that can be used to identify that person, none of the other useful properties of the numbers that make up a nominal scale are reflected in the attributes of the persons being measured.

An ordinal scale has all of the useful properties of a nominal scale, plus the ability to portray rank-order information. Thus, when the order of finish in a race is measured, the numbers assigned to each runner (first place, second place, and so on) serve to identify each runner *and* to indicate the order in which they finished. Interval scales, in turn, possess all the useful properties of nominal and ordinal scales, together with the ability to represent the size of the difference between persons or objects. Thus, when individuals receive interval-level attractiveness scores, these scores serve to (a) identify the persons being rated, (b) indicate their rank order in terms of attractiveness, and (c) indicate the relative similarities or differences in the attractiveness of the individuals being rated.

Finally, ratio scales possess all of the useful properties of nominal, ordinal, and interval scales, together with the property that ratios between scale values correspond to ratios between the attributes being measured. Thus, if three sections of drainage pipe are measured to be 10, 15, and 30 inches, these numbers (a) identify each pipe, (b) indicate which pipe is longest and shortest, (c) indicate which pipes are similar in length and which are relatively dissimilar in length, and (d) indicate that the longest pipe is three times as long as the shortest, and twice as long as the second shortest pipe.

Ratio scales, which represent the most useful and informative scales of measurement, are rare in psychology because a meaningful zero point is often difficult to define (in Chapter 9, we describe item response theory, which sometimes allows one to develop ratio scales). Interval scales are possible to develop in a wide range of settings, but in practice they are difficult to achieve. Many psychological tests appear to yield ordinal information and may exhibit some interval properties, but they do not always strictly fit the definition of interval scales (Coombs, Dawes & Tversky, 1970). Finally, many types of classification that appear to be qualitative in nature (e.g., assignment to a particular psychodiagnostic category), can be regarded as a quantitative measurement that employs a nominal scale.

Evaluating Psychological Tests

The aim of all psychological tests is to assign numbers (i.e., test scores) to individuals so that some attributes of those individuals are faithfully reflected by some properties of the numbers assigned. In Chapter 1 we noted that well-constructed psychological tests do this better than other available methods that are used in making decisions about people. It is appropriate to ask here just how we know (a) whether tests are any good and (b) whether tests are better than other measurement and decision-making techniques. For example, suppose that you take an intelligence test. How would you really know whether the test measured anything related to your level of intelligence? More important, how would you know whether that test did a better job of measurement than might have been done using another test, an interview, or some other measurement method?

Psychological tests are invariably imperfect, *as are all measurement devices;* the numbers assigned to individuals do not always correspond exactly to the attributes of those individuals. For example, John may receive a higher score than Mary on a test of spatial ability, yet he may, in fact, possess an equal level, or perhaps even a lower level, of spatial ability than Mary. Furthermore, some tests do a better job of measuring a particular attribute than others. Thus, if Richard receives a higher score than James on a 200-item, professionally developed reading test, we would conclude with more confidence that Richard is a better reader than if the test scores were obtained from a 5-item reading test published in a supermarket tabloid.

One of the central problems in psychological testing is to determine whether a specific test provides an adequate measure of a specific attribute. In other words, to determine how good a job the test does, it is critical to determine whether test scores really reflect the attributes of the persons being measured and if the test does meet some minimal definition of measurement. The evaluation of psychological tests as measurement instruments centers on two related issues: the reliability of the test scores and the validity of inferences that are made about individuals on the basis of the test scores.

Reliability

The consistency of test scores is of considerable importance in evaluating a test as a measurement instrument. A reliable test is one that yields consistent scores when a person takes two alternate forms of the test, or when he or she takes the same test on two or more different occasions. The importance of reliability can best be illustrated by examining the outcomes of an *unreliable* test. Table 3-3 shows the scores of three students on an unreliable vocabulary test given first on a Monday morning, and then again the following Wednesday.

This test does not appear to measure, in any consistent sense, *any* attribute of Judy's, Kevin's, and Scott's. It is safe to assume that the verbal ability of the three students did not change dramatically between Monday and Wednesday. Their scores, however, did change dramatically. The test given on Monday suggests that Kevin is best and that Scott is only slightly ahead of Judy. Wednesday's test results suggest that Judy is the best, and that Scott and Kevin are tied. In other words, *there is no consistent relationship between scores on this test and the attribute being measured.* Scores like this might occur if the test included very specialized terms (e.g., vocabulary items involving baseball on Monday's test; items involving history on Wednesday's test). Note that the test may

TABLE 3-3   SCORES ON AN *UNRELIABLE* VOCABULARY TEST

Student	Monday	Wednesday
Judy	49%	94%
Kevin	86%	38%
Scott	52%	38%

not even provide a nominal scale of measurement, since Scott and Kevin, who may differ dramatically in their verbal ability, received the same score on Wednesday.

Hence, reliability is the first requirement for good measurement. In order to provide an adequate measure of a particular attribute, a test must *at least* assign scores in a consistent fashion. Methods of defining, estimating, and increasing test reliability, therefore, are extremely important and have been the focus of a great deal of research. The topic of reliability is examined in Chapters 5 and 6.

Validity

Tests are used to make inferences about people. For example, if John receives a higher score on a spatial ability test than Mary, we may infer that he possesses more spatial ability than she. The validity, or correctness, of these inferences is a major concern in psychological testing.

There are two types of inferences that one might make on the basis of test scores. First, there are inferences regarding the attribute being measured. Test scores might be used to infer that one person is more intelligent, more outgoing, or more skilled in French than another. The validity of these inferences is referred to as *validity of measurement*. The central question in assessing the validity of measurement is, "Does the test adequately measure what it purports to measure?" A valid intelligence test, therefore, is one in which more intelligent individuals receive consistently higher scores than do less intelligent individuals.

Tests are not only used to measure specific attributes; they are used to make decisions. The decision to admit a college applicant on the basis of his or her test scores represents a second type of inference—the inference that a person with high test scores is more likely to succeed than a person with low test scores. It therefore is important to assess the validity of a test as a basis for making specific decisions. *Validity for decisions* is the second major facet of test validity; a test that is useful for making accurate decisions about individuals exhibits this type of validity. Chapters 7 and 8 examine validity of measurement and validity for decisions, respectively.

Reliability theory provides a set of procedures for determining whether tests are consistent in assigning scores to individuals. A test that is completely unreliable cannot measure *any* attribute. A reliable test measures something, but reliability theory does not provide any mechanism for determining *what* the test measures. In order to understand fully which attribute or set of attributes is being measured by a test, one must examine the validity of that test. Investigations of the reliability and validity of a test, then, help determine the adequacy with which a test measures a specific attribute of the persons who take the test.

Statistical Concepts

Why Statistics?

One of the authors of this book teaches a statistics course or two every year and often must answer questions such as, "What do statistics have to do with psychology?" One way to answer this question is to note that psychological measurement leaves us with lots of numbers, and that statistics give us a method for answering questions about the meaning of those numbers. For example, if Susan receives scores of 82, 78, and 75 on math, reading, and history tests, does this mean that she is really better at math than at reading or history? Since tests are imperfect measures, the answer might be yes and might be no. Statistics provide methods for answering questions like this.

Statistics can be used to describe test scores. There are statistics that answer the question, "How did people do on the test?"; other statistics answer questions like, "Did most people do the same, or were there large individual differences in test scores?" More important, statistics can be used to make inferences about the meaning of test scores. Statistical methods can help answer questions like, "Is Susan really better at math?" Statistics provide a method for communicating information about test scores and for determining what conclusions can and cannot be drawn from those scores.

Basic Concepts

There are three statistical concepts that are central to psychological measurement: *variability, correlation,* and *prediction.* Of the three, variability is the most basic; it is also the most central. Psychological measurement is concerned with individual differences, and the application of a test is nothing more than a method of expressing individual differences in a quantitative (numeric) form. If there are no individual differences, everyone should, on average, receive the same score on the test. To the extent that individuals really do differ, they will receive scores that differ. Statistical indices of variability allow us to measure and describe the extent to which test scores differ.

When we ask, "Is intelligence related to success in school?" in effect we are asking whether there is any correlation between the two variables. If people who receive high scores on intelligence tests also succeed in school, we can say that the two measures correlate. On the other hand, people who receive high scores on a math test may be no better or worse as golfers than those who receive low scores. In other words, there may be little or no correlation between scores on math tests and scores on the golf course.

Prediction is closely related to correlation but allows us to answer a somewhat more concrete question. Suppose you knew that Scholastic Aptitude Test (SAT) scores were related to college grades (correlation) and also knew that your brother had received scores of 600 and 550 on the verbal and quantitative portions of the test. What grade point average (GPA) would you predict for him? The statistical procedure of linear regression allows us to answer this sort of question.

In the sections that follow, we briefly discuss the statistical concepts used in measuring variability and correlation and in predicting scores on one measure (e.g., grade point average) on the basis of scores on another (e.g., SAT scores). (Those students who do not feel comfortable with statistics will probably find it worthwhile to turn to the Basic Statistics Review presented in Appendix D before going on in this chapter.)

Variability. If 100 students in an introductory psychology course take a test, you expect that some people will do well, that others will do less well, and that others will do poorly. You could describe the performance of the class as a whole in several ways, the simplest of which would be to report the average test score, or the *mean,* symbolized by $\bar{X}$. The mean provides a good summary, but it does not describe individual differences.

Some people did much better than average (their scores were higher than the mean), while others did much worse. It is useful to develop a statistic that measures the extent to which individuals differ. This is most easily done by computing the difference between each person's score and the mean (i.e., subtract the mean from each test score). This *deviation score* measures the extent to which each individual differs from the mean.

There are two basic principles used in developing most statistics:

1. Statistics are usually based on the average of several scores.
2. Statistics that are based on deviation scores usually work with squared scores rather than raw scores.

Both of these principles are used in defining the basic measure of variability, the *variance*. The variance is given by

$$\sigma_x^2 = \frac{\Sigma\,(X_i - \bar{X})^2}{N} \qquad [3\text{-}1]$$

where

$$\sigma_x^2 = \text{variance of } X$$
$$(X_i - \bar{X}) = \text{difference between each person's test score and the mean of the test scores (i.e., a deviation score)}$$
$$N = \text{number of persons.}$$

The variance is simply the average of the squared deviation scores. A large variance indicates that individual scores often differ substantially from the mean, and therefore from one another. A small variance indicates that most individuals received very similar scores, and therefore that most people are very close to the mean.

It may not be obvious why we invoked the second basic rule of statistics ("square everything") in defining the variance. The reason is simple. It can be shown algebraically that the average deviation score is always equal to zero, regardless of the amount of variability in test scores. Since a simple average of the deviation scores will not tell us anything about variability, we do the next best thing and look at the average of the *squared* deviation scores.

Squaring deviation scores allows us to develop a simple measure of variability. Unfortunately, squaring also changes the unit of measurement. For example, a person who receives a score of 30 on a test in which the mean is 50 has a deviation score of -20. That person's squared deviation score is 400. In order to restore the original unit of measurement, you simply need to take the square root. The square root of the variance is referred to as the *standard deviation* and is symbolized by σ_x. This measure of variability is widely used in psychological measurement and represents one of the most common measures of the variability of a set of scores.

One application of the standard deviation is to form standard scores, or *z scores*. Suppose you knew that your score on a psychology test was 20 points above the mean. This indicates that you did better than average, but does not indicate whether you did *much* better than average or only a little better than average. If most people's scores were within two or three points of the mean, your score would seem pretty spectacular, and you might expect a grade of A+. However, if the top of the score distribution were 200 points above the mean, your grade would be a C+ rather than an A+. It would be useful in this case to interpret your deviation score in comparison to other people's deviation scores. The z score does exactly this.

The z score is obtained by dividing a person's deviation score by the standard deviation. That is,

$$z = \frac{(X - \bar{X})}{\sigma_x}$$ [3-2]

A positive z indicates that you are above the mean, a negative z indicates that you are below the mean, and the size of z indicates, in standard deviation units, how far your score is away from the mean. Together with the normal curve, z scores can be used to provide direct and easily interpretable descriptions of test scores. For example, a z score of 1.0 indicates that you did better on the test than 84 percent of the people in the class. A z score of 1.65 indicates that you did better than 95 percent of the class. A z score of −1.25 indicates that you did better than only 10 percent of the class. The z transformation is discussed in more detail in Chapter 4.

Correlation. The simplest way to describe the relationship between scores is through the use of a scatterplot. A scatterplot is a graph showing the positions of a group of people on each of two variables. The X axis on the graph is used for one variable, the Y axis is used for the second variable, and each person's score is represented by a single dot. For example, consider the data in Table 3-4, which represent general aptitude test scores and grades of 12 undergraduate college students. In tabular form, the relationship between the two variables is not particularly evident. Figure 3-1 presents the same data in the form of a scatterplot. As can be seen in the scatterplot, it appears that grades tend to increase as test scores increase. However, the relationship is far from perfect; that is, it is

TABLE 3-4 GENERAL APTITUDE TEST SCORES AND GRADES FOR 12 UNDERGRADUATES

Person	Aptitude scores	Grades
A	50	3.1
B	60	3.7
C	20	1.6
D	30	3.4
E	80	4.0
F	50	2.2
G	50	3.7
H	30	1.9
I	30	2.5
J	70	2.2
K	20	2.5
L	70	3.1
$\bar{X}$	46.67	2.83
σ_x	20.59	.78

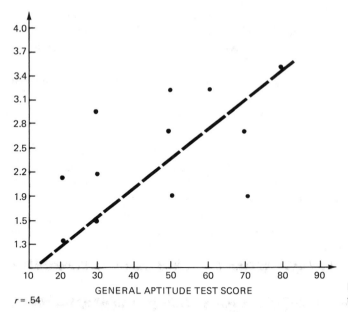

Figure 3-1   Relationship between Aptitude Test Scores and Grades

obvious that each increment in test score is not accompanied by a comparable increment in grade. There is a general trend to the data, but there are also some exceptions.

The relationship shown in Figure 3-1 is called a *positive correlation* because an increase in one variable is associated with an increase in the other variable. That is, the higher the test score, the higher grades tend to be. Although it is true that the majority of the correlations reported in measurement literature are positive, some variables tend to show opposite patterns. Such correlations are called *negative correlations* because an increase on one variable is associated with a decrease on the other variable. For example, among adults, age is negatively correlated with running speed—the older you are, the slower you are likely to run.

The simplest and most common measure of correlation is the *correlation coefficient,* symbolized by *r*. In order to compute *r*, multiply each person's z score on X (e.g., SAT-Verbal) by his or her z score on Y (e.g., grade point average), and take the average of these products. In other words,

$$r = \frac{\Sigma (z_x \times z_y)}{N} \qquad [3\text{-}3]$$

Once again, this statistic is a simple average. The question is why the average of z_x times z_y provides a measure of the correlation between X and Y.

It may not be immediately obvious why multiplying z scores has anything to do with the correlation between two variables. In fact, the link is simple. Correlation implies that people with high scores on X (large positive z) will also have high scores on Y, and that people with low scores on X (large negative z) will also have low scores on Y. The product of two large positive z's is a large positive number; the product of two large negative z's is *also* a large positive number. The r is simply the average of these numbers, so a large r indicates that people with high scores on X also have high scores on Y, and that people with low scores on X also have low scores on Y. In other words, the size of r indicates the extent to which two variables are correlated.

When two variables are not correlated, people with high scores on X will sometimes have high scores on Y ($z_x \times z_y$ is large and positive), will sometimes have average scores on Y (z_y is near zero, so z_x is near zero), and will sometimes have low scores on Y ($z_x \times z_y$ is large and negative). In this case, the average $z_x \times z_y$ (r) will be near zero, and once again, the size of r indicates the strength of the correlation between X and Y.

Correlation coefficients range in absolute value from 0 to 1. A correlation of 0 indicates that two variables are unrelated, and a correlation of 1 indicates that two variables are perfectly related. A positive correlation indicates that high scores on X are associated with high scores on Y (e.g., SAT scores and grades). A negative correlation indicates that high scores on X are associated with *low* scores on Y. This occurs most frequently when two variables are scored in opposite directions. For example, a high score is good in bowling, whereas a low score is good in golf. Since both variables are influenced by general athletic ability, one might expect a negative correlation between bowling scores and golf scores.

Prediction.   One of the practical uses of correlation is in prediction. If scores on one variable, such as performance on the job, are correlated with scores on another, such as a test of mechanical comprehension, one implication is that we can predict job performance from test scores. Many of the decisions we make about individuals are based (at least implicitly) on predictions. Colleges admit students most likely to succeed. Industries hire people who are predicted to perform well and screen out those predicted to fail. Clinical psychologists often base their treatment decisions on the predicted outcome of different types of therapy. The topic of prediction is therefore one of considerable practical importance.

The problem of prediction is complicated by the fact that predictors (X's) and the variables we wish to predict (Y's) are often on different scales of measurement. For example, the SAT, which yields scores ranging from 200 to 800, is often used to predict grade point averages, which typically range from 0.0 to 4.0. The technique used for making predictions must therefore take into account the scale of measurement of both X and Y as well as the extent to which X and Y are correlated. The technique referred to as *linear regression* accomplishes exactly this.

The predicted score on Y, based upon a person's score on X, is given by the equation

$$\hat{Y} = a + bX \qquad\qquad [3\text{-}4]$$

where

$$\hat{Y} = \text{predicted score on } Y$$
$$a = \text{intercept}$$
$$b = \text{slope or regression coefficient}$$
$$X = \text{score on the predictor}$$

In other words, your predicted score on Y is equal to your score on X multiplied by b, plus a constant, a.[2] The constant (intercept) allows us to adjust for different scales of measurement for X and Y. The regression coefficient, b, indicates the expected change in Y per unit change in X. For example, consider the equation shown below and illustrated in Figure 3-2:

$$\text{Predicted GPA} = (.5) + .005 \times \text{SAT-verbal.} \qquad [3\text{-}5]$$

A student with an SAT score of 550 would have a predicted GPA of 3.25. A student with a score of 650 would have a predicted GPA of 3.75, which is .5 (i.e., $100 \times .005$) units higher than that of the lower-scoring student.

The regression equation is a linear equation that predicts that every increase of one unit in X will result in an increase of b units in Y. However, the use of this form of prediction does not imply that the functional relationship between two variables is linear. Psychology abounds with relationships which are nonlinear. The field of psychophysics, which is concerned with the relationship between physical characteristics of stimuli and our perceptions of those stimuli, suggests that a variety of nonlinear functions is needed to describe these relationships. The linear form is used in prediction because it is the most simple and robust form available (Dawes & Corrigan, 1974; Yntema & Torgerson, 1961). In particular, many nonlinear relationships can be described very well using linear equations, simply by transforming the X and Y variables to different forms.

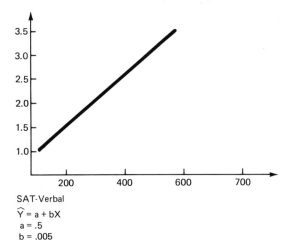

SAT-Verbal

$\widehat{Y} = a + bX$
$a = .5$
$b = .005$

Figure 3-2 Predicting Grade Point Average from SAT-Verbal Scores

Explaining Correlation: Factor Analysis

Mental tests often show moderate to high positive intercorrelations. Factor analysis represents an application of advanced statistical methods to the problem of explaining why two tests are correlated. Suppose, for example, that two tests designed to measure reading comprehension and vocabulary showed a correlation of .53. If someone asked you why these tests were correlated, you would probably say that their correlation is explained by the fact that they both measure pretty much the same thing—verbal ability.

[2] $b = r_{xy} \frac{\sigma_y}{\sigma_x}$; $a = \widehat{Y} - b\bar{X}$

Your explanation represents an application of inductive reasoning: You identify the more general, abstract, common variable of verbal ability by noting features the two tests seem to have in common. Factor analysis represents a statistical method of achieving the same result. Factor analysis attempts, through statistical means, to identify the basic underlying variables that account for the correlations between actual test scores. We call these basic variables that account for the correlations among test score *factors;* more than two tests may have the same factor in common, and it is possible that many factors will be needed to explain the intercorrelations among a large group of tests.

Table 3-5 shows the intercorrelations among four tests: a reading comprehension test (RC), a vocabulary test (VOCAB), a figure rotation test (FR), and an exploded figures test (EF). The figure rotation test is one that requires subjects to identify complex geometric figures presented from different vantage points in space. The exploded figures test requires subjects to identify three-dimensional figures in a disassembled state. If you were called upon to explain why the correlations between RC and VOCAB and between FR and EF are high, while all the other correlations are low, you would probably say that these four tests each measured one or two basic abilities, spatial ability and verbal ability, and that these two abilities were somewhat independent. The fact that RC and VOCAB are highly correlated suggests that they measure the same factor. The fact that RC and VOCAB show very low correlations with FR and EF suggests that the first two variables measure a *different* factor than is measured by the latter two variables.

When factor analysis is applied to the correlations shown in Table 3-5, the results are very similar to those suggested by our common-sense analysis of these correlations. The analysis suggests that there were two distinct factors; the factor loadings, or the correlations between the original four tests and these two factors, are shown in Table 3-6. In the table, both the reading comprehension and vocabulary show high correlations with the first factor and low correlations with the second; both the figure rotation and exploded figures tests show high correlations with the second factor and low correlations with the first. It seems sensible, therefore, to label the first *verbal ability* and to label the second *spatial ability.*

You might wonder why psychologists bother with such complex methods when the results are precisely what common sense would suggest. The answer, of course, is that in many cases the pattern of correlations among psychological tests is too complex for seat-of-the-pants methods to produce reliable and valid results. For example, when there are ten tests, one must examine 45 separate correlation coefficients among the tests. It is generally quite difficult to determine with any precision how many factors are needed to adequately explain the correlations among a number of tests, and it is often even more difficult to identify the factors themselves. To make matters worse, two psychologists

TABLE 3-5   CORRELATION AMONG TWO DEPTH PERCEPTION MEASURES, A READING COMPREHENSION TEST, AND A VOCABULARY TEST

	RC	VOCAB	FR	EF
Reading Comprehension (RC)	1.0			
Vocabulary (VOCAB)	.62	1.0		
Figure Rotation (FR)	.12	.09	1.0	
Exploded Figures (EF)	.04	.11	.76	1.0

TABLE 3-6   RESULTS OF A FACTOR ANALYSIS
OF THE CORRELATIONS SHOWN IN TABLE 3-5

	Factor loadings	
Variables	Factor I	Factor II
Reading Comprehension	.88	.09
Vocabulary	.76	.15
Figure Rotation	.04	.72
Exploded Figures	.20	.78

looking at the same correlation matrix are likely to disagree in their subjective assessments regarding the number and the identity of the underlying factors. Factor analysis provides an analytic method of determining the number of factors and the statistical characteristics of those factors.

At a more fundamental level, one might ask what is accomplished by carrying out a factor analysis. There are probably two answers: (a) the interpretation of data is simplified by reducing the number of variables and (b) the focus of research moves from specific tests to more general factors, which have many of the same characteristics of constructs. In the same way that the essential information conveyed by a large number of concrete, observable measures can be summarized and put into some ordered perspective by a small number of constructs, factors serve to summarize and organize the essential information conveyed by a large number of individual tests. One of the fundamental features of factor analysis is that the number of important, interpretable factors is always smaller than the number of tests, often considerably smaller. In our verbal-spatial ability tests example, all of the important information conveyed by four tests could also be conveyed by the two factors.

There are a number of methods of factor analysis, and they vary considerably in their mathematical sophistication and their usefulness. The most fundamental distinction is between *exploratory* factor analysis, in which the factors that provide the best statistical fit to the data are derived, and *confirmatory* factor analysis, in which factors are defined in terms of the specific hypothesis that is being tested by the experimenter. In general, confirmatory analyses are more useful than exploratory ones, but the applicability of these two techniques varies, depending on the specific area of inquiry. For example, psychologists know a great deal about the structure of cognitive abilities, which allows for the application of more powerful confirmatory methods of analysis. On the other hand, we do not yet know enough about some aspects of interpersonal attraction to form specific hypotheses about factors, and we must therefore restrict our efforts to exploratory factor analysis.

CRITICAL DISCUSSION:
Measurement Scales and Statistics

There is an apparent paradox in psychological research: Complex statistical procedures are often employed in analyzing fairly crude (e.g., ordinal-level) measures. If the measures are so crude, is there really any point to the sorts of statistical gymnastics that appear in psychological journals? Some writers say no (e.g., Siegel, 1956), but others say yes (Gaito, 1980; Lord, 1953). One way to resolve this controversy is to consider the different roles of measurement and statistics in psychological research.

The role of measurement is one of translation. That is, measurement allows us to express very diverse phenomena in a universal language—the language of numbers. The role of statistics is to draw information and inferences from those numbers. Statistics can be thought of as a set of rules for drawing conclusions from numbers. The important point is that *statistical conclusions are conclusions about the numbers themselves, not necessarily about the things or people that the numbers represent.* An example will help to illustrate this point.

Suppose that there were two day-care centers in town, and that one claimed to dramatically improve infants' intellectual ability by exposing them to three hours of flashcards each day. Teachers at this center design a measure, called the *Is Your Baby Better?* scale, and administer it at both facilities. The means and standard deviations obtained by administering the scale to 100 infants at each site are the following:

	With flashcards	Without flashcards
Mean	122	104
Standard Deviation	6.1	5.8

The differences between the scores are statistically significant. Does this mean that flash-cards work? If not, what does it mean?

It is useful to distinguish between the statistical and the substantive statistical conclusions implied by these results. The statistical conclusion that would be reached is that the mean scores do indeed differ, or more simply, that the *numbers* differ at the two day-care centers. This does not mean that flashcards really do improve intelligence. The substantive conclusion about the *meaning* of these numbers depends very much on the measure itself. Does this scale really measure infant intelligence? Maybe it measures flashcard knowledge, which may be quite distinct from intelligence. Is the scale at all reliable? Is the scale administered in an unbiased way at both centers? The statistical data presented here do not address these questions. In the chapters that follow, you may find it useful to keep in mind that statistical conclusions, even those drawn from complex analyses, are conclusions only about the numbers themselves. Careful attention to measurement, or to the meaning of those numbers, is required to make sense out of psychological research.

SUMMARY

Much of the public controversy over psychological testing is due to a failure to consider what *measurement* really means. As we noted in this chapter, it is a process of assigning people numbers that faithfully reflect important characteristics of the individuals being assessed. Measurement can range from the simple assertion that two people are consistently different to the assertion that person A has twice as much of an attribute as person B. In this chapter, we noted that there are a variety of scales of measurement, and that tests that do no more than indicate who has more or less of a particular attribute nevertheless provide valuable measurement.

Two concepts are basic to evaluating any test. First, it should yield consistent, or reliable, scores. Second, it should form the basis for correct, or valid, inferences about the persons being measured. Chapters 5–9 examine in detail the methods used in evaluating psychological tests. These methods require the application of a variety of statistics, particularly in assessing the variability of test scores and the relationships between test scores and other variables (e.g., the correlation between scores on scholastic ability tests and grades) as well as for predicting scores on other tests and measures on the basis of scores on particular tests. In reading research on psychological tests, you will encounter frequent references to the variance (and standard deviation) of test scores, to the correlations among scores, and the regression equations used in prediction. Advanced topics such as factor analysis will also be encountered. You do not have to be a statistician to follow this research; as long as you have a firm grasp of the concepts of variability, correlation, and prediction, you will find that even technical studies are relatively easy to follow.

CHAPTER 4

SCALES, TRANSFORMATIONS, AND NORMS

Psychological tests involve obtaining samples of behavior in order to measure attributes such as intelligence, motivation, risk taking, and psychopathology. The score on a scholastic test might reflect the number of questions answered correctly; the score obtained in an observation of mother-child interactions might be the number of times the mother smiles at her baby. This sort of behavior count is simple and concrete, but not necessarily informative. Suppose, for example, that you knew that a student has answered 27 questions correctly on a statistics exam or that a mother had smiled at her baby five times in 30 minutes. It would be impossible, without other information, to determine whether the student had done well or whether the mother is showing unusual warmth in dealing with her baby. In other words, *raw scores,* which represent simple counts of the behaviors sampled by the test or measuring procedure, do not always provide useful information. It is often necessary to reexpress or transform raw scores into some more informative scale.

We use the term "scale" to refer to the set of scores that might be reported for a test. For example, scores on a test of general mental ability might be reported on an IQ scale. Scales are very often transformations of the original raw scores. The goal of this chapter is to discuss the most widely used methods of transforming raw scores into more interpretable, and therefore more useful, scales.

TRANSFORMATIONS

The simplest transformation is one that expresses scores in terms of percentages rather than raw units. Going back to our example in which a student answered 27 test questions correctly, if you knew that there were 40 questions on the test, that student's score could be reexpressed (transformed) as a score of 67.5 percent. This simple transformation has the three characteristics that many of the most useful transformations exhibit:

1. It does not change the person's score; it simply expresses that score in different units.
2. It takes into account information not contained in the raw score itself—here, the number of items on the test.
3. It presents the person's score in units that are more informative or interpretable than the raw score.

Several of the transformations discussed in this section are more complex than the percentage-correct transformation but will nevertheless exhibit these three characteristics. One exception is the area transformation, in which transformed scores do not reflect all the properties of raw scores.

Linear Transformations

A linear transformation is one that takes the form shown in Equation 4-1:

$$\text{Transformed Score} = \text{Constant} + (\text{Weight} \times \text{Raw Score}) \qquad [4\text{-}1]$$

This equation has the same general form as the regression equation discussed in Chapter 3. As with regression equations, this form of a transformation guarantees a simple direct relationship between raw scores and transformed scores that can be depicted using a straight line, as in Figure 4-1. As illustrated by the figure, a raw score of 30 would equal a transformed score of 400.

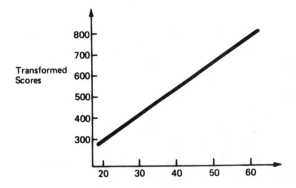

Transformed Score = 100 + 10 x Raw Score

Raw Score of 30 = Transformed Score of 400

Figure 4-1   A Linear Transformation of Raw Scores

One of the most familiar linear transformations is the z score. As discussed in Chapter 3, the z score that corresponds with a raw score value of X is given by

$$z = \frac{X - \bar{X}}{\sigma_x}$$ [4-2]

This may not look like a linear equation, but a little manipulation allows us to restate the z-score equation in the same form as Equation 4-1. That is,

$$z = (-\bar{X}/\sigma_x) + (1/\sigma_x) \times X$$ [4-3]

The z transformation is extremely useful for a number of reasons. First, the z score indicates each person's standing as compared to the group mean. Those with positive z scores received raw scores that were above the mean, whereas those with negative z scores received raw scores that were below the mean. Second, when the distribution of raw scores is reasonably normal, z scores can be directly converted to percentiles. Figure 4-2 illustrates the relationship between z scores and percentiles for the normal distribution.

For example, 84.1 percent of the scores in a normal distribution are below a z score of 1.0. Therefore, if you received a z score of 1.0, you could conclude that you received a better score than 84 percent of the people taking the test. Similarly, a z score of 0 indicates that you did better than half of the people taking the test. Most statistics texts include detailed tables for converting z scores to percentiles.

This interpretation of z scores is accurate only when scores are normally distributed. Micceri (1989) and Wilcox (1992) suggest that deviations from strict normality are common. However, the normal distribution is nevertheless a reasonable working approximation in most cases. More important, the deviations from normality that are most often seen do not greatly affect the relationships between z scores and percentiles. Even when the variable being measured has a distribution that is far from normal, the z score table still provides a working estimate of percentiles; unless the distribution is severely skewed (an abnormally large number of high or low scores), percentiles obtained from a z score table will generally be within 5 to 10 percent of the true percentile value. Thus, z scores are very useful in interpreting most psychological tests and measurements.

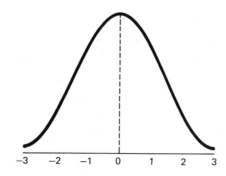

z score	−3	−2	−1	0	1	2	3
Percentage of Distribution below This Score	.1%	2.3%	15.9%	50%	84.1%	97.7%	99.9%

Figure 4-2 Relationship between z Scores and Percentile for Normally Distributed Variables

Variations of the z transformation.   There are two features of z scores that many people regard as undesirable. First, half of the z scores in a distribution will be negative. Second, z scores often have fractional values; even when they exceed $+1$ or -1, they must be carried to at least two decimal places to extract most of the information from each score. Several score transformations can be used to overcome these two disadvantages; T scores illustrate this type of transformation.

The T score is a simple transformation of z that takes the following form:

$$\text{T Score} = (z \text{ score} \times 10) + 50 \qquad [4\text{-}4]$$

For example, a z score of 1.30 could be reexpressed as a T score of 63. A z score of -1.97 could be reexpressed as a T score of 31. T scores have a mean of 50 and a standard deviation of 10, and thus have an effective range of 20 to 80. Scores up to five standard deviations away from the mean, which represent extraordinary extremes, will have T scores in the range of 0 to 100.

Area Transformations

A second type of transformation, referred to as an area transformation, changes the meaning of the score value. These transformations are based on the normal curve, and they change portions of the area under this curve to scale score values.

We have already mentioned one such area transformation, the percentile, or percentile rank. In order to show how this transformation relates to the concept of area, and also to show how it changes the meaning of the test score, we present in Figure 4-3 an example of a reasonably normal distribution of 100 test scores expressed in raw scores and percentiles. A test score of 3 represents the twenty-sixth percentile; a test score of 6 represents the seventy-sixth percentile.

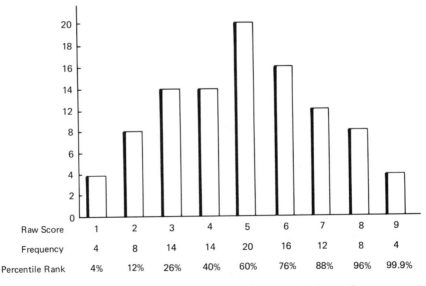

Raw Score	1	2	3	4	5	6	7	8	9
Frequency	4	8	14	14	20	16	12	8	4
Percentile Rank	4%	12%	26%	40%	60%	76%	88%	96%	99.9%

Figure 4-3   Test Scores Expressed as Raw Scores and as Percentiles

Notice how the percentile transformation changes the relationship between test scores. The difference between a test score of 1 and a score of 2 is the same as the difference between a 5 and a 6. The percentiles, however, differ considerably. Scores near the center of the distribution differ substantially in their percentile ranks (5 = 60 percent, 6 = 76 percent), while scores at the extremes have more similar percentile ranks (1 = 4 percent, 2 = 12 percent). This percentile transformation magnifies differences between individuals at the middle of the distribution and compresses the differences between individuals at the extremes.

Figure 4-4 illustrates two area transformations in relation to a normal curve, and it helps to clarify the way in which the concept of area is used to transform raw scores. The data in Table 4-1 are from a test in which scores are normally distributed, with a mean of 100 and a standard deviation of 15. A raw score of 80 has a percentile rank of 9.2, indicating that 9.2 percent of all scores are 80 or lower. Similarly, the table indicates that over 90 percent of the scores are 120 or lower. As we noted earlier, most statistics texts include tables that allow you to easily convert z scores (which are themselves transformations of raw scores) into percentile ranks. The transformation to percentile ranks is one of the most common and useful transformations of raw scores.

In addition to the two linear transformations illustrated in Figure 4-4 and the percentile transformation, Table 4-1 and Figure 4-4 include a second area transformation, the stanine. The stanine is a contraction of the term "standard nine" and represents one of the simplest transformations available; raw scores are transformed to a single digit, between 1 and 9. The stanine transformation uses the concept of area in a different sense than does the percentile rank transformation. The lowest 4 percent of the distribution receives a stanine of 1. The next lowest 7 percent receives a stanine of 2. The next lowest 12 percent receives a stanine of 3, and so on. Whereas the percentile rank transformation expresses raw scores directly in terms of the area in a specific part of the normal curve, the stanine transformation works by first computing where in the distribution each score lies and then transforming the percentile rank into a one-digit stanine.

You may have noted that when a variable is normally distributed, the stanine transformation does not greatly change the relationship between raw scores, except at

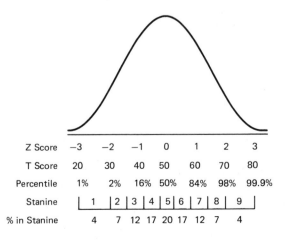

Figure 4-4 Linear and Area Transformation in Relation to the Normal Curve

TABLE 4-1   TRANSFORMATIONS OF DATA FROM A TEST WITH A MEAN OF 100
AND A STANDARD DEVIATION OF 15

Raw score	z score	T score	Percentile	Stanine
70	−2.0	30	2.3	1
80	−1.33	36	9.2	2
90	−.66	43	25.5	4
100	0	50	50	5
110	.66	56	74.5	6
120	1.33	63	90.8	8
130	2.0	70	97.7	9

the extremes. The difference between a stanine of 4 and a stanine of 5 is the same, in raw score terms, as the difference between stanines of 5 and 6.

EQUATING SCALE SCORES

There are many instances when it is not possible or desirable to use the same test across different groups of examinees or for the same group of examinees at different points in time. For example, a topic of recent interest is the decline in performance on tests such as the Scholastic Aptitude Test (SAT), Graduate Record Examinations (GRE), and other standardized aptitude measures. In these cases, scores of current examinees are compared to those of students who took these tests many years ago. For a variety of practical reasons (e.g., test security) the forms of the tests used today are not exactly the same as those used by the students in the past. The question is, then, how does one compare the performance across different groups of examinees when using different forms of the tests?

Another illustration that is relevant here occurs when comparing the level of performance of the same group of people at two or more points in time. For example, in many school settings, achievement tests are administered at the beginning and end of the school year as a way of assessing academic growth over that period of time. If the same test is used both times, a variety of factors (e.g., students' ability to remember questions) complicates the interpretation of test scores. Rather than using the same test twice, the tests given at the beginning and end of the year are likely to be alternate forms of the same achievement test. The question is, How can the test publisher be sure that both forms are equal in terms of their psychometric characteristics (difficulty, etc.)? The present discussion illustrates several procedures for equating scale scores across groups of examinees or forms of tests.

Equating Alternate Forms Administered to the Same Examinees

Perhaps the most common type of equating occurs where there are multiple forms of the same test and we want to make sure that the scores earned on the different forms are interpreted properly. The simplest way to equate two alternate forms of a test would be to distribute both forms of the test *randomly* to a large representative sample of examinees. The random assignment of forms to examinees or examinees to forms is crucial to the accuracy of this procedure. The next step would be to generate the descriptive statistics (mean, standard deviation) on both forms of the test. As the final step, a straightforward linear transformation (using z scores) can take place, equating a specific raw score from one test to the scale score it would equal on the second test.

As an illustration, assume that two different alternate forms of an ability test were developed and then administered to a sample of students. Forms A and B are randomly assigned to a large class of approximately 300 students—150 of each test form. After the tests have been scored, the following results are observed:

	Form A	Form B
Mean	64.72	67.69
Standard Deviation	12.66	10.83

Using the z transformation, 64.72 (i.e., $z = 0$) on form A equals 67.69 (i.e., $z = 0$) on form B. Taking various scores from form A, we can convert them to z scores and then transform each z to the appropriate "equivalent" score on form B. For example, a score of 70 on form A has a z value of .42, which is equal to a score of 72.24 on form B. To avoid confusion of interpretation, since the same scores on both forms are interpreted differently, we might find it desirable to further convert the scale scores from both test forms to one of the common linear transformations, such as T scores. As a final step, a table such as Table 4-2 can be prepared and placed in the interpretive and scoring manual of the test. As long as the two test forms do not differ radically in their mean, variability, and shape, the above procedure for equating the two forms works quite well.

TABLE 4-2 SCALE SCORE EQUATING FOR FORMS A AND B

Score on form A	z Score for form A	Equivalent score on form B	T Scores for both[1]
75	.81	76.43	58
74	.73	75.60	57
73	.65	74.73	56
72	.58	73.97	56
71	.50	73.11	55
•	•	•	•
•	•	•	•
•	•	•	•
55	−.77	59.35	42
54	−.85	58.48	41
53	−.93	57.62	40
•	•	•	•
•	•	•	•

[1]Note: $\bar{X} = 50$, $\sigma_x = 10$

Equating Alternate Forms Administered to Different Examinees

Assume that we want to develop a new form of test for a large psychology course but want to make sure that the interpretation of the results will be comparable to a similar test given five years earlier. Obviously, it is not possible to give the previous sample of examinees the new test. However, is possible to give the *new* sample of examinees a selection (i.e., mini-test) of items from the *old* test, together with the new test. In this case, we actually have three tests—the old test, the new test, plus the common set of items given to both groups of people. The mechanism for equating the new test form to the old test form is through this common collection of items, referred to as an anchor test. Although the technical details of the procedure are beyond the scope of this book, it is informative to describe the rationale behind the technique. The basic idea is that the information obtained from the anchor test provides data that allows one to equate the two test forms.

Consider the situation in Figure 4-5, where both old and new forms of a test (A and B) have 50 items, and the anchor test has 10 items. If people perform differently on test forms A and B, it might be difficult to determine whether this reflects differences in the people taking the test or differences in the tests themselves. The use of a common anchor test, which is taken by both groups of examinees, allows us to separate differences among examinees from differences between the test forms.

Consider the first situation shown in the figure, in which test scores differ but scores on the anchor test are approximately the same. The anchor test suggests that the groups are similar in terms of their ability, since the two groups receive similar scores, but that form A is easier than form B. In this case, scores on the two tests have to be interpreted differently. In particular, a score of 30 has a higher percentile rank for form B than for form A.

The opposite may occur. Situation 2 in the figure illustrates a case in which overall test scores are similar, but scores on the anchor test differ. The group of people taking form A scored higher on the anchor test than those taking form B; this suggests that the

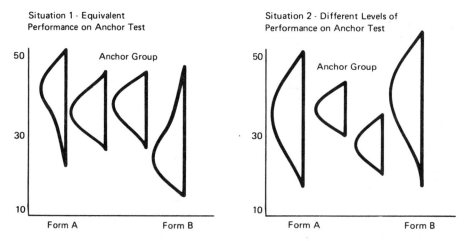

Figure 4-5 Using Anchor Tests to Equate Test Forms

group taking form A is systematically different than the group taking form B. Since their total test scores are the same, the logical conclusion is that form A must be more difficult than form B. If the tests were equally difficult, we would expect group A to do much better than group B. Based on the information provided by the anchor test, we can adjust the A and B scale score values so that a raw score of 30 on form A receives a higher scale score than does a raw score of 30 on form B.

The procedures described in the previous section and in this one are relatively simple. The technical literature on test development contains a variety of more sophisticated techniques that can be used in equating test scores. We have mentioned some simple methods in order to indicate the general principles involved in equating test scores. Additional information on score-equating procedures can be found in Angoff (1971). Students interested in detailed discussions of more recent advances in score-equating procedures can consult a special issue of *Applied Measurement in Education* (1990, Vol. 3), as well as Braun and Holland (1982), Dorans (1990), Fairbanks (1987), and Lord (1980).

Although test form equating may seem like a dry, technical topic, one must keep in mind that mistakes in equating can have enormous consequences. Perhaps the most widely discussed equating error was in the scoring of the Armed Services Vocational Aptitude Battery (ASVAB) (see Chapter 14). An equating error in the development of one of the ASVAB forms led to a massive influx of individuals who, had their tests been scored appropriately, would not have been judged qualified to join the armed services. When Congress was informed of the error, questions were immediately raised about how these supposedly unqualified people were performing in their jobs. It was only then that the Congress learned that there were no good measures of the job performance of enlisted personnel, that in fact the armed services did not really know how test scores related to job performance! One result was a massive research program on job performance in the military; the results of this project are summarized in a special issue of *Personnel Psychology* (1990, Vol. 43, No. 2).

NORMS

Scores on psychological tests rarely provide absolute, ratio scale measures of psychological attributes. Thus, it rarely makes sense to ask, in an absolute sense, how much intelligence, motivation, depth perception, and so on, a person has. Scores on psychological tests do, however, provide useful *relative* measures. It makes perfect sense to ask whether Scott is more intelligent, is more motivated, or has better depth perception than Peter. Psychological tests provide a systematic method of answering such questions.

One of the most useful ways of describing a person's performance on a test is to compare his or her test score to the test scores of some other person or group of people. Many psychological tests base their scores on a comparison between each examinee and some standard population that has already taken the test. The SAT, in which scores of each individual are compared to the scores of thousands of other high school students, provides an example of this approach.

When a person's test score is interpreted by comparing that score to the scores of several other people, this is referred to as a norm-based interpretation. The scores to which each individual is compared are referred to as *norms,* which provide standards for interpreting test scores. A norm-based score indicates where an individual stands in comparison to the particular normative group that defines the set of standards.

There are several different groups that might be used in providing normative information for interpreting test scores. For example, the raw score of an entry-level secretary on a typing speed test could be compared to (a) the scores of people in general, such as might be obtained in a random census survey; (b) the scores of experienced typists; or (c) the scores of other entry-level secretaries. The same raw score might be high (i.e., above the mean) when compared to people in general, low when compared to experienced secretaries, and near the mean when compared to other entry-level secretaries. We offer this example to illustrate two essential points: First, there is no single population that could be regarded as *the* normative group. Second, a wide variety of norm-based interpretations could be made for a given raw score, depending on which normative group is chosen. These two points suggest that careful attention must be given to the definition and development of the particular norms against which a test score will be interpreted.

Types of Norms

In some cases, norms may be developed that are national in scope, as in the case of large achievement test batteries. Results of such tests will be interpreted across the country in many different locations and by many different groups. In these instances, norm groups may involve many thousands of children, and tens of thousands of individuals may take the tests annually.

When developing local norms to be used in much smaller testing applications, the practical problems are considerably less complex. However, the usefulness of the norms in these local situations is not any less dependent on the care taken during each step in the norming process. For example, a small university may develop a faculty rating scale to be completed by students for purposes of deciding on raises, promotions, and/or tenure. Over several years there may be only a relatively small number of courses and instructors involved in the norming process. Later, when using the normative data to make evaluations of the teaching performance of current faculty, the data that are collected may involve 40 to 50 instructors. Although the logistics of compiling local norms are typically less complex than those involved when compiling national norms, the basic process is not really different. In developing local norms for interpreting test scores, the same care should go into defining and collecting data on the normative sample as is observed in large-scale testing programs.

Regardless of the scope of norms (e.g., national versus local), normative data can be expressed in many ways. Four of the most common forms are percentile ranks, age norms, grade norms, and profiles.

Percentile Ranks.   The most common form of norms is percentile rank, which represents the simplest method of presenting test data for comparative purposes. For example, one of the pieces of information on the score report form for tests such as the SAT is the percentile rank of the examinee's score. Thus, a person with a score of 500 might be in the fiftieth percentile. This percentile rank represents the percentage of the *norm group* that earned a raw score less than the score of that particular individual. For a test like the SAT, the appropriate norm group is the population of high school students who are considering applying for college. A score at the fiftieth percentile indicates that the individual did better on the test than 50 percent of the norm group.

It is possible to compare one's score to several different norm groups. For example, scores on the advanced tests on the GRE (i.e., subject matter tests such as chemistry or psychology) sometimes give the examinee several percentile ranks, depending on the specific norm group used. Thus, a particular score may have one percentile rank when compared to the norm group of all graduate school applicants, but a different percentile rank (perhaps lower) when compared to applicants electing to pursue graduate study in a particular academic field.

Table 4-3 illustrates norm data as they are typically presented in a percentile rank format; the table is an adaptation taken from the Norms Booklet for the Clerical Speed and Accuracy Test of the Differential Aptitude Tests. The purpose of the test is to see how fast and accurate examinees can be in a 100-item checking task. The score is simply the number of items that are correctly checked in three minutes. The norms table is based on both boys and girls who were tested at the beginning of grades 8 through 11.

The data in the body of the table represent the raw scores necessary to achieve various percentile ranks, depending on whether the student was a boy or girl, and depending on the examinee's grade. Several interesting conclusions can be drawn from these data. First, there seems to be a general increase in performance as one moves through the grades. Second, the very lowest percentile ranks have raw scores that could be classified as in or close to the chance range. Since this test has 100 items, each having 5 options, a chance score would be close to 20. One therefore would have to interpret the lower percentile ranks very carefully. Third, and perhaps more important, notice that often the scores for girls must be several points higher to achieve the same percentile rank as boys. This is true across the entire norm table. Simply stated, girls performed better on this test than the boys.

Age Norms. Many psychological characteristics change over time; vocabulary, mathematical ability, and moral reasoning are examples. Although there may be a general pattern of growth for these types of variables, often there are wide variations among people as to whether they grow at faster or slower rates.

An age norm relates a level of test performance to the age of people who have taken the test. For example, one edition of the Stanford-Binet Intelligence Test has a vocabulary subtest that consists of 46 items, arranged from the easiest to the most difficult. The procedure is to read each word and have the examinee give a definition. This procedure continues until the person is unable to correctly define several words in a row. This yields a score for the examinee that represents the number of words defined correctly. Table 4-4 presents some normative data from this particular vocabulary test. For example, for the *typical* child at age 6, the average number of correct definitions is about 18; for age 12, the number is about 28. Therefore, if an examinee correctly defined about 25 words, his or her performance is similar to the typical child who is ten years of age.

The principle involved in developing age norms is fairly simple: they can be developed for any characteristic that changes systematically with age—at least up to some age level. Second, we need to obtain a representative sample at each of several ages and

TABLE 4-3 CLERICAL SPEED AND ACCURACY TEST PERCENTILE NORMS FOR USE WITH MRC ANSWER SHEETS

				Raw Scores					
Percentile	B Grade 8 Fall	G Fall	B Grade 9 Fall	G Fall	B Grade 10 Fall	G Fall	B Grade 11 Fall	G Fall	Percentile
99	58–100	63–100	62–100	67–100	66–100	73–100	69–100	78–100	99
97	54–57	58–62	56–61	62–66	59–65	65–72	61–68	69–77	97
95	49–53	54–57	52–55	58–61	54–58	61–64	55–60	63–68	95
90	46–48	52–53	49–51	55–57	51–53	58–60	53–54	60–62	90
85	44–45	50–51	47–48	53–54	49–50	56–57	51–52	58–59	85
80	43	48–49	45–46	51–52	48	54–55	49–50	56–57	80
75	42	47	44	49–50	47	52–53	48	54–55	75
70	40–41	46	43	48	46	50–51	47	53	70
65	39	45	42	46–47	45	49	46	52	65
60	38	44	40–41	45	44	48	45	51	60
55	37	43	39	44	43	47	44	50	55
50	36	42	38	43	42	46	43	49	50
45	35	41	37	42	41	45	42	47–48	45
40	34	39–40	36	41	39–40	44	41	46	40
35	32–33	38	35	40	38	43	40	45	35
30	31	36–37	33–34	39	37	42	39	44	30
25	29–30	34–35	32	38	35–36	40–41	37–38	42–43	25
20	28	32–33	30–31	36–37	33–34	38–39	35–36	40–41	20
15	26–27	30–31	28–29	32–35	31–32	36–37	32–34	38–39	15
10	23–25	26–29	25–27	28–31	28–30	32–35	30–31	35–37	10
5	19–22	22–25	21–24	24–27	23–27	26–31	25–29	30–34	5
3	13–18	16–21	14–20	19–23	18–22	22–25	20–24	25–29	3
1	0–12	0–15	0–13	0–18	0–17	0–21	0–19	0–24	1

TABLE 4-4 TYPICAL SCORES ON VOCABULARY
TEST OF THE STANFORD-BINET AT DIFFERENT
AGE LEVELS

Age level	Test score
14	31
12	28
10	25
8	22
6	18

Source: Adapted from Thorndike, Hagen, and Sattler
(1986).

measure the particular age-related characteristic in each of these samples. For example, Figure 4-6 presents some hypothetical data showing performance on an intelligence scale at several different age levels. Looking at age 60 months, the seventy-fifth percentile rank is approximately 35, the fiftieth percentile is about 18, and the twenty-fifth percentile rank is approximately 8. Of those three values, the median is the most important because it shows what the typical performance level is at each age level. As can be seen, we can make linear interpolations between any two points if we choose. However, also of importance is the considerable overlap *between* different age levels. For example, note that the seventy-fifth percentile rank for 60 months is about 35 and that it is equal to approximately the median value for age 72 months. Thus, while the typical 60-month-old examinee does not perform as well as the typical 72-month-old examinee, *some* 60-month-old children do. While age norms tend to emphasize the average level at a given age, it is important to remember that there is considerable variability within the same age, which means that some children at one age will perform *on this test* similarly to children at other ages.

Grade Norms.   Another type of norm commonly used in school settings is called a grade norm. Grade norms are very similar to age norms except that the baseline on the graph (see Figure 4-6) is the grade level rather than age. These norms are most popular when reporting the achievement levels of school children.

A typical example of normative data in grade equivalent values is presented in Table 4-5. Table 4-5 shows data from the 1970 edition of the California Achievement Tests, in particular, the vocabulary subtest. The vocabulary subtest has two parts of 20 items each, and scores of these two parts are summed together. Thus, scores on this test could range from 0 to 40. This particular version of the test is typically appropriate for students in grades 2 through 4.

The interpretation of grade norms is similar to age norms. For example, based on Table 4-5, the *median* score for children just beginning the second grade (grade equivalent 2.0) is about 22, whereas the typical score for a beginning fourth grader (grade equivalent 4.0) is approximately 37. What happens if a student who is just beginning grade 2 earns a scale score of 37 on this test? In this case, the child would receive a grade equivalent score of 4.0. Does this mean that this child who is beginning second grade is achieving like a typical child who is beginning fourth grade? The answer to this question

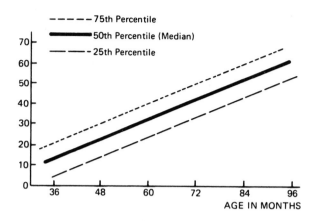

Figure 4-6 Age Norms for a Hypothetical Test

TABLE 4-5 GRADE EQUIVALENTS FOR VOCABULARY SCALE SCORES ON THE CALIFORNIA ACHIEVEMENT TEST

GE	VOCAB	GE	VOCAB	GE	VOCAB
0.6	0–12	2.6	29	5.1	
0.7	13	2.7	30–31	5.2	
0.8		2.8		5.3	39
0.9	14	2.9	32	5.4	
1.0		3.0	33	5.5	
1.1	15	3.1	34	5.6	
1.2		3.2		5.7	
1.3	16	3.3	35	5.8	
1.4	17	3.4		5.9	
1.5		3.5		6.0	
1.6	18	3.6	36	6.1	
1.7	19	3.7		6.2	
1.8	20	3.8		6.3	
1.9	21	3.9		6.4	40
2.0	22	4.0	37	6.5	
2.1	23–24	4.1		6.6	
2.2	25	4.2		6.7	
2.3	26	4.3		6.8	
2.4	27	4.4		6.9	
2.5	28	4.5		7.0	
		4.6	38	7.1	
		4.7			
		4.8			
		4.9			
		5.0			

Source: Adapted from the Examiner's Manual for the California Achievement Tests, Complete Battery, Level 2 Form A, 1970, McGraw-Hill, Inc. Reproduced by permission.

is both yes and no. It is yes in the sense that this second grader is obtaining a score on *this* test that we would expect a typical fourth grader to earn if he or she also took this version of the test. However, the answer is no in terms of saying that the second grader is at an overall achievement level of a student entering fourth grade. One needs to be extremely careful when interpreting grade norms not to fall into the trap of saying that just because a child obtains a certain grade equivalent value on a particular test, he or she is like a child of that grade equivalent level in all areas. In areas such as emotional and social growth, as well as in other achievement areas, the child may not perform at that grade equivalent.

Profiles. Many decisions made in psychological or educational settings do not simply involve comparing an examinee's score on a single test to a norm group. For example, with an achievement test battery that assesses several areas, interpretation rarely focuses only on one area. In general, interpretations are made in terms of comparisons among the different areas. That is, the relative strengths and weaknesses of an individual student are stressed and, if necessary, differential remediation may be suggested, depending on the areas of weakness. Also, in many instances, this pattern of strengths and weaknesses may be used to encourage and/or discourage an individual from pursuing certain occupational paths. The important point is that often we are interested in the *pattern* or *profile* of performance rather than performance on only one variable.

An illustration from the measurement literature that emphasizes profiles is the Strong-Campbell Interest Inventory (a more recent version of this same inventory is reviewed in Chapter 17). Complicated in its construction and scoring, the basic purposes of this interest inventory are (a) to help individuals more objectively identify their own occupational interest areas and (b) to allow comparisons to be made between their own interests and those of successful members of a wide variety of occupations. Table 4-6 presents a sample profile for a teenage boy. Note that three types of information are provided: scores on general occupational themes, high and low basic interests, and high and low occupations. The numbers provided are interpreted as standard scores with a mean of 50 and an approximate standard deviation of 10. Thus, scores considerably higher than 50 indicate strength or strong positive attraction to that area, whereas scores considerably lower than 50 indicate just the opposite.

The main purpose of the profile is to allow the examinee to compare his or her profile with patterns typical for individuals considered successful in different occupations. For example, in the table we can see the pattern of interests for this teenage boy next to the occupations for which he is most similar and dissimilar. In this particular case, the boy seems to favor scientific-academic interest areas and to shun business-related enterprises. It is very important to understand, as the manual for this instrument stresses, that the profile does *not* represent abilities. The most sensible thing to do is to use interest information to help make some preliminary occupational decisions.

Cautions for Interpreting Norms

Normative information can be misinterpreted in many ways. These range from using normative-data that was based on inappropriate target populations to simply misinterpreting the particular statistics underlying normative data. The most important of these potential sources of misinterpretation is when the norms provided in the test manual or in other types of articles are not based on samples that adequately represent the type of population to which the examinee's scores are to be compared. A careful reading of the technical manual generally assists in deciding whether the norms are at least close to

TABLE 4-6   INTEREST PROFILE FOR A TEENAGE MALE

General occupational themes			Five high occupational scales		
R	66	High	IR	Engineer	57
I	64	High	IRC	Computer Programmer	54
A	64	Very High	IRS	Math-Science Teacher	53
S	41	Moderately Low	IA	College Professor	53
E	42	Moderately Low	RIC	Cartographer	52
C	44	Moderately Low			

High basic interest scales			Five lowest occupational scales		
R	Adventure	71	ECS	Buyer	−6
R	Mechanical Activities	68	ECR	Agribusiness Manager	−3
I	Science	68	CE	Banker	1
R	Nature	65	C	Accountant	3
A	Writing	65	ES	Sales Manager	3
A	Music/Dramatics	64			
I	Mathematics	63			
R	Military Activities	62			
R	Agriculture	58			
A	Art	58			

Low basic interest scales			Coding		
E	Effective Management	35	R	=	Realistic
E	Merchandising	37	I	=	Investigative
C	Office Practices	40	A	=	Artistic
S	Teaching	40	S	=	Social
E	Sales	41	E	=	Enterprising
			C	=	Conventional

Source: Reproduced by special permission of the distributor, Consulting Psychologists Press, Inc., Palo Alto, CA, for the publisher, Stanford University Press, from the Strong-Campbell Interest Inventory, Form T325, of the Strong Vocational Interest Blank, by David Campbell and Jo-Ida Hansen. Copyright 1974, 1981 by the Board of Trustees of Leland Stanford Junior University.

those desired. However, many times even these statements can be misleading. One way to help to resolve this problem is to develop, over time, local norms on samples for which one has control over selection and testing.

A second difficulty in interpretation that was also mentioned in reference to grade norms should be reemphasized here. Grade norms, and to some extent age norms, can easily be seen as saying that the examinee *should* be performing at the tested level not only of that specific test but also in other areas and behaviors. It is fairly easy to assume mistakenly that a grade equivalent of 7.5 for a student who is actually in the latter part of the eighth grade means that he or she is only capable of acting, in all respects, like a typical student in the middle of the seventh grade. Since potential for misinterpretation in grade norms is high, one needs to exercise caution when using them and/or listening to interpretive information from others involving grade norms.

Another problem with normative data is that they can become out of date very quickly. Since the process of developing and norming a test is very time consuming and expensive, most large-scale tests are not renormed very often. This is also particularly true for less well known instruments. As major events happen at different points in time and have some important impact on society, then over time the norms on tests may no longer reflect the current performance levels of the population of interest. This would certainly be true for achievement batteries that are trying to reflect common content in the schools. Not only should norms be based on samples that represent adequately the target population, they also should be current.

An additional problem that may be encountered with normative data has to do with the size of the sample taken. Typically, when we look at the norms, there is a tendency to *assume* they are fixed and not subject to error. That is, the temptation is to think that if the same norm group were reexamined with the same test, their scores would produce the same pattern as expressed in the norms manual. However, if norm groups are small, there may be considerable sampling error. That is, if *another* group similar to the norm were tested to renorm the test, the distributions and data derived from the new group would not necessarily be the same as the first. If the size of the original group is sufficiently large (for example, for some large tests, the norms groups number into many thousands), changes in norms due to sampling error are generally too small to make a practical difference.

Finally, a special word needs to be said about profiles. Profiles are frequently used in school settings when strengths and weaknesses in achievement are discussed and also are utilized widely in the area of personality measurement. However, the interpretation of profiles generally implies looking at the *differences* among several subtest scores and then drawing some conclusions about the examinee based on those differences. As will be mentioned later in Chapters 6 and 22, there are some special problems encountered when interpreting difference scores because difference scores are not as dependable as scores on single tests. Thus, one should be especially aware of this problem when interpreting profiles and also should expect that the test manually will say something about this problem and suggest cautions when interpreting this type of data.

EXPECTANCY TABLES

There is a method of presenting normative data, referred to as an *expectancy table,* that is closely related to the concept of correlation. An expectancy table presents the relationship between test scores and some other variable, based on the experience of members of the norm group. For example, an expectancy table might present the likelihood of successful job performance as a function of scores on an employment test, as in Figure 4-7. In our example, a job applicant with a test score of 42 would have approximately a 90 percent chance of success on the job, whereas an applicant with a score of 8 would have a 35 percent chance.

In principle, there is no limit to the number of expectancy tables that could be developed; test scores could be related to any variable of interest. In general, however, expectancy tables are likely to be developed which relate in some meaningful way to the expected use of the test. For example, a college admissions test is likely to be accompanied by an expectancy table relating test scores to college success. These tables give a rough but concrete illustration of the implication of an individual's score on the test.

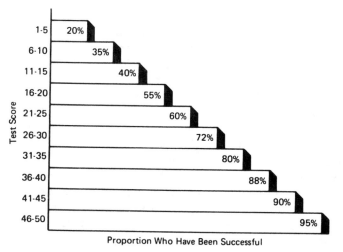

Figure 4-7 An Expectancy Table Relating Test Scores to Likelihood of Success on the Job

Constructing Expectancy Tables

Table 4-7 presents some data collected over several years on 207 students who had taken a math test prior to enrolling in a statistics course. In general, people who did well on the test also did well in the course; the correlation between pretest scores and course grades was about .70. The table presents a scatterplot of test scores in relation to course grades. An expectancy table can be constructed by converting the numbers in Table 4-7 to percentages, or probabilities. The question we seek to answer is, "What is the probability of receiving an A, B, C, and so forth, for a person with a specific score on the pretest?" To answer this, we take the total from each row in the scatterplot (8, 30, 39, and so on) and change the value within the row to proportions of the total. The resulting expectancy table is shown in Table 4-8. Looking at the lowest row of Table 4-7, note that there were a total of eight people with pretest scores of 24 or less. Of those eight, six, or .75 of them, earned an F in the course, and two, or .25 of them, earned a D. In Table 4-8, .75 and .25 values are placed in the F and D columns of the lowest row. The upper row, however, has .25 of the eight people earning B's and .75 of the people earning A's. Thus, given a test score on the predictor, one can estimate the probability of earning a specific grade in the course. For example, what was the probability of earning a B if a student got between 28 and 30 on the math test? Since 18 percent of the students with that type of test score get a B, the probability was .18.

Interpretation and Cautions

An expectancy table is an efficient way of communicating normative information related to predictions that might be based on test scores. For example, think about the situation where a counselor's book could be developed illustrating the relationship between performance on a measure such as the SAT and performance in many different universities. Thus, there might be an expectancy table for the University of Colorado, another for Michigan State, and so on. Not only could there be different tables for different universities, but separate tables could be developed for males and females, and perhaps for

TABLE 4-7 SCATTERPLOT BETWEEN MATH PRETEST SCORES AND GRADES IN A STATISTICS COURSE

	F	D	C	B	A	Raw total
40				2	6	8
37–39			8	18	9	35
34–36		4	18	17	4	43
31–33		11	19	14		44
28–30	3	14	15	7		39
25–27	8	13	9			30
24	6	2				8
	F	D	C	B	A	207

Grade in Statistics

TABLE 4-8 EXPECTANCY TABLE FOR TABLE 4-7

	F	D	C	B	A	Total
40				.25	.75	1.00
37–39			.23	.51	.26	1.00
34–36		.09	.42	.40	.09	1.00
31–33		.25	.43	.32		1.00
28–30	.08	.36	.38	.18		1.00
25–27	.27	.43	.30			1.00
24	.75	.25				1.00
	F	D	C	B	A	

Grade in Statistics

different departments (i.e., English, psychology) *within* the same university. It all depends on how the specific admission decisions are made.

The real advantage of utilizing expectancy tables is that they give people a simple way of understanding the relationship between test scores and probable levels of success. The stress of this book is on the use of test information in decision making, and providing an individual with one or more relevant expectancy tables may assist that person in making a better decision.

Although expectancy tables have many useful facets, we must be careful when interpreting information from expectancy tables. First, since correlational data can be somewhat unstable from sample to sample, it is important that the sample sizes be fairly large. As with other norms, errors due to sampling could make an important difference in how the data are interpreted. A second factor is the magnitude of correlation between the two variables. If the magnitude is high, then we could put more faith in the probabilities in the expectancy table. If the correlation between test scores and success is fairly low, the expectancy table may not be very useful. Finally, one needs to realize that the patterns of relationship between predictors and criteria can change over the years. Also, since there are probably a variety of factors that influence outcomes, it would be wise to not be too discouraged if expectancy tables suggest a low probability of performing well, or to be overly confident if the probabilities are high.

Cutoff Scores

In many settings where large numbers of individuals take tests (e.g., civil service examinations), it is necessary to set cutoff scores for passing applicants, for accepting or rejecting applicants, or for deciding which individuals should receive further assessment. For example, when jobs such as firefighter or police officer become available, it is common to have many more applicants than jobs. It is also common to start with a written examination and then proceed with a more intensive, and expensive, assessment procedure for those who exceed the cutoff score.

The process of setting cutoff scores on tests involves a complex set of legal, professional, and psychometric issues (Cascio, Alexander & Barrett, 1988). A variety of methods have been proposed, some of which are quite complex. The most widely accepted one, the Angoff method, is, however, quite simple. This method uses expert judges to rate for each test item the probability that a barely qualified or competent person will answer it correctly. For example, an expert examining a test for firefighters might judge that a barely competent firefighter would have a one in four chance of answering a particularly difficult item correctly, thereby give it a rating of .25. The cutoff score for the test is determined by the average of the item scores. If a barely competent person would be expected to answer about half of the items correctly, the score needed to pass that test will be at least 50 percent.

CRITICAL DISCUSSION:
Should Black IQ Scores Be Based on White Norms?

Scores on tests of general intelligence are often expressed in terms of an intelligence quotient (IQ). The IQ is a norm-based score that compares an individual's score to the scores in a particular normative population. Although there is some variation in the scales employed, most tests that report IQs employ a score distribution with a mean of 100 and a standard deviation of 15. Thus, an IQ of 110 indicates that the individual scored better than average (approximately in the seventy-fifth percentile). Scores below 100 indicate below-average performance.

One of the most serious controversies in the field of intelligence testing has to do with differences in the scores obtained by white and black examinees. The average score reported for blacks tends to be lower by about 15 points than the average score reported for whites. The reasons for the differences are the subject of considerable research and debate, but the implication is clear: More blacks will be labelled "below average" in intelligence than whites. Some critics have suggested that this difference in scores in part reflects the use of inappropriate norm groups (Williams, 1971). In particular, if scores of black examinees are compared to norms based almost exclusively on a white norm sample, the scores will give a biased, unrepresentative indication of blacks' performance.

Two facts are worth noting in the debate on test norms. If the (largely white) population norms are used to evaluate test scores, more than half of the blacks tested will be labelled "below average." On the other hand, if scores of black examinees are compared only to scores of other blacks, one half of all blacks will be labelled "above average" and one half will be labelled "below average." Which of these is correct?

In a sense, the debate over norm groups is misleading because *both* positions cited above are correct. Population norms indicate how well a person does relative to the population as a whole; subgroup norms indicate how well a person does relative to a particular group. Neither of these indicates the "real" level of intelligence; norm-based scores indicate relative, not absolute, performance. The question in evaluating norm-based scores is not which score is correct but, rather, which score is more useful. An example may help to clarify this point.

If a college student took a test of business knowledge, several different normative interpretations might be possible, some of which are illustrated in Table 4-9. The same test score might look quite good when compared to the general population (eighty-fifth percentile), but it might look bad when compared to successful businesspersons (thirty-fifth percentile). If this student were applying for admission to an MBA program, comparisons to business majors would be useful. On the other hand, comparisons to the general population would be most useful in answering the question, "How much does this person know about business?"

TABLE 4-9   POSSIBLE NORMATIVE INTERPRETATIONS
OF A TEST OF BUSINESS KNOWLEDGE

Norm group	Percentile rank
General Population	85th
College Population	60th
Business Majors	48th
Successful Businesspersons	35th

In our opinion, the choice of norm group does not have a pivotal impact on the IQ controversy. The norm group employed does not define *the* meaning of test scores; rather, each norm group provides another vantage point for interpreting test scores. In deciding whether black IQ scores should be based on white norms, you first need to determine what it is you want to know. If you want to know how a person did compared to black examinees, use black norms. If you want to know how a person did compared to white examinees, use white norms. Finally, if you want to know how a person did compared to the rest of the people who took the test, you should use norms based on the general population.

SUMMARY

Test scores can be difficult to interpret in their raw score form; knowing that a student answered 62 questions correctly on a multiple-choice test, for example, simply doesn't tell you much. To interpret test scores sensibly, one needs to consider other types of information, such as the total number of test items or the performance of other similar individuals who took the same test. Linear transformations, such as the z score or the T score, provide a simple means for comparing an individual's score to the scores obtained by others. Positive z scores (or T scores above 50) indicate above-average performance, and the larger the z (or T), the better one's relative performance. Area transformations such as the percentile rank or the stanine provide another simple way of describing a person's relative performance.

Alternate forms are available for many widely used tests, and it is important to guarantee that scores on different forms can be interpreted similarly. There is a vast and complex body of research on equating methods, but the basic principles are quite simple. Test-equating studies involve administering parts or all of several different forms to the same set of examinees and comparing their performance. When test forms are well equated, examinees should receive essentially the same scores on any form of the test.

Norms are critical to the interpretation of test scores. A variety of types of norms exist, and more than one set of norms might be used in interpreting test scores. Expectancy tables represent a special type of normative information, which can be used to illustrate the meaning of scores on tests used in admissions, personnel selection, and a variety of other individual and institutional decisions.

CHAPTER 5

RELIABILITY: THE CONSISTENCY OF TEST SCORES

Neither physical measurements nor psychological tests are completely consistent; if some attribute of a person is measured twice, the two scores are likely to differ. For example, if a person's height is measured twice in the same day, a value of 5'10¾₆" may be obtained the first time, and a value of 5'10¼₆" the second. A person taking the Scholastic Aptitude Test (SAT) twice might obtain a score of 1060 in the fall and 990 in the spring. A person taking two different forms of a test of general intelligence might obtain an IQ of 110 on one test and 114 on the other. Thus, test scores and other measures generally show some inconsistency. On the other hand, most test scores are not completely random. For example, one is unlikely to obtain a reading of 98.6° using one fever thermometer and a reading of 103° using another. Similarly, a child is unlikely to obtain a score of 95 percent on a well-constructed reading test and a score of 40 percent on a second, similar test. Methods of studying, defining, and estimating the consistency or inconsistency of test scores form the central focus of research and theory dealing with the reliability of test scores.

As stated in Chapter 3, measurement is the process of assigning numbers to persons so that some attribute of each person is accurately reflected in some attribute of the numbers. The reliability or consistency of test scores is critically important in determining whether a test can provide good measurement. For example, suppose you take a test of spatial visualization ability that provides a different score every time you take the test— sometimes your scores are very high, sometimes low, and sometimes moderate. Since spatial visualization ability is a fairly stable characteristic, this test cannot possibly be a reliable measure—the scores vary substantially, even though the attribute the test is designed to measure does not. In other words, in this case the numbers do not reflect the attribute they are being used to measure.

The practical importance of consistency in test scores is a direct result of the fact that tests are used to make important decisions about people. For example, many high schools require that students pass a competency test before they are allowed to graduate. Imagine what would happen if test scores were so inconsistent that many students who received low scores on one form of the test received high scores on another form of the same test. The decision to either grant or withhold a diploma might depend more on which form of the test the student took than his or her mastery of the high school curriculum.

This chapter presents a basic definition of test reliability and describes methods used in estimating the reliability or consistency of test scores. First, we describe sources of consistency and inconsistency in test scores. Next, we present a short outline of the theory of test reliability. Finally, we discuss methods of estimating the reliability of test scores, particularly as they relate to the different sources of consistency or inconsistency described in the first section of this chapter. Questions regarding the use of information about test reliability and factors affecting reliability are discussed in Chapter 6.

SOURCES OF CONSISTENCY AND INCONSISTENCY IN TEST SCORES

In understanding factors that affect the consistency of test scores, it is useful to ask, "Why do test scores vary at all?" For example, if I give a spelling test to a group of fourth graders, what factors are likely to lead to variability in test scores? Thorndike (1949) has prepared a list of possible sources of variability in scores on a particular test. This list, presented in Table 5-1, is a useful starting place for understanding factors that may affect the consistency or inconsistency of test scores.

The first category of factors that affect test scores lists some lasting and general characteristics of individuals. For example, we would expect some children to do consistently better than others on a spelling test because they are good spellers or because they are skillful in following instructions and in taking tests. The second category lists lasting but specific characteristics of individuals. For example, some children who are generally poor spellers might nevertheless know how to spell many of the particular words included in the test. If these children were given another test, made up of different words, they might receive very different scores. The third category lists temporary but general characteristics of individuals. For example, a child who is ill or very tired might do poorly this time around but might receive much higher scores if he or she is tested when healthy and well rested. The fourth category in the table lists temporary and specific characteristics of individuals. For example, the test may contain the words *Baltimore, Milwaukee,* and *Seattle.* A child who took the test shortly after looking at the sports section of the newspaper might have a temporary advantage on such a test. The fifth category lists some aspects of the testing situation that could lead to inconsistency in test scores. For example, if half the class took the test in a noisy, poorly lit room, we might expect their scores to be lower than they would have obtained under normal conditions. Finally, the sixth

TABLE 5-1 POSSIBLE SOURCES OF VARIABILITY IN SCORES ON A PARTICULAR TEST

I. Lasting and general characteristics of the individual
  A. Level of ability on one or more general traits, which operate in a number of tests
  B. General skills and techniques of taking tests ("test-wiseness" or "test naivete")
  C. General ability to comprehend instructions

II. Lasting but specific characteristics of the individual
  A. Specific to the test as a whole
    1. Individual level of ability on traits required in this test but not in others
    2. Knowledge and skills specific to particular form of test items
    3. Stable response sets (e.g. to mark A options more frequently than other options of multiple-choice items, to mark true-false items "true" when undecided)
  B. Specific to particular test items
    1. The "chance" element determining whether the individual does or does not know a particular fact
    2. Item types with which various examinees are unequally familiar (cf. item II.A.2 above)

III. Temporary but general characteristics of the individual (factors affecting performance on many or all tests at a particular time)
  A. Health
  B. Fatigue
  C. Motivation
  D. Emotional strain
  E. "Test-wiseness" (partly lasting; cf. item I.B. above)
  F. Understanding of mechanics of testing
  G. External conditions of heat, light, ventilation, etc.

IV. Temporary and specific characteristics of the individual
  A. Specific to a test as a whole
    1. Comprehension of the specific test task
    2. Specific tricks or techniques of dealing with the particular test materials
    3. Level of practice on the specific skills involved (especially in psychomotor tests)
    4. Momentary "set" for a particular test
  B. Specific to particular test items
    1. Fluctuations and idiosyncrasies of human memory
    2. Unpredictable fluctuations in attention or accuracy, superimposed upon the general level of performance characteristic of the individual

V. Systematic or change factors affecting the administration of the test or the appraisal of test performance
  A. Conditions of testing: adherence to time limits, freedom from distractions, clarity of instructions, etc.
  B. Interaction of personality, sex, or race of examiner with that of examinee that facilitates or inhibits performance
  C. Unreliability or bias in grading or rating performance

VI. Variance not otherwise accounted for (chance)
  A. Luck in selection of answers by sheer guessing
  B. Momentary distraction

Source: Adapted from Thorndike, R. L. (1949). *Personnel Selection*. Copyright © 1949 by John Wiley & Sons, Inc. Reproduced by permission.

category in the table lists some chance factors that may affect test scores. Some of the variability in scores will be due strictly to luck.

In most testing applications, we are interested in lasting and general characteristics of persons, such as spelling ability. Thus, in most cases the first category in Table 5-1 represents a source of consistency in test scores, and all of the remaining categories represent sources of unwanted inconsistency. However, this breakdown is not always quite so simple. For example, we might be interested in measuring a specific characteristic, such as a child's ability to spell *Baltimore* on May 30, 1993. In this case, we might conclude that elements from categories I, II, III, and IV would all contribute to consistency in measurement and that inconsistency in the child's performance on that particular item at the particular time the child is tested would largely be determined by elements from categories V and VI. The determination of whether each of the factors listed in the table contributes to consistency or inconsistency in measurement thus depends largely on what one is trying to measure. As will be seen in the sections that follow, the definition of reliability, as well as the methods used to estimate the reliability of test scores, ultimately depends on one's definition of precisely what attribute is being measured and of the sources of inconsistency in the measurement of that attribute.

GENERAL MODEL OF RELIABILITY

A perfect measure would consistently assign numbers to the attributes of persons according to some well-specified rule (e.g., if John is more anxious than Teresa, he should receive a higher score on an anxiety test than she does). In practice, our measures are never perfectly consistent. Theories of test reliability have been developed to estimate the effects of inconsistency on the accuracy of psychological measurement. The basic starting point for almost all theories of test reliability is the idea that test scores reflect the influence of two sorts of factors:

1. factors that contribute to consistency: stable characteristics of the individual or the attribute one is trying to measure
2. factors that contribute to inconsistency: features of the individual or the situation that can affect test scores but have nothing to do with the attribute being measured

This conceptual breakdown is typically represented by the simple equation

$$\begin{matrix} \text{Observed Test} \\ \text{Score} \end{matrix} = \begin{matrix} \text{True} \\ \text{Score} \end{matrix} + \begin{matrix} \text{Errors of} \\ \text{Measurement} \end{matrix} \qquad [5\text{-}1]$$

Or, more succinctly,

$$X = T + e \qquad [5\text{-}2]$$

where

$$X = \text{score on the test}$$
$$T = \text{true score}$$
$$e = \text{error of measurement}$$

There is an important distinction between the concept of true score as applied in Formula 5-2 and the notion of ultimate truth or perfect measurement. Thus, true scores on a measure of anxiety are *not* an indication of a person's "true" or "real" level of anxiety. Rather, the true score represents a combination of all the factors that lead to consistency in the measurement of anxiety (Cronbach, Gleser, Nanda & Rajaratnam, 1972; Stanley, 1971). As a result, the components that make up the true score part of a test will vary, depending upon what is being measured. Consider, for example, a test of mechanical aptitude given to a U.S. Air Force mechanic in a noisy, poorly lit room. As indicated in Table 5-2, the stressful conditions of measurement could be considered as either part of the true score or part of the error component, depending on whether the test is intended to measure mechanical aptitude in general or mechanical performance under stressful conditions.

Errors in measurement represent discrepancies between scores obtained on tests and the corresponding true scores. Thus,

$$e = X - T \qquad\qquad [5\text{-}3]$$

The goal of reliability theory is to estimate errors in measurement and to suggest ways of improving tests so that errors are minimized.

The central assumption of reliability theory is that measurement errors are essentially random. This does not mean that errors arise from random or mysterious processes. On the contrary, a sizable negative error in a score a person received on the Graduate Record Examination (GRE) could easily be accounted for if it were known that the person (a) had stayed up all night, (b) had a hangover, (c) was sitting next to a noisy air conditioner during the test, and (d) used the wrong part of the form to mark the answers. For any individual, an error in measurement is not a completely random event. However, across a large number of individuals the causes of measurement error are assumed to be so varied and complex that measurement errors *act* as random variables. Thus, a theory that assumes that measurement errors are essentially random may provide a pretty good description of their effects.

If errors have the essential characteristics of random variables, then it is reasonable to assume that errors are equally likely to be positive or negative and that they are not correlated with true scores or with errors on other tests. That is, it is assumed that

TABLE 5-2   DIFFERENT DEFINITIONS OF TRUE SCORE WHEN AN APTITUDE TEST IS GIVEN UNDER STRESSFUL CONDITIONS

	Test is used to measure	
	Mechanical performance in general	**Mechanical performance under stressful conditions**
Individuals' Mechanical Aptitude	True Score	True Score
Stressful Conditions of Measurement	Error	True Score
All Other Irrelevant Sources of Variability	Error	Error

1. Mean error of measurement $= 0$.
2. True scores and errors are uncorrelated: $r_{te} = 0$.
3. Errors on different measures are uncorrelated: $r_{e1e2} = 0$.

On the basis of these three assumptions, an extensive theory of test reliability has been developed (Gulliksen, 1950; Lord & Novick, 1968). Several results can be derived from this theory that have important implications for measurement. For example, Table 5-1 listed sources of variability in test scores that might contribute to the consistency or inconsistency of measurement. Reliability theory provides a similar breakdown by showing that the variance of obtained scores is simply the sum of the variance of true scores plus the variance of errors of measurement. That is,

$$\sigma_X^2 = \sigma_T^2 + \sigma_e^2 \qquad [5\text{-}4]$$

In effect, Formula 5-4 suggests that test scores vary as the result of two factors: (a) variability in true scores and (b) variability due to errors of measurement. If errors are responsible for much of the variability observed in test scores, test scores will be inconsistent; if the test is given again, scores may not remain stable. On the other hand, if errors of measurement have little effect on test scores, the test reflects mainly those consistent aspects of performance we have labelled true score.

The *reliability coefficient* (r_{xx}) provides an index of the relative influence of true and error scores on obtained test scores.[1] In its general form, the reliability coefficient is defined as the ratio of true score variance to the total variance of test scores. That is,

$$r_{xx} = \frac{\sigma_T^2}{\sigma_X^2} \qquad [5\text{-}5]$$

or, equivalently,

$$r_{xx} = \frac{\sigma_T^2}{\sigma_T^2 + \sigma_e^2} \qquad [5\text{-}6]$$

There are several interpretations of the reliability coefficient. Perhaps the most straightforward interpretation is that r_{xx} indicates the proportion of variance in test scores that is due to, or accounted for by, variability in true scores.

SIMPLE METHODS OF ESTIMATING RELIABILITY

The goal of estimating reliability is to determine how much of the variability in test scores is due to errors in measurement and how much is due to variability in true scores. The *parallel test* model suggests a strategy for accomplishing this goal. According to the parallel test model, it might be possible to develop two forms of a test that are equivalent in the sense that a person's true score on form A would be identical to his or her true

---

[1]Reliability theory deals with population parameters (e.g., ρ_{xy}) rather than sample statistics (e.g., r_{xy}). However, for the sake of simplicity, reliability formulas are presented in terms of r rather than ρ.

score on form B. If both forms of the test were administered to a number of people, differences between scores on form A and form B could be due only to errors in measurement. Thus, if there were large differences between scores on the two forms, one would conclude that measurement errors were a major source of variability in test scores. On the other hand, if scores on both tests were highly similar, one would conclude that measurement errors were small and that the test was highly reliable.[2]

The parallel test model provides a conceptual solution for estimating reliability but does not necessarily provide a *practical* solution. The reason for this is that strictly parallel tests are difficult to develop. Four practical strategies have been developed that incorporate many features of the parallel test method and that provide workable methods of estimating test reliability:

1. test-retest methods
2. alternate forms methods
3. split-half methods
4. internal consistency methods

The methods described here are most likely to be useful in situations where one is interested in measuring lasting, general characteristics of individuals, such as abilities or traits. In these situations, the attributes of the persons being measured represent the sole source of true score variance, and all other factors that affect measurement combine to represent the error component. As will be discussed in a later section, this sort of testing application is typical, but not universal. In many situations, the tester must identify explicitly the purpose and the uses of measurement in order to determine which factors affect true scores and error. In more complex testing applications, reliability theories that break a measure down into true score and random error components may not be sufficient; a more general and complex theory is presented later in this chapter. Nevertheless, for many testing applications, simple methods based upon classical reliability theory may be quite useful. Several of these methods are presented below.

Test-Retest Method

The test-retest method is one of the oldest and, at least at first glance, one of the most sensible methods of estimating the reliability of test scores. Reliability is concerned with the consistency of test scores; the test-retest method directly assesses the degree to which test scores are consistent from one test administration to the next. The test-retest method involves (a) administering a test to a group of individuals, (b) readministering that same test to the same group at some later time, and (c) correlating the first set of scores with the second. The correlation between scores on the first test and scores on the retest is used to estimate the reliability of the test.

The rationale behind this method of estimating reliability is disarmingly simple.

---

[2]The basic equations of reliability theory can also be derived from several models that do not depend on the concept of parallel tests (Lord & Novick, 1968; Nunnally, 1982).

Since the same test is administered twice and every test is parallel with itself, differences between scores on the test and scores on the retest should be due solely to measurement error. This sort of argument is quite probably true for many physical measurements. For example, if a tape measure is used to measure the length of a room and is then used to measure the same room a week later, any difference between the two measurements is likely to be entirely due to measurement error. Unfortunately, this argument is often inappropriate for psychological measurement, since it is often impossible to consider the second administration of a test a parallel measure to the first. Thus it may be inaccurate to treat a test-retest correlation as a measure of reliability.

There are several reasons why the second administration of a psychological test might yield systematically different scores than the first administration. First, the characteristic or attribute that is being measured may change between the first test and the retest. Consider, for example, a reading test that is administered in September to a class of third graders and then readministered in June. We would expect some change in children's reading ability over that span of time; a low test-retest correlation might reflect real changes in the attribute measured by the test. Second, the experience of taking the test itself can change a person's true score; this is referred to as *reactivity*. For example, students who take a geography test may look up answers they were unsure of after taking the test, thus changing their true knowledge of geography. Likewise, the process of completing an anxiety inventory could serve to increase a person's level of anxiety. Thus, the first test may serve as a catalyst that causes substantial change in true scores from one administration to the next. Third, one must be concerned with carry-over effects, particularly if the interval between test and retest is short. When retested, people may remember their original answers, which could affect their answers the second time around.

In addition to the theoretical problems inherent in the test-retest method, there is a practical limitation to this method of estimating reliability. The test-retest method requires two test administrations. Since testing can be time consuming and expensive, retesting solely for the purpose of estimating reliability may be impractical.

It is common to distinguish between reliability, which is the ratio of true to observed variance, and temporal stability, which refers to the consistency of test scores over time. If true scores are likely to change over time, this distinction is both theoretically and practically important. Thus, test-retest correlations are often thought of as stability coefficients rather than reliability coefficients. However, even when this distinction is drawn, there are problems with the test-retest technique. For example, it is not clear whether carry-over effects should be regarded as sources of measurement error or as sources of real stability (or instability) in measurement. Nor is it clear whether reactivity effects always contribute to true scores or to error. It could be argued that carry-over and reactivity effects are a natural aspect of the attribute being measured and should be taken into account in estimating stability. On the other hand, these effects may inflate (or deflate) one's estimate of the true stability of test scores, thus yielding inaccurate estimates of both reliability and stability.

The test-retest method is most useful when one is interested in the long-term stability of a measure. For example, research on the accuracy of personnel selection tests is concerned with the ability of the test to predict long-term job performance. Research in this area has therefore focused on the temporal stability of job performance measures (Schmidt & Hunter, 1977). The argument here is that short-term variations in job performance represent error when the purpose of the research is to predict performance over the long term.

Alternate Forms Method

The alternate forms method of estimating reliability is, on the surface, the closest approximation to the method suggested by the parallel tests model. The key to this method is the development of alternate test forms that are, to the highest degree possible, equivalent in terms of content, response processes, and statistical characteristics. For example, alternate forms exist for several tests of general intelligence; these alternate forms commonly are regarded as equivalent tests. The alternate forms method of estimating test reliability involves (a) administering one form of the test (e.g., form A) to a group of individuals; (b) at some later time, administering an alternate form of the same test (e.g., form B) to the same group of individuals; and (c) correlating scores on form A with scores on form B. The correlation between scores on the two alternate forms is used to estimate the reliability of the test.

The alternate forms method provides a partial solution to many of the problems inherent in test-retest methods. For example, since the two forms of the test are different, carry-over effects are less of a problem, although remembering answers previously given to a *similar* set of questions may affect responses to the present set of questions. Reactivity effects are also partially controlled; although taking the first test may change responses to the second test, it is reasonable to assume that the effect will not be as strong with alternate forms as with two administrations of the same test. The alternate forms method also may allow one to partially control for real changes over time in the attribute being measured. Since carry-over effects are less of a problem here than in the test-retest method, it may not be necessary to use a long interval between test administrations. It is feasible to administer the second form immediately after the first, which cannot be done in most test-retest studies.

Although the alternate forms method avoids many of the problems inherent in the test-retest method, there are still many drawbacks to this technique. For example, since two separate test administrations are required, the alternate forms method could be as expensive and impractical as the test-retest method. Second, it may be difficult and expensive to develop several alternate forms of a test. It is questionable that the expense involved in developing alternate forms and in administering two tests rather than one is justified solely for the purpose of assessing the reliability of the test. In addition, it may be difficult, if not impossible, to guarantee that two alternate forms of a test are, in fact, parallel measures. Thus, if alternate forms are poorly constructed, one might obtain low reliability estimates strictly as a function of the lack of equivalence between the two alternate forms.

Split-Half Methods

Split-half methods of estimating reliability provide a simple solution to the two practical problems that plague the alternate forms method: (a) the difficulty in developing alternate forms and (b) the need for two separate test administrations. The reasoning behind split-half methods is quite straightforward. The simplest way to create two alternate forms of a test is to split the existing test in half and use the two halves as alternate forms. The split-half method of estimating reliability thus involves (a) administering a test to a group of individuals, (b) splitting the test in half, and (c) correlating scores on one half of the test with scores on the other half. The correlation between these two split halves is used in estimating the reliability of the test.[3]

The split-half method avoids many of the theoretical and practical problems inherent in test-retest and alternate forms methods. First, this method allows reliability to be estimated without administering two different tests or administering the same test twice. Thus, whenever a multi-item test is administered, the split-half method could be used to estimate reliability. Since there is only one test administration, carry-over effects, reactivity effects, and especially the effects of change over time on true scores are minimized. Inconsistencies in scores obtained on two different halves of a test are therefore likely to reflect inconsistencies in responses to the test itself, rather than changes in the individual that may have occurred between administrations of two alternate forms, or between a test and retest.

There are several ways of splitting a test to estimate reliability. For example, a 40-item vocabulary test could be split into two subtests, the first one made up of items 1 through 20 and the second make up of items 21 through 40. One might suspect, however, that responses to the first half would be systematically different from responses to the second half, so that this split would not provide a very good estimate of reliability. For example, many vocabulary tests start with the easiest items, then become progressively more difficult. In addition, a person taking the test might be more fatigued during the second half of the test. In splitting a test, the two halves would need to be as similar as possible, both in terms of their content and in terms of the probable state of the respondent. The simplest method of approximating this goal is to adopt an *odd-even split*, in which the odd-numbered items form one half of the test, and the even-numbered items form the other. This guarantees that each half will contain an equal number of items from the beginning, middle, and end of the original test.

The fact that there are many ways a test could potentially be split is the greatest weakness of the split-half method. Consider, for example, the six-item test shown in Table 5-3. There are ten different ways that this test could be split,[4] and each split yields a somewhat different reliability estimate. In other words, the correlation between half A and half B may vary, depending on how the test is split. The question is, Which is *the* reliability of the test? Although the idea of forming an odd-even split generally makes sense, this particular method of splitting the test is somewhat arbitrary; there is no guarantee that the reliability coefficient obtained from this particular split will be the most reasonable or accurate estimate of the relative contribution of true scores and errors of measurement to the variability of test scores. Since it is difficult to make a strong argument in favor of one particular method of splitting a given test over another, it is difficult to decide which split-half reliability estimate to use.

---

[3]As we will note in Chapter 6, this correlation estimates the reliability of each half-test. Scores on the entire test will be more reliable than scores on either half; a correlation formula is used to estimate the reliability of the total test, given the correlation between the split halves.

[4]The number of possible splits rises geometrically as the length of the test increases. There are, for example, 126 different ways of splitting a ten-item test into two five-item halves.

TABLE 5-3 TEN POSSIBLE WAYS OF SPLITTING A SIX-ITEM TEST

Test items, half A	Test items, half B	Reliability estimate
1,2,3	4,5,6	.64
1,2,4	3,5,6	.68
1,2,5	3,4,6	.82
1,2,6	3,4,5	.79
1,3,4	2,5,6	.88
1,4,5	2,3,6	.81
1,5,6	2,3,4	.82
2,3,5	1,4,6	.72
2,4,5	1,3,6	.71
2,4,6	1,3,5	.74

Internal Consistency Methods

Internal consistency methods of estimating test reliability appear to be quite different from the methods presented so far. Internal consistency methods estimate the reliability of a test based solely upon the number of items in the test (k) and the average intercorrelation among test items ($\bar{r}_{ij}$). These two factors can be combined in the following formula to estimate the reliability of the test:

$$r_{xx} = \frac{k(\bar{r}_{ij})}{1 + (k - 1)\, \bar{r}_{ij}} \qquad [5\text{-}7]$$

Thus, the internal consistency method involves (a) administering a test to a group of individuals, (b) computing the correlations among all items and computing the average of those intercorrelations, and (c) using Formula 5-7, or an equivalent formula, to estimate reliability.[5] This formula gives a standardized estimate; raw score formulas that take into account the variance of different test items may provide slightly different estimates of internal consistency reliability.

There are both mathematical and conceptual ways of demonstrating the links between internal consistency methods and the methods of estimating reliability discussed so far. First, internal consistency methods are mathematically linked to the split-half method. In particular, *coefficient alpha,* which represents the most widely used and most general form of internal consistency estimate, represents the mean reliability coefficient one would obtain from all possible split halves [Cortina (In press) notes that alpha is equal to the mean of the split halves defined by formulas from Rulon (1939) and Flanagan (1937)]. In other words, if every possible split-half reliability coefficient for a 30-item test were computed, the average of those reliabilities would be equal to coefficient alpha. The difference between the split-half method and the internal consistency method is, for the most part, a difference in unit of analysis. Split-half methods compare one half-test to another; internal consistency estimates compare each item to every other item.

[5]Several similar formulas have been developed by Kuder and Richardson (1937), Cronbach (1951), and others.

In understanding the link between internal consistency and the general concept of reliability, it is useful to note that internal consistency methods suggest a fairly simple answer to the question, "Why is a test reliable?" Remember that internal consistency estimates are a function of (a) the number of test items and (b) the average intercorrelation among those test items. If we think of each test item as an observation of behavior, internal consistency estimates suggest that reliability is a function of (a) the number of observations one makes and (b) the extent to which each item represents an observation of the same thing observed by other test items. For example, if you wanted to determine how good a bowler someone was, you would obtain more reliable information by observing the person bowl many frames than you would by watching the person roll the ball once. You would also obtain a more reliable estimate of that person's skill at bowling from ten observations of the person bowling in typical circumstances than if you watched him bowl three times on a normal alley, then watched him bowl five times in a high-pressure tournament, and then watched him bowl twice on a warped alley. If every item on the test measures essentially the same thing as all other items, and if the number of items is large, internal consistency methods suggest that the test will be reliable.

Reliability Estimates and Error

Each of the four methods of estimating test reliability implies that different sources of variability in test scores might contribute to errors of measurement. Some of these are listed in Table 5-4. As the table shows, both the split-half and the internal consistency methods define measurement error strictly in terms of consistency or inconsistency in the content of a test. Test-retest and alternate forms methods, both of which require two test administrations, define measurement error in terms of three general factors: (a) the consistency or inconsistency of test content (in the test-retest method, content is always consistent); (b) changes in examinees over time; and (c) the effects of the first test on responses to the second test. Thus, while each method is concerned with reliability, each defines true score and error in a somewhat different fashion.

The principal advantage of internal consistency methods is their practicality. Since only one test administration is required, it is possible to estimate internal consistency

TABLE 5-4   SOURCES OF VARIABILITY THAT CONTRIBUTE TO ERRORS IN MEASUREMENT

	Method of estimating reliability			
	Test-retest	**Alternate forms**	**Split-half**	**Internal consistency**
Content Factors		Inconsistency of Test Content Nonparallel Tests	Inconsistency of Test Content Nonparallel Halves	Inconsistency of Test Content
Effects of First Test on Examinee Temporal Factors	Reactivity Carry-over True Change over Time	Reactivity Carry-over True Change over Time		

reliability every time the test is given. Although split-half methods can be computationally simpler, the widespread availability of computers makes it easy to compute coefficient alpha, regardless of the test length or the number of examinees. It therefore is possible to compute coefficient alpha whenever a test is used in a new situation or population. A low value for alpha could indicate that scores on the test will not be highly consistent and therefore may form a poor basis for describing the person or for making decisions about the person. However, as noted in the next section, an internal consistency estimate does not necessarily represent *the* reliability of a test. Indeed, test reliability often depends more on what one is trying to do with test scores than on the scores themselves.

THE GENERALIZABILITY OF TEST SCORES

Reliability theory tends to classify all the factors that may affect test scores into two components, true scores and random errors of measurement. Although this sort of broad classification may be useful for studying physical measurements, it is not necessarily the most useful way of thinking about psychological measurement (Lumsden, 1976). The most serious weakness in applying classical reliability theory is probably the concept of error. As Table 5-4 suggests, the factors that determine the amount of measurement error are different for internal consistency methods than for test-retest or alternate forms methods. We typically think of the reliability coefficient as a ratio of true score to true score plus error, but if the makeup of the true score and error parts of a measure change when we change our estimation procedures, something is seriously wrong.

The theory of generalizability presented by Cronbach and his colleagues (1972) represents an alternate approach to measuring and studying the consistency of test scores. In reliability theory, the central question is, "How much random error is there in my measures?" In generalizability theory, the focus is on our ability to generalize from one set of measures (e.g., a score on an essay test) to a set of other plausible measures (e.g., the same essay graded by other teachers). The central question in generalizability theory is, "What are the conditions over which I can generalize?" or "Under what sorts of conditions would I expect either similar or different results than the ones obtained here?" Generalizability theory attacks this question by systematically studying the many sources of consistency and inconsistency in test scores.

Suppose we wish to measure an individual's need for dominance, using a projective test administered by an individual clinician. We are concerned about the possibility that test results would be unreliable, and so we have three different psychologists test the person and, furthermore, repeat the test three times with each psychologist. Scores from such a procedure might look something like those depicted in Table 5-5 and Figure 5-1.

Is this test reliable? It depends on what we mean by reliability. For example, both psychologists B and C give fairly consistent scores over time, but C consistently differs from psychologists A and B. The three psychologists agree best in March but agree less well in January or May.

It would be possible to deal with the data in Table 5-5 using classical reliability theory. That is, we could simply treat the inconsistencies in test scores as random error. However, it might be more informative to examine systematic differences between psy-

TABLE 5-5   TEST RESULTS FOR THREE DIFFERENT PSYCHOLOGISTS, EACH
OF WHOM TESTS THE INDIVIDUAL THREE TIMES

Time of testing	Psychologist			
	A	B	C	Average
January	77*	88	70	83
March	86	86	74	82
May	92	84	72	82.6
Average	85	86	72	

*Note: Scores on this hypothetical test range from 1 to 100.

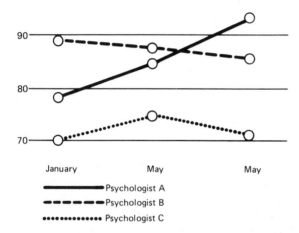

Figure 5-1   Test Scores from Table
5-5

chologists or between times, and to use this information describing circumstances under which one can or cannot generalize test scores. The statistical technique *analysis of variance* [see Cronbach et al. (1972) and Maxwell and Delaney (1990) for detailed descriptions of this method] provides a method for measuring the systematic effects of several variables (psychologists, times, etc.) on the consistency of measurements.

The analysis of variance provides statistical estimates of the variability in test scores associated with systematic differences in the ratings assigned by psychologists, and differences in the ratings obtained in January, March, and May. Figure 5-2 illustrates the breakdown of the variability of test scores in Table 5-5 into systematic and unsystematic sources. Average test scores in January, March, and May were quite similar. Therefore, the variability due to the time of testing is small. On the other hand, there were consistent differences between psychologist C and psychologists A and B. As a result, a larger proportion of the variability in scores is associated with differences between psychologists. Finally, a good deal of the variability is not systematically associated either with the psychologists or the time of measurement.

Analysis of the variance in test scores suggests that scores can be more accurately generalized over time (in the table, average scores obtained at each measurement were quite similar) than other psychologists (psychologists differed in terms of their average scores). Thus, the question, "Is this test reliable?" would be answered differently if one is

VARIABILITY OF TEST SCORES

Figure 5-2 Systematic and Asystematic Variability in the Test Scores Shown in Table 5-5

concerned with the stability of scores over time rather than with the stability of scores obtained by different psychologists.

Advantages of generalizability theory. Generalizability theory has been the focus of a great deal of research, but, until fairly recently it was not often used to deal with practical testing problems. Several reviews and texts (e.g., Brennan, 1983; Shavelson & Webb, 1981; Shavelson, Webb & Rowley, 1989) have brought generalizability theory to the attention of a wider audience, and the techniques of generalizability theory are being applied in a wider variety of research areas. We believe that the primary advantage of generalizability theory over the classical theory is conceptual rather than statistical. That is, generalizability theory forces you to think of reliability as a characteristic of the *use* of test scores rather than as a characteristic of the scores themselves. For example, this theory recognizes that you can often make more reliable decisions about peoples' *relative* standing (e.g., comparing two people in terms of verbal ability) than about their *absolute* level on a trait or attribute. Thus, as we have noted earlier, the same set of test scores might have several different levels of reliability, depending on the intended use of the scores. We believe that the uses of test scores are much more important than the scores themselves, and that generalizability theory is therefore a considerable improvement over the classical theory of reliability that has dominated the history of psychometrics.

The second major advantage of generalizability theory is that it provides answers to a variety of practical questions that cannot be answered using classical reliability theory. For example, companies that interview job applicants often have the appliant talk to several individuals, each of whom asks several questions. One company might use four people who each ask five questions, whereas another company might use two people who each ask ten questions. Generalizability theory could be used to determine which strategy for combining the number of persons and questions would yield the most reliable assessments.

CRITICAL DISCUSSION:
Generalizability and Reliability Theory

Cronbach and others (1972) note that classical reliability theory, which breaks test scores down into true score and random error components, is simply a special case of generalizability theory. The difference between the two theories is that the generalizability approach recognizes that error is not always random and that it often is useful to identify specific, systematic sources of inconsistency in measurement. Generalizability theory identifies both systematic and random sources of inconsistency that may contribute to errors of measurement.[6]

Classical theory is probably most useful in situations in which well-developed tests are given under highly standardized conditions. For example, college entrance examinations, such as the SAT, are given under nearly identical conditions nationwide. As long as test administration procedures are followed, it is unlikely that the location, the test administrator, or the time of year at which the test is administered will have substantial effects on test scores. Inconsistencies between one administration and the next are likely to be small, and when they do occur, they are likely to be a function of the test itself and of the individuals responding to the test. Thus, the assumption that consistency in test scores is due to the true score component, and that inconsistencies reflect essentially random error, is probably reasonable.

The more complex methods associated with generalizability theory are likely to be more useful when (a) the conditions of measurement are likely to affect test scores or (b) test scores are to be used for several different purposes. For example, in almost every type of measurement involving human judgment (e.g., interviews, ratings, many clinical tests), there is the possibility of bias. Some interviewers give higher scores to men than to women; attractive people often receive more favorable ratings on a number of dimensions than unattractive people; a clinician whose orientation is Freudian may give a different interpretation of a specific incident than a behaviorally oriented clinician. The point is, human judges could be considered "conditions of measurement," and in a wide variety of circumstances one might expect systematic differences in human judgment. We might also expect that measures of some attributes and traits will be more strongly affected by the physical conditions of measurement than others. For example, a person might receive different scores on a color discrimination test taken in a room with fluorescent light than in a room with natural light. Finally, we might expect some measures to be more stable over time than others (e.g., measures of basic values as opposed to opinions regarding the outcome of a future sporting event). If scores differ systematically according to when, where, or how the test was taken, these differences will affect the generalizability of test scores. They are not, however, random sources of error, and test theories that treat them as such will lead to erroneous conclusions.

Generalizability theory encourages us to ask questions such as, "In what situations is this test reliable?" rather than simply asking whether or not a test is any good. According to this theory, a test could be reliable for some purposes, but quite unreliable for others. Generalizability theory focuses our attention on what we wish to *do* with a test, rather than on the test itself.

SUMMARY

Although perfect measures of physical and psychological characteristics would be highly desirable, error-free measurement is impossible; *all* tests and methods of measurement are subject to some degree of error. Reliability theory provides a method for defining and estimating measurement error in specific testing applications.

---

[6]When there are no systematic differences in test scores associated with conditions of measurement (e.g., psychologists, time), classical theory and generalizability theory are mathematically identical.

In its most basic form, the classic theory of reliability states that all measures are made up of two independent components, namely, true score and error. The reliability coefficient is simply the percentage of the total variance in test scores that is due to the true score component. A variety of methods have evolved to estimate the reliability of specific tests and measures. These might involve multiple administrations either of the same or of equivalent tests, or they might be based on a single test administration. Internal consistency estimates are the simplest and most practical, and they are the most widely used.

Generalizability theory represents a sophisticated elaboration of the ideas present in the classic theory. Analyses of the generalizability of test scores begin with a description of the intended uses of test scores and the conditions of measurement; they proceed to define the true score and error components in terms of these two factors. The classic theory of reliability, which dominated the field for over 70 years, can be thought of as a special case of the broader theory of generalizability. Although analyses of test reliability are still conducted along the lines laid out in the classic theory, generalizability theory is becoming increasingly popular and is likely to replace the more traditional approach as the method of choice for defining and estimating reliability.

CHAPTER 6

USING AND INTERPRETING INFORMATION ABOUT TEST RELIABILITY

In the previous chapter, we discussed different methods of estimating the reliability of test scores. In this chapter, we show how information about reliability can be used in evaluating, interpreting, and improving psychological tests. First we discuss the relationship between reliability and the accuracy of test scores. While it may be obvious that reliable tests are more accurate than unreliable tests, it is difficult to describe on the basis of reliability information alone how much consistency one can expect in test scores. Next we discuss the relationship between reliability and the validity of inferences which are based on tests. Tests are used both to measure specific attributes of people and to predict their standing on important criterion variables (e.g., success in school, performance on the job), and the reliability of test scores affects the accuracy of both of these uses. We then discuss factors affecting the reliability of test scores. It is difficult to interpret reliability information accurately unless one knows *why* a test is reliable or unreliable. Finally we consider several special issues in the interpretation and use of information concerning test reliability.

USING THE RELIABILITY COEFFICIENT

The reliability coefficient provides useful information for evaluating tests. In addition to providing a general indication of the effects of true scores and error, the reliability coefficient can be used in two important ways: first, in establishing confidence intervals; and second, in estimating the effects of unreliability on the correlation between tests and criteria of interest (e.g., success in school).

The Standard Error of Measurement

The reliability coefficient provides a *relative* measure of the accuracy of test scores. Thus, a test with a reliability of .90 is more reliable than a test with a reliability of .80. However, the reliability coefficient does not provide an indication, in absolute terms, of how accurate test scores really are. For example, suppose a psychologist measured a child's intelligence and obtained a score of 110. Could we be confident that the score obtained was really higher than the average score expected on the test (100), or would we expect test scores to vary more than 10 points simply because of measurement error? Even if we knew that the test was highly reliable (e.g., a reliability coefficient of .93), we would not be able to answer this question. The reliability coefficient simply does not reveal, in concrete terms, how much variability should be expected on the basis of measurement error. In order to describe the accuracy of test scores concretely, we need to know more than the reliability of the test; we must also know the size of the *standard error of measurement*.

The standard error of measurement (SEM) is a function of two factors: (a) the reliability of the test (r_{xx}) and (b) the variability of test scores (σ_x). Thus, the standard error of measurement is given by

$$\text{SEM} = \sigma_x \sqrt{1 - r_{xx}} \qquad [6\text{-}1]$$

The standard error of measurement provides a measure of the variability in test scores expected on the basis of measurement errors. For example, imagine that a woman with an IQ of 100 was tested repeatedly with a standard intelligence test. Since tests are not perfectly reliable, she would not receive a score of 100 every time; sometimes she would receive a score higher than 100, and sometimes she would receive a lower score. The total distribution of her test scores might look something like the one shown in Figure 6-1. The standard error of measurement corresponds to the standard deviation of this distribution. In other words, the standard error of measurement indicates how much variability in test scores can be expected as a result of measurement error.

The standard error of measurement can be used to form confidence intervals, which in turn provide a concrete indication of how accurate test scores really are. For example,

| 85 | 90 | 95 | 100 | 105 | 110 | 115 |

Standard Error of Measurement = 4.7

Figure 6-1 Distribution of Scores Obtained by Repeatedly Testing a Woman with an IQ of 100

the scores shown in the figure have a mean of 100 and a standard error of 4.7. In a normal distribution, 95 percent of all scores fall within 1.96 standard deviations of the mean. Thus, we can form a confidence interval around the mean by multiplying the standard error by 1.96. For this woman, whose true IQ is 100, we would expect 95 percent of her test scores to fall within 9.2 (4.7 × 1.96 = 9.2) points of the mean. Thus, we would expect 95 percent of the test scores received by this woman to fall in the 90.8 to 109.2 range.

In this example, we formed a confidence interval around the mean of many (hypothetical) measurements. In most applications we have only one test score and we wish to know how much confidence could be placed in that particular score. This is done by forming a confidence interval around the person's *estimated true score* (Lord & Novick, 1968). For example, if a person received a score of 96 on the test illustrated in the figure, we would estimate his or her true score, then place confidence intervals around that estimate, rather than placing a confidence interval around the observed score. This distinction is important because of the phenomenon of *regression toward the mean:* Because of measurement error, the variability of test scores is larger than the variability of true scores. In other words, test scores are generally farther from the mean than true scores. For example, if a person receives a score of 80 on an intelligence test (with a mean of 100), his or her true score is probably larger than 80; a person with an observed score of 110 will receive an estimated true score between 100 and 110. Figure 6-2 illustrates the relationship between observed scores and estimated true scores for this hypothetical test.[1]

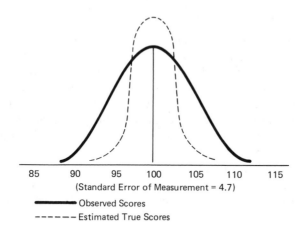

85   90   95   100   105   110   115
(Standard Error of Measurement = 4.7)
━━━━ Observed Scores
╌╌╌╌ Estimated True Scores

Figure 6-2 Distributions of Observed Scores and Estimated True Scores for a Hypothetical Test of General Intelligence

The estimated true score, together with the standard error of measurement, provides a concrete description of the accuracy of test scores. For example, suppose that a person received a score of 90 on the test illustrated in Figure 6-2. Suppose further that our best estimate (obtained from a regression equation) of this person's true score was 93. We could then be 95 percent confident that his or her actual true score falls within 9.2 points (4.7 × 1.96) of this score. In other words, if a person receives a score of 90, we can be confident that his or her true score falls within the range of 83.8 to 102.2. If the

[1]Methods of estimating true scores are discussed in Cronbach et al. (1972) and in Lord and Novick (1968).

standard error of the test were larger, the range in which we could be confident that true scores will fall would also be larger. For example, if the standard error was 7.5, the confidence interval for a test score of 90 would be 78.2 to 107.8.

The principal drawback of using the standard error to describe the accuracy of the test scores received by an individual is the fact that measurement errors are not always equally large for all test scores. On the contrary, it is generally assumed that measurement errors are small for extreme scores and largest for moderate scores. Ferguson (1981) discusses methods of calculating standard errors for different score levels. These methods, however, rest on debatable assumptions and are not universally accepted (Lumsden, 1976).

Reliability and Validity

Psychological tests are never perfectly consistent or reliable. Our failure to achieve perfect reliability in psychological measurement has implications for the validity of tests, both for the validity of measurement and for the validity of predictions (and decisions) based upon test scores. In a nutshell, lack of reliability places a limit on the validity of inferences drawn from test scores. Thus, a test that is not perfectly reliable cannot be perfectly valid, either as a means of measuring attributes of a person or as a means of predicting scores on a criterion. The rationale here is simple. A valid test is one that consistently assigns to persons numbers that reflect their standing on a particular attribute. An unreliable test, which provides inconsistent scores, cannot possibly be valid.

It is important to note that tests that *are* reliable are not necessarily valid. For example, consider the five-item "test of general intelligence" shown in Table 6-1. You would expect scores on this test to be almost perfectly consistent. For example, if a person took this test in January and then again in June, he or she would almost certainly give the same answers. However, we would not accept this test as a valid measure of intelligence, nor would we expect this test to provide accurate predictions of scholastic performance. Thus, consistency in test scores is no guarantee of validity in measurement or prediction.

Less-than-perfect reliability reduces the potential validity of measures. It follows, then, that if the reliability of psychological tests were increased, the validity of those tests would also be expected to increase. The question is, How much of an increase in test validity could we expect if measurement errors were somehow reduced or eliminated?

Spearman's (1904) original motivation for developing the true score theory of reli-

---

TABLE 6-1   A "TEST OF GENERAL
INTELLIGENCE" THAT WOULD BE HIGHLY
RELIABLE BUT NOT AT ALL VALID

---

1. In what month were you born? _____
2. What is your mother's first name? _____
3. 1 + 1 = _____
4. How many days are there in a week? _____
5. Which of the following is a *triangle*? _____
   a) □ b) △ c) ○

---

ability stemmed from a question very much like the one stated above. He reasoned that measurement errors would decrease, or attenuate, the correlation between two tests, X and Y (in other words, the validity of predictions). Thus, the correlation between unreliable measures of X and Y would be lower than the actual correlation between (perfectly reliable measures of) X and Y. He developed the *correction for attenuation* as a method of estimating the actual relationship between X and Y, given the correlation between two imperfectly reliable measures of X and Y. The correction for attenuation is given by the following formula:

$$r'_{xy} = \frac{r_{xy}}{\sqrt{r_{xx} \times r_{yy}}} \qquad [6\text{-}2]$$

where

r'_{xy} = correlation between x and y (r_{xy}), corrected for attenuation
r_{xx} = reliability of x
r_{yy} = reliability of y

The correction for attenuation provides an estimate of the correlation between perfectly reliable measures of X and Y. As Table 6-2 suggests, the correction can have a substantial effect on r_{xy}, particularly when the reliabilities of X and/or Y are low.

It is now common for researchers in many areas to routinely incorporate the correction for attenuation into their work. For example, research on the validity of tests used in personnel selection usually considers the effects of limited reliability in estimating the usefulness of these tests (Hartigan & Wigdor, 1989; Schmidt & Hunter, 1977; see Chapter 18 for a discussion of validity generalization research). However, although theoretically justified, the correction for attenuation is often criticized on practical grounds. In practice, the correction almost always overestimates the actual correlation between x and y (Lumsden, 1976). In addition, the correction formula assumes the impossible: that one can develop tests with no measurement error. Rather than estimating the correlation one would obtain using perfectly reliable measures, it is often useful to estimate how much

TABLE 6-2   CORRECTION FOR ATTENUATION

Observed r_{xy}	r_{xx}	r_{yy}	Corrected r_{xy}
.30	.90	.80	.353
	.70	.60	.462
	.50	.40	.671
	.40	.30	.867
.20	.90	.80	.235
	.70	.60	.308
	.50	.40	.447
	.40	.30	.578
.10	.90	.80	.117
	.70	.60	.154
	.50	.40	.223
	.40	.30	.289

improvement one would expect in r_{xy} if the reliability of either or both tests could be improved by a specific amount. For example, suppose that r_{xy} is equal to .40 for two tests with reliabilities of .70 and .75, respectively. How high would we expect the correlation between x and y to be if we could improve the reliabilities of each test to .90? Formula 6-3 is used to answer this question. The effect of changing the reliability of one or both tests on the correlation between x and y is given by

$$r'_{xy} = \frac{r_{xy}\sqrt{\text{new } r_{xx} \times \text{new } r_{yy}}}{\sqrt{\text{old } r_{xx} \times r_{yy}}}$$

[6-3]

where

r'_{xy} = correlation between x and y, corrected for change in the reliability of x and/or y

old r_{xx} and old r_{yy} = reliability of x and y at the time the test was given

new r_{xx} and new r_{yy} = new levels of reliability of x and y

Formula 6-3 is the most general form of the correction for attenuation. For example, if both tests could somehow be made perfectly reliable, the new r_{xx} and r_{yy} would be equal to 1.0, and Formula 6-3 would be mathematically identical to Formula 6-2. The most useful aspect of Formula 6-3 is that it allows us to estimate the effects of both raising and lowering the reliability of x and y on the correlation between x and y. Table 6-3 illustrates how a correlation of .40 between x and y would change as the reliability of x and y was either increased or decreased. As the table shows, the expected correlation between x and y would increase to .52 if highly reliable measures of x and y (e.g., r_{xx} and r_{yy} = .95) could be obtained but would decrease to .22 if less reliable measures of x and y (e.g., r_{xx} and r_{yy} = .40) were used.

TABLE 6-3 CHANGES IN r_{xy} AS A FUNCTION OF THE RELIABILITY OF x AND y
Original Test: r_{xy} = .40 r_{xx} = .70 r_{yy} = .75

Increasing reliability		Corrected	Decreasing reliability		Corrected
r_{xx}	r_{yy}	r_{xy}	r_{xx}	r_{yy}	r_{xy}
.75	.80	.43	.65	.70	.37
.80	.85	.45	.55	.60	.31
.85	.90	.48	.45	.50	.26
.90	.90	.50	.45	.45	.25
.95	.95	.52	.40	.40	.22

FACTORS AFFECTING RELIABILITY

In Chapter 5 and in the preceding sections of this chapter, we discussed methods of estimating the reliability of a test, along with several ways of using information concerning reliability. In our discussion of internal consistency estimates, we touched briefly on the question of *why* tests are or are not reliable. In this section we examine in more detail the factors that affect the reliability of psychological tests. Basically, there are four factors that affect the reliability of a test:

1. characteristics of the people taking the test
2. characteristics of the test itself
3. the intended uses of test scores
4. the method used to estimate reliability

Characteristics of the people taking the test. The first factor that affects the reliability of psychological measurement is the extent to which people taking the test vary on the characteristic or attribute being measured. As stated earlier, tests are designed to measure individual differences. If individuals do not differ very much on a particular attribute or trait, it is difficult to develop a reliable measure of that attribute. For example, imagine that you are a first-grade teacher trying to estimate individual differences in height of your students as they are seated at their desks. Since children at this age tend to be quite similar in height, this task would be quite difficult. On the other hand, a high school teacher would find this task much easier, since at that age there is a greater variation in students' heights. Thus, when individual differences are quite large, it is much easier to measure them.

The standard deviation provides a measure of variability, or the extent to which individuals differ. Thus, the larger the standard deviation, the more likely it is that a test will be reliable. However, a large standard deviation also implies that measures will, in an absolute sense, be inaccurate. Recall that the formula for the standard error of measurement (SEM) is

$$\text{SEM} = \sigma_x \sqrt{1 - r_{xx}} \qquad [6\text{-}4]$$

Formula 6-4 suggests a paradox. If individual differences are very small, test reliability probably will be low. However, the standard deviation also will be small, and thus the standard error of measurement will be small. Hence, it might be possible to have a test that is unreliable as a measure of individual differences but nevertheless provides an accurate measure of each person's standing on the attribute measured. The clearest example of this phenomenon would occur if everyone received the same score on a test. For example, if a group of physicists took a third-grade mathematics test, each of them would probably receive a score of 100. Since there are no individual differences in test scores, the test would have a reliability coefficient of 0.0; however, the standard error of measurement would also be 0.0. Thus, the test would be perfectly unreliable and perfectly accurate at the same time.

Because the variability of the attribute being measured affects test reliability, it is likely that many tests will show different levels of reliability, depending on the population in which they are used. For example, a test of general intelligence will be more reliable for the population in general than for a population of graduates of highly select colleges. It follows, then, that it will often be difficult to cite any figure as *the* reliability of a test. Tests will be more reliable in settings when individual differences are extreme, and less reliable in settings where individual differences are small.

Characteristics of the test.   Internal consistency formulas for estimating reliability suggest that two factors affect the reliability coefficient: (a) the correlations between items and (b) the number of items. This definition suggests that the reliability of a test can be increased in either of two ways: by increasing the correlations between items or by increasing the number of items. Thus, a test made up of 40 mathematics questions is likely to be more reliable than a 40-item test that covers mathematics, spatial visualization, baseball trivia, and knowledge of French grammar; and an 80-item mathematics test is likely to be more reliable than a similar 40-item mathematics test.

Since most well-developed tests are designed to measure one attribute or trait, the first strategy—that of increasing the homogeneity or consistency of the test items—is not always easy to implement. Therefore, the typical strategy for increasing the reliability of a test is to lengthen the test. Psychometric theory provides the *Spearman-Brown formula,* which can be used to predict the effect of lengthening a test on the reliability of that test. If the length is increased by a factor of n (e.g., double the length, or $n = 2$), the reliability of the new, expanded test is estimated by

$$\text{new } r_{xx} = \frac{n \times \text{old } r_{xx}}{1 + (n - 1) \text{ old } r_{xx}} \qquad \text{[6-5]}$$

where

$$\text{old } r_{xx} = \text{reliability of the original test}$$
$$\text{new } r_{xx} = \text{reliability of the lengthened test}$$

Table 6-4 illustrates the effects of lengthening a 20-item test with a reliability of .60. As shown by the table, it would be possible to substantially increase the reliability of the test by greatly increasing the number of items. Thus, adding 100 more items would raise the reliability from .60 to .90. It may, however, be exceedingly difficult and prohibitively expensive to add 100 extra items.

Formula 6-5 can also be used to predict the effect of decreasing the length of a test. For example, a 200-item test might be highly reliable (e.g., $r_{xx} = .95$), but it also might be too long for many applications. A short form of the same test might show acceptable levels of reliability and be much more practical. For example, a 50-item short form of this test would have an estimated reliability coefficient of .80.

In principle, the reliability of most psychological tests is under the control of the test developer. Internal consistency formulas imply that if a test is sufficiently long, it will be reliable, even if the average inter-item correlation is fairly small. For example, a 50-item

TABLE 6-4   EFFECTS ON RELIABILITY OF LENGTHENING
A 20-ITEM TEST WITH A RELIABILITY COEFFICIENT OF .60

Test length	n	Estimated reliability
40 items	2	.75
60	3	.81
80	4	.85
100	5	.88
120	6	.90

test in which the average inter-item correlation is .20 would have a reliability of .92. A 100-item test in which the average inter-item correlation is as small as .05 still would have a reliability of .84. Thus, in theory, there is really no excuse for an unreliable test. On the other hand, a large coefficient alpha is not by itself an indication of a good test if the number of items is large. As Cortina (In press) notes, even a poorly developed test will be reliable if it is sufficiently long. However, though it is theoretically possible to achieve a high level of reliability with any test simply by increasing its length, practical barriers may prevent implementing such a strategy.

First, long tests are more time consuming and expensive than short tests. The increase in reliability may not be worth the price, especially if tests are not used to make final decisions about people. Second, it often is quite difficult to write good test items. In addition, the new items added to the test must be substantively and statistically similar to the items already on the test; otherwise, the Spearman-Brown formula will not provide an accurate reliability estimate. Thus, in practice it may be quite laborious to lengthen many tests substantially.

Intended use of test scores.

In Chapter 5 we noted that tests might have different levels of reliability for different purposes. For example, suppose that school children take tests of general intelligence at a very early age (e.g., in first grade) and take the same test again many years later (e.g., on entering high school). The test might be highly reliable each time it is given but might show much less temporal stability. Thus, the test would be a more reliable indicator of the children's general mental ability at the time they took each test than it would be as an indicator of their long-term level of intelligence.

In general, the reliability of test scores is related to the breadth (versus narrowness) of the inferences that are made. For example, suppose a person takes a computer-presented test of spatial visualization that involves mentally rotating three-dimensional geometric shapes. This test would provide a more reliable measure of the person's present level of spatial visualization ability than of his or her ability ten years down the road. Test scores could probably be better generalized to other computer-presented tests than to similar paper-and-pencil tests. Finally, test scores might generalize better to other tests involving mental rotation than to tests that involve other spatial visualization tasks.

In sum, tests often show different levels of reliability for identifying individual differences at a specific point in time than for identifying individual differences across time. Tests are more reliable for identifying gross distinctions between individuals than they are for very fine distinctions. For example, one would expect a high degree of reliability for a mastery test (scored either pass or fail) of fifth-grade mathematics given to a sample made up of 50 second graders and 50 college sophomores. Almost everyone in the first group is likely to receive failing scores, and almost everyone in the second group is likely to receive passing scores. On the other hand, it might be difficult to reliably rank-order 100 Ph.D. candidates in terms of their general intelligence; for although there would be some standouts, this group would tend to be homogeneous. Finally, it is easier to make reliable inferences about stable characteristics of individuals than about characteristics that vary unpredictably. For example, it would be easier to develop a reliable measure of a person's basic values than of a person's mood state.

Methods Used to Estimate Reliability

Test-retest, alternate forms, split-half, and internal consistency methods of estimating test reliability each imply slightly different definitions of true score and error. For example, changes over time in the attribute being measured are considered sources of measurement error in estimating test-retest reliability. When split-half or internal consistency estimates are employed, the temporal stability of the attribute being measured is not a relevant factor.

In general, one might expect internal consistency estimates to be higher than alternate forms correlations, which in turn should probably be higher than test-retest reliability estimates. The reason for this is that more factors contribute to measurement error when test-retest or alternate forms methods are used than when internal consistency methods are used. For example, temporal instability and reactivity affect test-retest estimates but have no effect on internal consistency estimates. There are situations, however, where test-retest reliability can be expected to be higher than internal consistency estimates. For example, if people remembered all their responses to the first test, it would be possible to obtain perfect test-retest reliability, even if the internal consistency estimate was exactly 0.0.

The method used in estimating reliability should correspond with the way in which test scores are used. For example, if test scores obtained on one occasion are used to make inferences across long periods of time, it is important to estimate the temporal stability of test scores. If a clinic employs several different psychologists to score responses to the Rorschach inkblot test, it may be important to determine the extent to which test scores can be generalized across psychologists. There is no single figure that represents *the* reliability of a test, so the choice of an appropriate method for estimating and defining reliability is potentially very important.

SPECIAL ISSUES IN RELIABILITY

Psychometric theory typically has little to say about the content of a test; a reliability coefficient of .90 is generally interpreted in the same way, regardless of what the test measures or what type of items are included in the test. However, the proper methods of estimating and interpreting test reliability may depend on what the test measures. In particular, some ability and achievement tests measure speed of response, whereas others measure performance irrespective of speed. This distinction has important implications for the estimation and interpretation of test reliability.

A second issue of importance is the reliability of difference scores, or gain scores. In assessing training and educational programs, it is common practice to give a pretest before training, and a post-test after training. The difference between pretest and post-test scores is then used to measure the gain associated with training. Difference scores of this sort may present some special problems in terms of their reliability, as is discussed later in this section.

The final issue taken up is the reliability test batteries, or of composite scores. Very often, scores from a number of tests are combined to form a single composite score. For example, in making graduate admissions decisions, some psychology departments consider the total score on the Graduate Record Examinations (GRE). This total score represents the sum of individual scores on verbal, quantitative, and analytical tests, as well as a psychology test. It is important to determine the reliability of a total score such as this; reliability theory provides methods for doing so.

Speed Tests versus Power Tests

The most widely used type of test is one in which there is a correct answer for each of many individual test items. Tests of this sort are often administered under strict time limits. A person's score on such a test is therefore likely to be affected by two factors: (a) whether the person knew (or guessed) the answer to each item and (b) whether the person had enough time, or worked quickly enough, to respond to each item. Thus, it is not always possible to determine whether a low test score indicates that the person did not know the answers or that he or she worked too slowly (or was given too little time) to respond to all the questions.

In theory, the distinction is often made between *speed tests* and *power tests*. A speed test is one in which each of the items is trivially easy but is administered within such a strict time limit that it is impossible to answer all questions. For example, the examinee might be given 60 seconds for a 100-item test made up of questions such as those shown in Table 6-5. It is assumed that, given enough time, the person could answer every item correctly. However, the strict time limit makes it impossible to complete every item. Individual differences in test scores are thus a function of the speed with which the examinee responds to individual items—the faster the person works, the more items he or she will complete. In contrast, a power test is one in which speed in responding has no effect on the test score. For example, a 20-item introductory psychology exam administered with no time limit would probably be considered a power test. No matter how quickly (or slowly) the examinee works, the final score is determined by the person's knowledge of the material, together with his or her luck in guessing or having studied just the right material.

Split-half and internal consistency methods are inappropriate for estimating the reliability of speed tests. In fact, a pure test of speed should have a split-half reliability of nearly 1.00. For example, suppose that a secretary answered 68 items on a 100-items test of clerical speed. It is safe to assume that practically all items attempted would be answered correctly. An odd-even split of this test therefore should yield two halves, with scores of 34 on each half. Another, very slow examinee who only attempted 8 items

TABLE 6-5   ITEMS THAT MIGHT APPEAR ON A SPEED TEST

Item	Are A and B the same or different?		
	A	B	
1.	1376493	1376443	_____
2.	John K. Adams	John K. Adams	_____
3.	3749 Parkwood Ct.	3749 Parkwood Dr.	_____
4.	863-4587	863-4587	_____
5.	Sailing Master	Sailing Mister	_____

should receive scores of 4 on each odd-even split. Thus, the halves would almost be perfectly correlated, regardless of the true reliability of the test.

One alternative is to split the test time-wise rather than item-wise (Stanley, 1971). Thus, a 30-minute, 200-item speed test could be split into two 15-minute halves. When the number of items completed in the first 15 minutes is compared with the number completed in the last 15 minutes, these numbers should be consistently similar if the test is reliable.

Although the test-retest method is not recommended for most testing applications (Nunnally, 1978), this method is useful for assessing the reliability of speed tests. In a speed test, items are often trivial and fairly meaningless. It is precisely for this reason that the usual barrier to the use of test-retest method—subjects' tendency to remember their responses—tends not to be a problem with speed tests. When the test content is meaningful, subjects are likely to remember their responses to test items; when test items involve trivial perceptual or motor tasks, over time it becomes more difficult to remember or duplicate one's responses to a large number of test items. Thus, the test-retest method might be quite useful in assessing the reliability of a speed test, particularly in settings where it is difficult to obtain scores on separately timed half-tests.

Reliability of Difference Scores

In evaluating a training program, researchers often look at the difference between scores on a pretest and scores on a post-test. A counselor who wishes to know whether Kathleen is better in mathematics or in English may examine the difference in grades received in these two areas. In both cases, the examiner might be surprised to learn that the *change scores* or *difference scores* can show low levels of reliability, even when the two tests being compared are highly reliable.

Suppose we want to measure how much students have learned in a one-semester statistics course. We might give them a test at the beginning of the semester (X), then give them another, equivalent test at the end of the semester (Y), and compute the difference between the scores on the two tests ($D = X - Y$). This difference score (D) would have a reliability of

$$r_{DD} = \frac{\dfrac{r_{xx} + r_{yy}}{2} - r_{xy}}{1 - r_{xy}} \qquad [6\text{-}6]$$

where

r_{DD} = reliability of the difference between scores on X and scores on Y
r_{xx} = reliability of X
r_{yy} = reliability of Y
r_{xy} = correlation between X and Y

Examination of Formula 6-6 leads to a somewhat surprising conclusion: All other things being equal, *the higher the correlation between X and Y, the lower the reliability of the difference score.*

To understand this apparent paradox, one must remember that both X and Y are made up of true score and error. Thus,

$$X = T_x + e_x \qquad [6\text{-}7]$$

and

$$Y = T_y + e_y \qquad [6\text{-}8]$$

The difference between X and Y reflects two factors: (a) differences in true scores and (b) differences due to measurement error. If X and Y are highly correlated, the true score part of X must overlap considerably with the true score part of Y. As a result, there will be hardly any difference in the true scores on these variables. Differences between scores on X and scores on Y therefore will be due almost entirely to measurement error. Thus, the more highly correlated X and Y are, the less reliable their difference.

Our discussion of the reliability of difference scores has implications for both research and testing applications. For example, a comparison of pretest and post-test scores might be used to determine who has learned the most in a drivers' education course. If the pretest and post-test are comparable (and it would not make any sense to use completely different types of tests), scores on the two tests are likely to be positively correlated and difference scores will show low levels of reliability. Thus, in this case the measure of individual differences in the amount learned (post-test minus pretest) could be quite unreliable. Persons who appear to have learned quite a bit in this drivers' education course (large difference) could show little apparent gain in an equivalent course. This does not reflect instability in their ability to learn; rather, it is a reflection of the potential unreliability of measures of change or gain.

The problems inherent in the use of difference scores have led to a variety of statistical techniques for studying and measuring change (Cohen & Cohen, 1983; Collins & Horn, 1991; Harris, 1963). Although most researchers avoid the use of difference scores for measuring change, you will probably encounter several studies that still use them. In interpreting the results of these studies, it is very important to keep in mind the special problems posed by the typically low reliability of difference scores.

Reliability of Composite Scores

A difference score is obtained by *subtracting* the score on one test from the score on another. A composite score is obtained by *adding* the scores on several different tests. Whereas difference scores are often unreliable, composite scores are typically *more reliable* than the tests that make up the composite. In particular, the more highly correlated the individual tests, the higher the reliability of the sum of those tests.

The reliability of a composite, or summed score, is given by

$$r_{ss} = 1 - \frac{k - (k\bar{r}_{ii})}{k + (k^2 - k)\,\bar{r}_{ij}} \qquad [6\text{-}9]$$

where

$$r_{ss} = \text{reliability of the sum}$$
$$k = \text{number of tests}$$
$$\bar{r}_{ii} = \text{average test reliability}$$
$$\bar{r}_{ij} = \text{average correlation between tests}$$

For example, if three tests had reliabilities of .70, .75, and .80 and an average intercorrelation of .39, the reliability of the sum of the scores on these three tests would be

.85. If the average intercorrelation among these three tests was .65, the reliability of the sum would be .89.

The basic principles for determining the reliability of a composite score are exactly analogous to those involved in determining the internal consistency of a test. The more tests that are combined, and the higher the correlation between them, the higher the reliability of the composite. Adding together scores on several highly correlated tests achieves exactly the same objectives as adding together scores on several positively correlated test items to form a single test score. Each test can be thought of as an observation, or measurement, of a particular attribute, much in the same way that each test item is thought of as a separate observation. Highly correlated tests represent independent observations of similar attributes or of the same attribute. As noted in this chapter and in Chapter 5, the best method to assure reliability is to obtain as many observations as possible of the attribute that is to be measured.

HOW RELIABLE SHOULD TESTS BE?

All things being equal, a highly reliable test would always be preferable to a test with little reliability. However, all things are rarely equal; the most reliable test might also be the most expensive or most difficult to administer. Test reliability may be crucial in some settings (e.g., those in which major decisions are made on the basis of tests) but less important in others (e.g., where tests are used only for preliminary screenings). It is impossible to specify any particular figure as the minimum level of reliability needed for *all* testing applications, but rough guidelines can be established for some of the more common uses of tests.

High levels of reliability are most necessary when (a) tests are used to make final decisions about people and (b) individuals are sorted into many different categories based upon relatively small individual differences. For example, tests are used for placement in the armed forces—individuals can be assigned to any of a number of jobs based largely on their scores on the Armed Services Vocational Aptitude Battery. In this case, measurement error could have a significant effect on decisions (Murphy, 1984a). If the tests used in placement are unreliable, the decisions made regarding thousands of recruits also will be unreliable.

Lower levels of reliability are acceptable when (a) tests are used for preliminary rather than final decisions and (b) tests are used to sort people into a small number of categories based upon gross individual differences. For example, if several hundred people apply for a small number of places in a graduate program in clinical psychology, test scores might be used for preliminary screening, in which applicants who essentially have no chance of being admitted (e.g., the bottom 25 percent of the applicant pool) are screened out. If a test were used in this way, a high level of reliability would be desirable, but not essential.

Table 6-6 illustrates the levels of reliability typically attained by different types of psychological tests and measurement devices. There is, of course, some variability in reported levels of reliability. Thus, some standardized tests of intelligence report levels of reliability in excess of .95, whereas others report reliability estimates closer to .80. Nevertheless, clear differences exist in the levels of reliability achieved by different types

TABLE 6-6   LEVELS OF RELIABILITY TYPICALLY REPORTED FOR DIFFERENT TYPES OF TESTS
AND MEASUREMENT DEVICES

Typical reliability estimate	Test type	Interpretation
.95		Measurement errors have virtually low effect
.90	Standardized group tests of intelligence	High to moderate reliability
.85	Standardized achievement tests	
.80		
.75	Classroom multiple-choice tests	Moderate to low reliability
.70	Rating scales	
.65		Low reliability
.60	Some projective measures	
.55		
.50		True scores and error have equal effects on test scores

of tests. Most standardized tests of general intelligence report reliability estimates in the neighborhood of .90 (Jensen, 1980). For almost any testing application, this is likely to be regarded as a high level of reliability. Reliability estimates of .80 or more are typically regarded as moderate to high; a reliability coefficient of .80 indicates that 20 percent of the variability in test scores is due to measurement errors. For most testing applications, reliability estimates around .70 are likely to be regarded as low, although, as noted before, this level of reliability might be sufficient when tests are used for screening or for making preliminary decisions. Finally, reliability estimates lower than .60 usually are thought to indicate unacceptably low levels of reliability.

Generalizability theory encourages us to ask questions that go beyond the simple reliability tests. For example, Buckley, Cote, and Comstock (1990) reviewed research on measures of personality and attitudes, and they concluded that on average, 36 percent of the variance in these measures was due to measurement error, implying a reliability of .64. This does not mean, however, that the constructs measured by these tests account for the other 64 percent. Buckley and his colleagues (1990) also found that 22 percent of the variance in scores could be attributed to the method of measurement; they found, in addition, that only 42 percent of the variance in scores on measures of personality characteristics and attitudes was attributable to the traits these scales were designed to measure. Thus, in the case of the measures reviewed in this study, a reasonably decent level of reliability may say more about the extent of method bias than about the quality of measurement of personality and attitude scales.

CRITICAL DISCUSSION:
Precise but Narrow—The Bandwidth-Fidelity Dilemma

There are sometimes practical obstacles to maximizing the reliability of tests. For example, a test with a reliability of .90 might be twice as expensive to develop as a test with a reliability of .85. The gain in reliability might not be worth the cost. In addition to the occasional practical problems, there are some theoretical reasons why it may be impossible to achieve high levels of reliability in measuring a particular attribute or trait. In particular, there is an inevitable conflict between the goal of attaining precision (reliability) in measurement and the goal of attaining breadth. This conflict is referred to as the *Bandwidth-Fidelity Dilemma* (Cronbach & Gleser, 1965; Shannon & Weaver, 1949).

The terms "bandwidth" and "fidelity" come from communication theory. Bandwidth refers to the amount of information that is contained in a message, while fidelity refers to the accuracy with which that information is conveyed. The greater the amount of information to be conveyed (bandwidth), the less accurately it can be conveyed (fidelity). The greater the level of accuracy desired, the less information that can be conveyed. The trade-off between bandwidth and fidelity also applies to testing. For any given test, a choice must be made between measuring a very specific attribute with a high degree of accuracy or measuring a broader attribute with less accuracy. Consider, for example, a history test with 20 items. If all 20 items deal with eighteenth-century American history, one might obtain a highly reliable measure of each student's knowledge of that particular aspect of history. On the other hand, if the 20 items cover all areas of the world, from ancient times to modern, one would be able to measure each student's general knowledge of history, but one would not be able to obtain a very accurate or reliable measure of such a broadly defined area of knowledge.

The time and resources available for testing are typically limited. As a result, we sometimes have to sacrifice reliability and accuracy in measurement in order to measure traits and attributes that are broadly of interest. Thus, it may not be practical, even if it is technically possible, to attain high levels of reliability with every psychological test and measurement device.

SUMMARY

All other things being equal, highly reliable tests are preferable to less reliable ones. However, in most cases all other things are *not* equal, and it is important to consider carefully the implications of different levels of reliability. The standard error measurement, which is determined by both the reliability and the standard deviation of a test, is very useful for describing, in concrete terms, just how much faith can be put into test scores. Tests can be highly reliable, but nevertheless highly imprecise, in the sense that actual test scores can vary considerably from administration to administration.

The correction for attenuation illustrates very concretely the implications of different levels of reliability. When tests are unreliable, the correlation you obtain between test scores can severely underestimate the strength of the relationship between the characteristics the tests were designed to measure. The correction formulas presented here allow you to determine the effects of low reliability on the reported validity of tests. They also allow you to determine whether the time and effort needed to increase test reliability is likely to have a concrete payoff in terms of higher validity coefficients.

It is important to correctly estimate and interpret reliability in a number of special testing applications. These include testing applications that involve speeded tests, for which internal consistency methods may be appropriate, and scores that are based either on differences between scores on two different tests or on the sum of scores on two different tests. An important rule of thumb is that difference scores often show very low levels of reliability, whereas composite scores (i.e., those constructed by summing several different tests) may be highly reliable.

CHAPTER 7

VALIDITY OF MEASUREMENT: CONTENT AND CONSTRUCT-ORIENTED VALIDATION STRATEGIES

Two of the principal problems in psychological measurement are determining whether a test measures what it is supposed to measure and determining whether that test can be used in making accurate decisions. Suppose a psychologist devises a test and claims that it measures reading comprehension and can be used to predict success in graduate school. These claims would not carry much weight unless they were supported by evidence. Hence, the psychologist must present data to show that the claims are accurate, or *valid*. For example, if test scores are correlated with grades or with professors' evaluations of graduate students, it is reasonable to conclude that the test is a valid predictor of success in graduate school. If test scores are related to other measures of reading comprehension, or if the test provides a representative sample of tasks that measure reading comprehension, then the test probably does indeed measure what it purports to measure.

This chapter opens our discussion of validity. There are many ways in which tests can be used; as a consequence, there are many ways of defining validity. We begin this chapter by discussing in more detail the two major types of validity: (a) the validity of measurement and (b) the validity for decisions. The validity of measurement is the main focus of this chapter. Ways of defining and estimating the validity of decisions are discussed in the chapter that follows.

VALIDATION STRATEGIES

In the 1940s and the early 1950s, research on psychological measurement was characterized by a bewildering array of methods of defining and assessing validity. One of the many contributions of the American Psychological Association's *Technical Recommenda-*

tions for Psychological Tests and Diagnostic Techniques (1954) was the development of a fairly simple system for classifying procedures for assessing validity. The *Technical Recommendations* recognized four essentially different ways of defining validity:

1. content validity
2. construct validity
3. predictive validity
4. concurrent validity

These four categories are sometimes referred to as the four faces of validity.

For many years it was thought that different types of validity were appropriate for different purposes. For example, for educational testing, content validity might be called for; whereas for personnel testing, predictive validity might be needed. Landy (1987) referred to this approach to matching "types" of validity to specific testing applications as "stamp collecting." Today, it is recognized that these four "faces" represent four different strategies for validating the inferences that are made on the basis of test scores rather than four different types of validity (*APA Standards for Educational and Psychological Testing,* 1985). Rather than describing fundamentally different types of validity, researchers now agree that all validation strategies are designed to pursue the same basic goal: understanding the meaning and implication of test scores. Messick (1989) provides a succinct definition of validation as the "scientific inquiry into test score meaning." Nevertheless, there is some value in considering separately two different uses of the term "validity," which correspond to the two different ways in which tests are most often used—for measurement and prediction or for decision making. Both content and construct validation strategies represent approaches for determining whether a test provides a valid measure of a specific attribute.[1] In other words, these approaches define validity in terms of measurement—a test is valid if it measures what it is supposed to measure. Predictive and concurrent approaches examine the validity of predictions or decisions that are based on tests—a test is valid if it can be used to make correct or accurate decisions.

To illustrate the differences between validity of measurement and validity for decisions, consider the case of an organization that decides to use an inventory labelled Leadership Skills Profile to help select managers. First, you might ask whether this inventory really tells you anything about a person's leadership skills (validity of measurement). Second, you might ask whether people who receive high scores on this test turn out to be good managers (validity for decisions). The difference between these two aspects of validity is that in the first case, you are concerned with what the test measures, whereas in the second, you are interested in using the test to make predictions about a variable that is not directly measured by the test (i.e., success as a manager), but that you think is related to what the test measures.

---

[1]It is possible to include *all* validity research under the heading of construct validity. The rationale here is that all research on the validity of tests and measures is ultimately concerned with constructs and that any validation strategy may ultimately help to establish the relationship between the test and the construct. See Chapter 8 for further discussion of this point.

Guion (1991) notes that validity of measurement is not always necessary or sufficient to guarantee validity for decisions. A very good measure of leadership skills may be a poor predictor of performance as a manager, for leadership and day-to-day management are very different things. A poor measure of leadership might nevertheless allow you to identify good managers. It is therefore important to consider the two major aspects of the term "validity" separately.

ASSESSING THE VALIDITY OF MEASUREMENT

It is a simple matter to determine whether a homemade ruler provides a valid measure of length—simply take the ruler to the Bureau of Weights and Measures and compare it with a standard. This strategy won't work for evaluating the validity of a psychological test. The reason for this is simple, but fundamental to an understanding of methods of psychological measurement: For many of the characteristics that psychologists wish to measure (e.g., introversion, intelligence, reading comprehension), there are no universal standards against which test scores can be compared. In other words, if I measure Paula's general intelligence and come up with an IQ of 112, I cannot go to the Bureau of Weights and Standards to find out if I was right. Unfortunately, there is *no* external standard I can use to check this figure or to check scores from most other psychological tests. Rather than validating test scores against some external standard, psychologists must employ more indirect methods in determining the validity of tests. That is, psychologists must collect evidence from a variety of sources to demonstrate that tests measure what they are designed to measure.

In a sense, one's work is never done when attempting to establish the validity of measurement. There is no definitive way of proving that a given test *is* a measure of general intelligence, of reading comprehension, or of any other trait. Establishing the validity of a specific test is always partially subjective and depends on a researcher's judgment regarding the weight of the available evidence. Nevertheless, although the methods discussed in this chapter are both indirect and partially subjective, judgments regarding the validity of measurement can and should be based solidly on empirical evidence.

Both content and construct-oriented validation strategies involve the accumulation of evidence that suggests that the test actually measures what it purports to measure. Content validity is established by examining the test itself, while construct validity is established by examining the relationship between test scores and a variety of other measures.

CONTENT-ORIENTED VALIDATION STRATEGIES

One way to gather evidence for the validity of measurement is to examine the content of the test. A test that contains 25 addition and subtraction problems is probably a better measure of simple mathematical ability than a test that contains 10 questions about sports and no addition and subtraction problems. *Content validity is established by showing that the behaviors sampled by the test are a representative sample of the attribute being measured.* Thus, content validity depends both on the test itself and on the processes involved in responding to the test (Guion, 1977). For example, a paper-and-pencil test of job knowledge might not provide a valid measure of a worker's *ability* to do the job, even if it provides a valid measure of his or her *knowledge* of what to do in the job.

One can get a rough idea of a test's content validity simply by looking at test items. If all test items appear to measure what the test is supposed to measure, there is some evidence of content validity. The evidence is weak, but it is a start. In order to develop more detailed evidence of content validity, it is necessary to introduce the concept of content domain.

Content Domains

Every psychological test is a systematic sample from a particular *domain* of behaviors. A detailed description of the content domain provides the foundation for assessing content validity.

When you say, "I want to measure *X*," you have specified a particular content domain. A content domain represents the total set of behaviors that could be used to measure a specific attribute or characteristic of the individuals that are to be tested (Guion, 1977). For example, a test designed to measure performance as a baseball player could be constructed by sampling from the total domain of behaviors (running, fielding, hitting) involved in the game of baseball. The domain covered by a test might be very broad (e.g., reading comprehension), or it might be very narrow (e.g., addition problems involving decimals to two places, with sums less than 10). Regardless of its size, every content domain has a number of properties that are useful in assessing content validity.

First, as the name implies, a content domain has *boundaries*. There are a great many possible test items within these boundaries that could validly be used to measure a person's standing on the content domain; a detailed description of the content domain to be measured allows one to determine whether each test item lies within the boundaries of the domain. There is clearly a problem if a large number of behaviors sampled by the test are outside the boundaries of the domain one wishes to measure. Returning to an earlier example, a test that is made up of questions about sports will not provide a valid measure of simple mathematical ability. The test might provide an accurate measure of sports knowledge, but questions about sports fall outside the boundaries of the domain of mathematical ability.

Second, content domains are *structured*. That is, the contents of a content domain can often be classified into several categories. The description of such a content domain presented in Table 7-1 helps clarify the concepts of boundaries and structure of content domains. The domain described in the table has well-defined boundaries and structure. Because this domain is very concrete, it is possible to make some precise statements about the areas included in the domain and about the relative importance of each of those areas. This detailed description of the boundaries and structure of the content domain is essential in evaluating content validity.

It should be relatively easy to decide whether specific test items are within or outside the boundaries of the domain described in Table 7-1. It should also be easy to

TABLE 7-1 DETAILED DESCRIPTION OF A CONTENT DOMAIN

1. Domain to be measured: Knowledge of world history as covered in a standard seventh-grade course.
2. Areas included in this domain:

A. Issues	B. Areas	C. Time span
1. Social	1. Europe	1. 18th Century
2. Political	2. Americas	2. 19th Century
3. Cultural	3. Africa & Asia	

3. Relative importance of the areas covered.*

		Social	Political	Cultural
Europe	18th Century	5%	10%	3%
	19th Century	5%	8%	2%
Americas	18th Century	6%	17%	2%
	19th Century	9%	13%	5%
Africa & Asia	18th Century	2%	0%	0%
	19th Century	6%	5%	2%
				100%

*Note: These percentages reflect the relative amount of reading and lecture time dedicated to each area.

decide whether a test forms a representative sample of this content domain. As discussed in the section that follows, detailed comparisons between the boundaries and structure of the content domain and the structure of the test are at the heart of content validity.

Unfortunately, many content domains cannot be described in the level of detail shown in the table. It is very difficult to provide detailed descriptions of content domains such as "mathematical concepts" or "performance on mechanical tasks." These domains include a broad range of behaviors whose boundaries might be difficult to specify. It may therefore be very difficult to decide whether specific test items are within or outside of the boundaries of the domain. If the different areas or classes of behaviors included in the domain cannot be categorized, or if the relative importance of those areas cannot be decided upon, it may be impossible to determine whether the test provides a representative sample of the content domain.

Assessing Content Validity

There is no exact, statistical measure of content validity. Rather, content validity represents a judgment regarding the degree to which a test provides an adequate sample of a particular content domain (Guion, 1977). Judgments about content validity are neither final nor absolute; tests show various levels of content validity, and experts do not always agree in their judgments . Nevertheless, judgments about content validity are not arbitrary. A detailed description of the content domain provides a framework for the careful evaluation of tests and provides a method for systematic evaluation of the validity of measurement.

The basic procedure for assessing content validity consists of three steps:

1. Describe the content domain.
2. Determine the areas of the content domain that are measured by each test item.
3. Compare the structure of the test with the structure of the content domain.

Although this procedure appears to be simple, in practice it is difficult to implement. The principal difficulty is encountered at the first step, the description of the content domain. Outside of the area of classroom testing, it is often difficult to describe content domains in the level of detail shown in Table 7-1. For example, consider applying this strategy in assessing a test of verbal ability. Although it might be possible to decide what sort of tasks were or were not included in this content domain (boundaries of the domain), it would be exceedingly difficult to define in any detail the structure of this domain. In other words, it would be difficult to specify the relative importance or frequency of the different tasks that involve verbal ability. In this case, a test developer might have a general definition of the domain he or she wishes to measure but little detailed knowledge of the structure of that domain. It would be difficult to determine whether a specific test provided a representative sample of this domain; therefore, it would be difficult to argue on the basis of content alone that the test provides a valid measure of verbal ability.

A detailed description of the content domain yields a set of categories that can be used to classify test items. First, each test item can be classified as being within the boundaries of the domain or outside the boundaries of the domain. This type of classification is simple, but important; a test is not likely to show much content validity if the majority of the test items are clearly outside of the boundaries of the domain it is supposed to measure. Those test items that are within the boundaries of the domain can be further classified according to the areas of the domain they measure. For example, items on a history test designed to measure the domain described in Table 7-1 could be classified as dealing with social, political, or cultural issues, and further classified as dealing with European, American, or African and Asian history. In other words, the categories used to describe the content domain can also be used to classify each item on the test.

The final step in assessing content validity is to compare the content and structure of the test with that of the content domain. If none of the test items falls within the boundaries of the domain, then it seems clear that the test will show no content validity. Furthermore, if test items deal with only a specific portion of the domain, the test will not show substantial evidence of content validity.

Consider, for example, the tests described in Table 7-2. The domain we wish to measure is performance as a shortstop, which presumably includes hitting, base running, and fielding a variety of balls. Each of the two tests described in the table includes behaviors that are clearly within this content domain, yet neither of them provides a valid

TABLE 7-2 EXAMPLES OF TESTS THAT FAIL
TO ADEQUATELY SAMPLE A DOMAIN

The Domain: Performance as a shortstop in intermural softball
Test A: Hitting 40 pitches thrown in batting practice
Test B: Fielding 70 ground balls that are hit toward second base

sample of the domain. In this example, some combination of test A and test B might provide a better sample of this particular content domain and thus a better, more valid test. In general, a test that appears to provide a representative sample of the major parts of a content domain will be judged to show high levels of content validity. The closer the match between the structure of the test and the structure of the domain, the stronger the evidence of content validity. In order to demonstrate content validity, tests should sample all parts of the content domain and should devote the largest number of items to the larger, more important areas included in the domain, with comparatively fewer items devoted to less important aspects of the domain.

Response processes and content validity. Several researchers, notably Guion (1977) and Sackett (1987), have noted that assessments of content validity focus almost exclusively on the *content* of test items or assessment exercises. Questions of how stimuli are presented to subjects, how responses are recorded and evaluated, and what is going through the respondent's mind are rarely considered in studies that use content-oriented validity strategies. Failure to consider these issues adequately could be a serious mistake, as can be illustrated through an examination of the underlying logic of content-oriented validation.

The logic of content-oriented strategies of validation is that the test should provide a representative sample of the domain one wishes to measure. By this logic, validation efforts should be concerned more with the extent to which *responses* to items provide a representative sample of the domain of responses than with the extent to which stimuli are representative. After all, psychological tests are samples of *behavior* that are used to draw inferences about the domain of behaviors sampled. Therefore, a test that used unrepresentative stimuli but sampled the domain of responses well would be preferable to one that included representative stimuli but unrepresentative responses. An example of the latter is the work sample test, which is often used as a predictor, and sometimes as a measure, of job performance (see Chapters 20 and 21). Work sample tests ask respondents to carry out, under optimal conditions, a standard set of tasks that are part of the job; their performance on each task is carefully observed and scored. In terms of the stimuli employed, these tests are often highly representative and realistic. However, it is clear that these tests typically measure maximal rather than typical performance. That is, people typically perform their best on these tests and probably do not perform as well on the job, where they are not so closely monitored and not so free of distractions. It has long been argued that tests of maximal performance measure different things than tests of typical performance (i.e., how well a person *can* do a task versus how well he or she *does* it; see Cronbach, 1970, for an excellent discussion of the typical-maximal distinction). Research has shown that tests of typical versus maximal performance are not highly correlated (Sackett, Zedeck & Fogli, 1988). A content-oriented analysis of work sample tests would not account for this finding unless it considered the effects of a wide range of variables, such as the repondent's motivation to perform on responses to test items.

Outcome of a Content Validity Study

The principal outcome of a content validity study is a judgment about the adequacy with which the test samples a particular content domain. Lawshe (1975) has proposed a *content validity ratio* as a measure of the extent to which expert judges agree on content validity, but this statistic measures agreement rather than validity itself. To our knowledge, there is no single statistic that can be used to measure content validity.

Although there is no exact measure of content validity, it is clear that some studies provide more and better evidence for content validity than others. The key to deciding whether it is possible to make systematic and reliable judgments about content validity lies in the description of the content domain. The more detail provided about the boundaries and structure of the content domain, the more confidence that can be placed in judgments about content validity. If a test developer cannot clearly describe the boundaries and the contents of a particular domain, it is difficult to see how he or she could ever convincingly demonstrate content validity. However, even if we assume that the domain is well understood and that we can, with some confidence, establish that the test *is* a representative sample from the domain, we are still not out of the woods. Even if the right types of items are sampled, the way they are written may be confusing or the response formats used may be inappropriate. Thus, two tests that both show strong evidence of content validity will not necessarily produce identical scores. Although a test that is known to provide a representative sample of a particular domain is very likely to provide a valid and accurate measure of that domain, it is important to remember that a content validity study cannot, by itself, guarantee the validity of measurement.

Content Validity, Reliability, and the Validity of Decisions

You may have noted the strong similarity between our discussion of reliability and our discussion of content validity. Although reliability studies and content validity studies address somewhat different questions, reliability and content validity are conceptually similar (Cronbach et al., 1972). The difference is mainly one of emphasis. Reliability theory assumes that the test represents a sample from a domain of possible test items; this same assumption provides the basis for studies of content validity. The principal difference between a reliability study and a content validity study lies in the emphasis placed on providing a precise description of the domain. Reliability theory simply assumes that there is a domain and that the test could be lengthened by sampling more items from that domain. In a content validity study, the researcher must describe in detail *which* domain he or she wishes to measure. Thus, if a test provides a reliable measure of *some* domain but fails to measure the particular domain that is of interest, one might achieve a high level of reliability with little or no content validity.

It seems clear that content validity is important to understanding test scores. However, there is some controversy over whether content validity can be used to establish the validity of decisions based on test scores. A number of researchers have suggested that a content validity approach might be useful in determining whether specific tests could be used in applications such as personnel selection. The basic argument is as follows: (a) tests are used to predict performance on the job; (b) job performance requires certain abilities and skills; (c) if the tests require the same abilities and skills as those required on the job, then tests could be used to predict job performance; and (d) therefore, the validity of a test for selection decisions can be established by comparing the content of the test with the content of the job. This type of definition of content validity has been widely accepted both by industry and by the federal government. However, most experts agree that content validity is relevant only in determining the validity of measurement (does the test measure what it claims to measure?), not in determining the validity of decisions that are made based on test scores.

Carrier, Delessio, and Brown (1990) investigated the hypothesis that judgments about the content validity of tests would allow one to assess the validity of those tests as predictors of important criteria. Their results are sufficiently ambiguous to give comfort to the supporters *and* the detractors of content-oriented strategies of assessing validity for decisions. They found that expert judgments of content validity were significantly correlated with levels of criterion-related validity, but that these correlations were small. Their results suggest that content-related evidence is useful but not sufficient for assessing the criterion-related validity of psychological tests.

CONSTRUCT-ORIENTED VALIDATION STRATEGIES

Psychologists are keenly interested in measuring abstract attributes—happiness, intelligence, motivation, sociability. These things do not exist in the literal, physical sense; it is impossible to gather up a pound of happiness or a handful of intelligence. Nevertheless, they must be measured in order to apply, test, and extend psychological theories and principles.

The problem of measuring abstract attributes is by no means restricted to psychology. Physicists routinely measure unobservable properties of matter. Mass provides a good example of this type of property; mass itself cannot be seen or heard, yet this hypothetical property of objects is clearly important and clearly measurable. Attributes such as mass, happiness, or intelligence are referred to as *constructs*. They represent ideas *constructed* by scientists to help summarize a group of related phenomena or objects. For example, if a person tells the truth in a wide variety of situations, we might label that person as honest. Honesty is a construct; it cannot be *directly* observed, yet it is a useful concept for understanding, describing, and predicting human behavior.

Tests are often designed to measure psychological constructs. Some tests provide valid measures of important constructs, while others show little or no construct validity. Because constructs are abstract in nature, the process of determining whether a test provides an adequate measure of a specific construct is complex.[2] In order to describe the process of construct validation, we must first discuss the nature of psychological constructs.

Constructs

All constructs have two essential properties: They are abstract summaries of some regularity in nature, and they are related to or connected with concrete, observable entities or events. Gravity provides a good example of a construct: When apples fall to earth, the construct gravity is used to explain and predict their behavior. It is impossible to see gravity itself; all one sees is the falling apple. Nevertheless, it makes perfect sense to measure gravity and to develop theories that employ the construct gravity. It certainly

---

[2]Angoff (1988) reviewed the history of different definitions of validity and their relations to construct validation.

seems more sensible to deal with this abstract force we call gravity than to develop theories and methods that apply only to falling apples.

Constructs are essential to science. They represent departures from our immediate sensory experience that are necessary in order to form scientific laws (Margenau, 1950). They allow us to generalize from an experiment involving falling apples to situations involving a variety of falling objects. A construct such as gravity is related to a number of concrete objects and events. Thus, once I learn about gravity, I will be able to predict a wide variety of phenomena.

Constructs are not restricted to unseen forces, such as gravity, or to processes, such as learning. Rather, any group of similar things or events may serve to define a construct. Thus, most categories that we use to classify and discuss everyday objects or events are in fact constructs. For example, the color red is a construct. There are plenty of red things, some of which plainly vary in color, but the basic idea of red is an abstraction. Poverty, reading ability, and cognitive style are thus all labels for constructs (Cronbach, 1971).

Although constructs are themselves hypothetical abstractions, all constructs are related to real, observable things or events. The distinguishing feature of psychological constructs is that they are *always* related, directly or indirectly, to behavior or experience. Some constructs, such as aggressiveness, or achievement motivation, are thought of as causes of particular behaviors. Other constructs, such as pleasure or verbal ability or musical talent, refer to the ability to perform a number of related behaviors. As discussed in the section that follows, still other psychological constructs show no direct connection with observable behaviors; rather, they are connected with other constructs that are, in turn, connected with behavior or experience.

Psychological Constructs

Psychological measurement is a process based upon concrete, observable behaviors. Hence, a psychological test is nothing more than a sample of behaviors. To determine whether a test provides a good measure of a specific construct, we must translate the abstract construct into concrete, behavioral terms. The process of providing a detailed description of the relationship between specific behaviors and abstract constructs, referred to as *construct explication,* is the key to determining the construct validity of a test.

The process of construct explication consists of three steps:

1. Identify the behaviors that relate to the construct to be measured.
2. Identify other constructs and decide whether they are related or unrelated to the construct to be measured.
3. Identify behaviors that are related to each of these additional constructs and, on the basis of the relations among constructs, determine whether each behavior is related to the construct to be measured.

An example describing the three steps of construct explication is presented in Table 7-3. In the table the construct validity of a test designed to measure aggressiveness in school children is being examined. The first step in the process of construct explication is to describe behaviors that are related to aggressiveness. A child who assaults other stu-

TABLE 7-3 STEPS IN DESCRIBING THE CONSTRUCT "AGGRESSIVENESS IN SCHOOL CHILDREN"

1. Identify behaviors related to aggressiveness

Construct	Behavior

Aggressiveness ─── Assaults other students
Aggressiveness ─── Pushes to head of line
Aggressiveness ─── Dominates games

2. Identify other constructs and decide whether they are related to aggressiveness

Construct	Behavior

Need for Power

Aggressiveness ─── Assaults other students
Aggressiveness ─── Pushes to head of line
Aggressiveness ─── Dominates games

Honesty

3. Identify behaviors that are related to each construct and determine their relation to the construct to be measured

Construct	Behavior

Need for Power ─── Makes decisions in groups
Aggressiveness ─── Dominates games
Aggressiveness ─── Assaults other students
Aggressiveness ─── Pushes to head of line
Honesty ─── Refrains from cheating
Honesty ─── Tells truth to the teacher

Note: Constructs and behaviors that are related to one another are connected with a solid line. Unrelated constructs or behaviors are not connected.

dents, who pushes to the head of the line, or who dominates most games might be labelled aggressive. There are many other behaviors that might be considered as examples or manifestations of aggressiveness, and at this stage we should try to provide as many as possible. The more behaviors we are able to list, the clearer the picture will be of what we mean when we say "aggressiveness."

The second step in providing a detailed description of the construct aggressiveness is to identify other constructs that could sensibly be measured in the subject population and to determine whether each of these is related or not related to aggressiveness. For example, it is useful to identify other constructs, such as need for power, that are related to aggressiveness. It is also useful to identify constructs that are clearly *not* related to the specific construct to be measured. For example, the statement that the construct "aggressiveness" is unrelated to the construct "honesty" helps to define the boundaries of both aggressiveness and honesty.

The third step is to identify behaviors that are related to each of these additional constructs. For example, a child who always makes decisions for groups or who dominates games might exhibit a high need for power. A child who refrains from cheating and who tells the truth to his or her teacher might be labelled as honest. Because we have made some statements about the relationships between the constructs of honesty, need for power, and aggressiveness, it should be possible to state whether each of these behaviors is related or unrelated to aggressiveness. For example, if aggressiveness and need for power are related, it is plausible that some behaviors that indicate high levels of need or power (e.g., "dominates games") will also indicate high levels of aggressiveness. Similarly, if aggressiveness and honesty are unrelated, then knowing that a student refrains from cheating or tells the truth to the teacher reveals nothing about his or her level of aggressiveness.

The end result of the process of construct explication is a detailed description of the relationships among a set of constructs and behaviors. This system of relationships, referred to as a *nomological network,* provides a definition of what we mean by "aggressiveness" (Cronbach & Meehl, 1955). Because constructs are abstract in nature, it is impossible to provide a concrete, operational definition of a term such as "aggressiveness." The nomological network provides an alternative way of systematically describing constructs. In our example, aggressiveness is defined as a personal characteristic that is related to a large number of behaviors (e.g., assaulting others), but which is not related to other behaviors (e.g., refraining from cheating). Although a construct cannot be directly observed, it can be inferred from observable behaviors. To put this another way, we cannot say precisely what aggressiveness *is,* but we can describe how an aggressive child might act and we can make reliable and meaningful statements about children's level of aggressiveness by observing their behavior. The more detail included in descriptions of the nomological network, the more precision there will be in describing constructs.

Cronbach (1988, 1989) noted that applications of the methods described in Cronbach and Meehl (1955) have proved to be very difficult. He noted in 1988, "There is no hope for developing in the short run the 'nomological networks' we once envisioned" (p. 13). Thus, construct validity has a somewhat more limited goal than was once envisioned. Rather than embedding each test in a complex network of associations with many other constructs, most construct validity researchers now pursue the goal of determining what inferences about psychological constructs can and cannot be made on the basis of a test score and under what conditions those inferences are or are not valid (Cronbach, 1988).

Assessing Construct Validity

The goal of construct validation is to determine whether test scores provide a good measure of a specific construct. The process of construct explication provides a definition of the construct in terms of concrete behaviors. Although construct explication does not define precisely what a construct such as aggressiveness *is,* it does tell how that construct relates to a number of behaviors. A child who shows a high level of aggressiveness is likely to show certain behaviors (e.g., assaulting classmates) and is less likely to show other behaviors than a child who is low on aggressiveness. A well-developed nomological network, therefore, provides detailed information about the relationship between the construct and a large number of behaviors. This information can be used to describe the way in which a good measure of a construct can be *expected* to relate to each of these behaviors. A test shows a high level of construct validity if the pattern of relationships between test scores and behavior measures is similar to the pattern of relationships that can be expected from a perfect measure of the construct. An example will help to clarify this point.

Our explication of the construct "aggressiveness" (see Table 7-3) suggests that the following behaviors are directly related to the construct: (a) assaulting other students, (b) pushing to the head of lines, and (c) dominating games. In other words, we would expect measures of these behaviors to be positively correlated with a good measure of aggressiveness. The behavior "makes decisions in groups" was related to a construct (need for power) that was in turn related to aggressiveness; we might therefore expect measures of this behavior to show a positive correlation with measures of aggressiveness. Finally, the behaviors "refrains from cheating" and "tells truth to teacher" are not at all related to aggressiveness. We therefore might expect measures of these behaviors to be uncorrelated with a measure of aggressiveness. The correlations we would expect between measures of each of the behaviors and measures of aggressiveness are summarized in Table 7-4.

A detailed description of the construct provides a basis for describing the relationships to be expected between a good measure of that construct and a variety of behaviors. Actual test scores can be correlated with behavior measures, and the results can be compared with the pattern of results expected on the basis of our explication of the construct. The stronger the match between the expected correlations and the actual correlations between test scores and behavior measures, the stronger the evidence of construct validity.

Table 7-5 shows comparisons between expected and actual correlations for two tests designed to measure aggressiveness in school children. Test A appears to be a valid measure of the construct "aggressiveness"; the correlations between test scores and behavior measures are very similar to the correlations one would expect on the basis of our theory of aggressiveness. In contrast, the data suggest that test B is a poor measure of aggressiveness. Behaviors we would expect to correlate strongly with aggressiveness show weak and sometimes negative correlations with test scores. Other behaviors that have nothing to do with aggressiveness show fairly sizable correlations with

TABLE 7-4   THE EXPECTED CORRELATIONS BETWEEN A GOOD MEASURE
OF AGGRESSIVENESS AND MEASURES OF SPECIFIC BEHAVIORS

Behaviors	Relationship with aggressiveness	Expected correlation
Assaulting others	Direct	Strong Positive
Pushing in line	Direct	Strong Positive
Dominating games	Direct	Strong Positive
Making decisions	Indirect—related to need for power	Weak Positive
Refraining from cheating	None	None
Telling truth to teacher	None	None

TABLE 7-5   CORRELATIONS BETWEEN TEST SCORES AND BEHAVIOR MEASURES FOR TWO TESTS

Behaviors	Expected correlations	Actual correlations	
		Test A	Test B
Assaulting others	Strong Positive	.59	−.22
Pushing in line	Strong Positive	.70	.14
Dominating games	Strong Positive	.65	.02
Making decisions in groups	Weak Positive	.30	−.40
Refraining from cheating	None	.09	.56
Telling truth to teacher	None	−.04	.39
		(Test with *high* level of construct validity)	(Test with *low* level of construct validity)

test B. It appears fair to conclude that test B does not measure aggressiveness *as we have defined it.*

Construct validity depends upon a detailed description of the relationship between the construct and a number of different behaviors. The more we know about the construct, the better our chances for determining whether a test provides an adequate measure of that construct. One implication is that it will be easier to determine construct validity for measures of well-defined constructs than for measures of constructs that are loosely defined. If I define a new construct but have only a fuzzy idea of what that construct means, it follows that I will never be able to tell whether a given test provides a good measure of that construct.

A very sophisticated version of the validation strategy described here was applied by Mumford, Weeks, Harding, and Fleishman (1988) in their analysis of the relationships among student characteristics, course content, and training outcomes. Their study incorporated measures of six student characteristics, sixteen measures of course content, and seven measures of training outcomes. They articulated hypotheses about the relationships between each of these 29 measures and criterion variables, and they developed an integrated model that described the hypothesized relationships. This model allowed them to describe the relationships among the three constructs (i.e., characteristics, content, and outcomes) and to draw conclusions about the relative importance of individual versus situational variables in determining training outcomes.

Another example of this approach is in a study by Pulakos, Borman, and Hough (1988), in which experts were first asked to estimate the correlations they would expect between specific predictors and criteria. This allowed the authors to compare the estimated correlations with the correlations they actually found. Results of one study of army enlisted personnel, in which there were eight predictors and three criteria, are presented in Table 7-6. In this study, 83 percent of the obtained correlations were in the predicted direction. Although the observed correlations were typically smaller than the estimated correlations, 87 percent of the correlations were of the relative magnitude

TABLE 7-6 ESTIMATED AND OBTAINED CORRELATIONS FOR ARMY ENLISTED PERSONNEL

	Criteria					
	Technical skill		Personal discipline		Military bearing	
Predictors	Est.	Obs.	Est.	Obs.	Est.	Obs.
Technical	.38	.21	.11	.00	.09	−.18
Quantitative	.27	.17	.10	.06	.07	−.08
Verbal	.29	.16	.08	.04	.08	−.19
Speed	.16	.09	.07	.04	.06	.07
Achievement Orientation	.50	.23	.36	.03	.25	.17
Dependability	.36	.15	.54	.22	.31	.14
Adjustment	.34	.12	.44	.05	.19	.11
Physical Fitness	.16	−.01	.10	−.11	.54	.27

Note: Est. = Expert judge estimates; Obs. = Observed correlations, $N = 8,642$.

Source: From Pulakos, Borman, and Hough (1988). Reproduced with permission.

predicted by the experts (i.e., those predicted to be largest were, in fact, usually the largest). These results present strong evidence for the construct validity of the measures employed.

Methods of Construct Validation

Which methods are most appropriate for studying construct validity depend to a large extent on the construct we wish to measure. A combination of laboratory experiments, field experiments, questionnaires, and unobtrusive observations might be necessary to provide the data that underly construct validation. Statistics that deal with differences between control and experimental groups, with correlations between various measures, with individual variations, or with change over time might be used to test predictions that are based upon our description of the construct. Data about the reliability of a test under different conditions might contribute to our assessment of construct validity. In fact, it would be fair to say that *any* type of data or statistic might be useful in determining construct validity.

Although any method might be used to assess construct validity, a few methods seem to be most common. The most basic method is to correlate scores on the test in question with scores on a number of other tests. Here, the word "test" is used broadly to indicate any type of behavioral measure. We have already discussed this basic method in some depth and will return to a specialized application of this method in a later section. Another common method of studying construct validity involves the mathematical technique known as factor analysis (see Chapter 3). Factors are very much like constructs, and factor analysis provides an analytical method for estimating the correlation between a specific variable (a test score) and scores on the factor. Factor analysis also provides a compact summary of information about the relationship among a large number of measures. The description of a construct provides information about the expected relationships among variables; factor analysis helps determine whether this pattern of relationships does indeed exist.

A third common method of studying construct validity involves experimental manipulation of the construct that is to be measured. For example, a test designed to measure anxiety should show higher scores for subjects in an experiment who are led to expect shocks than for subjects who expect to fill out an innocuous questionnaire. On the other hand, if a study has nothing to do with anxiety, the control group and the experimental group would *not* be expected to receive different scores on the test of anxiety. A combination of experiments in which the construct of interest is manipulated and experiments in which that construct is *not* manipulated provides a powerful method for assessing construct validity.

A study by Flynn (1987) illustrates the use of archival data and reviews of existing research in construct validation. This study reviewed research from 14 nations documenting substantial rises in IQ scores over the last 30 to 40 years. Flynn (1987) noted that there are several correlates of increasing IQ scores, including increases in scientific achievement, superior performance in schools, and an increase in the number of individuals classified as "geniuses." He then surveyed selected newspapers, magazines, and educational journals in countries exhibiting substantial increases in IQ scores and looked for evidence of these phenomena (e.g., an increasing number of patents and inventions, news stories describing an increase in the number of geniuses). His survey showed no evidence of increases in scientific achievement, inventions, and so forth, to go along with the massive increases in IQ, leading him to question whether the IQ tests surveyed really measured intelligence.

Multitrait-Multimethod Approach

Campbell and Fiske (1959) outlined an approach that is very often used in assessing construct validity. They noted that if we use a number of methods to measure more than one trait or construct, the correlations among these measures will take the form of a *multitrait-multimethod matrix*. For example, the honesty, the aggressiveness, and the intelligence of a group of school children might be measured using three methods: teacher ratings, paper-and-pencil tests, and ratings from outside observers. The correlations among these three traits, measured by each of these three methods, are shown in Table 7-7.

A multitrait-multimethod study provides a great deal of data that is useful in assessing construct validity. First, since each of the constructs is measured using a number of different methods, it is possible to determine whether different methods of measurement produce comparable sources. The correlations between a test measuring honesty, teacher ratings of honesty, and observers' ratings of honesty indicate whether these three methods all measure the same construct. Correlations between different measures of the same construct are underlined in Table 7-7. The data suggest that different methods of measuring honesty, aggressiveness, and intelligence are in pretty close agreement—correlations between different measures of each of the three traits range from .52 to .82. Thus, there is evidence for *convergent validity*—multiple measures of each of the three constructs converge to yield similar results. The convergence of different methods serves

TABLE 7-7   A MULTITRAIT-MULTIMETHOD MATRIX

Method	Trait	Teacher ratings			Tests			Observers' ratings		
		Honesty	Aggressiveness	Intelligence	Honesty	Aggressiveness	Intelligence	Honesty	Aggressiveness	Intelligence
Teacher Ratings	Honesty									
	Aggressiveness	.43								
	Intelligence	.36	.32							
Tests	Honesty	.62	.03	.20						
	Aggressiveness	.22	.70	.13	.40					
	Intelligence	.10	.13	.64	.22	.30				
Observers' Ratings	Honesty	.59	.11	.02	.60	.20	.21			
	Aggressiveness	.14	.82	−.16	.13	.61	.23	.30		
	Intelligence	.21	.10	.72	.06	.19	.52	.49	.36	

Note: Convergent validity coefficients are underlined. Correlations between different constructs using the same method (e.g., teacher ratings) are enclosed in solid triangles. Correlations between measures of different constructs using different methods are enclosed in broken triangles.

to increase our confidence that we are, in fact, measuring the constructs we wish to measure. Therefore, convergent validity is the first link in establishing construct validity.

The correlations between different traits or constructs are enclosed within solid and broken triangles in Table 7-7. In designing a multitrait-multimethod study, the researcher will usually select a group of constructs that are *not,* in theory, strongly related. Therefore, correlations between measures of different traits should be small—certainly smaller than correlations between different measures of the same trait. The correlations between measures of different constructs or traits serve to indicate the *discriminant validity.* Constructs are chosen to be clearly different, and measures of those constructs should therefore not correlate highly. Since the correlations between measures of different constructs shown in the table are clearly smaller than the correlations between different measures of the same construct, there appears to be evidence for discriminant validity. That is, the three constructs being measured in this study seem to be discriminably different. Since the constructs intelligence, honesty, and aggressiveness are, in theory, unrelated, low correlations between measures of those constructs provide further evidence of construct validity.

The correlations enclosed in solid triangles represent measures of different constructs using the same method. For example, the table shows the correlations between teacher ratings of honesty, aggressiveness, and intelligence. The correlations between measures of different traits obtained using a single method (e.g., teacher ratings) are somewhat larger than the correlations enclosed in broken triangles, which represent correlations between different traits measured by different methods. This frequently found pattern indicates *method bias*. For example, the correlation between honesty ratings and intelligence ratings provided by the teacher is higher than any of the honesty-intelligence correlations that involve two different methods of measurement. When two different constructs are measured using the same method, we expect some correlation solely as a result of the common method of measurement. A multitrait-multimethod study allows us to estimate the effects of that bias.

The multitrait-multimethod approach is an efficient and informative method for studying several questions related to construct validity. This method suggests that a good test of a particular construct has three characteristics:

1. Scores on the test will be consistent with scores obtained using other measures of the same construct.
2. The test will yield scores that are *not* correlated with measures that are theoretically unrelated to the construct being measured.
3. The method of measurement employed by the test shows little evidence of bias.

The data from a multitrait-multimethod study can often be difficult to interpret; in the simple example presented here, there were 36 separate correlation coefficients to consider. A number of analytic methods have been proposed to simplify the interpretation of multitrait-multimethod matrices, ranging from the analysis of variance (Kavanaugh, MacKinney & Wolins, 1971; Stanley, 1961) to confirmatory factor analysis (Schmitt & Stults, 1986). In addition, sophisticated analytic methods have been developed for answering questions implicit in the multitrait-multimethod design, such as whether or not two tests measure the same construct (Turban, Sanders, Francis & Osburn, 1989).

Strong versus Weak Evidence of Construct Validity

Cronbach (1988, 1989) contrasted two different strategies for construct validation research. The weak version of construct validation involves collecting all the relevant evidence about the relationship between scores on a test and other measures. He dismissed this strategy as "*Dragnet* empiricism," in the sense that it involves collecting "just the facts," with little regard for their usefulness in understanding the test or the construct being measured. He criticizes most applications of the multitrait-multimethod design as mindless and mechanical; the selection of traits and methods is more often based on convenience than on compelling hypotheses.

In contrast, the strong version of construct validation involves testing your interpretation of test scores against other plausible hypotheses. Landy (1987) notes that all validation studies involve hypotheses testing, but it is clear that some hypotheses would allow you to gather strong evidence of construct validity and others would give only weak support for a particular interpretation of test scores. For example, suppose you were interested in evaluating the construct validity of situational interviews that are used in personnel selection (Latham, Saari, Pursell & Campion, 1980). This type of interview presents the interviewee with descriptions of several hypothetical situations he or she might encounter at work, then asks the interviewee what he or she should do in each situation. Research on criterion-related validity shows that these interviews predict subsequent job performance. A weak program of construct validation would involve gathering as much information as possible about variables that could conceivably be related to outcomes of these interviews (e.g., biographical data, performance data, and scores on standard interviews). A strong program of construct validation would start with specific hypotheses about what such an interview actually measures. Several possibilities come to mind. First, the interviews might measure a social desirability factor; people who know the desirable answer to the questions in these interviews might do well in them and also do well in jobs that require social interactions. Second, these interviews might measure general intelligence; people who are intelligent might be better able to diagnose the situations presented to them and arrive at the best response to each situation. Third, these interviews might measure some type of job knowledge; people with experience in similar situations might be best equipped to perform well in such an interview. A strong program of construct validation would incorporate measures of intelligence, social desirability, and prior experience, and it would determine the extent to which each could account for the situational interview's validity in predicting job performance.

A second difference between a strong and weak program of construct validation may be temporal. Weak construct validation research is often done after the fact (i.e., after the test has been developed) to determine just what an existing test or assessment procedure measured. Strong programs of construct validation often begin at the test development stage (Fiske, 1987; Frederickson, 1986). That is, a strong program of construct validation is easiest to carry out if the initial decision about what types of items, response formats, and so forth, to use are guided by your understanding of the construct you wish to measure. If the design of the test does not spring from the nature of the construct, it may subsequently be very difficult to demonstrate that it does indeed measure the construct of interest.

CONTENT AND CONSTRUCT VALIDITY

Content validity is typically determined by examining the sampling plan of the test and seeing whether the test provides a representative sample of the content domain. Construct validity is established by showing that the relationship between test scores and other observable measures is similar to the relationships that would be expected between the construct itself and those observable measures. Furthermore, content validity is typically determined for tests of very concrete domains, such as classroom tests, whereas construct validity is generally determined for tests designed to measure abstract attributes, such as aggressiveness or honesty. It would therefore seem that content and construct validity are very different, and perhaps mutually exclusive. Although there is some merit to this point of view, it is better to view content and construct validity as highly related. First, both represent approaches for determining the validity of measurement—for determining whether a test measures what it purports to measure. Second, the distinction between a construct and a content domain is not as fundamental as it might appear (Landy, 1987; Messick, 1988). A content domain represents a group of similar test items whose boundaries and structure are fairly well understood. Although in theory it may be possible to sample *all* the items in a content domain, in practice, test scores are used to estimate the hypothetical score on the domain. In other words, an individual's standing or score on a content domain is an abstraction, very much like a person's level of a construct such as honesty. Many researchers feel that most content categories *are* constructs (Cronbach, 1971).

The similarity between content domains and constructs suggests that both content- and construct-oriented approaches may be applicable in a variety of cases. Content validity can be determined whenever the boundaries and structure of a domain can be described in some detail. Construct validity can be determined whenever the researcher can provide a detailed statement about the relationship between the construct and a variety of concrete, observable measures. Both strategies provide evidence that the test measures what it is designed to measure; the combination of content and construct validity represents very strong evidence for the validity of measurement. It is never possible to say with complete certainty that test *X* measures construct *Y* or domain *Z*, but methods described here allow the accumulation of clear and compelling evidence that the test measures what it is supposed to measure. Content validity is established if a test *looks* like a valid measure;[3] construct validity is established if a test *acts* like a valid measure.

There are a few cases in which one must choose to follow either a content validity approach or a construct validity approach. For example, a good deal may be known about the boundaries and structure of a domain such as "knowledge of behavioral statistics," but nothing about how knowledge of statistics should relate to other observable traits or behaviors. In this case, there would be little choice—content validity would represent the most feasible approach for assessing the validity of measurement. On the other hand, one might have a very clear idea of how a construct such as "honesty" relates to a number of observable behaviors, yet be unclear as to the boundaries of the construct. Here, content validity would be out of the question; a construct validity approach would be the only one feasible. Both of these examples represent cases in which the theory of what is being measured has not been fully developed. In other words, both of these cases represent situations where because of a poorly developed theory of the domain or construct to be measured, it is impossible to say precisely what would represent a good test or a bad test. In these situations, it is difficult to demonstrate convincingly the validity of measurement.

---

[3]The term "face validity" is used to denote the layperson's judgment that a test looks like it measures what it is supposed to measure. Here, we are referring to a more detailed examination of the relationship between the test and the domain.

CRITICAL DISCUSSION:
Do Intelligence Tests Really Measure Intelligence?

There is considerable controversy over the validity of intelligence tests. In later chapters we review some of the evidence that bears on this controversy. It is useful here to consider the methods that are used to determine whether intelligence tests really measure intelligence. A brief review of these methods will illustrate the process by which the validity of measurement is determined.

A content validity strategy is not very useful in assessing the validity of intelligence tests. Intelligence is a very broad concept; it would be very difficult to draw up an exhaustive list of the types that could be used to represent intelligence. In other words, it would be nearly impossible to specify the boundaries and content of the intelligence domain.

Several research strategies have been used in assessing the construct validity of intelligence tests. All these strategies depend on key assumptions that are made in defining the construct "intelligence." In particular:

1. Intelligence is assumed to involve the processing, retrieval, and manipulation of information.

2. Activities that require complex information processing will draw more heavily on intelligence than will activities that represent simple information-processing tasks.

3. Intelligence is a general construct that is related to a wide range of specific cognitive abilities.

The use of digit span tests illustrates an application of the first two assumptions. For example, if I read to you a list of nine digits, more mental manipulation is required to repeat the list backwards from memory (you must store, retrieve, and mentally invert the list) than to repeat the list in its original order (here, you only store and retrieve the list). Since general intelligence involves the processing of information, it follows that mental tasks that involve more complex processes should be more highly correlated with intelligence tests than will tasks that involve simpler processes. In this context, a higher correlation can be expected between intelligence test scores and scores of tests that involve repeating digit spans backwards than between intelligence and simple digit span tests. Most good intelligence tests show exactly this pattern (Jensen, 1980). A new test that also showed this pattern of results would exhibit evidence of construct validity.

Another method of validating intelligence tests is to consider situations that, to different extents, involve general intelligence. For example, school places heavy demands on information-processing abilities, whereas in many social situations, individual differences in intelligence have very little bearing on behavior. We would therefore expect intelligence test scores to be highly correlated with success in school but to show much smaller correlations with measures of social skills. Once again, this is exactly the pattern of results found when validating most intelligence tests (see, however, Flynn, 1987).

A third method of validating an intelligence test is to correlate scores on that test with scores on other, well-validated tests of specific cognitive abilities, including other intelligence tests. This procedure may sound circular, but it does provide useful evidence. If there is solid evidence that tests X, Y, and Z are well-validated measures of intelligence, it follows that any new test of intelligence should yield similar scores to those obtained using the existing tests. If the new test has nothing in common with the existing, well-validated tests of intelligence, it would be difficult to conclude that the new test really measures intelligence. Higher correlations would also be expected between scores on intelligence tests and scores on tests of abilities that are, in theory, strongly related to intelligence (e.g., verbal ability) than between intelligence tests and tests of abilities thought to be minimally related to general intelligence (e.g., simple reaction time).

The best validation research employs multiple methods. It would be difficult to conclude on the basis of any single finding that a test *really* measures intelligence. Several well-researched intelligence tests present evidence from multiple sources and by multiple methods that test scores act the way that the construct itself is assumed to act. In other words, research involving diverse methods, research questions, and subject populations has provided evidence of the construct validity of these tests that is accepted by many psychologists.

Summary

To understand validation, it is important to keep in mind exactly *what* is validated. It is not the test that is validated but, rather, the inferences that are made on the basis of test scores. For example, if an individual receives a high score on an inventory designed to measure need for achievement, you might infer that he or she shows high levels of achievement motivation. You might also infer that he or she would do well in a management training course. The first type of inference concerns measurement, and this was dealt with in this chapter. The second type of inference involves a prediction about something other than the attribute that was directly measured, and this is dealt with in the chapter that follows.

Both content-oriented and construct-oriented strategies are used to assess the validity of measurement. Content-oriented strategies are based on the simple premise that tests are samples of behavior. Content-oriented validation strategies involve examining the degree to which the sample is representative of the broader domain you wish to measure. In applying this strategy, you must not only examine the test items but also consider the response processes and the behaviors elicited by the test. The greater the match between the behaviors actually sampled on the test and those that represent the domain you wish to measure, the greater your confidence in the validity of measurement.

Construct-oriented strategies start with construct explication, that is, the detailed description of exactly what the test is designed to measure. Psychological constructs are by definition linked to observable behaviors, and the process of construct explication involves describing those links in as much detail as possible. A successful construct explication will give you a very clear idea of how a good measure of the construct should relate to a wide variety of other measures, which in turn gives you a yardstick for evaluating your measure. If the test you are studying acts like a good measure, in the sense that it is related to other constructs and measures in the same way as the construct you have explicated, you can infer that it provides valid measurement.

Research provides no definite answers regarding the validity of measurement—you can never be 100 percent certain that your measure is a valid measure. However, the accumulation of evidence over several studies should increase your confidence that you are indeed measuring the content domain or the construct you intend to measure. As you will see in Chapters 13–22, most of the tests that are used to make important decisions about individuals are supported by large bodies of research, often applying many if not all of the methods of validation described in this chapter.

CHAPTER 8

VALIDITY FOR DECISIONS: CRITERION-RELATED VALIDITY

As noted in Chapter 1, a major reason for our interest in tests is that they are used to make important decisions about individuals. Tests do not always lead to correct decisions; but compared to other alternatives, they are thought to represent the most accurate, fair, and economical method of making decisions (Wigdor & Garner, 1982a). In fact, in settings where decisions must be made about large numbers of individuals (e.g., in screening military recruits), psychological tests often represent the *only* practical method of making systematic decisions.

The validity of tests as decision-making aids is a topic of great practical importance. The accuracy of decisions is directly linked to the validity of test scores—an invalid test can lead to decisions that are both ineffective, from the decision maker's point of view, and unfair, from the individual's point of view. The simplest method of determining whether a test can be used validly in making decisions is to correlate test scores with measures of success or of the outcomes of decisions. These measures are referred to as criteria; hence the term "criterion-related validity." The correlation between test scores and criteria provides a quantitative estimate of validity, which in turn can be used to obtain a detailed picture of the effect of testing on decisions. In particular, measures of criterion-related validity provide means to determine whether tests will serve to reduce particular types of decision errors and whether the gains in the accuracy of decisions are worth the costs of testing. This chapter presents a number of methods of estimating and interpreting the criterion-related validity of a test.

DECISIONS AND PREDICTION

Mathematical decision theory makes a formal distinction between a *decision,* which involves choosing a particular course of action, and a *prediction,* which involves estimating the value of some variable, such as success in school, on the basis of what is known about another variable, such as Scholastic Aptitude Test (SAT) scores. Criterion-related validity deals with the correlation between tests and criteria, or with the degree to which test scores can be used to predict criteria. Although a prediction is formally different from a decision, there are strong conceptual similarities between predictions and decisions. In fact, these are sufficiently strong that we will treat the correlation between test scores and criteria as synonymous with validity for decisions. An example will help to clarify both the similarities and the differences between predictions and decisions.

Assume that you are a personnel manager trying to pick the best three applicants for the job of master machinist out of the five shown in Table 8-1.

TABLE 8-1 MECHANICAL COMPREHENSION SCORES OF FIVE APPLICANTS

Applicant	Scores on mechanical comprehension test (100 = Perfect score)
A	98
B	82
C	81
D	43
E	29

Applicants A, B, and C have reasonably high test scores, while D and E have low scores. If you had no other information, you would probably predict that A, B, and C would perform well on the job, and you therefore would hire these three and reject D and E.[1] Prediction occurs when you try to estimate a person's score on a particular measure, such as a measure of job performance, on the basis of that person's score on some other measure, such as a mechanical comprehension test. Thus, you predict that applicants with high test scores will perform well on the job. You never *know* how someone will actually perform, but a good test allows you to make fairly accurate predictions. A decision represents some action that you take on the basis of your predictions. You hire someone because you predict he or she will perform well on the job; you select a particular course of psychotherapy because you predict that it will be most beneficial for a particular client; you place a child in a special remedial class because you predict that the class will provide a suitable learning environment for the child. Predictions are not

---

[1]Note that although it is *predicted* that A will be better than C, the same action is taken toward both (both are hired). This is one of the differences between prediction and decision.

always accurate, and therefore tests do not always lead you to make the correct decisions; however, the more accurate your predictions, the better your decisions will be.

The correlation between test scores and a measure of the outcome of a decision (the criterion) provides an overall measure of the accuracy of predictions. Therefore, the correlation between test scores and criterion scores can be thought of as a measure of the validity of decisions. As will be seen in a later section, thorough investigation of the effect of tests on decisions involves a number of factors in addition to the criterion-related validity of the test. Nevertheless, the *validity coefficient,* or the correlation between test scores and criterion scores, provides the basic measure of the validity of a test for making decisions.

CRITERIA

A *criterion* is a measure that could be used to determine the accuracy of a decision. In psychological testing, criteria typically represent measures of the outcomes that specific treatments or decisions are designed to produce. For example, workers are selected for jobs on the basis of predictions the personnel department makes regarding their future performance on the job; the job applicants who are actually hired are those who, on the basis of test scores or other measures, are predicted to perform at the highest level. Actual measures of performance on the job serve as criteria for evaluating the personnel department's decisions. If the workers who were hired actually *do* perform at a higher level than would have those who were not hired, the predictions of the personnel department are confirmed, or validated. In a similar way, measures of grade point average or years to complete a degree might serve as criteria for evaluating selection and placement decisions in the schools. A particular strategy for making college admissions decisions may be a good one if the students who are accepted receive better grades or complete their degrees in a shorter time than the applicants who were rejected would have done. Again, in a similar way, measures of adjustment or of symptom severity might be used to evaluate decisions regarding the choice of psychotherapy.

An example will help to illustrate the importance of developing appropriate criterion measures. For years, the military has used the Armed Services Vocational Aptitude Battery (ASVAB) in the selection and placement of new recruits. The principal evidence for the validity of the ASVAB has been the finding that ASVAB scores are consistently correlated with success in military training courses. However, the ASVAB was designed and has been used to predict performance on the job, not performance in training. Thus, until recently it was not proven that the ASVAB leads to correct decisions, although research on the validity of similar tests suggests that it does (Schmidt & Hunter, 1981). To correct this, the military undertook large-scale research efforts to develop measures of job performance and to assess the criterion-related validity of the ASVAB.

Unfortunately, the choice of criterion measures used in determining the validity of tests is often made in a careless or haphazard manner (Guion, 1965a). The key to choosing criterion measures is to determine the decision maker's goal. The goal of the personnel department is to select productive workers; the appropriate criterion for evaluating its decisions will be a measure of productivity. The goal of admissions directors is to select students who are capable of performing well in classes; measures of classroom performance will supply criteria for evaluating their decisions.

CRITERION-RELATED VALIDATION STRATEGIES

There are two general methods for assessing criterion-related validity: *predictive* and *concurrent* validation strategies. Predictive validity is recognized as the most accurate method of estimating validity, but is also recognized as presenting the most serious practical and ethical problems. Concurrent validity is a generic term which refers to a variety of more practical procedures for assessing validity. Barrett, Phillips, and Alexander (1981), Guion and Cranny (1982), and Schmitt, Gooding, Noe, and Kirsch (1984) note that the conceptual and empirical distinctions between predictive and concurrent validity are not necessarily fundamental. However, the two general approaches do raise different practical, ethical, and statistical issues and are therefore worth discussing separately. We should emphasize here that these two approaches represent different strategies for estimating the same quantity, the correlation between test scores and criterion scores. These two strategies differ in a number of practical and operational details, but not in their fundamental goals.[2]

The Ideal: Predictive Validation Strategies

The goal of a predictive validity study is to determine the correlation between test scores, which are obtained *before* making decisions, and criterion scores, which are obtained *after* making decisions. Personnel selection represents a typical setting in which a predictive validity study might be carried out; here, a decision must be made to hire or reject each applicant, and a measure of job performance serves as a criterion for evaluating that decision. In this setting, a predictive validity study consists of two simple steps:

1. Obtain test scores from a group of applicants, but *do not* use the test, either directly or indirectly, in making hiring decisions.
2. At some later time obtain performance measures for those persons hired and correlate those measures with test scores to obtain the predictive validity coefficient.

The predictive validity approach is thought of as an ideal for two conflicting reasons. From the scientific point of view, it represents the simplest and most accurate strategy for estimating the correlation between test scores and criterion scores in the population of applicants in general. Yet in another sense, this strategy is impractical, so although it is considered an ideal strategy for estimating validity, it is not a realistic one. The distinguishing feature of the predictive validity approach lies in the fact that decisions are made about applicants *without* using the test for making decisions, either directly or indirectly.

[2]A third strategy, referred to as synthetic validity, has been used to infer or estimate the validity of both tests and test batteries (Guion, 1965b). This strategy provides logical estimates of validity based on the tests' ability to predict various components of the criterion.

The advantage of the predictive validity approach is that it provides a simple and direct measure of the relationship between scores on the test and performance on the criterion for the population of applicants in general. If the test *were* used to select applicants, the correlation between test scores and performance measures (which are collected at some later time) would indicate the validity of the test in the population of people with high test scores (those selected using the test), rather than the validity of the test in the population in general. In most decision situations, the goal is to select those most likely to succeed out of the total population of applicants. In order to estimate the validity of a test for this type of decision, an estimate of the correlation between test scores and performance scores must be obtained for *all* applicants. Most practical methods for estimating the validity of decisions involve correlating test scores and criterion scores in some preselected population (e.g., present workers) and therefore fall short of the ideal predictive validity approach.

Practical objections. The key to the predictive validity approach is the requirement that the population in the validity study be similar to the general population of applicants. The only effective way to carry out a predictive validity study is either to make the same decision for everyone (e.g., hire all applicants) or to make decisions on a random basis (e.g., flip a coin). It is understandable that decision makers object to an approach that forces them to abandon, albeit temporarily, any system of selection in order to guarantee that the sample of people selected is representative of the population of applicants. It is impractical to hire people, admit them to school, or assign them to different types of therapy on a random basis. Of course, if the present system has little or no validity, decisions based on a table of random numbers are not likely to be any worse. Still, as a matter of practical politics, it is difficult to envision many people accepting an *explicitly* random system, such as would be necessary in a true predictive validity approach.

Ethical objections. An incorrect decision has negative consequences for both the individual and the decision maker. For example, an organization that hires a worker who has little chance of success on the job is likely to incur substantial losses in terms of training costs and lost productivity. The individual also incurs some serious costs—failure on the job is a very negative experience and may contribute to depression or to loss of self-esteem, not to mention the monetary loss incurred when the employee is subsequently dismissed. Likewise, the psychologist who adopts a predictive validity approach would have to tolerate a number of failures that are probably preventable, with sometimes serious consequences to the clients involved. Thus, the predictive validity approach puts the decision maker in the ethically precarious position of selecting some people who he or she believes are very likely to fail (i.e., those with low test scores).

The Practical Alternative: Concurrent Validation Strategies

The practical alternative to a predictive validity strategy is simply to obtain both test scores and criterion scores in some intact, preselected population and to compute the correlation between the two. Since many research designs of this type call for obtaining test scores and criterion scores at roughly the same time, they are known as *concurrent* validation strategies. As Guion and Cranny (1982) point out, the delay between obtaining test scores and obtaining criterion is not really the most fundamental difference between predictive and concurrent validity. The most fundamental difference is that a predictive validity coefficient is obtained in a random sample of the population about whom decisions must be made, whereas a concurrent validity coefficient is generally obtained in a preselected sample (e.g., present employees, students already accepted into college, patients in therapy) that may be systematically different from the population in general.

Guion and Cranny (1982) describe a number of common concurrent strategies for estimating the validity of a test for predicting scores on a specific criterion; three of these are especially common and can be described in simple terms (see also Sussman & Robertson, 1986). First, one can give the test to individuals who have already been selected (e.g., current workers, college freshmen) from the applicant population and obtain the criterion measure at approximately the same time the test is given. The correlation between test scores and criterion measures is a validity estimate. Next, one can select among applicants using the test (X), following up with a criterion measure (Y) at a later time. Finally, it is possible to use data from personnel files as measures X and Y. In all these designs, the correlation between test scores and criterion scores can be used to estimate the validity of the test, yet the population in which both the predictor and the criterion are measured may be systematically different from the population of applicants in general. The population of workers at a plant or students in a college is much more selective than the population who applied for jobs or who applied for school, since there are typically large numbers of applicants who receive low scores on tests and interviews and hence do not pass the selection process. The fact that the population in a concurrent validity study is significantly more selective than the population of applicants in general has a potentially serious effect on the correlation between test scores and criterion scores. The nature and the extent of this effect are discussed later in this section.

Although in applied settings concurrent validity is much more common than predictive validity, the predictive approach is generally preferred over the concurrent validity approach. The correlation between test scores and criterion scores in some preselected, intact population is in theory not likely to be the same as the correlation between test scores and criterion scores in the population in general. Yet it is the latter correlation that is most important in assessing the validity of decisions. In most cases, tests are used to make decisions about very general populations; the validity of a test in a highly select population will not necessarily reveal much about the validity of the test for making selection decisions.

Advantages. Three factors favor a concurrent validity approach. First, concurrent studies are practical. It is not necessary to select randomly or to allow a significant time lag between testing and criterion measurement in order to obtain concurrent validity coefficients. Second, concurrent validity studies are easier to conduct than predictive studies. In a concurrent study, it might be possible to obtain test scores and performance measures and to correlate them in a single day; a predictive study might last for months or even years. Third, although test theory suggests that concurrent validity coefficients seriously underestimate the population validity, concurrent validities are in fact often similar in size to predictive validities (Barrett, Phillips & Alexander, 1981; Schmitt et al., 1984). Although there may be considerable theoretical differences between a predictive study and a concurrent study, the outcomes of these two types of studies are often sufficiently similar to justify the more practical concurrent validity approach.

Statistical problems. Research designs that use the correlation between test scores and criterion measures in a highly selective population to estimate the validity of a test for making decisions in the population in general give rise to a number of statistical problems. By far the most serious problem in concurrent designs is the *range restriction* that occurs when people are selected according to their test scores (i.e., only those with high test scores are selected). Range restriction could have a substantial effect on the correlation between test scores and the criterion.

Range restriction also occurs in criterion measures. In work settings, people who perform very poorly are likely to be fired, whereas those who perform well are likely to be promoted. In school, students with consistently low grades are likely to fail or drop out. In clinical settings, clients are not likely to continue treatments that clearly are not working. As a result, the range of criterion scores is likely to be much smaller in an intact, preselected group (workers at a plant, students already admitted to college) than in the population in general.

Range restriction serves to reduce the correlation between test scores and criterion measures. Consider the scattergrams shown in Figure 8-1. In the population of applicants, A, there is a substantial correlation between the test and the criterion. If people are selected on the basis of their test scores, the range of the predictor is directly restricted. Scattergram B shows the effect of selecting those with test scores above 60. It suggests that the correlation between test scores and criterion measures is much smaller in the group whose test scores are above 60 than in the population in general. Range restriction in the criterion has a similar effect. Scattergram C shows the relationship between test scores and criteria for those with *criterion* scores above 60; the correlation between test scores and criteria also is obviously smaller than the population correlation. Finally, scattergram D depicts the correlation between test scores and criteria when there is range restriction in *both* the predictor and the criterion; here the concurrent validity coefficient drops to nearly zero. Direct selection of applicants on the basis of test scores serves to restrict the variability of test scores. Indirect selection on the basis of criterion measures (e.g., promotion of high performers) serves to restrict the variability of criterion scores. In either case, range restriction has a potentially dramatic effect on the correlation between test scores and criteria. Since range restriction often occurs in a concurrent validity study, it is critical to estimate its effects on the correlation between test scores (X) and criterion scores (Y). Guion (1965a) presents the following formula, which can be used to estimate the correlation between X and Y that would be obtained if there were no range restriction in the predictor (e.g., no selection):[3]

$$r_c = \frac{r(\sigma u/\sigma res)}{\sqrt{1 - r^2 + r^2\,(\sigma^2 u/\sigma^2 res)}} \qquad [8\text{-}1]$$

[3]A variety of more complicated formulas exist to correct for direct or indirect range restriction on X, Y, or both.

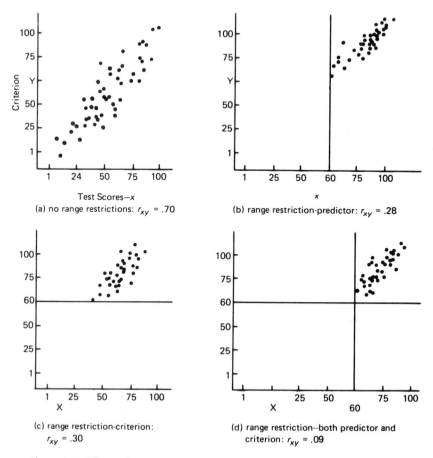

Figure 8-1 Effects of Range Restriction on the Correlation between Test Scores and Criterion Measures

where

r_c = estimate of the population r, correcting for range restriction
r = sample correlation coefficient
σu = standard deviation of the sample on the predictor *before* range restriction
σres = deviation of sample after range restriction

The effects of range restriction can be graphically illustrated by computing estimates of the true correlation between a test and a criterion under varying degrees of range restriction. Table 8-2 shows the best estimate of the population correlation coefficient if the r obtained in a range-restricted sample is equal to .30. As the table shows, when range restriction is minimal (e.g., when σ_x is reduced from .8 to .7), its effects are minimal. However, when range restriction is extensive, the correlation in the restricted sample may seriously underestimate the true r. One implication of Formula 8-1 is that the correlation between test scores and a criterion measure is not likely to be large if a

TABLE 8-2   EFFECTS OF RANGE RESTRICTIONS IN THE PREDICTOR X

Standard deviation of X before range restriction	Standard deviation of X after range restriction	Estimated population correlation if the sample $r = .30$
.8	.7	.33
.8	.6	.38
.8	.5	.45
.8	.4	.53
.8	.3	.64
.8	.2	.78

concurrent study is carried out in a setting which is very selective, that is, when only those with extremely high test scores are represented. Formula 8-1 implies that concurrent validity coefficients will generally *underestimate* the validity of the test and that the underestimation may be severe when range restriction is extensive.

Conceptual problems.   Tests are most often used in an attempt to discriminate superior applicants from marginally acceptable or unacceptable applicants. Specifically, the goal of tests in most selection decisions is to screen out probable failures (see Landy, 1978). A predictive validity study provides a measure of how well a test can accomplish this goal; a concurrent validity study may not. A concurrent study typically contains very few, if any, marginal or poor performers. Because a concurrent study is carried out in a preselected population made up of people who are probably performing at acceptable levels (or better), the correlation between test scores and criterion scores measures the validity of the test in discriminating acceptable performers from superior performers. Therefore, a concurrent validity coefficient does not necessarily reveal much about the validity of decisions. If the population in a concurrent validity study is significantly different from the population of applicants in general, it is possible that a concurrent study will not provide a useful estimate of validity for decisions.

There is a second problem with most concurrent studies. The population in a concurrent study often differs from the population of applicants in a number of ways, and some of these differences could have important implications for the correlation between test scores and criteria. For example, a concurrent validity study conducted in a work setting generally includes a number of workers who have extensive experience on the job. The abilities that contribute to a new worker's performance may be completely different from the abilities that determine an experienced worker's performance. Therefore, a test that predicts the performance of experienced workers may not be as useful in predicting the performance of a new worker.

CONSTRUCT VALIDITY AND CRITERION-RELATED VALIDITY

Virtually any validation strategy can provide information about the construct validity of a test or assessment device. Researchers have moved from thinking that there were fundamentally different types of validity toward a unitary definition of validity, in which all validation *is* construct validation (Angoff, 1988; Cronbach, 1988; Landy, 1987; Messick, 1988; see also *Standards for Educational and Psychological Testing,* 1985). Although this unitary definition of validity is useful for organizing and thinking about validation research, the statement that all validity research is concerned (at least implicitly) with construct validity can be confusing. Consider the example of a personnel selection research project in which the researchers want to determine whether a particular test (e.g., the Wonderlic Personnel Test) predicts supervisory judgments about job performance. This appears to be a very practical question, without any of the abstract subtleties of a construct validity study. In fact, however, construct validity is at the heart of a study of this type.

Binning and Barrett (1989) suggest a framework for describing and analyzing validity studies, which can be used to show how the study described previously involves construct validity. The essential features of this framework are illustrated in Figure 8-2.

In Figure 8-2, actual measures are enclosed in rectangular boxes, and constructs are enclosed in elongated circles. In a typical validation study the finding of interest is thought to be the relationship between the actual test and the actual criterion measure (i.e., the arrow between the two boxes). It should be clear, however, that the real concern of the study is the relationship between the predictor and the criterion construct, represented in Figure 8-2 by the heavy arrow. That is, your concern as an applied psychologist is not to predict *ratings* of job performance but, rather, to predict actual job performance. Ratings are used as an operational criterion because you believe, or have evidence to suggest, that they are related to the construct of job performance.

What about the predictor construct (i.e., cognitive ability)? The predictor construct enters into a validation study of this type through the selection of actual tests or predictors. There are several links involved here. First, the predictor construct of ability is believed to be linked to the criterion construct of performance (construct-to-construct link). Second, the actual predictor (the Wonderlic) is thought to be linked to the predictor construct of ability (measure-to-construct link). The combination of these two links suggests that the Wonderlic will be related to performance ratings, which, in turn, will provide evidence for the link between that test and the construct of job performance.

The framework presented here suggests that any *scientific* validation effort will involve constructs on both the predictor side and the criterion side. That is, operational measures of both the predictor and the criterion should be selected on the basis of the constructs they are thought to measure. While it would be possible to select predictor tests and/or criteria without considering the criteria they represent (e.g., you might try

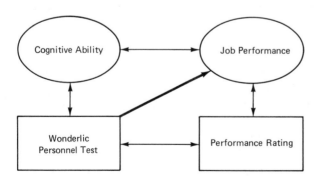

Figure 8-2   Inferences in the Validation Process

out a test that happens to be handy, or use the same criteria some other person has used in the past), a study of this sort would be little more than an exercise in data analysis. A well-designed validity study will always involve inferences about psychological constructs, regardless of the particular validation strategy employed.

Validity Evidence from Meta-Analyses

Novice researchers are often disappointed to find that no matter how original their ideas seem, it usually turns out that someone else has already done a study similar to the one they are designing. There are tens of thousands of studies in the published literature in psychology, and it is not unusual to find hundreds on a given topic [e.g., Ones, Viswesvaran, and Schmidt's (In press) review of the validity of paper-and-pencil integrity tests included over 180 studies, yielding 665 validity coefficients across over 575,000 observations; this review is discussed in Chapter 18]. For any specific test, several studies may be available; and for general classes of tests (e.g., cognitive ability tests), there may be several hundred.

The term "meta-analysis" refers to methods for combining research results from a large number of studies (Hedges & Olkin, 1985; Hunter & Schmidt, 1990). For example, if 50 studies have already been done on the validity of the Wonderlic Personnel Test (see Chapter 18 for a discussion of this test and of meta-analyses of validity studies for similar tests) as a predictor of job performance, the results of those studies can be averaged to give an overall estimate of the validity coefficient. The technical procedures involved in meta-analysis are more complex than computing the mean across all studies; corrections for attenuation and range restriction might be applied, and the results of each study might be weighted by its sample size. Nevertheless, the basic idea of meta-analysis, that the results of previous research should be considered in evaluating the criterion-related validity of any test or group of tests, is a simple one that has gained broad professional acceptance.

One reason for placing our discussion of meta-analysis in a section dealing with construct validity is that a clear specification of the construct is often critical for performing and interpreting a meta-analysis. It is rare for there to be large numbers of studies that use *precisely* the same tests and criterion measures, and it is necessary to make judgments about which studies should be grouped together. Returning to the example above, the studies examining correlations between scores on the Wonderlic Personnel Test and measures of job performance might include a variety of specific performance measures ranging from sales figures to supervisory ratings. The decision to group all those studies into the same analysis should be based on a careful assessment that they all represent operational measures of the same basic construct—job performance.

Meta-analyses are increasingly common in virtually all areas of psychology; they are also encountered in fields such as medicine (Olkin, 1992). One of the first steps in evaluating the criterion-related validity of virtually any test (especially commercially available tests or scales that have been in use for some period of time) should be a visit to the library. For many types of tests and criteria, the odds are good that a meta-analysis has already been conducted or that the literature exists that will enable you to conduct one yourself. The results of previous studies will not always address the particular research question you have in mind, but they should prove useful in giving you some guidance in interpreting the results of your own validity study. For example, if your study shows that a test is uncorrelated with an important criterion, but 30 other studies of the same test have shown correlations in the .40 to .60 range, you might expect there to be a flaw in your study that makes your particular findings difficult to interpret or generalize.

We do not believe that meta-analyses of existing research should replace carefully conducted validity studies. If they did, there would soon be nothing left to meta-analyse! However, it is silly to ignore the results of previous validity research, especially if other researchers have already examined the validity of your particular test for predicting the same type of criterion. Meta-analyses provide a means of systematically examining existing research; this examination should be useful in evaluating the criterion-related validity of virtually any measure.

INTERPRETING VALIDITY COEFFICIENTS

A criterion-related validity study provides an estimate of the correlation between test scores and criterion measures. Theoretically, this correlation could range in absolute value from 0.0 to 1.0. In practice most validity coefficients tend to be fairly small—a good, carefully chosen test is not likely to show a correlation greater than .5 with an important criterion, and, in fact, validity coefficients greater than .3 are not all that common in applied settings. The correlations would almost certainly be higher if more reliable tests and criterion measures were used. Nevertheless, the levels of criterion-related validity achieved by most tests are rarely in excess of .6 to .7.

The figures shown in Table 8-3 provide a representative picture of the size of the validity coefficients often observed in personnel selection research. These correlations represent average validity coefficients computed across a number of studies, with a total N of over 140,000 (Schmidt, Hunter & Pearlman, 1981). At first glance, these average validities look quite discouraging—the average of the correlations is .269. The squared correlation coefficient (r^2) indicates the percentage of the variance in the criterion that can be accounted for by the predictor. An average criterion-related validity of .269

TABLE 8-3   AVERAGE CRITERION-RELATED VALIDITIES
ACROSS A NUMBER OF CLERICAL JOBS

Test	Job proficiency criteria[a]	Training criteria[b]
General Mental Ability	.24	.43
Verbal Ability	.19	.39
Quantitative Ability	.24	.43
Reasoning Ability	.21	.22
Perceptual Speed	.22	.22
Spatial/Mechanical	.14	.21
Clerical Aptitude	.25	.38

[a]Note: e.g., performance ratings

[b]Note: e.g., training course grades

Source: Schmidt, Hunter, and Pearlman (1981).

indicates that approximately 7 percent of the variability in job proficiency measures and measures of performance in training can be accounted for (on the average) by test scores. Stated another way, 93 percent of the variability in performance *cannot* be accounted for by tests.

It is important to keep in mind that the values presented in Table 8-3 represent uncorrected coefficients. If corrected for attenuation *and* for range restriction, they could be substantially larger; corrected values in the .50's are often reported for tests of this sort (Hunter & Hunter, 1984). Nevertheless, even a validity of .50 would indicate that tests accounted for only 25 percent of the variance in the criterion (i.e., if $r = .50$, $r^2 = .25$). In most settings where tests are used to make important decisions, they account for relatively small percentages of the variability in criteria. Critics of testing (e.g., Nairn et al., 1980) have used this point to support their argument that tests are worthless. In fact, things are not as bad as the typically low values of r and r^2 might suggest. The validity of a test as an aid in making decisions should be judged by evaluating the effects of tests on the accuracy of decisions. The validity coefficient does not in itself provide a complete measure of the effects of tests on decisions. In some situations, tests that are extremely accurate predictors lead to only marginal increases in the quality of decisions. In other situations, a test that shows a very low level of criterion-related validity may nevertheless contribute greatly to improving the quality of decisions. The effect of a test on the quality of decisions is affected by a number of factors that may be unrelated to the criterion-related validity of that test.

Tests and Decisions

The validity coefficient is only one of many factors that determines the degree to which a test may improve or detract from the quality of decisions. To fully evaluate the effect of a test on decisions, one must also consider the *base rate* and the *selection ratio* of a decision.

The base rate refers to the level of performance on the criterion in the population at large. For example, if 95 percent of all applicants perform successfully in a college course, the base rate is .95. If only 12 percent of the applicants to a psychology program successfully complete their degrees, the base rate is .12. Thus, the base rate indicates the percentage of the population who can be thought of as potential successes.

The selection ratio represents the ratio of positions to applicants. If 30 people apply for three jobs, there is a 10 percent selection ratio; if 10 prospective students apply for an incoming class of 9, there is a 90 percent selection ratio. Thus, the selection ratio indicates the degree to which the decision maker (e.g., personnel manager, admissions director) can be selective in his or her decisions.

Outcomes of decisions. A decision represents some action taken with regard to a specific individual. A decision may involve accepting or rejecting a college applicant, or it may involve assigning or not assigning a client to a specific course of psychotherapy. Because predictions are never perfect, each decision may have many possible outcomes. In college admissions, some applicants who are accepted might turn out to be poor students, and others who were rejected might have been excellent students. A clinician might assign some clients to a course of therapy which is less than optimal. Nevertheless, the goal is to make the largest possible number of correct decisions—to accept potential successes and reject potential failures. A valid test should aid in accurately predicting both success and failures and should therefore contribute to the quality of decisions. Figure 8-3 presents a schematic representation of the decision process.

Tests, interviews, application blanks, and the like, present information about each individual. The formal or informal rules used in making decisions comprise a *strategy*. For example, a college admissions office might decide to accept all applicants with a B+ average and with SAT scores over 550. This strategy leads to a *decision*—accept or reject—for each applicant. Furthermore, there are a number of possible *outcomes* of this decision. Some students who are accepted will succeed, others will fail. Some students who were rejected would have succeeded, and others would have failed.

The decision to accept an applicant is usually based upon the prediction that the applicant will succeed; the decision to reject an applicant implies a prediction of failure, or at least of a lower level of success. One way to evaluate the accuracy of decisions is to compare predictions with the outcomes of decisions. Figure 8-4 presents a cross-tabulation of predicted criterion scores with actual criterion scores. This type of a table described all the possible outcomes of a decision. One possible outcome is a *true positive* (TP): a person who is predicted to succeed and who actually does succeed. Another possible outcome is a *true negative* (TN): a person who is predicted to fail (rejected) and who actually would have failed had he or she been accepted. True positives and true negatives represent accurate, correct decisions; they represent cases in which people who will succeed are accepted and those who will fail are not accepted. One of the principal goals of psychological testing is to increase the frequency of these correct decisions.

Another possible outcome of a decision is the *false positive* (FP): some of the people who are accepted turn out to be failures. Since the decision to accept a person who later turns out to be a failure implies the prediction that that person would succeed,

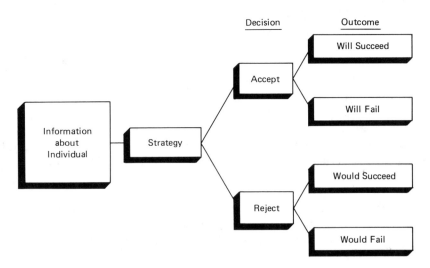

Figure 8-3 The Decision Process

Source: Adapted from Wiggins, 1973, p. 227.

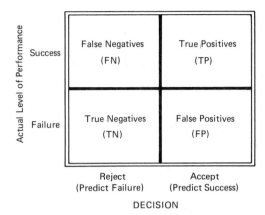

Figure 8-4 diagram:

Actual Level of Performance

	Reject (Predict Failure)	Accept (Predict Success)
Success	False Negatives (FN)	True Positives (TP)
Failure	True Negatives (TN)	False Positives (FP)

Reject
(Predict Failure)

Accept
(Predict Success)

DECISION

Figure 8-4 Possible Outcomes of a Decision

the decision represents an error that is produced as the result of a false prediction. Finally, there are *false negative* (FN) decisions, in which an applicant who would have succeeded, given the change, is rejected. False negatives are also decision errors in that they also lead to the wrong course of action for a specific applicant.

Base rates and decisions.   One of the factors that strongly affects the outcomes of a decision is the *base rate* (BR), or the number of potential successes in the population of applicants. If 90 percent of those who apply are likely to succeed, it should not be too difficult to select a highly successful group. With a base rate of 90 percent, random selection will on the average lead to successful applicants being chosen nine times out of ten. Indeed, when the base rate is very high, it may be difficult to devise a test that leads to significantly better decisions than would be reached by flipping a coin. If the base rate is 90 percent, there may not be very much room for improvement.

A very high base rate practically guarantees a large number of true positive decisions. Unfortunately, it may also lead to a number of false negative decisions. Consider a group of 200 people who apply for 100 positions. A base rate of 90 percent means there are 180 potential successes in this group. Since there are only 100 positions, even the best strategy will result in rejecting 80 potential successes (false negative decisions). While an extremely high base rate may help to maximize the number of true positives, it may also lead to a number of decision errors, particularly false negative decisions.

Tests are often used to predict criteria that have very low base rates (Murphy, 1987b). For example, Wiggins (1973) discusses applications of personality tests to screen out draftees because of psychiatric disability. The base rate for severe psychiatric problems is undoubtedly low; it is likely that fewer than 5 percent of the population would be screened out of military service because of psychiatric disorders. Since the base rate is very low, most of the population are, in fact, negatives (no presence of psychiatric disorder). Because positives (those with psychiatric disorders) are very rare, any decision procedure that attempts to isolate this rare group is likely to classify falsely a number of negatives (no disorder) as positives (disorder present). In other words, with a very low base rate, false positive decision errors become much more likely. On the other hand, a low base rate practically guarantees a large number of true negatives. If there are very few psychiatric cases in the population, few people will be screened out by the test, and most of those not screened out will belong to the large group that does *not* exhibit psychiatric disorders.

In general, tests are more likely to contribute to the overall quality of decisions when the base rate is around .50. When the base rate is extremely high, there is not much room for improvement in terms of locating true positives and there is little chance of avoiding a substantial number of false negatives. When the base rate is extremely low, a number of false positives is likely. When the base rate is around .50, there is a greater possibility of minimizing decision errors and it may be possible to make very accurate decisions if a test with sufficient validity can be found.

Selection ratio and decisions.

The second factor that affects the quality of decisions is the *selection ratio* (SR), or the ratio of applicants to openings. If 100 people apply for 99 openings at a college, the college cannot be very selective. As a consequence, it doesn't really matter what strategy the college follows, the result will always be pretty much the same. Contrast this with the situation in which 100 people apply for one opening. Here, the validity of the decision strategy has a marked influence on the quality of the decision. A perfectly valid strategy will lead to selection of the best applicant; an invalid strategy could lead to selection of the worst. When the number of openings is large relative to the number of applicants, the selection ratio is high. For example, when ten people apply for eight positions, the selection ratio is equal to .8. In the extreme case where the number of applicants is equal to the number of openings, the selection ratio is equal to 1.0. In this case, there is no choice but to accept everyone.

When the number of openings is small relative to the number of applicants, the selection ratio is small. A small selection ratio indicates that there are few constraints on the decision. For example, if ten people apply for two openings, the selection ratio is .20, which means that eight out of every ten people who apply can be turned down. Of course, if there is no system for selecting among applicants, the freedom to turn down eight out of ten may not represent any real advantage. However, if there is a valid system for making decisions, a low selection ratio allows selection of the "cream of the crop." In fact, when the selection ratio is sufficiently low, a test with very modest validity still can contribute significantly to the accuracy of decisions.

Taylor and Russell (1939) published a series of tables that dramatically illustrate the effect of the selection ratio on the accuracy of decisions. Taylor-Russell tables indicate the proportion of successes that can be expected, given the validity of the test, the base rate, and the selection ratio. One of the Taylor-Russell tables is shown in Table 8-4; validity coefficients are shown at the side of the table, the selection ratio is shown at the top, and the expected proportion of successes are shown in the body of the table. Several points should be noted in examining the table. First, if the test has a validity of .00, the expected level of success is exactly equal to the base rate, regardless of the selection ratio. In other words, a test with no validity yields essentially random decisions. Next, at very high selection ratios (e.g., SR = .90), the expected level of success using an extremely accurate test is not much higher than the level of success one would expect with a validity of .00. Finally, at very low selection ratios, a test with a reasonably low level of validity still could lead to substantial increases in the proportion of "successes"; when a

TABLE 8-4 TAYLOR-RUSSELL TABLE SHOWING THE EXPECTED PROPORTION OF SUCCESSES WITH A BASE RATE OF .50

Validity	Selection ratio									
	.05	.10	.20	.30	.40	.50	.60	.70	.80	.90
.00	.50	.50	.50	.50	.50	.50	.50	.50	.50	.50
.10	.54	.54	.53	.52	.52	.51	.51	.51	.51	.50
.20	.67	.64	.61	.59	.58	.56	.55	.53	.53	.52
.30	.74	.71	.67	.64	.62	.60	.58	.56	.54	.52
.40	.82	.78	.73	.69	.66	.63	.61	.58	.56	.53
.50	.88	.84	.78	.74	.70	.67	.63	.60	.57	.54
.60	.94	.90	.84	.79	.75	.70	.66	.62	.59	.45
.70	.98	.95	.90	.85	.80	.75	.70	.65	.60	.55
.80	1.00	.99	.95	.90	.85	.80	.73	.67	.61	.55
.90	1.00	1.00	.99	.97	.92	.86	.78	.70	.62	.56
1.00	1.00	1.00	1.00	1.00	1.00	1.00	.83	.71	.63	.56

highly valid test is used in a situation characterized by a low selection ratio; one is able to select successes essentially 100 percent of the time.

It is important to select successes, but the overall quality of a decision strategy is affected not by the number of successes only but by the combination of *all* of the possible outcomes of the decision. For example, with a low selection ratio a number of *potential* successes might also be turned down (false negatives). Taylor-Russell tables do not provide a complete picture of the effects of the base rate or the selection ratio on all the outcomes of a decision; the selection ratio, the base rate, and the validity of the test interact in a complex way to affect all the outcomes of decisions. Nevertheless, the Taylor-Russell tables do provide important information for interpreting validity coefficients.

The effect of base rates, selection ratios, and test validity on outcomes. The outcomes of decisions are determined by the base rate, the selection ratio, and the validity of the test. To explain the interaction of these three factors, we first show how the base rate and the selection ratio determine the number of true positives, true negatives, false positives, and false negatives that would occur if one were making decisions on a random basis. Random decisions represent a baseline against which decisions that involve tests can be compared. A test is not useful unless it leads to significantly better, more accurate decisions than would be made without using tests.

When decisions are made on a random basis, the number of true positives, true negatives, false positives, and false negatives can be computed directly from the base rate (BR) and the selection ratio (SR). The probability of a true positive [P(TP)] is given by

$$\text{Probability of a True Positive Decision When Decisions Are Made at Random} = \text{Base Rate} \times \text{Selection Ratio} \qquad [8\text{-}2]$$

With a base rate of .60 and a selection ratio of .50, 30 percent of the decisions made at random will be true positives. The probability of each other outcome can be solved by subtraction, as shown in Figure 8-5.

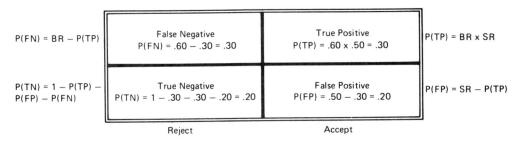

Figure 8-5 The Outcomes of Random Decisions with a Base Rate of .60 and a Selection Ratio of .50

Thus, the probability of a false negative is equal to the base rate minus the probability of a true positive [P(TN) = .60 − .30 = .30]; the probability of a false positive is given by the selection ratio minus the probability of a true positive [P(FP) = .50 − .30 = .20]. Finally, the probability of a true negative is given by 1 minus the sum of the other three probabilities [P(TN) = 1 − .30 − .30 − .20 = .20]. In other words, when the base rate is .60 and the selection ratio is .50, 50 percent of all random decisions will be correct (TP and TN), and 50 percent of the random decisions will be incorrect (FP and FN). These figures represent a baseline against which decisions involving tests can be evaluated.

When a valid test is used to make decisions, the probability of a true positive increases from P(TP) = BR × SR to

$$P(TP) = BR \times SR + r_{xy} \sqrt{BR(1 - BR)SR(1 - SR)}$$ [8-3]

This formula shows that the use of a test increases the probability of making true positive decisions and that the increase in the likelihood of true positive decisions is a function of the validity of the test (r_{xy}), adjusted by a scaling factor [$\sqrt{BR(1 - BR)SR(1 - SR)}$]. Thus, when the validity of the test is equal to .00, the probability of a true positive is exactly the same as when decisions are made at random. Whenever the test has a validity greater than .00, true positives are more likely when the test is used to make decisions than when decisions are made at random. As a consequence, both false positives and false negatives are less likely when decisions are based on a valid test than when decisions are made at random.

Figure 8-6 shows how decision errors decrease as test validity increases. With a base rate of .50 and a selection ratio of .40, 50 percent of all random decisions will be either false positives or false negatives, both of which represent decision errors. When a test with a validity of .40 is used to make decisions, the proportion of correct decisions rises from 50 percent to 68 percent; when a test with a validity of .70 is used, the proportion of correct decisions rises to 72 percent. As shown by the figure, a valid test increases both the number of true positives and the number of true negatives, while decreasing both false positives and false negatives.

As stated at the beginning of this section, the interpretation of validity coefficients is surprisingly complex. The meaning of a validity coefficient cannot be fully understood unless one understands the context in which a test will be used. A test with a validity of .70 may not be very useful if the base rate or the selection ratio is very high. On the other hand, a test with a validity of .10 might lead to a considerable increase in the accuracy of

	Random Decisions		Using a Test with a Validity of .40		Using a Test with a Validity of .70	
	FN .30	TP .20	FN .21	TP .29	FN .19	TP .31
	TN .30	FP .20	TN .39	FP .11	TN .41	FP .09

Figure 8-6 Outcomes of Random Decisions and Decisions Based upon Tests with a Base Rate of .50 and a Selection Ratio of .40

decisions if the selection ratio is low. Therefore, it makes little sense to say that a validity coefficient of .20 is bad or that a validity of .50 is good. It depends largely on the contexts in which tests will be used.

Tests and the Bottom Line—Applications of Utility Theory

Throughout this book we focus on the impact of psychological tests on decisions that must be made about individuals. The principal justification for the use of psychological tests is that they allow better decisions to be made than would be made without tests. The question is, how much better? Utility theory provides a method of answering this question.

According to utility theory, correct decisions (true positives, true negatives) are valued, while incorrect decisions (false positives, false negatives) are to be avoided, or have a negative value. Utility theory suggests that two things must be known before the impact of psychological tests can be assessed: (a) how many additional correct decisions will result if tests are used and (b) how much value is placed on good decisions. Methods described earlier in this chapter can be applied to the first question—if the base rate, selection ratio, and validity coefficient are known, the effect of tests on decisions can be determined easily. The trick, then, is to determine the value of outcomes.

One way to determine value is to make a judgment as to what will be gained by making a good decision instead of a bad one. This approach has been widely used in personnel selection and has provided estimates of the financial impact of tests on selection decisions. For example, it is possible to estimate, in dollar terms, the value of the products, goods, and services provided by a superior worker, an average worker, and a poor worker. These estimates can be used to determine the standard deviation of job performance, measured in dollar terms (Judiesch, Schmidt & Mount, 1992). Since a valid selection test will lead to an increase in the number of superior workers and a decrease in the number of poor workers hired, it is possible to use judgments of the value of performance to provide estimates of the financial impact of valid selection decisions.

Utility theory provides a method for estimating, in dollar terms, the gain (per year) in productivity that will result if valid tests are used in personnel selection. This gain is estimated by

$$\text{Productivity gain} = K \, r_{xy} \, SD_y \, \bar{Z}_s \qquad [8\text{-}4]$$

where

K = number of persons selected

r_{xy} = validity coefficient

SD_y = standard deviation of the criterion

$\bar{Z}_s$ = average (standard) test score among those selected

Utility estimates have suggested that the use of psychological tests in areas such as personnel selection could lead to substantial gains in performance. For example, Hunter and Hunter (1984) estimate that the use of cognitive ability tests in selection for entry-level federal jobs could lead to a productivity gain of over *$15 billion* per year. Hunter and Schmidt (1982) estimate that the nationwide gain associated with the use of psychological tests in personnel selection could exceed $80 billion per year.[4]

There are two problems with utility equations such as Formula 8-4. First, they typically overestimate increases in utility (Cronshaw & Alexander, 1985; Murphy, 1986). Second, they ignore the costs associated with incorrect rejection decisions (false negatives; Boudreau, 1991). However, application of this branch of utility theory has greatly increased our understanding of the impact of psychological tests on the quality of decisions made daily by organizations and institutions.

Formula 8-4 suggests that several factors affect the overall quality of decisions. First, of course, is the validity of the test (r_{xy}). Second is the standard deviation of the criterion (SD_y); the larger this standard deviation, the larger the potential gain associated with the use of tests. The rationale here is straightforward. A large standard deviation indicates substantial differences in criterion scores; a small standard deviation indicates that everyone performs at pretty much the same level. If individual differences in performance are large, the quality of selection decisions makes a great deal of difference, but if everyone performs at about the same level, decisions will not affect criterion scores greatly. Finally, the average test score among those selected ($\bar{Z}_s$) affects utility. The organization that is able to attract the "cream of the crop" among applicants gains more than another organization that is able to attract only mediocre applicants (Murphy, 1986). The utility score given by Formula 8-4 represents a complex combination of the characteristics of the applicant pool, the selection ratio, and the decisions of individual applicants.

CRITICAL DISCUSSION:
Values and Validation

We have presented validity and utility as related but distinct topics. Messick (1988; 1989) suggests a different framework, in which values are taken explicitly into account in the process of validation.[5] The central idea in this framework is that we need to consider both the *inferences* made on the basis of test scores (these are the focus of traditional validity models) and the *actions* taken as the result of test scores. Thus, in this framework the

---

[4]More recent analyses (e.g., Hartigan & Wigdor, 1989) imply much smaller productivity gains.

[5]Cronbach (1988) identifies several perspectives on validation, three of which incorporate value or societal concerns: (a) functional—the worth of the test, (b) political—the acceptability of test outcomes, and (c) economic—the contribution of the test to productivity.

validation process might take into account (a) the construct validity of the test, (b) the relevance or utility of the test, (c) the value implications of test scores, and (d) the potential and actual social consequences of test use. The unique aspect of this framework for understanding validity is that both the values that underly testing (e.g., whether or not it is valuable to predict college grade point average for applicants) and the social consequences of testing (e.g., a selection test that includes many geometric items will lead to the selection of more males than females) are an integral part of validation, rather than concerns that should be addressed by someone other than the scientist investigating validity.

The appropriateness of including social consequences in the definition of validity is somewhat controversial. For example, the fact that on average females receive lower scores than males on the mathematical portion of the SAT is taken by some critics as evidence of the *invalidity* of the test. Virtually any test that produces socially undesirable outcomes is likely to be attacked in this manner (Jensen, 1980; Seymour, 1988; Sharf, 1988).

Messick's (1988) framework is somewhat more sophisticated than the simplistic one suggested by these critics—that tests whose consequences are socially undesirable are necessarily invalid. Messick suggests that we must consider whether the social consequences of a test are a reflection of the test or a reflection of the actual phenomenon being measured. For example, there is clear agreement among testing specialists that there are real differences in the average intelligence levels of different subgroups in the population (see special issues of the *Journal of Vocational Behavior*, 1986, December; and 1988, December, for reviews of this evidence). A test of intelligence that *failed* to reflect this real difference would probably be judged invalid in Messick's framework. On the other hand, if undesirable social consequences are the result of the test rather than of the phenomenon being measured or predicted, this should be considered in evaluating the validity of a test.

One of the advantages of Messick's framework is that it encourages us to consider values in the selection of criteria. That is, a researcher applying this framework might not be satisfied with a test if its use not only led to increases in one criterion (e.g., average GPA) but also led to substantial decreases in other relevant criteria (e.g., the representativeness of students admitted). As we noted at the beginning of this chapter, the selection of appropriate criteria is the first and most important step in criterion-related validity studies. Messick's framework may be a very useful tool for accomplishing this end.

SUMMARY

The success of psychological tests in predicting a wide range of important criteria (e.g., academic achievement, performance on the job, outcomes of therapy) helps to explain both their importance and their acceptance. In later chapters we will review evidence of the validity of several types of tests; the aim of this chapter has been to describe the process of collecting and interpreting criterion-related validity evidence.

Both predictive and concurrent validation strategies have been described. Although there are important theoretical differences between these methods, it is not unusual to obtain similar validity estimates from each, especially if factors such as range restriction can be adequately accounted for.

While it is possible to obtain valid predictors without considering the constructs that tests are designed to measure (strategies for developing such tests are described in Chapter 10), a clear assessment of the constructs involved is usually the first step in a criterion-related validity study. In particular, careful attention must be given to the constructs your criteria are chosen to represent. In too many studies, criteria are chosen on the basis of convenience (e.g., grade point average is an easily obtained metric of academic success, even though it fails to capture many critical aspects of the construct), rather than substantive theory. An examination of the criterion construct is especially important in conducting and interpreting meta-analyses; for a poorly defined meta-analysis might include many irrelevant studies and may not adequately answer your particular research question.

Validity coefficients cannot be sensibly interpreted without considering the context in which tests are likely to be used. Two features of the testing context, the base rate (BR) and the selection ratio (SR), are critically important, and depending on the BR and SR, a test with high validity may make either a great or a very small contribution to the quality of decisions. In certain situations (e.g., a low SR), tests with modest validity coefficients can nevertheless make a substantial contribution.

Utility theory provides a way of combining information about the validity of the test, the context in which tests will be used, and the value of the good or poor decisions that might result from use of the test. This approach allows you to estimate in very concrete terms what will happen if you decide either to use or to discard tests in making particular decisions.

CHAPTER 9

ITEM ANALYSIS

Many of the most widely used tests contain a number of multiple-choice items, each of which is designed to measure the same attribute or the same content. The best example is the familiar test of scholastic aptitude. There is usually a correct or preferred answer to each item, and each item is scored as correct, 1; incorrect, 0. The total test score is simply the sum of the scores on all of the items. In the last four chapters, properties of test scores, such as reliability and validity, were discussed. This chapter will deal with the relationship between characteristics of individual test items and the quality of the test as a whole. Some test items contribute to reliability and validity; "trick" questions or ambiguous items may detract from the overall quality of a test.

The term "item analysis" refers to a loosely structured group of statistics that can be computed for each item in a test. Although many item analyses incorporate common methods of analysis, there are as many "recipes" for item analysis as there are for chili. The exact choice and interpretation of the statistics that make up an item analysis is determined partly by the purpose of testing and partly by the person designing the analysis. Nevertheless, there are some very general issues that are addressed in almost every item analysis. This chapter suggests a set of general questions that should be asked when examining individual test items and shows how information from an item analysis can be used to improve tests.

PURPOSE OF ITEM ANALYSIS

Item analysis can help increase our understanding of tests. Close examination of individual tests is essential to understanding *why* a test shows specific levels of reliability and validity. The reliability coefficient reveals something about the effects of measurement error on test scores. Validity coefficients reveal something about the accuracy of predictions that are based on test scores. A good item analysis can often be very informative when tests are unreliable or when they fail to show expected levels of validity. An item analysis can show *why* a test is reliable (or unreliable) and may help in understanding why test scores can be used to predict some criteria but not others. Item analysis may also suggest ways of improving the measurement characteristics of a test.

Tests are sometimes limited in their reliability or validity because they contain items that are poorly worded or that are "trick" questions requiring complex mental gymnastics. Other items may look fine but don't actually measure the construct of the content domain that the test is designed to assess. The reliability and validity of a test can generally be improved by removing such items. At first glance, this seems to run counter to one of the basic propositions of reliability theory: The longer the test, the better. Actually, there is no conflict between the policy of removing poor items and the goal of maximizing reliability. Reliability theory assumes that all test items measure the same thing. Item analysis helps locate items that don't meet this assumption, and removing them can improve the reliability of tests.

Critical Features of Test Items

The question that should be asked when examining each test item is, "Does this item do a good job of measuring the same thing that is measured by the rest of the test?" Different computer programs contain a variety of statistics that bear upon this general question. Attempts to answer this question usually draw upon information provided by three types of measures: distractor measures, difficulty measures, and item discrimination measures.

In examining each item of a test, the first and most natural question to ask is, "How many people chose each response?" There is only one answer; the rest are referred to as distractors. Therefore, examining the total pattern of responses to each item of a test is referred to as *distractor analysis*.

Another natural question is, "How many people answered the item correctly?" To answer this question, an analysis is made of *item difficulty*. A third question is, "Are responses to this item related to responses to other items on the test?" Answering this question entails an analysis of *item discrimination*. In the sections that follow, we present several common procedures for analyzing the total pattern of responses to an item, the difficulty of an item, and the interrelationships among responses to different test items.

DISTRACTOR ANALYSIS

Typically, there is one correct or preferred answer for each multiple-choice item on a test. A lot can be learned about test items by examining the frequency with which each of the incorrect responses is chosen by a group of examinees.

Table 9-1 shows data on a single item that was part of an introductory psychology test. The table shows that most of the students answered the item correctly. A fair number of students chose either *b* or *c*; very few chose *d*. Although the calculation of the percentage of examinees choosing each response may not appear to have accomplished anything profound, it constitutes a fairly complete and potentially informative distractor analysis. The percentages convey a great deal of information about the skill with which the item was written.

A perfect test item would have two characteristics. First, people who "knew" the answer to that question would always choose the correct response. Second, people who did not know the answer would choose randomly among the possible responses. This means that some people would guess correctly. It also means that each of the possible incorrect responses should be equally popular.

For the test item shown in the table, responses *b*, *c*, and *d* served as distractors. Fifty-five percent of the students answered this item correctly. If this were a perfect test item, we might expect the responses of the other 45 percent of the students to be equally divided among the three distractors. In other words, we might expect about 15 percent of the students to choose each of the three incorrect responses.

TABLE 9-1   ITEM FROM INTRODUCTORY PSYCHOLOGY TEST

Item 42. Paranoid schizophrenia often involves delusions of persecution or grandeur.
Which secondary symptom would be most likely for a paranoid schizophrenic:
(a) auditory hallucinations
(b) motor paralysis
(c) loss of memory
(d) aversion to food

	Number choosing each answer	Percent choosing each answer
Correct Response	a 47	a 55
	b 13	b 15
	c 25	c 29
	d 1	d 1

What To Look for in a Distractor Analysis

We can compute the number of people expected to choose each of the distractors using the simple formula

$$\text{Number of persons expected to choose each distractor} = \frac{\text{number of persons answering item incorrectly}}{\text{number of distractors}} \qquad [9\text{-}1]$$

Thirty-nine people answered the item incorrectly. We therefore would expect 13 people to choose each distractor. In fact, 13 people chose response *b*. More people chose response *c* than would be expected, and fewer chose *d*.

When the number of persons choosing a distractor significantly exceeds the number of expected, there are two possibilities. First, it is possible that the choice reflects partial knowledge. For this example, someone who knows a bit about psychosis might know that both auditory hallucinations and memory loss are plausible symptoms for a variety of disorders. Therefore, for someone with such partial knowledge, the answer to this question might be a toss-up between *a* and *c*. A second, more worrisome possibility is that the item is a poorly constructed "trick" question. If one more of the distractors is extremely popular among students who have a good knowledge of the domain covered by the item *and* if the identification of the correct response hinges upon some extremely obscure or subtle point, the item is not likely to be a valid measure of the content domain. There are some situations in which extremely difficult or subtle items are desirable, such as those in which the intent is to measure individual differences among people at the high end of a score distribution (e.g., competitors for a scholarship). However, in most situations, these types of items do not contribute to the overall quality of a test. For most tests, the presence of items with extremely popular distractors is likely to *lower* the reliability and validity of the test.

Some distractors are extremely unpopular. Response *d* for the test item shown in the table is an example. The number of people who actually chose this response is considerably smaller than the number one would expect by chance. The presence of an extremely unpopular or implausible distractor affects a number of important item characteristics. The most obvious effect of an unpopular distractor is that it lowers the difficulty of the item. If a person knows nothing whatsoever about the domain being tested, the probability of choosing the right answer on an item with four possible choices is one in four. If one of those choices is obviously incorrect, it can be eliminated. Thus, if I don't know anything about paranoid schizophrenia but am able to eliminate response *d* as utterly implausible, the probability of guessing correctly has been raised from one in four to one in three.

ITEM DIFFICULTY

Difficulty is a surprisingly slippery concept. Consider the following two items:

1. $(6 \times 3) + 4 = $ _____
2. $9\pi[ln(-3.68) \times (1 - ln(+3.68))] = $ _____

Most people would agree that item 2 is more difficult than item 1. If asked *why* item 2 is more difficult, they might say that it involves more complex advanced procedures than the first. Consider next another set of items:

1. Who was Savonarola?
2. Who was Babe Ruth?

Most people will agree that item 1 is more difficult than item 2. If asked *why* item 1 is more difficult, they might say that answering it requires more specialized knowledge than item 2.

As these examples might suggest, there is a strong temptation to define difficulty in terms of the complexity or obscurity of the test item. Yet if you were to look at any test you have recently taken, you would likely find yourself hard pressed to explain precisely *why* some items were more difficult than others. The only common thread running throught the "difficult" items may be the fact that when you took the test, you did not know the answers to these questions.

The psychologist doing an item analysis is faced with a similar problem. Some test items are harder than others, but it is difficult to explain or define difficulty in terms of some intrinsic characteristics of the items. The strategy adopted by psychometricians is to define difficulty in terms of the number of people who answer each test item correctly.[1] If everyone chooses the correct answer, the item is defined as an easy item. If only one person in 100 answers an item correctly, the item is defined as a difficult item.

Measuring Item Difficulty

The most common measure of item difficulty is the percentage of examinees who answer the item correctly, or the *p value*. An item's *p* value is obtained using the following formula:

$$p \text{ value for item } i = \frac{\text{number of persons answering item } i \text{ correctly}}{\text{number of persons taking the test}} \qquad [9\text{-}2]$$

The use of *p* values as a measure of item difficulty has several interesting implications. First, the *p* value is basically a behavioral measure. Rather than defining difficulty in terms of some intrinsic characteristic of the item, with this method difficulty is defined in terms of the relative frequency with which those taking the test choose the correct response. Second, difficulty is a characteristic of both the item and the population taking the test. A math problem that is very difficult when given in a high school course will be very easy when given in a graduate physics course.

Perhaps the most useful implication of the *p* value is that it provides a common measure of the difficulty of test items that measure completely different domains. It is very difficult to determine whether answering a particular question about history involves knowledge that is more obscure, complex, or specialized than that needed to answer a math problem. When *p* values are used to define difficulty, it is very simple to determine whether an item on a history test is more difficult than a specific item on a math test taken by the same group of students.

Effects of Item Difficulty on Test Scores

When everyone in a class chooses the wrong answers to a particular test item, there is usually an uproar, and, with luck, the offending item will be dropped from the test. Although infuriated students may not see the problem in technical terms, there is a sound psychometric basis for dropping such an item.

As stated in Chapter 1, one of the basic assumptions of measurement is that there

---

[1]As we will note later, item response theory provides a more sophisticated definition and measure of difficulty.

are systematic individual differences in the construct or the content domain being measured. Tests represent a method of quantifying these differences. When nobody chooses the correct answer (a p value of .0), there are no individual differences in the "score" on that item. Note that the same is true when *everyone* chooses the correct response (a p value of 1.0). This suggests one of the most important principles of item analysis. An item with a p value of .0 or a p value of 1.0 does not contribute to measuring individual differences and thus is almost certain to be useless.

When we compare the test scores of two people, we are typically interested in knowing who had the highest score or how far apart the two scores were. A test item with a p value of .0 or 1.0 has no effect on the differences between scores received by two subjects—dropping all of the test items with p values of .0 or 1.0 from a test will not affect the rank order or the size of the differences between different people's scores. Test items with p values of .0 or 1.0 may affect the test mean but have no effect whatsoever on the test's reliability or validity, nor on the decisions based upon the test scores.

Item difficulty has a profound effect on both the variability of test scores and the precision with which test scores discriminate among different groups of examinees. The effects of difficulty on the variance of test scores are fairly obvious when p values are extreme. When all the test items are extremely difficult, the great majority of the test scores will be very low. When all items are extremely easy, most test scores will be extremely high. In either case, test scores will show very little variability. Thus, extreme p values directly restrict the variability of test scores.

The variability of test scores is maximized when p values average around .5. In fact, test scores are more variable when *all* the p values cluster around .5 than when there is some range of p values. Since most tests are designed to measure some construct or attribute over a range of possible scores, some variability in test scores is to be expected. When tests are designed for the general measurement of some continuous variable (e.g., intelligence, need for achievement), there is little doubt that items with p values near .5 are preferred over extremely easy or extremely difficult items. In most analyses of item difficulty, items with p values near .5 should be considered optimum.

Some tests are not designed to provide equally good measurement at all points on a continuum. For example, a simple reading comprehension test may be used to screen out people whose reading ability is below some minimal level required on a job. If the job demands that the workers be above the twentieth percentile in a general reading ability, it makes little difference whether the worker reads at a high school, college, or post-graduate level. A test will be maximally effective in making this type of screening decision if the item difficulties correspond roughly with the cutting point. In order to decide whether each applicant is above or below the twentieth percentile, a test that consist of items with p values near .2 would be best (Lord, 1952). If the objective is to screen the very top group of applicants (e.g., medical admissions), the test should be composed of very difficult items.

ITEM DISCRIMINATION

Every item can be thought of as a separate test. Some items do a pretty good job of measuring the same thing that is measured by the test as a whole. Some items measure nothing at all (i.e., items with p values of .0 or 1.0); others measure the wrong thing altogether. One of the principal aims of item analysis is to discover which items best measure the construct or attribute the test was designed to measure.

If the test and a single item both measure the same thing, one would expect people who do well on the test to answer that item correctly and those who do poorly to answer that item incorrectly. In other words, a good item *discriminates* between those who do well on the test and those who do poorly. In this section, we discuss three statistics that can be used to measure the discriminating power of an item: the discimination index, the item-total correlation, and inter-item correlations.

Discrimination Index

The method of *extreme groups* can be applied to compute a very simple measure of the discriminating power of a test item. If a test is given to a large group of people, the discriminating power of an item can be measured by comparing the number of people with high test scores (e.g., those in the top 25 percent of the class) who answered that item correctly with the number of people with low scores (e.g., the bottom 25 percent) who answered the same item correctly. If a particular item is doing a good job of discriminating between those who score high and those who score low, more people in the top-scoring group will have answered the item correctly.

The item discrimination index, D, is based on the simple rationale described above. The first step in computing this index is to select an upper group and a lower group. Customarily, these extreme groups are made up of either those with scores in the upper and lower 27 percent or those with scores in the upper and lower 33 percent of the group taking the test (Cureton, 1957). For all practical purposes, these extreme groups can include anywhere from 25 percent to 35 percent of the examinees; any breakdown within this range yields similar discrimination measures. Once extreme groups are formed, the next step is to calculate the percentage of examinees passing each item in both the upper group and the lower group. The item discrimination index is simply the difference between these two percentages.

An example will help clarify the item discrimination index. A 40-item test was given to 100 students. The 27 students with the highest test scores formed the upper group, and the 27 with the lowest scores formed the lower group. The percentage of those in the upper group and the percentage of those in the lower group passing each item on the test were then computed. Data from four of these items are presented in Table 9-2.

Recall that the p value is a measure of item difficulty. The data in the table suggest that both items 1 and 2 were substantially more difficult for the lower group than for the upper group. The logic of the D statistic is simple. The test itself was, by definition,

TABLE 9-2   PERCENT PASSING

Item	Upper group	Lower group	D
1	71	42	29
2	60	24	36
3	47	42	5
4	38	61	−23

substantially more difficult for the lower group than for the upper group. If an item and a test both measure the same thing, the item should also be more difficult for the lower group than for the upper. The D statistic provides a simple but efficient measure of the discriminating power of each test item (Engelhart, 1965).

Item 3 does not show much discriminating power. The D value for this item is very small, reflecting the fact that the item was about equally difficult in the upper and lower groups. The statistics for item 4 are even more discouraging. This item shows plenty of discriminating power, but in the wrong direction. A negative D index indicates that an item is easier for people who do poorly on the test than for those who do well on the test. This is the exact opposite of what would be expected if the item and the test were measuring the same thing. The D values suggest that both item 3 and item 4 are poor test items. The small D value for item 3 suggests that it does not make any discriminations between those who do well on tests and those who do poorly. The negative D value for item 4 suggests that the item discriminates, but in the wrong direction. One goal of test construction is to generate items that, like items 1 and 2, allow for valid discrimination between high and low scorers.

Shortcuts in computing D.   The procedure for computing D described in the previous section is fairly simple, but there are even simpler methods available. The general formula for the D statistic is

$$D = \frac{U}{n_u} - \frac{L}{n_l}$$ [9-3]

where

U = number of people in the upper group who passed the item
n_u = number of people in the upper group
L = number of people in the lower group who passed the item
n_l = number of people in the lower group

In many cases, the upper group and the lower group are equal in size. In this case, where $n_u = n_l$, Formula 9-3 reduces to

$$D = \frac{U - L}{n}$$ [9-4]

where

$$n = n_l = n_u$$

Thus, in many cases D can be obtained by computing the difference between the number of people in the upper group who pass an item and the number in the lower group who pass the same item, and dividing by n.

Item-total correlation.   The discrimination index is a simple statistic that provides a good deal of information on the degree to which a particular item and the total test measure the same thing. There is a more familiar statistic, the *item-total correlation*, that provides the same sort of information. As the name implies, this statistic represents the simple correlation between the "score" on an item (a correct response usually receives a score of 1; an incorrect response receives a score of 0) and the total test score. This correlation is often referred to as a *point-biserial* correlation. Years ago, when computers were not available, there was some real utility in developing simple computational formulas for different types of correlations. Since computers are now readily available, there is no good reason to treat an item-total correlation differently than any other correlation. Thus, we will avoid the term "point biserial" and emphasize that the item-total correlation is a simple correlation coefficient.

The item-total correlation is interpreted in much the same way as the item discrimination index, *D*. A positive item-total correlation indicates that the item successfully discriminates between those who do well on the test and those who do poorly. More important, a positive item-total correlation indicates that the item measures the same thing that is being measured by the test. An item-total correlation near zero indicates that the item does not discriminate between high and low scores. A negative item-total correlation indicates that the scores on the item and scores on the test disagree. Those who do well on an item with a negative item-total *r* do poorly on the test.

The principal advantage of the item-total correlation is its familiarity. It is the simple correlation between item scores and test scores. Therefore, it is easy to test the statistical significance of an item-total correlation. It also is easy to make judgments about practical significance. If the item-total *r* is .40, we know that the item can account for 16 percent of the variability in test scores. An item discrimination index of .40 cannot be reexpressed in such concrete terms. Finally, item-total correlations are directly related to the reliability of a test (Nunnally, 1978).

Inter-item correlations. When conducting an item analysis, it makes sense to compute the correlations among all test items. The resulting inter-item correlation matrix is packed with information. First, it is possible to compute the reliability of a test given the average inter-item correlation and the number of items on the test. This is a useful fact, but this property of inter-item correlations is not the most important. The most important use of inter-item correlations is in *understanding* measures of item discrimination. Up to this point, we have not said *why* a particular item might show high or low levels of discriminating power. It might be obvious that items that show large positive item-total correlations also will show positive correlations with the most test items. It is not always obvious why other test items show low item-total correlations. Examination of the inter-item correlations can help us understand why some items fail to discriminate between those who do well on the test and those who do poorly.

If the item-total correlation is low, there are two possible explanations. First, it is possible that the item in question is not correlated with any of the other items on the test. In this case, the item should be either substantially rewritten or discarded altogether. The second possibility is that the item shows positive correlations with some test items but correlations near zero, or perhaps even negative correlations, with other items on the test. This would occur, for example, if the test measured two distinct attributes. Thus, a mathematics test that contained several complexly worded problems might measure reading comprehension as well as mathematical ability. Reliability theory suggests that such a test, in which different items measure different things (and thus are uncorrelated), would not provide consistent measurement.

INTERACTIONS AMONG ITEM CHARACTERISTICS

An item analysis yields three types of information: (a) information about distractors, (b) information about item difficulty, and (c) information about item discrimination power. These three types of information are conceptually distinct, but empirically related. Thus, examining distractors reveals something about difficulty; item difficulty directly affects item discriminating power. In this section, we briefly describe ways in which item characteristics interact.

Distractors and Difficulty

A multiple-choice item which asks the year in which B. F. Skinner published *The Behavior of Organisms* could be very difficult or very easy depending on the distractors. Consider these two versions of the same item.

  A. In what year did Skinner publish *The Behavior of Organisms*?
    a) 1457
    b) 1722
    c) 1938
    d) 1993
  B. In what year did Skinner publish *The Behavior of Organisms*?
    a) 1936
    b) 1931
    c) 1938
    d) 1942

Even a person who knows very little about the history of psychology is likely to find version A to be an easy item. On the other hand, version B is likely to be extremely difficult. The difficulty of an item is greatly affected by the plausibility of the distractors. If the examinee knows *nothing* about the domain being tested, any distractor might be equally plausible. In general, however, people taking tests have some knowledge of the domain and are not fooled by ridiculous distractors. On the other hand, examinees usually have an imperfect knowledge of the domain and therefore may be fooled by extremely plausible distractors. Some items are extremely difficult because of one or two extremely popular distractors. In either case, it may be possible to substantially change the item's difficulty by rewriting some distractors.

Difficulty and Discrimination

The level of difficulty places a direct limit on the discriminating power of an item. If everyone chooses the correct response ($p = 1.0$), or if everyone chooses an incorrect response ($p = .0$), item responses cannot possibly be used to discriminate between those who do well on the test and those who do poorly. When the p value is near .0 or near 1.0, the ability to discriminate between individuals is restricted.

Table 9-3 shows the *maximum possible* value of the item discrimination index (D) for test items at various levels of difficulty. The table shows that items with p values near .50 have the maximum potential to be good discriminators. It is important to keep in mind that a p value near .50 does not *guarantee* that an item will be a good discriminator. Extreme p values place a direct statistical limit on the discriminating power of an item. When the p values are near .50, there are no statistical limits on discriminating power. Nevertheless, a poor item with a p value of .50 is still a poor item.

TABLE 9-3 MAXIMUM VALUE OF THE
ITEM DISCRIMINATION INDEX (D)
AS A FUNCTION OF ITEM DIFFICULTY

Item p value	Maximum D
1.00	.00
.90	.20
.80	.40
.70	.60
.60	.80
.50	1.00
.40	.80
.30	.60
.20	.40
.10	.20
.00	.00

Distractors and Discrimination

It is difficult to write a good test item. There usually is no problem in writing the stem of the question or framing the correct response; the trick is to write good distractors. The lack of discriminating power shown by test items often can be attributed to poor distractors. The presence of one or more completely implausible distractors serves to lower the difficult of an item. As discussed in the previous section, items that are extremely easy have little or no potential for making valid discriminations. The same is true of extremely difficult items.

Distractors should be carefully examined when items show negative D values or negative item-total correlations. When one or more of the distractors looks extremely plausible to the informed reader *and* when recognition of the correct response depends on some extremely subtle point, it is possible that examinees will be *penalized* for partial knowledge. Consider, for example, the following item:

Reviews of research on the effectiveness of psychotherapy have concluded that

    a. psychotherapy is never effective.

    b. psychotherapy is effective, but only in treating somatoform disorders.

    c. psychotherapy is effective; there are no major differences in the effectiveness of different types of therapy.

d. psychotherapy is effective; behavioral approaches are consistently more effective than all others.

Choice *c* is correct. A student who is familiar with research on psychotherapy, but whose professor is strongly committed to praising the virtues of behavior therapy, might mistakenly choose *d*. Those examinees who have no inkling of the correct answer may choose randomly and do better than those who have some command of the domain being tested but who do not recognize the correct response. This sort of an item will not contribute to the overall quality of the test. Rather, it is a source of measurement error and should be either revised or removed. The revision of one or more distractors may dramatically increase the discriminating power of poor items.

THE ITEM CHARACTERISTIC CURVE

Tests are usually designed to measure some specific attribute, such as verbal ability. The more of this attribute a person has, the more likely the person will answer each test item correctly. The *item characteristic curve* (ICC) is a graphic presentation of the probability of choosing the correct answer to an item as a function of the level of the attribute being measured by the test. The item characteristic curve serves as the foundation of one of the most powerful theories in modern psychometrics, item response theory (or latent trait theory). The ICC also summarizes much of the information conveyed by item analysis, and suggests how this information might be used to understand the relationships between the attribute being measured and test responses (Lord, 1977; Lord & Novick, 1968; Rasch, 1960).

Figure 9-1 shows an item characteristic curve for a "good" item on a test of verbal ability. This theoretical ICC plots the probability of answering the item correctly against a person's level of verbal ability. As verbal ability increases, the probability of choosing the correct answer increases dramatically. This suggests that the item is a fairly good measure of verbal ability.

The item characteristic curve is a graphic summary of the key features of a test item: its difficulty, its discriminating power, and the probability of answering correctly by

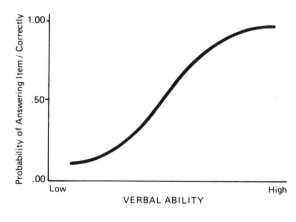

Figure 9-1   Item Characteristic Curve for Item *i* on a Verbal Ability Test

guessing. The mathematics involved in estimating the mathematical parameters of this curve are complex, requiring both large samples and sophisticated computer algorithms (Drasgow & Hulin, 1991). However, you can gain an appreciation of the basic ideas behind the ICC by simply graphing the probability of a correct response as a function of the total test score. Figures 9-2, 9-3, and 9-4 illustrate such graphs.

Suppose an item was not a very good discriminator. What would a graph of the relationship between item responses and total test scores look like? Figure 9-2 shows such a graph for a very difficult item that shows little discriminating power. Notice that the difficulty of the item (i.e., as indicated by the probability of a correct response) decreases, though only slightly, as the total test score increases. That is, people who did well on the test have a *slightly* higher chance of doing well on this item than those who did poorly on the test. If you compare this graph to the one shown in Figure 9-1, which represents an ICC for an item with high discriminating power, it should be clear how the steepness or *slope* of the graph indicates discriminating power. A steep upward slope indicates that people who did well on the test (or who possess a large amount of the ability measured by the test) are *much* more likely to respond correctly to the item than people who did poorly on the test. A flatter slope, as in Figure 9-2, indicates a weaker relationship between test scores and responses to the particular item illustrated in the graph. Figure 9-3 shows an item with *negative* discriminating power (the item-total r for this item is $-.24$). In this graph the curve slopes downward, indicating that people who did well on the test are *less* likely to do well on this particular item.

Graphs of this type can also be used to illustrate item difficulty. Figure 9-4 shows graphs of the relating item scores to total test scores for three items that show similar discriminating power, but that differ in difficulty. Item C is the most difficult, item B is moderately difficult, and item A is the least difficult. The position of the curve gives a

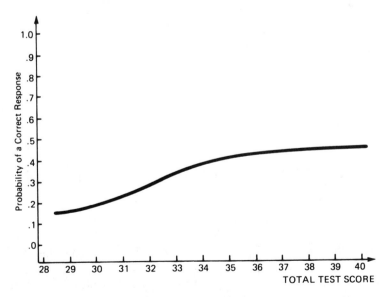

Figure 9-2 Graph of Item versus Test Score for an Item with Little Discriminating Power ($p = .24$; item-total $r = .03$)

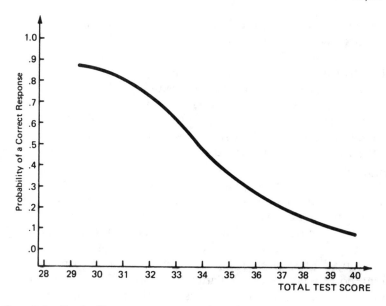

Figure 9-3   Graph of Item versus Test Score for an Item with Negative Discriminating Power ($p = .52$; item-total $r = -.24$)

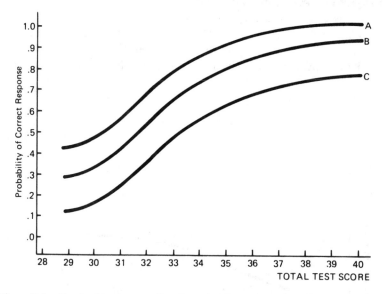

Figure 9-4   Graph of Item versus Test Score for Three Items That Vary in Difficulty

good indication of the difficulty of each item. For the most difficult items, the curve starts to rise on the right-hand side of the plot (high total test scores). This is simply a graphic illustration of the fact that the probability of answering a difficult item correctly is low for most examinees and rises only in the top group of those taking the test. For the easier items, the curve starts to rise on the left-hand side of the plot (low total test scores); the probability of answering an easy item correctly is high for everyone but the very bottom group of examinees.

It is important to keep in mind that the graphs in Figures 9-2, 9-3, and 9-4 are *not* true item characteristic curves. As we noted earlier, the estimation of ICCs is mathematically complex and beyond the scope of this text. These graphs do, however, provide a reasonable approximation of the ICC, and they make it possible for test developers and test users who do not have access to the sophisticated methods used in estimating ICCs (e.g., psychology students doing class research projects) to gain an appreciation of the powerful ideas behind this technology.

Item Characteristic Curves and Item Response Theory

Traditional item analysis procedures supply us with good measures of discrimination and difficulty. If item characteristic curves simply provided alternate measures of these vital item characteristics, they would hardly be worth the trouble. There are, however, some unique advantages associated with ICCs. In particular, they illustrate the basic ideas that underlie item response theory.

Item response theory was constructed to explain and analyze the relationship between characteristics of the individual (e.g., ability) and responses to individual items (Hulin, Drasgow & Parsons, 1983; Lord, 1980; Thissen & Steinberg, 1988; Weiss, 1983). Reliability and validity theories typically concentrate on test scores and only peripherally deal with individual items. Thus, item analysis represents a sort of ad hoc follow-up analysis when used in the context of explaining reliability or validity. Item response theories, on the other hand, are developed precisely for the purpose of understanding how individual differences in traits or attributes affect the behavior of an individual when confronted with a specific item.

Item response theory starts with a set of assumptions about the mathematical relationship between a person's ability and the likelihood that he or she will answer an item correctly. These assumptions form a basis for item characteristic curves, which represent a combination of assumptions regarding underlying relationships and the empirical outcomes of testing. To the extent that these assumptions are true, item response theory allows precise inferences to be made about underlying traits (e.g., ability) on the basis of observed behavior (e.g., item responses).

One of the principal advantages of item response theory is that it provides measures that are generally *sample invariant*. That is, the measures that are used to describe an item characteristic curve do not depend on the sample from which test data are drawn. The same is not true for standard item analysis statistics. The same reading test that is difficult (low *p* values) for a group of fourth graders may be less difficult and more discriminating for a group of sixth graders but extremely easy for a group of eighth graders. The invariance of measures obtained using item response theory is thought to be important, since it allows characteristics of items to be analyzed without confounding them, as traditional item analyses do, with the characteristics of the people taking the test.

Item response theory and test-taking behavior.   Most proponents of item response theory focus on the technical advantages of this approach, such as sample invariance, or on the fact that this approach allows you to tackle issues that are very difficult to handle in traditional item analysis (applications of this theory to three such issues are described in the section follows). In our opinion, the real advantage of item response theory may be conceptual rather than mathematical. Unlike the traditional approach to item analysis, this theory encourages you to think about *why* people answer items correctly.

The most widely cited model for responses to typical test items suggests that there are really two things that explain a correct response: luck and ability. The mathematical methods used in constructing ICCs under this model include a parameter that represents the susceptibility of the item to guessing, another that represents the role of ability in item responses, and a third that represents item discriminating power. Item response theory defines difficulty in terms of the level of ability needed to answer the item correctly, with a given level of probability. In contrast, the traditional definition of difficulty says nothing about what makes an item difficult or easy. Thus, traditionally an item is difficult if most people answer incorrectly and easy if most people answer correctly. Item response theory states that a difficult item is one that requires a high level of ability to achieve a correct answer, while an easy item is one that can be answered by people with lower ability levels.

In addition to providing a better definition of item difficulty than the traditional approach, this theory provides a better definition of discriminating power. In item response theory, discriminating power is defined in terms of the relationship between item responses and the construct the test is designed to measure. Thus, if individuals who are very high on spatial ability are more likely to answer an item on a spatial ability test than individuals who are low on that ability, the item shows high discriminating power. The traditional approach links item responses to total test scores rather than to the construct the test is designed to measure. One implication is that traditional item discrimination statistics are only as good as the test itself. If the test is a poor measure of the construct, the relationship between item scores and total test scores may tell you little about the worth of the item.

Item response theory has become the dominant theme in modern psychometric research. In several of the chapters that follow (e.g., Chapters 11, 15, and 16) we will discuss contemporary applications of item response theory to practical testing problems. Some of the more specialized applications of the theory are described below.

Practical Applications of Item Response Theory

Although the mathematical complexity of item response theory has to some extent stood in the way of its widespread use, there are several advantages unique to item response theory that explain why this approach has become increasingly popular. First, as mentioned earlier, the theory produces measures of item difficulty, discrimination, and so on, that are invariant across different samples of people who take the test. Second, item response theory can be applied to solving several problems that are difficult to solve using traditional approaches. Three examples are noted here: (a) an approach that uses distractors in estimating ability, (b) an approach that tailors the test to the individual examinee, and (c) approaches for analyzing and constructing specialized tests.

Getting information about ability from distractors.   In traditional item analysis, an answer is either right of wrong. It makes no difference which distractor is chosen—a right answer receives a score of 1 and a wrong answer receives a score of 0. In fact, some distractors are probably better answers than others in that some reflect partial knowledge while others will be chosen only if the person has little or no knowledge.

Item response theory suggests that *any* response made to an item could provide information about one's knowledge or ability. Rather than concentrate solely on the correct response, the theory encourages construction of a separate ICC for each possible response to a multiple-choice item, distractors as well as the correct response. Figure 9-5 shows a set of item characteristic curves for the possible responses to a single test item. Choice *a* (the correct response) shows positive discriminating power; one of the distractors (choice *c*) also shows some positive discriminating power. Choice *d* is extremely unpopular and therefore shows no discriminating power, whereas choice *b* shows negative discriminating power.

Figure 9-5 suggests that alternative *c* is nearly as good an answer as alternative *a*, although it shows less discriminating power. On the other hand, both *b* and *d* are bad choices. In particular, the lower a person's ability, the higher the probability that the person will choose *b*. Rather than scoring the item either right or wrong, an examinee might receive nearly full credit for choosing *c*, and might receive the lowest score for choosing *b*.

Tailored testing.   Tests are usually constructed for a fairly diverse audience. For example, a test of general mathematical ability might contain several easy items, several items of moderate difficulty, and several very difficult items. For any individual taking the test, many of the items may be inappropriate and uninformative. For example, someone who is gifted in mathematics will find most of the items very easy and will be challenged only by the most difficult items. Someone who has great difficulty with mathematics will find most of the items too difficult and will do better than chance only on the easiest items. Rather than constructing a long test that contains some items appropriate for each ability level, it would be better to construct tests tailored to the ability level of

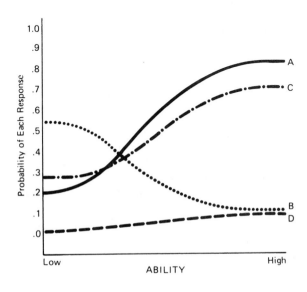

Figure 9-5   Item Characteristic Curve for Each Response to a Multiple-Choice Item

the person taking the test. Developments in microcomputer technology and in psychometric theory have made this possible (Urry, 1977).

One of the most interesting applications of item response theory is in computerized tailored testing. For any individual, a test is most precise if the difficulty of each item corresponds with his or her level of ability. Item response theory can be used to help tailor tests to individual examinees. When an individual takes a test at a computer terminal, it is possible to estimate his or her ability at each step of testing and then to select the next item to correspond with the person's estimated level of ability. For example, the first item on a tailored test might be moderately difficult. If an examinee passes that item, the computer may select a more difficult question for the second item on the test. If a person fails that item, the next item selected for the test might be less difficult. Tailored testing allows a great deal of precision within a fairly short test. This type of testing is discussed in more detail in Chapter 11.

Item analysis for specialized tests.   For the most part, this chapter has dealt with tests designed to measure some attribute or construct over a reasonably wide range (e.g., scholastic aptitude tests). In this type of measurement, three general principles can be applied in evaluating item analyses:

1. Incorrect responses should be evenly distributed among distractors.
2. Item difficulties should cluster around .50.
3. Item-total correlations should be positive.

There are a number of situations, however, in which these guidelines do not apply. Screening tests and criterion-keyed tests are outstanding examples.

Screening tests are those that are used to make preliminary decisions or to make decisions as to whether or not persons exceed some minimum level of knowledge or proficiency needed to qualify for a position. For example, a bus driver must achieve a minimum level of visual acuity and depth perception in order to qualify for a license. However, visual acuity beyond this minimum does not make the person a better bus driver; rather, subminimal vision disqualifies applicants. Screening tests also are useful when the number of applicants greatly exceeds the number of positions, as is often the case in graduate admissions. A medical school that receives large numbers of applications and that never accepts applicants from the bottom half of the pool would benefit greatly if test scores could be used reliably to screen out this lower group.

A criterion-keyed test is one in which there are no right or wrong answers; it is a test in which a person's score is determined by the similarity of his or her responses to the responses of some known group. For example, the Minnesota Multiphasic Personality Inventory (discussed in Chapter 20) was constructed in such a way that examinees' responses could be compared with those of people diagnosed as schizophrenic, paranoid, and so forth. To the extent that a person's responses are similar to those previously diagnosed as schizophrenic, a diagnosis of schizophrenia would be indicated.

Item response theory is particularly useful in analyzing both screening tests and criterion-keyed tests. For example, consider a test designed to screen out the lower half of the applicant pool for medical school. An ideal item for this test would have an item characteristic curve similar to that shown in Figure 9-6. The curve would be very steep at the point about which the school wished to discriminate (the middle of the ability distribution), with a low probability of answering correctly among the low group and a high probability of answering correctly among the high group. A short test made up of items such as this would be effective for this type of preliminary screening.

In designing a criterion-keyed test, several ICCs could be developed relating item responses to different criteria. For example, Figure 9-7 illustrates how a particular item response might be related to the likelihood of being diagnosed as depressed, schizophrenic, or paranoid. This figure suggests that the item discriminates well for diagnoses of depression and schizophrenia but is unrelated to diagnoses of paranoia. Further, the ICCs indicate that individuals who answered yes to the item "I disliked school" are likely to be diagnosed as depressed but are unlikely to be diagnosed as schizophrenic.

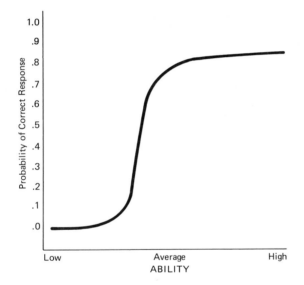

Figure 9-6 An Item Ideally Suited for Screening the Upper from the Lower Half of the Ability Distribution

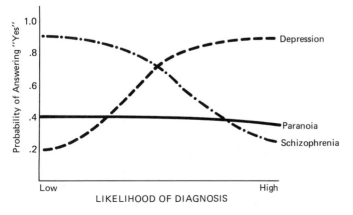

Figure 9-7 ICC's Relating Responses to the Item "I Disliked School" to Psychiatric Diagnosis

CRITICAL DISCUSSION:
Using Item Response Theory to Detect Test Bias

As we noted in Chapter 2, the question of whether or not tests or test items are biased against minorities, females, and others is a very important one, and it is the focus of a great deal of controversy. One reason for this controversy is that there are many ways of defining and detecting test item bias (Berk, 1982; Holland & Thayer, 1988). These methods range from the very simple, in which a test item is regarded as biased if different groups receive different scores or have different passing rates, to the very complex, in which bias is defined in terms of the relationship between the item and some external criterion. There is a growing consensus among testing experts that measures based on the item response theory are among the best measures of test item bias (Drasgow & Hulin, 1991; Thissen, Steinberg & Gerrard, 1986).

Although the mathematics of item response theory are quite complex, the application of this approach to the analysis of test item bias is based on a fairly simple idea—that the relationship between item scores and the construct being measured by the test is an important consideration, especially when bias in measurement (as opposed to bias in prediction) is at issue. Examination of item characteristic curves, and the statistics that describe these curves, provides a set of methods for detecting item bias. Figure 9-8 illustrates an item that has different measurement characteristics; that is, it is biased against males, while favoring females. As you can see, the item is more difficult for males but does not discriminate those males with low levels of ability from those with high levels of ability. In contrast, the item is less difficult and is a better discriminator for females.

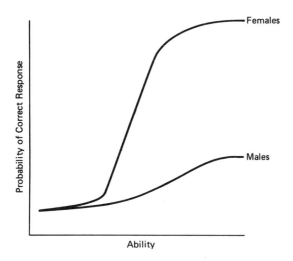

Figure 9-8   ICC for a Biased Test Item

One of the many advantages of using ICCs and item response theory in the analysis of test item bias is that it illustrates very clearly how items are biased; such an analysis can predict the probable consequences of using particular items on a test. For example, items like the one illustrated in Figure 9-8 would have two effects. First, males would get lower test scores (i.e., the items are more difficult for males). Second, the test would not measure the construct in question as well for males as for females (i.e., it has lower discrimination for males).

Summary

Scores on psychological tests usually represent the sum, average, or some other function of responses to individual items. This chapter has focused on multiple-choice items, where one of several choices is correct, but the concepts discussed here apply equally to other types of testing (e.g., personality items that have no "correct" response). In understanding responses to these items, and the contribution of information from each item to the total test score, it is important to consider the responses to distractors, the difficult of the item, and its discriminating power. Distractors that attract an unusually small or large number of responses may need to be rewritten; doing so is likely to improve the item substantially. Items that are too difficult or too easy (i.e., answered incorrectly or correctly by almost all examinees) contribute little to the overall value of the test. Finally, items that show high discriminating power, defined in terms of a D value or an item-total correlation, are likely to provide useful measures of the same thing measured by the test as a whole.

Item response theory provides a sophisticated and powerful alternative to the traditional methods of item analysis and scoring. The item characteristic curve provides a graphic summary of an item's difficulty, discriminating power, and susceptibility to guessing. This theory provides not only elegant solutions to problems difficult to attack in terms of traditional methods but also sensible definitions of the concepts of difficulty and discrimination. Rather than defining them in terms of the people taking the test (i.e., the p value) or the other items on the test (i.e., the item-total r), the theory defines them in terms of the relationship between the ability or attribute measured by the test and the responses individuals make to test items. This approach has come to dominate modern psychometric research, and it opens the way for sophisticated new testing strategies.

CHAPTER 10

THE PROCESS
OF TEST DEVELOPMENT

This chapter opens our discussion of the application of the principles of psychological measurement outlined in previous chapters. Up to this point we have studied the basic concepts of psychological testing without reference to their application in specific testing situations. In this chapter we examine the process of test development and highlight some of the problems test developers face as they attempt to measure various psychological traits, attitudes, and behaviors.

Test development can be broken down into three distinct stages. The first stage involves test construction. Issues such as item writing, scale construction, response sets, and selection of test format are of primary interest here. Next, new tests are standardized for use on particular target populations, norms are developed, and considerable research is undertaken to establish estimates of the tests' reliability and validity. Finally, with the passage of time, tests need to be revised to keep them contemporary and current, both with respect to norms available and item content. This chapter is therefore divided into three sections that deal with these aspects of test development.

CONSTRUCTING THE TEST

Item Writing

The first step in the test construction process is to generate an item pool. Although test items form the basic building blocks of tests, little attention has been given to item writing in comparison to other aspects of the test development process (e.g., scale construction and response sets). Why this is so is not completely clear. Perhaps it is because item writing has often been seen as much more of an art than a science. Given this view, test developers have often elected to rely on statistical item analysis procedures to help them identify and eliminate poor items rather than to focus on how to improve the item-writing process itself. They appear to be laboring under the assumption that through much trial and error in writing, eventually subsets of items can be identified that will measure the trait in question.

There are some common issues that arise in item writing, however, that merit discussion. For example, item length can sometimes be a problem. Examinees may get confused if an item is so long that the major point is missed as it is read. Another critical variable in the item-writing process involves the vocabulary used in the test items. Test developers need to be aware of the reading level of the target group for whom the test is intended. Likewise, the wording of items needs careful consideration to avoid the use of double negatives and possible ambiguity in responding. Items such as "I do not read every editorial in the newspaper every day," from the California Psychological Inventory, often create uncertainty on the part of examinees. Should they respond true to this statement if they agree? What would a false response imply? Table 10-1 presents additional hypothetical examples of poorly written as well as well-written items.

One additional factor that test developers have increasingly taken into account in item writing concerns the presence of sexist, racist, or other offensive language. Although blatantly offensive language is relatively easy to detect and eliminate, subtle linguistic nuances are often overlooked and not perceived as offensive by the developer. A case in point involves interest tests that use occupational titles containing reference to only one sex, for example, using the term "mailman" instead of "mail carrier" or "fireman" rather than "firefighter." Even though such gender-specific language does not appreciably affect most interest test scores, if it promotes sexist attitudes or causes some people to react negatively to testing, then it needs to be eliminated. The best method for eliminating problems inherent in written items is to try them out on sample populations. Test developers generally begin with a large item pool and weed out unacceptable items until a satisfactory subset is identified.

Item Content

One of the factors that leads to differences in the interpretability of tests stems from the nature of the item content used in their construction. Some test developers use a particular theoretical belief system to guide them in the creation of test items. Generally, test

TABLE 10-1   EXAMPLES OF POORLY WRITTEN AND WELL-WRITTEN ITEMS

Poorly written items	Well-written items
It is not acceptable to say no when asked to give to charity.	It is considered bad manners to turn down a request for a charitable donation.
I do not believe that all our laws are good for the citizens of this country.	I think that some laws are harmful to particular citizens.
If you ask, people will not tell you what they are thinking most of the time.	I believe that people tend to keep their real thoughts private.

constructors draw upon one particular theory of personality, career interests, or intellectual ability and translate the ideas of that theory into test items.

Allen Edwards adopted this item-writing strategy in developing his personality test, the Edwards Personal Preference Schedule (EPPS). Working from a theory of personality outlined by Murray (1938), Edwards directly translated many of the manifest needs postulated in the theory into behaviorally worded test items. For example, Murray theorized that the need for autonomy often influences people to do things on their own or seek a lifestyle characterized by independence and unconventionality. Edwards took this concept of autonomy and translated it into such test items as "I like to avoid situations where I am expected to do things in a conventional way" and "I like to avoid responsibilities and obligations." You can easily see how these items directly reflect the theorized need. One particularly interesting feature of test items generated from theory is that what they are measuring is often relatively transparent. Because of their transparent nature, these items are usually quite easy for examinees to "see through." Thus examinees answer them as they would like to appear rather than as they actually are.

The other approach used in item writing is much more atheoretical and does not rely on theory to guide the selection of item content. In this method, test developers generate a large item pool with very diverse item content. Often there is no common theme that binds the items together. The trick is to create items that will differentiate how one group responds from how another group responds. The Minnesota Multiphasic Personality Inventory (MMPI) was developed using primarily this approach. Because such items often bear little theoretical significance, they are generally much less transparent than theory-based items and consequently much less subject to examinee distortion. Table 10-2 gives a comparison between several EPPS and MMPI items and shows how easy it is to detect what theoretical items are measuring in comparison to items generated without regard to theory.

TABLE 10-2   THEORETICAL AND ATHEORETICAL ITEMS CONTRASTED: EXAMPLES
FROM THE EPPS AND THE MMPI

Items from the EPPS	Items from the MMPI
I would like to write a great novel or play. (Scale: Achievement)	I enjoy detective or mystery stories. (Scale: Hysteria)
I like to avoid responsibilities and obligations. (Scale: Autonomy)	I almost never dream. (Scale: Psychasthenia)
I like to be the center of attention in a group. (Scale: Exhibition)	I have never had a fit or convulsion. (Scale: Depression)
I like to be in love with someone of the opposite sex. (Scale: Heterosexuality)	I enjoy a race or game better when I bet on it. (Scale: Masculinity/Femininity)
I like to keep my letters, bills, and other papers neatly arranged and filed according to some system. (Trait: Order)	I am so touchy on some subjects that I can't talk about them. (Scale: Schizophrenia)

Item Response Alternatives

The types of item response alternatives used in psychological testing vary widely. Some self-report measures, such as the Personality Research Form, employ a simple true-false response format. Others, such as the Tennessee Self-Concept Scale, employ a multiple-choice answer format where examinees respond on a five-point Likert scale, indicating how truthful statements are about them. Projective tests, such as the Rorschach and the Rotter Incomplete Sentences Blank, rely on a free response format on the part of the examinee.

Sometimes the purpose of the test dictates the type of answer format. Consider the Wide Range Achievement Test, which assesses spelling ability by having the examinee print the correct spelling of a word spoken orally by the examiner. In contrast, the spelling subtest of the Differential Aptitude Test asks test takers to indicate whether or not stimulus words are spelled correctly. While both are tests of spelling ability, the former relies on auditory spelling, whereas the latter stresses visual recall skills. Consequently, an examinee may score quite differently on these two measures because a variation in the response format changes the nature of the task.

By far the most popular format in objective testing has involved the use of multiple-choice items. Use of this item format provides several advantages over other formats. First, test item scoring is easy and rapid. Second, the error in the measurement process associated with guessing is reduced as the number of alternatives in the item is increased (e.g., a four-alternative item produces a 25 percent probability of a correct response due to guessing; a five-alternative item reduces the chances of guessing a correct answer to 20 percent). Finally, no examiner judgment is involved in the scoring of multiple-choice items.

The multiple-choice item format has its shortcomings, however. It is often difficult to write alternative statements for items that function as good distractors. Another problem with multiple-choice items is that they may contain transparent cues that signal the correct response. This occurs when articles such as "a" or "an" are used in the wording of multiple-choice items in a manner that gives the examinee a definite clue as to the correct choice. Similarly, sometimes the tense of verbs used in the stem and in an alternative may aid the test taker in identifying the keyed response. An example of a multiple-choice item that signals the correct response alternative is shown in Table 10-3.

Scale Construction

Each item on a psychological test represents an observation of some particular behavior or trait. By grouping similar items together, test developers can generate multiple observations of the same behavior or trait. As we have seen in Chapters 5 and 6, increasing the

TABLE 10-3   CUEING THE CORRECT
RESPONSE IN A MULTIPLE-CHOICE ITEM

The car featured in the movie *Rain Man* was a
(a) Allante (Cadillac)
(b) Roadmaster (Buick)
(c) Escort (Ford)
(d) Aries (Dodge)

number of behavioral observations increases the reliability of our estimates of that variable. However, item grouping can be done in various ways, resulting in psychological scales that have different characteristics and require different interpretations. Traditionally, three scaling methods have been used in developing psychological tests.

Rational scales.   Historically the oldest method of scaling, the "rational" method of scale construction implies that there is some underlying thought, belief, or rationale that is used as the basis for selecting items and grouping them together into a scale. This is precisely what test developers do when they draw upon a particular theoretical system to guide them in selecting a set of items to measure a specific theoretical idea. For example, when Edwards (1957) wanted to measure various manifest needs within people and study how they affected behavior, he followed Murray's theoretical ideas about needs and created scales consisting of items reflecting Murray's concepts. The advantage of rationally derived scales is that test developers can then draw upon theory to make predictions about behavior because the scales have been designed to measure the theory's concepts.

Rationally derived scales can also have some severe shortcomings. It is obvious that the usefulness of such scales is tied to the validity of the theory upon which they are based. If the theory is sound and leads to accurate predictions about how people will behave, then scales based on that theory should lead to valid and meaningful predictions also. Likewise, if the theory is not substantiated, then scales based on that theory are likely to have questionable validity. Another potential problem arises from the transparent nature of scales constructed using the rational approach. For example, it is not difficult to understand what the item "I have often felt like taking things that do not belong to me" measures. Consequently, sophisticated examinees can distort their responses, either consciously or unconsciously, so as to appear in a particular light.

Empirical scales.   Empirically derived scales rely on criterion-keying for their validity. With this method, well-defined criterion groups are administered a set of possible test items. Items that statistically differentiate the groups are included on the test. For example, a group of male adult schizophrenics diagnosed by clinical interview might be contrasted with a group of normal, emotionally well-adjusted male adults. Both groups would be given the same set of items, but only those that clearly separated the schizophrenics from the criterion group would be retained. While this procedure produces reasonably valid tests, it does not permit any analysis of *why* the criterion groups differ on such items. The major testing purpose served, then, is to discriminate one group from another, rather than to understand the underlying theoretical reasons for their differences.

In contrast to rational tests, empirical tests are generally difficult to dissimulate because the content of the items that may differentiate groups is not readily apparent. An example would be an item from the MMPI such as, "I enjoy detective or mystery stories," which if answered false suggests a tendency toward denial. However, it is very difficult to determine its psychological significance from merely reading or responding to this item.

Factor-analytic scales.   The final method of test construction employs factor-analytic procedures as the basis for item selection. In this method, the correlations among items are examined to determine which factors account for most of the variability in responding on the test. Once the groups of items constituting each of the factors has been identified, they often are labelled by perusal of the item content within the group. Because these groupings were determined by statistical analysis rather than theoretical determination, it is often very difficult to capture the essence of the scales formed by such item groupings or their relationship to clinically useful concepts.

Another problem with factor-analytically derived tests stems from the variability in item groupings obtained when different methods of factor analysis are used to construct the scales. The strength of this method, however, is that it yields instruments with psychometric properties generally superior to those constructed by either of the other two methods.

Response Sets

To measure various psychological traits, test developers often employ self-report inventories that ask examinees to share information about themselves. However, some examinees believe that the information being requested is too personal or embarrassing to report. Sometimes they may even feel coerced into completing an inventory and then decide not to complete it accurately. On other occasions they find the questions stated in such vague terms that they are unsure about how to respond in order to present an accurate reflection of their thoughts, feelings, attitudes, or behaviors. In such instances as these, test takers may consciously distort their responses, guess at items when they are stated in vague terms, answer items carelessly, or even unintentionally mismark their answer sheets. Factors such as these add unwanted error variance to test scores and confound the interpretation process. Whenever individuals respond to something other than the actual item content when being tested, the validity of the information obtained is of questionable value. Therefore, better psychological tests have built-in methods of detecting these sources of extraneous variance so that they can be potentially minimized or even eliminated in the interpretation process.

Social desirability.   One of the most pervasive and problematic response sets is social desirability. The effects of this response tendency on measures of personality have been stated most cogently by Allen Edwards (1964). His research demonstrated that people from various backgrounds, educational levels, and cultures generally agree as to which behaviors are socially desirable and which are undesirable. From his analysis of various personality tests, he concluded that many of those tests did not accurately measure the traits they were designed to assess but, rather, provided indices of individuals' propensities for giving socially approved responses. He stated that the rate of endorsement of personality test items was a linearly increasing function of the items' social desirability values. Thus, Edwards was arguing that when examinees respond to personality test items, they do not attend as much to the trait being measured as to the social acceptability of the statement. Consequently, Edwards has proposed that this tendency to give desirable answers is itself a personality trait that is probably more manifest than other traits. Unless controlled or eliminated, the effects of social desirability were postulated to mask the appearance of other dimensions of personality under investigation.

Researchers have tried various methods of controlling the effects of this response set. The most common methods have been to pair items of equal desirability ratings in an ipsative format, to select neutral items that are neither strongly positive nor strongly negative on the social desirability dimension, or to statistically adjust test scores to eliminate any such effects. This latter method is accomplished by devising a special scale to assess the tendency for examinees to give socially desirable responses and then statistically correcting their other test scores for this distorting factor. However, none of these methods has proven particularly successful in controlling or eliminating the effects of this response set. Nevertheless, authorities in the testing field still do not agree on how severe this problem is or how invalidating its effects are.

Random responding.   This response set usually results when examinees fail to attend to the content of test items and respond randomly either because they are unmotivated or incapable of completing the task accurately. Examinees often give random responses on an inventory when they do not want to be evaluated or when they are incapable of validly taking the test (e.g., unable to read the questions or too disturbed to attend to the task). For example, students referred to counseling because of disciplinary infractions might be unwilling to cooperate with any testing efforts, perhaps viewing them as an infringement of their rights. In such cases, their testing results would be of limited clinical value.

To help prevent the clinician from attempting to interpret such results and arriving at faulty conclusions, test constructors often include scales on their tests designed to identify this response pattern. The typical form of these scales includes items that tend to be universally true or false for everyone. If the respondents attend to the content of these items, they will answer them in the expected direction. If a random response pattern is utilized, however, then by chance they will endorse too many of these items in the opposite direction of the population and produce a score on the scale that is highly suggestive of random responding. Sample items from such a scale taken from the Personality Research Form are shown in Table 10-4.

Not all tests have special scales for detecting random responding. Wise test users generally familiarize themselves with the overall picture generated by random test proto-

TABLE 10-4   SAMPLE ITEMS FROM THE INFREQUENCY SCALE OF THE PERSONALITY RESEARCH FORM

Item	Response
I was born over 90 years ago.	True
I try to get at least some sleep every night.	False
I make all my own clothes and shoes.	True
Sometimes I feel thirsty or hungry.	False
I rarely use food or drink of any kind.	True
I have no sense of touch in my fingers.	True
I am able to breathe.	False
I have never ridden in an automobile.	True

Source: From Douglas Jackson, *Personality Research Form*, Copyright © 1967, 1974, 1984 by Douglas N. Jackson. Reprinted by permission of Sigma Assessment Systems, Inc., 1110 Military Street, P.O. Box 984, Port Huron, MI 48061-0984.

cols by experimentally completing a number of answer sheets with random responses. Once the general pattern of scores resulting from a random response set is known, similar score patterns when encountered can be interpreted with caution, and follow-up information on the motivational level of the examinee can be obtained.

The potential problem raised by this response set can be demonstrated by the Psychological Screening Inventory, a short diagnostic instrument used to aid the clinician in conceptualizing the difficulties of clients and determining the seriousness of their pathology. Unfortunately, randomly completed inventories strongly resemble those of seriously disturbed people. Figure 10-1 presents a validly completed psychotic profile and a randomly generated one. Unless clinicians are aware of such potential interpretive problems with an instrument, they are likely to arrive at invalid conclusions and possibly inappropriate referrals for treatment.

Dissimulation. This response set generally refers to completing an inventory in such a manner so as to appear overly healthy (faking good) or overly disturbed (faking bad). It is produced by the conscious efforts of the respondent to produce a picture that is distorted or dissimulated from reality. This response set is most operative in situations where testing is being done as part of a selection process for jobs, promotions, awards, and the like, or for decision-making purposes relative to the establishment of diminished capacity as part of a defense against culpability in a criminal matter. In both cases invalid

Figure 10-1   Graphs of a Random and a Psychotic Response Pattern

conclusions could be drawn if this conscious distortion effort were unknown to the clinician.

Personality tests differ greatly with respect to how successfully they address this problem. Some tests, like the MMPI, are quite sensitive to detecting dissimulation, while others, like the EPPS, have no built-in checks for this response set. However, the lack of scales to check for faking in some inventories may not be a serious problem. First, corrections for response distortion rarely help (Hogan, 1991; Nicholson & Hogan, 1990); if faking is suspected, there may be no good way of estimating what the score would have been without faking. Second, recent research suggests that while personality tests are often fakable, this may not greatly affect their correlations with other tests and measures, and therefore faking may not diminish their validity as predictors of future behavior (Hough, Eaton, Dunnette, Kamp & McCloy, 1990).

Response Style

Response style refers to a general tendency to either agree or disagree with statements without attending to their actual content. The tendency to generally agree has been labelled acquiescence; the tendency to disagree is often referred to as criticalness. Both are considered to be problematic when operative in psychological assessment instruments because client responses are then quite likely to be based on these response tendencies rather than on the specific content of test items. For example, if John gives an agree response to the items "I prefer to not eat meat" and "I believe that eating meat is morally wrong," the clinician cannot unambiguously determine if John really holds philosophical beliefs in common with vegetarians or if he merely tends to agree with whatever is stated regardless of the content. The potential effects of this problem increase as the imbalance in the number of true and false keyed responses on the test increases. If there are equal numbers of positive and negative responses keyed on the test, then any tendency to acquiesce or be critical will not influence the test score markedly. When this balance is not maintained, then profile scores may be affected by these responding styles.

The seriousness of this problem in personality testing has long been debated by experts in the field (Edwards, 1970; Jackson, 1967; Rorer, 1965). Some believe that the effects of acquiescence or criticalness are seen only on those items that are ambiguous for the examinee. When the item content is perceived as unclear or confusing, then the response given will likely depend on the examinee's internal preference for agreeing or disagreeing. An example of an ambiguous item would be the statement, "I think Lincoln was greater than Washington." There are few clues as to what this item is measuring or what the interpretation of a true or false response might be. On the other hand, clear, unambiguous items such as "I hated my mother" are not likely to induce an acquiescent or critical response, but rather a response directed at the content of the item.

Unfortunately, some experts in testing state that the most useful items are those that are less obvious and transparent. Use of these subtle items does invite the operation of response styles, however. An example in which this problem has occurred is the F scale measuring authoritarianism developed by Adorno, Frenkel-Brunswik, Levinson, and Sanford (1950).

Norming and Standardizing Tests

In Chapter 4 we covered some of the general concepts related to both test standardization and norming. We saw that due to the problems inherent in the measurement of psychological traits (i.e., the difficulty in establishing a zero point for most traits), we need to use the differential performance of various comparison groups to give test scores meaning. We also discovered the importance of standardizing testing procedures so that additional sources of error could be eliminated from the measurement process. In this chapter we want to expand our discussion of these two essential features of psychological tests to see how they are actually employed in the construction of psychological tests.

Norming Psychological Tests

Selecting and testing appropriate norm groups for psychological tests is both a difficult and very expensive task. As we learned in Chapter 4, selecting samples that represent the target population for which the test is intended can be quite complicated. Ideally, good comparison groups would provide a representative sample of the population in question, being neither too specific and limited nor too broad and nonapplicable for meaningful score interpretation. While tests having norm groups consisting of only students living on the East Coast might by very useful for interpretation locally on the East Coast, their value in other parts of the country would be somewhat suspect. On the other hand, tests that employ very general norm groups representative of the United States at large might not be very useful for providing meaningful score interpretation on a more regional basis. Consequently, several different norm groups are usually established for tests so that users can choose the most appropriate comparison group for their particular purpose.

Steps in Developing Norms

Defining the target population. As we have seen, a primary concern in the development of norms is the composition of the normative group. A general principle in developing norms is that the composition of the normative group is determined by the intended use of the test. For example, most tests of mental ability are designed to assess an individual's ability relative to others in the population. Here, the appropriate normative group is people in general; norms based on a sample of Ph.D. candidates will yield inappropriately low scores.

Consider a second example. Testing organizations such as Educational Testing Service produce professional exams like the Law School Admission Test (LSAT) or Test of English as a Foreign Language (TOEFL). In the case of the LSAT, the target population is those college students who aspire to or plan on applying for entrance to law school. In the case of the TOEFL, the target group is composed of those students whose native tongue is not English but who anticipate studying abroad where the language of instruction is English. In both situations, the appropriate comparison groups are those for which the test is used in making admission decisions. To compare the performance of the test taker (e.g., prospective law school student) to data based on an inappropriate norm group (e.g., high school dropouts) makes little sense. In the worst case, incorrect decisions can be made about some of the applicants if an inaccurate or inappropriate comparison norm group is used. A critical first step in the development and interpretation of norms is to ensure that the target group on which they are based is relevant and appropriate.

Selecting the sample.   Once the test developer has determined the appropriate target group from which to obtain norms, a second important step is to obtain a representative sample from each of these groups. In theory, selecting the sample should be relatively simple, but in practice there are numerous pitfalls. The key in the process is to obtain samples that are a representative cross-section of the target population. For example, assume that the target population for norm development for an achievement testing program consists of beginning and end-of-year students in the seventh, eighth, and ninth grades. To construct norms, we need a method of obtaining samples from each of these grades taken at both the beginning and end of the year that are representative of all students (in the United States, for example) in these grades at these times of the year.

There are a variety of sampling techniques one could use to obtain a representative sample. However, some techniques could be nearly impossible to implement. For example, a random sample of seventh, eighth, and ninth graders would be completely impractical. Even if one could identify a certain number of *schools* at random, it is not certain whether the officials at each school would cooperate. Participating in a norming effort takes a lot of time on the part of the school and also disrupts the normal activities; a substantial percentage of the schools may decide against allowing outsiders to use valuable instructional time.

The method most likely to be used when developing large-scale norms is a variation of cluster sampling. The first step is to identify regions of the country that should be represented (Northeast, Southwest, etc.). After identifying regions, subdivisions may be further made into rural and urban areas. Then, based on the overall plan for how many students are needed, a decision is made as to how many school systems within the various regions and rural/urban areas would be needed to obtain the desired number of participants. The last step would be to select the systems at random and convince as many as possible that it would be to their benefit to participate in the norming project. Within each system one then tries to sample as many of the total number of seventh, eighth, and ninth grade students as possible.

Standardization

After item selection, scale development, and norming have been completed, test developers need to standardize as much of the testing procedure as possible. The goal is to eliminate as many extraneous variables as possible from affecting test performance. Some of the factors that play a role in the determination of an examinee's test performance come immediately to mind. These include such things as test-taking instructions, time limits, scoring procedures, and guidelines for score interpretation.

Other factors are not so intuitively obvious, however. Factors such as the physical surroundings in which the testing is done, the health of examinees, the time of the test administration, and many other tangentially related variables may also play a significant role in affecting test scores. For example, what effect would attending a late-night party have on test performance? Would depression significantly affect the scores an individual might get on an interest test? Is performance affected by the temperature, lighting, or interior design of the testing room? Does testing performance vary as a function of the time of day, day of the week, or month of the year when the test is given? And what effect might a noisy air-conditioner have? While all these conditions could conceivably affect scores on a test, it would be impossible to try to account for all of them.

The practical solution is to standardize the test administration process. Standardization involves keeping testing conditions as invariant as possible from one administration to another. By adhering to strict rules of test administration and scoring, many of these extraneous sources of variance can be eliminated, thus permitting more meaningful interpretation of testing results. This is particularly important when norms are used in the interpretation process. Unless testing conditions remain essentially invariant, valid comparisons of individual test scores to test norms are virtually impossible.

While standardizing testing procedures would not appear to be difficult, many practical problems arise. Items that are selected for inclusion on tests become outdated or obsolete. When this occurs, it is important to remove them to keep the test current. Since the test was normed and standardized using the original items, this raises serious questions about using these original norms for score interpretation. Test developers have circumvented this problem by substituting new items that have similar item characteristics for the out-of-date ones. This ensures that the new items discriminate at approximately the same level as their predecessors and, therefore, help keep the testing task as standardized as possible.

A similar problem is encountered in the standardization of ability tests, such as the Scholastic Aptitude Test or the Graduate Record Examinations. It would be useful to compare the performance of students not only with their peers but also with other students from earlier years. Unfortunately, however, the actual test content is not invariant from one test administration to another. Changes occur because dated items are eliminated and many items are dropped because they were on forms of the test that have been released to the public for inspection. In order to permit valid score comparisons with older norm group performances, statistical item replacement is again utilized to maintain a standardized testing procedure.

TEST PUBLICATION AND REVISION

Writing the Manual

The next step in the test development process is the preparation of a manual. It is here that the test developer outlines the purpose of the test, specifies directions for test administration and scoring, and describes in detail each of the steps in its development. Pertinent information concerning the reliability and validity of the test needs to be included so that users can evaluate the test both with respect to its psychometric characteristics and its applicability to various assessment situations.

Manuals also need to contain detailed information about the norming process. Test developers need to inform the user how the norm groups were selected and how the testing was done. They must provide a thorough description of the samples employed (e.g., the number tested, the age, the race, the sex, and the geographical location). The inclusion of only partial data in this section of the manual makes score interpretation difficult and open to serious error.

When a test manual is initially written, it usually contains only minimal data containing the psychometric characteristics of the test. Much of the research work done up to that time has been conducted solely by the test's author. After the test has been published, other researchers begin to experiment with its use and report their findings. These data frequently lead to modifications of score interpretations as the meaning of certain scales becomes more refined. Similarly, new data are reported on the test's reliability and validity. These data must then be assimilated into new editions of the manual. Keeping the manual up-to-date is a critical step in the test development process, but, unfortunately, it is often not done in a timely manner.

Revising the Test

When should a test be revised? There is not a clear answer to this question. In part, it depends on the timelessness of the content. For example, the Revised Minnesota Paper Form Board Test (MPFB) employs geometric designs to measure an aspect of mechanical aptitude. Items consisting of only two dimensional geometric figures, such as those on the MPFB, are virtually always contemporary and do not become dated.

Many tests, however, contain items that need updating to keep them current. The Strong Interest Inventory illustrates this point. An early revision of the Strong contained an item that referred to the *Literary Digest*. This item remained on the inventory until it underwent a revision over 30 years later. The problem with this item was that the *Literary Digest* went out of business during the Great Depression of the 1930s. Consequently, individuals responding to this item 10 or 15 years later probably had little or no awareness of what the item meant. What effect this may have had on the usefulness of this item in identifying interests is unknown, but it is much more likely that it was negative rather than positive. It is obvious that more frequent revisions are necessary when item content is so definitively dated.

Another factor that influences the timing of test revisions is their popularity. Tests that have generated a great deal of user interest are usually subjected to considerable research activity. This leads to the establishment of a substantial data base that adds valuable information about the meaning of test scores and their generalizability. These new data often suggest item content modifications, changes in test administration procedures, or alterations in test scoring. The dilemma that test developers face, however, is that to make the indicated revisions entails renorming the test. Scores on the newly revised test cannot legitimately be compared to the older test norms. Since renorming is both expensive and time consuming, a decision must be made between retaining the less perfect older test or revising it. Often the revision process is put off until the number of significant modifications required warrants the added costs associated with renorming.

Interpretation and cautions.   While tests that have been recently revised to take into account current research findings and eliminate dated item content are often superior to older, less up-to-date tests, it needs to be stated that some very old, infrequently revised tests still work as well as more contemporary tests. The variables they measure are stable, enduring, and apparently sufficiently robust to overcome any technical short-comings in the tests. Sometimes even dated item content continues to produce the desired assessment outcomes despite significant developments and changes in our society. As we noted above, the Strong Interest Inventory underwent few revisions during the first 40 years of its existence. While some of the items containing dated item content negatively affected test scores, others had no appreciable effect. Consider the item "Pursuing bandits in a sheriff's posse." While this item may have been apropos in the 1920s or 1930s, it certainly is dated today. However, research (Hansen & Campbell, 1985) has shown that this item still has good validity today. Apparently, the interest dimension measured by this item is not affected by the dated content of the item. The point to be made here is that not all tests can be judged by their age. Newer is not always better.

CRITICAL DISCUSSION:
Should Tests Be Normed Nationally, Regionally, or Locally?

There is no definitive answer to this question. It depends on the purpose for which the testing is being done. Consider the following example. Maria is in the tenth grade in one of the city's four high schools. Maria's counselor is concerned that her grades are not as good as they should be. Is Maria not studying? Are her below-average grades due to a reading deficit, to some other learning problem, or are they really reflective of her ability? In order to try to answer this question, Maria is given a general intelligence test to determine how she compares to other students. The question arises as to what would be the most meaningful comparison group? Should she be compared to other members of her class? Would it be more beneficial to see how she performs relative to other tenth graders in the city? Perhaps she should be compared to the other tenth graders in the state or even nationally. The choice of which norm group to use is dictated by the specific question to be addressed.

    If Maria's counselor wanted to evaluate her performance relative to that of her classmates, then the most appropriate choice would be a locally developed norm group consisting of other tenth graders at her high school. Even using a citywide norm group might not give the most useful information if there were substantial differences among the schools in the city. This might be especially of concern if one school drew heavily from a section of the city where English was a second language. Certainly regional or national norms would be less useful because Maria's counselor would not know how the average tenth grader in her school scored compared with the national norms. Knowing that Maria is above or below the national mean would not permit an analysis of Maria's score in relation to that of her class.

    Ideally, Maria's counselor would have locally developed norms on the intelligence test so a direct, meaningful comparison could be made between how she scored on the test and how her classmates scored. Unfortunately, local norms frequently do not exist, and so test users must select norm groups that match the characteristics of the local situation as closely as possible. Interpretive errors can arise, however, when this substitution is made.

    How specific must local norms be? Sometimes even norms based on the general local population are not adequate for the assessment task. For example, if College X wishes to use a scholastic aptitude test to select students for admission into the engineering program, local norms based on all entering freshmen at College X may not provide sufficient information. A student may perform above the mean for all entering freshmen at

College X yet still be considerably below the mean for those who enter the engineering program. Even within the same college, subgroups of students may be quite different. Use of a more general norm group tends to mask these differences that may be of central importance. Consequently, in this situation, the most appropriate norm group would consist of only enrolled engineering students at College X rather than the more broadly constructed universitywide freshmen population.

There are testing applications that call for more general comparison groups. School administrators are often called upon to show that the educational experience being provided for students is effective. One way to demonstrate this is to compare the performance of local students with regional or national norms. Using large, general norm groups for score interpretation reduces the regional and local variability that exists among students and often yields less biased and more meaningful conclusions to be drawn from the data. Frequently, national norm groups become a constant standard against which to assess progress. Using regional or national norms in this manner, school districts look more closely at the *change* in group performance from one year to another in comparison to the norm rather than looking at the absolute level of performance attained. In either case, the assessment goals of the user are better served with broad rather than specific norm groups.

Despite this discussion, most test manuals advise users to develop their own local norms whenever possible. We would support this position as long as the purpose of testing is consistent with the use of locally generated norms. As we have seen, however, this is not always the case. We believe that the selection of which norm group to use should always be based on the testing decision to be made. Whether locally developed norms serve this function best depends on the application.

SUMMARY

The process of test development begins with the basic element of all tests, namely, the items themselves. Test constructors first generate a large item pool from which they refine, modify, and reject items generally through statistical analysis of examinees' responses until they arrive at a final set of items that appear to satisfy their requirements. Although this crucial step in the developmental process has not been researched as thoroughly as other aspects of the test construction process (i.e., scale building and norming), attention has been given to several aspects of item writing, such as item length, reading difficulty, and cultural bias, that appear to affect how people respond to test items.

There are many different strategies used in developing tests. The choice of a particular method often depends on the test development philosophies of test authors, while the item response format is often a matter of author preference or determined by the nature of the trait being measured. The two most popular methods of determining item content are (a) to base all test items on a particular theoretical basis and (b) to construct items that are not theory related but reflect extremely diverse activities, behaviors, values, symptoms, and attitudes. Each method has its strengths and weaknesses. The multiple-choice item format is by far the most frequently used, but it is not necessarily superior to other formats and can have serious shortcomings.

Once test items have been chosen, they are usually grouped into scales that intend to provide the user with multiple observations of specific attributes or traits. The three principal scaling methods in use produce either rational scales, empirical scales, or factor-analytic scales. Rationally derived scales are theory based; they allow the generation of specific, testable hypotheses but permit examinees to easily distort their scores. Empirical derivation produces scales with enhanced validity characteristics that are robust and less subject to examinee distortion than rational scales. Empirical scales have little or no link to theory, however, and therefore make causal interpretation of score differences very difficult or even impossible. Factor-analytically derived scales have superior psychometric characteristics, are preferable for research use, but rarely lead to practical, clinically useful information.

A number of factors other than item content affect the responses examinees give to test items. Examples include the social desirability of items, carelessness, conscious attempts at distortion, and personality style. Test constructors attempt with varying degrees of success to control for the effects of these response sets either by creating testing formats that reduce their action or by devising statistical correction formulas that can be applied to test scores to account for their presence.

To give test scores meaning, norms are employed to provide points of reference to aid in the interpretation process. Care must go into the selection of samples used in the norming of tests. Factors such as gender, age, geographical location, race, ethnicity, and socioeconomic status need to be considered in choosing appropriate normative groups. The usefulness of a test is often a function of the representativeness of the norm groups provided in the test manual.

The problem of standardizing test procedures and materials to eliminate the effects of extraneous factors on examinee performance has always been a challenge to test developers. There are probably countless factors that might influence test performance, and it is not feasible to attempt to account for all of them. Through explicit standardization of the process and procedures of testing, test developers hope to control or eliminate as many of these factors as possible. The chapter ends with a discussion of the process of test publication and revision.

CHAPTER 11

COMPUTERIZED TEST ADMINISTRATION AND INTERPRETATION

This chapter discusses the increasingly important role of computers in the administration and interpretation of psychological tests. Computers have long been used in test scoring, but until the 1980s their role was largely restricted to recording answers and computing test scores. Computers are now used for a much wider variety of purposes in psychological testing, and there is clear evidence that computer-based testing is beginning to replace traditional paper-and-pencil methods of test administration in many contexts. Furthermore, computers are an increasingly important tool for interpreting test scores, to the extent that some systems of computerized test interpretation seem designed to replace psychologists and other testing professionals in interpreting scores on a variety of tests and inventories.

This chapter explores a number of issues that arise out of the use of computers in administering and interpreting psychological tests. First, the use of a computer keyboard rather than a pencil and paper as a method of responding to test items can change the test taker's strategy for taking the test; it can also change the psychometric characteristics of test scores in unexpected ways. It is not always clear whether responses to a particular set of test items have the same meaning when administering via computer versus paper and pencil. Second, the use of computers in testing provides an opportunity to apply highly sophisticated strategies for adaptive testing, in which tests are tailored to individual respondents. In particular, computerized testing systems allow you to apply the powerful tools of item response theory (described in Chapter 9) to the development and scoring of adaptive tests. This chapter will examine the advantages of this method of testing.

Computerized test interpretation systems make it possible to obtain detailed narrative descriptions of the possible meaning of test scores. For example, individuals responding to inventories designed to assess psychopathology might receive narrative reports that seem highly similar to psychological diagnoses. The possibility that these computer-generated reports might replace or overrule the clinical assessments of psychologists, psychiatrists, and other mental health professionals has generated a great deal of debate. This chapter examines the technical, practical, and ethical issues in the debate over computerized test interpretation.

Finally, this chapter examines the use of computerized testing programs to detect unusual or invalid patterns of responses to test items. For example, ability test scores can be inflated if examinees have opportunities to guess when answering items. Responses to personality and interest inventories may be affected by "faking" on the part of examinees, that is, by examinees' distorting scores to purposely look good or bad on a particular test. Methods of dealing with guessing, faking, and other response sets exist (some of these were reviewed in Chapter 10), but none of the most widely used methods is completely satisfactory. Computer-based testing provides an opportunity to apply a variety of more sophisticated approaches to the problems created by guessing, faking, and other invalid response patterns.

USE OF COMPUTERS IN TESTING: A TAXONOMY

As the introduction of this chapter suggests, the phrase "computerized testing" can refer to a wide variety of ways in which computers might be used in psychological testing. Hartman (1986) suggested that the involvement of computers in testing and assessment can be classified on a continuum similar to that shown in Figure 11-1. At the simplest level, computers might be used as a simple data-storage device. In cases where it is important to retain responses to individual items or scores of many individuals, the use of computers to store data is a practical necessity; large-scale testing programs can generate mountains of paper, and the storage and retrieval of hard copies of test responses or testing files can be surprisingly difficult. Although computers are clearly important in this type of testing, we will not use the phrase "computerized testing" to refer to testing programs in which computers are used merely to read answer sheets or store item responses and test scores. The use of computers solely as data-storage devices does not change the test or its use in any essential way, whereas the use of computers for adminis-

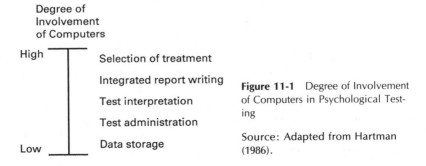

Figure 11-1 Degree of Involvement of Computers in Psychological Testing

Source: Adapted from Hartman (1986).

tering or interpreting tests, or for selecting treatment options, represents a potentially fundamental change from traditional testing practices.

As we noted earlier, computers can be used either to administer the same test that is given via paper and pencil or to administer similar but shorter tests that are specifically tailored to each individual examinee. Computer administration may affect the scores obtained from the test, although evidence we will review later in this chapter suggests that computerized versions of specific tests are often essentially equivalent to their paper-and-pencil counterparts. In fact, many computer-administered tests are interpreted in exactly the same way, often using the same norms, as the paper-and-pencil version.

Whereas computerized test administration might represent nothing more than an evolution in testing technology, computerized test interpretation represents a sharp break with the past. Traditionally, the interpretation of test scores has been thought to require specialized training and has represented one of the more important activities of professional psychologists (Wade & Baker, 1977). The use of computerized interpretation systems as an adjunct to, or a replacement for, clinical judgment is therefore a controversial proposal. Computerized reports are especially controversial when issued in the form of narrative statements. It is common for test interpretation services to offer narrative reports that appear to explain the meaning and implications of scores on tests and inventories such as the Minnesota Multiphasic Personality Inventory (MMPI); these reports are sometimes constructed so that it would be difficult to tell whether they were generated by a person or a machine. The fact that computers can generate narrative reports or diagnoses that are, on the surface, indistinguishable from clinical diagnoses raises a number of troubling questions that will be examined later in this chapter.

The highest level of computer involvement in testing is where the computer not only interprets test scores but also "decides" on the appropriate treatment, therapy, training program, and so on. In principle, a person seeking counseling, advice, or treatment might bypass psychologists, physicians, or other professionals altogether by simply taking a battery of tests and being directed to appropriate types of medication, therapy, training, and so on, by computer algorithms. At the moment, this possibility is more theoretical than real; we do not know of any existing programs in which assessments are done and in which important treatment decisions are made solely by computer. Nevertheless, the possibility exists that such systems could be designed and implemented.

COMPUTERIZED TEST ADMINISTRATION

The growing use of computers in psychological testing represents only one aspect of the increasing use of computers in measurement of all kinds. For example, Allran (1989) described computerized systems for measuring physical strength and endurance. Computerized sensors are rapidly replacing mechanical measurement devices in automobile engines and motors of all sorts. However, psychological measurement represents a special case in which the use of computers might change the meaning of test scores. That is, it is possible that people taking psychological tests might respond differently to a computerized test than to a traditional paper-and-pencil test. This concern is especially acute in computerized adaptive testing (which is reviewed in the following section of this chapter), where the test might be considerably shorter and more tightly focused (i.e., containing only those items appropriate for the examinee's ability level) than traditional tests.

The first issue in automated testing is whether the computer format itself affects responses to the test. In other words, do people receive similar scores on a paper-and-pencil version as on a computer-presented version of the same test? Surprisingly, few studies have been conducted on this issue, and most of these have featured small samples and inconclusive results. Nevertheless, studies by Elwood (1969), Johnson and Mihal (1973), and Katz and Dalby (1981) suggest two important conclusions. First, test scores obtained using computer-presented tests are highly correlated with scores on paper-and-pencil tests. Second, there is evidence that people view computerized tests more positively than equivalent paper-and-pencil tests. Third, there is some evidence that cultural differences might be smaller on computerized tests than on paper-and-pencil tests (Johnson & Mihal, 1973). It appears possible, then, that computers could be used to present many ability tests with little loss in the accuracy or acceptability of testing.

Although the evidence suggests that presentation of ability test items on a computer screen, as opposed to a sheet of paper, does not substantially affect the characteristics of the test, the same may not be true of other types of tests and inventories. Davis and Cowles (1989) found that subjects responding to computerized measures of anxiety and locus of control seemed to "fake good"; that is, they seemed to give responses indicating lower levels of test anxiety than they gave to paper-and-pencil versions of the same basic inventory. They speculated that the novelty and apparent scientific rigor of computerized tests might prompt people to answer differently than they would to a more familiar paper-and-pencil test.

Although computerized tests are often equivalent to paper-and-pencil tests, research on the effects of test format suggests that several factors could lead to differences. Mazzeo and Harvey's (1988) review suggested that differences between the two test types might depend on factors such as whether the test was speeded, whether it contained graphics, whether items were based on long reading passages that were difficult to display along with the item on the screen, and whether the computerized tests allowed respondents to omit or return to items. Green (1988) outlined a number of ways in which computerized administration could affect the strategies used to respond to items. Finally, Fleishman (1988) noted that computerized tests are often assumed to be equivalent to paper-and-pencil tests, despite the absence of any research on their actual equivalence, and that the standards for developing computerized tests are often considerably lower and less well defined than the standards for paper-and-pencil tests. These studies suggest that test publishers should conduct separate norming and equating studies whenever they introduce computer-administered versions of standardized tests.

Computerized testing is a worldwide phenomenon that is growing rapidly (international research on this topic is presented in *Applied Psychology: An International Review,* Vol. 36, No. 3–4). For example, the armed services of each of the members of the North Atlantic Treaty Organization (NATO) have developed computerized tests, although the United States is the only NATO member that has developed operational computerized adaptive tests to date. For test developers, the question is not *whether* they should develop computerized tests but, rather, *how* they should use the capabilities of the computer to improve their tests. As we will note later in this chapter, there are still many instances in which paper-and-pencil tests will be the test of choice. Nevertheless, you can expect to see more and more use of computers in administering and interpreting tests in the near future.

Unique Advantages of Computerized Tests

Although there are many areas in which practicality constraints may lead you to choose paper-and-pencil tests over computer-administered tests, computerization presents some potentially unique advantages. Computerization has changed not only *how* you give tests but also *what* you measure with tests. For example, it is relatively easy to measure response latency, or the time needed to respond to each item. The increasing graphic capabilities of computers make it possible to measure spatial and perceptual abilities that were virtually impossible to measure with paper-and-pencil tests. Perhaps the most promising direction for computerized testing, however, will arise out of the current interactions between cognitive psychologists, test developers, and computer programmers (Embertson, 1985; Hofner & Green, 1985; Jones & Applebaum, 1989; Ronning, Glover, Conoley & Witt, 1987).

Hofner and Green (1985) note that computational models are becoming increasingly popular in many areas of psychology, including perception, memory, language acquisition, and reasoning. In the area of intelligence, Sternberg's (1985) triarchic theory includes computational components as part of the definition of intelligence. Psychological tests in all these areas are likely to be presented via computer; in most cases, the processes that these theories describe cannot be adequately measured with conventional tests.

Computerization is most likely to be necessary when the tasks presented in the test require precise timing, stimulus control, dynamic graphic presentation, or limited exposure to the material in each test item. These variables are critical to many theories of cognition, and they can also be relevant to theories of personality and psychopathology (Hofner & Green, 1985). As the influence of cognitive psychology on psychometrics increases, we are more and more likely to see computerized psychological tests that have sophisticated features such as the measurement of response latency or the dynamic presentation of test items.

COMPUTERIZED ADAPTIVE TESTING

An adaptive test is one in which the questions are tailored specifically to the individual being examined. For example, an adaptive test of general mental ability will include items that are neither too easy nor too difficult for the respondent. As a result, when two individuals of different ability take the same version of the same test, they might respond to completely different sets of questions. The idea of adaptive, or tailored, testing has a long history in the area of ability testing. In principle, all the various methods of adaptive testing are similar to the method employed when the Stanford-Binet Intelligence Scale is administered by an individual examiner. First, the examiner (or the computer) must use some data to estimate the subject's ability. On the basis of this estimate, test questions must be chosen that seem appropriate for that ability level, omitting questions that are too easy or too difficult for the subject in question. Using the Stanford-Binet, the clinician first estimates the entry level on the basis of vocabulary test scores, then establishes a subject's ceiling level on the basis of test responses. Computerized adaptive testing provides an alternative strategy that includes continually estimating a subject's level of ability, choosing specific items that are appropriate for that level, and using responses to those items to revise and sharpen the estimate of a subject's ability (Weiss & Davinson, 1981).

A variety of adapative testing strategies exist. The simplest method is to start testing with a moderately difficult item. If a person fails this first item, it is followed by an easier item. Testing proceeds in this manner, always following a correct answer with a more difficult item, and an incorrect answer with an easier item. This strategy is adaptive at every stage of testing but presents some difficulties in scoring.[1] A similar strategy is to divide the test into two or three sections, as in Figure 11-2. Examinees who do well in the first section of the test are routed to the more difficult items in Section 2; examinees who show average or poor performance are routed to the less difficult items in Section 2. Similarly, a person's performance on the second section of the test determines which items he or she will encounter in the third section of the test. A person who correctly answers most of the difficult items in Section 2 might go on to the most difficult items in Section 3. Examinees who either do poorly on the difficult items or well on the easy items in Section 2 might go on to the less difficult items in Section 3.

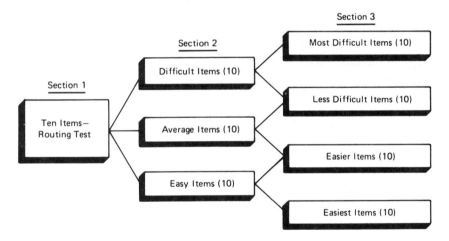

Figure 11-2   An Adaptive Test with Three Sections

The most sophisticated strategy for computerized adaptive testing involves applying latent trait theory or item response theory to intelligence testing (Urry, 1977; Urry & Dorans, 1981). The theory provides methods of estimating the difficulty of the item, the discriminating power of the item, and the probability of guessing the correct answer to that item, independent of the sample being tested. Once these item parameters are known, the theory provides procedures for (a) estimating the subject's ability on the basis of his or her response to each item, (b) choosing the optimal test items on the basis of that

---

[1]These difficulties are resolved if indices based on item response theory are employed.

estimate, and (c) revising that estimate on the basis of responses to each new item. Because the computer continually reevaluates its estimate of the subject's ability and selects optimal items, it is possible to achieve high levels of accuracy in providing estimates of a person's ability using an extremely small set of test questions.

Comparability of Adaptive and Traditional Tests

Much of the recent research comparing computerized and paper-and-pencil tests has examined computerized adaptive tests (CAT). Two reasons explain why these tests might yield different scores than those obtained from more traditional tests. First, they are presented via computer, which means that examinees do not have opportunities to scan ahead, go back and change answers, and so on. Second, they are adaptive, typically requiring fewer items and less variability in item difficulties than traditional tests. However, research suggests that CAT tests are often highly comparable to their paper-and-pencil counterparts. For example, Henly, Klebe, McBride, and Cudeck (1989) showed that scores from the CAT versions of several subtests from the Differential Aptitude Tests were highly correlated with scores from the traditional test. Cudeck (1985) demonstrated similar results for the CAT and traditional versions of the Armed Services Vocational Aptitude Battery (ASVAB). Mead and Drasgow (1992) analyzed scores from 115 tests in 356 different content areas. Their study showed high levels of equivalence (i.e., correlations between CAT and paper-and-pencil versions in the .90 range) for power tests, but lower equivalence (i.e., correlations in the .60 range) for highly speeded tests. When speed of response is a critical variable, details as trivial as the layout of the answer sheet (e.g., fill in bubbles versus shade the area between two lines) can markedly affect scores. It is no surprise that computerized administration of highly speeded tests, in which you must respond using a keyboard or a mouse, presents special problems.

Advantages of Computerized Adaptive Testing

There are several reasons why computerized adaptive tests might be preferred over traditional tests. First, these tests are highly efficient in the sense that they yield highly reliable and precise scores with a small number of items (Drasgow & Hulin, 1991; Schoonman, 1989; Weiss, 1983). Because they require a smaller number of items than traditional tests, they can also be administered in less time. As we will note below, this time savings can often have a substantial impact on the overall cost of testing.

Second, it is much easier to maintain test security with CAT than with traditional testing. There are, unfortunately, many individuals and groups who make their living by helping people cheat on admission tests, personnel selection, and licensing tests. We are not talking about the various schools that offer coaching on tests such as the Scholastic Aptitude Test or the Graduate Record Examination. Although their tactics are occasionally questionable, these schools are not in the business of pirating the test. Rather, we are referring to individuals or groups who help people obtain unauthorized copies of tests, who sell answers to tests, or who help individuals cheat on tests. In traditional testing the same test is given to thousands of individuals, and once one copy has been obtained, or once someone has memorized the items on that test, test security has been breached. In CAT there often is no hard copy of the test to steal, and an individual who takes the test in order to memorize the items will be exposed only to a small number of potential test items. In contexts where there is a strong incentive to cheat, the added security of CAT is a very important advantage.

When only a small number of tests are given (e.g., when the tests are given by an individual clinician), computerized testing can be an expensive proposition, in part because of the necessary investment in computer hardware and maintenance (Schoonman, 1989). However, in some large-scale testing programs, CAT can be highly cost-effective. Even though a large-scale CAT program requires the purchase of many computers, the savings in testing time can easily offset the expenses of computerization. The armed services' project to develop and implement a computerized adaptive form of the ASVAB (CAT-ASVAB) provides a vivid illustration.

The ASVAB is currently administered in schools and in a number of military testing sites. Because the test takes several hours, it is impractical to bring examinees from a long distance to take the test; the combined travel time and testing time would require an expensive overnight stay. Therefore, there is a need for a large number of testing sites throughout the nation. If the testing time could be cut—which can be accomplished with CAT—the number of testing sites could also be cut, and the savings mount up quickly. The saving of applicants' time also deserves consideration. Anyone who has taken an all-day multiple-choice exam can appreciate the advantage of measuring the same thing with a much shorter test.

COMPUTER-BASED TEST INTERPRETATION

The use of computers to aid in the interpretation of test scores can take many forms. In its simplest form a computer program might merely retrieve and display information about the reliability and accuracy of test scores (e.g., when error bands are reported around scores) or about the various norms that might be used to interpret tests. In its most extreme form it might involve a completely automated testing, diagnosis, and treatment system. Most programs for computer-based test interpretation (CBTI) represent some compromise between the use of the computer solely as an information-retrieval system and the use of the computer as a replacement for the psychologist, physician, and so on, whose responsibility it is to give and interpret tests.

Applications of CBTI

The first widely used CBTI systems were developed in the 1960s to aid clinicians in interpreting scores on the MMPI (Moreland, 1990).[2] Although most CBTI systems are still used in interpreting scores on measures of personality and psychopathology, several systems have also been developed for interpreting scores on tests of intelligence and ability (Kramer, 1988), for interpreting structured clinical interviews (Spitzer, Williams, Gibbon & Furst, 1990), and for diagnosing neuropsychological problems (Adams & Brown, 1986). More than 400 CBTI services and systems are now commercially avail-

---

[2]This inventory, as well as computerized systems for interpreting its scores, is described in Chapter 21.

able, and this number is likely to continue to grow (Butcher, 1987; Conoley, Plake & Kemmerer, 1991).

CBTI development.   Kramer (1988) describes two basic strategies for developing CBTI systems, the clinical approach and the actuarial approach. Systems that follow the clinical approach attempt to codify clinical experience and judgment into a set of decision rules. For example, if clinical experience suggests that elevated scores on a particular scale (e.g., the hysteria scale on the MMPI) are associated with a particular psychological disorder, the computer program might include commands to notify the test user of this possible diagnosis whenever an individual's test score is above a specific cutoff value. Actuarial strategies are similar in nature, but they use information about the statistical associations between test scores and diagnoses, as opposed to clinical experience or judgments, to create decision rules. A program that follows the actuarial approach might examine the known correlates of test scores and notify the test user whenever specific diagnoses are statistically predicted on the basis of test scores. Most CBTI systems seem to follow the clinical strategy, in which the computer is programmed to mimic the judgment of the clinician, rather than the actuarial approach, in which the computer functions more like a statistician (Moreland, 1990).

Vale, Keller, and Bentz (1986) provide a clear description of the process of developing a CBTI system for personnel testing in industry. Their study is somewhat of a rarity; the processes used to develop most CBTI systems, and the decision rules that characterize the computer programs, are often treated as closely guarded secrets. From a business standpoint, this makes perfect sense; once the basic workings of a computer program become common knowledge, that program can easily be duplicated, so that the test interpretation service loses much of its commercial value. From a scientific and professional standpoint, however, this secrecy presents a number of problems, some of which will be noted in the sections that follow.

Guidelines for the use of CBTI.   In 1986 the American Psychological Association developed *Guidelines for Computer-Based Tests and Interpretations.* This set of guidelines, which grew out of the more general *Standards for Educational and Psychological Testing,* is designed to encourage responsible use of computerized test interpretation services. However, there are good reasons to believe that many users and CBTI developers are either not aware of or not in compliance with the APA guidelines (Farrell, 1989). Because of the secrecy that surrounds commercial CBTI development, it is often difficult to determine whether the interpretations offered by various services conform to the technical requirements of the guidelines. The potential for abuse by individual test users is an even more worrisome problem. For example, we know of a case in which a licensed psychologist performed a "diagnosis" on an individual by simply reading him the narrative report provided by a commercial test interpretation service, informing him that he was suffering from organic brain damage and probably from depression and schizophrenia, among other things. The only basis for his statements was that the computer printout said that this was the appropriate interpretation of scores from the one test that the individual had taken.

Conoley, Plake, and Kemmerer (1991) suggest that users of CBTI systems should at a minimum be competent in the use and interpretation of the test in question without the aid of a computer program. That is, users should be sufficiently knowledgeable about the test to recognize when the computer-generated report is either correct or in error. Thus, the role of CBTI should be to act as an aid to the clinician, not as a substitute. A well-developed CBTI system might alert clinicians to aspects or implications of test scores that they had not fully considered, or they might provide some independent collaboration of the clinician's interpretation.

The CBTI Controversy

The controversy of CBTI involves several separate issues. First, the validity of computerized interpretations is often in doubt. Second, it is possible that both test users and the individuals who take tests may place undue weight on computer-generated reports. Third, the use of computerized interpretations as a substitute for professional judgment raises a number of ethical questions.

CBTI validity.   Several reviewers note that CBTI systems are extremely difficult to validate (Conoley et al., 1991; Moreland, 1990; Snyder, Widiger & Hoover, 1990). Because the computer algorithms are often proprietary in nature (i.e., the company that develops the CBTI system is unwilling to reveal how interpretative reports are generated), there may be no way to know when or whether the interpretations generated by a particular program are valid. Also, the lack of good criteria makes validity research difficult. If you are going to try and validate computer-generated reports, you need some well-defined standard that defines the "correct" interpretation of each person's test scores. This is sometimes done using the method of extreme groups, in which computer-generated test interpretations for groups of people with relatively severe and clearly defined psychological problems (e.g., diagnosed schizophrenics) are compared to those of people in general. However, this method provides only a limited view of the validity of CBTI systems, since it is often difficult to assemble identifiable groups that correspond to all the diagnostic interpretations that might be included in a computerized report.

Conoley and his colleagues (1991) suggest that the trend toward easy-to-read narrative reports probably compromises the validity of computer-based interpretations. In order to generate a natural-sounding report in simple English, it is sometimes necessary to make a large number of statements or predictions, each of which may be based on relatively little evidence. One broad rule of thumb that might be used in estimating the validity of a computerized interpretation is that the more it says about you, the less likely it is to be true.

Vale, Keller, and Bentz (1986) reported an interesting strategy for validating computerized interpretations. Their CBTI system involved generating a library of interpretative statements judged by experts to be appropriate for different test-score levels. In particular, they generated verbal descriptions of the meaning of test scores at the tenth, twenty-fifth, fiftieth, seventy-fifth, and ninetieth percentile on each of the several scales included in their test battery. Their validation strategy represented a variation on the retranslation methods sometimes used in developing rating scales (see Chapter 19 for descriptions of these methods). They gave the tests to a group of individuals and then asked an independent group of experts, individuals who had not been involved in constructing the CBTI system, to read the computer-generated reports and to estimate the test scores received by the individuals described in each report. The relatively high level of accuracy in reconstructing test scores from narrative reports suggests that the two methods of conveying information about performance on the test (i.e., numerical score versus narrative interpretation) were highly equivalent.

Do CBTI reports receive undue weight?

Several authors have expressed concern that computer-generated test interpretations might be given undue weight by both test users, such as clinicians who may defer to the computer's interpretation, and test takers (Matarazzo, 1983, 1986; Skinner & Pakula, 1986). Computer-generated reports might have an aura of objectivity and scientific credibility that cannot be matched by the best professional. That the validity of these reports is often uncertain makes the possibility that they will receive undue weight very worrisome.

Although the idea that computer-generated reports might be seen as more accurate and credible than similar interpretations obtained from human judges seems very reasonable, research suggests that these reports are *not* seen as more credible or accurate (Andrews & Gutkin, 1991; Honacker, Hector & Harel, 1986). One possibility is that computers have become so commonplace in modern society that reports of this type have lost their novelty and aura of scientific certainty. Anyone who has worked with computers quickly learns the limitations of this technology—the phrase "garbage in, garbage out" is still the best description of many computer analyses—and the idea that computers can be trusted to arrive at the right answer in psychological assessment may be an anachronism.

Professional ethics and CBTI.

The standards of professional practice in psychology clearly prohibit using a computerized test interpretation service as a replacement for the informed judgment of a qualified psychologist. Although this restriction may sound a bit self-serving (i.e., psychologists have decided that machines cannot replace psychologists), it is an essential safeguard against potential abuse of computerized test interpretation. First, computerized interpretations often fail to convey information about the limitations of any specific test. Whereas a computer-generated report might be based on scores on one test taken at a single point in time, clinical judgment is supposedly based on many forms of assessment and on data not easily included in a CBTI system (e.g., the client's behavior and demeanor in a clinical interview). Second, complete reliance on CBTI provides no protection against completely and obviously faulty interpretations of test scores.

Matarazzo (1986) raised an interesting ethical issue in his critique of computerized test interpretations. An individual clinician who interprets a test is ethically responsible for the professional interpretation of that test, and he or she is bound by a strict set of ethical guidelines. (See Appendix B and *Guidelines for Computer-Based Tests and Interpretations,* 1986.) There is no individual who has comparable responsibility when a test is sent to a computerized scoring service. The use of computerized test interpretations often fails to include the sorts of safeguards that are implicit in the set of ethical standards that bind licensed psychologists. Probably the best solution is to incorporate *both* the professional judgment and standards and the power of computerized scoring by using computerized test interpretations in conjunction with clinical interpretations by qualified professionals, rather than relying on computerized test interpretations alone.

DETECTING INVALID OR UNUSUAL RESPONSE PATTERNS

In theory, responses to test items should be determined by two factors: (a) the individual's standing on the construct being measured and (b) random measurement error. This is the central assumption of the classical theory of reliability reviewed in Chapter 5. However, test responses can be influenced by specific response patterns that have nothing to do with what the test is designed to measure and that do not fit the usual definition of measurement error. For example, an individual taking a multiple-choice examination might make a series of lucky guesses and as a result receive an unrealistically high grade. A person taking an interest inventory or a personality inventory might engage in faking, that is, distorting his or her responses to present a specific impression (e.g., giving socially desirable responses). A person might simply be careless in filling out an answer sheet (e.g., filling in the wrong column of bubbles). It is important to develop methods of detecting and correcting for such invalid or unusual response patterns.

In paper-and-pencil testing, the methods that could be used to deal with invalid response patterns are necessarily somewhat simple and crude. For example, many ability and achievement tests include corrections for guessing in their scoring formulas; the correction is determined from a simple equation that takes into account the number of response options on each question and the total test score. The use of computers in testing makes it possible to apply a wide range of sophisticated detection methods and correction procedures that are either impossible or impractical to apply to paper-and-pencil testing.

Waller (1989) notes that traditional corrections for guessing do not adequately distinguish between random and partial-knowledge guessing. Random guessing occurs when the item is very difficult for the examinee—when he or she has virtually no idea of the true answer. Partial-knowledge guessing occurs when the examinee knows enough about the topic or about the type of question to eliminate some but not all of the response alternatives.[3] The application of item response theory, a strategy used in most computerized adaptive tests, makes it possible to reliably discriminate between these two types of guessing and to apply different correction factors depending on the degree of partial knowledge used in responding to questions.

Both signal detection theory (Lanning, 1989) and item response theory (Drasgow & Guertler, 1987) have been successfully applied to the problem of detecting inappropriate responses (e.g., random or inconsistent responding). Although these methods are difficult to apply to tests with small numbers of items (Reise & Due, 1991), they are applicable to a wide range of computerized adaptive tests.

Finally, computerized testing may be useful in detecting faking on personality and interest inventories. Research by Holden and his associates (Holden & Fekken, 1988; Holden, Fekken & Cotton, 1991; Holden & Kroner, 1992) and by George and Skinner (1990) suggests that response latencies, or the time it takes to respond to individual

---

[3]Some of the strategies taught at test-coaching academies are, in effect, ways to move from random to partial-knowledge guessing. For example, if you know that on a particular test "None of the above" is virtually never the correct answer, you can eliminate that response option regardless of your knowledge or lack of knowledge of the topic covered by a question.

items, might be useful in detecting faking. Interestingly, responses may be *faster* when people are faking. The rationale here is that people can immediately recognize the socially desirable response, and if they are trying to present a favorable front rather than answering honestly, they do not have to spend as much time thinking about the items.

Although it seems easier to detect and deal with invalid or unusual response patterns to computerized tests than to paper-and-pencil tests, computerization is not the final solution to invalid responses. The best approach to invalid response patterns may be to use multiple methods of measurement and assessment. Consistency in results across several methods of assessment might be a better indicator of careful and honest responding than any of the existing statistical or empirical indices.

CRITICAL DISCUSSION:
The Barnum Effect and Computerized Test Interpretation

Suppose you complete a personality inventory and receive a computerized report that says:

YOU ARE A WARM PERSON, BUT OCCASIONALLY INTROSPECTIVE. YOU WORK HARD AND SOMETIMES ARE DISAPPOINTED WHEN OTHERS DO NOT PUT IN AS MUCH EFFORT AS YOU. YOU ARE KIND AND GENTLE, BUT FIRM IN YOUR DEALINGS WITH PEOPLE WHO TRY TO TAKE ADVANTAGE OF YOU.

Does this feedback sound accurate? Many individuals will say yes and rate this description as a highly accurate description of their personality, even if the description has nothing to do with their own personalities or their test scores. Psychologists have labelled the tendency to agree with bogus personality feedback that is vague and generally positive as the "Barnum effect." Several researchers have expressed concern about the Barnum effect in computerized test interpretation, that is, the possibility that people will accept virtually any statement on a computerized report as accurate, regardless of its validity or relevance (Guastello, Guastello & Craft, 1989; Guastello & Rieke, 1990; Prince & Guastello, 1990).

While the Barnum effect may be a problem in computerized test interpretation, it can also be a problem in dealing with the test interpretations provided by a psychologist. There is evidence that the Barnum effect is just as potent when a clinician provides vague and global feedback as when a computer provides exactly the same feedback (Dickson & Kelly, 1985; Furnham & Schofield, 1987). Indeed, some of the concerns that have been raised about the validity of computerized test interpretations apply equally to the test interpretations done by licensed professionals (Murphy, 1987a). Therefore, although you should be wary of accepting a computerized test interpretation at face value, the same advice might apply to accepting the interpretations of clinicians who do not use computers.

SUMMARY

As we noted earlier, the question is not *whether* to use computers in psychological testing but, rather, *when* and *how*. The use of computers in psychological testing ranges from the mundane (e.g., using computers to present the same test that is now done on paper) to the highly controversial (e.g., using computers to make diagnoses). In general, computerized tests and computerized adaptive tests seem closely parallel to their paper-and-pencil counterparts. Computerization can affect highly speeded tests, and perhaps some personality inventories, but for ability and achievement tests, the computer is probably the best medium for presenting the test. There are still cases in which the practical advantages of paper-and-pencil testing outweigh the efficiency and security of computerized tests. For example, the full computerization of some large-scale scholastic tests would be very costly. However, it is likely that many testing programs will steadily move from paper-and-pencil formats to computerized adaptive testing.

Computer-based test interpretation is likely to remain controversial. The professional publications that many psychologists read are crammed with ads for test interpretation services, and the claims that some of these ads make are difficult to believe. On the other hand, we are quickly approaching a time in which the interpretation of psychological tests *without* the aid of computers may be a thing of the past (Murphy, 1987a). The challenge ahead of us is to develop optimal strategies for using computerized test interpretation systems.

Finally, computerization opens the possibility that the many technical advances that have dominated the psychometric literature in the past decade, especially developments in item response theory, will make their way into the mainstream of psychological testing in education, industry, and clinical settings.

CHAPTER 12

MEASURING PSYCHOLOGICAL ATTRIBUTES

Throughout this book we have focused on the use of tests for making decisions about individuals. In this chapter we introduce the major types of tests that are used to make these decisions. In particular, we focus on the use of cognitive ability measures, interest measures, and measures of personality in making decisions about individuals and in helping individuals to make their own decisions.

The aim of this chapter is to present a general introduction to these three types of tests. We discuss in general terms the nature of ability, interests, and personality, and we note the implications of differences in these three types of attributes for psychological measurement. We also present the historical foundations of modern ability, interest, and personality measurement, in each case highlighting the impact of practical demands on the development of tests and testing strategies. Finally, we describe general strategies for psychological testing in each of the three domains and outline characteristics one might look for in a good measure of ability, interest, or personality.

PSYCHOLOGICAL ATTRIBUTES AND DECISIONS

Some psychological attributes are more relevant than others to the problem of making decisions about individuals. In part, this depends on the nature of the decision. For example, in choosing a course of psychotherapy for a client, measures of the person's mathematical ability may not be very useful or relevant, although the same measures might by very useful and relevant in general academic admissions and placement decisions. Nevertheless, some types of psychological tests are likely to be more broadly useful in making decisions than others.

There are several ways of classifying the broad domain of psychological testing. One useful dimension is the extent to which the attributes being measured are relatively stable or relatively fluid. Adult intelligence is an example of a stable attribute; attitudes and moods are examples of fluid attributes. In general, stable attributes are more likely to be relevant for making decisions about individuals, particularly if those decisions have a long-term impact (e.g., college admissions).

A second useful dimension for classifying psychological attributes is the type of behaviors through which those attributes are manifest. For example, individual differences in general intelligence are manifest in the performance of cognitively demanding tasks. Individual differences in political beliefs are manifest in how someone votes or in his or her choice of reading matter. Individual differences in interests are manifest in each person's satisfaction with, or reaction to, different choices (e.g., choice of an occupation) or activities. Some behaviors are more relevant to decision makers' goals than others.

Several areas in psychological measurement are *not* broadly relevant to making decisions about individuals, either because of their fluid nature or because of their limited relevance to important criteria. For example, there is a large body of research on attitude measurement that is important but is not highly relevant to decision making. The same can be said for research on measurement of mood, of beliefs, of values, or of narrowly focused abilities or skills (e.g., artistic aptitude). The three domains that *are* most relevant to decision making are the domains of ability, interest, and personality. General mental ability contributes to performance in a variety of domains, particularly scholastic performance and performance of cognitively demanding tasks. Interests have a substantial bearing on a person's satisfaction with, or reactions to, his or her situation. Personality involves consistency in a person's behavior in a wide range of situations. All three domains represent stable attributes, and all three involve behaviors that are broadly relevant to the goals of both decision makers and the individuals who are the focus of those decisions.

INTELLIGENCE—GENERAL MENTAL ABILITY

The Nature of Intelligence

The first question that must be faced in measuring intelligence is whether there *is* any such thing as intelligence. It should not be difficult to convince a layperson that intelligence exists; there are clear differences in the way in which people who are commonly labelled "intelligent" and "retarded" deal with the problems of everyday life. The importance of intelligence and the influence of intelligence on behavior clearly show up when individuals are confronted with novel or complex situations. Everyday observation, however, is not sufficient to determine whether intelligence is a *scientifically* valid and useful construct. The primary scientific basis for asserting that general intelligence exists and that individual differences in intelligence have some impact on behavior is the observation that there is a positive correlation between almost every reliable measure that calls for mental processing, retrieval, or manipulation of information and almost any other measure that involves cognitive activity. In other words, a person who performs very well on one cognitive test, such as a reading comprehension test, is likely to perform well on a number of other cognitive tests including maze tests, analogy tests, and digit-symbol substitution tests (Eysenck, 1979; Guttman & Levy, 1991; Humphreys, 1979; Jensen, 1980). Furthermore, virtually any combination of scores from ordinary paper-and-pencil tests that involve active information processing (in which scores are positively weighted) yields essentially identical estimates of general cognitive ability (Ree & Earles, 1991). The combined evidence clearly indicates that people differ along some general continuum, which is usually labelled intelligence.

It seems reasonable to conclude that people differ in terms of their general levels of intelligence and that these differences have implications for a variety of behaviors. It is more difficult to arrive at a widely acceptable definition of intelligence that is both precise and useful. Historically, psychologists have shown little agreement in their definitions of intelligence. Both Neisser (1979) and Miles (1957) have provided incisive commentaries on the difficulties in defining psychological constructs such as intelligence. We do not claim to offer a definition that resolves all outstanding controversies, but we do offer some principles that should be considered in developing intelligence tests.

First, intelligence is a construct, not a thing (Humphreys, 1979; Eysenck, 1979). Thus, it is impossible to arrive at a definition of the "essence" of intelligence; it can be defined only in terms of the behaviors that indicate various levels of intelligence. It makes much more sense to try to specify what an intelligent person *does* than to try to decide what intelligence *is*. Second, intelligence cannot be defined strictly in terms of one type of behavior but, rather, must be defined in terms of a variety of behaviors that pose cognitive demands. Thus, a test that includes only one type of content, such as a vocabulary test, is not likely to represent an adequate measure of intelligence. Finally, intelligence should, by definition, be related to success in a variety of cognitively demanding endeavors (e.g., school, training programs, work). This correlation need not necessarily be perfect, or even high, but a measure that shows no such correlation is not likely to be a good measure of intelligence.

The concept of general mental ability—a term many prefer to the value-laden term "intelligence"—refers to the existence of systematic individual differences in the performance of tasks that involve the manipulation, retrieval, evaluation, or processing of information. There is some evidence that general mental ability is related to very basic cognitive and physiological processes (Jensen, 1980; Sternberg, 1977, 1984), but it is not yet clear whether mental ability can be meaningfully described in terms of these underlying processes. At present, then, definitions of general mental ability must be presented in terms of behaviors rather than in terms of hypothetical causes of those behaviors. Since general mental ability is defined as a consistent facet of performance in all cognitively demanding tasks, it follows that if two individuals differ in their general mental ability, this difference will be consistent across several different types of information-processing tasks.

Specific mental abilities differ from general ability in that they refer to performance in a specific type of task. For example, people who show equivalent levels of general mental ability might nevertheless differ in their performance on a wide range of tasks involving, for example, the mental rotation of objects, the identification of objects presented from unusual perspectives, and the solution of three-dimensional mazes. The consistent differences in the performance of this type of task might be interpreted as differences in spatial ability.

Several theories have been developed to help identify the different types of mental ability and to clarify the relationships among different abilities. The theories developed by Spearman, Thurstone, and Vernon help to illustrate the concepts of general and specific abilities. Guilford's theory represents a very different way of organizing the domain of mental ability.

Two-factor theory. The starting point for Spearman's theory (1904, 1927), as well as a number of the theories which followed, is the observation that scores on any two cognitively demanding tests almost invariably show a positive correlation (Allinger, 1988; Humphreys, 1979; Jensen, 1980). Spearman accounts for this fact by positing that scores on every cognitive test are influenced by a person's standing on a *general intellectual factor,* or level of *g,* and that correlations among test scores can be explained entirely by the fact that different tests provide partial measures of the same general intellectual factor, *g.* Spearman recognized that scores on each test are also influenced by measurement error (*e*), and that each test also measured some specific factor (*S*) that was unique to each test and independent of one's level of general intelligence. For example, scores on a verbal comprehension test are determined largely by one's level of general intelligence, but they are also affected by one's specific ability to perform verbal comprehension tasks, independent of one's general intelligence.

Spearman's theory has several important implications. First, since specific factors (*S*'s) are unique to individual tests, the theory suggests that important or meaningful individual differences in test performance are due solely to individual differences in general intelligence, *g.* Second, the theory implies that a good intelligence test will be highly *g-loaded*; that is, the influence of a specific factor or of measurement error will be minimized. The third and most important implication is that a good measure of *g* will successfully predict performance of *all* cognitively demanding tasks. The theory clearly suggests that the development of a good measure of *g* will lead to a substantial payoff, since a test with a high *g* loading should predict an extremely wide range of "intelligent" behaviors.

Thurstone and group factors. While admitting the importance of a general intellectual factor, many psychologists object to the notion that the correlations between psychological tests could be *completely* explained in terms of their relationship to *g.* Thurstone (1935; 1938) noted that there are factors common to groups of tests, labelled *group factors,* that are related to *g* but clearly not identical to *g.* For example, tests of reading comprehension, verbal analogies, simple addition, and subtraction involving fractions all will be positively correlated as a consequence of their relationship to *g.* Yet we would expect higher correlations between the two verbal tests and between the two numerical tests than we would between a verbal test and a numerical test. In Thurstone's terms, we would say that the first two tests share a group factor, labelled verbal comprehension, whereas the third and fourth tests share a different group factor, labelled numerical ability. These group factors are somewhat independent of one another, but both are related to *g.*

Thurstone (1938) suggested that intelligence could best be understood in terms of seven group factors, or *primary mental abilities,* defined as

Verbal Comprehension—vocabulary, reading comprehension, verbal analogies, and the like.

Word Fluency—the ability to quickly generate and manipulate a large number of words with specific characteristics, as in anagrams or rhyming tests.

Number—the ability to quickly and accurately carry out mathematical operations.

Space—spatial visualizations as well as ability to mentally transform spatial figures.

Associative Memory—rote memory.

Perceptual Speed—quickness in perceiving visual details, anomolies, similarities, etc.

Reasoning—skill in a variety of inductive, deductive, and arithmetic reasoning tasks.

Since these mental abilities are seen as at least somewhat independent, it might be possible for two people who are identical in their level of *g* to differ dramatically in terms of their strengths and weaknesses in primary mental abilities. Thus, the most practical implication of Thurstone's theory is that intelligence should be measured at the level of primary mental abilities; the measurement of a single general factor would obscure much of the information conveyed by these seven group factors. While Spearman might argue that our attention should be focused on measuring *g*, Thurstone and his followers suggest that intelligence tests should be developed to tap each of a number of factors.[1]

Vernon's hierarchical model.   Vernon (1960; 1965) suggests that in a sense both Spearman and Thurstone are right. Vernon's model suggests a general factor, *g*, that pervades all tests of intelligence and that can be broken down into two broad categories, called *major group factors.* There are two major group factors, verbal-educational and spatial-motor, which can be further divided into minor group factors, such as verbal or spatial factors; in some respects, these minor group factors resemble primary mental abilities. Minor group factors, in turn, summarize patterns of association among individual tests. Vernon's hierarchical model is represented in Figure 12-1.

Hierarchical models of intelligence imply that tests designed to measure *g* and tests designed to measure more specific aspects of intelligence both have their place. The choice of a specific level in the hierarchy should be determined by the purpose of testing rather than by personal preference. For example, a psychologist interested in arriving at a very general classification of children might choose a measure of *g*, whereas another psychologist who is interested in selecting people to mechanical abilities might focus on that minor group factor. According to hierarchical theories, there is no reason to argue about the primacy of *g*, or of group factors. Hierarchical theories allow for many levels of organization, depending on the purpose of measurement.

---

[1]In his later years, Spearman accepted the necessity of group factors; however, he never completely abandoned his original assertion that intelligence tests should be designed to measure *g*.

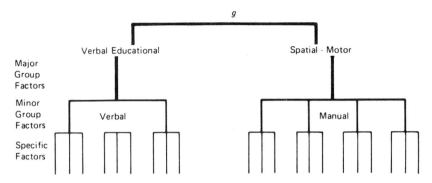

Figure 12-1   Vernon's Hierarchical Model

Guilford's structure of intellect model.   Guilford's (1967; 1988) model represents a strong departure from the theories discussed so far in that Guilford does not accept the existence of a general intellectual factor, either in the basic sense, as proposed by Spearman, or in the sense of a higher-order factor, as proposed by Vernon (1965). Rather, Guilford proposes that intelligence is organized according to three dimensions:

1. Operations—what a person does.
2. Contents—the material on which operations are performed.
3. Products—the form in which information is stored and processed.

There are six types of operations, five types of content, and six types of products. Guilford proposes that each combination of a specific operation, a specific type of content, and a specific type of product defines a unique type of intelligence. In other words, there are 180 different types of intelligence, defined by all possible combinations of six operations, five types of content, and six types of product. Later versions of the theory proposed even more types of intelligence. The structure of intellect model is typically as shown in Figure 12-2.

Although Guilford and Hoepfner (1971) claim to have identified 98 of the 180 factors suggested by the model (see also Guilford, 1988), the theoretical and practical implications of Guilford's model are somewhat in doubt (Allinger, 1988; Bachelor, 1989; Ulosevich, Michael & Bachelor, 1991). To date, Guilford's model has not greatly affected the practice of intelligence testing.

Fluid and crystallized intelligence.   Cattell (1963) has suggested two related but conceptually distinct aspects of general intelligence: *fluid* and *crystallized* intelligence. Fluid intelligence is defined as the ability to see relationships, as in analogies and letter and number series; fluid intelligence primarily deals with reasoning ability. Crystallized intelligence, on the other hand, refers to an individual's acquired knowledge and skills; in a sense, crystallized intelligence refers to the size of one's store of factual knowledge. As one might expect, fluid and crystallized intelligence measures tend to be highly correlated, reflecting the fact that people high in fluid intelligence find it easier to quickly build

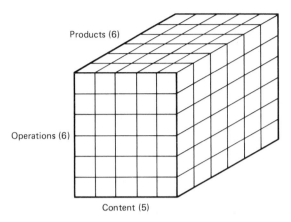

Figure 12-2 Guilford's Structure of Intellect Model

up a large store of factual knowledge (Jensen, 1980). Nevertheless, these two types of intelligence are *conceptually* distinct, and there is evidence that they show different developmental trends (Horn, 1985; Horn & Cattell, 1967).

Cognitive processes in intelligence. Sternberg (1977; 1980; 1981b; 1982; 1985) has proposed a very different structure of the domain of intelligence. His theory notes that mental activities can be broken down into components, and that different sorts of components are used to acquire information, to carry out specific mental tasks, and to plan, monitor, and evaluate general mental processes. The theory suggests that adaptation to one's environment is a critical measure of intelligence (Sternberg, 1984), a proposition that has been suggested previously by many others (e.g., Mercer, 1979).

Early theories of the cognitive processes involved in intelligence tended to focus on elementary information-processing operations, or the ways in which we perceive, encode, store, and retrieve information (Jensen, 1980). More recent theories have worked from a broader base. For example, Sternberg's (1985) triarchic theory of intelligence features three subtheories. His componential theory, which is concerned with *how* intelligent behavior is generated, deals with the basic cognitive processes involved in knowledge acquisition and performance. His contextual theory deals with *what* behaviors are intelligent in what contexts. His experiential theory deals with *when* a given behavior is intelligent. As we will note in this chapter, cognitive theories are having an increasing impact on the design of tests of intelligence (Hunt, 1982; Sternberg, 1984). Broad-based theories, such as Sternberg's (1985), may fundamentally alter the way in which we develop, interpret, and use tests of general intelligence.

Historical Foundations of Intelligence Testing

Today, intelligence testing represents a multimillion-dollar industry. It may therefore come as a surprise that intelligence testing is a relatively modern phenomenon. The term "mental test" did not appear in its modern sense until 1890. The first test that provided a standardized and reasonably valid measure of general intelligence did not appear until 1908. In fact, the term "intelligence" is relatively modern. Prior to 1900, psychologists (the few who then existed) and philosophers generally did not distinguish intelligence from a number of other human characteristics, such as consciousness, human nature, or soul (Matarazzo, 1972). The concept of intelligence as a general cognitive ability therefore received scant coverage in the writings of early psychologists.

The early development of theories of intelligence and of tests designed to measure general intelligence centered mainly in England and France in the early 1900s. In England the pioneering work of Galton provided both the impetus and the tools for the systematic study of individual differences. In France changing attitudes toward the insane and the mentally retarded provided the impetus for developing practical measures of mental ability. These events helped set the stage for the intelligence-testing movement.

Measurement of individual differences.   The contributions of an English biologist, Sir Francis Galton, to scientific psychology are of singular importance. Galton's interest in psychology was secondary to his interest in heredity, and today the theories of intelligence that appeared to pervade his work have been largely repudiated. His contribution is not in terms of *what* he found but, rather, in terms of his development and synthesis of systematic methods of measuring individual differences. Galton and his students, notably Pearson, developed several of the basic procedures used today in the analysis of individual differences.

James McKeen Cattell helped to bring the study of individual differences to the United States. Although a student of Wundt (an experimentalist who had little patience with the study of individual differences), Cattell was influenced by Galton and developed a set of sensorimotor tests that were used to measure the intellectual level of college students. His tests were similar to Galton's and included measures of strength, reaction time, sensitivity to pain, and weight discrimination. In an article describing these procedures, Cattell (1890) was apparently the first to use the term "mental test." Although the tests included in his battery would probably no longer be described as "mental," the nomenclature stuck, and the term "mental test" was soon commonplace.

The 1890s saw a flurry of mental tests of the sensorimotor type. A number of early studies, most notably Wissler (1901), dealt a fatal blow to these mental tests by showing that sensorimotor tests of the type employed by Galton and Cattell were highly unreliable and, worse, showed little or no correlation with other measures of intelligence, such as teachers' estimates of examinees' intellectual level. By this time, however, practical methods of measuring intelligence were being developed successfully in France.

The classification of the mentally retarded.   Prior to the nineteenth century, treatment of the mentally retarded and the insane frequently was callous and occasionally barbaric; mentally disturbed persons were subject to confinement, neglect, and ridicule. Humanitarian movements in the nineteenth century helped to change attitudes toward the mentally disturbed and spurred the development of humane and effective methods of treating mental disorders.

One of the first tasks in effectively caring for these patients was the proper classification of mental disorders and deficiencies. At the simplest level, uniform procedures had to be developed for differentiating the insane, who suffered from emotional disorders, from the mentally retarded, who typically suffered from an intellectual deficit. As early as 1838, Esquirol, a French physician, pointed out that there were many degrees of retardation and suggested that an individual's use of language was critical in distinguishing among different degrees of retardation. Esquirol's work anticipated many later developments in measuring intelligence using tests predominantly verbal in content.

The work of another French physician, Seguin, was especially important in providing an impetus for the development of intelligence tests. Seguin rejected the widely held belief that retardation was incurable and demonstrated that sensorimotor training could be highly beneficial for retarded children, particularly those with less profound levels of retardation. Seguin's success in training retarded children opened a number of alternatives for children who were not intellectually capable of responding to normal schooling; it also demonstrated the practical need for a standardized measure of general intelligence. Seguin's work was instrumental to a decision by the French Ministry of Public Instruction, nearly 50 years later, to commission the development of a method of quickly and accurately measuring general intelligence.

Individually administered tests.   The early mental tests were often nothing more than batteries of psychomotor tests that bore little relation, either theoretically or empirically, to everyday behavior or to success in school. Binet was among the early critics of such tests, insisting intelligence would be measured better by sampling performance in a variety of more complex tasks that involved functions such as memory, comprehension, and judgment (Binet & Henri, 1895). In 1904 the Ministry of Public Instruction appointed Binet to a commission charged with studying procedures for educating the mentally retarded.[2] One of the primary tasks of this commission was to develop practical measures for identifying school children who were intellectually unable to profit from education in the public schools and, within this group, to identify children who would be most likely to benefit from special education. In 1905 Binet, in collaboration with Simon, developed the first scale to provide a practical and reasonably valid measure of general intelligence, the 1905 Binet-Simon scale (Binet & Simon, 1905).

The 1905 Binet-Simon scale contained 30 items, or tests, arranged in order of difficulty. Although there were a few psychomotor tasks included in this test, most items called for the use of language, reasoning, or comprehension. For example, the first item called for the child to follow a moving object with his or her eyes. Item 11 asked the subject to repeat three spoken digits. Item 20 asked the subject to tell how two common objects were alike, whereas item 30 required the subject to define a set of abstract items (Matarazzo, 1972). The 1905 scale had a number of appealing features: Item difficulties were determined empirically; there was a clear ordering of item difficulties; and there was a broad sampling of the domain of activities requiring intelligence. However, the 1905 scale suffered from a number of drawbacks, the most serious being the lack of any precise method of scoring the test or of interpreting total scores.

The first revision of the Binet-Simon scale appeared in 1908. In the 1908 scale, a few unsatisfactory items from the earlier scale were dropped and a number of new items were added, bringing the total number of items on the 1908 Binet-Simon scale to 58. The most important revision, however, had to do with the way in which item difficulty was established and the way in which test scores were interpreted. It is well known that very young children (3 to 4 years old) almost always perform well on tasks similar to those

---

[2]Binet and his associates in the Society for the Psychological Study of the Child were instrumental in initiating this committee. For an excellent, concise history of Binet's work, see Matarazzo (1972).

sampled by the easiest items on the Binet-Simon test, but that they almost always fail the more difficult items. Similarly, somewhat older children (7 to 8 years old) generally pass all the simplest items and perform well on tests of moderate difficulty but almost always fail the most difficult items. In effect, the age at which a typical child first masters a particular task provides an indirect indication of the difficulty of the task. Binet took advantage of this fact to group test items in terms of age levels and to express an overall test score in terms of a *mental level,* defined as the age of a normal child receiving the same test score as the examinee.

Although Binet performed the somewhat neutral term "mental level," the term "mental age" is more common. The method of expressing intelligence test scores in terms of mental age represented a tremendous breakthrough. Whereas previous attempts at measuring intelligence had yielded scores whose interpretations were not immediately obvious (e.g., on the 1905 scale, was a score of 22/30 good, average, or poor?), the score yielded by the 1908 Binet-Simon was concrete and understandable. A score of 7 years meant that the examinee's performance resembled that of a typical 7-year-old. The use of an age scale contributed significantly to the popularity of intelligence tests (Goodenough, 1949; Matarazzo, 1972).

Binet's tests were developed to be used with children. Noting the need for a comparable test for adults, David Wechsler, a psychiatrist at Bellevue Hospital, developed the Wechsler-Bellevue Intelligence Scale. This test was administered on an individual basis to adults and required them to respond to a variety of verbal and performance-oriented items. This test was the forerunner of the highly successful Wechsler Adult Intelligence Scale and of later tests developed by Wechsler for assessing children's intelligence.

The intelligence quotient. Since 1908 the Binet-Simon test has undergone many revisions, some of which are discussed in Chapter 13. One of the most influential, carried out by Terman (1916) at Stanford University, resulted in the Stanford-Binet Intelligence Test, in which the intelligence quotient (IQ) first appeared. The IQ was developed to deal with certain difficulties inherent in the 1908 Binet-Simon. For example, if a child received a mental age of 7, this had different implications, depending upon the age of the child taking the test. A 5-year-old receiving a mental age of seven was performing ahead of the level expected for most 5-year-olds; a 7-year-old with a mental age of 7 was showing completely normal performance; and a 12-year-old with a mental age of 7 showed a potentially serious intellectual deficit. To aid in the interpretation of mental age scores, the intelligence quotient was formed by dividing the mental age by the chronological age, as in Formula 12-1:

$$IQ = (MA/CA) \times 100 \qquad\qquad [12\text{-}1]$$

where

$$
\begin{aligned}
IQ &= \text{intelligence quotient} \\
MA &= \text{mental age} \\
CA &= \text{chronological age}
\end{aligned}
$$

(The ratio of MA/CA is multiplied by 100 in order to remove decimal points.)

When a child is performing at exactly the level reached by other children of the same age, the child's mental age is exactly equal to his or her chronological age, yielding an IQ of 100. Thus, 100 indicates normal, or average performance. When the child's mental age is *lower* than his or her chronological age, the IQ is *less than* 100, indicating substandard performance. When a child's mental age is *higher* than his or her chronological age, the IQ is *greater than* 100, indicating above-average performance.

Although an IQ score based on mental age has many useful features, this type of IQ measure leads to a number of difficulties. First, there is the technical problem induced by the fact that performance does not show equal levels of variability at all ages. Thus, a 4-year-old with an MA of 5 receives the same IQ score (125) as an 8-year-old with an MA of 10, but it is not clear whether they both show the same degree of superior performance relative to their age group. This problem can be partially dealt with in the test development process, but it does not represent the most serious problem in the use of an IQ score based on mental age. The most serious problem occurs when one tries to measure the intelligence of adults.

Mental age does not increase steadily throughout a person's entire life; an average 85-year-old is not likely to solve many problems that are beyond the grasp of an ordinary 84-year-old. While there is evidence that many adults continue to add to their score of factual knowledge throughout their entire lives, it seems clear that the *rate* of development in basic cognitive abilities decreases sharply with age (Eysenck, 1979). In effect, an IQ score based on mental age penalizes the older examinee. While chronological age is progressing at a steady rate, mental age soon levels off. As a consequence, the IQ = MA/CA formulation invariably suggests that as people get older, they steadily become less intelligent. In other words, if you lived long enough, your mental age IQ would invariably reach zero!

Because of the problems mentioned above, mental age is no longer used in computing IQ scores. On modern tests, a *deviation* IQ score is computed. The deviation IQ is obtained by computing standard scores on a specific intelligence test and then converting those scores to a scale with a mean of 100 and a standard deviation of 15. For example, a person whose test score is two standard deviations above the mean (approximately ninety-eighth percentile in a normal distribution) receives a deviation IQ score of 130. Someone whose score is one standard deviation below the mean receives an 85, while a person whose test score is exactly equal to the mean receives an IQ score of 100. This system preserves many of the desirable features of the mental age IQ without some of the flaws. First, a score of 100 indicates average or normal performance. Second, a score above 100 indicates above-average performance, while a score below 100 indicates below-average performance. Third, the size of the difference between the mean score (100) and a person's IQ score indicates, in a very concrete way, the relative standing of the person's score. Intelligence test scores tend to follow a nearly normal distribution; as a consequence, tables of the normal curve can be used to translate deviation IQ scores into percentiles that indicate what percentage of the population would be expected to receive higher or lower test scores.

Standardized group testing.   The standardized, machine-scored intelligence tests that are used widely today are quite different from Binet's tests. The Stanford-Binet and similar tests represent complex social interactions in which examinees are faced with challenging tasks. They must be administered on an individual basis by specially trained psychologists, and they require considerable care and professional judgment in their administration and interpretation. Several psychologists, most notably Otis, began in the early 1900s to develop simpler tests that could be administered under standard conditions to groups of examinees.

The real impetus for the development of group tests, however, came with America's entry into World War I. Prior to the war, the American army had been small and somewhat insular. When our entry into the war led to a sudden influx of high numbers of men, along with an expansion in the complexity of the army and the size of the chain of command, it soon became apparent that the traditional, somewhat haphazard methods of classifying and placing new soldiers—particularly for identifying promising officer candidates—would simply not be sufficient. Hence, some reasonably simple and economical method of classifying recruits was needed. The American Psychological Association had volunteered its services to the war effort, and an APA committee, headed by Yerkes and including psychologists such as Otis and Terman, was assigned the task of developing a practical method of measuring the intellectual level of a large number of soldiers. Their efforts led to the development of two tests, Army Alpha and Army Beta. Army Alpha was a written test that could be administered to large groups of recruits and that provided a rough measure of general intelligence. Army Beta, a nonverbal test designed for illiterates and for recruits who spoke little or no English, could also be administered in groups and used simple pictorial and nonverbal instructions.[3]

Although today there is some debate as to the precise value and validity of Army Alpha and Army Beta (Gould, 1981), the tests were perceived as being useful at the time. They provided at least a rough classification of men, which was of considerable utility in making the large number of selection decisions necessary at that time.

The apparent success of the army's group tests did not go unnoticed in business circles and educational settings. Soon after the war the demand arose for similar tests in civilian settings, and many psychologists were happy to fill the bill. By the mid to late 1920s, intelligence testing was widespread, particularly in the schools. Uncritical enthusiasm for group intelligence testing did not fully abate until the 1960s, and even today standardized group intelligence tests still are used on a routine basis in a number of settings where their validity and utility are questionable. This issue is discussed in later chapters.

Characteristics of a Good Test of General Mental Ability

In describing a general strategy for assessing intelligence, we attempt to synthesize some of the theoretical and practical knowledge contained in our survey of the development of intelligence tests and of theories of intelligence to describe a general strategy for measuring intelligence. The purpose of this section is to provide a set of guidelines for evaluating tests that purport to measure intelligence. Some tests embody all of the essential characteristics expected in a good intelligence test, while others seem to lack them entirely. This is not to say that every test that follows the strategy described here is a good test and that every test that fails to follow this strategy is a bad one. Nevertheless, we think it is

---

[3]Gould's (1981) account suggests that the administration of Army Beta was neither simple nor standardized but was a rather harrowing and confusing experience for many people taking the test. The validity of Army Beta scores is doubtful.

possible to describe the general characteristics of a good measure of intelligence and to use this information in evaluating tests.

The strategy we describe is geared toward measuring general intelligence, although the strategy also might apply when measuring one of Vernon's (1965) major group factors. Measures of specific intellectual abilities follow the same basic rules of test construction as do measures of nonintellectual abilities or measures of specific personality variables.

Broad sampling of tasks.

The first principle for measuring general intelligence is that the test should include a broad sampling of cognitively demanding tasks. Every test is a sample of behavior, and since the domain of intelligence is extremely broad, any test of intelligence should feature a similarly broad sample of the domain. One should be very cautious in using a test that claims to measure intelligence but that contains only one type of item (e.g., a vocabulary test, a verbal analogies test, a digit-symbol substitution test). A test that consists exclusively of reading comprehension items is a reading comprehension test, not necessarily a test of general intelligence. Binet was the first to successfully apply the broad sampling principle; the tasks included in this test ranged from simple sensorimotor tasks to questions involving complex abstract concepts.

Broad sampling of cognitive domain may be achieved by including items that tap many different aspects of the domain. For example, a good test of intelligence might include items that measure many (or all) of Thurstone's primary mental abilities. A broad sampling of items and subtests serves to increase the content validity of a test of general intelligence.

Intelligence tests are not information tests.

There is a longstanding distinction between aptitude tests and achievement tests in psychological testing. Achievement tests are used widely in educational settings. They measure one's mastery of a specific branch of knowledge or of a specific content area. Classroom tests are good examples of achievement tests; professional licensing exams are another. Aptitude tests are more general in nature and designed to measure cumulative knowledge, skills, and abilities that have developed as a result of the subject's life experience. The distinction between aptitude and achievement is now recognized as being one of emphasis rather than as the fundamental distinction, as was once assumed (Anastasi, 1982; Angoff, 1988; Jensen, 1980). Indeed, there are some psychologists who maintain that there is no useful distinction between aptitude tests and achievement tests (Humphreys, 1978). In our opinion, the distinction still is useful in terms of describing types of items that should or should not appear on tests of general intelligence.

It seems clear that intelligence tests should not contain a large number of achievement-type items. In other words, intelligence tests should *not* predominantly measure knowledge of specific facts. Scores on these items typically reflect some combinations of the amount and quality of schooling, together with the level of crystallized intelligence. Although the amount of information at one's disposal is clearly related to the level of general intelligence, knowledge of specific information does not provide a good *measure* of intelligence. Most intelligence tests are designed to measure something broader and more important than the size of one's store of facts. They are designed to measure and predict performance on a wide variety of tasks in which the knowledge of specific facts may be of little importance.

It is impossible to design a test that does not call for any prior knowledge; all intelligence tests call for some knowledge of specific facts. Critics of intelligence testing have seized upon this point to argue that since the specific facts that are important and relevant to one culture may be less important in another, the tests are inherently culturally unfair. In our opinion, this argument carries much more weight for tests in which knowledge of specific facts is likely to materially affect one's test score. In most good intelligence tests, knowledge of specific facts is likely to have little impact on test scores. Intelligence tests that are in reality achievement tests will tend to be much more prone to cultural bias.

Indifference of the indicator. One of the fundamental principles espoused by Spearman (1923) was that of the "indifference of the indicator." Basically, this principle means that on a good test of intelligence, the content of specific items should be irrelevant, since the test is designed to measure the process by which terms are answered. For example, consider a verbal analogies test, in which all of the analogies address relationships among parts of the body, as in

Hand is to arm as foot is to _____?

The principle of indifference of the indicator is upheld if the content of each analogy can be changed without changing the *essential* characteristics of the test. For example:

Uncle is to cousin as father is to _____?

The important of this principle is that the measurement of intelligence is not restricted to a particular type of item or a particular content area. Rather, any item that poses a cognitively challenging task is a potential candidate for inclusion on an intelligence test. On the other hand, items that presuppose detailed knowledge of some specialized domain are not as likely to provide good measures of intelligence, and an intelligence test that is *irrevocably* tied to one specific type of item or one specific domain of knowledge is not likely to be a good measure of intelligence.

Sufficient sample of items. In psychological testing, there is a built-in conflict between practical and theoretical considerations when determining the length of a test. Test theory shows that the longer the test, the more reliable the test; yet long tests are more time consuming and more difficult to administer than short tests. It may not be possible to specify the optimal length of an intelligence test, but several factors argue against extremely short tests. First, of course, is the concern for the reliability of a short intelligence test. A second and more important concern is the breadth of coverage of a very short test. It may be quite difficult to achieve both reliability and content validity with a small item sample.

It is difficult to draw the line between a short test and a long test. This difficulty is exacerbated by the fact that abbreviated versions of several existing intelligence tests are known to be highly reliable and highly correlated with their longer counterparts. Nevertheless, we suggest that a good test should feature at least a dozen or so of each type of test item. Certainly, a five-item test of general intelligence that features one reading comprehension item, two vocabulary questions, an addition problem, and a subtraction problem should be suspect. A good test should include a sufficient sampling of each of many types of tasks. This is particularly important if subscale scores (e.g., verbal, quantitative) are to be computed.

INTERESTS

The Nature of Interests

Strong (1943) defined an interest as "a response of liking" (p. 6). It is a learned affective response to an object or activity; things in which we are interested elicit positive feelings, things in which we have little interest elicit little affect, and things in which we are totally disinterested elicit apathy or even feelings of aversion. For example, some people enjoy (are interested in) opera, other people can take it or leave it, and still others hate it.

Interests are different from abilities. The fact that you like opera does not make you an opera singer. However, interests and abilities tend to show some similar patterns. People often learn to like things they do well and learn to dislike things they do not do well (Strong, 1943). One practical distinction between abilities and interests is in terms of the variables that they tend to predict. Measures of ability tend to predict measures of performance or efficiency. Interests are typically related to persistence and satisfaction rather than to performance. Thus, although the fact that a person is extraordinarily interested in opera does not necessarily indicate that he or she will succeed as an opera singer, it does indicate that the person would be happy as an opera singer (the audience, however, might not be so happy).

Interests can be used to predict choices, especially when there are few external constraints. For example, when a person goes to a bookstore, his or her interests (together with the price of the book) have a substantial impact on the choices of which book to buy. Even in decisions that have substantial consequences, such as choosing a career, interests have a substantial effect. A person who hates to work with figures is not likely to choose a career in accounting, even if very lucrative jobs are available.

Interests differ in terms of their specificity. The typical conception of interests is that they are tied to specific objects or activities, such as interest in baseball, interest in ships, or interest in dentistry. However, very broad domains of interest have been identified; examples include scientific interests, masculine interests, and humanitarian interests. Within the occupational domain, interests in specific occupations (e.g., air traffic controller), in broad occupational fields (e.g., medical jobs), and in general types of fields (e.g., business) have been assessed. To date, measures of specific interests have been more useful than measures of general interests in predicting future choices and future satisfaction (Super, 1973).

A distinction is typically made between interests and values; values are regarded as more general and more resistant to change than interests. Super (1973) has suggested that interests and values are best defined in a sort of means-end relationship. Thus, values are objectives one seeks in order to satisfy a need, while interests are linked to specific activities through which values can be obtained. Examples of the work values proposed by Super are quality of life, material outcomes, self-expression, and behavior control.

Expressed versus inventoried interests. Early research on interest measurements led to the conclusion that people were unaware of, or could not adequately verbalize, their interests. The principal support for this conclusion was the finding that scores on interest inventories did a better job in predicting future satisfaction than did "claimed" interests, which were obtained by simply asking persons to name things in which they were interested. The assumption that people could not identify their interests led to, or at least reinforced, the development of complex, indirect methods of interest measurement.

More recent research has forcefully questioned the assumption that people cannot describe their own interests validly (Dolliver, 1969; Slaney & Russell, 1981; Zytowski & Borgan, 1983). This research suggests that expressed interests show comparable levels of validity in predicting future choices and satisfaction to that achieved by well-constructed interest inventories. It may well be the case that "claimed" interests are valid interests. Nevertheless, interest inventories continue to serve a useful purpose, especially when used for counseling. Inventories help to clarify interests and alert clients to specific aspects of their interests that may be unknown to them. For example, even if a person knows exactly the activities in which he or she is interested, inventories provide valid comparisons that could not be carried out by the person being assessed. No matter how much the client knows about his or her interests, the person is probably not sufficiently well informed to validly compare them to those of accountants, physicians, forest rangers, and so on. Interest inventories provide such comparisons.

Historical Foundations of Interest Measurement

The history of interest measurement is concerned largely with the assessment of vocational interests. Although research in interests broader than those linked to occupations can be traced back to Thorndike (1912), *applications* of interest measures have been linked almost exclusively to vocational counseling.[4] In fact, it is fair to say that measures developed in the years following World War I have provided the foundation for the modern field of vocational guidance and counseling (Zytowski & Borgan, 1983).

The first standardized vocational interest inventories were developed between 1916 and 1923 at the Carnegie Institute of Technology (now Carnegie Mellon University). E. K. Strong, a member of the Carnegie group, moved on to Stanford, where he supervised a student (K. Cowdery) whose thesis dealt with differentiating lawyers, engineers, and physicians in terms of their interests. The success of Cowdery's study encouraged Strong to undertake a broader line of research, attempting to differentiate many or all occupations in terms of patterns of interests (Strong, 1943). The result of this research was the Strong Vocational Interest Blank. This test, now known as the Strong Interest Inventory (SII), represents one of the most widely used, widely researched tests in existence (Zytowski & Borgan, 1983).

At the same time that Strong was developing and perfecting his test, G. F. Kuder

---

[4]There are, for example, over 200 vocational interest inventories currently in use.

developed a similar test. Although both tests use a person's descriptions of his or her own interests to predict occupational adjustment and satisfaction, the approaches followed by these two researchers differed in important ways. Strong used the responses of people in general as a point of reference and determined how the responses of particular groups (e.g., carpenters, dentists, pilots) differed from this reference group. Kuder's approach was a bit more straightforward: He simply determined the extent to which a person's responses were similar to those of each occupational group. Strong's tests assume that responses that are similar to an occupational group *and* different from those of people in general tell the most about occupational interests. Kuder's tests assume that any response could provide information about a person's occupational interests, even if that response is not unique to that one occupation. To date, there is little evidence that one method is qualitatively better or worse than the other.

There are two generic approaches to measuring vocational interests, the actuarial approach and the trait-and-factor approach. The tests developed by Strong and Kuder are good examples of the actuarial approach, which searches for consistencies in interest data without necessarily explaining them. Thus, if we knew that most carpenters liked football, but that most lawyers like baseball, we could (actuarially) state that interest in football is related to carpentry and that interest in baseball is related to the law. The trait-and-factor approach, on the other hand, represents an attempt to explain or outline the substance of vocational interest.

The earliest practitioners of vocational counseling were advocates of the trait-and-factor approach (e.g., Parsons, 1990). This approach gradually lost its popularity, in part because of the very visible success of the actuarial approach. However, in recent years, the trait-and-factor approach has reemerged. The dominant theory of vocational choice is the one developed by Holland (1973), who suggests that vocational interests can be broken down into six basic types: realistic, investigative, artistic, social, enterprising, and conventional. Interests in specific occupations or occupational clusters can be predicted on the basis of these broad factors or themes.

Modern revisions of the SII have successfully combined the actuarial approach with the trait-and-factor approach. The SII has retained the traditional (actuarial) occupational scales but also includes measures of basic interests and of Holland's occupational themes. Thus, it is now possible to give both specific and general feedback in the process of vocational counseling. The addition of general dimensions to the SII greatly increases the usefulness of this measure as a counseling tool.

Characteristics of a Good Interest Measure

As noted above, there are two basic approaches to interest measurement, the trait-and-factor approach and the actuarial approach. Because of the two fundamentally different approaches, two very different sets of criteria can be developed for evaluating interest measures.

Actuarial approach.   Actuarial measures compare a person's interests to those of members of specific groups and attempt to predict satisfaction with various activities or occupations. The first requirement for an actuarial measure is criterion-related validity. Thus, if a vocational interest measure indicates that a person's interests are very similar to the interests of carpenters, the most crucial issue in assessing validity is whether or not the person's interests *are* similar to those of carpenters.

A number of interest inventories have demonstrated their validity statistically. However, empirical demonstrations, particularly if they are somewhat dated, are not always convincing. An interest inventory that successfully assessed vocational interests 30 years ago might be outdated today. However, the best actuarial instruments are subject to constant research and frequent revision. In general, it is necessary to periodically check and revise the normative bases of interest measures; a measure which has not been revised or renormed for a long time should be used with caution.

Actuarial measures vary considerably in the breadth of the questions asked and of the scores provided. In general, interest inventories are most likely to prove useful when the questions span several different domains and when scores are provided that illustrate several different kinds or levels of interests. For example, the SII asks questions about areas such as work-related interests, preferences for activities, and preferences for types of people, and it provides scores for specific occupational interests (e.g., carpenter, psychologist, policeman), general vocational interests, and broad vocational themes. Such a test is much more useful than a test that samples only a limited domain of interests or provides only a limited range of information.

Trait-and-factor approach.

With actuarial tests such as the SII, construct validity is not really a relevant concern. In the actuarial approach, no attempt is made to determine which underlying variables or constructs are measured; using this approach, interest measures are judged solely in terms of their ability to predict. When the trait-and-factor approach is followed, however, construct validity is directly relevant.

The principles for evaluating inventories designed to measure a specific interest or group of interests are similar to those that would be followed in evaluating a measure of a specific cognitive ability or personality dimension. First, the interest must be sufficiently well defined to permit an assessment of the relationship between test items and the construct being measured. Second, the relationship between the interest being measured and the other relevant constructs must be spelled out in sufficient detail to allow a detailed assessment of construct validity.

Holland's (1973) theory of vocational choice can be used to illustrate the application of both of these principles. The theory describes in detail the content of each of six broad vocational themes and, more important, describes in detail the relationships among these themes. This allows one to (a) specify item content that is relevant to each theme and (b) compare the empirical relations among measures of the six themes to the theoretical relationships among the constructs themselves.

The most obvious prerequisite for a good trait-and-factor measure is the existence of a reasonably detailed theory or rationale that outlines the set of factors to be measured, the relations among these factors, and the relationships between these factors and behaviors such as occupational choice. As noted in Chapter 7, the better the surrounding theory, the more likely that convincing evidence regarding construct validity will be developed successfully.

PERSONALITY

The Nature of Personality

Frank (1939) noted that "an initial difficulty in the study of personality is the lack of any clear-cut conception of what is to be studied" (p. 389). More modern reviewers suggest that the situation has not fundamentally changed in the intervening years (Carson, 1989; Pervin, 1985; Rorer & Widigor, 1983). There still is some uncertainty over what personality is, over the usefulness of the term "personality," and over the contribution of personal factors, as opposed to environmental factors, to the understanding of behavior.

A definition of personality must take into account several facts. First, individuals are unique in the sense that no two people are exactly alike in terms of temperament, behavior, or preferences. Second, individuals do not behave in identical ways in all situations. A person behaves differently at a football game than he or she would in church. Third, although individuals are unique and are not completely consistent across situations, there is considerable commonality in human behavior. That is, although there are great differences in detail, many people show similar patterns of behavior. The description of broad personality types may allow us to group individuals meaningfully in a way that accurately describes some important behavior patterns.

In theory, there are two extreme positions that could be put forth to explain behavior, the purely trait-oriented position and the purely situational position. The former concentrates solely on the person and ignores the situation in which behavior occurs, whereas the latter ignores the person and concentrates solely on the situation. Neither position represents a fruitful or even adequate description of personality (Carson, 1989; Pervin, 1985). A more comprehensive definition that considers both the person and the situation has been suggested by Pervin (1980). Personality is defined as the set of characteristics of a person or of people that account for consistent patterns of response to situations.

Consistency in behavior.   During the 1970s and 1980s, the dominant issue in research on personality was the debate over the consistency of behavior across situations (Bem & Funder, 1978; Epstein, 1980; Mischel & Peake, 1982). This controversy can be traced back to the 1930s, and probably has roots as old as those of psychology (Maddi, 1984; Pervin, 1985). The core issue in this debate was whether persons do in fact behave in relatively consistent fashions across a wide range of situations.

If we accept (in its most extreme form) the argument that behavior is not at all stable across situations, it would make no sense to measure personality, interests, ability, or any other individual difference variable (Rorer & Widigor, 1983). The data do not support this extreme interpretation, but neither do they support the opposite extreme, that behavior is *completely* stable across situations.[5] The heart of the person-situation debate is not which factor is completely dominant but, rather, how much emphasis should be placed on consistency versus inconsistency.

---

[5]Pervin (1985) notes that few if any of the participants in this debate argue strictly for the person or for the situation and that nearly everyone accepts some consistency and some situational control.

Maddi (1984) notes the distinction between absolute and relative consistency. A person may be consistent, relative to others, without being absolutely consistent in his or her behavior. For example, if we observe a person attending a friend's wedding, attending a football game, and attending a scientific conference, that person's behavior might change from setting to setting. This apparent inconsistency does not necessarily mean that behavior is unstable. A person who is more outgoing than another at a wedding will also probably be more outgoing at a football game or at a scientific conference. Thus, when compared to the behavior of others in the same situation, the individual might be highly consistent.

Personality psychologists appear to have reached a consensus that individual behaviors are unstable but that broad patterns of behavior show some consistency (Epstein, 1980) and that persons show more relative than absolute stability in their behavior (Maddi, 1983; Pervin, 1985). This suggests that personality measures may provide a useful means of predicting individual differences in general patterns of behavior, but that to accomplish this, both the personality dimension(s) measured and the behavior being predicted must not be too narrow or specific.

Traits.   Although the study of personality is not the same thing as the study of traits (Pervin, 1985), the trait approach has provided much of the language and framework used in describing personality. For example, if a person always tells the truth, returns a wallet full of money he or she has found, and files accurate tax returns, we might label that person as honest.

There are three different ways of thinking of traits: (a) traits are causes of behavior, (b) traits are illusions, in the mind of the beholder, and (c) traits are descriptive summaries. The causal approach uses traits to explain behavior. Thus, if asked why a person returned the wallet full of money, one might answer, "Because he is honest." The difficulty with this approach is its circularity—a person is labelled honest if he or she does honest things; these same honest behaviors are then explained by the fact that the person is honest.

The second approach—that traits exist in the mind of the beholder rather than in external reality—is based on several lines of research in the areas of perception, judgment, and memory (Chapman & Chapman, 1969; Hakel, 1974; Shweder & D'Andrade, 1980). This research suggests that we perceive, store, and retrieve information about others' behavior in terms of coherent wholes and units that are very much like traits; hence, some of the coherence we see in others' behavior is imposed by us rather than being a reflection of external reality.

While the research cited above does suggest that traits are in part a function of how we process information about behavior rather than reflections of behavior itself, it does not necessarily suggest that traits are wholly illusory. A more widely accepted conclusion is that there is some consistency or structure to behavior, and that traits are merely descriptions of related behavior patterns. Thus, when a person is described as honest, this trait name is a summary term describing an array of related behaviors. The term "honest" is equivalent to saying that the person has done many things in the past that indicate a high regard for the truth and that in the future similar behaviors are expected in similar sets of circumstances.

The use of traits as descriptive rather than as causal terms has several appealing features. First, the descriptive approach avoids the circularity inherent in the causal approach. Second, the descriptive approach is potentially dynamic. For example, if someone was very aggressive from grade school to college but became comparatively meek as an adult, the causal approach would find it difficult to explain this in terms of underlying traits. However if traits are regarded as merely descriptive, there is no problem in stating that a person was aggressive in one phase of his or her life and meek in another.

Personality taxonomies. Although many personality psychologists believe that it is useful to measure traits, there has been a long history of disagreement about *what* traits to measure. A quick look through the textbook used in any personality course shows that different theories have emphasized very different sets of traits; as you will see in Chapter 20, various personality inventories also seem to tap quite different aspects of personality. Until the 1980s there was no broad agreement about what traits best summarized the domain of personality.

There is now some consensus that the domain of human personality can be characterized in terms of the five factors listed in Table 12-1; these factors are often referred to as the "big five" (Digman, 1990; McCrae & Costa, 1985, 1986, 1987, 1989). These five factors are highly robust and have been replicated in a number of studies using different methods of measurement (e.g., paper-and-pencil inventories, interviews, peer ratings) and in different linguistic and cultural groups. There are personality inventories specifically designed to measure these five factors (e.g., the NEO Personality Inventory; Costa & McCrae, 1992); but perhaps more important, several of these five factors seem to be present in many, if not most, well-designed personality inventories (Barrick & Mount, 1991). Thus, this taxonomy provides a basis for organizing and comparing studies involving a wide range of personality inventories.

As you might expect, given the long history of disagreement over the basic structure of personality, this taxonomy is not universally accepted. There are still controversies over the meanings, and the names, of several of the factors, particularly the factor Openness to Experience. There are also several studies showing that factors not in this taxonomy are important predictors of a variety of criteria (e.g., performance on the job;

TABLE 12-1   THE FIVE-FACTOR MODEL OF PERSONALITY

Factor	Definition
Extroversion	People high on this dimension are sociable, gregarious, assertive, talkative, and active
Emotional Stability	People *low* on this dimension are anxious, depressed, angry, emotional, embarrassed, and insecure
Agreeableness	People high on this dimension are courteous, flexible, trusting, good-natured, cooperative, and tolerant
Conscientiousness	People high on this dimension are dependable, careful, thorough, responsible, hard-working, and persevering
Openness to Experience	People high on this dimension are imaginative, cultured, curious, original, and artistically sensitive

Hough, Eaton, Dunnette, Kamp & McCloy, 1990; Tett, Jackson & Rothstein, 1991). Nevertheless, this taxonomy appears to provide a good starting point for describing what personality inventories should measure, and it helps to organize the previously fragmented body of research on personality and its correlates.

Historical Foundations of Personality Measurement

Systematic efforts to describe and categorize human character can be traced back to the ancient Greeks (Eysenck & Eysenck, 1969). From antiquity, differences in temperament were ascribed to the excessive influence of one of the four "humors": a sanguine personality reflected strong blood, a melancholic personality reflected the influence of black bile, a phlegmatic personality reflected the influence of phlegm, and a choleric personality reflected an overabundance of yellow bile. This fourfold classification represented both a taxonomy of personality types and a theory regarding the causes of individual differences in personality, and it persisted well into the nineteenth century.

Early psychological investigations of personality were tied closely to the study of psychopathology; many of the major developments in personality assessment can be traced back to such research. For example, Ketschmer's early taxonomy suggested that personalities could be described on a continuum from schizophrenic to manic depressive (Eysenck & Eysenck, 1969). The link between personality testing and the assessment of psychopathology has remained strong throughout the history of personality measurements. Tests designed solely to predict psychopathology are still often described as personality tests.

As psychology gradually emerged as a discipline separate from both philosophy and medicine, theories of personality became increasingly concerned with understanding and describing the structure of everyday behavior. Thus, by the 1930s, research in personality moved beyond its early focus on abnormal behavior and returned to the general problem of describing and classifying personality types. The 1930s and 1940s were a period of "grand theories" of personality, which attempted to explain broad consistencies in behavior in relatively universal terms. More recent research is characterized by a "middle level" approach (Maddi, 1984), in which more narrow aspects of behavior are the focus of research and theory.

Methods of personality assessment. The development of objective measures of personality has many parallels to contemporary developments in intelligence testing. In the latter stages of World War I it was recognized that psychological assessments might be useful in predicting, and possibly alleviating, cases of shell shock, or "war neurosis." Woodworth developed the Personal Data Sheet, a self-report questionnaire, in an effort to screen out individuals highly susceptible to shell shock. Although his test was developed too late to be widely used for wartime purposes, many of the test development methods developed by Woodworth were applied by later researchers. In particular, Woodworth pioneered the procedure of determining an item's validity by contrasting the responses of normal individuals with those of individuals diagnosed as mentally ill.

The most outstanding application of the method suggested by Woodworth is the Minnesota Multiphasic Personality Inventory (MMPI). The MMPI was developed in the late 1930s and early 1940s in an attempt to provide an objective aid for the diagnosis of psychopathology. It still is one of the most widely used measures in both clinical diagnosis and in research on personality.

The decade following World War I witnessed a development of several *projective* measures of personality (Dubois, 1970). Projective methods are ones that give the subject an abstract or unstructured stimulus, such as an inkblot or an incomplete sentence, and require the subject to interpret the stimulus and respond. The assumption of the projective method is that the individual's "private world" is revealed by the way he or she organizes and interprets unstructured or ambiguous situations (Frank, 1939). Probably the earliest projective method was the method of free verbal association popularized by Carl Jung. Here, subjects were given a list of stimulus words (e.g., sister) and asked to give their first response to each one. The most widely known projective technique was developed by Rorschach (1921), who used subjects' responses to inkblots as a diagnostic tool. Other projective methods developed during this decade included the sentence completion technique and the use of children's drawings in the assessment of personality (Dubois, 1970). Later decades would see the continuing development of projective methods, such as the Thematic Apperception Test (TAT).

As noted earlier, the 1930s and 1940s were a time of grand theories of personality that attempted to explain an extraordinarily wide range of behaviors within a single theoretical framework (Zucker, Aranoff & Rabin, 1984). Although these grand theories did not last, they did influence personality psychologists to develop measures that were broader than those concerned exclusively with psychopathology. Examples are provided by the factor-analytic research of Guilford and Guilford (1934; 1939), Cattell (1957), and Eysenck (1960). Early factor-analytic research on personality provided the conceptual basis for several modern multifactor personality inventories that attempt to describe multiple aspects of personality that are relevant to everyday life as well as to understanding psychopathology.

Perhaps the best exemplar of a broad, integrated attempt to describe and assess personality is the work of Murray. First at Harvard's Psychological Clinic, and later working with the United States Army's Office of Strategic Services (OSS) in assessing candidates during World War II, Murray led teams of psychologists in assessing individuals. Murray's work stressed a holistic view and used multiple measures to study individuals' perceptions, cognitions, emotions, and actions and form an integrated assessment. The methods employed by the OSS are described in some detail in Chapter 22.

Characteristics of a Good Personality Measure

As noted earlier, there is no clear-cut conception of what personality is, and as a result it is difficult to determine whether a specific test represents an adequate measure of personality. However, it is possible to specify some general principles for evaluating measures of personality. Two issues are especially relevant: their interpretability and their stability.

Interpretability.   Personality inventories differ substantially in what they attempt to measure. Some attempt to measure a single, narrowly focused dimension; others attempt to measure several dimensions that together span a broad domain of behavior; still others attempt to measure a small set of very general or global dimensions. One of the first principles in evaluating a personality inventory is that the results must convey information about the individual that can be interpreted reliably by various users. In other words, personality tests that are reasonably specific in terms of what they are trying to measure are likely to prove more useful than tests that are vague.

In considering the interpretability of personality measures, the bandwidth-fidelity dilemma referred to in Chapter 6 must be kept in mind. Tests that attempt to provide broad statements about the person may provide information which is relevant for understanding a wide range of behaviors, but they also provide information that is vague and potentially unreliable. For example, Eysenck (1976) suggested that the basic dimensions underlying personality were introversion-extraversion and neuroticism-stability. Because of their generality, measures of either of these dimensions would be quite useful, but it also would be difficult to describe precisely what is meant by the terms "introversion" and "stability." On the other hand, tests that measure one narrowly focused dimension of personality provide precise, interpretable information that is relevant to only a particular subset of behavior.

One of the best compromises between bandwidth and fidelity is found in the multifactor personality inventories that grew out of the work of Guilford, Cattell, and others. These inventories combine breadth and depth by providing scores on multiple well-described dimensions that, taken together, span a fairly broad domain of behaviors. This is not to say that multifactor inventories are the only useful personality tests. Rather, these inventories represent one method of dealing with the inevitable trade-off between the breadth of the domain being measured and the interpretability of test scores.

Stability.   Stability can be defined in two different ways, both of which are relevant for evaluating personality measures. First, there is the stability of scoring rules, which affects inter-judge agreement. In general, objective measures have simple and significantly more stable scoring rules than are possible with projective measures. As noted earlier, the existence of stable rules connecting the behavior of the examinee to the score he or she obtains is essential in order to achieve valid measures of personality, or of any other attribute.

The second meaning of stability—stability across situations—refers to both the test scores and to the attribute being measured. As the person-situation debate suggests, not all personality measures are consistent across situations. In fact, there are reasons to believe that almost any personality measure would yield inconsistent scores across *some* situations (Maddi, 1984). It is critical, then, to assess the degree to which a particular personality measure yields consistent scores *across the range of situations in which it will be used.* The relative stability of two different personality measures can vary, depending on the situations in which they are applied.

All other things being equal, a personality measure that yields consistent scores across the entire range of situations normally encountered would be preferable to another measure that was completely situation-bound. However, few measures are likely to be either completely impervious to situations or completely determined by situations. As a result, careful attention must be given to the range of situations in which a test will be used.

An examination of the dimensions measured might also contribute to the assessment of stability. Some personality dimensions are by definition unstable, in the sense that they can be strongly tempered by a single act or by a small set of behaviors. For example, if a person is happy six days of the week and sad once in a while, we use the trait "happy" as a consistent and generally quite accurate description of that person's behavior. On the other hand, if a person who has been regarded as honest tells one or two lies, one's evaluation of that person's honesty shifts dramatically. Other dimensions might be unstable in a different sense, in that they represent classes of behavior that occur in most but not all situations. For example, a person might be very outgoing at work, but quiet at home. Although this behavior is inconsistent in the absolute sense, it is nevertheless predictable.

It is essential that personality measures exhibit levels of stability that are consistent with their intended uses. Thus, there must be a stable, reliable relationship between the behavior of an individual and the score he or she receives. Second, the behavior being measured must show some consistency over a specific (but possibly implicit) range of situations.

CRITICAL DISCUSSION:
Do Different Test Formats Give Unique
Interpretive Information?

There are two major schools of thought concerning how psychological tests should be developed. One school maintains that a test score should reflect how an examinee has performed in relation to other people who have taken the same test. This testing philosophy has given rise to the *normative* test format, where norm or comparison groups are used. The intent of this testing format is to answer such questions as, "Does Melanie like artistic activities more than other women?" "Is José more outgoing than his peers?" and "Did Melinda respond on the test like other severely depressed adult women?"

Proponents of the other school of test construction have focused their attention more on the individual test taker and the interrelation of his or her various psychological traits. They have been more interested in examining how strong the preferences are for specific attributes within individuals. This testing strategy led to the development of the *ipsative* format that centered on the individual as the focal point for score comparisons. Some of the types of questions that are addressed using this test format are "Is Trudy more interested in science or business?" "Is Ted more likely to be angry or depressed when frustrated?" and "Will Heidi prefer security or advancement when seeking employment?" In each of these cases the point of comparison is within the individual and not between the individual and other people.

The interpretive difference between these two test construction strategies lies in the type of information each provides. Normative tests give an indication of the absolute strength of attributes, since an external reference point (the norm group) is used for comparison purposes. Ipsative tests, on the other hand, give an indication of the relative strength of attributes within the individual, since the central comparison here is how the examinee ranks the strength of his or her attributes.

The standard item format for ipsative tests is to present the examinee with a choice between two or more attributes in each test item. The subject's task is to choose which of the alternatives is preferred. Usually the attributes being measured by the test are paired, requiring the examinee to choose one trait over another in each item. A rank-ordering of all traits results, but it is impossible to determine the absolute strength of each attribute. It can be concluded that trait A is stronger than trait B, since it was chosen more often, but not how strong traits A and B are—both could be very strong, neutral, or very weak. For example, a food preference test might give a choice between spinach and liver. The subject might choose spinach over liver, although he or she may strongly dislike both.

In contrast, normative tests usually permit the examinee to indicate a preference for each item independently. This item format produces test scores that more nearly reflect the absolute level of an attribute within an individual. Following the example above, if the examinee can indicate the degree of preference of spinach and liver, he or she will probably respond with strong disliking for both.

The use of either item format has its advantages and disadvantages. Ipsative tests permit the user to clearly specify which traits are strongest and which are weakest for an individual. Their disadvantage lies in the fact that there is no way to determine how strong or weak the traits are. Another major weakness of ipsative tests is that their scales are not independent of one another, which makes their use in research very limited. Normative tests, on the other hand, give more precise information about the actual level of trait strength but do not always permit the user to know the examinees' preferences among traits of nearly equal strength. An attractive feature of normative tests is that they do allow for independence among scales and therefore are used widely in research.

Which format is the best? This question has never been answered satisfactorily. Each format provides its own unique information about the examinee. It is our opinion that the choice between them should depend on the appraisal question being addressed. If intra-individual information is desired, then ipsative measures would be most desirable. If inter-individual information is desired, then normative measures should be selected.

SUMMARY

Tests, scales, and inventories have been developed to measure a wide range of psychological attributes ranging from attitudes and values to abilities and skills. The domains of cognitive ability, interests, and personality are particularly relevant to the process of making decisions about individuals and helping them make decisions about themselves, and these are reviewed in this chapter.

There are a number of different structural theories of intelligence or mental ability; these theories differ in terms of the importance of general versus specific abilities and in terms of the number of specific types of intelligence proposed. Most ability tests are based on some version of a hierarchical model in which both general cognitive ability and a number of specific types of ability are seen as important.

A survey of the history of intelligence testing shows the strong practical bent of this type of testing. The development of individual and group tests arose in response to the problems encountered in classifying schoolchildren and military recruits. The intelligence quotient was developed to make the interpretation of these tests simpler. Today ability testing is a multimillion-dollar industry in the United States alone, and it is highly important in many other countries.

We suggested several general principles for evaluating intelligence tests. First, they should include a broad sampling of tasks and should not rely too heavily on items that measure factual knowledge. Second, item content is probably less important than the processes used to answer items. Third, the sample of items should be sufficiently large to provide some basis for making inferences to this broad domain.

Interest measurement has largely revolved around the assessment of vocational interests. Interest measures have been developed using both actuarial and trait-and-factor approaches, and they have included both self-report and more indirect strategies of measurement. A variety of types of measures have been shown to be useful, particularly when based on either current, well-constructed samples (i.e., actuarially developed tests) or well-articulated theories of vocational interest (i.e., trait-and-factor tests).

Personality measurement has been hindered by disagreements over the consistency of behavior and over which factors should be included in an adequate description of normal personality. In recent years, both debates have been to some extent resolved; most researchers believe that behavior is sufficiently stable to allow meaningful measurement, and that the five-factor theory provides a reasonable taxonomy of personality. The best measures of personality are likely to provide both consistent and stable measures of some or all of these key traits.

CHAPTER 13

ABILITY TESTING: INDIVIDUAL TESTS

The measurement of ability represents one of the most widespread applications of psychology in everyday life (Wigdor & Garner, 1982). Ability tests range from those that tap the general mental ability we refer to as intelligence, to those that tap specific abilities, such as spatial visualization. Measures of general intelligence have broadest application in that they are used in educational, clinical, and work settings as aids in making a wide variety of decisions. Hence this chapter and the two that follow concentrate most heavily on measures of general intelligence and less on tests of more specific abilities.

Jensen (1969) has noted that "intelligence, like electricity, is easier to measure than to define" (p. 5). Although it may at first seem paradoxical, psychologists have developed a number of reliable and valid measures of general intelligence in the absence of a totally satisfactory definition of the construct that these tests are designed to measure. The *Ninth Mental Measurements Yearbook* (1985) provided descriptions and reviews of 77 separate intelligence tests. Sixty-one of these were designed to measure general intellectual level, while the other 16 measured specific mental abilities. Thirty-two of the general intelligence tests could be administered in groups and could be scored by clerks or by machine; the remaining 29 must be administered individually by a specially trained examiner.[1] A thorough review of all these tests would be counterproductive, since many of them are either highly specialized or poorly constructed, and thus rarely used. We therefore describe outstanding exemplars of the major types of intelligence tests.

---

[1]The more recent *Tenth Mental Measurements Yearbook* (1989) and *Eleventh Mental Measurements Yearbook* (1992) review smaller numbers of intelligence tests.

In this chapter we discuss tests that are administered to a single individual by a trained psychologist. Although this type of test dominated the early history of intelligence testing, today standardized tests that can be administered in groups are much more common. In the chapter that follows, we discuss several widely used group intelligence tests.

THE ROLE OF THE EXAMINER

As discussed in Chapter 1, a psychological test is nothing more than a standardized sample of behavior. It is relatively easy to ensure standardization in objective tests given to large groups of examinees, such as scholastic tests, since they generally feature simple instructions, multiple-choice questions, and machine-scoreable answer sheets. In an individual test of intelligence, however, a good deal of professional training and skill are required to achieve an acceptable degree of standardization. First, whereas most group tests require the subject to work alone on a well-structured task, an individual mental test requires social interaction between the examiner and the subject. This has several implications. At the simplest level both a written test and a psychologist administering an individual test can be thought of as stimuli that prompt responses on the part of the subject. A written test provides a standard set of stimuli to all subjects, while a psychologist presents a somewhat unique stimulus in each case. Even if the examiner's overt behavior can be partially standardized, evidence suggests that characteristics of the examiner, including age, sex, race, physical attractiveness, social skills, and nonverbal communication skills, affect a subject's responses during the test (Tagiuri & Petrillo, 1958). Even more important, an individual test represents a social interaction. The behavior of the examiner may change in response to the subject's behavior. For example, if a child refuses to answer a relatively easy question, the examiner may have to depart from his usual testing format in an attempt to elicit the child's cooperation. From the subject's point of view, the social nature of the individual test affects his or her perception of the task in several important ways. In an individual test, the subject must respond to a *person* rather than to a question. A shy examinee may respond in a hesitant manner, and might be less willing to employ partial knowledge in making informed guesses while being closely observed by a psychologist. Furthermore, the reactions of the examiner to responses to earlier questions could provide subtle cues that affect responses to later questions.

For the reasons cited above, individual mental testing is typically undertaken only by psychologists who have received extensive professional training. The psychologist's first job is to establish and maintain rapport with the person being tested. The examiner must elicit the subject's interest and motivation to perform well on challenging and demanding tasks; he or she must also ease any anxiety the subject might have about performing the tasks in the presence of a psychologist. With young children, tests can be presented as a game, but children tend to become easily bored or frustrated when confronted with problems they cannot solve or tasks they cannot comprehend. Adults are likely to be apprehensive and possibly resentful in testing situations in that an intelligence test represents a possible blow to one's self-esteem. In addition, many adults view a visit to a psychologist in a fairly negative light and may initially be defensive and suspicious.

In order to obtain a valid measure of intelligence, the person taking the test must come to believe that the examiner is trustworthy and nonjudgmental and must view the test as an interesting but nonthreatening task. It takes special skills and training to build and maintain this type of rapport without destroying the standardized nature of the test. A certain amount of training also is necessary to develop a smooth and confident manner in handling the test materials. Many individual tests require subjects to manipulate objects, complete picture series, solve puzzles, or respond to verbal queries, and the psychologist must be careful to observe standard procedures in handling the different sections of the test. An examiner who appears to be nervous, who fumbles in presenting test materials, or who fails to present materials in a standard fashion is not likely to obtain an accurate measure of the subject's intelligence.

The most important objective of the specialized training psychologists undergo before administering intelligence tests is the development of sound professional judgment in scoring responses to test questions. Individual intelligence tests often employ open-ended questions such as, "What would you do if you found someone's wallet in the street?" Although test manuals provide extensive guidelines for evaluating responses to this type of question, the evaluation of responses to open-ended questions is necessarily subjective, and a thorough understanding of the purpose and nature of each section of an intelligence test is required to ensure standardization in scoring.

Judgments about the quality of responses to open-ended questions are doubly critical, since they can affect the testing process as well as the test scores. A number of individual mental tests are constructed so that the choice of questions and the sequencing of subtests are partially dependent on the subjects' responses to previous questions. The successors to Binet's early tests provide a good example: The examiner must score the test as he or she goes along to decide when to stop testing. A mistake in scoring could result in an incomplete or improperly sequenced test.

The final aspect of the psychologist's role in individual mental testing lies in the interpretation and communication of test results. While group tests of mental ability are sometimes given as part of a routine testing procedure (e.g., the Scholastic Aptitude Test), individual tests generally are given with some particular purpose in mind. Individual testing is both expensive and time consuming, and a person is not likely to be referred for individual testing unless his or her behavior seems to indicate an unusually high or low level of intelligence. Parents who bring a child to a psychologist for testing are apt to have certain expectations about the results of the test and are likely to interpret results that are ambiguously presented in light of those expectations. Similarly, an agency that refers a child or an adult for testing does so on the basis of hypotheses about the subject's level of intelligence, and these hypotheses tend to color their interpretations of testing reports. It is the psychologist's responsibility to clearly describe the results of the test, the significance and the limitations of those results, and the courses of action the results suggest.

INDIVIDUAL TESTS OF GENERAL MENTAL ABILITY

The Stanford-Binet

As mentioned in Chapter 1, the major impetus for the development of intelligence tests was the need to classify (potentially) mentally retarded school children. The scales developed for this purpose by Binet and Simon in the early 1900s were the forerunners of one of the most successful and most widely researched measures of general intelligence, the Stanford-Binet Intelligence Scale. The Stanford-Binet is used widely in assessing the intelligence of children and young adults, and it is one of the outstanding examples of the application of the principles of psychological testing to practical testing situations.

The scale developed by Binet and Simon in 1905 consisted of a set of 30 problems, varying from extremely simple sensorimotor tasks to problems involving judgment and reasoning. The basic strategy followed in this test and in its many revisions was to observe the subject's reactions to a variety of somewhat familiar, yet challenging tasks. Terman and Merrill (1937) neatly summarize Binet's procedures, noting that this type of test is "not merely an intelligence test; it is a method of standardized interview which is highly interesting to the subject and calls forth his natural responses to an extraordinary variety of situations" (p. 4).

There have been several major revisions of Binet's original scales; of these, the most recent might also be the most important. The Fourth Edition of the Stanford-Binet, released in 1986, represents a major advance on many fronts. First, for the first time the selection and design of the tests included in the Stanford-Binet is based on a well-articulated theory of intelligence. Second, the Stanford-Binet leans less heavily on verbal tests than has been true in the past—of the 15 sections, 11 involve quantitative reasoning, visualization, or short-term memory. Third, as is described in the section that follows, the test includes specific procedures to quickly and accurately adapt test content and testing procedures to the capabilities of the individual examinee.

Each of the subtests of the Stanford-Binet is made up of open-ended questions or tasks that become progressively more difficult. The examples of items similar to those found in the vocabulary, comprehension, and copying subtests presented in Table 13-1 help convey the basic nature of the test.

Characteristics of the Stanford-Binet. Like many other tests of general mental ability, the Stanford-Binet samples a wide variety of tasks that involve the processing of information and measures an individual's intelligence by comparing his or her performance on these tasks to the performance of an appropriate norm group. Unlike most intelligence tests, the Stanford-Binet has employed a well-developed theory of intelligence to guide the selection and development of subtests. Drawing on the work of Vernon (1965), Cattell (1963), Sternberg (1977, 1981a), and others, the authors of the Stanford-Binet have formulated a three-level hierarchical model of cognitive abilities and have used this model in selecting subtests and in scoring the Stanford-Binet.

The theoretical model used in developing the Stanford-Binet is shown in Figure 13-1. At the highest level is *g*, or general mental ability. This ability can be broken down into crystallized ability, fluid/analytic abilities, and short-term memory. Crystallized ability can be further broken down into verbal and quantitative reasoning abilities. Finally, specific tests can be related to each of the abilities in this hierarchical model.

In earlier versions of the Stanford-Binet, IQ was computed by comparing an individual's mental age to his or her chronological age. In the current revision, the term "mental age" has been dropped, and "IQ" has been replaced by "Standard Age Score" (SAS). The SAS is determined by comparing an individual's performance on each subtest with the performance of others in the same age group. Thus, an 8-year-old who performs better than most other 8-year-olds receives a high SAS, and one who performs worse

TABLE 13-1   ITEMS SIMILAR TO THOSE USED IN STANFORD-BINET

Vocabulary Test
Define the following terms.

Level

A	ball
E	coin
J	debate
P	prevaricate

Comprehension Test
Answer the following questions.

Level

A	Why do houses have doors?
D	Why are there police?
I	Why do people pay taxes?
O	Why do people belong to political parties?

Copying Test
Copy the following figures.

Level

A	○
C	⌐
F	△
I	▱

than most eight-year-olds receives a low SAS. The Standard Age Score has the same meaning as an IQ; as with IQ scores derived from earlier versions of the Stanford-Binet, the mean and standard deviation of the SAS distribution are 100 and 16, respectively. Thus, a SAS of 116 indicates a level of general intelligence that is higher than approximately 85 percent of an individual's peers (i.e., one standard deviation above the mean).

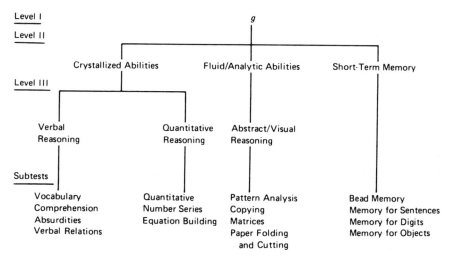

Figure 13-1   Theoretical Model for Stanford-Binet

Although "SAS" has the same general meaning as "IQ," the new term is both more precise and less value-laden, and it may make it easier to communicate both the meaning and the limitations of test scores.

Administration and scoring of the Stanford-Binet.   Throughout its history the Stanford-Binet has been an adaptive test, in which an individual responds to only that part of the test that is appropriate for his or her developmental level. Thus, a young child is not given difficult problems that would lead only to frustration (e.g., asking a 5-year-old why we have a Constitution). Similarly, an older examinee is not bored with questions that are well beneath his or her age level (e.g., asking a 10-year-old to add 4 + 5). Subtests in the Stanford-Binet are made up of pairs of items that are progressively more difficult. A child taking the test may respond only to a few sets of items on each subtest.

Historically, one of the examiner's major tasks has been to estimate each examinee's mental age in order to determine the level at which he or she should be tested. The recent revision of the Stanford-Binet includes an objective method of determining each appropriate level for each examinee, through the use of a *routing test.*

Test 1 of the Stanford-Binet is a 46-item vocabulary test that is used to determine the starting level for each of the remaining 14 subtests. A child taking this test starts with an item that is likely to be easy for his or her age level; a very young child starts with the easiest items, whereas an older child might start in the middle of the test. In each of the 15 tests of the Stanford-Binet, the examiner must first determine the child's *basal level,* that is, the lowest point at which the child correctly answers both items at two consecutive levels. Most children pass their first set of vocabulary items, but if either of the two items is failed at the entry level, the examiner drops back a level and continues working backward until the basal level is reached. This basal level can be regarded as a minimum estimate of the examinee's performance level.

Once the basal level has been determined, the examinee is given successively more difficult items until he or she fails three out of four items at two consecutive levels. The higher of these levels represents a *ceiling level,* or a maximal performance level.[2] This level is then used, together with the examinee's chronological age, to determine the entry level for each of the remaining tests. For example, assume that a 12-year-old examinee reaches his ceiling level at items 35–36; using a chart similar to Figure 13-2, the examiner could then determine that the examinee should start with item set M on each of the remaining tests.

Once the entry level for the remaining tests has been determined, the basal age and the ceiling age must be determined individually for each of the 14 tests. The procedure is essentially identical to that used with the vocabulary test—the basal level is the lowest level at which an examinee consistently passes items, and the ceiling level is the lowest level at which the examinee consistently fails items. Three examples of this process are presented in Table 13-2.

Raw scores on each of the 15 tests are converted to subtest SAS, scaled with a mean of 50 and standard deviation of 8, by comparing raw scores to the norm table for the group closest in age to the person being tested. Because cognitive development is rapid for young children, separate norm tables are developed at intervals of approximately four

---

[2]In the Stanford-Binet vocabulary test, this level is labelled the critical level.

C.A.	3-4	5-6	7-8	9-10	11-12	13-14	15-16	17-18	19-20	21-22	23-24	25-26	27-28	29-30	31-32	33-34	35-36	37-38	39-40	41-42	43-44	45-46
2-0 to 2-5	A	A	A	A	B	B	C	C	D	D												
2-6 to 2-11	A	A	A	B	B	B	C	C	D	D	E	E										
3-0 to 3-5	A	A	B	B	C	C	C	D	D	E	E	F	F									
3-6 to 3-11	A	B	B	C	C	D	D	D	E	E	F	F	G	G								
4-0 to 4-5	B	B	C	C	D	(D)	E	E	E	F	F	G	G	H	H							
4-6 to 4-11	B	B	C	C	D	D	E	E	F	F	G	G	H	H	I							
5-0 to 5-5	B	C	C	D	D	E	E	F	F	F	G	G	H	H	I							
5-6 to 5-11	C	C	D	D	E	E	F	F	G	G	G	H	H	I	I							
6-0 to 6-5	C	C	D	D	E	E	F	F	G	G	H	H	I	I	J							
6-6 to 6-11	C	D	D	E	E	F	F	G	G	H	H	H	I	I	J							
7-0 to 7-5	C	D	D	E	E	F	F	G	G	H	H	H	I	I	J	J						
7-6 to 7-11	C	D	D	E	E	F	F	G	G	H	H	I	I	J	J	K	K					
8-0 to 8-11	C	D	D	E	F	F	G	G	H	H	I	I	J	J	K	K	L	L				
9-0 to 9-11	C	D	D	E	F	G	G	H	H	I	I	J	J	J	K	K	L	L				
10-0 to 10-11	C	D	D	E	F	G	H	H	I	I	J	J	K	K	K	L	L	M	M			
11-0 to 11-11	C	D	D	E	F	G	H	I	I	J	J	K	K	L	L	L	M	M	N	N		
12-0 to 12-11	C	D	D	E	F	G	H	I	I	J	J	K	K	L	L	L	M	M	N	N	O	
13-0 to 13-11	C	D	D	E	F	G	H	I	J	J	K	K	L	L	M	M	M	N	N	O	O	P
14-0 to 14-11	C	D	D	E	F	G	H	I	J	J	K	K	L	L	M	M	N	N	O	O	P	P
15-0 to 15-11	C	D	D	E	F	G	H	I	J	K	K	L	L	M	N	N	N	O	O	P	P	
16-0 to 16-11	C	D	D	E	F	G	H	I	K	K	L	L	M	M	N	N	O	O	O	P	P	Q
17-0 to 17-11	C	D	D	E	F	G	H	I	K	K	L	L	M	M	N	N	O	O	P	P	Q	Q
18-0 and over	C	D	D	E	F	G	H	I	K	L	L	M	M	N	N	O	O	P	P	P	Q	Q

Directions: The entry level is found at the intersection of the examinee's chronological age (C.A.) and the highest pair of items administered on the Vocabulary Test. For example, an examinee whose C.A. is 4-2 and whose highest pair of items administered on the Vocabulary Test is 13-14 would begin the remaining tests at Level D as shown above.

C.A. is recorded in years and months. The C.A. for a child who is 9 years, 5 months, and 16 days old would be 9-6. The C.A. for a child who is 9 years, 5 months, and 15 days old would be 9-5.

Figure 13-2 Determining Basal and Ceiling Levels

Source: From Thorndike, Hagen, and Sattler (1986). Copyright © 1986 by The Riverside Publishing Company, 8420 W. Bryn Mawr Avenue, Chicago, IL 60631. Reprinted by permission.

months for children between the age of 2 and 6. For example, there is a separate norm table for children 27 to 31 months old, for children 31 to 35 months old, and so on.[3] Norms are provided at intervals of six months for children age 6–12 and one year for ages 12–18. For adults, there is a five-year interval for 18–23 and a ten-year interval for ages 23–33. Tables are provided for transforming subtest SAS scores into SAS scores for each of the four areas (verbal, abstract/visual, quantitative reasoning, and short-term mem-

[3]We have rounded the ages somewhat. For example, one table refers to ages 27 months, 16 days, to 31 months, 15 days.

TABLE 13-2 ENTRY-LEVEL CHART, AGES 6–13

Level	Item		Level	Item		Level	Item
F	P/F 11.		F	(P)/F 11.		F	P/F 11.
	P/F 12.	**Basal Level**		(P)/F 12.			P/F 12.
G	P/F 13.		G	(P)/F 13.		G	P/F 13.
	P/F 14.			(P)/F 14.			P/F 14.
Entry Level H	(P)/F 15.		H	(P)/F 15.	**Basal Level** H	(P)/F 15.
Basal Level	(P)/F 16.			P/(F) 16.			(P)/F 16.
I	(P)/F 17.	**Entry Level** I	(P)/F 17.	I	(P)/F 17.
	(P)/F 18.			P/(F) 18.			(P)/F 18.
J	P/(F) 19.		J	(P)/F 19.		J	P/(F) 19.
	P/(F) 20.	**Ceiling Level**		P/(F) 20.			(P)/F 20.
K	(P)/F 21.		K	P/(F) 21.		K	P/(F) 21.
	(P)/F 22.			P/(F) 22.			P/(F) 22.
					Ceiling Level		
Ceiling Level L	P/(F) 23.		L	P/F 23.	**Entry Level** L	(P)/F 23.
	P/(F) 24.			P/F 24.			P/(F) 24.
M	P/(F) 25.		M	P/F 25.	M	P/F 25.
	(P)/F 26.			P/F 26.			P/F 26.

This examinee started at Level H. She passed the first four items at two consecutive levels, which means that the basal level has been established at Levels H-I. The examiner continued testing until the examinee failed three out of four items at two consecutive levels (Levels L-M). This is the examinee's ceiling level. Testing stops at this point.

This examinee started at Level I. He failed Item 18, so the examiner had to go <u>below</u> the entry level to find the basal level. The examinee passed two consecutive levels, Levels F-G, to establish his basal level. The examiner then proceeded to the first level <u>above</u> the entry level and continued testing until the examinee failed three out of four items at two consecutive levels (Levels J-K). This is the examinee's ceiling level. Testing stops at this point.

This examinee started at Level L. A basal level was not established, so the examiner dropped back <u>below</u> the examinee's entry level to Item 22. The examiner gave items in reverse order until the examinee passed four items at two consecutive levels to reach her basal level. The examiner then reviewed the scoring and found that the examinee had failed three out of four items at Levels K-L to reach her ceiling level. Testing stops at this point.

Source: From Thorndike, Hagen, and Sattler (1986). Copyright © 1986 by The Riverside Publishing Company, 8420 W. Bryn Mawr Avenue, Chicago, IL 60631. Reprinted by permission.

ory), and for transforming the area SAS scores into a composite SAS that reflects general mental ability. Both the area SAS scores and the composite (general) SAS are scaled with a mean of 100 and a standard deviation of 16.

    Evaluation of the Stanford-Binet. One of the principal strengths of this test lies in the continuity between the present Stanford-Binet and the original scales developed by Binet and Simon. The tasks used to tap intelligence have not changed fundamentally over the last 75 years. More important, both the fundamental definition of intelligence as an ability which involves reasoning, comprehension, and judgment, and the age-referenced measurement of intelligence have remained constant features of the Stanford-Binet throughout its many revisions. It seems likely that each successive revision has done a better job of measuring the same set of constructs as was measured by preceding versions of the test. This stands in sharp contrast to many other tests, in which a revision seems to change the character of the test entirely. The continuity of the Stanford-Binet has two implications. First, longitudinal research that measures a person's intelligence at different revisions of the Stanford-Binet is both possible and informative. Since each revision measures the same constructs, changes in test scores tend to indicate real developmental changes in intelligence rather than changes in the test itself. Second, the considerable body of research on the reliability, validity, and interpretation of earlier versions of the Stanford-Binet is clearly relevant to the present version of the test.

There is considerable evidence for the reliability of the Stanford-Binet. The correlations between Forms L and M of the 1937 revision (alternate-form reliability coefficients) are greater than .90 for nearly all age levels. The fourth edition of the Stanford-Binet shows even more impressive levels of reliability. Internal consistency reliabilities for the 15 subtests average .88; the composite SAS shows a reliability of .95 or greater at all age levels (Thorndike, Hagen & Sattler, 1986). While there is evidence that the test is somewhat less reliable for very young children (i.e., ages 2½ to 5½) and for children with very high IQs (i.e., above 140), it seems clear that the test very rarely shows low levels of reliability, regardless of the age or IQ of the subjects being measured (McNemar, 1942). Thus, there appears to be a relatively small amount of error variance in Stanford-Binet scores.

There also is considerable evidence for the content, construct, and criterion-related validity of the Stanford-Binet. First, the test is particularly valid as a predictor of academic success. The correlations between the Stanford-Binet and grades, teacher ratings, and achievement test scores typically fall between .40 and .75 (Jensen, 1980). Second, the test is highly correlated with a number of other well-validated ability tests (Carvajal, Gerber, Hewes & Weaver, 1987; Carvajal, Hardy, Smith & Weaver, 1988; Carvajal & Weyand, 1986; Laurent, Swerdlik & Ryburn, 1992; Thorndike et al., 1986). Third, inspection of the test suggests considerable content validity. At all age levels, the test samples a broad array of items related to judgment and reasoning. All these factors provide strong evidence that the Stanford-Binet provides a valid measure of the construct of general intelligence.

Historically, the Stanford-Binet has been regarded as one of the best individual tests of a child's intelligence available. The recent revision of the Stanford-Binet may increase its relevance in adult testing. This test draws upon a long history of development and use and has successfully integrated theoretical work on the nature of intelligence. It is likely that the Stanford-Binet will remain a standard against which many other tests of general mental ability are judged.

The Wechsler Adult Intelligence Scale

In its earlier versions, the Stanford-Binet provided an age-linked scale of intelligence. A series of tests developed by David Wechsler represent examples of an alternate strategy for measuring intelligence, a *point scale* (Edwards, 1972). Rather than developing separate tests that are maximally appropriate for highly specific age ranges, Wechsler designed tests made up of items that are appropriate for a wide range of ages. In Wechsler's tests a subject receives a certain number of points for each item answered correctly. In this respect, Wechsler's tests are similar to the more familiar group tests of intelligence— a subject often takes the entire test, and the IQ is determined primarily by the number of items answered correctly. The first in a series of tests developed by Wechsler was the Wechsler-Bellevue Intelligence Scale (Wechsler, 1939). The primary impetus for the development of this test was the growing awareness that the Stanford-Binet, which was designed primarily for children, did not at that time provide an adequate measure of adult intelligence. Not only was the use of mental age inappropriate in measuring adult intelligence, but as Wechsler pointed out, the content of Stanford-Binet items was typically oriented toward the interests and concerns of school children rather than those of adults. In addition, Wechsler noted that adults often were penalized by the emphasis on speed of response characteristic of many Stanford-Binet items. Older persons often work more slowly than young children, and adults do not always take instructions to work quickly at face value. To overcome these faults, the Wechsler-Bellevue was designed as an adult-oriented point scale of intelligence that placed little emphasis on speed.

The Wechsler-Bellevue was replaced in 1955 by the Wechsler Adult Intelligence Scale (WAIS) (Wechsler, 1955, 1958). The WAIS, which is similar in content but technically superior to the Wechsler-Bellevue, is by far the most widely used individual test of adult intelligence (Matarazzo, 1972). In 1981 the WAIS was revised, and is now referred to as the Wechsler Adult Intelligence Scale–Revised, or WAIS-R. As with the earlier revision, the 1981 revision represents a technical improvement rather than a broad-based change in the WAIS.

Characteristics of the WAIS-R.   The WAIS-R includes 11 separate subtests. Six of the subtests make up the Verbal scale, and the remaining five make up the Performance scale. A person taking the WAIS-R receives a full-scale IQ score, a verbal IQ score, and a performance IQ score, as well as scaled scores on each of the subtests. The 11 subtests which make up the WAIS-R are described briefly below.

VERBAL SCALE

1. *Information.* Contains 29 items covering knowledge of general information that is neither specialized, esoteric, nor academic in nature. The information covered in this test is the type an adult could reasonably be expected to acquire in our culture.

2. *Digit Span.* The examiner reads aloud a list of three to nine digits, which the subject must repeat. This test, which represents one of the most common measures of intelligence, requires the subject to reproduce lists of digits both in the order in which they were presented and in reverse order. The test measures short-term memory.

3. *Vocabulary.* A list of 35 words is presented, both orally and in writing. The subject must define or explain each word.

4. *Arithmetic.* Contains 14 simple problems that can typically be solved without paper and pencil (e.g., how many inches are there in 4½ feet?). This is thought of as a reasoning test rather than a quantitative performance test.

5. *Comprehension.* The subject responds to 16 open-ended questions by explaining why certain things should be done, or by describing what he or she would do in certain situations. This subtest, which is quite similar to a number of the Stanford-Binet tests, reveals the subject's level of understanding or insight.

6. *Similarities.* The subject responds to 14 open-ended questions by telling how two things are alike. This test seems to correspond best to Spearman's suggestion that the ability to see relations is a critical indicator of *g*.

PERFORMANCE SCALE

7. *Picture Completion.* Is comprised of 20 cards containing pictures in which some critical detail is missing. The subject must tell what is missing.

8. *Picture Arrangement.* Ten sets of three to six cards, when arranged in their proper order, tell a story. Each set of cards is presented out of sequence, and the subject must deduce the underlying story in order to put the cards in their correct sequence.

9. *Block Design.* A set of nine cards with geometric designs in red and white correspond to a set of wooden blocks whose sides are painted red, white, or red and white. The subject must arrange from four to ten blocks to duplicate the figure on the card. This test appears to measure nonverbal intelligence.

10. *Object Assembly.* This test consists of four flat cardboard representations of common objects that have been cut up to form a jigsaw puzzle, which the subject must assemble. Since the objects are extremely familiar (e.g., a hand) and the number of pieces is small, this is an extremely easy test that shows low correlation with other subtests, but that may provide clinically useful data relative to the subject's comprehension of simple tasks if the test score is low.

11. *Digit Symbol.* This is basically a code-substitution test, and it represents one of the oldest, best-established psychological tests. A subject is given a code sheet that pairs nine symbols (e.g., [) with digits. The subject is given a long list of digits and, using the code sheet, is required to substitute the appropriate symbol for each digit. This is a strictly timed test; the total number of symbols that are provided within $1\frac{1}{2}$ minutes determines the subject's subtest score.

Examples of several WAIS-R items are shown in Figure 13-3.

Administration and scoring of the WAIS-R.   Like the Stanford-Binet, the WAIS-R must be administered on an individual basis by a specially trained psychologist. Although the administration and scoring of some subtests (e.g., arithmetic) is a relatively simple matter, many of the subtests, especially those comprised of open-ended questions, call for informed professional judgment in scoring responses. As with the Stanford-Binet, a large part of the examiner's job is to establish and maintain rapport with the person taking the test.

The 11 subtests of the WAIS-R are given separately, alternating the verbal and performance subtests. The examinee first completes the information subtest, then the picture completion subtest, then the digit span subtest, then the picture arrangement subtest, and so on. In each subtest, items are arranged in order of difficulty, with the

Picture Completion

Picture Arrangement

Figure 13-3   Sample Items from the WAIS-R

Source: Simulated items from the Wechsler Adult Intelligence Scale–Revised. Copyright ©
1981, 1955 by The Psychological Corporation. Reproduced by permission. All rights reserved.

easier items at the beginning of each subtest and the more difficult items given later. For
most subtests, it is neither necessary nor useful to administer all test items to every
subject. Instead, a fairly easy item is given first, and a subject who answers that item
correctly receives credit for that item *and* for all the easier items of the subtest. If the
subject fails the first item, the examiner adminsters all the easier items in order to
determine what types of problems the subject can or cannot solve. Similarly, if a subject
consecutively fails a number of the moderately difficult items, the examiner concludes

the subtest rather than administering the most difficult items. The rationale for this procedure is that subjects tend to lose interest in testing if they are forced to respond to a number of items that are either insultingly easy or impossibly difficult for them.

The WAIS-R manual includes tables that are used to transform raw scores on each of the subtests to standard scores with a mean of 10 and a standard deviation of 3. These standardized subtest scores provide a uniform frame of reference for comparing scores on the different sections of the WAIS-R. For example, if a person receives a score of 16 on the digit span test and 9 on the block design test, one might reasonably infer that that person is relatively better at the functions measured by the digit span test than at those measured by the block design test. The question of interpreting differences in subtest scores is a complex one, and it is discussed in a later chapter that deals with clinical assessment.

Scores on the verbal scale, the performance scale, and the full scale are obtained by adding the standard scores on the six verbal subtests, the five performance subtests, and all eleven subtests, respectively. The manual provides tables for converting verbal, performance, and full-scale scores into deviation IQs based on a mean of 100 and a standard deviation of 15. The Stanford-Binet IQ is based on a standard deviation of 16; one consequence of this difference is that people with above-average scores tend to receive higher scores on the Stanford-Binet than on the WAIS-R, while those with below-average scores tend to do better on the WAIS-R than on the Stanford-Binet.

Evaluation of the WAIS-R.   Like the Stanford-Binet, the WAIS-R is a carefully developed test with many appealing features. Adequate norms exist for stable and sensible interpretations of most of the scores produced by the WAIS-R. In addition, there is consistent evidence supporting the reliability of the WAIS and the WAIS-R. Full-scale IQs typically show split-half reliabilities in excess of .95, whereas the reliabilities of the verbal IQ and the performance IQ are typically in the .90 and .95 range. Individual subtests typically exhibit lower levels of reliability, but subtest reliabilities lower than .70 are fairly rare.

The content, rationale, and procedures of the WAIS-R are basically the same as those of the WAIS. For this reason, research on the validity of the WAIS provides a good basis for estimating the validity of the WAIS-R. Matarazzo (1972) has summarized research on the criterion-related validity of the WAIS that suggests that WAIS scores are correlated significantly with a number of criteria of academic and life success, including grades and measures of work performance and of occupational level. There are also significant correlations with measures of institutional progress among the retarded.

The criterion-related validities of the WAIS are typically smaller than Stanford-Binet validities. In part, this may reflect the fact that intelligence is a more important source of individual differences in children's performance in school than in adults' performance in college or on the job. This is because motivation and experience tend to be more important determinants of adult performance.

An examination of the WAIS-R itself suggests at least some degree of content validity. The test samples a variety of cognitively demanding tasks, and while some tasks are more clearly related to the construct of general intelligence than others, all of the subtests seem to fit the domain of intelligence. There are two lines of evidence for construct validity, internal and external. The consistently high correlations between

WAIS scores and scores on other tests of general intelligence (Cooper & Fraboni, 1988), such as the Stanford-Binet, provide external evidence of construct validity, and a number of factor-analytic studies provide internal validity evidence. The classification of subtests into verbal and performance categories was done on theoretical rather than empirical grounds (Edwards, 1972). Factor analysis of the WAIS and of similar tests designed by Wechsler to measure children's intelligence at preschool and school-age levels support the performance/verbal distinction (Cohen, 1957a, 1957b, 1959; Geary & Whitworth, 1988; Kaufman, 1975; Wallbrown, Blaha & Wherry, 1973). These factor analyses do not produce identical results, but all the analyses do agree on two fundamentals: (a) the presence of a strong general factor and (b) the presence of at least two major group factors, one of which is predominantly verbal in nature, and the other a perceptual-performance factor. Thus, the calculation of a verbal IQ, a performance IQ, and a full-scale IQ seems empirically justifiable.

Because the WAIS-R is a point scale in which most of the items on all of the subtests are administered to all examinees, the total testing time tends to be longer for the WAIS-R than for the Stanford-Binet. One strategy for decreasing the amount of time needed to administer the WAIS-R is to develop short forms of the test. Silverstein (1968, 1970) has shown that short forms of the WAIS can be developed either by eliminating up to nine of the subtests, or by eliminating a number of items from each subtest. Scores on short forms developed using either of these two strategies show substantial correlations (i.e., in the .80 to .90 range) with full-scale IQs. Thus, although it is usually recommended that the full test be administered, it is possible to obtain quick and reasonably accurate measures of adult IQ using part of the WAIS or the WAIS-R.

The Wechsler Intelligence Scale for Children

The Wechsler-Bellevue and the WAIS represent the most successful application of individual point scales as measures of adult intelligence. In the years following the widespread adoption of his adult intelligence test, Wechsler applied a similar strategy to developing individual point scales for measuring the intelligence of children.

The Wechsler Intelligence Scale for Children (WISC) was developed in 1949 to measure the intelligence of children between 5 and 15 years of age; the scale was basically a downward extension of the Wechsler-Bellevue. Many of the WISC items were taken directly or adapted from Form II of the Wechsler-Bellevue, although all of these items were independently restandardized on a large sample of children. The revised version of the WISC, the WISC-R, was released in 1974. As with the WAIS, this revised version is fundamentally similar but technically superior to the WISC. A new edition of the test (WISC-III) was recently released. Like the previous revision of WISC, WISC-III represents an increasingly sophisticated variation on the same theme as the original WISC. It includes updated items, modernized artwork, better norms, and more extensive validation research, but it is nevertheless highly simliar to the original version of WISC.

Characteristics of WISC-III.   WISC-III consists of 12 subtests, divided into two scales (the Verbal Scale and the Performance Scale), as shown below.

VERBAL SCALE

1. Information
2. Similarities
3. Arithmetic
4. Vocabulary
5. Comprehension
6. Digit Span (an alternate test that may be substituted for one of the verbal tests)

PERFORMANCE SCALE

7. Picture Completion
8. Picture Arrangement
9. Symbol Search
10. Object Assembly
11. Coding
12. Mazes (an alternate test that may be substituted for coding)

The subtests of the WISC-III are basically similar to those of the WAIS-R and contain questions and tasks appropriate for children. The most significant difference in the domain sampled by the two tests is the inclusion of the mazes subtest in the WISC.[4] This subtest asks the child to solve a series of paper-and-pencil mazes within specific time limits.

Administration and scoring of the WISC-III. The administration of the WISC-III is similar to that of the WAIS-R. The child starts with a verbal scale subtest (information), then goes on to a performance scale subtest (picture completion), and continues alternating verbal and performance subtests until the test is completed. The examiner has the option of substituting the mazes subtest for the coding subtest and may also substitute the digit span subtest for any one of the verbal scale subtests if special circumstances (e.g., handicaps) make it impossible to administer that particular test. Although in practice many psychologists tend to administer no more than ten subtests (Edwards, 1972), since only ten tests are needed to compute IQ scores, it is probably best to administer all twelve tests. Although supplementary tests need not be used in computing IQ scores, they may provide clinically useful data, particularly for children whose test scores are very low (Anastasi, 1982).

Like the WAIS-R, raw scores on each of the WISC subtests are transformed into standard scores, with a mean of 10 and a standard deviation of 3. The WISC-III yields verbal, performance, and full-scale deviation IQs based on a mean of 100 and a standard deviation of 15. The WISC-III manual also provides tables for estimating the child's *test age;* procedures for interpretation of these test-age scores are very similar to those for the mental age scores provided by the Stanford-Binet.

---

[4]The coding subtest of the WISC is an easier version of the digit-symbol test of the WAIS-R.

Evaluation of the WISC-R and WISC-III.   Like the WAIS, the WISC-R and the WISC-III are both highly reliable tests. Verbal, performance, and full-scale IQ scores typically show split-half and test-retest reliabilities in excess of .90, and most individual subtests show reliabilities of .70 and higher. There is also evidence for the construct validity of the WISC-R. Factor analyses of the WISC-R support the classification of subtests as measures of verbal and performance IQ (Kaufman, 1975). Logical analysis of the contents of individual subtests also supports this classification (Bannatyne, 1974). Furthermore, the verbal, performance, and full-scale IQs obtained from the WISC-R show substantial correlations (*r* in excess of .70) with scores on the Stanford-Binet. Finally, there is considerable evidence for the criterion-related validity of the WISC-R. Kaufman (1979) notes that the correlations between WISC-R full scale IQs and measures of academic achievement (e.g., grades, teacher ratings) are typically in the .50 to .60 range, and that validities in the neighborhood of .70 are often attained when the WISC-R is used to predict performance in elementary school. A comparison of the processes used to develop WISC-R and WISC-III suggests that WISC-III will show similar levels of criterion-related and construct validity.

Both the WISC-R and WISC-III appear to be excellent individual measures of children's intelligence. Although testing with the WISC-R or WISC-III is often more time consuming than with the Stanford-Binet, it is possible to develop short forms that very accurately predict full-scale scores (Silverstein, 1968, 1970). As with the WAIS-R, the WISC-R and WISC-III are well-standardized, widely used tests that serve as outstanding exemplars of an individually administered point scale of intelligence.

The Wechsler Preschool and Primary Scale of Intelligence

The WPPSI was developed in 1968 to measure the intelligence of children between the ages of 4 and 6½. A revision (WPPSI-R) has made it possible to test children ages 3 to 7. The WPPSI is in part a downward extension of the WISC—except for three new subtests, nearly half of the items on the WPPSI were taken directly from the WISC.

Characteristics of the WPPSI-R.   Like the WISC and the WAIS, the WPPSI is composed of a number of subtests grouped into a verbal scale and a performance scale. The content of the WPPSI-R is generally quite similar to that of the WISC-R, although considerably simpler. Several features of the WPPSI-R were designed to make it easier to test young children; these include more reliance on verbal instructions and responses, as well as the use of very colorful and attractive testing materials.

As with the WAIS and WISC, the revision of the WPPSI did not involve fundamental changes in the test but, rather, technical refinements, especially expanded content, and more extensive standardization. Thus, research on the WPPSI probably provides a conservative estimate of the reliability, validity, and utility of the WPPSI-R.

Administration and scoring of the WPPSI-R.   The administration and scoring of the WPPSI is highly similar to that of the WAIS and the WISC in that a child alternately completes verbal and performance subtests. The sentences subtest may be substituted for any of the verbal tests if circumstances demand, or it may be used as a supplementary test. Raw scores on each subtest are transformed to standard scores (M = 10; SD = 3), and verbal, performance, and full-scale IQs are expressed on a scale with a mean of 100 and a standard deviation of 15.

The WPPSI differs from the WAIS and the WISC primarily in the nature and demands of the examiner's role. Using the WPPSI, the examiner must actively maintain a very young child's interest in a series of challenging and potentially frustrating tasks. Children at this age are more likely to become bored and less likely to be motivated to expend significant effort than are older children who are tested with the WISC.

Evaluation of the WPPSI-R. Like the WAIS-R and the WISC-R, the WPPSI-R is highly reliable. Verbal, performance, and full-scale IQs typically show reliabilities near .90, whereas subtest reliabilities typically approach .80. Both factor analyses and correlations with other intelligence tests provide evidence for the construct validity of the WPPSI (Wallbrown, Blaha & Wherry, 1973). Although there is some evidence for the criterion-related validity of the WPPSI, data regarding the predictive power of the WPPSI are relatively sparse. There are a number of potential explanations for the relative lack of criterion-related validity data; perhaps the simplest is that it is difficult to locate appropriate criterion measures for preschool children.

All three of Wechsler's current tests (the WAIS-R, the WISC-III, and the WPPSI-R) are viewed by many as among the best individual measures of intelligence. It is not entirely clear whether all the subtests of each test are equally necessary, particularly if the intent is to measure a person's general intelligence. However, each subtest has been chosen carefully to provide potentially unique data on a subject's intellectual functioning.

The Kaufman Assessment Battery for Children

The Kaufman Assessment Battery for Children (K-ABC) is a recent addition to the domain of individual tests of mental ability (Kaufman & Kaufman, 1983a, 1983b). Nevertheless, it has already been the focus of extensive research[5] and was used with over 1 million children in its first four years of distribution. This test is noteworthy for several reasons. First, like the fourth edition of the Stanford-Binet, the K-ABC is based on a well-articulated theory of intelligence that is grounded strongly in research in neuropsychology and cognitive psychology. Second, the test is designed to minimize the cultural bias that is thought to exist in many intelligence tests. Third, the test attempts to separate fluid and crystallized intelligence (see Chapter 12) and to provide diagnostic information that helps determine *why* children perform well on some tasks and poorly on others.

Characteristics of the K-ABC. The K-ABC is designed for assessing children ages 2½ to 12½. The test consists mostly of nonverbal items (e.g., pictorial diagrams) that require children to perform a variety of information processing tasks. The battery is divided into a mental processing section designed to measure fluid intelligence and an achievement section designed to measure crystallized intelligence, or acquired knowledge (Kaufman, Kamphaus & Kaufman, 1985). The mental processing scales are divided

---

[5]The fall 1984 issue of *Journal of Special Education* (Vol. 18, No. 3) was devoted to the K-ABC.

into tests of two fundamentally different types of information processing; sequential processing and simultaneous processing. Sequential processing occurs when problems are solved in a step-by-step fashion; examples are the digit span test of the WISC-R and everyday mathematics problems. Simultaneous processing occurs when multiple pieces of information must be organized and integrated to solve a problem; problems such as Ravens' Progressive Matrices and comprehending the meaning of a paragraph are examples. The achievement scales measure vocabulary, reading comprehension, general knowledge, and knowledge of arithmetic.

The claim that the K-ABC is less prone to cultural bias than other intelligence tests rests partly on the content of the test and partly on its organization. As noted earlier, K-ABC items are predominantly nonverbal. In fact, it is possible to administer several sections of the test in such a way that neither verbal instructions nor verbal responses are necessary. These nonverbal tests are particularly useful for assessing language-impaired children. The mental processing scales, which are regarded by the test authors as the best measure of intelligence (Kaufman et al., 1985), minimize dependence on knowledge of facts or school-related skills and attempt to tap basic information-processing abilities.

Administration and scoring of the K-ABC.   The K-ABC incorporates flexible procedures for administration that are designed to guarantee fair and accurate assessments for all children. In particular, the first three items on the mental processing subtests can be used to "teach the task." The examiner is encouraged to use alternate wording, guidance, or even a foreign language to communicate task expectations to an examinee who fails *any* of the first three items (Kaufman & Kaufman, 1983a). This flexibility may be particularly important in testing children from minority cultures, who do not always understand the tasks presented to them by examiners.

Like the Stanford-Binet, the K-ABC is partially adaptive to the developmental level of the child taking the test. For example, 12 subtests are administered to children 7 or older, but only seven subtests would be administered to a 2½-year-old. Some subtests featuring simple recognition tasks are reserved for preschool children (age 2½ to 4), whereas tests that involve reading are administered only after age 5. Total test administration time ranges from 40–45 minutes for younger subjects to 75–85 minutes for older subjects.

In addition to scores on individual subtests, five global-scale scores are reported, each using a scale with a mean of 100 and a standard deviation of 15 (i.e., a deviation IQ scale). First, an achievement score that represents the child's level of crystallized intelligence is reported. Four different scores that relate to the level of fluid intelligence are reported. A nonverbal score is reported for those subtests that do not involve use of language by either the examiner or the subject. Separate scores are reported for sequential processing and simultaneous processing tasks. Finally, a mental processing composite score, which represents a weighted composite of sequential and simultaneous scores, is reported. This mental processing composite is most closely identified with the child's level of fluid intelligence.

Evaluation of the K-ABC.   Extraordinary care has been taken in the development of the K-ABC, both in selection of information processing tasks that reflect our current understanding of several aspects of cognition and intelligence, and in the administration of the test items themselves (Coffman, 1985; Kaufman, et al., 1985). The result has been a test that is technically excellent in many respects. First, test scores show high levels of reliability; internal consistency reliabilities average near .80 for individual subtests, and above .90 for the five global-test scores (Kaufman & Kaufman, 1983b). Second, the mental processing composite is positively correlated with several measures of school achievement and shows an average correlation of .70 with the WISC-R full scale IQ (Kaufman et al., 1985). Finally, factor analyses of the K-ABC suggest that the fundamental organization of the mental processing tests (sequential versus simultaneous) is empirically justified, offering some evidence of construct validity (Kaufman & Kamphaus, 1984). However, other researchers have questioned the extent to which the hypothesized factors are in fact measured by the K-ABC (e.g., Strommer, 1988).

The principal attraction of the K-ABC is its claim to measure separately fluid and crystallized intelligence, and to further separate fluid intelligence into sequential and simultaneous processes. There is some doubt about these claims (Merz, 1984; Page, 1985); it is not clear whether the mental processing composite really measures fluid intelligence or, indeed, whether there is any such thing as fluid intelligence (Guilford, 1980). Nevertheless, the fact that this test is anchored in cognitive and neuropsychological theory is of definite merit. Until recently the psychology of intelligence and the technology of intelligence testing seemed to exist independently. The recent revision of the Stanford-Binet and the emergence of the K-ABC are clear signs of a fundamental and long-awaited change in the nature of intelligence testing. In part, as a result of its strong theoretical base, the K-ABC has proved especially useful in special populations, such as the gifted or the neurologically impaired.

The Individual Intelligence Test as a Clinical Interview

Individual tests of intelligence are expensive and time consuming, and they admit at least some subjectivity into the evaluation of a subject's intelligence. Although tests like the Stanford-Binet, the WAIS, the WISC, and the WPPSI appear to be both reliable and valid, several group tests of intelligence, which are relatively simple to administer and score, show comparable levels of reliability and validity. The continuing popularity of individual tests of intelligence can be explained partly by the conviction held by many psychologists that these tests not only measure intelligence, but provide important data on the way in which individuals deal with a variety of demanding tasks (Rapaport, Gill & Schafer, 1968). It is possible that a skilled clinician can learn a great deal about the person being tested by observing his or her responses to the different tasks that make up each particular test.

There are at least two sorts of behavioral data that might emerge from an individual test of intelligence. First, there is the subject's general reaction or approach to testing. The person may be excited or may be bored; he or she may respond hesitantly or may guess impulsively. The observation of this general orientation to testing may be critical in interpreting test scores. Two people of equal intelligence may receive very different scores if one approaches the test in a relaxed, confident manner while the other is anxious or hesitant in responding to questions.

The second type of behavioral data that can be gathered in individual tests is the data produced by incorrect responses. On a multiple-choice test, errors are not terribly informative, except in their impact on the total test score. The open-ended nature of many individual tests allows for a qualitative analysis of erroneous responses (Rapaport, Gill & Schafer, 1968; Robb, Bernardoni & Johnson, 1972). For example, both "Scott" and "Santa Claus" are incorrect responses to the question, "Who was the first man to fly over the North Pole," but the two answers indicate very different things. The first response probably indicates partial knowledge, since Scott was a polar explorer, whereas the second answer could indicate a flippant attitude or a bizzare view of the world, especially if given by an adult. Errors on performance tests may shed considerable light on problem-solving strategies—a child who completes a large number of digit symbol substitutions but makes many errors is approaching the task differently than another child who completes fewer substitutions but makes no errors.

In addition to observing test behavior, a clinician obtains important information from test scores. Very childlike behaviors from a 10-year-old with an IQ of 76 have different implications than identical behaviors from a 10-year-old with an IQ of 114. The IQ score helps to determine which types of behaviors one would expect in response to cognitively challenging situations. Tests which provide scores for a number of subtests, such as the WAIS, may be especially useful. Both Rapaport, Gill, and Schafer (1968) and Robb, Bernardoni, and Johnson (1972) provide extended discussion of *scatter analyses* of WAIS scores, in which clinical interpretations are assigned to sizable differences in WAIS subtest scores. For example, Rapaport, Gill, and Schafer suggest that the picture completion score being markedly lower than the vocabulary score is a possible indicator of pre-schizophrenia or of a paranoid condition. Over the last 20 years there has been a good deal of research on scatter analysis, much of which suggests complex statistical limitations on the information that could be obtained from comparisons among intelligence subtest scores. Because this literature is more relevant to the clinical interpretation of intelligence tests than to the tests per se, we defer discussion of scatter analysis to Chapter 21.

INDIVIDUAL TESTS OF SPECIFIC ABILITIES

Although individual tests of general intelligence have been both extensively researched and widely used, the techniques of individual testing have been used only sparingly in measuring more specific abilities. In part, this may be a concrete indication of the trade-offs involved in individual assessment. Individual testing is time consuming and expensive. Although the expense may be justified when assessing broad constructs such as intelligence, it is not likely to be justified in assessing specific aptitudes that are relevant in a narrower range of situations.

One area for which individual tests have been developed is in the assessment of aptitudes relevant to Piaget's developmental theories. A particular concern of Piaget's theory is the development of children's ability to comprehend basic features of their world, such as the conservation of matter. Because many Piagetian concepts are relevant in assessing the level of comprehension exhibited by young (e.g., preschool age) children, standardized group tests are not feasible. An example of an individual test of one Piagetian concept is presented below.

Concept Assessment Kit—Conservation

This test is designed to measure young children's (age 4 through 7) comprehension of the concept of conservation. Different forms of the test present the child with pairs of objects which are the same with respect to the amount of matter they contain, their length, or their area. One of these is then changed spatially, and the child is asked whether the amount of matter (area or length) is still the same in the two objects. The child receives one point for each set of objects if he or she answers yes, and another point for correctly explaining, in response to a prompt from the examiner, why they are still the same.

Each of the three forms of the test yields two scores (correct answer and correct explanation) in each of six areas that correspond to the dimensions varied on the form (e.g., length, area, number). Each form can be administered and scored in 20 minutes or less.

Although the test has demonstrated an acceptable level of reliability, reviews of this test have not been positive (De Vries & Kohlberg, 1969; Hall & Mery, 1969; Smock, 1970). First, the test has been criticized on the basis of the limited information provided by a numerical score. Piaget's methods usually have included in-depth observations which take into account the difficulty of the task and the potential subtleties of responses. Attempts to standardize Piagetian tasks and to provide simple scoring guidelines may sacrifice the essential nature of these tasks (De Vries & Kohlberg, 1969). In a related point, the test has been criticized for insufficient sampling of the domain covered by conservation tasks. Although there is some evidence for both content validity and criterion-related validity (Ayers, 1972), the test has not been accepted widely as a valuable measure of Piaget's concept of conservation.

CRITICAL DISCUSSION:
Testing Minorities

The question of whether intelligence tests are equally fair, valid, and useful for white and minority examinees has been the focus of considerable research and debate (McShane & Cook, 1985; Oakland & Parmelee, 1985). Part of the controversy has to do with the administration of individual tests of ability. If minority children are assessed by white examiners, will the resulting test scores validly reflect the children's intelligence? Will the same children receive different (probably higher) scores when tested by someone of their own race? If so, which scores are more credible?

In general, the question of whether white examiners can fairly assess minority subjects has revolved around three issues: language, expectations, and orientation to testing. First, it is assumed that white and minorities may speak different dialects so that a variety of communication problems may result. Second, it is assumed that white examiners have low expectations for the minority individuals they test and that these expectations might directly affect the performance of the individuals being tested. Finally, it is assumed that minority examinees might approach the testing situation very differently when interacting with a white examiner than when interacting with a minority examiner. It may be easier to establish rapport and to maintain a high level of interest and motivation if the examiner is of the same race and social class as the person being tested.

Of the three issues described above, the last—the subject's orientation to the testing situation—is probably the most serious. There is little evidence that language differences between whites and minorities pose a serious problem in individual assessment, nor is there clear evidence as to the effects of examiners' expectations (Oakland & Parmelee, 1985). There are, however, reasons to believe that white and minority examiners may evoke different reactions from minority subjects.

Rather than focusing exclusively on the examiner's race or social class, it might be more profitable to focus on his or her training and professionalism. Well-trained psychologists generally do a good job in establishing rapport, but they should also be able to recognize situations in which they are not establishing rapport, since psychologists have an ethical obligation to discontinue testing if they cannot establish adequate testing conditions. Unfortunately, the testing field is not made up solely of well-trained professionals; many persons who administer psychological tests are woefully unqualified. A great many of the difficulties in fairly and accurately testing minorities could be minimized by ensuring that competent professionals carry out the assessments.

There is no guarantee that any examiner, white or minority, will do a professional job of assessment. There are, however, practical steps that the consumers of test information can take to maximize the likelihood that minorities will be tested fairly. The most obvious is to see that the assessment is carried out by a licensed psychologist. What is the examiner's background and experience? Is the examiner a diplomate of the American Board of Professional Psychology? A second step is to inquire about the assessment methods themselves. Are important decisions based on a single test score or on multiple, independent assessments? What steps are taken to guarantee rapport? The use of qualified examiners employing multiple assessment methods may provide a remedy to many of the problems that currently exist in testing minorities.

SUMMARY

Individually administered tests of general mental ability are important in both historical and practical terms. This type of test made it possible to reliably and validly measure intelligence, and they addressed a number of practical needs, especially in the field of education. All the various versions of the Stanford-Binet are built on Binet's original insights that (a) the type of problem a child of normal intelligence can reliably solve varies with age and (b) highly intelligent children can solve problems that are usually appropriate for older children, whereas less intelligent children's performance seems like that of a younger child. The current version of the Stanford-Binet represents one of the well-validated measures of intelligence available and serves as a benchmark against which many other tests are evaluated.

Binet's original tests were developed expressly for children. David Wechsler developed comparable tests for adults (i.e., the WAIS and WAIS-R). The concepts involved in the WAIS were subsequently applied to testing school-age children (i.e., the WISC-R and WISC-III) and even preschoolers (i.e., the WPPSI-R). All the tests in this series have shown consistent evidence of reliability and validity; because this test provides scores on several separate subtests as well as on the verbal and performance sections, it is widely used by psychologists in diagnosing specific types of learning problems (see Chapter 21).

The Kaufman Assessment Battery for Children (K-ABC) is a psychometrically sophisticated battery that was designed to reflect current thinking in cognition and neuropsychology; it was also designed to minimize cultural bias. While there is clear agreement that this battery provides good measurement of intelligence, it is less clear whether the other goals of the K-ABC have been fully met. Nevertheless, it is a useful assessment instrument.

The most critical question in evaluating the tests described in this chapter may be not about the tests themselves but, rather, about the examiner. All these tests require a highly trained examiner, and scores on all of them can be affected by the behavior, demeanor, and possibly appearance of the examiner. The chapter that follows reviews tests in which the role of the examiner is less central.

CHAPTER 14

ABILITY TESTING: GROUP TESTS

Although most people take one or more tests that measure general intelligence or cognitive ability at some time in their lives, the individual tests described in the previous chapter are not the most common type of ability test. Most of us are tested in school, using one or more of the widely distributed group tests of general cognitive ability or scholastic ability, such as the Scholastic Aptitude Test (SAT). This sort of test typically includes a large number of multiple-choice questions that are answered on a machine-scorable answer sheet and is often given to large groups of people. In principle, however, there is no reason why this sort of test could not be given to a single individual.

Group tests have many important features that set them apart from individual tests of mental ability. Most of these features are a direct result of the fact that these tests are designed so that they can be administered to groups of individuals rather than being administered on a one-to-one basis. First, in individual testing the examiner's role is both complex and central to the proper administration and scoring of the test. In a sense the examiner is an integral part of the individual test. The examiner's role in a group test is more distant and routine. His or her primary responsibilities typically include carrying out routine paperwork, issuing standard instructions, maintaining strict adherence to the time limits of each section of the test, and supervising the distribution and collection of test materials. In group testing, the examiner must be as unobtrusive as possible, limiting his or her activities to proctoring and answering an occasional procedural question. It is this simplification of the examiner's role that makes large-scale intelligence testing possible.

Second, the differing roles of the examiners in individual versus group tests may have a significant effect on the responses of those being tested. In an individual test, the examinee is responding to a *person,* whereas in a group test the examinee is responding to a *question.* The individual examiner may give off cues that either inhibit the response of a shy subject or allow another subject to infer the correct answers to specific questions. A paper-and-pencil test provides a standard, identical stimulus to each person being tested. Even more to the point, a paper-and-pencil test provides a relatively anonymous format for responding to questions in which one is not entirely sure of the answer. In face-to-face testing, a person may be reluctant to guess or may feel that a specific answer will not meet with the examiner's approval. The multiple-choice format employed by most group tests encourages guessing whenever one's partial knowledge can be used to eliminate one or more implausible choices.

Third, the use of a multiple-choice format may alter the cognitive process used in answering questions. An open-ended question poses a relatively unstructured task, in which the respondent must discover the optimal response. A multiple-choice question may involve psychological processes ranging from recognition memory to inductive and deductive reasoning, depending on the content of the question and of the choice of possible answers. In addition to differences in the cognitive processes involved, individual and group tests may differ in the problem-solving strategies needed to respond effectively to each type of test. In a group test, the optimal strategy may be to eliminate incorrect alternatives; this strategy does not apply to most individual tests.

ADVANTAGES AND DISADVANTAGES OF GROUP TESTS

Group testing presents two principal advantages: standardization and efficiency. A group test provides the same stimulus to each person. Test examiners' manuals include extensive, detailed instructions for creating and maintaining standard test conditions, so that the test is essentially identical, both in its content and administration, regardless of where and when it is given. Objective (often computerized) scoring systems guarantee that a specific test will receive the same score, regardless of who scores the test. As discussed in Chapter 1, one of the things that separates a psychological test from other types of behavioral samples is its standardized nature. In many respects, a group test presents a closer approach to the ideal, completely standardized behavior sample than is possible with an individual test.

Group tests are qualitatively more efficient than individual tests. For individual intelligence tests, an examiner might need hundreds of hours to administer and score 100 tests. For group intelligence tests, the number of people being tested has very little impact on the total time and expense involved in administration and scoring. It is clear that without group tests, intelligence testing would never have developed into the large-scale industry that it is today. Whether widespread use of intelligence tests is a good thing or a bad thing is debatable; this issue is examined at the end of this chapter. What is beyond debate is the impact of group tests on the evolution and application of intelligence testing.

Group tests present several disadvantages. First, the impersonal nature of group testing makes it difficult, if not impossible, to collect data on test behavior. An individual test allows one to observe *how* a person responds to specific challenges and also provides a wide range of cues that may be useful in interpreting test scores (e.g., some subjects may be anxious or impulsive in their response). A group test simply provides data on the number of questions answered correctly. Although it is also possible to gather information about a subject's ability by examining incorrect responses (see Chapter 9), this is rarely done. It generally is impossible to determine with any precision *why* a person chose a particular (correct or incorrect) response to any given question on a multiple-choice group test. The inability to collect qualitative data on a person's test performance may limit the value of the information provided by a group test.

The second major disadvantage of group tests is a function of the test format. As noted earlier, multiple-choice questions probably call for different psychological processes than the open-ended questions typically used in individual testing, and many critics suggest that the functions measured by multiple-choice questions have little to do with intelligence. Hoffman (1962) and Ryan (1979) have argued strongly that multiple-choice questions foster rote learning and penalize original, creative thinkers. However, empirical research provides little if any support for the notion that group tests measure knowledge of specific facts and that they fail to measure important intellectual functions that presumably could be measured using other procedures (Jackson, 1984; Jensen, 1980). The more important question of whether comparable psychological processes are involved in responding to different types of problems has not yet been resolved. Some of the evidence that bears upon this question is presented in Chapter 15.

MEASURES OF GENERAL INTELLIGENCE

Several group tests designed to measure general intelligence also provide information about more specific aptitudes, in much the same way as the WAIS-R provided verbal, performance, and full-scale IQs. Some of these tests are short forms designed for only rough classification, but several technically excellent tests exist that give highly accurate measures with minimal effort on the part of the examiner. Two tests, the Multidimensional Aptitude Battery and the Cognitive Abilities Tests, are good examples.

Multidimensional Aptitude Battery

Jackson (1984) noted that although the WAIS and the WAIS-R are extremely well developed and useful tests, several factors restrict their more widespread application. First, they must be administered on an individual basis by a highly trained examiner. Second, there is some subjectivity in the scoring of the tests, in that numerous judgments must be made regarding the appropriateness of specific answers. Third, these tests do not have sufficient "floor" or "ceiling"; that is, they do not differentiate well at either the high or the low ends of the score distribution. Over a period of more than ten years, Jackson and his co-workers developed and refined the Multidimensional Aptitude Battery (MAB), a test that retains many of the best features of the WAIS-R and has substantially overcome all the disadvantages cited by Jackson.

The MAB can best be described as a machine-scoreable counterpart of the WAIS-R. In essence, Jackson and his co-workers translated the WAIS-R into a form that is suitable for group testing. Like the WAIS-R, the MAB is divided into a verbal section and a performance section; the subtests on the MAB duplicate 10 of the 12 WAIS-R subtests. Thus, the verbal section of the MAB is made up of information, comprehension, arithmetic, similarities, and vocabulary subtests. The performance section includes digit symbol, picture completion, spatial visualization, picture arrangement, and object assembly subtests.

Unlike the WAIS-R, which features a free response format, the MAB is made up of multiple-choice questions. Examples of the types of questions employed are shown in Table 14-1. In the development of the MAB, careful attention was given to comparability with the WAIS-R. Evidence regarding the technical adequacy and the construct validity of the MAB, as well as its comparability with the WAIS-R, is reviewed below.

The MAB has shown levels of reliability comparable to the WAIS-R. Subtest reliabilities, estimated by test-retest, split-half, and internal consistency methods, are typically in excess of .70 and often in excess of .80. Reliabilities for the verbal, performance, and full-scale scores are uniformly high, typically in the neighborhood of .95 (Vernon, 1985). Factor analysis has been used in assessing the construct validity of the MAB. In general, factor-analytic studies have provided strong evidence of the usefulness of providing separate scores in the verbal and performance sections and the comparability of the MAB verbal and performance factors to the same factors derived from the WAIS-R (Vernon, 1985).

Jackson (1984) noted the consistently high correlation between the MAB and the WAIS-R. In fact, the correlation between the WAIS-R and the MAB ($r = .91$) is generally higher than the correlation between the WAIS and other well-constructed tests of general intelligence, and even higher than the correlation between the WAIS and the Wechsler-Bellevue (Jackson, 1984). The consistency, both in terms of content and of test scores, between the MAB and the WAIS is sufficiently high to allow for a meaningful

TABLE 14-1   SAMPLE ITEMS FROM THE MULTIDIMENSIONAL APTITUDE BATTERY

Picture Completion—Choose the letter that begins the word describing the missing part of the picture.

A.   L
B.   E
C.   B
D.   W
E.   F

The answer is **Light** so **A** should be marked.

Arithmetic—Solve the following problem.
1. If it costs $8 for two students to go to the theatre, how much will it cost for three students?
A. $10   B. $16   C. $12   D. $4   E. $6

The answer is **C**, $12, therefore one should mark **C**.

Source: Copyright © 1983 by Douglas N. Jackson. Published by Research Psychologists Press, Inc., P.O. Box 984, Port Huron, MI 48060. Reproduced by permission.

comparison between test scores. In fact, MAB scores can be reported in terms of WAIS-R IQ units.

Administration of the MAB.   The MAB consists of two batteries, verbal and performance, each of which includes five separately timed tests. The number of multiple-choice questions on each test ranges from 20 to 50. There is a seven-minute time limit for each of the ten tests. Including instructions and practice items, each battery can be administered in 45–50 minutes.

Test items are arranged in increasing order of difficulty on each of the ten tests. There is no guessing penalty, and individuals are encouraged to attempt as many items as possible. Nevertheless, the short time limit guarantees that scores on most of the tests will reflect speed as well as power factors.

Tests can be easily hand scored, or alternately they can be sent to the publisher for machine scoring. The profile of scores obtained from this test includes T scores for each of the ten subtests, as well as verbal, performance, and full-scale IQs.

Evaluation of the MAB.   There is every indication that the MAB is comparable to the WAIS-R in all major aspects (Reynolds, 1988). It appears that Jackson and his associates have retained the appealing features of the WAIS-R, such as its broad coverage and its usefulness in assessing adult populations, while achieving the practical advantages of a group-administered test. Jackson (1984) cautions that the transition from individual to group testing could affect some examinees' responses and may entail the loss of valuable observational data (see also Silverstein, 1988). Nevertheless, it is clear that the MAB presents an appealing and highly practical alternative to the WAIS and the WAIS-R.

The Cognitive Abilities Tests

The Cognitive Abilities Tests represent two distinct group tests of general mental ability that are widely used in testing school children.[1] The first set is composed of the Primary Batteries, Primary 1 for students in kindergarten and first grade, and Primary 2 for students in grades 2 and 3. All directions for the Primary batteries are given orally; no reading is required to respond to the pictorial items on these tests. The Primary Batteries are made up of four subtests:

1. *Oral Vocabulary,* in which the child must identify pictures of specific objects or animals.
2. *Relational Concepts,* in which the child must correctly identify specific relations (e.g., indicate which of four pictures depicts a ball *under* a chair).
3. *Multimental,* in which the child must pick out the picture that does not belong in a specific set or series.
4. *Quantitative Concepts,* in which the child must indicate which picture exemplifies a specific quantitative concept (e.g., find the box with *two* sets of sticks in it).

[1]The Cognitive Abilities Tests represent revisions of the Lorge-Thorndike Intelligence Tests.

The Primary Batteries yield a single overall score, which is interpreted as a deviation IQ.

The second set of Cognitive Abilities Tests is contained in the Multilevel Edition, which is divided into eight overlapping levels (A through H) and is designed to be administered in grades 3 through 12. The Multilevel Edition includes ten subtests, which provide verbal, quantitative, and nonverbal scores.[2]

VERBAL BATTERY	**QUANTITATIVE BATTERY**	**NONVERBAL BATTERY**
1. Vocabulary	5. Quantitative Relations	8. Figure Analogies
2. Sentence Completion	6. Number Series	9. Figure Classification
3. Verbal Classification	7. Equation Building	10. Figure Synthesis
4. Verbal Analogies		

Each subtest in the Multilevel Edition is made up of multiple-choice items arranged in order of difficulty. Students in the lower grades attempt items that are at or near the beginning of each subtest (easier items), whereas students in the higher grades complete the same number of items but start at a later, more difficult point in the test. For example, a third-grade student would be tested at level A and on the vocabulary subtest would attempt items 1–25. A fifth-grade student would be tested at level C and would attempt items 11–35. All levels of each subtest have a common time limit, allowing one to test students at different levels simultaneously. The total testing time for the Multilevel Edition is 98 minutes.

The Cognitive Abilities Tests are similar in many respects to both the WISC-R and the Stanford-Binet. First, the Multilevel Edition yields verbal, quantitative, and nonverbal scores, which in turn represent weighted sums of subtest scores. Although the term "IQ" is avoided, the Standard Age Scores that are reported for the three batteries look very much like deviation IQ scores. Standard Age Scores are reported on a normalized standard scale with a mean of 100 and a standard deviation of 16. Second, the use of both the Primary and the Multilevel Batteries allows the examiner to adapt the test to the level at which the examinee is most likely to be functioning. Like the Stanford-Binet, the examiner selects items that are neither too easy nor too difficult for the subject being tested. Thus, a child being tested does not respond to all items, but only to those that are appropriately difficult.

Evaluation of the Cognitive Abilities Tests. The Cognitive Abilities Tests have a long history of development and successful application. All three batteries have shown high levels of reliability; alternate form reliabilities of .85 to .95 are typical. In addition, the test manual provides estimates of the standard error of measurement for each test battery as a function of both the score level and the examinee's age. Although it is widely known that the precision of scores on many tests varies as a function of both of these variables, information regarding variation in standard error levels is rarely provided. The availability of this information for the Cognitive Abilities Tests is a definite asset.

The Cognitive Abilities Tests have shown consistently high correlations with other aptitude and achievement tests (Sax, 1984); these correlations provide some evidence of

[2]Tests in the Nonverbal Battery employ neither words nor numbers.

construct validity. Another piece of relevant information can be obtained from factor analyses of the tests. In general, this research does not support the idea that scores on three separate batteries are useful (Hopkins, 1978; Sax, 1984). There is some evidence that the Verbal Battery measures something that is distinct from the Nonverbal and Quantitative Batteries, but it is not clear whether any further meaningful distinctions can be made.

In summation, because the Cognitive Abilities Tests are adaptive to subjects' developmental level, are relatively simple to administer, and show evidence of technical adequacy, they are an appealing alternative to many more complicated or expensive tests of general mental ability.

SCHOLASTIC TESTS

The most widely used group tests of general intellectual level are those used in college and graduate school admissions. Most common are the SAT (Scholastic Aptitude Test) and the Graduate Record Examinations (GRE), which are administered to many thousands of high school and college students each year. These tests have a number of characteristics in common: Both are composed of large numbers of multiple-choice questions, both provide measures of a number of different aspects of general scholastic aptitude (i.e., both provide verbal and quantitative scores), and both are typically administered to very large groups. Although similar in content, the two tests are designed for different purposes and hence are described separately.

Scholastic Aptitude Test

The SAT is one of the most technically outstanding tests of general intellectual level. It is administered on a nationwide basis by the College Entrance Examination Board. Although the test is specifically designed as an aid in making admissions and placement decisions for prospective college students, the test can be validly regarded as a measure of general intelligence, since it primarily measures comprehension and reasoning ability rather than knowledge of specific facts. Several sample SAT items are shown in Table 14-2.

The SAT yields separate verbal and mathematical scores. Since several new forms of the test, which may vary in both length and difficulty, are prepared each year, raw scores are not reported. Rather, standard scores based on a mean of 500 and a standard deviation of 100 are reported. Test score norms are anchored to a standard reference group of college applicants from 1941; thus, an SAT score of 500 is equal to the score that would be expected for the average applicant in 1941 rather than the average score of the particular group taking the test that year. The use of a standard reference group greatly facilitates the comparison of test scores from year to year (Cronbach, 1970). A score of 600 indicates the same degree of relative superiority to the level of performance expected from this standard group, regardless of which form of the test is administered.

In addition to the mathematical and verbal scores of the regular SAT, many applicants receive scores on achievement tests for specific fields such as English or biology. Scores on these separate achievement tests are also expressed on the 500-point standard scale (SD of 100). Although verbal, mathematical, and achievement test scores are

TABLE 14-2   SAMPLE SAT ITEMS

2m

COW:BARN :: (A) Pig:mud (B) chicken:coop
(C) camel:water (D) cat:tree
(E) horse:racetrack

In the figure above, a 5-meter pole and a 3-meter pole are tied together so that the length of the overlapping portion is 2 meters. What is the length *x* of the two poles combined in this way?
(A) 4 m
(B) 5 m
(C) 6 m
(D) 7 m
(E) 8 m

Source: SAT questions selected from *Taking the SAT, College Entrance Examinations Board* (1983). Reprinted by permission of Educational Testing Service, the copyright owner of the test questions. Permission to reprint the above material does not constitute review or endorsement by Educational Testing Service or the College Board of this publication as a whole or of any other questions or testing information it may contain.

reported in comparable units, comparisons among test scores received by a specific individual are not at all simple. For example, a verbal score of 550 and a mathematical score of 510 do not necessarily indicate that the student is higher in verbal than in mathematical ability. Differences between test scores are to some extent influenced by measurement error, so SAT score reports typically include graphic illustrations of confidence intervals and counsel against interpreting apparent differences in test scores when these intervals overlap. At a more fundamental level, the simple comparison of test scores implies that they are absolute rather than relative measures. A verbal score above 500 indicates that the subject's verbal performance is better than the average expected in the 1941 standard sample. A mathematical score of 450 indicates that the subject did not do as well as the average 1941 applicant would be expected to do on this test. Although these sorts of relative scores are very informative for making comparisons between persons, they are less useful for comparisons between an individual's score on one test versus another.

One criticism of tests such as the SAT is that they do not measure important skills, particularly skill in reasoning and expression. In partial response to these criticisms, the Test of Standard Written English (TSWE) was added to the SAT in 1974. TSWE items assess usage and sentence construction through multiple choice questions. For example, an item might provide four different versions of a phrase in a particular sentence and ask which one is correct, or which is clearest or best. Although considerable effort has gone into the development of TWSE, the validity and usefulness of this section of the SAT exam is not well established.

A major revision of the SAT was undertaken in 1990; the new SAT will be introduced in 1994. The revised SAT is divided into two parts; (a) SAT-I: Reasoning Tests, which are designed to assess verbal and mathematical reasoning, and (b) SAT-II: Subject Tests, which are designed to assess skill and knowledge in writing and in 18 specific subject areas (e.g., subject tests from areas such as literature, history, mathematics, and science). The new SAT will include the use of essays (in the writing test) and the use of open-ended questions in the mathematical reasoning section, in which students must solve problems and fill in answers rather than responding solely to multiple-choice questions.

The new SAT will rely more heavily on questions that require reasoning and critical thinking (e.g., long reading passages that call for comparisons or synthesis) and less heavily on simple vocabulary (e.g., items asking for antonyms have been dropped), simple calculation (e.g., the use of calculators will now be permitted), or factual knowledge. This change in the content of questions and in response formats is certainly in keeping with the current educational emphasis on critical thought rather than rote memorization. It is not yet clear whether these changes will affect the validity and usefulness of the new SAT. On the one hand, the new test probably assesses important cognitive skills that were not assessed in the previous SAT. On the other hand, scores on some sections of the new test may be influenced by the subjectivity of graders (i.e., the essay portions of the essay test must be evaluated by readers who cannot be totally objective) or by students' different levels of comfort and skill with using calculators, as well as the possibility that some students may not have calculators. It may be several years before the effects of the changes to the SAT can be assessed adequately.

The American College Testing Program (ACT) represents an alternative to the SAT. ACT scores are reported on a 36-point scale, with a mean of approximately 18 and a standard deviation of approximately 7. The ACT is more closely tied to what is learned in school than is the SAT and has traditionally been considered technically inferior to the SAT (Anastasi, 1982). However, in 1989, the Enhanced ACT Assessment System was introduced. The Enhanced ACT incorporates a number of technical and conceptual improvements over previous ACT tests; examples of improvements include reading tests that more heavily emphasize reasoning skills and tests of science reasoning. Although the ACT is still inferior to the SAT as a measure of general intelligence, the ACT system has many appealing features.

Two features distinguish the Enhanced ACT Assessment system from the SAT. First, the ACT represents an integrated assessment system that includes tests of four basic competencies that are critical for success in college (english usage, mathematics usage, social studies reading, and natural sciences reading), as well as including measures of basic interests. ACT assessments may, therefore, be more useful for counseling students (see Chapter 16) than the aptitude scores that result from the SAT. Second, the ACT is more closely tied to secondary school curricula than the SAT. Proponents of achievement tests as alternatives to ability tests find this feature attractive. However, as we note in a later section, the ability-achievement distinction may not be as useful as it appears.

Graduate Record Examinations

The SAT is designed to assist in undergraduate admissions and placement decisions. The GRE, which are administered by the Educational Testing Service, serve a similar function in graduate admissions and placement decisions and are also used in assigning scholarships, fellowships, and traineeships. Like the SAT, the GRE is given several times each year.[3]

---

[3]As the result of test disclosure ("Truth in Testing") laws, the GRE is offered less frequently in some states than in others.

The GRE include both an aptitude test and advanced achievement tests in several disciplines. Although these tests have traditionally been referred to as the GRE Aptitude and the GRE Advanced tests, the Educational Testing Service recently adopted the titles GRE General Test and GRE Subject Test for two sections of the GRE because these titles are thought to provide clearer descriptions of the purpose and scope of each test. The GRE General Test provides verbal ability, quantitative ability, and analytic ability scores; these three scores are thought to reflect verbal comprehension and quantitative skills, as well as ability in logical reasoning. Verbal items include analogies, sentence completions, and reading comprehension. Quantitative items include questions dealing with simple algebra and geometry, as well as quantitative comparisons and data interpretation. Analytic items include syllogisms, interpretations of logical diagrams, and groups of related statements from which one must abstract specific rules. Examples of verbal, quantitative, and analytic items are presented in Table 14-3.

GRE Subject (Advanced) Tests are given in 20 different fields, including biology, geography, music, psychology, and Spanish. Like the SAT, scores on the GRE are reported on a standard scale, with a mean of 500 and a standard deviation of 100. These scores are anchored to a specific reference group who took the test in 1952. Thus, a verbal score of 500 is equal to the average raw score that would have been expected in the reference group. A score of 500 on the music test is the score expected from a person taking this test who has an average aptitude (general) score of 500. Since some disciplines are more selective than others, direct comparisons of scores on different subject tests may be misleading. A score of 600 in sociology could indicate a higher level of (relative)

TABLE 14-3   SAMPLE GRE ITEMS

The _____ science of seismology has grown just enough so that the first overly bold
theories have been _____.
(A) magnetic . . accepted
(B) fledgling . . refuted
(C) revolutionary . . analyzed
(D) predictive . . protected
(E) exploratory . . recalled

The average of x and y is 20. If z = 5, what is the average of x, y, and z?
(A) 8⅓ (B) 10 (C) 12½ (D) 15 (E) 17½

If Ramón was born in New York State, then he is a citizen of the United States.
The statement above can be deduced logically from which of the following statements?
(A) Everyone born in New York State is a citizen of the United States.
(B) Every citizen of the United States is a resident either of one of the states or of one of the territories.
(C) Some people born in New York State are citizens of the United States.
(D) Ramón was born either in New York or in Florida.
(E) Ramón is a citizen either of the United States or of the Dominican Republic.

Source: GRE test questions selected from GRE Information Bulletin, 1986–87. Published for the Graduate Records Examinations Board by Educational Testing Service. Copyright © 1986 by Educational Testing Service. Reprinted by permission. Permission to reprint the above material does not constitute review or endorsement by Educational Testing Service of this publication as a whole or of any other testing information it may contain.

performance than a score of 620 in physics. Similarly, direct comparisons among the verbal, quantitative, analytic, and subject scores of a single applicant are difficult to interpret. Verbal and quantitative scores of 480 and 550, respectively, do not necessarily indicate that a person performs better, in an absolute sense, on quantitative than on verbal tasks. Rather, GRE scores indicate levels of intellectual ability relative to a fixed reference group.

Starting in 1992, a computerized version of the GRE General Test was offered at test sites in nearly 100 metropolitan areas. Computerization makes it possible to offer the GRE at virtually any time—the initial plans include offering the GRE three days a week, essentially every week of the year, as opposed to the current schedule, in which it is offered five days a year—and to obtain immediate scoring. The initial testing system consists of a presentation of the same test as is available on paper via the computer, but there are plans for the quick adoption of an adaptive form of the test, which should substantially cut the time needed to take the GRE.

Evaluation of the GRE and the SAT.   Although the GRE and the SAT are prepared by different agencies for different purposes, both tests are similar in many fundamentals. First, both represent outstanding examples of careful, professional test development. Test items are extensively screened, edited, and pretested before being included in either test. As a result, both tests are highly reliable (internal consistency reliabilities are consistently above .90), and both are consistently accurate predictors of a variety of measures of academic success. Manuals for both the SAT and the GRE provide detailed information on the interpretation and use of test scores; it is particularly noteworthy that both manuals discuss the limitations of test scores and clearly indicate that these scores should not be the *sole* basis for academic decisions.

The most fundamental similarity between the SAT and the GRE is in terms of the processes presumably involved in answering questions correctly. The great majority of the questions, whether verbal, quantitative, or analytical, require reasoning and comprehension rather than knowledge of specific, and possibly obscure, facts. In some cases, items rely upon verbal comprehension; in others, upon deducing quantitative relationships; and in others, upon symbolic logic. In almost every case, however, the subject is required to *actively* process, manipulate, and evaluate a good deal of information in order to arrive at the correct answer to a specific question.

Although critics suggest that the multiple-choice format limits a test to a simple exercise of rote memory, there is little reason to believe that a student can do well on the SAT or the GRE without superior reasoning and comprehension abilities. On the other hand, there is the possibility that intelligent students who are unfamiliar with the demands of multiple-choice group tests may do poorly on either test. It is possible that revisions to the format of the SAT will diminish the importance of this factor, at least for that test.

Both the SAT and the GRE have been criticized as potentially biased measures; most of this criticism has been directed at the SAT, which is much more widely used. The root of this criticism is the problem noted in Chapter 2, that different groups systematically receive different scores on most tests of general cognitive ability. For example, both gender differences (Holden, 1989) and race differences (Crouse & Trusheim, 1988) in SAT scores have been the focus of controversy, including several lawsuits. Most test researchers agree that the differences in scores are not solely a result of test bias and that the tests are reasonably good measures of ability and scholastic aptitude for males, females, whites, and minorities. The issue of whether or not the tests should be used in contexts where differences in scores exist is taken up later in this chapter.

Ability versus Achievement Tests

Psychologists and educators have traditionally distinguished between ability (or aptitude) tests and achievement tests. It is not clear that the ability-achievement distinction is a useful one. (There is a similar debate over fluid versus crystallized intelligence, as can be seen in Guilford, 1980.) For example, research on achievement tests often demonstrates the influence of broad ability factors on achievement scores (Jones & Applebaum, 1989). Nevertheless, it may be useful to distinguish between these two types of tests, at least with regard to the different goals they serve.

The traditional distinction between ability and achievement tests is that the latter is geared toward specific knowledge or skills that are acquired over a restricted span of time. For example, a person taking a course in auto mechanics may be tested at the end of the semester on the specific knowledge and skills the course was designed to impart. Ability tests, on the other hand, refer to broad and general abilities that are acquired over long spans of time. Verbal ability or spatial ability are examples. If we think about ability versus achievement tests in terms of the goals of the two types of tests, a somewhat different picture emerges. Achievement tests are *retrospective* in their purpose. That is, they are designed to assess changes in knowledge and skills acquired in the relatively recent past. In academic settings, achievements are used primarily to determine what a person has learned or mastered, although they may also be useful for determining whether that person is ready to go on to more advanced levels in a particular discipline. In work settings, achievement tests are used to determine whether or not specific training objectives have been met. Ability tests are *prospective* in their purpose. That is, they give an indication of how well a person is likely to perform now and in the future in a variety of tasks. They are not tied to specific educational or training experiences but, rather, to broader, more general, and more long-lasting developmental experiences. It is important to note that achievement tests can be used to make predictions of the future (e.g., advanced placement tests) and that ability tests can be used to help diagnose previous deficiencies in performance. Nevertheless, the distinction between the two types of tests that is outlined here is, in our opinion, useful in understanding the research literature on ability versus achievement testing.

Jones and Applebaum (1989) review a number of reports by the National Research Council and other groups that examine achievement tests. A common thread running through virtually every report is that standardized tests that employ multiple-choice response formats are not sufficient to tap critical areas of achievement. The most common criticism of this format is that it puts a premium on the recognition of details and puts too little emphasis on critical thinking skills. There is an increasing call for more open-ended and free-response questions like those incorporated in the new SAT, together with proposals to develop computerized tests that incorporate information such as response latency in diagnosing students' problem-solving skills.

We do not believe that changing response formats is the answer to the current deficiencies of achievement tests. Although the multiple-choice format is undoubtedly restrictive, it is clearly possible to measure things other than recognition of trivial details with multiple-choice items. For example, multiple-choice items in the Multidimensional Aptitude Battery or in sections of the Graduate Record Examination clearly call for reasoning and problem solving and cannot be adequately answered through rote memorization of facts. Alternatives to multiple-choice questions will contribute to the expense and difficulty of testing and will almost certainly lead to decreased levels of reliability.

The use of achievement tests to certify student progress and teacher competency is a somewhat mixed blessing. On the one hand, there is the perennial complaint that when these tests are required, the emphasis in instruction will shift in such a way that teachers teach to the test (Jones & Applebaum, 1989). On the other hand, without some systematic assessment of competency and achievement, we may find that neither teachers nor students know the material. The most critical determinant of the contribution of these tests is their validity. If the tests used to certify competency are themselves poor measures of the domain of knowledge or skill being tested, it is hard to see how achievement testing will contribute to the quality of education. Valid tests of achievement, on the other hand, may allow you to accurately assess the progress of individuals as well as the success of various teaching and training strategies.

To date, research on the validity of achievement tests has usually relied on content-oriented validation strategies. That is, the validity of achievement tests has usually been assessed by comparing the test with the educational or training curriculum. The current emphasis on testing understanding and problem-solving abilities suggests that content-oriented strategies will no longer be adequate.[4] As with other tests, the appropriate validation strategy for achievement tests will have to take into account the types of constructs measured by different response modes, as well as the relationships of those constructs to achievement in specific subject areas or domains. Research on the construct validity of tests of educational achievement is still somewhat rare, but it is likely to become more common in the near future.

MULTIPLE APTITUDE BATTERIES

The major advantage of group tests is their efficiency. They allow the collection of a large amount of information, under carefully standardized conditions, in a short period of time. This approach makes it possible to achieve several different goals. First, it is possible to measure a single dimension, such as general intelligence, with a wide variety (and a large number) of questions, thus ensuring some degree of reliability as well as construct validity. Alternately, it might be possible to obtain measures of several distinct abilities, each with a reasonable degree of reliability and within a time frame that is not substantially greater than that often needed to assess general intelligence. This is exactly the strategy followed by several multiple aptitude test batteries. Rather than measuring several aspects of a more general ability, these batteries attempt to measure several distinct abilities in their own right. Whereas the measurement of several distinct abilities

---

[4]Many researchers would argue that a purely content-oriented strategy never was adequate, and that construct validation has always been required for tests of this type.

could be both cumbersome and unreliable if individual testing methods were employed, the measurement of several distinct abilities in a single test battery is, in principle, no more difficult than the measurement of a single ability.

The Armed Services Vocational Aptitude Battery

The Armed Services Vocational Aptitude Battery (ASVAB), which is probably the most widely used paper-and-pencil test in existence, illustrates both the strengths and weaknesses of multiple aptitude test batteries. This test, which is administered annually to over 1.5 million individuals, is used by the armed services to screen potential recruits and to assign recruits to different jobs, training programs, and career areas. The use of a multiple aptitude battery rather than a single test of general intelligence provides the best chance for successfully meeting the complex set of demands placed on the ASVAB.

The ASVAB consists of a battery of ten separate subtests, which are listed in Table 14-4. These subtests range from 15 to 84 items and feature a mix of speed and power tests administered with time limits ranging from 3 to 36 minutes. The entire test can be administered in three hours.

TABLE 14-4 SUBTESTS OF THE ARMED SERVICES VOCATIONAL APTITUDE BATTERY

---

1. General Science—25 items measuring general knowledge of the physical and biological sciences.
2. Arithmetic Reasoning—30 items which involve simple calculation, but which call for the ability to determine the appropriate analysis.
3. Word Knowledge—35 vocabulary items.
4. Paragraph Comprehension—15 items assessing subjects' understanding of several short paragraphs.
5. Numeric Operations—speed test made up of 50 problems involving simple calculation.
6. Coding Speed—speed test made up of 84 items asking the subject to substitute numeric codes for verbal material.
7. Auto and Shop Information—25 items measuring knowledge of automobiles, tools, shop terminology, and shop practices.
8. Mathematics Knowledge—25 items measuring knowledge of high school–level mathematics.
9. Mechanical Comprehension—25 items measuring understanding of basic mechanical principles.
10. Electronics Information—25 items measuring knowledge of electric principles and electronic terminology.

Scores on the individual subtests are combined to produce seven separate composite scores:

ACADEMIC COMPOSITES

1. Academic Ability: Word Knowledge, Paragraph Comprehension, and Arithmetic Reasoning
2. Verbal: Word Knowledge, Paragraph Comprehension, and General Science
3. Math: Mathematics Knowledge and Arithmetic Reasoning

OCCUPATIONAL COMPOSITES

4. Mechanical & Crafts: Arithmetic Reasoning, Mechanical Comprehension, Auto & Shop Information, and Electronics Information

5. Business & Clerical: Word Knowledge, Paragraph Comprehension, Mathematics Knowledge, and Coding Speed

6. Electronics & Electrical: Arithmetic Reasoning, Mathematics Knowledge, Electronics Information, and General Science

7. Health, Social & Technology: Word Knowledge, Paragraph Comprehension, Arithmetic Reasoning, and Mechanical Comprehension

Several other composites are computed by the individual services. Thus, there is a potential for obtaining a large amount of information about both specific aptitude and about major groups of aptitudes that are thought to be relevant to successful performance in training and in a wide variety of jobs within the armed services.

Administration and use of the ASVAB.   There are several noteworthy features to the ASVAB program. First, the ASVAB is usually given by professional test administrators from the Department of Defense or the U.S. Office of Personnel Management. This guarantees a level of standardization of testing procedures that is impossible to meet with many other tests. Second, considerable care has gone into the procedures used for disseminating and interpreting ASVAB scores. The ASVAB is given most often in schools, and extensive efforts are made to provide counselors with relevant information about each student's scores, as well as detailed normative information that can be used to interpret those scores. A student who has taken the ASVAB receives reports listing his or her percentile score on each composite. The counseling department of the school receives a more extensive report on each student and also receives a Military Career Guide, which provides expectancy charts for each of approximately 130 clusters of occupations in the various services. This guide indicates the probability that a student with a particular set of scores will qualify for at least one job within each of the clusters. Since many military jobs have clear parallels in the civilian sector, this guide provides a counseling tool that is broadly useful.

In contrast to many other tests, the ASVAB is part of a well-integrated program that includes continual research in all the branches of the armed services on the technical adequacy and practical usefulness of the test, specific procedures for using the test in both selection (i.e., screening recruits) and job placement, and extensive provisions for using the test as a counseling tool (Katz, 1987). For example, students who take the ASVAB now receive a sophisticated workbook that helps them assess their career interests and determine which military careers best match their abilities and interests. Even if those students decide not to pursue military careers, this type of vocational information can be highly useful in choosing a civilian career.

Evaluation of the ASVAB.   Evaluations of the technical adequacy of the ASVAB have not been completely favorable (Cornbach, 1979; Murphy, 1984a; Weiss, 1978). Although several specific issues have been raised by different reviewers, most of them revolve around the way test scores are calculated and reported rather than around features of the test itself. Recall that the ASVAB is a *multiple* aptitude battery designed to assess several *different* aptitudes. This is reflected, in part, by the fact that there is no overall ASVAB score. Unfortunately, scores on the individual subtest are not reported to individuals or to counselors. Only the seven composites described earlier are reported. The critical question, then, is whether these composites represent discriminably different pieces of information. Examination of the composites themselves and of the technical manual of the test suggests that they do not (Prediger, 1987).

As can be seen from examining the composites, the same tests appear in many different composites. For example, the arithmetic reasoning subtest appears in five of the seven composites. Furthermore, the composites are so highly correlated with one another that their scores essentially are redundant. The average intercorrelation among the seven composite scores is .86; corrected for attenuation, the average intercorrelation is an astounding .92. The only reasonable conclusion is that the composites do *not* provide information about different sets of aptitudes and that, in fact, any one of the composites could be substituted for another with little loss of information. Murphy (1984a) suggested that the composites, particularly the academic ability composite, provide information about the individual's general aptitude but do not provide information about multiple aptitudes.

Although the ASVAB has shown evidence of reliability and criterion-related validity, it nevertheless fails the acid test of a multiple aptitude battery. The ASVAB does not provide the information about multiple abilities needed for successful job placement. For most of its major goals, the military would do just as well with a short test of general intelligence (Murphy, 1984a). Recent research (e.g., Zeidner & Johnson, 1992) suggests that it might be possible to obtain more useful information for classification from the ASVAB if different scoring methods are used. Although the ASVAB is highly "g-loaded" (Hunter, Crosson & Friedman, 1985; Thorndike, 1985), there is evidence that it *can* provide information about several separate abilities (Welsh, Kucinkas & Curran, 1990). However, the process of making even minor changes in a program such as ASVAB is a daunting one, and it is not clear whether the sort of technical solution offered by Zeidner and Johnson (1992) will be applicable in a testing program as complex as ASVAB.

The General Aptitude Test Battery

The General Aptitude Test Battery (GATB) was developed in 1947 by the Department of Labor and is presently used by the U.S. Employment Service for making job referrals in literally hundreds of jobs. The GATB, which is available in at least 12 different languages and is used in over 35 countries (Droege, 1984), rivals the ASVAB in terms of the frequency with which it is used to make decisions about individuals. The GATB measures nine aptitudes using 12 separate tests; the tests and the aptitudes measured are listed in Table 14-5. The test is also available in a nonreading form, in which tests are administered orally, or by using nonverbal materials (e.g., a number comparison test is used in place of the name comparison test); separate versions of the test are available for deaf examinees and wheelchair-bound examinees.

Like the Stanford-Binet and the WAIS, the GATB includes both verbal and performance tests (e.g., assembly and disassembly tasks). As a result, the administration of the GATB is somewhat laborious and complex; the test typically takes over two hours to

TABLE 14-5 APTITUDES MEASURED BY THE GENERAL APTITUDE
TEST BATTERY

Aptitude	Tests
G—General Learning Ability	Vocabulary
	Arithmetic Reasoning
	Three-Dimensional Space
V—Verbal Ability	Vocabulary*
N—Numerical Ability	Computation
	Arithmetic Reasoning
S—Spatial Aptitude	Three-Dimensional Space
P—Form Perception	Tool Matching
	Form Matching
Q—Clerical Perception	Name Comparison
K—Motor Coordination	Mark Making
F—Finger Dexterity	Assemble
	Disassemble
M—Manual Dexterity	Place
	Turn

*Note: As with ASVAB, the same GATB test might be used in measuring
several different aptitudes.

administer. Factor analyses of the GATB suggest that the test measures three general factors: (a) a cognitive factor representing general learning ability, verbal ability, and numerical ability; (b) a perceptual factor representing spatial aptitude, form perception, and clerical perception; and (c) a psychomotor factor representing motor coordination, finger dexterity, and manual dexterity (Hunter, 1983a). The perceptual factor is almost perfectly correlated with a combination of the other two factors, suggesting that the test measures two basic abilities, cognitive and psychomotor.

Use of the GATB. The GATB is a central part of the U.S. Employment Service's job referral program (Delahunty, 1988; Hartigan & Wigdor, 1989). This referral program includes many elements besides the GATB, such as counseling and workshops, but scores on the GATB can have a pivotal impact on an applicant's chance to be considered for jobs.

The GATB referral system consists of four steps: (a) intake—registration and orientation, (b) assessment—testing and evaluation of credentials, (c) file search—location of appropriate job opportunities, and (d) referral. Employers make the final decisions about individuals referred by the Job Service, but because the referral process is designed to locate qualified candidates, individuals who are referred very often receive job offers.

The U.S. Employment Service has the complex task of referring the most qualified individuals for the job *and* attempting to ensure that individuals who have been traditionally disadvantaged by standardized testing (e.g., minority group members, individuals with disabilities) have an opportunity to compete for these jobs. During the 1980s various schemes for computing and reporting scores separately for members of different ethnic and racial groups were proposed and implemented (Hartigan & Wigdor, 1989). This type of race norming led to significant controversies, lawsuits, and a moratorium on the use of the GATB by several agencies. As a result of the Civil Rights Act of 1991, the practice of race norming (i.e., reporting scores in terms of percentiles within one's own racial or ethnic group) has been discontinued. As we were completing this edition, the question of whether the moratorium on the use of the GATB would be lifted or modified was not yet resolved.

Evaluation of the GATB. GATB reliabilities are comparable to those of other similar tests, such as the ASVAB (Hartigan & Wigdor, 1989). The validity of the GATB has been researched in hundreds of separate studies. Validity generalization procedures led Hunter (1983c) to conclude that the GATB is valid in all jobs for which it is used, and that GATB validities are higher in more complex or demanding jobs than in simpler jobs. Hunter (1983b) also concluded that the GATB was fair to minorities and that the inclusion of a psychomotor composite helps to reduce the adverse impact of this test (i.e., it reduces differences between the average scores of different groups).

The most controversial issue in the evaluation of the GATB has been its utility (see Chapter 19). The GATB referral process was developed and adapted, in part, because of research suggesting that the use of the GATB in job referral could lead to extraordinarily large gains in productivity. The most frequently cited figure is in the neighborhood of $80 billion. It is now clear that a figure such as this is wildly inflated (Hartigan & Wigdor, 1989) and that the use of GATB will not by itself generate this level of productivity. Nevertheless, the use of GATB may help employers locate the most qualified applicants, and in the long run could result in productivity gains that far exceed the cost of testing and referral.

Ability Testing and Cognitive Research

In the last 20 to 30 years, the "cognitive revolution" has swept through most areas of psychology. Research on cognitive processes has come to dominate fields as diverse as motivation (see a special section on motives and goals in human performance, *Psychological Science, Vol. 3,* No. 3) and psychotherapy (where cognitively oriented therapies have emerged). The relatively new field of cognitive science provides an exciting integration of psychological, neurological, and computational models of human thought and brain function. However, the recent explosion of knowledge regarding cognitive processes has had relatively little influence to date on the ability testing. Despite all the advances in cognitive research, the "best" tests of cognitive ability still follow the basic philosophy and measurement strategies developed by Binet at the turn of the century and by the research team that developed Army Alpha during World War I.

There are at least three areas in which you might expect that cognitive research *would* have a substantial impact on ability testing. First, cognitive researchers have reached some consensus that many higher-level cognitive processes, which presumably include those involving mental abilities, can be best understood through a "mental architecture" that includes three components: (a) working memory, (b) declarative memory, and (c) procedural memory (Lord & Maher, 1991). Working memory is that part of memory that is currently activated, whereas declarative and procedural memories store factual information and information about how to do things, respectively (this is a substantial simplification, but it gives a flavor of these three key concepts). Some existing tests (e.g., the K-ABC) and many tests currently being developed (e.g., computerized tests being developed by the armed services) include measures of working memory; other tests (e.g., the fourth edition of the Stanford-Binet) have been revised to partially accommodate this description of cognitive function. However, few existing tests provide meaningful assessments of all three components.

Second, there have been a number of theories of intelligence that attempt to identify multiple types (e.g., Gardner, 1983) or components (e.g., Sternberg, 1984, 1985) of intelligence. Although some tests have been proposed or developed, none of these has proved completely satisfactory, and there is no indication that they will replace current tests of ability (Sternberg, 1981b, 1991).

Third, applied researchers (e.g., Ackerman, 1987; Murphy, 1989b) have become increasingly interested with *how* ability translates into performance on a variety of tasks. Several theories suggest that general mental ability, which is critical to the acquisition of task knowledge, is more critical when the task is new or novel than when an individual has had a chance to practice the task. Although this research does not suggest different ways in which ability should be measured, it does suggest that ability tests should be used in different ways—in particular, to identify those most likely to acquire knowledge and understanding of the task quickly.

Lohman (1992) suggests three reasons why cognitive research has had relatively little impact on ability testing. First, the decomposition of complex, real-world tasks into their basic cognitive components has proved much more difficult than anyone anticipated. Thus, it is often difficult to determine exactly which aspects of the theory apply to which tasks. Second, it is difficult to replace existing psychometric tests with experimental tasks that are designed to measure the same abilities or processes. This problem is related to the first (the difficulty of matching the theory to the task); even when psychometric researchers and cognitive researchers use the same terms, they are not always referring to the same phenomena. Third, measures of speed of response (or latency), which are so central to many cognitive theories, are easier to obtain than to interpret. This is because of the well-known speed-accuracy trade-off (Ackerman & Humphreys, 1990). That is, increasing the speed of responses usually results in a decrease in accuracy. If examinees believe that accuracy is important, they tend to respond more slowly; if they believe that speed is important, they tend to be less accurate. Speed of response often has more to do with subjects' orientation to the test than with their basic cognitive processes.

Finally, Sternberg (1991) suggests that practical constraints may prove the most difficult barrier to translating advances in cognitive research into new methods of testing. Test publishing is a big business, and it is difficult to convince publishers of the need to make radical changes in their tests, especially when the familiar testing methods "work" so well. As you saw in Chapter 11, however, developments in computerized testing may open the door for translating advances in cognitive research into new methods of measuring cognitive ability.

CRITICAL DISCUSSION:
The Case against Large-Scale Testing

The Scholastic Aptitude Test provides an illustration of a large-scale testing program. Here, several thousand students answer hundreds of multiple-choice items that tap areas ranging from vocabulary and reading comprehension to inductive and deductive reasoning. This type of testing has been the focus of extensive criticism (Gross, 1963; Hoffman, 1962; Nairn et al., 1980; Ryan, 1979). Although many specific arguments have been raised in this debate, the case against large-scale testing boils down to two essentials: (a) this type of testing does not measure the right variables, and (b) this type of testing does not provide truly useful information.

In arguments over what group tests measure or fail to measure, the multiple-choice response format is frequently cited as the culprit. Some critics argue that multiple-choice items penalize creative thinkers (Hoffman, 1962), while others argue that they measure knowledge of specific facts, but not of general abilities (Ryan, 1979). In general, research does *not* support either of these criticisms (Jensen, 1980; Wigdor & Garner, 1982). It is possible, however, that the psychological processes involved in answering multiple-choice items might be difficult from those involved in answering the types of open-ended questions that are used in many individual ability tests. Even here, however, the evidence does not suggest that multiple-choice items yield scores that are very different than might be obtained with other test formats—*scores* from tests made up exclusively of multiple-choice items are generally highly correlated with scores from similiar tests that include *no* multiple-choice items (Jackson, 1984; Wigdor & Garner, 1982). Thus, it is difficult to argue that the use of multiple-choice items seriously distorts the measurement of ability.

The best argument *against* large-scale testing is that there may not be good arguments *for* large-scale testing. Tests such as the ASVAB are probably not as useful as they are expensive (Murphy, 1984a). Even the SAT, a test with an impressive level of validity, may not be all that useful. There is evidence that SAT scores have only a minor impact on college admission decisions (Gottfredson & Crouse, 1986) and that the use of these tests might have a very negative effect on minority applicants that, for them, outweighs the potential benefits of the test. Even Jensen (1980), a staunch advocate of testing, recommends against the routine practice of giving tests by the thousands and then deciding what to do with test information. We suspect that if consumers gave more thought to how test information was to be used, fewer tests would be given.

SUMMARY

The development of standardized tests of mental ability that could be administered to groups of examinees has fundamentally changed the face of the testing industry. As we saw in Chapter 12, this type of test was developed to meet a very specific need, namely, the screening of large numbers of military recruits in World War I. The apparent success of this type of testing encouraged psychologists to bring this technology into civilian settings.

The primary difference between individual and group tests is that with the former, examinees respond to an examiner, who must interpret and score their responses, whereas with the latter, they respond directly to test items. This makes it relatively easy to provide highly standardized conditions of measurement, which tends to increase reliability and validity. On the other hand, a heavy reliance on simple response formats (usually, multiple-choice) may limit the value of a test.

We described the Multidimensional Aptitude Battery, which represents an ingenious adaptation of the WAIS-R for group administration. This test has retained most of the positive features of the WAIS-R and is substantially easier to administer. We next described the Cognitive Abilities Tests, which are widely used in testing school children. This chapter described three scholastic tests, the Scholastic Aptitude Test, the Enhanced ACT Assessment System, and the Graduate Record Examinations, which should be familiar to many of you. These tests, which are used in making academic admissions decisions, measure both general abilities and more specific competencies or areas of content expertise.

The Armed Services Vocational Aptitude Battery and the General Aptitude Test Battery represent two of the most widely used cognitive test batteries in existence. Both tests are designed to provide information about general as well as specific abilities, but it is not clear that either has been fully successful in both roles. Nevertheless, there is clear evidence that these tests are useful for making important decisions.

We noted that the influence of cognitive psychology on psychological testing has been disappointingly small. Current theories of cognition differ in a number of ways from the theories of intelligence that have driven the development of several widely used tests, but to date little progress has been made in translating cognitive principles into useful tests. We review several reasons for the currently limited impact of cognitive research on psychological testing.

CHAPTER 15

ISSUES IN ABILITY TESTING

As discussed in Chapter 1, the apparent success of early tests in classifying recruits during World War I led to a boom in civilian intelligence testing in the 1920s and 1930s, and laid the foundation for the large-scale intelligence testing industry that exists today. Since its inception, however, large-scale intelligence testing has been the focus of sustained public controversy (Cronbach, 1975). Although conflicts between test specialists sometimes revolve around technical or esoteric issues, the primary issue which has fueled the bitter public debate over IQ testing has been the fact that the average test scores for minority groups tend to be lower than average test scores for whites. Furthermore, this difference between the means of white and minority test scores on an intelligence test is generally about the same size as the standard deviation of the test, or approximately 15 points.

The difference in average test scores means that there will be *relatively* few minorities who receive high test scores and that minorities will be overrepresented among those receiving low scores on the test. As a result, if tests are used as the *sole* method of making decisions, fewer minorities will be selected into schools, jobs, and training programs than if decisions are made at random or if quotas are imposed. In very selective contexts (e.g., prestigious schools), the use of tests as the sole means for making decisions effectively rules out most minority applicants.

A number of possibilities have been suggested to account for the difference between white and non-white test scores. Hereditarians suggest that genetic factors are partially responsible for individual differences in intelligence test scores. The extreme hereditarian position goes further, suggesting that differences between white and non-white test score means are attributable primarily or solely to genetic differences between whites and non-whites (Schockley, 1972).

Environmentalists suggest that test score differences can best be understood in terms of differences in the environments, particularly in the cultures of white and minority examinees. Extreme environmentalists go further, suggesting that standard intelligence tests are valid only for middle-class whites, and that these tests cannot provide valid or useful measures for minorities, who presumably are brought up in a culture that is significantly different from that of middle-class whites. In 1968 the Black Psychological Association called for a moratorium on the use of psychological tests in classifying disadvantaged students on the grounds that these tests showed substantial cultural bias; Jackson (1975) labelled psychological testing as a "quasi-scientific tool for perpetuating racism" (p. 88).

Most psychologists view both extreme hereditarianism and extreme environmentalism as fundamentally incorrect. There is a good deal of evidence to suggest that intelligence is affected by both heredity and environment, and that both factors must be taken into account in understanding individual or group differences in scores on intelligence tests. Nevertheless, the debate between the environmentalists and the hereditarians has helped call our attention to three issues that are explored in depth in this chapter: (a) bias and fairness in mental testing; (b) culture-fair, or culture-reduced, testing; and (c) the heritability and the modifiability of IQ.

BIAS AND FAIRNESS IN MENTAL TESTING

There is a widespread belief that cognitive ability tests are biased and that the use of these tests in educational placement, academic admissions, and personnel selection results in decisions that are fundamentally unfair. One line of evidence that suggests that tests are biased is the existence of systematic differences in test scores as a function of socioeconomic status, sex, and race (Jensen, 1980; Linn, 1982). Researchers on test bias have reported that, in general,

1. test scores from children and adults in the middle and upper classes tend to be higher than those of children and adults in the lower socioeconomic classes.
2. whites tend to receive higher scores than minorities.
3. males receive systematically higher scores on some tests and systematically lower scores on other tests than females.[1]

These differences have been attributed by some authors to test bias and have been cited as an example of the unfair nature of tests (Jackson, 1975; Williams, 1974).

The debate about bias and fairness in mental tests has been hampered by a lack of agreement over basic terms. For example, if whites receive higher scores on a given test than minorities, is this an indication of bias, lack of fairness, both bias and unfairness, or

[1]For a variety of perspectives on the debate over IQ, race, and social class, see Eckberg (1979), Flynn (1980), Herrnstein (1971), Jensen (1980), Joseph (1977), Kamin (1974), and Scarr (1981).

neither of these? It is useful at the outset to define bias and fairness in terms that are accepted by most psychologists.

Defining Bias and Fairness

In our everyday language, bias and fairness seem to be closely related, if not identical, concepts. It seems obvious to most people that a biased test is unfair and that an unbiased test is fair. In the context of testing and decision making, however, bias and fairness represent fundamentally different concepts. In some instances, a biased test may lead to decisions that are regarded widely as fair, whereas an unbiased test may lead to decisions that are condemned universally as unfair. It is important, therefore, to distinguish between the two concepts.

Simply put, bias is a statistical characteristic of the test scores, or of the predictions based upon those scores.[2] Thus, *bias is said to exist when a test makes systematic errors in measurement or prediction*. For example, if test scores indicate that males perform better in verbal reasoning tasks than do females, when in fact they both perform equally well, the test provides a biased measure of verbal reasoning. If a test used in college admissions systematically overpredicts the performance of males and underpredicts the performance of females, that test functions as a biased predictor.

Fairness refers to a value judgment regarding decisions or actions taken as a result of test scores. For example, in selecting firefighters, most cities use some combination of cognitive ability tests, interviews, and tests of physical strength. Quite frequently the group of applicants selected is predominantly male, even though many females may have applied for the job. Some people regard this situation as fundamentally unfair, since females are largely excluded from this job. Others regard the same situation as completely fair, reasoning that the tests select the best-qualified applicants, regardless of sex. The question of whether the situation is fair depends entirely on one's assessment of what *should* be done. People who believe that firefighters should be representative of the population in general will regard this situation as unfair; those who believe that persons with the highest scores should be hired will perceive it as fair.

Table 15-1 lists some major differences between bias and fairness. First, bias is a characteristic of the numbers (test scores or predicted criterion scores), whereas fairness is a characteristic of people's actions or decisions. The principle implied here is that numbers are morally and philosophically neutral. People's actions or decisions can be fair or unfair; numbers may be accurate or inaccurate, but they cannot be fair or unfair.

Second, bias is a statistical concept, whereas fairness is a judgment based on individual values. The third and fourth defining characteristics of bias and fairness flow directly from this second characteristic. Because bias is a statistical issue, it can be defined empirically and its existence can be determined scientifically. By examining test data, one can determine the extent to which a test provides biased measures or biased predictions. Fairness, on the other hand, involves a comparison between the decisions that were made and the decisions that "should have" been made. The question of which decisions should have been made depends upon the decision maker's values, as well as features of the

---

[2]Sheppard (1982) defines bias as a property of the test *or* the way the test is used.

TABLE 15-1   DEFINING CHARACTERISTICS OF BIAS AND FAIRNESS

Bias	Fairness
• Refers to *test scores* or to *predictions* based on test scores.	• Refers to *actions* taken or decisions made.
• Is based on *statistical* characteristics of scores or predictions.	• Is a *value judgment* regarding outcomes.
• Is defined *empirically*.	• Is defined in *philosophical* or *political* terms.
• *Can* be scientifically determined.	• *Cannot* be scientifically determined.

situation in which decisions were made. Values, in turn, reflect philosophical and political considerations rather than empirical ones. As a result, fairness *cannot* be determined by scientific methods. Scientific methods can be used to reflect precisely what *was* done, but they cannot determine what *should have* been done.

Because bias and fairness are defined in different terms, it follows that a biased test will not necessarily lead to unfair decisions, and that decisions based upon unbiased tests are not necessarily fair. For example, an unbiased test of upper-body strength could be used to select firefighters. Since such a test would systematically screen out women applicants, many people would regard this outcome as unfair. The same test could be used to select among applicants to dental school, since dentists must occasionally exert physical force. However, in this case the use of a test that effectively screened out women would be regarded as unfair by almost everyone. On the other hand, it may be regarded as fair to increase the number of minorities hired in a job they have traditionally been denied. In this case, a biased test might achieve this end more readily than an unbiased one.

Types of Test Bias

As noted in Chapters 7 and 8, tests can be used for two general purposes: to measure a particular characteristic or attribute and to predict scores on some criterion or outcome measure. The major types of test bias parallel these two major uses. Thus, it is useful to distinguish between *bias in measurement* and *bias in prediction.*

Bias in measurement occurs when the test makes systematic errors in measuring a specific characteristic or attribute. For example, several psychologists claim that IQ tests may be valid for middle-class whites, but that they are not reliable or valid for blacks or other minorities (Joseph, 1977; Williams, 1974). There is evidence that employment interviews provide biased measures of the applicants' characteristics; they are, for example, typically biased in favor of attractive applicants (Arvey, 1979).

Bias in prediction, on the other hand, occurs when the test makes systematic errors in predicting some criterion or outcome. It is often argued that tests that are used in academic admissions and in personnel selection underpredict the performance of minority applicants and that the tests therefore have an adverse impact on minority admissions and hiring. In other cases, tests might be useful predictors with one group (e.g., males) but be markedly less accurate when used to predict the performance of some other group.

Detecting Bias in Measurement

At one time it appeared that test bias could be assessed by obtaining expert judgments (see our Critical Discussion entitled "Are Judgments of Item Bias Useful?"). There is now consensus that it is virtually impossible to assess the degree to which an item is biased simply by examining its content. The only time that judgmental methods seem to work is when test items contain *highly* specialized knowledge that is available to some examinees but not to others. For example, an intelligence test that contained nothing but items dealing with terms used in musical notation would probably be biased in favor of music students. For all practical purposes, though, psychological tests are virtually never so transparent in their biases that experts can accurately judge or predict test bias or test item bias. Therefore, methods more sophisticated than those based on armchair judgments are necessary to detect bias.[3]

The methods used in investigating construct validity may be adapted to determine whether a test measures the same thing or whether it measures substantially different things for different groups in the population. For example, suppose that you believed that a scale labelled a test of general intelligence provided a good measure of cognitive ability for whites, but when it was used with minorities simply measured familiarity with white middle-class culture. To test this hypothesis, you might identify several variables known to be related to general intelligence. Examples include grades in school and performance on problem-solving tasks. You might also identify several variables that reflect familiarity with white middle-class culture. Examples include number of years in suburban versus inner-city schools and ability to correctly identify terms and figures uniquely identified with white middle-class culture. If the test measures substantially different things for whites and minorities, you would expect systematic differences in the relationships between test scores and known correlates of intelligence and cultural familiarity. That is, if the test really *did* measure different things for whites and minorities, you might find correlations similar to those shown in Table 15-2.

This method of assessing bias in measurement involves examining external correlates of test performance. It would also be possible to test the hypothesis that the test measures substantially different things in different groups by examining internal evidence: the scores on the test itself. One indicator of bias in measurement would be the presence of a *group × item interaction* in the difficulty of test items. A group × item interaction occurs when the *relative* difficulty of test items varies across groups. Table 15-3 illustrates a short test for which a group × item interaction might be expected. The interaction described in the table can be more clearly described by graphing the results from the white and minority samples. Figure 15-1 shows, in graphic terms, the group × item interactions. As can be seen from the figure, the item that is easiest for white examinees (Jane Austen) is most difficult for minorities, whereas the item that is easiest for minorities (Amiri Baraka) is most difficult for whites. It appears here that the test measures exposure to "classic" literature for whites, but measures exposure to modern black literature for minorities. If the test measured the same thing for both groups, items that were relatively difficult for whites would also be relatively difficult for minorities.

[3]A variety of methods of detecting bias are discussed in a handbook edited by Berk (1982).

TABLE 15-2   HYPOTHETICAL RESULTS SUPPORTING THE HYPOTHESIS OF BIAS IN MEASUREMENT

	Correlations with test scores	
Known correlates of intelligence	**White sample**	**Minority sample**
School grades	.48	.03
Problem-solving scores	.39	.10
Known correlates of familiarity with white, middle-class culture		
Number of years in suburban schools	.04	.44
Accuracy in identifying terms and figures unique to this culture	.20	.59

TABLE 15-3   AN EXAMPLE OF GROUP × ITEM INTERACTION

Question	Percent correct	
Identify one work by each of the following authors:	**White Sample**	**Minority Sample**
Jane Austen	.50	.20
Peter Straub	.42	.43
Amiri Baraka	.15	.47

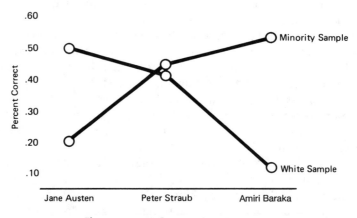

Figure 15-1   A Group × Item Interaction

Evidence Regarding Bias in Measurement

Research on differential validity most clearly addresses the question of whether tests measure different things for different groups, in that it deals with the relationship between test scores and other variables of interest. At one time the hypothesis that ability tests were differentially valid for predicting criteria such as grades in school, performance on the job, or success in training was widely accepted (Arvey, 1979; Guion, 1965a). The basis for this belief was the fact that many ability tests showed significant correlations with relevant criteria when used with whites, but showed nonsignificant validity coefficients when used with minorities. Although some researchers have maintained that differential validity occurs in specific settings (Katzell & Dyer, 1977; Schmitt, Mellon & Bylenga, 1978), the consensus of most testing specialists is that differential validity is *not* a widespread phenomenon (Cleary, Humphreys, Kendrick & Wesman, 1975; Hartigan & Wigdor, 1989; Linn, 1982).

It appears that many instances of "differential validity" are in fact the result of inappropriate comparisons. Tests of the significance of a correlation coefficient depend largely on the sample size. Because samples of minority examinees are, by definition, likely to be much smaller than samples of white examinees, the same correlation coefficient will often be deemed significant in the large white sample, but not significant in the smaller minority sample (Boehm, 1977; Hunter, Schmidt & Hunter, 1979; Schmidt, Berner & Hunter, 1973). When differences in sample size are taken into account, one rarely finds convincing evidence that ability tests provide substantially better predictions of relevant criteria for some racial or ethnic groups than for others.

Examination of research evidence dealing with group differences in the reliability or the validity of cognitive ability tests provides little support for the hypothesis that bias in measurement is widespread (Cleary et al., 1975; Jensen, 1980). Research using more sophisticated methods of analysis, including analytic methods of comparing factor structures and applications of the item response theory, also suggests that bias in measurement is somewhat rare (Drasgow & Kanfer, 1985; Hulin, Drasgow & Parsons, 1983: See Wainer & Braun, 1988 for discussions of methods of detecting bias), although it is sometimes reported (Thissen, Steinberg & Gerrard, 1986). It is possible, however, that these tests are biased in the predictions they make.

Detecting Bias in Prediction

Regardless of whether a test provides a biased or an unbiased measure of examinees' cognitive ability, there is a good possibility that the test will provide biased predictions. For example, an academic ability test might routinely overestimate the future academic performance of males and underestimate that of females. In this case, females will be at a disadvantage if the test is used to make academic selection or placement decisions. It is also possible that a test will be highly accurate in predicting the performance of whites, but at the same time it will show relatively little accuracy in predicting the performance of minorities, even though the test does not systematically overpredict or underpredict performance levels for either group. In this case, a high-scoring member of a minority group will be at a considerable disadvantage, since his or her performance on the test will not necessarily lead to a prediction of high performance on the criterion, whereas the high-scoring white applicant will be predicted to perform at a high level.

The typical method of predicting a person's score on the criterion on the basis of his or her score on a test is to use a regression equation (see Chapter 4). That is, the predicted criterion score ($\hat{Y}$) is given by the equation

$$\hat{Y} = a + bx \qquad [15\text{-}1]$$

where

$$\hat{Y} = \text{predicted performance}$$
$$x = \text{test score}$$
$$a = \text{the intercept}$$
$$b = \text{the slope of the regression line}^4$$

Bias in prediction exists when the regression equations used to predict a relevant criterion in two or more separate groups differ in terms of their intercepts, their slopes, or their standard errors of estimate.

Regression equations are affected by a number of parameters, most notably the test mean ($\bar{X}$), the mean on the criterion ($\bar{Y}$), the standard deviations of X and Y, and the correlation between X and Y. Bartlett and O'Leary (1969) have illustrated the effects of differences in each of these parameters or predictions. For example, consider the situation depicted in Figure 15-2, where whites and minorities show equal levels of criterion performance ($\bar{Y}$), equal levels of variability in test scores and in performance (σ_x and σ_y), and equal levels of test validity (r_{xy}). However, the mean test score among whites is higher than the mean test score for minorities. In this situation, the intercepts of the white and minority regression equations differ, and the test will yield biased predictions. Whites and minorities who earn the same test score will receive different predictions regarding their performance on the criterion.

The situation depicted in the figure is of broad concern, since many groups in the population are known to differ in terms of their average test scores. In particular, average scores on most cognitive ability tests are higher for middle-class whites than for minorities or for members of lower socioeconomic classes. *Unless these differences in test scores reflect systematic (and comparable) differences in criterion performance, ability tests will yield biased predictions.* Bias in prediction could arise as a result of a number of factors: differences in test scores, differences in criterion performance, differences in the variability of test scores or performance, or differences in test validity. In any case, bias in prediction could affect the decisions made about individuals. Since systematic differences are known to exist in the average scores received by whites and minorities on most cognitive ability tests, the possibility of bias in prediction must be seriously examined.

Evidence Regarding Bias in Prediction

The methods for detecting bias in prediction are fairly straightforward—simply compute a separate regression equation for predicting criterion scores in each group, and compare

---

[4]The formulas for the regression equation are

$$\hat{Y} = a - bx$$

where

$$a = \bar{Y} - b\bar{X}$$
$$b = r_{xy} \times \frac{\sigma_y}{\sigma_x}$$

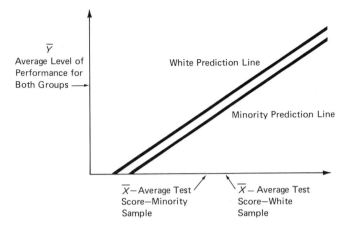

$\overline{Y}$
Average Level of
Performance for
Both Groups —→

White Prediction Line

Minority Prediction Line

$\overline{X}$ —Average Test
Score—Minority
Sample

$\overline{X}$ — Average Test
Score—White
Sample

Figure 15-2 A Biased Prediction: Groups Show Equal $\bar{Y}$, but Different $\bar{X}$

the equations.[5] We can therefore move directly to an examination of the empirical evidence regarding bias in prediction.

First, it is clear that the question of whether differential validity exists is relevant to understanding both bias in measurement and bias in prediction. If the correlation between test scores and criterion measures differs across groups, it is almost certain that the slope of the regression line will also differ. Evidence reviewed earlier in this book suggests that differential validity is not a widespread phenomenon. It appears, likely, therefore, that differences in slopes and intercepts, when they occur at all, will reflect differences in the means and standard deviations of both tests and criterion measures, rather than reflecting differences in test validity. There is evidence that these parameters vary across groups, and that some degree of bias in prediction therefore may be present.

In general, the slopes of regression equations computed separately for males and females or for whites and minorities appear to be similar (Arvey, 1979; Jensen, 1980). In other words, within each group, individuals with high test scores are likely to receive high scores on a number of relevant criteria, and the difference in performance between persons with high test scores and persons with low test scores is roughly equivalent across groups. Bias in standard errors also is relatively infrequent, although in some cases groups who tend to perform most poorly also will have the smallest standard errors. However, there is evidence of a fairly consistent difference in the intercepts of regression equations computed separately for whites and minorities (Cleary et al., 1975; Hartigan & Wigdor, 1989; Gael, Grant & Richie, 1975; Linn, 1982). In particular, regression equations computed separately for whites and minorities tend to have similar slopes, but different intercepts, with the white intercept typically higher than the minority intercept. This pattern of results is illustrated in Figure 15-3.

As illustrated by the figure, if separate regression equations are used for whites and minorities, a lower criterion score will always be predicted for a minority group member than for a member of the white sample who has received the same test score. On the

[5]There are statistical tests for determining whether differences between regression equations are significant.

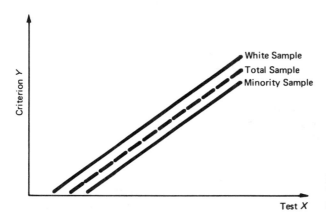

Figure 15-3 Prediction Equations That Differ in Intercept, but Not in Slope

other hand, if the regression equation computed for the total sample is used for everybody, whites and minorities who receive the same test score will receive the same predicted criterion score.

Throughout the 1960s and 1970s it was believed widely that ability tests *underpredicted* the performance of minorities. This view is no longer accepted. Linn (1982) notes that

> whether the criterion to be predicted is freshman GPA in college, first year grades in law school, outcomes of job training, or job performance measures, carefully chosen ability tests have *not* been found to underpredict the actual performance of minority group persons. (p. 384)

In fact, the reverse may be true. If the minority group intercept is lower than the intercept for whites, as is often the case, the use of the total sample's regression equation to predict criterion performance will tend to *overpredict* the performance of minority group members. This overprediction bias is likely to be small (Cleary et al., 1975). Nevertheless, attempts to reduce intercept bias may actually be unfavorable to minorities. The use of separate regression equations is likely to result in the selection of fewer rather than more minorities if similar selection standards are enforced in each group (Linn, 1982; Jensen, 1980).

Difficulties in Research on Bias and Fairness

Research on bias and fairness in testing is difficult for a number of reasons. First, there is no clear consensus about the precise meaning of terms such as "unbiased" or "fair," particularly when the debate over bias and fairness goes outside the scientific community. One of the recurring problems in psychological research is that it deals with concepts and terms that are somewhat familiar to the general public. Thus, terms like "bias," "fairness," "intelligence," and so forth, have excess meaning—they convey things to the general public that are not part of their scientific definition. As a result, widespread agreement about many of the topics addressed in this section is virtually impossible because the critical terms in the debate over bias and fairness in ability testing mean different things to different people.

Research on bias and fairness is not only difficult to communicate to the general public; it is also quite difficult to do. One of the surprising difficulties in doing research on the effects of race and gender on test scores arises because the demographic characteristics of test takers are frequently unknown. For example, Wainer (1988) noted that many students taking the Scholastic Aptitude Test (SAT) do not respond to questions about their race or ethnic identity. The data suggest that the number of students who do not respond is nearly as large as the total number of responses from black, Asian-American, Mexican-American, Puerto Rican, and Native American respondents *combined*. He goes on to show that failure to identify one's race or ethnic origins is more common in some groups than in others, and that this could have a substantial effect on the interpretation of test results.

Another difficulty in doing research on bias and fairness is the sensitivity of the questions raised. Research on race and gender, particularly as they may affect scores on cognitive ability tests, is so sensitive a topic that many researchers seem to have concluded that we should not continue to do research in this area. There are many reasons for this conclusion. First, there is the possibility that research will be misinterpreted or that research findings will somehow exacerbate the already disadvantaged status of women and minorities. Second, researchers who examine race or gender differences and publicly discuss their results are often subject to harassment and abuse (Gordon, 1988). For example, Scarr (1988) describes the experiences of Arthur Jensen, a psychologist who suggested that intelligence tests were not biased, and that racial differences in test scores *might* be partially genetic in origin, noting that Jensen "was harassed, threatened, and driven into virtual protective custody by colleagues, students, and other radicals who resented his hypothesis" (p. 57).

Scarr (1988) has noted that we probably do more harm than good by trying to avoid sensitive issues, such as race and gender, in psychological research. It is patronizing for investigators (almost always white and usually male) to decide a priori that some research questions about minorities or females are best left unexplored; among other things, this decision makes it difficult to investigate the strengths of underrepresented groups and their ways of functioning well. Scarr does, however, suggest that the way in which research questions are phrased and conceptualized must take into account the sensitive nature of the questions. For example, she suggests that research questions framed in terms of what is wrong with, what is deficient in, or what is in need of change for women and minorities are at best offensive and, at worst, inflammatory.

The bottom line in considering research on race and gender-related variables may be its value orientation. If the middle-class mainstream is held up as an ideal and point of comparison, research on race and gender can easily fall into the "what is wrong with these people" frame of mind. On the other hand, research on how and why members of different groups in the population perform important tasks and roles in society is both valuable and important, especially if this research avoids the trap of labelling group differences in terms of the failure of one group to meet another group's standards.

Are there remedies for test bias?   As we noted in Chapter 2, whenever two groups receive systematically different scores on a test that is used to make important decisions, important societal consequences can follow. For example, blacks receive lower scores than whites on some tests used for admission to medical schools (Gordon, 1988). If the test results dictate decisions, the result will be proportionately fewer black doctors. Females receive lower scores on tests of mathematical ability than males (Burton et al.,

1988). If test scores are used to determine who receives scholarships, fewer females will receive them. Thus, there is considerable interest in methods of reducing test bias.

One possible solution is to change the content of the test to reduce the influence of potentially irrelevant cultural factors on test scores. The next section of this chapter reviews research in this area, and shows that this strategy is not effective in reducing group differences in test scores. A more direct route to reducing group differences is in the test development stage. That is, you might develop tests with the specific objective of reducing group differences in test scores. This is the strategy implicit in the "Golden Rule" agreement.

The "Golden Rule" refers to a court settlement between the Golden Rule Insurance Company and the Educational Testing Service (ETS) regarding tests developed for insurance licensing exams. According to this settlement, ETS agrees to take steps in test development to reduce the differences in the mean scores received by black and white examinees. Specifically, ETS agrees to give priority in item selection to those test items for which the passing rates of blacks and whites are similar (Type 1 items) and to use items in which the white passing rates are substantially higher only if the available pool of Type 1 items is exhausted. Proponents of this type of solution note that the same thing is sometimes done to reduce sex bias in ability tests.

Although it may look appealing, the strategy implied by the "Golden Rule" agreement has been criticized (Committee on Psychological Tests and Assessments, 1988). First, this strategy is not necessarily effective. As the report cited above notes, a test developed according to this procedure may have exactly the same impact as a test developed in a standard fashion. Although this method of test development will reduce the *size* of the difference between scores received by whites and blacks, it does not necessarily change the rank ordering of individuals taking the test. Second, and more important, this procedure is likely to reduce the reliability and validity of the test. Using this procedure, the contribution of items to the technical adequacy of the test is no longer the primary criterion for selecting items. Rather, items will be selected primarily on the similarity of scores received by different groups. The "Golden Rule" procedure may reduce the reliability, validity, and utility of the test without increasing minority examinees' chances to compete effectively for jobs, academic admissions, and so forth.

There is clear agreement in the scientific community that it is possible to at least partially separate the effects of real differences in the attributes measured by tests from the effects of irrelevant biases in the analysis of test items (a variety of methods for detecting bias are reviewed in Berk, 1982; Hulin et al., 1983; and Ironson & Subkoviak, 1979). There is also clear agreement that differences in test scores are not due solely to irrelevant test bias (Gottfredson, 1986, 1988; Jensen, 1980; Reynolds & Brown, 1984). Rather, group differences in scores on cognitive ability tests reflect real differences in cognitive ability. There is considerable controversy over the meaning, causes, and modifiability of these differences, but there is little doubt that some of the differences in test scores reflects real differences in ability. One implication of this is that changing tests will not make the problem of test bias go away.

Rather than simply changing tests, we may need to change the way in which we use tests. For example, a controversy arose over the way in which the General Aptitude Test Battery (GATB) should be used by the U.S. Employment Service to refer applicants to job opportunities (Hartigan & Wigdor, 1989). The Department of Labor favored a scoring method that would statistically remove group differences in scores, resulting in more referrals for minority applicants. The Department of Justice favored a scoring method that would retain group differences, resulting in fewer referrals for minorities. A panel of the National Academy of Science suggested a compromise method that would give both minority and nonminority candidates a chance, by referring all candidates who would qualify under *either* scoring method. Subsequently, the Civil Rights Act of 1991 ruled out the application of this particular approach, but the principle that methods of scoring tests to reduce bias might be developed is still a valid one.

A second strategy for reducing the effects of test bias is to employ multiple methods of assessment. Test bias is most likely to be a societal problem when a single test score determines each person's fate. The use of a broad array of assessment devices that measure many important attributes may provide the ultimate safeguard against the possibility that irrelevant biases in test scores will unfairly handicap individuals taking the test.

CRITICAL DISCUSSION:
Are Judgments of Item Bias Useful?

One method that has been used to determine whether a test or a test item is biased is to assemble a panel of expert judges. If the concern is that items might be biased against a particular group (e.g., females, blacks), the panel will often contain members of that group. Research on these judgments of test or item bias clearly shows that this method is *not* effective for detecting bias; judgments about the extent to which an item is biased rarely correspond to *any* of the widely accepted measures of bias (Jensen, 1980; Shepard, 1982). Although panels of judges may not be useful in detecting bias, they may nevertheless serve an important function. They may be critical in ensuring the *acceptance* of psychological tests by both test users and examinees.

We are not suggesting here that the use of panels of experts to assess test and test item bias is nothing more than window dressing. On the contrary, these panels serve two very real functions. First, they are helpful in screening for items or tests that might be offensive to different segments of the population (Shepard, 1982). Second, they provide some assurance of due process. That is, the use of panels of experts, particularly panels that include members of minorities or other underrepresented groups, increases the likelihood that the concerns of these groups will be heard and taken into account. There is considerable evidence in research on perceptions of justice that the use of procedures that are apparently fair and reasonable increases the acceptability of the outcomes of those procedures (Folger & Greenberg, 1985). As Cronbach (1988) points out, a test that is technically excellent, but unacceptable to users, is worthless as an aid in making practical decisions. Practices such as the review of tests and test items by members of underrepresented groups may increase the acceptability of tests to those groups and to society in general.

CULTURE-REDUCED TESTING

The most common definition of cultural bias refers to "differences in the extent to which the child being tested has had the opportunity to know and become familiar with the specific subject matter or specific processes required by the test item" (Eells et al., 1951,

p. 58). For example, it is often assumed that white middle-class children have greater exposure to the cultural activities, such as symphony concerts or reading of classic literature, than do minority children, and that questions such as, "What is an oboe?" or "Who wrote *Crime and Punishment?*" will therefore be culturally biased against minorities. Even clearer examples of apparent cultural bias are provided by items in which the "correct" answer may vary from culture to culture. The Wechsler Intelligence Scale for Children–Revised (WISC-R) and the Stanford-Binet include questions such as, "What should you do if a younger child hits you"; in some cultures, the "correct" answer may be different from the answer one would expect from an intelligent, white middle-class child.

Test items that are highly academic in nature are often judged to be culturally biased. The underlying assumption in this assessment is that the school environment is an integral part of the white, middle-class culture. The curriculum planners, the teachers, the textbook authors, and the administrators of school systems are generally white, and the academic environment is assumed to be more foreign to the culture of many minorities—particularly to those living in the ghetto—than it is to whites. As a result, items that deal primarily with academic knowledge are likely to be judged culturally biased against minorities. Finally, verbal items are more likely to be regarded as biased than nonverbal items. The rationale here is that verbal items are likely to be presented in standard English, which more closely resembles the everyday language of middle-class whites than that of many minorities, particularly those in lower socioeconomic levels of society.

A composite picture emerges of a test that is likely to show (apparent) cultural bias. A test made up of items that deal with objects or events peculiar to the white, middle-class experience, that are interpreted differently by people from different subcultures, that tap academic as opposed to practical knowledge, or that are primarily verbal in nature may be regarded as culturally biased against minorities. By implication, a test that deals with universal symbols or objects and that is primarily nonverbal rather than verbal is less likely to be judged as culturally biased.

Before describing several tests designed or used to reduce apparent cultural bias, we must first discuss terminology. Cattell (1940) was among the first to develop what was referred to as a "culture-free" intelligence test. His choice of terms was in many ways unfortunate, since it is difficult to imagine any test in which culture has no effect whatsoever. Learned behavior is, by definition, a function of culture, and it therefore seems pointless to refer to any test as completely "culture-free." It is somewhat more accurate to describe many tests aimed at eliminating apparent cultural bias as "culture-fair," a term used by Cattell himself in the Culture Fair Intelligence Test. The problem with the term "culture-fair" is that there is often disagreement regarding the "fairness" of specific items for members of different cultures and subcultures, and the test developer may not be the best judge of what is fair. The same argument can be made, of course, in reference to judgments about the degree of cultural bias shown in test items, since these judgments are often subjective rather than data based (Jensen, 1980).

Rather than labeling a test "culture-free" or "culture-fair," it is more productive to locate the test on a continuum that ranges from heavily "culture-loaded" to highly "culture-reduced." A culture-loaded test is one that deals with objects, situations, beliefs, or lore peculiar to one particular culture or subculture. A culture-reduced test is one that deals with objects, information, or symbols that are universal, in the sense that members of any of the cultures or subcultures being tested would have equal familiarity and experience with the content and the demands of the test items. Some characteristics of tests that appear to be culture-loaded and culture-reduced are presented in Table 15-4.

Intelligence tests vary considerably in their apparent cultural loading. Perhaps the most highly culture-loaded test that purports to measure intelligence is the Black Intelligence Test of Cultural Homogeneity, or the BITCH (Williams, 1972). This test was developed in part to demonstrate the insidious effects of culture loading. The BITCH is basically a vocabulary test that measures knowledge of black ghetto slang and is made up of items similar to the following (the correct answers are starred):[6]

1. Running a game
   a. writing a bad check
   b. looking at something
   c. directing a contest
   d. getting what one wants*
2. Cop an attitude
   a. leave
   b. become angry*
   c. sit down
   d. protect the neighborhood

TABLE 15-4 SOME CHARACTERISTICS OF CULTURE-LOADED AND CULTURE-REDUCED TESTS

Culture loaded	Culture reduced
Paper-and-pencil tests	Performance test
Reading required	Purely pictorial
Written response	Oral response
Speed tests	Power tests
Verbal content	Nonverbal content
Recall of past-learned information	Solving novel problems

Source: Adapted from Jensen, 1980, p. 637.

The BITCH, by design, represents an extreme example of culture loading. An examination of this test therefore helps to clarify several of the issues in the debate on culture-loaded tests. First, this test convincingly demonstrates that it is possible to produce sizable differences in test scores by culturally loading the test. Blacks tend to receive considerably higher scores on the BITCH than do whites (Matarazzo & Weins, 1977), and test reviewers have suggested that middle-class whites might gain considerable insight into the debate on culture loading by taking a test such as the BITCH, which is biased in favor of a subculture. Second, it is clear that the type of intentional culture loading employed in the construction of the BITCH is *not* representative of intelligence tests in general. There are a number of clear differences between standard intelligence

[6]Reprinted from *Psychology Today,* May 1974, p. 101.

tests and this particular culturally loaded test. Taken together, these differences suggest that the BITCH is not merely a mirror-image of tests like the WAIS or the SAT and that whatever cultural bias operates in the latter tests does so in a much more subtle manner than in an obviously culture-loaded test such as the BITCH.

The clearest difference between the BITCH and standard intelligence tests lies in the type of items included in the different tests. The BITCH is made up exclusively of items measuring knowledge of a vocabulary employed in a specific subculture, and it does not contain any items that call for the *active* processing of information (e.g., problem-solving tasks). Most tests of general mental ability are made up of items that tap a variety of cognitive functions, both those involving information retrieval (e.g., vocabulary tests) and those involving active information processing. There appears to be little or no evidence that the BITCH provides a valid measure of the intelligence of blacks or whites (Cronbach, 1978; Jensen, 1980; Matarazzo & Weins, 1977).

The conclusion we reach when examining the BITCH is that the *blatant* cultural bias built into this particular test probably does not exist in standard intelligence tests. It is possible, however, that subtler forms of culture loading exist in many of the widely used intelligence tests, and it is this possibility that has contributed to widespread interest in developing culture-reduced tests of intelligence.

Performance Tests and Quantitative Tests

Although rarely developed for the specific purpose of culture-reduced testing, performance scales and quantitative subtests are standard features of many intelligence tests. For example, the Stanford-Binet includes a variety of nonverbal and performance subtests. The Wechsler Adult Intelligence Scale, the WISC, and the Wechsler Preschool and Primary Scale of Intelligence all contain performance scales as well as verbal scales. Both the GRE and the SAT contain quantitative (mathematical) as well as verbal sections, and the GRE also includes an analytic section. While none of these performance or quantitative tests necessarily meets *all* the requirements suggested by various authors for achieving a truly culture-reduced test, these tests all seem to be closer to the culturally reduced than to the culturally loaded end of the continuum.

Many proponents of culture-reduced tests suggest that differences in the test scores obtained by minority and white examinees are due largely to the fact that IQ tests are culturally loaded in favor of whites. This position implies that differences between minority and white test score means should be smaller on performance and quantitative tests, which appear to be culture-reduced, than on verbal tests, which appear to be culture-loaded. This hypothesis has been extensively researched but to date has received little empirical support.

Several large-scale studies clearly indicate that the difference between white and minority test score means is *at least* as large for nonverbal tests of intelligence (performance tests as well as quantitative tests) as it is for verbal tests of intelligence. For example the Coleman report, *Equality of Educational Opportunity* (Coleman et al., 1966), provides test data from over 600,000 school children in over 4,000 schools. This report shows that the differences between white and black mean IQs are comparable for verbal and nonverbal IQ tests, and in fact that these differences are generally a bit larger for nonverbal than for verbal tests. McGurk's (1975) review of 25 studies that compare verbal and performance test scores (mostly WISC, WAIS, or Wechsler-Bellevue scores) of whites and blacks reached a similar conclusion: Black-white differences in performance IQs are generally equal to or larger than differences in verbal IQs.

In response to the Association of Black Psychologists' call for a moratorium on intelligence testing, the Scientific Affairs Board of the American Psychological Association appointed a group of experts to investigate the issue of test bias. Their report included the conclusion that minority/white score differences on nonverbal tests were comparable to differences in scores on verbal intelligence tests, and that these differences were "quite general and not narrowly restricted to specific skills involving standard English" (Cleary, Humphreys, Kendrick & Wesman, 1975, p. 16). The fact that minority/white test score differences are equally large for verbal and nonverbal intelligence tests suggests that the cultural-bias hypothesis in its simplest form is incorrect. There can be little doubt that cultural and subcultural differences affect all behavior, including test behavior, and it seems plausible that some tests may be unfairly easier for some people than for others. However, it appears that test score differences are not the result of the predominantly verbal nature of IQ tests, nor are they a reflection of knowledge or understanding of a small set of culturally specific facts. Hence, although cultural bias probably does exist, it is not a simple phenomenon that lends itself to a simple solution.

Raven's Progressive Matrices

Raven's Progressive Matrices, probably the most widely used culture-reduced tests, have had a long and distinguished history. Factor analyses carried out in Spearman's laboratory in the 1930s suggested that tests made up of simple pictorial analogies showed high correlations with a number of other intelligence tests and, more important, showed high loadings on Spearman's g.

Raven's Progressive Matrices are made up of a series of multiple-choice items, all of which follow the same basic principle. Each item represents a perceptual analogy in the form of a matrix. There is some valid relationship that connects items in each row in the matrix, and there is also some valid relationship that connects items in each column of the matrix. Each matrix is presented in such a way that a piece of the matrix, located in the lower right-hand corner, is missing. The subject must choose from among six or eight alternatives the piece that best completes each matrix. An example of a Progressive Matrix item is presented in Figure 15-4.

There are three forms of Raven's Progressive Matrices. The most widely used form, the Standard Progressive Matrices, consists of 60 matrices grouped into five sets. Each of the five sets involves 12 matrices whose solutions involve similar principles, but which vary in difficulty. The principles involved in solving the five sets of matrices include perceptual discrimination, rotation, and permutations of patterns. The first few items in each set are comparatively easy, but the latter matrices may involve very subtle and complex relationships.

The Standard Progressive Matrices are appropriate both for children above 5 years of age and adults; because of the low floor and fairly high ceiling of this test, the Standard Matrices are also appropriate for most ability levels. For younger children (ages 4 to 10), and for somewhat older children and adults who show signs of retardation, the Coloured Progressive Matrices seem to be more appropriate. This test consists of three sets of 12

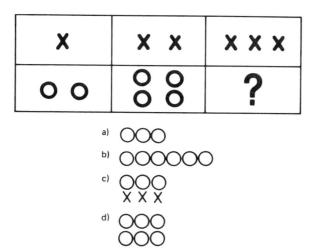

Figure 15-4 Type of Item Included in Raven's Progressive Matrices

matrices that employ color and are considerably less difficult than those that make up the Standard Progressive Matrices.

Finally, the Advanced Progressive Matrices are appropriate for intellectually advanced subjects who find the Standard Matrices too easy. The Advanced Matrices are made up of three sets of 12 matrices, many of which involve extremely subtle principles in their solutions. The test effectively discriminates among those who receive extremely high scores on the Standard Progressive Matrices.

Evaluation of Raven's Progressive Matrices.   One of the principal attractions of this series of tests is its combination of factorial purity, together with its minimal culture loading. A number of factor analyses of Raven's Progressive Matrices suggest that the only variable that is reliably measured by the test is Spearman's *g*; there is little evidence that spatial visualization or perceptual abilities significantly affect test scores. The test appears to measure abstract reasoning ability independently of one's factual knowledge or prior experience. Thus, the test appears to be unique in following Spearman's principles for measuring *g* (induction of relations, indifference of indicators), while at the same time meeting many of the desired characteristics of a culture-reduced test (simple instructions, abstract nonverbal item content, independence from previously learned material).

Scores on the Progressive Matrices are typically reliable (reliabilities generally range from .70 to .90) and show evidence of both construct and criterion-related validity. Progressive Matrices scores generally show correlations of between .50 and .75 with other intelligence tests, and correlations closer to .80 are sometimes reported (Burke, 1972). Progressive Matrices scores are also correlated with a variety of measures of academic success, although the validities tend to be lower than those typically found with more standard intelligence tests. Finally, the Progressive Matrices show some evidence of content validity.

At first examination, the Progressive Matrices appear to violate our suggestion in Chapter 12 that an intelligence test should comprise a variety of item types. Although all the items on each of these tests are in matrix format, it seems clear that the test in fact samples a wide variety of problem types by varying the principles that govern each matrix. Thus, a person must successfully solve a considerable variety of logical inference problems in order to obtain a high score on the test. The Progressive Matrices provide an excellent demonstration of the plausibility of measuring Spearman's *g* with a culture-reduced test.

Comparisons of the scores of whites and minorities on Raven's Progressive Matrices provide further evidence that the cultural bias hypothesis, in its simplest form, is incorrect. The Progressive Matrices are clearly culture-reduced tests, yet comparisons between test scores of whites and minorities show that the average score of white examinees is consistently higher than the mean score obtained by minorities. Furthermore, the difference between white and minority test score means is typically as large for the Progressive Matrices as for standard (culture-loaded) intelligence tests (Jensen, 1974; Veroff, McClelland & Marquis, 1971).

Adaptive Behavior Inventories

Although most general intelligence tests sample a broad array of intellectually challenging problems, there is considerable justification for the complaint that the domain sampled by these tests is nevertheless too narrow to provide an adequate measure of how well a person is able to function in society. In most day-to-day situations, it might be very difficult to detect any difference between the behavior of someone with an IQ of 93 and that of another person with an IQ of 108. A low IQ score *may* suggest poor performance in a variety of scholastic or intellectual endeavors, but it does not necessarily indicate an inability to cope with the normal demands of day-to-day life. Some people with high IQs function poorly in society, and many people with low IQs function well.

Adaptive behavior inventories represent an attempt to develop broad measures of a person's effectiveness in coping with the normal demands of day-to-day life. These inventories typically represent standardized interviews with persons having frequent contact with the subject (e.g., parents, teachers, siblings), and are aimed at assessing the effectiveness of the subject's reactions to the natural or social demands of his or her environment. These inventories are particularly useful in the diagnosis of mental retardation (Kaufman, 1979). The use of IQ scores as the *sole* criterion for classifying children as mentally retarded is clearly inappropriate, particularly in the case of minority children. Some children with low IQ scores have difficulties with every phase of their lives, whereas others might show deficits in school settings only. Inventories such as the American Association for Mental Deficiency's *Adaptive Behavior Scale* (Lambert, Windmiller, Cole & Figueroa, 1975) help to provide a broader base for diagnosis by including a great deal of information about the subject's social competence.

Mercer (1973, 1978) has been concerned with the inappropriate labelling of the mentally retarded, particularly among minorities, on the basis of IQ tests, and has developed several adaptive behavior inventories to provide more complete assessments of competence in dealing with one's environment. For example, the inventory described in Mercer (1973) consisted mainly of a household interview, usually with a parent, covering a variety of items from the Vineland Social Maturity Scale (Doll, 1965) and the Gesell Developmental Scales (Gesell, 1948a, 1948b, 1956), together with several original items. Examples of items included in the Mercer inventory are presented in Table 15-5.

As the table illustrates, the domain sampled in this test is much broader and less

TABLE 15-5   SAMPLE ITEMS FROM MERCER (1973) INVENTORY

Age in months

7–9	Does _____ recognize a stranger?
13–15	Does _____ walk when only one hand is held?
22–24	Does _____ usually unwrap or peel candy, gum, bananas before eating them?
36–47	Does _____ button clothing without help?
49–59	Can _____ turn pages one at a time?

Age in years

7	Does _____ tie shoe laces?
8–9	Does _____ count by two to twenty?
10–11	Does _____ look up telephone numbers and make telephone calls?
14–15	Does _____ usually give vent to rage by words rather than physical violence or crying?
16–49	Does _____ ever travel to nearby towns alone?

academic than the domain sampled by the Stanford-Binet or the WISC. This type of adaptive behavior inventory is not a substitute for a standard intelligence test but represents an invaluable *supplement* to an intelligence-testing program. Standard intelligence tests provide psychometrically refined measures of behavior in response to a particular class of problems that involve reasoning, comprehension, or a broad base of factual knowledge. Adaptive behavior inventories provide a less-refined but broader sample of behavior in response to the types of problems encountered in everyday life.

The System of Multicultural Pluralistic Assessment.   The culmination of Mercer's research on the assessment of children from a variety of subcultures (i.e., black, Hispanic, Anglo) is the System of Multicultural Pluralistic Assessment (SOMPA) (Mercer & Lewis, 1978). The SOMPA represents an assessment package appropriate for children between the ages of 5 and 11 that includes (a) the WISC-R, (b) interviews with parents, (c) individual interviews with the subject, (d) a medical history, (e) sensorimotor and perceptual testing, and (f) the Adaptive Behavior Inventory for Children, which measures adaptive behavior in family and community settings. Socioeconomic background information may be entered into regression equations to transform WISC-R IQ scores into a standard score referred to as an Estimated Learning Potential (ELP). The ELP indicates the level of test performance in comparison with children of similar racial and socioeconomic background; it is designed, not to predict performance in regular public school, but to estimate the extent to which a child might benefit from programs that are appropriate for or tailored to the child's cultural background.

While there are some questions about the value of ELP scores (Kaufman, 1979), there is little doubt that the SOMPA provides a wealth of data that may be useful for corroborating or modifying the interpretation of scores on standard intelligence tests. These data may be particularly critical for classifying children whose academic deficit is noticeable but not debilitating. Inappropriately labelling a child "retarded" could have serious social and emotional consequences (Mercer, 1973). Scores on intelligence tests provide hypotheses regarding the effectiveness with which a child deals with both the academic and nonacademic demands of daily life. A broad-based assessment package such as the SOMPA provides a means to test these hypotheses more thoroughly before diagnosing and labelling the child.

CRITICAL DISCUSSION:
Intelligence and Adaptive Behavior

The problem of what is or is not intelligent behavior has been the focus of a great deal of debate and disagreement in psychology. One way of defining "intelligent behavior" is to say that it is the set of behaviors that allow one to adapt to one's environment. This definition has been adopted by many psychologists, ranging from those critical of standard intelligence tests (Mercer, 1973; Mercer & Lewis, 1978) to information-processing theorists (Sternberg, 1985). Similar definitions are implicit in several models of skill acquisition (Ackerman, 1987) and performance (Murphy, 1989b).

Although defining intelligence in terms of adaptation to one's environment is intuitively appealing, there are serious problems with this definition. In particular, the phrase "adapting to one's environment" can be hopelessly ambiguous. The reason for the ambiguity is that "environment" can be defined at several different levels, and different levels of the environment might imply different "types" of intelligence (Gardner, 1983). For example, a child's environment might be defined in terms of his or her family, neighborhood, playmates, classes, and so forth. At any given point in time, a person may occupy several different environments, and behavior that is adaptive in one environment may not be adaptive in another.

One potential solution to the problem of defining intelligent behavior in terms of multiple environments is to recognize that environments differ greatly in their salience or importance. Thus, intelligent behavior might be defined as behavior that helps a person adapt to his or her most important environment. Unfortunately, it is seldom clear which environment *is* most important. Proponents of standard intelligence tests would probably argue that school represents the single most important environment, at least for children, and that existing tests provide very good measures of adaptation to that environment. Proponents of multicultural assessment (e.g., Mercer & Lewis, 1978) would probably argue for a broader definition. Nevertheless, we see some value in shifting the question from "what is intelligence" to "what environments define intelligent behavior." The latter question helps to focus the debate on *why* intelligence is being measured, rather than on whether one definition or the other is correct.

HERITABILITY, CONSISTENCY, AND MODIFIABILITY OF IQ

Individual differences in many physical characteristics, such as height or hair color, are largely determined by genetic factors. Tall parents tend to have tall sons and daughters, although the offspring may not be quite as tall as the parents.[7] The question of whether genetic factors are in any way responsible for individual differences in general intelligence, and if so to what degree, is central to the current controversy over intelligence and intelligence testing.

Interest in the possible genetic basis of intelligence can be traced back to the earliest

---

[7]This is because of regression to the mean.

days of intelligence testing. Galton's (1869) pioneering work on individual differences was largely motivated by his interest in heredity. One hundred years later the possible influence of genetic factors on intelligence became an issue of heated public debate when Jensen (1969) suggested that scientists must consider the hypothesis that differences between white and minority IQ scores are the result of genetic factors. The outcry was immediate, and the debate over possible genetic factors in intelligence has been intense and bitter ever since.

This section deals with three interlocking issues: heritability, the consistency of IQ, and the modifiability of IQ. Heritability studies attempt to estimate the degree to which both genetic factors and environmental factors contribute to individual differences in intelligence. The mix of genetic and environmental influences will, in turn, affect the degree of consistency and modifiability of IQ. The heritability debate suggests that it is important to both estimate the precise degree of consistency and to understand the way in which IQ may change over one's lifetime. A related issue is the question of whether, and under what conditions, IQ can be systematically modified.

Heritability of IQ

The available evidence makes it clear that both genetic factors (DeFries & Plomin, 1978) and environmental factors (Carroll & Maxwell, 1979) have some impact on individual differences in intelligence. However, neither genetic nor environmental factors by themselves can account for 100 percent of the variation in scores on intelligence tests. The issue, therefore, is not *whether* genetic and environmental factors account for some of the variability in test scores, but *how much* influence each of these factors exerts.

In theory, the total variance in test scores in a single population can be broken down into two components: (a) the variability that is due to all combinations of genetic factors and (b) the variability that is due to all of the various combinations of nongenetic or environmental factors (Li, 1975). Symbolically,

$$\sigma^2_T = \sigma^2_G + \sigma^2_E \qquad [15\text{-}2]$$

where

$$\sigma^2_T = \text{total test score variance}$$
$$\sigma^2_G = \text{variance due to, or explained by, genetic factors}$$
$$\sigma^2_E = \text{variance due to nongenetic or environmental factors}$$

Heritability is defined as the proportion, or the percentage of, the variability in test scores that can be accounted for by genetic factors.[8] Symbolically,

$$h^2 = \sigma^2_G / \sigma^2_T \qquad [15\text{-}3]$$

where

$$h^2 = \text{heritability of the trait being measured by the test}$$

---

[8]The reader may note the similarity between the heritability equations and the basic equations defining reliability, in which observed score variance is broken down into true score and error components.

Geneticists make a distinction between broad and narrow heritability. *Broad heritability* includes the effects of *all* genetic factors, including gene dominance and assortive mating (the fact that people do not marry at random, but tend to marry others with some similar genetic characteristics). Narrow heritability refers to the proportion of additive (nondominant) genetic variance under conditions of random mating (Jensen, 1975). Broad heritability estimates, which are debated by psychologists, can be interpreted as the squared correlation between genotypes (sum total of all genetic factors) and test scores in a specific population.

The basic data used in estimating heritability comes from comparisons of intelligence test scores obtained by related and unrelated persons. Members of the same family tend to have more similar IQs than members of different families who are raised in similar environments. Furthermore, the similarity between test scores increases as genetic similarity increases; brothers have more similar scores on intelligence tests than do cousins. The most illuminating data comes from studies of twins. Identical (monozygotic) twins have an identical genetic inheritance, whereas fraternal (dizygotic) twins are no more similar genetically than siblings who were born at different times. The intelligence scores of identical twins are highly correlated—and this correlation remains high even when the twins are raised apart—whereas the correlation between the IQs of fraternal twins is lower than that of identical twins.

Several complexities enter into the estimation of heritability. First, siblings or twins are not merely genetically similar; they share very similar environments. At least some of the correlation between the IQs of family members *must* be due to their similar upbringing and experience. Second, in studies where twins or siblings are raised apart, it still is likely that related persons will experience more similar environments than unrelated persons picked at random. It is unlikely that one monozygotic twin will be adopted by a white, middle-class family and that the other will be adopted by a family of poor, inner-city blacks. At an even subtler level, it has been shown that a person's appearance affects the reactions of others. As a result, identical twins may experience similar social environments solely as a result of their nearly identical appearance.

Finally, the determination of genetic similarity is not always simple. In particular, it is inappropriate to assume that all apparently unrelated persons are equally dissimilar in terms of genetic makeup. Unrelated persons are similar with respect to some genetic factors and dissimilar with respect to others. To complicate matters further, some genes or combinations of genes may be relevant to intelligence, whereas others may be completely irrelevant.

Several methods have been proposed for estimating the heritability of intelligence (Jensen, 1972, 1975; Li, 1975; Loehlin, Lindzey & Spuhler, 1975). Many of these methods are statistically complex, and involve a variety of assumptions about the correlation between genetic effects and environmental effects. There is considerable variability in the size of heritability estimates, but the body of available evidence suggests that the broad heritability of intelligence is between .3 and .5 for adults, and probably larger for children (Cronbach, 1975; Jensen, 1975, 1980; Plomin & Rende, 1991; Vandenberg & Vogler, 1985). Heritability estimates are higher for tests that measure general, as opposed to specific, abilities (Jensen, 1986). In other words, heritability studies suggest that *in the population,* between 30 and 50 percent of the variability in adult intelligence test scores might be explained by genetic factors. This does not mean that 50 percent of an *individual's* intelligence is genetic. In fact, heritability studies do not attempt to estimate the causes of an individual's intelligence; and even when heritability is very high in the population, genetic factors provide only a rough prediction of an individual's IQ.

A table in Jensen (1980, p. 245), which presents confidence intervals for estimating individual genotypic values, is particularly illuminating. If heritability is equal to 50 percent, individuals with identical genetic backgrounds might differ by as much as 29 IQ points without exceeding the bounds of chance (95 percent confidence interval). Even with a heritability of 75 percent, genetically identical individuals might be expected to differ by as much as 25 IQ points.

The most widespread error in interpreting heritability studies is the assumption that high heritability means that IQ is fixed at birth and is not modifiable. Heritability indicates the degree to which, *under present conditions,* genetic factors and environmental factors contribute to individual differences in intelligence; it says nothing about the relative importance of genetic factors if the environment were changed in some important way. Therefore, a heritability of 100 percent does not indicate that the trait being measured is fixed and immutable, but that under present conditions, environmental factors do not contribute to individual differences. For example, height has a heritability coefficient of nearly 1.00, yet there is considerable evidence of massive changes in height over the years (Angoff, 1988; Crow, 1969). This is attributable to several changes in the environment, including improved diet and better medical care. Similarly, changes in environment could have a substantial effect on intelligence regardless of the size of the heritability coefficient for intelligence. Viewed in this light, the heritability index is not a measure of the genetic nature of intelligence but, rather, is an index to which sociocultural conditions, as they presently exist, contribute to individual differences in intelligence (Cronbach, 1975; Li, 1975).

To understand the true nature of heritability ratios, one need only consider what would happen if everyone were raised in identical environments. If the environment were strictly controlled, then the only remaining source of variability would be genetic, and eventually 100 percent of the variability in test scores would be explained by genetic factors. Similarly, it might be possible to put individuals in environments that are so dissimilar that genetic differences would have a comparatively small effect on their behavior. Therefore, heritability studies reflect the influence of both genetic and environmental variations.

The idea that genetic factors contribute to intelligence is no longer controversial (Plomin & Rende, 1991), although controversies still rage over the extent of the genetic contribution and its implications. Recent research suggests that genetic factors are also important determinants of personality, psychopathology (e.g., schizophrenia, affective disorders, autism), alcoholism, temperament, and even attitudes (e.g., job satisfaction) (Bouchard, Lykken, McGue, Segal et al., 1990; Plomin & Rende, 1991; Tellegen, Lykken, Bouchard, Wilcox et al., 1988). Recent advances in behavioral genetics research hold significant promise for increasing our understanding of how *both* genetic and environmental factors affect intelligence, personality, and behavior.

Consistency of IQ

As noted in the previous section, the fact that intelligence shows a fairly high degree of heritability does not indicate that an individual's intelligence is a fixed, immutable quantity. If we accept the conclusion that intelligence may be modifiable, several questions emerge. First, under normal conditions, are intelligence test scores stable or do test scores change dramatically over the course of a person's life? Second, under what conditions might we expect systematic changes in intelligence? This section deals with the first of these questions.

Longitudinal and cross-sectional studies suggest a substantial period of stability in IQs, ranging from early childhood to fairly late adulthood. For example, Rees and Palmer (1970) assessed children at ages 6, 12, and 17 and showed correlations ranging from .75 to .83 between intelligence test scores at these three ages. Furthermore, fewer than 23 percent of the children tested showed a *maximum* change of greater than 20 points when their lowest recorded IQ was compared with their highest recorded IQ obtained in three testings; over 58 percent showed maximum changes of 15 points or less. Large-scale longitudinal studies by Harnquist (1968), Hopkins and Bracht (1975), and Magnusson and Backteman (1978) showed IQ correlations ranging from .73 to .78 over age intervals of 13–18 years, 10–16 years, and 10–15 years, respectively. A number of longitudinal and cross-sectional studies combine to show that intelligence scores are comparably stable between age 18 and middle adulthood (Matarazzo, 1972; Wechsler, 1958).

Intelligence scores show much less stability in very early childhood and in late adulthood. Lewis (1973) has shown that there is little or no consistency in test performance in the first two years of life and concludes that infant intelligence is neither stable nor measurable. The stability in test scores in later life has been researched much more widely, and there is some evidence to suggest a systematic change in IQ with age. Normative data from the WAIS show that full-scale IQ scores are at their highest around age 20–35, then decline steadily until age 60, and finally decline precipitously past age 60. This pattern is shown in Figure 15-5.

At first examination, the figure suggests that past age 35 or so, a person's intelligence declines steadily. There are, however, several problems with this interpretation. First, longitudinal studies, in which the same individuals are measured at a number of different ages, yield consistently different results than do cross-sectional studies, in which individuals of different ages are all tested at the same time (Nesselroade & Reese, 1973; Schaie & LaBouvie-Vief, 1974; Schaie & Strother, 1968). Whereas cross-sectional studies typically show steady and sizable declines in IQ scores from middle to late adulthood,

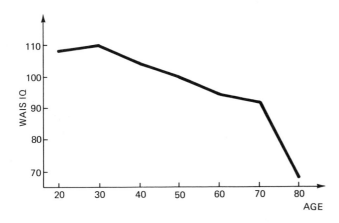

Figure 15-5 Average WAIS IQ by Age

Source: Adapted from Doppelt & Wallace, 1966, p. 323

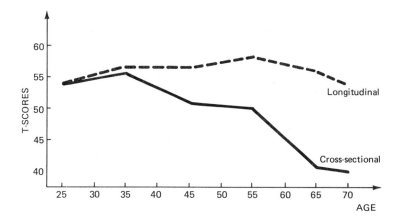

Figure 15-6 Trends in Test Scores from Cross-Sectional and Longitudinal Studies

Source: Adapted from Schaie & Strother, 1968, p. 675

longitudinal studies typically show very modest declines that begin much later in life. This pattern is illustrated in Figure 15-6.

The interpretation suggested by Schaie and LaBouvie-Vief (1974) is that the apparent decline in IQ shown in cross-sectional studies reflects generational or cohort differences rather than declines in individual intelligence over time. IQs provide relative rather than absolute measures of intelligence, and in comparison with an increasingly younger population that is tested during periods of rapid technological and cultural change, the *relative* performance of older examinees may decline in the absence of any absolute change in performance. In other words, if the normative group becomes increasingly smarter and better educated, the relative performance of *any* particular individual is likely to decline.

Although there are methodological problems in interpreting apparent cross-sectional declines in intelligence, there are also difficulties in longitudinal studies (Flynn, 1984; Nesselroade & Reese, 1973). One very real problem is that of (literal) subject mortality. The individuals who remain in a study beyond age 70 may differ systematically from those who drop out at the early stages. Thus, it is not clear whether longitudinal results are representative of the population in general. Second, it is not always possible to use identical or even comparable tests at different points in time (Flynn, 1984).

Taking methodological problems into account, however, the literature on age-related declines in intelligence suggests that the real decline in general intelligence with age is gradual in nature and starts later in life than was previously assumed (Birren & Schaie, 1977; Schaie, 1974). Intelligence appears to be relatively stable well past age 60, and it may not show noticeable declines until several years later. Thus, although scores on intelligence tests do not describe a fixed aspect of an individual's makeup, there is considerable evidence for the consistency of IQ over a large portion of the life span of typical individuals.

Modifiability of IQ

The disparity between the IQs of white, middle-class children and those of minorities has been a source of deep concern for over 20 years. In the 1960s several large-scale remedial programs to increase the IQ scores of minority children were suggested. Most notable was Project Head Start, which is featured in the Critical Discussion at the end of this chapter. The question we consider here is whether it is possible to change (increase) a person's IQ. We think that there is evidence that general cognitive abilities *can* be significantly increased, although it appears clear that changes cannot be expected as the result of short, simple, or faddish interventions.

Programs that appear to have met with success in increasing participants' cognitive abilities or basic academic skills share several features in common. First and foremost is the careful attention paid to the psychology of learning. Early programs, including many of the pilot programs included in the early years of Project Head Start, often featured untested strategies for improving basic skills that had little scientific or experiential basis. The successful programs described in Bloom (1976) and Hunt (1975) feature close attention to the processes involved in solving various problems, along with careful consideration of principles of learning and principles of reinforcement. A closely allied feature of successful programs is the careful analysis of the tasks that must be performed in the process of analyzing and solving problems (Whimbey, 1980). These programs are also likely to feature multiple, realistic criteria rather than vague and perhaps unattainable goals. The lack of realistic goals was a principal problem with some intervention programs. It was overly optimistic to assume that a few weeks of preschool instruction, which varied considerably from location to location, would result in dramatic increases in a wide range of ability and achievement measures. Finally, successful programs are likely to consider both the cognitive and the affective prerequisites to successful compensatory learning (Bloom, 1976). Changes in basic cognitive skills do not come about strictly as a result of learning particular facts, but rather may involve changing attitudes and habits as well as adapting individuals to standard learning environments.

In principle, IQ appears to be modifiable. It is clearly not a simple matter to dramatically raise IQ scores on any large-scale, long-term basis. However, a score on an intelligence test is not a fixed indicator of inborn capacity but, rather, is a sample of present behavior. Problem-solving skills can be learned, and other aspects of intelligent behavior can be acquired and reinforced, given the appropriate social environment. There probably are some genetic limitations on the degree to which IQ could be changed through changes in the environment; it is unlikely that everyone could be a genius, no matter how favorable the environment. Nevertheless, most IQ differences that are of concern are those that are well within the normal range (in the statistical sense), and these might be systematically modified by optimal structuring of the learning environment.

The most convincing evidence of the modifiability of IQ comes from studies of long-term changes in average scores on intelligence tests. For example, Flynn (1984) documented massive IQ gains in the United States over the period 1932–1978; some of these changes had been obscured in previous research by inconsistencies in the norming of different tests. Similarly, Humphreys (1989) reported evidence of substantial increases in IQ for the periods 1917–1942 and 1942–1960. In an extensive review of studies from 14 nations, Flynn (1987) documented increases of 5 to 25 points in IQ (on an IQ scale with a mean of 100 and a standard deviation of 15) in a single generation. The exact causes of these changes are difficult to identify but undoubtedly include improvements in the environment (e.g., better nutrition) as well as improvements in education. The important point is that it is possible to observe very large changes in IQ for a group or nation over a relatively short period. Therefore, you cannot assume that current differences in ability levels of different groups in the population are fixed and permanent.

CRITICAL DISCUSSION:
Project Head Start

In the 1960s the federal government embarked on a wide-ranging War on Poverty. One of the goals of this set of programs was to reduce the gap between educational opportunities afforded affluent and poor (mainly minority) Americans (Zigler & Valentine, 1980). Project Head Start represented one part of this effort.

Project Head Start refers to a number of different educational interventions designed to prepare poor and minority children to compete more effectively in school. Although the specifics of the different programs varied from location to location and have changed significantly over the years, the general theme tying them together was an effort to reach preschool children and to equip them with the knowledge, skills, abilities, and orientation necessary to perform well in school. It was thought that this program would allow educators to catch and remedy problems early, and that as a result the children who participated would perform at a level more similar to that attained by their more affluent peers.

Tests of general intelligence served as the main criterion in early evaluations of Head Start programs (Boehm, 1985). Many of these programs did result in gains in IQ of three to four points that persisted up to four years after participation in the program, but there was little evidence of long-term gains sufficiently large to make any difference in the children's school performance (Bouchard & Segal, 1985; Payne, Mercer, Payne & Davinson, 1973). The apparent failure of Project Head Start in its early years, together with other data, led to Jensen's (1969) controversial conclusion that "compensatory education has failed" (p. 2).

The initial disappointment with Project Head Start does not, in fact, imply that IQ cannot be changed. First, IQ data collected over different time spans and from different tests can be very difficult to interpret (Flynn, 1984); hence, it is not clear whether all Head Start programs really failed. Second, the actual content of Head Start programs varied considerably from site to site, making an evaluation of the project as a whole suspect. Third, the project was, in its early years, chronically underfunded, and it was subject to meddling by well-intentioned but uninformed legislators and administrators.

Over the years, evaluations of the potential contributions of Project Head Start have changed dramatically, to the point that it is one of the few remnants from the War on Poverty that is still evaluated positively by both conservatives and liberals. In part this is due to improvements in the program, and in part it is due to the adoption of more realistic goals; the programs under Head Start are now more likely to be evaluated in terms of how well they prepare children for future success in school than in terms of their impact on overall IQ.

SUMMARY

There are persistent differences in the average scores received by several racial and ethnic groups on standardized tests of mental ability; the reasons for these differences, their meaning, and the strategies for reducing these differences have been the focus of substantial research and discussion. To understand this research, it is first necessary to distinguish between bias and fairness. Bias is a statistical characteristic of test scores. Systematic differences in test scores, particularly in the regressions between test scores and important criteria, indicate that a test is biased. The assessment of fairness requires a value judgment in which the outcomes of tests are compared to the outcomes that most closely reflect a person's values and preferences. There is no necessary connection between bias and fairness; a biased test can be used fairly, and an unbiased test can be the source of obvious unfairness.

A variety of techniques for evaluating bias in measurement and bias in prediction were discussed. On the whole, well-developed tests rarely show bias in measurement. The bias in prediction that these tests show tends to be small, and often the bias is in the opposite direction than that suggested by critics of tests. Although standardized tests might not be seriously biased, the differences in test scores obtained by different groups are often large enough to motivate the search for alternative test types. Attempts to use nonverbal tests to reduce differences in test scores have not been successful, and increasing attention has been devoted to measures of adaptive behaviors.

Research on the heritability and consistency of IQ leads to several general conclusions. First, there appears to be a substantial genetic component to intelligence (and probably to several facets of personality). Second, IQ shows a high degree of consistency, such that scores obtained relatively early in life might provide a reasonable approximation of intelligence levels throughout one's lifetime. However, this does not mean that it is impossible to modify intelligence. Statements about heritability and stability tell us as much about the environment as about genetics, and large changes in the environment can lead to large changes in such highly heritable and stable traits as height and body type. The same is probably true for intelligence.

CHAPTER 16

TESTS AND EDUCATIONAL DECISIONS

In the first part of this book, we examined important characteristics of all tests, and reviewed the basic psychometric properties that are essential in the development of psychological tests. In the second section of the book, we looked at how those principles of psychological measurement are applied by psychologists. Specifically, we surveyed various types of psychological attributes that are typically measured, namely, aptitudes, interests, and personality traits. We examined in some depth the assessment of both general ability and special aptitude. We concluded with a discussion of test bias and offered a few suggestions to ensure the fairness of testing. Now, in this final section of the book, we turn our attention to specific applications of psychological testing. We examine some of the questions that often are faced in applied situations and see how tests are used to make various clinical decisions.

This section is divided into three units corresponding to the specific types of settings that rely most heavily on psychological testing. Chapters 16 and 17 form a unit on the use of psychological measurement in educational settings. The focus is on some of the decision-making questions faced in educational environments and on some of the major testing instruments available to meet those needs. Chapters 18 and 19 deal with the role of psychological testing in business and industrial settings. In these chapters, the discussion focuses on how specific job performance and selection questions are addressed through the use of psychological testing. Chapters 20, 21, and 22 focus on personality testing and diagnostic testing, with specific reference to how such tests are used in clinical assessment.

As we begin this third section, we focus on how ability and interest tests are used in making educational decisions both at the individual and the institutional levels. The types of decisions made at each of these levels often demand different kinds of information, however. At the college and university level, administrators need information about the academic abilities of prospective students in order to make appropriate admissions decisions. They are interested in selecting those students who have the ability to succeed and eliminating those who are likely to fail. At the primary and secondary school levels, educators are usually more interested in identifying those students who have special educational needs. At this level, standardized tests are used to identify both those who are especially intellectually gifted and those who may be in need of specific remedial help. Tests are also used in making decisions about how to best group students within a school system so that the instructional level chosen will be appropriate for their developmental level.

While institutions are usually concerned with admissions and selection decisions, individuals want information about their interests, strengths, and weaknesses to help them plan for their educational and vocational futures. Examiners are interested in knowing what kinds of skills they possess, what they are capable of learning, and what course of study and type of work they should pursue.

In this chapter we discuss how tests are used in making the decisions that confront both individuals and institutions. We begin by examining the central role testing plays in making institutional decisions. Next, we focus on how tests are used by individuals in making decisions about their own educational goals. Finally, we discuss the impact of psychological testing on both the individual and society as it relates to career planning and the effective use of human resources.

APPLICATIONS IN INSTITUTIONAL DECISION MAKING

Admissions Decisions

Since the turn of the century, colleges and universities have been interested in finding cost-effective, efficient ways of selecting students. This institutional need has given rise to the development and, eventually, large-scale implementation of aptitude testing programs designed to provide post-secondary schools with information about how successful students are likely to be if admitted to various programs of study. These programs rely on the premise that scholastic aptitude tests can effectively measure those abilities that are required to learn the types of materials usually encountered in academic courses.

These testing programs have not been without their critics, however. Issues have been raised about their possible bias in favor of middle-class, white students, their inability to predict academic performance accurately, the overreliance placed on such tests in making academic decisions, and the alleged ease with which test scores can be inflated through coaching. Nevertheless, many admissions decisions are based, at least in part, on such standardized aptitude tests. Consequently, few prospective students entering post-secondary educational programs escape coming into contact with these assessment instruments. Therefore, we will examine how such tests are used in making institutional decisions and how efficient they are in the process.

How are aptitude tests like the American College Test (ACT), Scholastic Aptitude

Test (SAT), and Graduate Record Examination (GRE) actually used by institutions? The answer varies with the school in question. Some institutions rely more heavily on test scores than others. Typically, however, test scores are combined with data on past academic performance in a regression equation statistically designed to yield the highest possible predictive equation for potential academic success. The rationale for this approach has been that past academic history alone does not always accurately reflect the actual potential of the individual, since extraneous factors such as family difficulties, social problems, health concerns, or motivational deficits may be operative in lowering performance levels.

Should institutions be using scholastic aptitude tests as aids in the admissions process? Do they really provide any critical data? How well do they work? These are the issues that we will now discuss by examining some of the criticisms levelled against admissions tests and their use and by evaluating the impact of these tests on higher education.

Retaking Scholastic Aptitude Tests.   Because of the perceived importance of aptitude tests in the selection process, students have often retested in an effort to improve their scores. Whether they are likely to show significant score gains has been a matter of some controversy (ACT, 1988; College Entrance Examination Board, 1987). Data reported by the College Entrance Examination Board on SAT retesting (College Entrance Examination Board, 1987) indicated that on the average, students who tested as juniors and again as seniors showed gains on their verbal and math scores of only 19 and 20 points, respectively. Given the standard error of measurement on the SAT, such gains are of questionable interpretable value. In only about 5 percent of the retest cases did score gains approach the magnitude of 100 points or more.

Similarly, research conducted by Wilson (1987) on the long-term stability of GRE scores tends to support the notion that students show only modest increases in their test scores as a result of retest. He studied 3,614 test takers who took the GRE on two occasions more than five years apart. His results revealed gains of approximately 40 points on the verbal section and 17 points on the math portion of the test.

There are instances when substantial score gains are more likely to occur, however. Information provided by ACT (1988) suggests that students who experienced difficulty with test directions on the day of the test, were highly anxious and unable to concentrate, were under considerable emotional stress, or were physically ill when they initially tested will probably achieve a somewhat lower score than they deserve. Likewise, students who have had limited or no experience taking standardized multiple-choice tests may perform substantially below their capacity because of their inability to employ successful test-taking strategies. Under such circumstances, retesting may substantially improve scores.

Admission of the educationally disadvantaged.   Scholastic aptitude tests have been severely criticized for being biased toward white, middle-class students. Critics point to the substantial body of research that shows that educationally disadvantaged students, often from minority groups, typically do not perform as well on aptitude tests as their white peers. They argue that it is this differential in performance that leads to underrepresentation of minorities in colleges, graduate programs, and professional schools.

On the other hand, proponents of scholastic aptitude testing have countered with research showing that although educationally disadvantaged students do score lower on such tests than their peers, they also achieve lower grades in school. They contend that scholastic aptitude tests substantially predict actual school performance just as they were designed to do. The educational deficits reflected in lower test scores are assumed to be the same ones that are related to poorer performance in the actual school setting. Some researchers (e.g., Manning, 1976) have even presented data suggesting that in some cases, tests like the Law School Admissions Test may, in fact, *overpredict* rather than *underpredict* actual school performance for some minority groups. Thus, the controversy rages on concerning to what extent aptitude tests are biased against minority students. The data would appear to indicate that bias is present, but whether it is the result of poor test construction or merely reflective of educational inequities in society has yet to be clearly resolved.

Should scholastic aptitude tests be used in making admissions decisions, or not? There are strong arguments for both points of view. It appears to us, however, that such tests are probably likely to enjoy widespread use by institutions until some other selection tool becomes available. Although the report of the National Academy of Sciences (Wigdor & Garner, 1982) suggested that the role aptitude testing plays in making admission decisions has been overrated, there are still no reasonable alternatives to their use.

We believe that the problem with using them does not really reside within the tests themselves. The research data seem to suggest that tests of scholastic aptitude actually accomplish what they were designed to do, namely, to pick out those who are most likely to perform well in school. The difficulty appears to be much more a societal concern involving how these tests are used. It is precisely at this level that institutions need to abandon rigid admission policies based on aptitude scores and select a more diverse student body, knowing that some students will need additional supportive services to achieve their educational goals. Thus, selection tools such as scholastic aptitude tests can be used either to maintain the status quo or move beyond it to create more opportunities for all segments of our society.

Prediction efficiency.   How well do scholastic aptitude tests work? A great many studies have been undertaken to determine the validity of scholastic aptitude tests for predicting future academic performance. Typically, researchers have compared grades in high school against admission test scores to see which would predict future college performance most accurately. The evidence has shown consistently that past academic history is superior to aptitude testing in predicting future school achievement. In general, the correlation between former grades in school and future grades is usually between .40 and .50, while test scores only manage correlations with future grades in the .30 to .35 range.

Should institutions continue to use test scores for making admissions decisions? Certainly, the amount of variance in academic grades that is accounted for by scholastic test scores is not very impressive (approximately 10 to 15 percent). Nevertheless, a small portion of the variance that is accounted for is unique to these tests and not assessed by past academic history alone. Because both sets of data do contribute some unique information, most institutions now combine them into a regression equation in order to maximize their ability to predict future grades. Utilizing such statistical procedures, the correlations obtained between predictor and criterion are often increased substantially (e.g., $r = .55$ to $.60$).

Tests produce their most impressive predictive successes when used with individuals who have performed poorly in school for reasons other than lack of ability. Similarly, testing provides a way of more equitably assessing students who come from very localized educational systems; in these cases, identical grade records tend to vary in meaning from one school system to another. In both instances, institutions can make more informed admission decisions based on the tested ability levels of those students.

Effects of coaching.   Because of the presumed importance of test scores in institutional decision making, many people have sought help from various "coaching clinics," hoping to learn how to take the tests so as to get the best score. These commercial ventures report gains in test scores ranging from 1.0 to 2.5 standard deviations (e.g., 100–250 points on the SAT or GRE). In addition to formal coaching, many students purchase one or more of the many self-help study books to better prepare themselves for taking the exam. Computer software is also available that allows students to diagnose their academic deficiencies and strengthen their skills with the expectation of improving their performance. Some recent reviews have suggested that coaching can have a significant impact on test scores (Owen, 1985), although the validity of these claims has been questioned (Wigdor & Garner, 1982).

Two corporations, Educational Testing Service and American College Testing Program, are actively involved in the testing controversy. They have conducted much research on the efforts of coaching and exam preparation on actual test performance. Most of their research has reported much more modest gains than suggested by their critics. Data from research on the SAT suggest that average score improvement after coaching is more in the range of a one-fourth to a one-third standard deviation, or 25 to 35 points. The most conservative evaluation to be made, given the data reported from all sources, is that the probability of *some* improvement in scores is quite high; *how much* improvement is another matter. Undoubtedly there is considerable inter-individual variation in score improvement. Those who claim very large gains in test performance have probably seen outstanding increases for some individual students. However, when aggregate data from a large population of students are considered, the gains are generally much less exciting. These data suggest that most students will achieve gains in their test scores no greater than 40 to 50 points as a result of coaching.

It is our belief that those individuals who are most apt to benefit from coaching or tutoring are those whose academic skills are rusty or nonexistent. Therefore, people who have been out of school for a period of time or who are particularly deficient in one or more essential academic skill area, such as written communication or mathematics, will probably benefit most. In addition, it is possible that the practice and basic skill building involved in coaching will improve their ability to handle additional course work.

Selection Decisions

Identification of exceptionality.   Institutions have long had a need to identify those individuals who are at either end of the ability continuum. One group of students needing rather early detection and remedial work concerns those who experience developmental delays in their maturation. The earlier these people can be identified and provided with learning environments designed to stimulate their intellectual and emotional development, the more likely it is that they will be able to maximize their talents. Aptitude tests are employed to make these decisions, while recognizing that some decisional errors will inevitably occur. Typically, the inaccurate decisions that are usually made are more likely to be false negative errors (i.e., individuals being classified as less able than they are) rather than false positive errors (i.e., students being classified as more talented than they really are). Consequently, even when errors are made, it is likely that those students who have been misclassified will be given special remedial treatment until the errors are detected. Thus, all who need special educational intervention will not be overlooked. However, testing errors can lead to the potential loss of educational opportunities and possible stigma for the students involved.

A second area of exceptionality that is receiving considerable attention today involves the identification of intellectually gifted students. Institutions need to identify those talented individuals who will benefit most from an enriched educational curriculum. In order to properly challenge these students, more demanding and complex learning environments need to be made available. Failure to provide adequate stimulation often leads to poor motivation and performance on the part of gifted students. They often become discouraged and fail to channel their talents in productive directions. Again, ability tests play a major role in the identification of these specially talented people.

Classroom selection. Perhaps one of the more inventive uses for aptitude tests in educational settings has been their application to the problem of tracking in the classroom. In this case, students are grouped according to ability in order to provide instruction that is consistent with their ability level. This application of aptitude testing seeks to maximize the motivation of students and minimize their frustration by placing them in classes where the material presented is neither too easy (and therefore boring) nor too difficult (which often leads to frustration). While tests are far from perfect tools in accomplishing this purpose, they are helpful aids in the decision-making process. The biggest danger in their use is that administrators may rely on them too heavily, without taking into account other important data that are essential to sound decision making. Certainly this is the case when talented students with a history of performing very well academically are not placed in more challenging class sections because of low test scores resulting from some extraneous factor, such as test anxiety or emotional upset.

Evaluation Decisions

Standardized ability tests have long played a major role in evaluating the effectiveness of educational programs. Achievement tests such as the *Iowa Tests of Basic Skills,* the *Iowa Tests of Educational Development,* and the *California Achievement Test* are typically administered to students within an institution to determine how they are performing in relation to their peers across the country. Strengths and weaknesses among students are noted, but from an institutional perspective, administrators are more interested in evaluating whether the curriculum has the breadth and depth characteristic of other programs. Administrators who give these tests are, therefore, very concerned about the overall effectiveness of their instructional program.

This institutional application of achievement testing has recently raised some troubling issues. Several years ago, a West Virginia physician, Dr. John Cannell, noted in a report that school children in West Virginia were reported to be above the national norm in their performance on a standardized ability measure. Because West Virginia has a very high illiteracy rate, he decided to investigate the issue further. He subsequently found that not only West Virginia but also every one of the 50 states had reported that the achievement scores of their school children were above the national average on standardized test batteries. This rather startling finding has been coined the "Lake Wobegon Phenomenon" after author Garrison Keillor's mythical town where all the children are above average.

How can everyone be above the national average? From our earlier study of the meaning of test scores, we know that theoretically this is impossible (i.e., 50 percent must be above the mean, and 50 percent below). The findings reported by Cannell have since been confirmed by an independent study conducted by the U.S. Department of Education. The answer to this paradox lies in the characteristics of the national norm group against which student performance is compared. Because of the great expense involved in renorming standardized tests on a yearly basis, test companies usually rely on well-developed norm groups that are often five or more years old. Consequently, when student performance is compared with the "national norm" it is really being compared with the performance of students who took the test several years earlier. It is therefore quite possible for everyone to be above the average because the comparison group is not composed of students taking the current test.

Why would we necessarily see an improvement in scores when a new test group is compared with the older norm group? One factor is that teachers often "teach to the test." That is, they note what content is covered on the various standardized tests in use at their school and then modify their teaching to cover that material in their classes. Curricula are often modified by administrators to better reflect the test content so that students will have exposure to the material and consequently perform well when tested. This "curriculum alignment" (Shanker, 1988) process probably accounts for much of the "Lake Wobegon Phenomenon."

The unresolved issue that testing and curriculum experts are now debating is whether teaching to the test and curriculum alignment are reasonable methods of attaining educational goals. Proponents claim that modifying curricula to reflect test content ensures that our educational programs are up-to-date and responsive to the needs of society. Critics, on the other hand, claim that as long as we use test content to guide our teaching, we jeopardize our ability to effectively evaluate how well we are really teaching. With all of the external pressures from people outside the school system to show positive educational progress, it appears as though teaching to the test will probably continue.

CRITICAL DISCUSSION:
The National Assessment of Educational Progress

American schools are frequently criticized on the grounds that students no longer attain basic skills (e.g., literacy, a working knowledge of mathematics) and that we are falling behind other nations in terms of educational attainment. Although some of these criticisms are probably justified, it is in fact quite difficult to sensibly evaluate the quality of our schools or the attainments of our students.

The National Assessment of Educational Progress (NAEP), which started in 1969, represents a systematic effort to assess what American students know and can do. A special issue of the 1992 *Journal of Educational Statistics* provides a detailed discussion of the NAEP program, which involves a complex sampling plan for both students and test items. In 1990, for example, over 145,000 students in more than 20 distinct samples provided data for NAEP. NAEP employs highly sophisticated applications of item response theory to provide consistent scaling of proficiency across a wide range of grades and content areas.

NAEP provides assessments of proficiency in science, mathematics, and reading. This assessment does not report scores for individual students, schools, or school districts; rather, it estimates proficiency at a national level. It also provides proficiency levels in individual participating states. On the whole, the results of NAEP do *not* support the idea that students are declining in their proficiency. Math proficiency was higher in 1990 than in the late 1970s. Performance in science declined in the 1970s but improved in the 1980s. For 9- and 13-year-olds, science proficiency levels in the 1990s were similar to those in the 1970s; although for older students, proficiency levels have dropped somewhat. Reading proficiency is at least as high, and for some age groups higher, now as in the 1970s.

The technical descriptions of the NAEP methods make it clear just how difficult it is to determine whether students are really improving or declining in their skills. Most comparisons of different nations, different school districts, different states, or trends over time confound real differences in proficiency with differences in curriculum, differences in the student population, and differences in the tests used to estimate performance. Although most people seem to believe that our educational system is failing, the data from careful assessments, such as that provided by NAEP, suggest that the picture is not so simple, and perhaps not so grim.

APPLICATIONS IN INDIVIDUAL DECISION MAKING

Although it is difficult to completely separate institutional from individual applications of testing in decision making, we have chosen the target or purpose for which the testing is done as our point of reference in making this distinction. Up to this point our focus has been on how tests are used by institutions to help make administrative decisions. Now we shift our focus to how tests are employed in the educational and career decisions made by the individual.

As students progress through the educational system, they encounter many decision points. Questions arise such as whether to prepare for college or to take vocationally relevant course work. Likewise, they face decisions about how much formal education to pursue, what academic major to select, which electives to take, and what career path to follow. How are psychological tests applied to these individual decision-making tasks? How useful are they? These are some of the issues that are examined here.

Educational Planning

Selecting an appropriate educational program is an extremely important goal in our society, yet many people are reluctant to seek help. They try to avoid a lengthy trial-and-error process, opting instead to narrow their alternatives to a small, manageable number of possibilities that seem to have potential for success and personal satisfaction. Testing often plays an important role in such decisions. We use several case studies to illustrate how psychological tests can affect educational and vocational decisions.

Take the case of Bob, who is a college sophomore currently taking a liberal arts curriculum. Although he came to college somewhat undecided about what he wanted to pursue, he felt little pressure to make a commitment until now. In the past it seemed that most decisions had been made for him. He had few choices open to him as he progressed through elementary and junior high school. In high school he simply followed a college preparatory program, since he knew that he was going on to college. Bob's hope was that as he got involved in college, the decision-making process would get easier. Unfortunately, he became more rather than less confused.

Bob sought help from the counseling center on campus and was administered two interest tests as part of the counseling process. What he learned from the test results was that he shared a similar interest pattern with people engaged in certain business occupations. Specifically, Bob's tests indicated a rather strong interest in the aspect of business that was people-oriented. He immediately began to think about selling, but his counselor pointed out to him that his strong secondary pattern of interest in art and design, combined with his business interests, would suggest a career in advertising. Although Bob was aware that he liked to draw at times, he had not pursued art with much interest because he was certain that he lacked sufficient ability to be successful as an artist. The thought of combining art with business and taking an introductory advertising course to check out his ability level was intriguing. Encouraged by the data supplied by these tests, Bob decided to explore advertising further.

How useful was this test data for Bob? Why had he not gravitated toward business or advertising on his own? Bob, like many of us, had some stereotypic ideas about business that kept him from taking any course work in that field. He had just assumed he would not like business. What the testing did for Bob was to give him some important information about how his interests compared to the interests of people in various jobs who were quite satisfied with their work. Although the tests did not reveal any major surprises about what he liked or disliked, they did help him reconsider his thinking about business and rekindle his interest in art.

Sometimes the issue in question is not so much interest as ability. For an example, consider the case of Dawn, who always had an interest in mechanical activities. She grew up with three brothers and learned to repair just about anything that was mechanical, including her bicycle and her car. As she approached college, however, she questioned whether she could successfully major in mechanical engineering. To assist Dawn in deciding about her future college plans, she was given a mechanical aptitude test. Coupled with other data, such as her excellent grades in math and science during high school and her scholastic aptitude test scores, the results of the mechanical aptitude test suggested that she had a better than average chance of completing that major.

Sometimes testing results do not coincide with an individual's current plans or past experience. Bill, for instance, was a second-semester sophomore with a C average who recently had begun to experience severe problems in his math course. As his course work was becoming more difficult, Bill was studying more and more, yet finding it harder to keep up. Because he had always been an A and B student in high school, Bill attributed his failing marks in math to the quality of the instruction he was getting and his lack of background in math (i.e., his high school had only required one year of math). Bill's math professor suggested he take some tests to see if he had a learning disability.

The results of a battery of both aptitude and achievement tests administered to Bill revealed that his current academic difficulty was probably due to his being less intellectually able than his peers. Interest testing was then done to help him formulate some alternatives to his current plans. He eventually decided to cut back to a part-time basis, monitor his progress for another semester, and reevaluate his educational plans at that time.

Sometimes too much reliance can be placed on tests, causing costly delays in the educational development and career planning of the individual. Bonnie was not a very motivated student. She did enough to get by but rarely applied herself beyond the bare minimum. She had other priorities in her life besides school. She worked at various part-time jobs throughout high school and spent considerable time with her steady boyfriend.

When Bonnie was a sophomore in high school, she was given an ability test and an interest inventory to help her set some educational and career goals. Her interest scores indicated that she liked working with people and doing artwork and mechanical-technical activities. The results of the ability test, however, indicated that she did not have the aptitude for college work. Since this was consistent with her mediocre grades in school, her counselor advised her to take the vocationally oriented track and to not consider attending college.

Now at age 24, Bonnie is a divorced, single parent of a three-year-old son. She is finding it difficult to live on her minimum wage as a hospital ward clerk, and so she has decided to reconsider attending college. During career counseling, she discovered that she was much brighter and more academically able than prior testing and school grades had shown. Both she and her counselor decided that lack of motivation and a poor self-concept were probably responsible for her marginal performance in the past. She was therefore encouraged to pursue her career ambition of becoming an occupational therapist. Had less weight been given to the earlier ability testing data, she might have gone to college much sooner.

In all four of the above cases, testing played a key role in helping individuals make important decisions about their educational plans. Testing provided either unique, new information or confirmation of past or present plans.

Career Planning

Perhaps one of the most frequent applications of individual testing in educational settings involves career decision making. Throughout their life spans, people are faced with decisions about what type of work to pursue. At an early developmental age, there is a need for general areas to be identified so that further exploration can be undertaken. During young adulthood, the need is often for more specific information concerning the probabilities of both success and satisfaction in various careers. Persons undergoing mid-life career changes present another problem. They are searching for support and encouragement in the change process and are seeking data that either reinforce or contraindicate their plans. At all stages of development, then, testing can play a significant role in the vocational decision-making process. Three case studies illustrate this role.

Megan, a high school sophomore, has been wondering what she should do after she finishes school. She has recently been thinking about taking some secretarial classes and going to work after graduation. As part of the career counseling process in her high school, Megan was given an interest test revealing that she had a rather definite preference for science. What had happened, however, was that Megan had never considered herself college material and therefore had not pursued science in school. When further ability testing was done, she learned that college was within her reach if she wanted to try. This information opened a whole new set of alternatives for her that she would not have explored without the use of tests.

Juan, on the other hand, was facing a mid-life crisis. He was a 32-year-old high school history teacher, but he was becoming increasingly disenchanted with teaching. He had entered the field partly by accident. As a student in college, Juan had not known exactly what he wanted to do. After taking a variety of courses for two and a half years, he decided to major in history because he had more hours in that area than in any other and he had always liked to study it. As he approached graduation, he realized that there were not too many jobs for history majors, so he completed the necessary hours in education to become a teacher. Now, ten years later, he thought he wanted a change.

Testing revealed that Juan's choice of teaching was quite consistent with his interests. Test data indicated that he had a rather clearly defined interest in social science and education. Further discussion with Juan indicated that the major source of his dissatisfaction was not his choice of work, but job-related factors, such as the new principal recently hired at his school. Using this information, Juan decided to remain in teaching because he had enjoyed it in the past but consider changing to a new school system.

Our final case is David, a college junior majoring in biological science with plans to go on to veterinary school. David began thinking that he might need a back-up plan in case he was unsuccessful in gaining admission to the veterinary program. Even though he had always received excellent grades, he knew that admission to that field was very competitive. David found that his test results were very supportive of his veterinary goal, but that they were also consistent with a number of other medically related fields as well as with computer-oriented work. The test results helped David to take several additional computer courses as electives while completing his major in biological science. In this way, he would leave college with an employable skill to fall back on if he were not able to gain acceptance into veterinary school. This course of action gave him an alternative to his current vocational plans should he need it in the future.

This chapter has illustrated a number of ways in which psychological tests are used in making educational and career decisions, both on an institutional level and on an individual level. In both cases, tests often have significant impact on the decisions made. While tests do not provide infallible data, they can be useful tools enabling decision makers to gather systematic information relatively quickly and accurately. Finally, as several clinical case studies illustrated, tests of ability and interest often form the basis for much decision making in the educational and career area.

Having already examined aptitude tests in a previous chapter, we turn our attention in the next chapter to a review of major interest inventories, including how they were constructed, what kind of information they provide, and how well they work.

CRITICAL DISCUSSION:
What Is Criterion-referenced Testing?

Criterion-referenced testing is not a new idea. It closely resembles the concept mastery approach to testing that has been used in educational settings for years. The essence of criterion-referenced testing lies in comparing the test performance of examinees to some objectively stated goal or standard of achievement to determine how much examinees have learned or at what level they are able to perform the tasks in question.

Our focus throughout this book has been primarily on norm-referenced tests. How do they differ from criterion-referenced tests? The answer lies in the frame of reference that each uses to give meaning to test scores. In the case of norm-referenced tests, the scores that examinees receive are compared to the scores of other people taking the same tests. The focus is not on how many items were answered correctly but, rather, on whether the number answered correctly was greater or less than that of a comparison group. Criterion-referenced tests, on the other hand, use a specified content area as the basis for comparison. These tests are designed to measure how much of the content area has been learned, mastered, or performed. Consequently, the focus is on the absolute number of items correctly answered in relation to the total number of correct responses on the test, rather than on the number responded to correctly relative to a comparison group.

Criterion-referenced tests have been used most extensively in educational settings where the instructional goal consists of clearly defined, objective content. For example, they are particularly well suited as aids in making decisions about the level of math or spelling proficiency attained by examinees, or the English reading fluency found among a class of foreign students. In addition, they have been used rather extensively in conjunction with computer-aided instruction. For example, criterion-referenced tests are frequently used to determine how much students have learned in a particular subject, so that a structured program of instruction can be given. Then, following a specified learning period, testing is done again to measure the amount of gain achieved by the students as a result of the instruction. The ease with which students' progress can be monitored through the use of computers enables educators to employ criterion-referenced tests to tailor instructional programs to each student's individual needs.

While criterion-referenced tests have been increasingly utilized in educational decision-making situations, they are not likely to supplant the premier role played by norm-referenced tests in psychological assessment. There still are several significant problems that plague developers of criterion-referenced tests and prevent their wide-scale application. For instance, there is the rather thorny issue of what constitutes an acceptable level of mastery for the attribute in question. Should mastery be defined as achieving a score of 100 percent on the test? Should answering 80 percent of the items correctly be considered adequate mastery of the material? Should the required level of mastery change as a function of other student characteristics, such as intelligence, sex, or grade level? Answers to these difficult questions are not yet readily available.

Finally, another problem involving criterion-referenced tests concerns how to evaluate them adequately. The methods reviewed earlier in the book for estimating the reliability of psychological tests do not work with criterion-referenced tests. For example, it has been shown that reducing the variability among test scores influences the size of the correlation coefficient that is employed in estimating the reliability of tests. However, in the case of criterion-referenced tests, which have an established level of mastery that everyone eventually attains through additional instruction, the amount of intersubject variability becomes zero. With such a restricted range of scores, our correlational techniques for estimating reliability do not work. Currently, other ways of establishing the reliability of criterion-referenced tests are being investigated (Ferguson & Novick, 1973; Hambleton & Novick, 1973).

SUMMARY

Colleges, universities, and professional schools have long had a need to find methods of identifying academically able students to be admitted to their institutions. Historically, they have turned to academic aptitude testing programs to provide them with predictive information about the academic potential of student applicants. Although institutions differ on how much emphasis should be placed on academic aptitude test scores, there has been solid support for including them along with past academic record in some type of regression equation as an aid in making admissions decisions.

Students often retake academic aptitude tests in an effort to raise their scores. Although significant score improvement occurs in a few isolated cases, the majority of research indicates that only modest gains are usually achieved.

Critics have raised substantive issues about the use of academic aptitude tests in making admission decisions for educationally disadvantaged students. Claiming clear evidence that such tests are biased toward the majority group, they contend that such tests discriminate against certain subgroups and prohibit their entry into post-secondary education. Although the bulk of the research suggests that academic aptitude tests predict academic success for disadvantaged students about as well as others, it was suggested that institutions may want to modify their use of test scores in working with certain subgroups in an effort to create greater equality among all groups within our society.

Others question the continued use of scholastic aptitude tests in admissions decisions because they account for so little of the variance in students' grades. Typically, scholastic aptitude scores correlate in the .30 to .35 range with first year grades. Proponents counter that although it is small, the contribution that scholastic aptitude tests make in predicting grades is unique and should not be disregarded.

Because scholastic aptitude tests can have such a profound affect on people's lives, many individuals attend special coaching clinics, tutoring sessions, or preparation classes to help them maximize their score. Although some students do improve their test scores dramatically, most people do not substantially improve their scores.

In addition to admissions decisions, scholastic aptitude tests are also utilized to identify individuals with specialized educational needs, to group students according to ability levels for program-planning purposes, and to evaluate the overall effectiveness of educational programs. Because our society places such a heavy premium on academic excellence, there has been the temptation to misuse the data generated from scholastic testing to support various political or personal aims.

Finally, academic testing is frequently used in clinical counseling situations to help people make realistic decisions about their futures. Several examples were discussed showing how testing can be employed to confirm people's plans, alert them to possible future problems or difficulties, and suggest new, unexplored career avenues for possible consideration.

CHAPTER 17

INTEREST
ASSESSMENT

In the preceding chapter, we showed how psychological tests are used in educational and vocational decision making. Now we examine the field of interest measurement to see specifically how interest tests fulfill their function. In this chapter, we examine four widely used measures of interest to see how they are constructed, what they can tell us about individuals, how well they exhibit the characteristics of a good test, and how they are used in making clinical decisions. In each case, a sample test profile and interpretive discussion is presented to demonstrate how the test is actually utilized.

The four interest tests chosen for review are the Strong Interest Inventory (SII), the Kuder Occupational Interest Survey (KOIS), the Career Assessment Inventory (CAI), and the Jackson Vocational Interest Survey (JVIS). Each test was selected for a particular reason.

The SII enjoys the heritage of being one of the oldest psychological tests currently in use and has been a dominant force in the field of interest measurement. No survey of interest tests would be complete without an in-depth look at the SII. The KOIS was included because it represents a divergent test construction philosophy and because it also has a rather long and rich history of research and use in the field. The CAI bears many similarities to the SII, but its unique contribution is its ability to measure the interests of people at the lower socioeconomic levels in our society. Finally, the JVIS was included because it is a relatively newly developed test that incorporates several contemporary test development techniques and offers the attractive feature of being hand-scoreable, unlike any of its predecessors. While other tests could have been selected for review, we believe these four provide a good overview of the entire field of interest measurement.

This chapter is arranged so that the four tests can be compared and contrasted quite easily. Each test is discussed from the same basic four perspectives, namely, its purpose, its manner of construction, its psychometric characteristics, and its application in both counseling and industrial settings.

THE STRONG VOCATIONAL INTEREST INVENTORY

The field of interest measurement as we know it today has its roots in the work of Edward K. Strong. Strong was a psychologist who taught at Carnegie Institute of Technology in Pittsburgh from 1919 to 1923. During that time a seminar was being held at Carnegie in which a 1,000-item pool of interest items was developed. A young graduate student, Karl Cowdery, completed a dissertation under Strong in which he found that the choices people made on a paper-and-pencil interest test could be used to accurately discriminate which occupations they entered. Cowdery never pursued this line of research further, but Strong continued investigating this phenomenon for more than 30 years. As McArthur (1992) has pointed out, Strong began by studying the interests of men in life insurance sales, although his first published scale measured the interests of personnel managers. His original inventory, the Strong Vocational Interest Blank, came out in 1926, with the manual appearing in print in 1927.

Strong was an incredibly compulsive, organized, motivated, and dedicated person. He spent many years gathering samples of occupational groups to be tested with his instrument. However, at the beginning he believed that only males should be considered because females produced demonstrably different responses to the items than did males and chose different career paths. Eventually Strong decided to devise a separate form for women with the same basic format, but with certain unique items. In 1933 he published the first women's form of the test. Strong later revised both the men's and women's forms of the test in 1938 and 1946, respectively.

About midway through the decade of the 1950s, Strong wanted to revise his test once again. He was getting on in age, however, and enlisted a young graduate student at the University of Minnesota at that time, David Campbell, to help him with the project. Strong eventually died, and Campbell eventually completed this next set of revisions. The men's form was completed in 1966, followed by the women's form in 1969. Neither of these revisions remained in use for long, however. With the advent of the women's movement, earlier assumptions about the career paths of women being uniquely different from those of men were challenged and eventually abandoned. With the increasing number of women entering the labor market and the change in thinking about the role of women, having two separate, gender-specific forms seemed inappropriate. Consequently, Campbell combined the men's and women's forms into one test, publishing it as the Strong-Campbell Interest Inventory in 1974. Since then the inventory has been revised, first in 1981 and then again in 1985. Currently known as the Strong Interest Inventory (SII), it is a direct descendent of the original instrument first published by Edward K. Strong.

Construction of the SII

Strong originally believed that the way to build an interest inventory was to contrast the responses of a specific occupational criterion group with those of a general, nonspecific, people-in-general group to determine a unique set of items that differentiated the two groups. Strong's method of developing occupational scales was to administer his inventory to workers in various occupations who met certain criteria of occupational satisfaction (e.g., were employed at least three years in their current job, reported being satisfied with their work, etc.). Strong then compared their responses to those of a general reference group. When he found items that were significantly preferred more or less often by a group of occupational workers than by the general reference sample, he combined them into an interest scale for that occupation. For example, if artists significantly endorsed an item such as "I like to attend symphony concerts" more often than did members of the general reference sample, then Strong included that item on the artist scale. Similarly, if artists marked the item "I like mathematics" significantly less often than the general reference group, then that item was also included on the artist scale since it still distinguished artists from the reference group.

It should be noted that the essential characteristic of occupational scale items is that they were designed to *differentiate* the interests of occupational groups from those of a general reference group. Items strongly preferred or rarely liked by both an occupational group and the general reference group did not qualify for inclusion on an occupational scale. This is graphically shown in Figure 17-1. While people in occupation X indicated a strong preference for hunting, so did the vast majority of the general reference group. In contrast, only about 35 percent of occupation X members said they liked gardening. However even a significantly smaller percentage of the general reference group indicated a preference for gardening. Consequently, because gardening discriminated between the two groups and hunting did not, only the former would appear on the scale for occupation X, despite the fact that workers in occupation X clearly like to hunt.

The composition of the general reference group posed a very difficult problem for Strong. He initially experimented with several groups that were chosen to represent

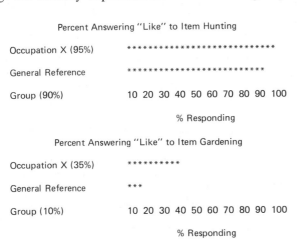

Figure 17-1 Comparison between Two Items and Their Ability to Discriminate between Groups

cross-sections of various socioeconomic strata and vocational interest areas. His studies revealed that the composition of the group was crucial in discriminating between the interests of various occupational groups. For example, he found that if he selected a general comparison group of skilled workers consisting of carpenters, plumbers, printers, and the like, he was able to locate numerous items that differentiated the interests of professional people from those of the skilled workers reference group, but he could not differentiate among the professions. Doctors, lawyers, and business executives all appeared to have similar interests with one another but had clearly distinguishable interests from those of the comparison group. His major concern, however, was that he could not separate the interests of one professional group from another group of professionals.

In contrast, Strong found that using the skilled worker reference group did allow him to rather easily differentiate one skilled group from another. Carpenters appeared to have quite different interests from plumbers or printers and other skilled workers. He concluded that as the similarity between the members of occupational groups and the general reference group increased, the discriminating power of the test increased. His conclusions are summarized in Table 17-1. With this discovery in mind, Strong, who was primarily interested in gaining maximum separation among business and professional occupations, decided to select a general comparison group that was biased toward this occupational level. Therefore the SII provides better separation among business and professional occupations than it does among occupations at lower socioeconomic levels. However, recent attempts to extend it to include more nonprofessional and technical occupations have been undertaken (Hansen, 1992).

TABLE 17-1 ADVANTAGES AND DISADVANTAGES OF STRONG'S USE OF DIFFERENT GENERAL REFERENCE GROUPS

Composition of General Reference Sample Used	Advantages and Disadvantages
Sample of workers at the unskilled level	Able to distinguish clearly among workers in unskilled jobs (i.e., construction laborers differed from assembly line workers, window washers differed from farm laborers, etc.).
	Could only distinguish all professionals from unskilled workers, but could not separate among professionals (i.e., groups such as doctors, lawyers, and engineers could not be clearly distinguished from one another, but as a group could be discriminated from unskilled workers).
Sample of workers at the skilled level	Able to distinguish clearly among workers in skilled jobs (i.e., electricians differed from sheet metal workers, plumbers responded differently than carpenters, etc.).
	Could only distinguish all professionals from skilled workers, but could not separate among professionals.
Sample of workers at the business and professional level	Able to distinguish clearly among workers employed in different professional or business occupations (i.e., ministers differed from bankers, professional artists differed from psychologists, etc.).
	While workers in different areas at the business and professional level could be differentiated from one another, workers at the skilled and unskilled levels all tended to show similar interests and could not be differentiated from one another.

The format of the Strong consists of 325 items covering occupations, school subjects, work-related activities, amusements and hobbies, types of people, preferences between different activities, and personal characteristics. Table 17-2 presents several items similar to those included on the SII. The "like," "indifferent," or "dislike" responses a person makes on the inventory are scored by computer and analyzed in reference to five types of scales: administrative indices, special scales, theme scales, basic interest scales, and occupational scales.

Administrative indices.   The administrative indices reveal information about the type and pattern of choices made by the examinee. They are designed to alert the counselor to possible interpretive problems that might moderate the validity of the results or greatly reduce their usefulness. Several scales are included in this group. One scale, the total response indicator, signals the number of items accurately read by the scoring machine. If the number of items omitted is very large, the validity of the results is doubtful. The most common reasons for omitting items seem to be that examinees either are unfamiliar with the terminology used in an item or mark the answer sheet so lightly that the optical reader scanning the sheet fails to pick up some of their responses.

A second validity indicator, the number of infrequent responses marked on the test, provides a check for proper completion of the inventory. Questionable response patterns are suggested when examinees give unusually large numbers of infrequent responses on the test. Invalid profiles due to questionable response patterns often result from poor motivation on the part of examinees, deficiencies in reading ability, confusion about test directions, or language difficulties. In all cases, the detection of such problems is essential in preventing erroneous interpretations from being communicated to the individual.

Finally, a response distribution matrix indicating the percentages of "like," "indifferent," and "dislike" responses enables the counselor to detect other interpretive problems. For example, individuals giving many "indifferent" responses may have trouble making decisions in general and consequently have not clearly differentiated their interests. The usefulness of the SII in such cases may be more to point out their indecision than to measure specific occupational interests. Likewise, unusually large response per-

---

TABLE 17-2   SAMPLE SII ITEMS

Mark *Like, Indifferent,* or *Dislike* next to the following items

1. Operating machinery _____	7. Sociology _____
2. Being a forest ranger _____	8. Contributing to charities _____
3. Chemistry _____	9. Buying merchandise for a store _____
4. Doing research work _____	10. People who assume leadership _____
5. Dramatics _____	11. Regular hours for work _____
6. Magazines about art and music _____	12. Thrifty people _____

Source: Reproduced by special permission from the *Strong Interest Inventory of the Strong Vocational Interest Blanks* of the *Strong Interest Inventory of the Strong Vocational Interest Blanks®*, Form T325. Copyright 1933, 1938, 1945, 1946, 1966, 1968, 1974, 1981, 1985 by the Board of Trustees of the Leland Stanford Junior University. All rights reserved. Printed under license from Stanford University Press, Stanford, CA 94305. Reproduced by special permission of the publisher, Consulting Psychologists Press, Inc., Palo Alto, CA 94303. Further reproduction is prohibited without the publisher's consent.

centages in either of the other two categories can cause significant modifications in the interpretability of the test results.

Special scales.   While various special scales have been developed over the years and have been included on earlier revisions of the inventory, only two remain on the current SII. The Academic Comfort (AC) scale provides information about whether an examinee's interests are similar to those of people who persist in formal academic settings in pursuit of college or professional degrees. It was developed by selecting items on the inventory that differentiated those with no college education from college graduates. Research has shown that as the amount of formal education increases, the score on the AC scale also increases (Hansen & Campbell, 1985). As a general rule, people who have artistic and scientific interests and who do not have strong preferences for outdoor, technical, and business activities produce high scores on this scale, enjoy school, and often pursue advanced degrees. On the other hand, those who endorse the opposite type of interests usually do not enjoy formal educational environments, score lower on the AC scale, and if they do pursue advanced degrees, do so more out of need than interest.

As with other scales on the SII, the AC scale was intended to measure not ability but interests. It has been found, however, that occupational groups do differ appropriately on the scale, depending on the amount of formal education and therefore ability required of workers. When measured directly, however, the correlation between AC scores and ability as measured by grades has usually been found to be quite low, ranging between .10 and .30 (Hansen & Campbell, 1985).

The Introversion-Extroversion (IE) scale provides a measure of the degree of interpersonal contact desired in an occupation. It was developed by comparing the interests of a sample of outgoing, gregarious people with a sample of quiet, reserved, less social people. The rationale on which this scale is based is that individuals who like close contact with people will probably find work settings requiring considerable interpersonal contact to be the most enjoyable. Conversely, those who favor less interpersonal interaction probably will enjoy working by themselves or in settings with minimal interpersonal contact.

Theme scales.   As more and more occupational groups were added to the inventory, it became desirable to categorize the occupations into some system. Strong experimented with several different classification systems but essentially chose one based on the intercorrelations among the occupational scales. This system continued in existence from the mid-1920s until the 1974 revision. While this classification system worked fairly well, there were always a few occupations that could be classified in more than one group because they shared a number of similarities with various diverse groups (for example, the veterinarian scale correlated about as well with the scientific group as it did with the outdoor and technical group). In 1974, when the male and female forms of the SVIB were combined into one form, a new classification scheme was needed, since both older forms had some different occupational groupings. The theoretical system of John Holland (Holland, 1973) was chosen to provide the new organizational schema.

Holland's system postulated that six major interest areas were identifiable that described both work environments and types of people. Holland stated that environments were determined principally by the people who inhabited them. Therefore, the optimal vocation choice involved the matching of people with their appropriate environmental type. Holland further postulated that a hexagon best represented the relationship that exists among these six interest areas. A description of each of his six types is presented in Table 17-3. The actual empirical relationships among the types is shown in Figure 17-2.

Inspection of the intercorrelations among the six types suggests that those that are nearest one another along the hexagon are most similar. As the distance along the hexagon increases, the relationship diminishes. Consequently, the least similar areas are

TABLE 17-3   DESCRIPTION OF THE SIX HOLLAND TYPES

R-Theme: People scoring high here usually are rugged, robust, practical, physically strong; they usually have good physical skills, but sometimes have trouble expressing themselves or in communicating their feelings to others. They like to work outdoors and to work with tools, especially large, powerful machines. They prefer to deal with things rather than with ideas or people. They enjoy creating things with their hands.

I-Theme: This Theme centers around science and scientific activities. Extremes of this type are task-oriented; they are not particularly interested in working around other people. They enjoy solving abstract problems, and they have a great need to understand the physical world. They prefer to think through problems rather than act them out. Such people enjoy ambiguous challenges and do not like highly structured situations with many rules. They frequently are original and creative, especially in scientific areas.

A-Theme: The extreme type here is artistically oriented, and likes to work in artistic settings that offer many opportunities for self-expression. Such people have little interest in problems that are highly structured or require gross physical strength, preferring those that can be solved through self-expression in artistic media. They resemble I-Theme types in preferring to work alone, but have a greater need for individualistic expression, and usually are less assertive about their own opinions and capabilities. They describe themselves as independent, original, unconventional, expressive, and intense.

S-Theme: The pure type here is sociable, responsible, humanistic, and concerned with the welfare of others. These people usually express themselves well and get along well with others; they like attention and seek situations that allow them to be near the center of the group. They prefer to solve problems by discussions with others, or by arranging or rearranging relationships between others; they have little interest in situations requiring physical exertion or working with machinery. Such people describe themselves as cheerful, popular, and achieving, and as good leaders.

E-Theme: The extreme type of this Theme has a great facility with words, especially in selling, dominating, and leading; frequently these people are in sales work. They see themselves as energetic, enthusiastic, adventurous, self-confident, and dominant, and they prefer social tasks where they can assume leadership. They enjoy persuading others to their viewpoints. They are impatient with precise work or work involving long periods of intellectual effort. They like power, status, and material wealth, and enjoy working in expensive settings.

C-Theme: Extremes of this type prefer the highly ordered activities, both verbal and numerical, that characterize office work. People scoring high fit well into large organizations but do not seek leadership; they respond to power and are comfortable working in a well-established chain of command. They dislike ambiguous situations, preferring to know precisely what is expected of them. Such people describe themselves as conventional, stable, well-controlled, and dependable. They have little interest in problems requiring physical skills or intense relationships with others, and are most effective at well-defined tasks. Like the E-Theme type, they value material possessions and status.

Source: From the report of the *Strong Interest Inventory* of the *Strong Vocational Interest Blank.* Form T325. Copyright © 1933, 1946, 1966, 1981, 1985 by the Board of Trustees of Leland Stanford Junior University. Reproduced by permission.

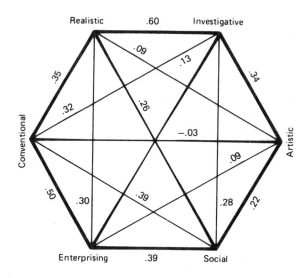

Figure 17-2 Intercorrelations between General Occupational Themes

Source: From the Manual for the Strong Interest Inventory, p. 29. Copyright © 1985 by Consulting Psychologists Press. Reprinted by permission.

those that lie diagonally across from one another. For example, people with conventional interests do not share much in common with artistic individuals, nor do scientists have many interests in common with people in business.

To adopt Holland's system for use on the SII, it was necessary to select a group of items that reflected each of the six personality types. Twenty items were subsequently selected for each type and organized into six theme scales. A general reference sample of both men and women were tested on these six scales to establish a norm group for comparison purposes. This norming of the six theme scales permits the user to formulate a picture of the examinee's interests and personality style in reference to that of a general male and female comparison group.

Basic interest scales.   The basic interest scales were designed to provide specific information about the "likes" and "dislikes" of the respondent. These scales consist of small numbers of items that are reasonably homogeneous with respect to their content. Each scale focuses on a narrow, concentrated interest area. For example, if examinees gave "like" responses to such items as "making a speech," "being a radio announcer," "interviewing people for a job," or "meeting and directing people," they would score high on the public speaking scale. Likewise, a preference for such items as "dentist," "pharmacist," and "surgeon" would lead to a high score on the medical service scale. For all of the basic interest scales, norms are reported on both males and females representing the general population.

Occupational scales.   The occupational scales are the oldest and most researched scales on the inventory. They were designed to provide information about the degree of similarity between the examinee's interests and those of selected occupational criterion groups. Each occupational scale was empirically derived by comparing the responses given by a sample of workers in an occupation with those given by a general, nonspecific sample of people and selecting only those items that significantly differentiated the two groups. The resulting items composing each scale are heterogeneous with respect to item content. For example, physicians indicated a definite preference for playing golf, which differentiated them from the general reference group. While this item does not reflect an occupationally relevant preference, it did significantly differentiate physicians from men in the general population and was therefore included on the physician's occupational scale. On the other hand, the item pertaining to math was highly preferred by both psychologists and the general male reference group. Because this item failed to differentiate the two groups, it was not included on the psychologist scale.

After a group of items were selected that significantly differentiated the occupational criterion groups from the general reference group, the criterion groups were scored on their own scales to determine precisely how many items would be endorsed by members of each group. Means and standard deviations were then computed for each scale and these raw scores transformed into T-score distributions. Thus, a score of 50 represents the number of items endorsed by the average member of each criterion group.

Over the history of the SII, more and more occupational groups have been tested, normed, and added to the profile. Finding adequate samples of both men and women for every occupation has often been very difficult, however. Some occupations, such as dental hygienist and home economics teacher, have traditionally been so dominated by women that locating a sufficient number of male occupational therapists to develop a male scale has been almost impossible. Likewise, other occupations have proven to be as problematic for women (e.g., agribusiness manager).

This raises the issue of why separately normed groups for the two sexes are needed. It would certainly be more efficient to report only one combined male-female group for each occupation. Unfortunately, because of the differences in interests between men and women, combined groups have not been used by most test authors. Researchers have tested various ways to handle this problem, but the resulting attempts have often been laden with sex bias.

Sex bias. The issue of sex bias in the measurement of interests historically was addressed only on a superficial level until the women's movement brought widespread attention to it. Prior to the 1970s, there was evidence that men and women differed in their interests even if employed in the same job. Consequently, some researchers in the field of interest measurement felt that the way to deal with this discrepancy was to have separate but equal inventories for the sexes. Unfortunately, this solution created additional problems because the inventories for men and women were rarely equal.

Generally, there were far more occupational criterion groups available on the male form of the test than on the female form of the test. The rationale for this discrepancy was that there were so few opportunities for women in historically male-dominated occupations that there was no need to include these occupations on the female form of the Strong.

Solving this problem has become a very complex issue. To simply compare both sexes with a combined group of both men and women is unacceptable, given the empirically determined sex differences in interests that have been shown in several studies (Johansson & Harmon, 1972; Spokane, 1979). To develop both male and female criterion groups for each occupation has been the most popular solution. The difficulty with this strategy, as we have already seen, is that in certain cases there are so few workers of one sex in an occupation that finding a representative sample from which to construct a reliable and valid scale has been virtually impossible.

With the advent of feminism, it seemed plausible that as more and more men and women entered nontraditional occupations, the differences in interests between men and women would gradually disappear. As our culture moved toward androgyny, this seemed to be a realistic hope. However, some data (Hansen & Campbell, 1985) have suggested that this is not the case. The differences which have existed in the past appear to be either remaining unchanged or increasing. Therefore, we are still in need of separately normed scales at the present.

Interpretation of the SII

To illustrate the SII, we focus our attention on the profile reproduced in Figure 17-3. This profile was generated from the responses of John B., a 22-year-old employed male who was thinking about entering college after working at various laboring jobs since graduating from high school.

From an inspection of the validity indicators, we can see that he responded to all but one of the items on the test and did not mark an inordinantly large number of infrequently given responses. Both of these indicators suggest that John's SII results probably give an accurate picture of his vocational interests. Next, we learn from the special scales that he did not indicate a particular preference for either working closely with people in face-to-face interpersonal encounters or working alone in less people oriented activities. Given his academic comfort score, it is not surprising that college was not his first choice after high school. John simply did not indicate many interests in common with people who enjoy school and pursue advanced degrees. His desire to attend college now is probably more influenced by his drive to get ahead than by his interest in educational matters.

The administrative indices provide some additional information about John. The low level of "like" responses given to the occupations listed on the inventory suggest that he may have rather clearly defined interests that are quite specific in nature. The overall distribution of his choices among the three response alternatives further reinforces the hypothesis that these results are probably valid for John.

The theme scales reveal that in general, his interests are strongest in business with much less interest in artistic, outdoor, mechanical, and social service activities than shown by most men. He demonstrates a slight preference for those aspects of business that are detail oriented and would probably find jobs requiring data management, accountability, or economic forecasting more desirable than jobs requiring high levels of interpersonal contact, such as sales or personnel management.

The basic and occupational scale scores are in agreement with the other parts of the profile and confirm his interests in business-oriented activities. The overall pattern of his scores on the SII is quite consistent with career choices in business fields such as accounting, information processing, data control, and finance. He would very likely be satisfied pursuing a job in any one of those areas. On the other hand, one of the additional strengths of the inventory is that it also indicates areas that John should probably avoid. Because of the strong dissimilarity between his interests and those of workers in artistic professions, social service careers, scientific fields, and technical-outdoor jobs, if he chose to enter one of those areas, he would probably fail to find a satisfying outlet for his interests, would become disenchanted with his work, and would eventually search for a different career.

Evaluation of the SII

Over the nearly 60-year span since it was first published, the SII has undergone extensive research on such issues as the stability of interests over time, the usefulness of interest scores in differentiating the members of one occupational group from another, and the predictability of future occupational entry on the basis of test results. Volumes have been written about this work; only the major findings are reviewed here.

Reliability. The most frequently employed methodology for measuring the reliability of the SII has been to administer the inventory on two occasions separated by an interval of time (i.e., test-retest reliability). The test-retest studies that have been conducted have produced results unparalleled in other areas of psychological testing. Interests as measured by the various forms of the SII have remained exceptionally stable over considerable intervals of time.

The two variables that appear to affect the stability of the inventory most are the length of time between testings and the age of the individual when initially tested. With intervals as short as one week, the stability of the profile is reported to be over 90. As the time interval increases, the reliability of the inventory decreases. Conversely, as the age of examinees when first tested increases, the stability of test scores generally increases. Campbell (1971) has shown how these two variables affect the reliability of the inventory. This information is summarized in Table 17-4.

Validity. The validity of the SII has generally been assessed by two methods. One method involves checking whether different occupational groups can be differentiated clearly from one another on the basis of their interest profiles. As discussed earlier, this type of study is designed to establish the concurrent validity of a test. A second method concerns whether interest scores are predictive of eventual occupational choice and career satisfaction (i.e., predictive validity).

Assessing how successfully the SII discriminates between people in different occupations has been studied using two different methods. In one method, researchers examine how criterion groups score on occupational scales other than their own. For example, attention might be focused on whether chemists actually score as high or higher on their own scale than other occupational groups. Campbell (1971) has reported data on a number of SII occupational groups and shown that in general criterion groups tended to score highest on their own scales. When exceptions did occur, they were usually in understandable directions. As in the example above, when the chemist occupational scale was studied, it was found that physicists actually scored higher on the chemist scale than did the average chemist (the mean score for physicists was 54 as opposed to 50 for chemists). This finding is not too surprising, however, given the similarity in interests among members of these occupational groups.

In the other, more frequently used method of establishing concurrent validity, comparisons are made between the response distributions of the general reference group

Figure 17-3 SII Response Profile

Source: Reproduced by special permission from the *Profile for the Strong Interest Inventory of the Strong Vocational Interest Blanks* of the *Strong Interest Inventory of the Strong Vocational Interest Blanks*®, Form T325. Copyright 1933, 1938, 1945, 1946, 1966, 1968, 1974, 1981, 1985 by the

Figure 17-3 (continued)

TABLE 17-4 MEDIAN TEST-RETEST CORRELATIONS FOR THE MEN'S OCCUPATIONAL SCALES
FOR VARYING AGES AND TEST-RETEST INTERVALS

Age at first testing	Test-retest interval					
	Two Weeks	1 Year	2–5 Years	6–10 Years	11–20 Years	20+ Years
17–18	—	.80	.70	.65	.64	—
19–21	.91	.80	.73	.67	.67	.64
22–25	—	—	.78	.69	.75	.72
26+	—	—	.77	.81	.80	—

Source: From Campbell D. P., *Handbook for the Strong Vocational Interest Blank*, p. 82.
Copyright © 1971 by Stanford University Press. Reproduced by permission.

and each criterion group to determine the percentage of overlap between the distributions. If occupational scales discriminate well, then there should be a small amount of score overlap with the general reference group. That is, members of the general reference sample should not score very high on any occupational scale. If the general reference group does generate high scores on an occupational scale, then the items on that scale are not differentiating the interests of criterion group members from those of a general sample of workers, and therefore it has little concurrent validity. Data presented by Hansen and Campbell (1985) on the amount of score overlap indicate that, on the average, approximately one third of the scores from the criterion group distributions overlap with those of the general reference group. The amount of overlap appears to vary as a function of how clearly defined the occupational groups are with respect to interests and specific worker tasks. For example, farmers, artists, and chemists show less overlap and are more clearly defined occupational groups than are college professors and elementary teachers, which show much larger score overlap.

The predictive validity of the SII generally has been assessed by administering the inventory to different samples of people prior to occupational entry and following them up later to determine in which careers they eventually became employed. Several problems have plagued this line of research. First, it is often difficult to determine if the occupations entered were predictable from earlier inventory results because current job titles may not have appeared on the original test profiles. Some researchers have dealt with this problem by simply comparing the individual's current occupation with a scale score from the original testing that most closely resembles the current occupation. Others, however, have held that this arbitrary decision process on the part of researchers tends to artificially inflate the predictive validity estimates for the inventory. They believe that only direct-scale comparisons should be done and all other data discarded when predictive studies are conducted. Depending on the strategy selected, researchers have differed somewhat in their conclusions concerning the inventory's predictive validity.

Strong (1955) reported that people tested with his inventory eventually entered occupations for which they had shown an interest when previously tested. Specifically, he stated that the chances were about two in three that people would be in occupations predicted earlier by high test scores on corresponding occupational scales. He also stated that the chances were only about one in five that individuals would be in occupations in which they had shown little interest when tested.

Other researchers (Dolliver, Irvin & Bigley, 1972) have suggested that the two-in-three estimate of the predictive efficiency of the SII is probably an overestimate, since their data indicated that the number of correct predictions was more in the vicinity of one in two. On the other hand, they reported that the one-in-five estimate for low scores was probably an underestimate. They reported that only one in eight people were later in occupations on which they had received low scores when tested. Regardless of which is the most accurate estimate of the predictive validity of the test, both indicate that it is quite useful in predicting future occupational entry.

Other factors have also been studied that appear to moderate the predictive efficiency of the SII. For example, McArthur (1954) found that socioeconomic status had an effect on the test's predictive power. He suggested that people from very wealthy families often chose careers less on the basis of interest and more on the basis of opportunities generated by the family's position. Consequently, the SII was found to be more predictive for middle-income people than for those of extremely high socioeconomic status. Brandt and Hood (1968) found that psychological adjustment also played a role. They reported that the test was more predictive for well-adjusted people than for those with emotional problems. Finally, Campbell (1966) demonstrated that the predictive validity of the SII was higher for those who had well-defined interests when initially tested. Thus, it is apparent that there are a number of factors that affect the overall validity of this test.

Applications of the SII

The SII has long been used as a major tool in helping people plan their educational and vocational futures. It was designed specifically for this purpose. It allows people to compare their interests with those of individuals already in the world of work, providing them with important information necessary to make more informed career choices. This application of the test has been by far the most common, and many experts in the field agree that the SII appears to accomplish this goal quite well (Borgen, 1988).

The SII has also been used rather extensively in selection situations where employment decisions need to be made, the rationale underlying its use in such cases being that job satisfaction is important for productivity. As we have noted, the SII does predict actual job entry and eventual satisfaction. Therefore, it has been used in selection situations to predict which potential employees are most likely to be satisfied with their work. Selection decisions have thus been based in part on these interest test scores. The use of the inventory for this purpose is somewhat controversial, however.

THE KUDER OCCUPATIONAL INTEREST SURVEY

The field of interest measurement has also been significantly affected by the work of Frederick Kuder. His interest inventories date back to 1939. The first editions of his test analyzed preferences in broad areas such as literary, scientific, mechanical, and social service fields. Later editions of the instrument began to depart from these broader areas and to report scores in relation to specific criterion groups.

The Kuder Occupational Interest Survey (KOIS) represents the latest in the line of interest inventories developed by Kuder. His instruments differ from those of E. K. Strong in two major ways. First, Kuder believed that the best way to assess interests was to use a forced-choice, ipsative item format (e.g., two or more alternatives in each item from which examinees must choose their response). Consequently, he employed a paired-comparison item format on his surveys. As discussed before, this strategy for scale construction produces test results that reveal *relative* strengths and weaknesses within an individual rather than the *absolute* level of a trait or factor within the individual.

Second, Kuder did not share Strong's conviction that the best way to measure interests involved comparing criterion groups with a common comparison group consisting of men or women in general. In place of this method, Kuder chose to use the actual average responses of each criterion group to determine the items for each of the scales on his survey. Thus, he was not interested in identifying only those items that differentiated a criterion group from a general comparison group, such as is the case with the SII, but in selecting all the items actually endorsed by members of a criterion group. His contention was that this method of scale construction provided superior separation among criterion groups and therefore improved the overall validity of the inventory.

Construction of the KOIS

The KOIS maintains the use of the ipsative item format that earlier versions of the test also used. It presents items in a trichotomous format, with instructions to select from each set of three alternatives the one that is most preferred and the one that is least preferred. In effect, a ranking of the three alternatives is thus obtained for each item. A sample of items similar to those on the survey is reproduced in Table 17-5. Descriptions of each of the scales on the KOIS follow.

TABLE 17-5   SAMPLE KOIS ITEMS

The directions state that in each group of three activities, examinees are to choose one that they would "most" like to do and one which they would "least" like to do by filling in the appropriate circle. One item in each group of three should be left blank, indicating that it is between the "most" and "least" preferred activity.

	M	L
1. Visit an art gallery	M	L
Browse in a library	M	L
Visit a museum	M	L
2. Collect autographs	M	L
Collect coins	M	L
Collect stones	M	L

Source: From the Kuder Form DD Occupational Interest Survey, Revised. Copyright © 1985 by Science Research Associates, Inc. Reproduced by permission.

Verification scale.   This scale was designed to assess whether examinees properly filled out their surveys. Each of the items on this scale is composed of three alternatives, only one of which is commonly selected by most people. For example, an item contributing to an examinee's score on the verification or V scale may include the following three choices: "be introduced to everyone at a big party made up of strangers," "be introduced to a few people at the party," or "not be introduced to people at the party." Examinees giving a "most like" response to either of the first or third choices have responded in a rather unique and statistically infrequent direction.

If a substantial number of infrequently endorsed responses are given throughout the test, the validity of the resulting scores becomes suspect. That is, the probability would be greatly increased that the test scores may have resulted from other factors than item content alone. Such factors as careless marking of the answer sheet, failure to follow the test directions, or random responding are often the cause of suspicious verification scores. However, all questionable verification scores need to be followed up to determine their cause, since examinees with rather unique interest patterns that are quite different from those of most people may generate verification scores that resemble those of an invalid profile.

Vocational interest estimates.   A recent addition to the KOIS is the vocational interest estimate (VIE) scales. These broadly defined interest areas provide an overview of the examinee's interests, broken down into ten major interest fields. In many ways, the VIE scales rather closely resemble the theme scales on the SII. In fact, Zytowski (1985) has shown how these ten interest fields can be reclassified into Holland's system of six by grouping several of the related areas together (e.g., the outdoor and mechanical areas can be combined to form Holland's realistic theme; the artistic, musical, and literary areas together compose Holland's artistic theme).

Occupational scales.   The occupational scales on the KOIS are similar to those on the SII in that they are designed to reflect the similarity between the respondent's interests and those of employed workers. The people chosen to represent the various occupational groups had similar demographic characteristics as those used in the construction of the SII; namely, their average age was 45 years, they had been employed in their current occupation for at least 3 years, and they were reportedly very satisfied with their work.

The occupational scales differ from those on the SII in that they were constructed to reflect all the interests and noninterests of occupational groups rather than just those that differentiated them from a general comparison group. The significance of this difference is that the occupational scales on the Kuder contain larger numbers of high base-rate items (i.e., those given very frequently by most people) than do the comparable scales on the SII. You will recall that in the case of the Strong, high base-rate items were essentially eliminated from the occupational scales by the use of a general comparison group in the development of the scales. This difference often means that examinees produce higher interest scores on the Kuder than on the SII because of the presence of these high base-rate items.

Kuder has maintained that his method of scale construction gives a more accurate picture of the similarity between examinees' interests and those of workers in various occupations than does the method employed on the SII because it permits a direct comparison of all interests and not just a unique subsample. There is little evidence at present, however, to substantiate that one method is clearly superior to the other.

On the Kuder the occupational scale scores are reported as correlation coefficients measuring the relationship between the individual's interests and those of workers in various criterion groups. The scores are arranged on the profile in descending order of magnitude, rather than grouping them according to any particular theoretical system such as that proposed by Holland and used on the SII. Kuder believed that the most meaningful arrangement of scores would show a listing of people's interests from strongest to weakest, without regard to the type of interests indicated. This is in keeping with the overall ipsative nature of the inventory that stresses the relative position of inventory scores.

While the ranking of the occupational scale scores is of greatest importance on the Kuder, their magnitude is also important. Keeping in mind that correlation coefficients range from .00 to 1.00 in magnitude and increase exponentially, it is rare for occupational scales to exceed values in the mid .70s. In fact, most criterion group members obtain scores ranging between .45 and .75. Therefore, users of the Kuder have found that scores below .45 on the occupational scales are indicative of minimal interest in those areas.

One additional feature of the occupational scales on the KOIS is that they span a much wider spectrum of the world of work than does the SII. This permits the user to assess interests not only at the business and professional level but also at the skilled level. This has persuaded some users to select the Kuder over the SII when time is a consideration and additional testing at lower socioeconomic levels is desirable.

College major scales.   The development of a special set of scales to measure academic interests represented an innovation on the KOIS that was not available on earlier Kuder inventories. These scales were designed to measure the similarity between the respondents' interests and those of college seniors majoring in various academic disciplines. They are of particular value in working with adolescents and young adults because the college major scales were developed with individuals from a similar age group. This is in contrast to the occupational scales that are composed of workers who average 45 years of age. Because of the developmental nature of interests, the availability of peer-criterion groups for score interpretation with younger examinees has been welcomed.

As can be seen from the profile reproduced in Figure 17-4, there are 22 male and 17 female college major scales on the KOIS. Because of the differences in the number and type of college major scales reported for males and females, their usefulness in cases of students with nontraditional interests has been questioned. Nevertheless, their addition to the profile has represented a useful innovation in interest measurement.

Experimental scales.   Eight additional scales have been included on the Kuder to provide supplemental administrative information useful in determining the overall validity of the profile. These scales can be found in the lower right-hand corner of the example in Figure 17-4. The M and W scales were designed to be used with the MBI and WBI scale to indicate whether examinees completed the inventory with an open and truthful

Kuder Occupational Interest Survey Report Form

Name

Sex MALE **Date**

Numeric Grid No. SRA No. 00102

1 Dependability: How much confidence can you place in your results? In scoring your responses several checks were made on your answer patterns to be sure that you understood the directions and that your results were complete and dependable. According to these:

YOUR RESULTS APPEAR
TO BE DEPENDABLE.

2 Vocational Interest Estimates: Vocational interests can be divided into different types and the level of your attraction to each type can be measured. You may feel that you know what interests you have already — what you may not know is how strong they are compared with other people's interests. This section shows the relative rank of your preferences for ten different kinds of vocational activities. Each is explained on the back of this report form. Your preferences in these activities, as compared with other people's interests, are as follows:

Compared with men		Compared with women	
HIGH		HIGH	
MECHANICAL	83	MECHANICAL	99
AVERAGE		MUSICAL	80
MUSICAL	75	AVERAGE	
CLERICAL	67	SCIENTIFIC	58
SCIENTIFIC	49	CLERICAL	55
LOW		LOW	
ARTISTIC	23	COMPUTATIONAL	18
SOCIAL SERVICE	19	OUTDOOR	18
OUTDOOR	17	ARTISTIC	11
COMPUTATIONAL	11	SOCIAL SERVICE	06
LITERARY	06	LITERARY	04
PERSUASIVE	01	PERSUASIVE	01

3 Occupations: The KOIS has been given to groups of persons who are experienced and satisfied in many different occupations. Their patterns of interests have been compared with yours and placed in order of their similarity with you. The following occupational groups have interest patterns most similar to yours:

Compared with men		Compared with women	
NURSE		ENGINEER	.59
ELEM SCH TEACHER		DENTIST	.58
OPTOMETRIST		COMPUTR PRGRMR	.56
PHOTOGRAPHER		OCCUPA THERAPIST	.55
PHYS THERAPIST		BANKER	.55
DENTIST		ARCHITECT	.54
BUYER		ACCT, CERT PUB	.53
SCIENCE TCHR, HS	.53		
X-RAY TECHNICIAN	.53	THESE ARE NEXT MOST SIMILAR:	
		AUDIOL/SP PATHOL	.49

THESE ARE NEXT MOST SIMILAR: (Compared with men)

POSTAL CLERK	
AUDIOL/SP PATHOL	
TRAVEL AGENT	
TV REPAIRER	
MATH TCHR, HS	
COMPUTER PRGRMR	
ENGINEER	
COUNSELOR, HS	
BRICKLAYER	
SUPERVSR, INDUST	
PODIATRIST	
LIBRARIAN	
MATHEMATICIAN	
AUTO SALESPERSON	
BOOKSTORE MGR	
ARCHITECT	
FILM/TV PROD/DIR	
FLORIST	
METEOROLOGIST	
PLUMBING CONTRAC	
PHARMACIST	
POLICE OFFICER	
WELDER	
BANKER	
PLANT NURSRY WKR	
PAINTER, HOUSE	
MACHINIST	
LAWYER	
AUTO MECHANIC	
PRINTER	

THE REST ARE LISTED IN ORDER OF SIMILARITY:

SOCIAL WORKER	
FORESTER	
INTERIOR DECOR	
PHYSICIAN	
CHEMIST	
ELECTRICIAN	
ACCT, CERT PUB	
INSURANCE AGENT	
REAL ESTATE AGT	
CLOTHER, RETAIL	.56
PERSONNEL MGR	.54
BLDG CONTRACTOR	.53
PHARMACEUT SALES	.53
BOOKKEEPER	.52
PSYCHOLOGIST	.50
CARPENTER	.50
PLUMBER	
VETERINARIAN	
STATISTICIAN	
RADIO STATION MGR	
MINISTER	.49

Compared with women MOST SIMILAR, CONT.

PHYS THERAPIST	.52
X-RAY TECHNICIAN	.52
VETERINARIAN	.52
PHYSICIAN	.52
ELEM SCH TEACHER	.52
DENTAL ASSISTANT	.52
SECRETARY	.51
MATH TEACHER, HS	.51
FLORIST	.51
EXTENSION AGENT	.51
INSURANCE AGENT	.50
SCIENCE TCHR, HS	.50
FILM/TV PROD/DIR	.49
NURSE	.49
BOOKKEEPER	.49
BANK CLERK	.49
BEAUTICIAN	.49
DIETITIAN	.49

THE REST ARE LISTED IN ORDER OF SIMILARITY:

LIBRARIAN	.48
COUNSELOR, HS	.48
OFFICE CLERK	.47
COL STU PERS WKR	.47
SOCIAL WORKER	.47
BOOKSTORE MGR	.47
PSYCHOLOGIST	.47
INTERIOR DECOR	.47
NUTRITIONIST	.46
RELIGIOUS ED DIR	.46
DEPT STORE-SALES	.46
JOURNALIST	.46
LAWYER	.46
	.45
	.46
	.46
	.46
	.45
	.45
	.45
	.45

Compared with men REST, CONT.

	.49
	.49
	.48
	.47
	.47
	.47
	.46
	.46
	.46
	.45
	.45
	.45
	.45
	.45

LIBRARIAN	.43
	.43
ARCHITECTURE	.43
FOREIGN LANGUAGE	.42
FORESTRY	.40
BUSINESS ADMIN	.40
AGRICULTURE	.40
BIOLOGICAL SCI	.39
PREMED/PHAR/DENT	.39
SOCIOLOGY	.38
ANIMAL SCIENCE	.57
ART & ART EDUC	.37
SERV ACAD CADET	.37

Compared with women (Occupations)

TRUCK DRIVER	.41
SCHOOL SUPT	.41
EXTENSION AGENT	.40
FARMER	.37
JOURNALIST	.35

4 College Majors: Just as for occupations, the KOIS has been given to many persons in different college majors. The following college major groups have interest patterns most similar to yours:

Compared with men

ELEMENTARY EDUC	.55
MUSIC & MUSIC ED	.55
ENGINEERING	.54
PHYSICAL EDUC	.54
MATHEMATICS	.51
PHYSICAL SCIENCE	.50

THESE ARE NEXT MOST SIMILAR:

ARCHITECTURE	.49
FOREIGN LANGUAGE	.49
FORESTRY	.48
BUSINESS ADMIN	.48
AGRICULTURE	.46
BIOLOGICAL SCI	.45
PREMED/PHAR/DENT	.45
SOCIOLOGY	.45
ANIMAL SCIENCE	.44
ART & ART EDUC	.44
DRAMA	.44

THE REST ARE LISTED IN ORDER OF SIMILARITY:

ECONOMICS	.43
PSYCHOLOGY	.43
HISTORY	.40
POLITICAL SCI	.36
ENGLISH	.33

Compared with women

PHYSICAL EDUC	.58
MATHEMATICS	.52
THESE ARE NEXT MOST SIMILAR:	
MUSIC & MUSIC ED	.51
HEALTH PROFESS	.50
HOME ECON EDUC	.48
BUSINESS EDUC	.48
ELEMENTARY EDUC	.48
BIOLOGICAL SCI	.48
THE REST ARE LISTED IN ORDER OF SIMILARITY:	
FOREIGN LANGUAGE	.45
NURSING	.44
HISTORY	.44
DRAMA	.41
ART & ART EDUC	.41
PSYCHOLOGY	.41
SOCIOLOGY	.38
POLITICAL SCI	.36
ENGLISH	.35

Experimental Scales.

		V-SCORE	55		
M	.52	MBI	.13	MBI	.13
S	.53	F	.52	M	.47	WBI	.13
				D	.64	W3	.65

7-3881

Figure 17-4 KOIS Profile

Source: From the Kuder Form DD Occupational Interest Survey, Revised. Copyright © 1985 by Science Research Associates, Inc.

attitude. This is accomplished by comparing an examinee's responses to those of men and women who took the inventory under two separate sets of instructions. On one occasion the instructions were to respond in a truthful and genuine manner (M and W scales), while on a second testing the instructions were to respond so as to create the best possible impression of themselves (MBI and WBI scales). Consequently, examinees giving overly flattering pictures of their interests are likely to score higher on the "best impression" scales rather than on the other set of scales representing more genuine responses.

One of the additional uses of the M and W scales is to assess how similar the respondent's interests are to those of adult males and females. Women and men who have atypical interests for their sex often score higher on the opposite-sex scale. This information often alerts the user to expand the exploration process with those examinees to include many nontraditional interest areas that may not have shown up on the profile. It is interesting to note that the M and W scales are really quite similar to the male and female general comparison scales encountered on the SII.

The remaining four scales were designed to give the user information about the developmental stage of a person's interests. The F and M scales were constructed by having a group of fathers and mothers respond to the inventory under the normal instructional set. The S and D scales were constructed by having the sons and daughters of those fathers and mothers also complete the inventory in the usual manner. By comparing the respondent's scores on these scales, users can determine whether the person's interests are more like those of a younger age group or more like those of older adults. The assumption underlying these scales is that if the examinees' interest patterns resemble those of adolescents and young adults, their inventoried interests are probably somewhat unstable and will undergo additional change. In contrast, examinees showing interests more like those of older adults are seen as having more well defined career interests less subject to change.

Interpretation of the KOIS

The sample profile reproduced in Figure 17-4 can be used to illustrate the interpretation process. This profile was generated by Tom, a 34-year-old male seeking vocational counseling. We begin the interpretation by checking the verification score to see if the results are likely to represent a valid picture of Tom's interests. Since there is a high probability that scores above .45 represent valid interest profiles, we assume that Tom's profile gives an accurate picture of his interests.

Next we can look at the vocational interest estimates to get an overall summary of the results. Tom's scores indicate that he has above-average interests in mechanical activities and below-average interests in artistic, social service, outdoor, computational, literary, and persuasive areas.

The occupational scales reveal that Tom has ranked his interest in social service and allied-health occupations highest, and he has completed the survey in a manner consistent with employed workers in those areas. His interests in technical and mechanical fields are also strong, but probably secondary to those in the social and health-related fields. It is interesting to note that Tom rejected few occupational possibilities, as evidenced by the lack of many low occupational scores.

The college major scales show a pattern of ranking most similar to college seniors pursuing various programs in education. The similarity to seniors in some of the sciences and engineering probably reflects Tom's mechanical and technical interests. The academic areas of least interest to Tom appear to be in the social and behavioral sciences.

The experimental scales reveal that Tom has fairly traditional male interests. He also apparently responded to the test in an open and honest manner, without a conscious attempt to dissimulate his results in a particularly favorable way. We can also see that his interests resemble those of older adults and therefore are likely to be rather stable. There are no indications that his results should not be taken as an accurate reflection of his overall vocational interests.

Evaluation of the KOIS

Since the publication of the KOIS in 1966, a number of studies have been conducted in an attempt to establish its psychometric characteristics. Much of this research is reported either in the *Manual* (Kuder, 1970, 1979) or in his book on interest measurement (Kuder, 1977).

Reliability. Two primary types of studies have been done to assess the stability of Kuder scores. As stated earlier, since the Kuder has an ipsative format, the order of the occupational scales is extremely important. Consequently, the ordering of the scales should remain stable over time if the inventory is to be of use in vocational counseling.

One hundred independent determinations of the stability of Kuder scores for both high school seniors and college students of both sexes were computed in order to check whether the ordering of scores would remain the same over time (Kuder, 1970). The results indicated that over a two-week interval, the median correlation coefficient was .90 for all comparisons. Other groups have been similarly tested, with the majority of test-retest coefficients being above .90. Longer time intervals up to three years have been used with engineering students. The resulting reliability estimates ranged from .35 to .98, clustering just under .90 for most groups.

The second group of studies conducted to assess the reliability of the Kuder involved the consistency of differences among scores on pairs of scales when tested over time. Of concern here is whether the differences between occupational scores remain constant or change as time passes. Data reported in the manual (Kuder, 1970) indicate that the separation between occupations remains quite constant, as indicated by test-retest correlation estimates ranging from .84 to .92.

Validity. The validity of the KOIS generally has been assessed in two different ways. First, attention has been given to the frequency with which members of one occupational group actually score higher on a scale other than their own (i.e., concurrent validity). Based on large samples, the general finding has been that such errors of classification occur approximately 6 percent of the time.

Similar concurrent validity research also has been designed to determine how well the occupational scales differentiate between groups. Much of this research has focused on the 30 core occupational groups selected to represent the domain of occupations covered on the KOIS. For each of these 30 groups, 100 employees were selected. All 30 groups were scored on all 30 scales. The resulting matrix revealed that many groups did not score highest on their own scale. However, the scales on which they did score highest tended to reflect similar interest dimensions (e.g., school superintendents often scored higher on the personnel manager scale; social workers often scored higher on the clinical psychologist scale, etc.). This data would seem to suggest some occupational groups can readily be separated on the basis of interest with a high degree of accuracy, while others are more alike and therefore more difficult to separate.

A third demonstration of concurrent validity involves studies comparing criterion group members' highest scores with the scores they generated on their own occupational scales. As with the reliability studies, the 30 core groups composed of 100 workers each were used. The results showed that 64 percent of the time, workers' scores on their own occupational scales were within .009 points of their highest scores. Thus, while the KOIS appears to do a reasonable job of differentiating the interests of various occupational groups, this separation is not perfect.

Research on the predictive validity of the KOIS is more sparse. As has been shown, demonstrations of predictive validity are of utmost importance to users of interest inventories. Unfortunately, much of the research on predicting job satisfaction and occupational entry from inventory scores has been done on earlier forms of the test (McRae, 1959; Lipsett & Wilson, 1954). These earlier results have suggested that the likelihood of being dissatisfied in a career is about three times greater if the career chosen was not consistent with previously measured interests. Since these findings were obtained for other forms of the Kuder, however, they cannot be unequivocally extended to the KOIS.

Two more recent predictive studies (Zytowski, 1976; Zytowski & Laing, 1978) have shed some additional light on the validity of the KOIS. Using data gathered on the Kuder Preference Record–Occupational, an earlier version of the KOIS with identical items, these researchers reported that, on the average, the accuracy of predicting eventual career selection was comparable to that of other instruments. Specifically, about 50 percent of the persons in the longitudinal sample were in careers consistent with their top five occupational scores when tested earlier.

Applications of the KOIS

The addition of college major scales on the inventory has been an important attraction for users who desire a direct measure of academic interests. These scales have been used widely to assist students in making important educational decisions, such as course selection and choice of major.

Because of the extended socioeconomic level of occupations provided by the KOIS, it also has found extensive use in those applied settings where the career objectives of people are likely to encompass a rather large span of the world of work. This situation is most often encountered in such settings as vocational-training schools, junior colleges, mental health centers, employment agencies, and within employee development offices in business and industry. Here, the primary decisions to be made involve placement of people into specific areas of training, educational programming, or employment, based on their inventoried interests.

CAREER ASSESSMENT INVENTORY

The Career Assessment Inventory (CAI) was developed by Charles Johansson and first published in 1975 by National Computer Systems, Inc. It was originally designed to measure the interests of those people considering careers not requiring a four-year college degree. Rather than being targeted at the business and professional level, as is the SII, the CAI was intended to assess the interests of workers at the skilled, semi-skilled, and unskilled levels of the occupational hierarchy. This is still true today for the *vocational version* of the test. However, an expanded form of the CAI, the *enhanced version* (Johansson, 1986), adds a number of professional-level occupations to the test and so extends its applicability to occupations requiring four-year degrees as well.

Although the item content on the CAI rendered it quite susceptible to sex bias, much careful consideration was given to this issue throughout its development. In order to eliminate sex bias as much as possible, several notable strategies were employed in the development of the CAI. First, gender-specific occupational titles were avoided in favor of more gender-neutral titles. Second, broad career exploration by both sexes was encouraged by choosing a representative cross-section of those careers at the nonprofessional end of the occupational spectrum. Finally, a rather novel procedure has been used in the development of the occupational scales on the current revision of the test. Rather than relying on the established method of developing gender-specific occupational scales (i.e., creating separate male and female scales for each occupation), Johansson (1984) initiated the use of combined-gender occupational scales, thus eliminating the need for separate male and female scores for each occupational group. These three test development procedures have significantly reduced the effect of sex bias on the inventory.

The overall format of the CAI as well as its derivation closely resemble that used in the construction of the SII. The development of the CAI included two substantial modifications, however, which improved its psychometric properties. First, the item response format was expanded to include a five-point continuum ranging from "very much like" to "very much dislike." Sample items are shown in Table 17-6. This response format enables examinees to make finer discriminations among their preferences than was possible with the three-point scale provided on the SII. Second, the CAI does not contain as many different types of items as does the SII. Of particular interest here is the fact that the CAI has dropped the ipsative-formatted section on dyadic preferences (e.g., respondents decide between two statements they would prefer—"produce an item" or "sell an item"),

TABLE 17-6 SAMPLE CAI ITEMS

201. Be a Bank Cashier .... L l I d D	226. Be a Driving Instructor .... L l I d D
202. Be a Bartender .... L l I d D	227. Be an Electrician .... L l I d D
203. Be a Barber .... L l I d D	228. Be an Elementary School Teacher .... L l I d D
204. Be a Bill Collector .... L l I d D	229. Be a Farmer .... L l I d D
205. Be a Biologist .... L l I d D	230. Be a Fashion Designer .... L l I d D

Source: From Johansson, *Career Assessment Inventory*. Copyright © 1973, 1982 by National Computer Systems. Reprinted by permission.

which always has created complex statistical problems for those desiring to establish reliability and validity estimates.

Construction of the CAI

As with the SII, scores on the CAI are organized into four classes of scales for purposes of interpretation. The theme, basic interest, and occupational scales provide a hierarchical analysis of interests into general areas of interests, more specific interests, and very specific interests, respectively. The fourth class of scales—the administrative indices and special scales—principally provide a check on the validity of the inventory results.

Administrative indices and special scales.   One scale contained in this group—the number of infrequently given responses—involves a measure of whether or not the examinee correctly followed the directions for filling out the answer sheet and was able to comprehend the written material on the instrument. A second scale—the number of total responses—simply alerts the user if too few responses were given or scored to produce a valid picture of the examinee's interests. Finally, the CAI also contains a response patterning section analogous to that on the SII that reveals the percentages of all response types given on the inventory. Once again, this array is intended to give information about potential choice problems faced by examinees, such as approach-approach problems (e.g., many interests present, all of which are very desirable), undifferentiated interests (e.g., no clearly defined likes or dislikes), or avoidance-avoidance problems (e.g., strong dislike shown for a major portion of activities surveyed by the CAI).

Several special scales recently have been included on the CAI that are very analogous to the IE and AC scales on the SII. They provide data on whether examinees like to have close contact with others on their jobs, and whether they enjoy formal educational settings, as is characteristic of those who obtain advanced training and academic degrees. In addition to these two scales, a third scale has been added to assess the variety among a respondent's interests, and a fourth scale to measure the degree to which examinees prefer artistic and social activities in comparison to mechanical and outdoor work.

Theme scales.   As has been previously described, Holland's theoretical system for classifying occupations provides the basis for grouping the remaining scales on the inventory. The theme scales give the user an overview of the examinee's interest in each of the six Holland areas. As with the theme scales on the SII, they are composed of 20 items chosen to represent each of the Holland types.

Basic interest scales.   The basic interest scales were constructed to measure the domains of interest assessed by the CAI. Their development was based on the intercorrelations among items on the inventory. Items that were related highly to one another and judged to fit logically into psychologically meaningful categories were grouped into basic interest scales. They differ from those on the SII in that they are generally much more homogeneous and show substantially higher intercorrelations. Their purpose, however, is the same—namely, to indicate areas of specific interest.

Occupational scales.   The occupational scales on the CAI were constructed in much the same manner as those on the SII. Workers were tested from various occupational groups within the skilled, semi-skilled, and unskilled levels of the workforce, and their responses were compared to those of either a general male or female reference sample representing a cross-section of all the criterion groups of the CAI. Those items differentiating criterion-group response from those of the general male and female reference samples were then selected for inclusion on the occupational scales. The major difference between the SII and the CAI involves how the item-selection process was done. While the SII forms separate occupational scales for each sex, on the CAI only those items common to both male and female scales were retained to form a combined-sex scale for each occupation. Following item selection, the scales were then normed for each criterion group, and the raw scores transformed to T scores to facilitate the interpretation process.

Just as with the SII, scores on the occupational scales indicate the degree of similarity between the examinee's responses to the CAI and the responses of each occupational criterion group. The assumption upon which these scales is based is that as the degree of similarity in interest increases, the likelihood of career satisfaction also increases. This follows from the fact that the members of each criterion group were selected primarily because they had indicated they were satisfied with their jobs, and therefore examinees showing similar interest patterns should experience satisfaction if they made the same occupational choices.

Interpretation of the CAI

The sample profile for the CAI appears in Figure 17-5. It reflects the interests of Bill, age 21, who is currently considering taking some vocational courses at the local vocational technical school but is uncertain as to which career path to pursue. He has spent the last three years since graduation from high school working on a factory assembly line.

The validity indicators in Bill's case all appear to be within normal limits and do not suggest the presence of any unusual test-taking attitudes on his part. His distribution of "like," "indifferent," and "dislike" responses appears to be sufficiently well-differentiated to preclude any special decision-making difficulties on his part. Furthermore, he seemed quite clear about his preferences, given the small number of "indifferent" responses he indicated.

The special scales reveal that Bill does not like to work closely with people but, rather, prefers working in environments with minimal interpersonal contact. His level of interest in academic activities resembles that of people who pursue limited formal education beyond high school or vocational school. Bill indicated some diversity among his interests, although they are focused mainly in the outdoor and technical area.

The theme and basic interest scales reveal that Bill has indicated a rather clear preference for agricultural, electronics, carpentry, and mechanical activities. With the exception of some interest in science, Bill showed little interest in any of the other areas on the CAI. His scores on the occupational scales also reflect this same pattern. His interests resemble those of workers in various outdoor and technical occupations, with little similarity to those of persons in business or social service fields.

Figure 17-5 CAI Profile

Source: From Johansson, *Career Assessment Inventory*. Copyright © 1973, 1982 by National Computer Systems. Reprinted by permission.

Evaluation of the CAI

Much of the research on the psychometric properties of the CAI has come from the efforts of its developer, Johansson. Estimates of the test-retest reliability of the instrument have compared favorably with those reported for the SII and the Kuder. Median test-retest correlations reported in the *Manual* (Johansson, 1984) on the theme, basic interest, and occupational scales have all ranged from the high .70s to the mid .90s, dropping in magnitude as the amount of time between testings increased from a week to seven years.

Studies on the validity of the CAI have been limited to examining its separation among occupations (demonstrations of concurrent validity) and its relationship to other interest inventories (demonstrations of construct validity). In assessing its concurrent validity, the percentage of overlap between various criterion groups and the reference sample of tradespeople-in-general has been computed. In moving to the use of combined-gender occupational groups on the 1982 revision of the CAI, there was some loss in the power of the occupational scales to separate the interests of the criterion groups from those of the general reference sample. Although this has increased the percentage of score overlap, the amount of overlap remains comparable with that reported for other interest inventories, such as the SII. Thus, the evidence tends to support reasonable concurrent validity for the CAI.

Studies examining the intercorrelations of like-named scales on the CAI and other interest inventories have generally produced median coefficients in the .60's. There are some important anomalies, however, (e.g., the female beautician SII scale and the female cosmetologist CAI scale) that produce much lower correlation coefficients, suggesting that they are apparently tapping different aspects of the workers in that occupation. While this is weak evidence for the construct validity of the CAI, it does offer some encouraging data supporting its current use. Unfortunately, no predictive validity research has been reported on the inventory to substantiate its use in predicting eventual occupational entry. Demonstrations of its predictive validity will be needed before the CAI can claim a permanent place among the established measures of career interests.

Applications of the CAI

Because it was designed to measure the interests of lower-socioeconomic workers, the CAI is not utilized as much in college settings as the SII and the KOIS. It is employed much more often as an aid in educational planning at the junior-college and especially vocational-technical school level. Many high school counselors find it extremely useful in career counseling with students considering entering the world of work immediately after graduation.

The CAI is also utilized in making personnel decisions in business and industry. The information provided by the inventory has proven to be of value in screening new employees for job openings and facilitating the transfer of currently employed workers to other areas within the organization. Additionally, it has been used to assist in the outplacement of workers displaced by changes in company policy or by a slow economy. In this latter case, the adult workers involved are often older and therefore not likely to return to school to complete an advanced degree or seek post-graduate professional training. The CAI is quite well suited to help them consider a mid-life career change within their financial and educational limitations.

JACKSON VOCATIONAL INTEREST SURVEY

The Jackson Vocational Interest Survey (JVIS), first published in 1977, represents a relatively new attempt at interest measurement. One of its unique features is that it allows for both hand and machine scoring, which is a very attractive feature when time and financial constraints are present. An advantage of machine scoring, however, is that it allows for computation of certain scales not available with the hand-scored version. Thus there is some loss of interpretive information when the JVIS is not machine scored.

Because of its relative newness, many of the test construction methods employed in the development of the JVIS were quite sophisticated and advanced. Consequently, Jackson was able to create an instrument with superior psychometric properties. Additionally, great care was taken during its development to suppress the effect of the acquiescence response set that pervades many interest inventories that require examinees to indicate an attraction or aversion for a set of stimulus items.

Construction of the JVIS

The JVIS consists of 289 vocationally relevant activities arranged in an ipsative format. The items are grouped into 34 basic interest scales on the basis of their interrelationships. Each of the scales was designed to reflect the interest dimension designated by its scale name. In addition, inter-scale correlation was minimized in an effort to maximize the amount of discrimination possible among interest patterns.

For each of the 289 items, examinees select either an A or B statement, indicating their preferred choice. The items are arranged such that an item from one of each of 17 basic scales in the A group is paired with an item from each of the 17 basic scales in the B group. Table 17-7 shows several sample items from the test. Thus, scales within a group are never directly compared with each other. Rather, they can be compared with one another only in reference to how frequently each was chosen when compared to a different common set of scales. Consequently, the JVIS can be thought of as an instrument composed of two separate sets of scales, virtually forming two independent ipsative measures.

All the basic interest scales on the JVIS were developed by employing the rational method of scale construction, where items are developed according to the theoretical ideas of the author, unlike the three inventories reviewed previously, which utilized an empirical method of scale construction. Jackson chose a rational approach based on research showing that scales derived rationally, purified by internal consistency checks, were more stable and valid than those derived empirically (Goldberg & Slovic, 1967; Ashton & Goldberg, 1973). More importantly, however, rationally derived scales permit a direct and meaningful interpretation of their content, and Jackson believed such scales therefore were more useful in counseling.

TABLE 17-7   SAMPLE JVIS ITEMS

A.	Artistically painting sets for a play.
B.	Playing records and having young students sing along.
A.	Acting in a television comedy.
B.	Teaching youngsters how to write.
A.	Spending spare time 'playing' with difficult algebra problems.
B.	Correcting spelling errors on a pupil's lesson.
A.	Weaving rugs with unusual designs.
B.	Buying and selling stocks for a client.
A.	Memorizing lines for a play.
B.	Investigating the possibility of buying foreign bonds.
A.	Developing unusual mathematical problems for use in a textbook.
B.	Studying a company's history of financial growth.
A.	Crafting unusual picture frames.
B.	Ordering new supplies for a store.
A.	Starring in a low-budget movie.
B.	Serving as administrative assistant to the head of a large firm.
A.	Studying the proof of a complex mathematics problem.
B.	Corresponding with customers by mail.

Source: From *Jackson Vocational Interest Survey.* Copyright © 1977 by Douglas N. Jackson. Reproduced by permission of Sigma Assessment Systems, Inc., 1110 Military Street, P.O. Box 984, Port Huron, MI 48061-0984.

Work role scales.   The 34 basic interest scales on the JVIS are composed of two different types. The first group, called the work role scales, bear some resemblance to both the basic interest and the occupational scales encountered on other interest inventories. They resemble the basic interest scales in that they were intended to measure specific interests rather than the degree of similarity between an examinee's interests and those of various occupational groups. Thus, the mathematics work role scale indicates whether individuals like math per se rather than whether they share interests in common with mathematicians. On the other hand, they function somewhat like the occupational scales in that research has shown that various occupational groups do score highest on the work role scale associated with their area of activity. For example, lawyers score highest on law and engineers score highest on engineering.

Work style scales.   The other group of basic interest scales is quite unique in that they were designed to measure preference for working in environments demanding particular modes of behavior, such as stamina, dominant leadership, security, and the like. The interest measured by this group of scales cuts across a number of careers and so are more broad in their scope. The additional information they provide helps form a more complete picture of the examinee's personal characteristics.

Additional scales.   If the JVIS is machine scored, several additional groups of scales are provided. The first of these is the general occupational theme scales. The JVIS provides scores on ten basic themes, which are very analogous to the theme scales on other instruments. Although the scale names are not always comparable, they can be grouped together to produce a list very similar to Holland's six themes.

Another group of scales provides data on the similarity between the examinee's interests and those of college students majoring in various academic disciplines. Finally, a third cluster of scales indicates the degree of similarity between an individual's interests and those of workers in a variety of careers. These latter scales are comparable to the occupational scales characteristic of other interest inventories.

Interpretation of the JVIS

Figure 17-6 presents the JVIS profile of Linda, a 35-year-old mother of two, returning to the workforce after an absence due to childrearing. The following description of her results demonstrates what type of information can be gained from the survey.

Linda's results suggest that she does not enjoy artistic activities as much as the majority of women. Instead, her interests appear to be much more in the sciences. She appears to like medical and allied-health work but may not seek out positions involving considerable social service activity. She will probably choose jobs requiring more technical skill and less direct interpersonal contact if she elects a medical career.

Linda has indicated generally that business is a lower priority for her than it is for most people. She has less interest in sales, clerical work, finance, and managerial activities than in most other areas on the JVIS. Should she enter a business field, the probability is low that Linda will find the work rewarding or satisfying, and it is highly likely that she will leave the field within a few years after entry.

When compared to various occupational patterns established for the JVIS, Linda's results resemble those of radiological and medical technologists, physicians, and other health professionals. Given her preference for high levels of job security, Linda would probably find a career in the medical area quite consistent with her work style.

Evaluation of the JVIS

One of the outstanding features of the JVIS involves its strong psychometric characteristics. Extensive research was undertaken as part of its development, but only highlights are presented here.

Reliability. Several different series of studies have been conducted to establish the reliability of the JVIS. First, data reported by Jackson (1977) on its test-retest reliability when used with college students revealed that the coefficients ranged from a low of .73 to a high of .91 over a short time span. Studies have not been done with time intervals longer than a few months, so its long-term stability remains unknown.

A second research strategy for establishing the reliability of the JVIS has been to check the stability of individual profiles over time. Obviously, if the highest scale score suddenly became the lowest on retesting, the stability of the survey would be suspect. Jackson (1977) has reported data from two separate studies that indicate that the rank ordering of the profile remains quite stable even over intervals up to six months.

Figure 17-6 JVIS Profile

Source: From *Jackson Vocational Interest Survey*. Copyright © 1977 by Douglas N. Jackson. Reprinted by permission of Sigma Assessment Systems, Inc., 1110 Military Street, P.O. Box 984, Port Huron, MI 48061-0984.

Validity.   Research activity designed to establish the validity of the JVIS generally has taken two main directions. One avenue has been to employ rather sophisticated factor analytic techniques to confirm that the content of the scales does measure the psychological variables that they were designed to assess. Much of the data reported by Jackson (1977) appears to substantiate the construct validity of the scales. This is particularly important for the JVIS, where direct interpretability of the scales is relied upon so heavily.

The second important avenue of research has been concerned with demonstrating validity for the occupational clusters. Once again, most of the research in this area has attempted to show that the occupational clusters have concurrent validity (i.e., workers in various occupations score highest on those scales that would be expected on an a priori basis). Few predictive validity studies have been reported to date to substantiate that the JVIS is useful in predicting occupational entry; however, most of the available research suggests that future studies will probably establish that relationship.

Applications of the JVIS

The JVIS has been used mostly with college students as an aid in curriculum selection and career planning. Additional sources of career information are given on the computer-generated profile to facilitate the career exploration process of examinees. The JVIS has not been used very extensively outside of educational settings. This may be due to the fact that it is such a new interest inventory, but it may also reflect that much of its scale derivation work utilized college students as subjects rather than employed adults. It remains to be seen whether the JVIS will begin to be used in other career counseling situations outside academia, such as for personnel selection or for placement in industry.

CRITICAL DISCUSSION:
Should Interest Tests Be Used in Personnel Selection?

Much controversy has arisen over the issue of whether interest tests should be used in personnel selection. Proponents of their use cite the vast literature indicating that interest tests predict eventual vocational choice and level of career satisfaction. They argue that since satisfied workers are most likely to remain in their chosen field of work, reduced employee turnover would save companies money that would otherwise be diverted to the selection and training of new employees.

On the other side of the controversy, critics argue that although interest tests have proven validity to predict which career fields an individual is likely to pursue, their validity rests on the assumption that examinees give genuine, unbiased responses to the test. They further state that it is inconceivable that potential job applicants are unbiased in responding to interest tests, since they are seeking the position for which they are being tested. Consequently, they are likely to respond to the test items as they believe a "good" employee of the company would. Critics cite several research studies (Wallace, 1950; Steward, 1947; Strong, 1943; Steinmetz, 1932) that have shown that interest tests results can be biased and distorted when test takers make conscious efforts to do so.

However, the issue is by no means resolved. Other studies (Campbell, 1971; Abrahams, Neumann & Githens, 1968; Stephenson, 1965) have suggested that real-life intentional distortions may not be as serious as those induced experimentally. Nevertheless, both Kirchener (1961) and Gray (1959) have argued that applicants for jobs can significantly alter their interest test scores.

While the use of testing in personnel selection has been questioned seriously by its critics, few have suggested other selection devices as reasonable alternatives. Perhaps one way to deal with the problem of biased or faked scores on these tests is to create scales to detect this type of response set. If the extent of the tendency to bias the test results could be determined, then a statistical correction factor could be applied to the results in order to obtain a more realistic appraisal of the applicant's career interests.

The controversy is likely to continue, however, until future research demonstrates that interest tests can be used validly in the selection process, or until other valid, cost-effective alternatives to interest testing are discovered.

SUMMARY

In this chapter, we have reviewed and analyzed four major interest measures in common use today. We examined in some detail how they were constructed and what information they provided to users. Sample cases and their associated profiles illustrated how these tests are used in clinical decision-making situations. Finally, each test was evaluated to determine how closely it reflects the characteristics of a good test outlined in the first section of this book. Table 17-8 provides a summary of this information as an aid in reviewing the tests covered in this chapter.

TABLE 17-8 COMPARISON OF CHARACTERISTICS OF VARIOUS INTEREST INVENTORIES

Test	Item Format	Item Content	Types of Scales	Benefits & Limitations
Strong Interest Inventory	Normative format with three choices: like, indifferent, and dislike	Items range from occupational titles to personal characteristics	Theme scales, basic scales, occupational scales, special scales, and admin. indices	*Advantages* oldest and most researched, good with business and professional-level occupations *Limitations* Poor discrimination among skilled and lower-level occupations, uses some unfamiliar job titles
Kuder Occupational Interest Survey	Ipsative format with examinees ranking their most- and least-preferred activity from a group of three	Items consist only of work-related activities	Vocational interest estimates, occupational scales, college major scales, and research scales	*Advantages* college major scales, gives ranking of interests for the examinee *Limitations* Reports scores in hard-to-compare correlation coefficients, ipsative format forces client rankings

Career Assessment Inventory	Normative format using seven-point Likert scale from most to least preferred	Items range from occupational titles to school subjects	Theme scales, basic scales, occupational scales, special scales, and admin. indices	*Advantages* Provides measure of skilled, semi-skilled, and unskilled-level of interests, uses combined-gender reference groups
				Limitations Has limited representation of occupations in several of Holland's groups
Jackson Vocational Interest Inventory	Ipsative format pairing two activities in each item	Items consist only of specific activities	Work role scales, work style scales, and additional scales	*Advantages* Permits hand scoring, newest and most technically advanced in item selection and scaling
				Limitations Little research yet to assess its validity

CHAPTER 18

PSYCHOLOGICAL MEASUREMENT IN INDUSTRY: ISSUES IN PREDICTION

In work settings ranging from small businesses to large corporations, from local, state, and federal agencies to the various arms of the military, decisions must be made regarding hiring, placement, training, promotion, raises, and the like. For the most part, personnel decisions involve either predictions or evaluations of job performance. Workers are hired, promoted, or placed in new jobs in order to achieve maximal levels of productivity; accuracy in prediction of job performance is therefore the cornerstone of successful personnel administration. Similarly, organizational rewards are in part based upon evaluations of *past* performance. The allocation of promotions, raises, bonuses, and awards depends upon evaluations of past and present performance. The accurate measurement of present and past performance is therefore central to many decisions regarding the allocation of organizational rewards. This chapter deals with the prediction of future performance; the measurement of present and past performance is discussed in Chapter 19.

Before discussing the actual tests that are used in industry to predict job performance, it is useful to consider the context of testing, or the extent to which psychological tests are used for making work-related decisions.

EXTENT AND IMPACT OF PERSONNEL TESTING

If one adopts a broad definition of the term "test," a definition that includes interviews and work samples as well as traditional paper-and-pencil tests, then it is safe to conclude that personnel testing is almost universal. An interview of some sort precedes nearly every job offer, and those candidates who are not interviewed are almost certain to have filled out a standard job application, which in some cases could be used as a form of test. If the definition of the term "test" is narrowed to include only paper-and-pencil measures used to assess candidates' abilities, skills, and achievements, the assessment of the extent to which tests are actually used in industry and the public sector changes somewhat. Friedman and Williams (1982) estimate that two thirds of the companies in the United States use written tests as aids in making selection and promotion decisions, although very few companies rely exclusively on tests of this type. Written tests are less common in Great Britain; approximately 50 percent of the British companies surveyed by Miller (1975) used written tests for selection and placement. Since the introduction of validity generalization procedures (discussed later in this chapter) and utility analysis (see Chapter 8), both of which suggest that selection tests are highly effective, testing appears to have increased.

The use of written tests is much more common for office positions than for production and sales jobs. In particular, candidates for clerical jobs represent the most heavily tested group of applicants in the private sector. Between 60 percent and 80 percent of the companies that use written tests use clerical tests. Testing is also common for positions involving highly specific skills or abilities (e.g., master electrician).

The fact that a test is given, and that test scores may be entered into an applicant's file, does not necessarily mean that the tests will be used in making personnel decisions. Tenopyr (1981) notes that although a number of tests may be given to each applicant, there is very little evidence that scores on written tests actually have a major impact upon personnel decisions. Private employers tend to rely heavily on interviews, credentials, and recommendations in making selection decisions, and they may pay little attention to scores on standardized tests.

Testing in Government and the Military

Written tests are very widely used for selection and placement in the federal government; they are used somewhat less, although still extensively, by state, county, and local governments. For the most part, civil service hiring is done using a merit system, in which applicants must receive high scores on competitive examinations in order to be considered for the job. Nearly 90 percent of all federal employees work in jobs that are filled using the merit system; for state, county, and local employees, the figure is nearer to 80 percent (Friedman & Williams, 1982). Figures from fiscal year 1978 provide a concrete indication of the scope of the federal government's testing program. That year there were over 1,600,000 applicants for federal jobs at all levels. Almost 700,000 of those applicants took at least one written test in the process of attempting to qualify for the prospective jobs (Friedman & Williams, 1982). Testing in the civilian and military sectors of the federal government has continued to grow since the time these figures were obtained.

The military represents the largest consumer of employment tests. Although the military workforce is considerably smaller than the workforce in the private sector or in civilian government, tests are used so widely and so frequently in the military that the total number of tests used per year far exceeds the total figure for either the private sector or civilian government. For example, over 1.5 million people per year take the Armed Forces Vocational Aptitude Battery (ASVAB). In addition to this basic test, the military uses over 900 separate skill classification tests. Finally, a large amount of basic and applied research on the validity of tests is carried out by the military.[1]

The military faces very different testing problems from those encountered in the private sector. Testing in the private sector is often designed to select from a pool of applicants the persons most qualified for a specific job. Although the military does set minimum selection standards, much of its testing is used in making placement rather than selection decisions. In other words, the military must plan carefully to use the talents, skills, and abilities of its recruits effectively. As a result, tests used in the military are likely to stress a combination of aptitudes and skills that are useful across a broad range of military jobs. Military testing very often includes the use of wide-ranging test batteries, such as the ASVAB, together with tests of skills that are necessary for specific military assignments.

Occupational and Professional Licensing

There are over 2,000 occupations that may require licensing or certification, ranging from accountants to physical therapists; in some states up to 25 percent of the workforce consists of licensed practitioners. Both oral and written tests are frequently used as part of the certification process. Testing for a license or a professional certificate therefore represents a fairly large scale activity.

A sizable array of state, local, and nongovernmental licensing boards exists. For the most part, examinations are prepared by board members, although national examinations prepared by professional testing agencies are becoming increasingly common (Friedman & Williams, 1982). Tests which are prepared by licensing boards vary extremely in quality; locally prepared exams almost always are technically inferior to nationally prepared ones (Wigdor & Garner, 1982a). Finally, licensing boards do not always demonstrate, or even investigate, the content, construct, or criterion-related validity of their exams. It is likely that many of the tests currently used in professional and occupational licensure are of limited validity.

Viewed as a whole, testing for professional licensure and occupation certification is in a state of near chaos (Murphy, 1988). National tests are used widely in some occupations but do not exist for many others. Licensing requirements typically vary from state to state, and the licensing exams used in different states and localities for the same occupation may show little overlap. Although testing for professional and occupational certification represents a potentially important application of psychological testing, as yet the available measurement technology is not being used to its fullest potential.

PREDICTING PERFORMANCE

Psychological tests provide information about those skills, abilities, experiences, and characteristics of individuals that can be used to predict job performance. One of the striking features of personnel testing is the diversity of techniques used to obtain predic-

---

[1]Unfortunately, little of this research is published in widely accessible journals; most validity studies are described in technical reports whose circulation is sporadic (for examples, see Vinberg & Joyner, 1982).

tor data. In part, this range is a reflection of the diversity of the world of work; "performance" as a middle manager is a very different thing than "performance" as a bus driver, and the abilities, skills, and experiences that contribute to performance in one job may be less relevant in another. The diversity of measurement techniques is also a reflection of the apparent diversity of factors that affect job performance. Depending on the job in question, performance may be a function of basic cognitive or noncognitive abilities (e.g., verbal comprehension, manual dexterity), previous experience, social skills, specific task-oriented skills (e.g., the ability to type 40 words per minute), levels of motivation, or some combination of all these factors.

Some testing techniques (e.g., paper-and-pencil tests, interviews) *appear* to be more appropriate than others for assessing specific attributes of the individual that might help predict job performance. For example, it is often assumed that basic cognitive abilities are best measured by paper-and-pencil tests, whereas the interview might be best for evaluating social skill. Other examples are shown in Table 18-1. The question of whether specific measurement techniques (e.g., interviews) are *in fact* most effective for assessing specific skills, abilities, knowledge, or personal characteristics is an emprical issue; we return to this question at the end of this section.

Paper-and-Pencil Tests

There is considerable overlap between the paper-and-pencil tests used in industry and those used in other settings, such as educational or clinical testing programs. In particular, the tests of general intelligence that are used widely in personnel selection and placement are essentially similar to those used in many other contexts. General intelligence tests used in industry are most typically group-type tests and are likely to be relatively short, but otherwise they do not differ in essential ways from other group tests of intelligence. The Wonderlic Personnel Test, a 50-item multiple-choice test that includes verbal, mathematical, pictorial, and analytic items, is a good example of the kind of intelligence test likely to be used in personnel testing and selection. This test has demonstrated high levels of reliability (alternate form reliabilities typically exceed .90) and is significantly correlated with measures of performance in a wide variety of jobs (Murphy, 1984b). There is also considerable evidence that scores on this brief test are very highly correlated with scores on more complex tests, such as the Wechsler Adult Intelligence Scale (WAIS) (Dodrill & Warner, 1988). The Wonderlic is now available in a computerized version designed to assess both ability and personality factors; the validity of the newer test is not yet well established.

TABLE 18-1 METHODS OF OBTAINING JOB-RELEVANT INFORMATION

Information desired	Method most likely to be used
Basic abilities, aptitudes	Paper-and-pencil Test
Social skills, motivation	Interview
Background experience	Application Blank, References, Background Checks
Current performance	Work Sample Test
Holistic evaluation	Assessment Centers

Several test batteries are widely used in personnel selection and placement; examples include the General Aptitude Test Battery (GATB) and the Armed Services Vocational Aptitude Battery (ASVAB). These test batteries provide measures of specific aptitudes that are relevant to work. More important, these tests are dominated by the same general factor that dominates other ability tests. That is, scores on these tests are strongly influenced by the respondent's level of general mental ability. This is critical for the simple reason that general mental ability is recognized as the single most important predictor of performance in a wide variety of jobs. That is, there is no other predictor that shows comparable levels of validity in an equally wide range of settings. (Evidence supporting this conclusion is reviewed in a special issue of *Journal of Vocational Behavior,* Vol. 29, No. 3.) As we will note later in this chapter, other predictors sometimes fare as well as tests of general mental ability, but no other technique for predicting job performance matches the overall effectiveness of tests of general mental ability.

Although intelligence tests used in industry are not fundamentally different from the tests used in other contexts, there are several tests of specific skills and aptitudes that are used almost exclusively in personnel selection and placement. Outstanding exemplars include several clerical tests and tests of mechanical comprehension.

Clerical Tests. Outside of the military, clerical workers represent the most widely tested category of workers. Approximately two thirds of all companies use written tests as aids in making hiring and promotion decisions, and between 60 percent and 80 percent of these companies use clerical tests.[2] These tests vary considerably in their emphasis, ranging from tests that sample one highly specific facet of clerical work to tests that tap several broadly defined abilities thought to be necessary to perform clerical jobs.

The Minnesota Clerical Test is an example of a test that measures a highly specific clerical function. The Minnesota Clerical Test is composed of two subtests, Number Comparison and Name Comparison. Both subtests are made up of long lists of pairs of numbers or pairs of names, in which each pair is either identical or differs in some minor detail. Examples of items similar to those used on the Minnesota Clerical Test are shown in Table 18-2.

A person taking this test must read each pair of names or numbers, compare them, and mark each pair which is identical. There is a very strict time limit, and the total score is determined by the number of pairs checked. Although there is some deduction for errors (checking a nonidentical pair, failure to check an identical pair), scores on the Minnesota Clerical Test are determined almost entirely by speed. In fact, this test is a perfect example of a speed test—if there were no time limit, almost anyone who understood the test instructions would answer all the test items correctly.

The Minnesota Clerical Test is a reliable measure of perceptual speed and accuracy; test-retest reliabilities typically exceed .70. There is also evidence of consistent positive correlations between scores on this test and supervisory performance ratings. However, questions may be raised about the importance of perceptual speed and accuracy in most clerical jobs. Although filing and data-retrieval tasks are frequently performed by clerical workers, there is little evidence that individual differences in perceptual speed contribute greatly to the variability in job performance. Thus, although the Minnesota Clerical Test

---

[2]Many of these companies also test nonclerical workers.

TABLE 18-2   ITEMS SIMILAR TO THOSE
ON THE MINNESOTA CLERICAL TEST

Number comparison	
1. 34796	34796
2. 246738	246638
3. 594327	594321
4. 6674532	6674532
5. 47948672	47948672

Name comparison	
1. Mitchell Tools	Mitchell Tools
2. Anderson, J. A.	Andersen, J. A.
3. Biloxi, Miss.	Biloxi, Miss.
4. Gleason's Motors	Gleson's Motors
5. McNally, John	McNally, John

possesses a certain amount of face validity (i.e., it *looks* like tasks often performed by clerical workers), it is not clear whether the criterion-related validity of this test is due to the importance of perceptual speed in job performance or to the overlap between perceptual speed and general intelligence.

This test shows a number of similarities to the tasks used by many cognitive psychologists to assess intelligence (Hunt, 1982). It is possible that the performance-related abilities measured by this type of a test are more cognitive (e.g., speed of mental operations, speed in comparing messages) than perceptual (Jensen, 1980).

Tests of mechanical comprehension.   A variety of skilled and semi-skilled blue-collar jobs call for an understanding of basic mechanical principles, as well as the ability to predict the outcome of mechanical activities, or to reason backwards from effects to probable mechanical causes. Examples of this job class include repair jobs of all types, machinists, many types of construction workers and laborers, and, of course, mechanics. Although mechanical knowledge and mechanical reasoning ability are not completely distinct from general intelligence, there is some utility in employing measures of mechanical comprehension rather than measures of academic intelligence in many blue-collar jobs. Measures of mechanical comprehension have face validity as well as a solid record of criterion-related validity (Ghiselli, 1966).

The Bennett Mechanical Comprehension Test is an outstanding example of an occupational test of basic mechanical knowledge and mechanical reasoning. The Bennett is available in two alternate forms (Forms S and T); each is a 68-item test designed to be administered using a 30-minute time limit. The pictorial multiple-choice items on this test vary widely in difficulty but share a common theme. The respondent is required to apply simple principles of physics and mechanics in responding to questions concerning the operations of common machines, tools, and vehicles. Examples of items from the Bennett are presented in Figure 18-1.

The Bennett Mechanical Comprehension Test has been shown to be highly reliable (internal consistency of reliabilities range from .81 to .93) and has shown respectable levels of criterion-related validity. Scores on the Bennett typically have shown correla-

Figure 18-1   Sample Items from Bennett Mechanical Comprehension Test

Source: From the Bennett Mechanical Comprehension Test. Copyright 1942, 1967–1970, 1980 by The Psychological Corporation. Reproduced by permission. All rights reserved.

tions of approximately .30 with measures of performance in training courses and with measures of job proficiency in studies involving machinists, mechanics, and machine operators (Ghiselli, 1966). Because of its well-documented reliability, validity, and simplicity, the Bennett is one of the most popular tests of mechanical comprehension. However, as Wing (1992) noted, one criticism of the Bennett is that it "just looks old"; if you look at the sample items in Figure 18-1, you will probably agree. It is not clear whether the appearance of the test influences the way in which individuals respond, but you can make the case the individuals will not take the test as seriously if most or all of the items represent items no longer found in a modern workplace.

Personality inventories.   The use of personality inventories as predictors of job performance has been a subject of controversy for nearly 30 years. An influential review by Guion and Gottier (1965) concluded that the research available at that time did not support the validity of personality measures as selection instruments. Although the intentions of Guion and Gottier (1965) were to encourage better research on the relationship between personality and job performance, almost the opposite happened. For the two decades that followed Guion and Gottier (1965), the accepted wisdom in personnel psychology implied that personality was not really relevant to job performance and that personality scales should not be used in selecting among job applicants. As a result of three recent reviews (Barrick & Mount, 1991; Hough, Eaton, Dunnette, Kamp & McCloy, 1990; Tett, Jackson & Rothstein, 1991), this view has changed.

There is evidence that a variety of personality characteristics are consistently related to job performance, including three of the "big five": agreeableness, conscientiousness, and openness to experience. Average validities for measures of these traits typically fall in the .15–.25 range, which, though not as high as validities demonstrated by cognitive ability tests, is clearly large enough to suggest that personality inventories can make a worthwhile contribution. Although measures of these and other personality characteristics are susceptible to faking (e.g., job applicants may distort their responses to appear more dependable or agreeable than they really are; see Chapter 10), response distortion does not appear to substantially affect the validity of personality inventories as predictors of performance (Hough et al., 1990). It is likely, therefore, that organizations will increase their use of personality measures in personnel selection, particularly in jobs where dependability, integrity (integrity tests are discussed later in this chapter), or responsibility are thought to be critical determinants of success.

Application Blanks

Standardized application blanks, which include questions dealing with the applicant's personal and work history as well as questions about his or her present status (e.g., age, address, marital status), have been used in industry since at least 1894 (Owens, 1976). Although application blanks are used routinely in almost every organization, these are not always recognized as tests. This is unfortunate, since it is well known that information from standard application blanks (background data, or "biodata") can be used to successfully predict job performance. In fact, biodata has consistently been shown to be one of the best, if not *the* best, predictors of job performance (Mumford, Uhlman & Kilcullen, 1992; Owens, 1976; Reilly & Chao, 1982).

There are two different strategies for using background data to predict job performance: (a) the development of empirical keys, or systems for scoring application blanks, and (b) the assignment of persons to groups that are homogeneous with respect to biographical information but differ in terms of expected job performance. The empirical keying strategy is the older of the two; to date, many of the papers reporting substantial correlations between background data and job performance have followed this strategy. However, more recent research on the use of background data in predicting job performance has moved in the direction of theories that classify persons on the basis of their patterns of past behavior, and that predict future performance on the basis of those classifications (Mael, 1991; Mumford et al., 1992, Owens & Schoenfeldt, 1979).

The empirical method of scoring biographical information blanks rests on the assumption that "successful" workers (defined in terms of performance, tenure on the job, salary, etc.) systematically differ from "unsuccessful" workers in a number of ways, and that at least some of the variables on which they differ are measured by standard application blanks. If an applicant's responses to a biographical information blank are highly similar to those of successful workers, and dissimilar from those of unsuccessful workers, success would be predicted for that applicant. On the other hand, a person whose responses are highly similar to those of the unsuccessful group would be predicted to fail. Thus, it is possible to assign to each person's total set of responses to a standard application blank a score that measures the degree to which the responses are similar to those given by successful workers, as opposed to those given by unsuccessful workers. There is considerable evidence that biodata scores of this type can be used to predict both job performance and turnover (Cascio, 1976; Reilly & Chao, 1982).

The simplest method of scoring application blanks is the "horizontal percentage" method described by Stead and Shartle (1940), which is similar to the method used in scoring the Strong Interest Inventory. The first step in applying the horizontal percentage method is to divide a pool of current or past workers into "success" and "failure" categories. Next, the number of successes and failures who endorse each possible response on an application blank is compared. A weight is computed for each possible response to each of the items on the application blank; this weight corresponds to the proportion of successes in the group of workers who endorsed that particular response.

Table 18-3 illustrates the process. In the group of workers described in the table, 60 had previous employment experience. Fifteen of these were failures, yielding a success rate of 25 percent. The item weight for the response "Yes" to the question, "Have you ever been employed?" is therefore 25. The item weight for the response "No" is 50 (25 successes out of 50 workers with no previous experience, or 50 percent). Using this same method, weights are developed for each of the possible responses to the item "Education" and to any other items contained in the application blank. The applicant's total score for the application blank is then computed by summing the weights assigned to each response chosen by the applicant. As a further illustration, an applicant who indicated "Yes" and "Grade School" in response to the two questions shown in the table would receive a total score of 45, whereas an applicant who indicated "Yes" and "College" would receive a score of 105. Another applicant who indicated "No" and "High School" would also receive a score of 105.

The item weight reflects the proportion of successes among those who endorsed a particular response. If there are many successes and few failures among those who give the same responses to a demographic item (e.g., "Post-Graduate"), the item discriminates successes from failures and receives a large weight. If there are many failures and few successes (e.g., "Grade School"), the item discriminates failures from successes and receives small weight. The total score therefore reflects the degree to which an applicant's responses are similar to those of the successful group. The total score is large if the applicant endorses many items with large weights—those chosen frequently by successes but infrequently by failures. The total score is low if the applicant endorses many items with low weights—those endorsed most frequently by failures.

There are many problems with the purely empirical approach to scoring biographical information blanks. First, the theroetical base of this method of scoring is sorely lacking. There is generally no attempt to determine *why* some items should receive large weights and others small weights. The determination of weights is done on a strictly empirical basis, and if the success rate in one group (e.g., males) is lower than in another, new applicants from that group will be penalized. This procedure creates some potentially explosive problems, since it presents the clear appearance of discrimination. Furthermore, the lack of any theoretical base makes it very difficult to explain why someone is penalized for membership in certain groups. Although equal employment opportunity laws make it unlikely that someone will be denied a job solely on the basis of membership in the "wrong" demographic group, the logical implication of the purely empirical strategy is to do precisely that—to select some groups and reject others, without necessarily being able to explain how group membership affects jobs performance.

There are also statistical difficulties with the purely empirical approach. Empirically derived scoring systems take advantage of *any* relationships between group membership and success, even those that are due to chance or to insufficient sampling. It is therefore necessary to "cross-validate" empirically derived scoring keys by demonstrating the valid-

TABLE 18-3 ILLUSTRATION OF THE HORIZONTAL PERCENTAGE METHOD

Item	Responses	Number of successes	Number of failures	Total	Success rate	Weight
Have you previously been employed?	Yes	15	45	60	15/60 = 25%	25
	No	25	25	50	25/50 = 50%	50
Education	Grade School	5	20	25	5/25 = 20%	20
	High School	20	25	45	25/45 = 55%	55
	College	20	5	25	20/25 = 80%	80
	Post-graduate	13	2	15	13/15 = 93%	93

Illustrative total scores

Responses to biographical information blank	Weights	Total score
Experience, grade school	25 + 20 =	45
No experience, high school	50 + 55 =	105
Experience, college	25 + 80 =	105
Experience, Post-graduate	25 + 93 =	118

358

ity of those keys in several independent samples (Darlington, 1968; Murphy, 1983; for a critical review of cross-validation methods, see Mitchell & Klimoski, 1986). A surprising number of studies fail to cross-validate empirical scoring keys (Schwab & Oliver, 1974). Many scoring keys are developed on a completely empirical basis, with little theory either to guide the researcher's initial hypothesis or to alert researchers to possibly spurious results. Results from a single sample will seriously overestimate the validity of an empirical scoring key, and it is unlikely that a useful validity estimate can be obtained unless the key is cross-validated in another, independent sample.

Another concern is the stability of empirical scoring keys. There is evidence that the validity of empirically scored biographical information blanks systematically deteriorates over time, and that a key that is highly valid one year may show little or no validity in ensuing years (Wernimont, 1962).

Owens and his associates developed an alternative strategy for predicting behavior on the basis of background data (Owens & Schoenfeldt, 1979). This approach, referred to as the Developmental-Integrative Model, involves sorting people into a small number of groups that are relatively homogeneous with respect to a wide variety of background data. The data used in classifying individuals includes standard demographic measures as well as measures pertaining to facets of one's life experience, such as academic achievement, group participation, financial responsibility, family adjustment, and situational stability (Baehr & Williams, 1967). The underlying assumption of this approach is that people whose background and experience is fundamentally similar will show similar patterns of behavior in the future, whereas people whose backgrounds are different will behave differently. There is considerable evidence to support this assumption; people who differ in basic patterns of background data are also likely to differ in social attitudes, goals, personality orientation, and levels of achievement (Owens, 1971). Even more to the point, persons who differ in basic patterns of background data are likely to differ in job performance and in the rapidity of job turnover (Brush & Owens, 1979).

There has been considerable progress in identifying the constructs that underly responses to biodata items (Mael, 1991; Mumford et al., 1992); this research is likely to help explain *why* biodata items are so successful in predicting future performance. The emergence of construct-oriented models represents a definite advance in the use of biodata in predicting job performance. Rather than examining individual responses to an application blank in an attempt to differentiate good from poor performers, this approach encourages researchers to classify persons into groups with similar life histories and to search for differences in performance among those groups. The classification of persons rather than items allows one to take into account considerable amounts of data from different sources, rather than relying on an arbitrary classification of present or past workers into successes or failures. At a more fundamental level, these models provide a scientific rationale for the use of background information in predicting job performance. The model encourages one to view biodata as an indicator of what a person *has* done, which in turn provides a solid basis for predicting what the person *will* do. However, the same problems that are present in empirically based uses of biodata may also be present here. Any use of biodata in making decisions about individuals ultimately rewards some people and penalizes others for their demographic characteristics (race, sex, income, etc.). This practice is regarded by many, including the authors of this book, as fundamentally unfair and, as will be noted later, may violate the civil rights of applicants.

The Employment Interview

Although there is considerable diversity in the types of tests used in making personnel selection decisions, there is one nearly universal component of all systematic personnel selection strategies—the interview. Surveys suggest that well over 95 percent of all employers use interviews as part of the selection process, and that the number of interviews conducted yearly may run as high as 20 *per person hired* (Landy & Trumbo, 1980). Not only is the interview widespread; it also appears to have a substantial effect on selection decisions; The majority of the firms surveyed by Miner and Miner (1978) identified the interview as the single most important component of their selection program. More recent studies (e.g., Ahlburg, 1992) attest to the continuing popularity of the interview. It is therefore no surprise that the employment interview has been the focus of a tremendous amount of research.

Research on the interview has been reviewed by Wagner (1949), Webster (1964, 1982), Ulrich and Trumbo (1965), Schmitt (1976), and Arvey and Campion (1982). Overall, these reviews paint a fairly dismal picture. First, there is little consistent evidence for the reliability of the interview; although individual interviews are sometimes consistent in their ratings, agreement between different interviewers is almost always low. Second, there is little evidence for the validity of the interview; validity coefficients in the teens are typical (Hunter & Hunter, 1984; Reilly & Chao, 1982), although some reviewers have reported higher correlations between interview outcomes and performance measures (Wiesner & Cronshaw, 1988).

The interview is especially prone to a number of systematic sources of error that, together with the limited reliability of the interview, serve to lower the overall validity of the interview. For example, the sex, age, race, and physical attractiveness of the applicant all appear to affect the outcomes of interviews unduly (Arvey, 1979b). Furthermore, the effects of these variables on interviewers' ratings are not necessarily uniform but, rather, tend to vary as a function of the job in question. For example, attractiveness may work in one's favor for some jobs, but it may work against one in others (Heilman & Saruwatari, 1979).

Upon studying the *incremental* validity of the interview, the picture becomes even more depressing. The interview is generally used in conjunction with a number of other selection tests (i.e., biodata, paper-and-pencil tests), and there is *very* little evidence that the interview adds to the validity of selection decisions. In other words, there is little reason to believe that decisions made with tests and interviews are any better than decisions made using tests alone. In fact, given the potential of bias in the interview, there are undoubtedly circumstances in which the use of a selection interview *reduces* the validity of selection decisions.

Given the consistently negative evidence with regard to the reliability and validity of the interview, the continuing popularity of this technique is surprising. Arvey and Campion (1982) suggest several reasons why interviews retain their popularity (see also Dawes, Faust & Meehl, 1989).

First, interviewers rarely receive concrete feedback on the accuracy of their decisions and therefore are likely to overestimate the validity of their recommendations. Research on hindsight bias and on a phenomenon referred to as the "illusion of validity" suggests that people systematically overestimate the accuracy of their own decisions

(Einhorn & Hogarth, 1978). As a result, interviewers are biased toward believing that interviews they conduct *do* provide a firm basis for making selection decisions, and are likely to discount the volume of research suggesting that interviews are not particularly valid.

Second, the interview is often regarded as more practical than alternatives that may be technically superior. Most people believe they are good interviewers. It therefore appears to be quite easy to set up a valid interview program—one must merely decide on a handful of starter questions and appoint someone to conduct the interviews. Empirical research suggests almost the opposite: that interviews are not likely to yield useful information unless they are carefully structured and unless interviewers are carefully trained (Mayfield, Brown & Hamstra, 1980). However, empirical research has historically had little effect on interview practice, and it is unlikely that research of this type will lead to qualitative improvements in interview techniques.

Third, the interview represents a chance to "sell" the organization to the applicant. The interviewer does not merely collect information but provides the applicant with a glimpse of the organization and may serve a critical function in the applicant's decision to accept or reject an offer.

It appears unlikely that the interview will disappear as a standard employment practice; over 30 years of research demonstrating biases as well as low levels of reliability and validity has hardly put a dent in the popularity of this selection technique.[3] It is therefore important to determine optimal ways of using the interview to increase the validity of selection decisions. Several suggestions have been made.

First, it is highly inefficient to use the interview as a method of obtaining routine background information (e.g., address, education); an application blank is better suited for this purpose (Tucker & Rowe, 1977).

Second, it is clear that interviews should be carefully structured (Arvey & Campion, 1982; Campion, Pursell & Brown, 1988; Schwab & Heneman, 1969; Wiesner & Cronshaw, 1988). Latham, Saari, Pursell, and Campion (1980) have recommended an extremely structured interview format, referred to as a "situational interview," in which examinees are asked to describe how they would behave in several hypothetical but critical situations. For example, an applicant for a baker's job might be asked what he or she would do if two oven thermometers gave readings that varied widely. Responses are independently rated by multiple interviewers, and composite ratings are used to make decisions about examinees. Although this structure may not be optimal in all settings, it represents a clear advance over the unconnected series of spontaneous questions that an untrained interviewer tends to ask. It is possible that increasing reliance on more structured interviews accounts in part for reports of increasing validity (Wiesner & Cronshaw, 1988).[4]

Third, interviews should focus on behaviors, rather than attitudes or skills (Janz, 1982; Motowidlo, Dunnette, Carter, Tippins, Werner, Griffiths & Vaughan, 1992; Orpen, 1985). There is evidence that a clear focus on behavioral information increases the reliability and criterion-related validity of measures obtained on the basis of interviews.

---

[3]Tenopyr and Oeltjen (1982) note that research on the reliability and validity of the interview is becoming increasingly rare, perhaps as a result of the limited impact of existing research.

[4]Differences in the design of interview research may account for some of the apparent increases in validity coefficients reported in recent research (Dreher, Ash & Hancock, 1988).

Fourth, it is reasonably clear that the interview is better for measuring some attributes of applicants than others. For example, interviews may not be appropriate for measuring basic cognitive abilities. In addition, since an interview represents a relatively short sample of behavior, this technique may not be appropriate for measuring traits or personality characteristics that are manifest only over a long period of time, such as honesty or dependability (McCormick & Ilgen, 1980). Rather, the interview is probably optimal for measuring characteristics such as social skills, which are manifest during the period of the interview itself and which are exceedingly difficult to measure using other testing techniques.

Work Sample Tests

Wernimont and Campbell (1968) distinguish between two strategies for predicting future job performance: the use of signs and the use of samples. An example of the former is when a paper-and-pencil test of mechanical comprehension is used to predict performance as a machinist. The applicant's level of mechanical comprehension is viewed as a sign, or probably a causal agent, in determining future job performance. Thus, people who receive high scores are predicted to perform better than those who receive low scores, based upon the assumption that ability is one of the signs of performance. The latter strategy, which involves using a sample of present performance to predict future performance, is considerably simpler and more direct. The use of signs assumes the existence of some theory regarding the relationship between the characteristics that are measured and job performance; the use of samples of present performance to predict future performance involves the simpler assumption that performance shows some consistency across time and tasks. Wernimont and Campbell (1968) argue that predictions of future behavior that are based upon samples of the characteristic behavior of individuals are likely to be more accurate than predictions that are based on measures of specific skills, ability, or knowledge (signs). Reviews by Asher and Sciarrino (1974) and Reilly and Chao (1982) provide at least partial support for this argument.

Work sample tests range from those that involve relatively simple tasks, such as a five-minute typing sample, to those involving complex samples of performance, such as those obtained using flight simulators. There are two common features to all work sample tests that should be examined in evaluating those tests. First, every work sample test puts the applicant in a situation that in some way is essentially similar to a work situation and measures performance on tasks reasonably similar to those that make up the job itself. Second, every work sample *differs* in important ways from the job in which it will be used. Even when the tasks are identical to those required on the job, it is reasonable to expect that examinees, who are trying to impress their prospective employers, will show higher levels of motivation in work sample tests than they will on the job. Thus, it is most reasonable to regard a work sample as a measure of *maximal* performance rather than a measure of *typical* performance. This is an important distinction because measures of maximal performance are not necessarily correlated with measures of typical performance (Sackett, Zedeck & Fogli, 1988).

When tests are used as signs of future performance, criterion-related validity is a function of the content or construct validity of both the test and criterion, as well as the validity of the theory linking a particular ability or set of abilities to performance. When a sample of present behavior is used to predict future performance, validity is primarily a function of the representativeness of the work sample. Thus, Asher (1972) hypothesized that the criterion-related validity of a work sample test would be highest when the point-to-point similarity between the test and the job itself was maximized. A later review by Asher and Sciarrino (1974) provided strong support for this hypothesis—the greater the similarity between the content of the work sample test and the content of the job, the more accurate the test will be in predicting job performance.

The principle that validity is maximized when the test most closely resembles the job itself provides useful guidance for designing work sample tests for many blue-collar and clerical jobs. It is often possible to have candidates perform the actual tasks that comprise the job (e.g., operating specific machines, typing, filing, retrieval); and if an adequate job analysis has been performed, it should be a reasonably simple matter to determine the match between the test and the job. However, as we noted in Chapter 7, assessing the content similarity between the test and the job can sometimes involve complex questions about the examinees' motivation and state of mind when responding to the test versus performing their jobs.

Managerial work sample tests.

Managerial work sample tests.   Although it is more difficult to develop a comprehensive and valid work sample test in managerial jobs than in many nonmanagerial jobs, the potential payoff of a valid managerial work sample test is considerable. Managerial effectiveness is not the simple result of possessing one or two key traits or abilities but is the result of a complex interaction between characteristics of the individual and characteristics of the situation. Samples of behavior in situations that seem to capture many of the salient characteristics of day-to-day management are thus particularly valuable in predicting performance as a manager (Cascio, 1982).

Probably the most widely used type of managerial work sample test is the *in-basket* (Fredericksen, 1962). As its name implies, an in-basket test is a simulation which presents the applicant with the types of memos, letters, notes, and other materials found in a typical manager's in-basket. The applicant is given background information on the job and is instructed to play the role of a new manager in the job. In response to the materials in the in-basket, the applicant is required to write letters, memos, agendas, and so forth, indicating how he or she would respond to the information in the in-basket. The applicant's responses can be scored in terms of their overall appropriateness, the order in which the applicant responds to items, the responses to specific critical pieces of information, or some combination of these factors.

Although in-basket tests vary considerably in content, generally being tailored to individual jobs and organizations, there is considerable consistency in the results achieved using this type of test. Brass and Oldham (1976) and Wollowick and McNamara (1969) report correlations ranging from .24 to .34 between ratings obtained from in-basket tests and a number of measures of managerial performance and effectiveness. Furthermore, there are clear differences between the in-basket responses of management trainees and those of experienced managers. Trainees tend to choose strategies for solving the problems posed in the in-basket that are less flexible, less feasible, and less effective than those chosen by experienced managers (Lopez, 1966). Research also suggests that the in-basket test effectively discriminates promising managerial candidates from applicants who are less likely to succeed. However, more recent research (e.g.,

Schippman, Prien & Katz, 1990) has questioned the reliability and validity of scores obtained from in-basket tests. On the whole, we believe that carefully constructed in-basket tests can yield useful information but that the construction of these tests is more difficult than it at first appears. Like other types of tests, it is probably easier to produce a bad in-basket test than a good one.

Another popular managerial work sample test is the leaderless group discussion (Bass, 1954). There is an exceedingly simple simulation, yet one that has considerable potential for measuring characteristics of potential managers important for successful job performance but not readily measured using other types of tests. In a leaderless group discussion, a group of participants is asked to carry on a discussion of a specific, usually job-related topic for a period of time. For example, a group of applicants might be told to conduct a 45-minute discussion of "career planning." By design, there is no formal discussion leader. There may be several raters who observe the discussion, but these raters do not participate in any way. Group members are therefore responsible for initiating, maintaining, and directing the group discussion.

It should be obvious that this procedure provides some information about aggressiveness, ability to provide structure, and leadership—inevitably, some group members take active or controlling roles, whereas others have little to say (Bass, 1954). This technique has also been used to assess characteristics such as persuasiveness, self-confidence, resistance to stress, oral communication ability, and interpersonal skills (Wollowick & McNamara, 1969).

Both Bass (1954) and Wollowick and McNamara (1969) suggest that the leaderless group discussion technique shows levels of reliability and validity comparable to those shown by other personnel tests. To some extent reliability and validity depend upon the characteristics the leaderless group discussion is used to measure. This technique seems particularly appropriate for measuring the tendency or ability to impose structure on a relatively ambiguous and unstructured situation but may be less suitable for measuring specific skills or knowledge. The combination of the leaderless group discussion with other types of managerial work sample might be particularly useful (Lopez, 1966).

Assessment Centers

The assessment center is not, as its name might imply, a place, nor is it a single, unified method of predicting job performance. Rather, an assessment center is a structured combination of assessment techniques that is used to provide a wide-ranging, holistic assessment of each participant. This technique is most likely to be used in making managerial selection and promotion decisions, although assessment centers are also employed for many other jobs.

The assessment center as it exists today is a lineal descendent of the multiple assessment procedures used by German and British psychologists in World War II and adopted by the American Office of Strategic Services (OSS) as aids in selecting agents and operatives (OSS, 1948). By the early 1970s over 1,000 companies had experimented with this method, prompting Hinrichs (1978) to refer to the assessment center as "one of the more phenomenal success stories of applied psychology" (p. 596).

Although the assessment centers used in different organizations differ widely in terms of content and organization, there are several features that nearly all assessment centers share in common and that are distinctive to this approach (Bray, Campbell & Grant, 1974; Bray & Grant, 1966; Finkle, 1976). These include the following:

Assessment in groups. In an assessment center, small groups of participants are assessed simultaneously. Since group activities and peer evaluations are an integral part of most assessment centers, it would be impossible to use this technique to its fullest advantage in assessing a single individual.

Assessment by groups. The assessment team may be made up of managers, psychologists, consultants, or some mix of these three groups. Each participant's behavior is observed and evaluated by a number of different assessors, and the final ratings represent the assessment team's consensus regarding the individual being evaluated.

The use of multiple methods. Assessment center activities might include ability tests, personality tests, situational tests, interviews, peer evaluations, and performance tests. The central assumption of this method is that each test has its strengths and weaknesses, and that a combination of diverse tests is necessary to capitalize on the strengths of each individual test.

The use of situational tests. Although the specific tests used vary from organization to organization, nearly every assessment center uses some type of work sample or situational test. Both the in-basket and the leaderless group discussion tests are popular, as are other role-playing exercises.

Assessment along multiple dimensions. The end result of an assessment center is a consensus rating along each of several dimensions. For example, candidates going through an assessment center at AT&T are rated on 25 dimensions, including organizational planning, resistance to stress, energy, and self-objectivity (Thornton & Byham, 1982). Each exercise in the assessment center typically provides information relevant to one or more dimensions, and ratings of a specific dimension (e.g., energy) might reflect data obtained from several different exercises.

The appeal of assessment centers is a function of the face validity, practicality, and, to a lesser extent, the empirical evidence documenting the criterion-related validity of this technique. In contrast to several paper-and-pencil tests that might be used in selection, the assessment center *appears* valid. The exercises included in many assessment centers resemble essential features of the manager's job, and the assessment team typically includes a number of actual managers. As a result, managers are much more likely to react favorably to an assessment center than to other, more objective selection tests (Finkle, 1976). In addition, an assessment center is likely to be surprisingly practical, since it does not generally require the extended service of psychologists or other testing specialists. Although early assessment centers relied upon psychologists to form their assessment teams, it is now clear that trained managers are every bit as good as psychologists for most assessment tasks,[5] and that participation in assessment centers is often highly beneficial for the managers who serve as assessors (Finkle, 1976; Greenwood & McNamara, 1967). Thus, although assessment centers involve a complex set of activities,

[5]The interpretation of projective tests would be an exception.

a major portion of the assessment tasks may be carried out by members of the organization, rather than by outside consultants.

Psychometric evaluations of the assessment center generally have been favorable. Inter-rater reliabilities of assessment center ratings show considerable variability, but are generally in the .60 to .95 range (Schmitt, 1977). Sackett and Hakel (1979) report comparable levels of temporal stability in assessment ratings. Evidence for the validity of the assessment center has also been consistently positive (Borman, 1982; Finkle, 1976; Gaugler, Rosenthal, Thornton & Bentson, 1987; Hinrichs, 1978; Howard, 1974; Huck, 1973; Thornton, 1992). For example, Borman (1982) reported a correlation of .50 between composite assessment ratings obtained at the beginning of an army recruiter training course and later performance in training. Data presented by Hinrichs (1978) suggest comparable levels of validity in predicting advancement within organizations. What is more important is that the validity of assessment center ratings for predicting promotion appears to *increase* as one moves into higher levels of management.

Finally, assessment centers appear to be fair and relatively unbiased methods of making selection and promotion decisions. In a carefully balanced study, Huck and Bray (1976) showed that assessment centers showed nearly identical levels of validity for white and black employees in predicting job performance and potential for advancement; furthermore, it showed that the regression equations for whites and blacks did not differ significantly.

Although an impressive body of evidence supports the validity of the assessment center method, Klimoski and Strickland (1977) have raised important questions about interpretations of the validity evidence. They note that assessment centers, which consist largely of managers (acting as assessors) making evaluations of participants, are validated against performance ratings and promotions, both of which are managers' on-the-job evaluations of these same participants. Thus, studies documenting the validity of the assessment center method do little more than demonstrate that one set of managerial ratings of a particular person (assessment ratings) are positively correlated with another set of managerial ratings (performance ratings and promotability ratings) of the same person. It is possible that assessment center ratings are "valid" because they share the same biases that affect performance ratings and promotion judgments. Thus, one hypothesis that would account for the validity of the assessment center method is that the same "fair-haired boys" who receive high ratings in a managerial assessment center will receive high performance ratings and quick promotions on the job, irrespective of their actual effectiveness. While it is unlikely that the validity of assessment centers is totally illusory (a product of shared biases), it is likely that biases inherent in *all* ratings tasks inflate the validity of the assessment center method (Cascio, 1982).

COMPARATIVE ASSESSMENT OF PERSONNEL TESTS

The availability of paper-and-pencil tests, interviews, biographical information blanks, work samples, and assessment centers as alternative methods of predicting job performance leads to the question of which method is best. Reilly and Chao's (1982) review provides an excellent starting point for this comparative assessment. They examined research on alternatives to standard ability tests and focused on eight alternative methods of predicting future job performance: biodata, interviews, peer evaluations, self-assessments, reference checks, academic performance, expert judgments, and objective tests. They evaluated each technique in terms of its criterion-related validity, practicality, and likelihood of providing unbiased predictions of future performance. Their review suggests that only biodata and peer evaluations show levels of validity that are in any way comparable to the validity of paper-and-pencil tests. They also suggest that none of the alternatives shows comparable levels of validity with less adverse impact against minority applicants and that when the issue of practicality is considered, paper-and-pencil tests are by far the best single selection device. A report by the National Academy of Sciences (Wigdor & Garner, 1982) reached a similar conclusion: that in employment testing there are no known alternatives to standard ability tests that are equally informative, equally fair, and of equal technical merit (see also Hartigan & Wigdor, 1989; Hunter, 1986; Hunter & Hunter, 1984).

Although standard ability tests appear to be the best aids available for making selection decisions, it is unrealistic to expect that ability tests will be used as the sole method of making selection decisions. Managers' distrust of paper-and-pencil tests, and their attachment to alternative selection devices (e.g., the interview) is not likely to be significantly affected by reviews of the research literature. Alternatives to paper-and-pencil tests are here to stay; the question is not whether they should be used but, rather, how they might best be combined with standard ability tests to maximize accuracy in predicting performance.

Surveys of personnel managers (Ahlburg, 1992; Dankin & Armstrong, 1989) reveal two depressing findings. First, personnel and human resource professionals are often unaware of the most basic findings of research on the validity of various personnel assessment and selection methods. For example, personnel managers in several countries, including the United States, consistently rank cognitive ability tests as among the *least* valid and useful tools for selection, and they rank interviews as among the *most* valid and useful tools for selection. The available body of research, which includes literally thousands of studies conducted in a wide variety of settings, shows that the opposite is true. Second, even those individuals who *know* which techniques have been shown to have the most or the least validity (e.g., individuals holding recent graduate degrees, who would have had extensive exposure to this research) do not seem to translate their knowledge into concrete action. That is, even when they are aware of the relevant evidence, well-trained personnel managers are more likely to use techniques such as the interview or assessments of experience, which they know to show less validity in most settings than ability tests or other relatively objective assessment methods. It appears that personnel managers' habit of using less valid methods is a difficult one to break.

The most general suggestion we can make is that each type of selection test is probably optimal for obtaining specific sorts of information about the applicant (see Table 18-1). In designing a selection program, it would be best to decide first what information is needed, and then select the tests, interviews, or other methods that are most appropriate for obtaining it.

Our second suggestion is that each type of selection should be used *only* for a specific purpose. The interview provides a good example of a test that can be used for a broad variety of purposes, including gathering background information, making inferences about specific cognitive abilities, or arriving at a holistic evaluation of the applicant; yet it should be used *almost exclusively* for assessing characteristics such as social skills and motivation.

Our third and final suggestion is that conflicts between different tests (e.g., high test scores but poor interview ratings) should be used to guide further inquiries about the applicant. If different methods are used to assess truly different aspects of each individual's qualifications, conflicts should be expected rather than avoided, and these conflicts should be used to provide the basis for more in-depth evaluations.

CRITICAL DISCUSSION:
Can Graphology Predict Occupational Success?

Graphology, or the analysis of handwriting, is surprisingly common in personnel selection. It is routinely used in Europe and in Israel, and it has been used by over 3,000 American firms (Ben-Shakar, Bar-Hillel, Bilu, Abba & Flug, 1986; Levy, 1979; Rafaeli & Klimoski, 1983). There has been virtually no research supporting the validity of graphology for predicting job performance or occupational success; the few methodologically strong studies that have been done suggest that graphology does not work and that the predictions of graphologists may be no better than predictions made by chance (Ben-Shakar et al., 1986). Why, then, is graphology so widespread?

One reason for the popularity of graphology is face validity. Graphology is used primarily to make inferences about the writer's personality, and handwriting seems to the lay audience a very reasonable indicator of personality, especially when it is analyzed according to a complex and arcane set of rules (Murphy, 1993). The idea that personality is revealed in one's face, mannerisms, and so forth, is a recurring theme in Western literature, and the use of handwriting to analyze personality is a simple extension of this theme.

Another reason for the apparent validity of graphology, in the eyes of consumers, is that it makes predictions that are both vague and difficult to verify, a characteristic this alleged science shares with astrology. Graphologists typically make holistic assessments and describe candidates with terms such as "honesty" or "insight," and it is very difficult to prove or disprove these assessments. It is notable that graphologists refuse to predict some easily verifiable characteristics of writers, such as their gender (Ben-Shakar et al., 1986). Untrained individuals can predict a writer's gender approximately 70 percent of the time, and if graphology has any validity whatsoever, graphologists should be able to do even better in predicting gender.

A third reason for the acceptance of graphologists is that some of their predictions *are* valid. For example, graphologists involved in personnel selection will often ask a candidate to write a brief biographical essay and will base their recommendations on a graphological analysis of this document. Research has demonstrated that the validity of these readings is due to the *content* of the biographical essay and not to graphological analysis of the handwriting. That is, untrained individuals given the same information contained in these essays can make predictions that are as valid as those of the graphologists. All in all, the available evidence does not support the use of graphology in personnel selection or placement.

Assessing Integrity

Dishonesty in the workplace, ranging from employee theft and white-collar crime to the unauthorized use of equipment, materials, and supplies (e.g., making personal long-distance calls from the office, taking home tools and materials), is extremely costly; estimates of the costs of employee theft alone often exceed $40 billion per year. Employers are therefore very interested in evaluating the honesty or integrity of job applicants and incumbents.

The whole question of assessing honesty or integrity is highly controversial. First, it is not clear whether honesty is a stable trait, or whether it is primarily determined by situational factors (Murphy, 1993). Second, the methods used in the past to assess or infer honesty were often seen as coercive and inaccurate. For example, prior to the Employee Polygraph Protection Act of 1988 banning the practice, the polygraph (often called the "lie detector") was widely used to screen job applicants. Research on this method of assessing honesty suggested that it was both inaccurate and highly offensive. Third, honesty is a uniquely valued characteristic, and assessment methods that brand some people as dishonest may provoke extreme reactions. Suppose, for example, that you apply for the job of master machinist. You will probably react differently to the news that you did not get the job because you did not possess a sufficient degree of fine visual discrimination ability than to the news that you were turned down because you are dishonest!

As a result of the controversy over integrity testing, these tests have been the focus of a great deal of recent research. The tests, as well as the research on the validity of these tests, are described below.

Integrity Tests

Although paper-and pencil integrity tests have been in existence since at least the 1950s (Ash, 1976), their widespread use is relatively recent. O'Bannon, Goldinger, and Appleby (1989) report that these tests are used by 10 to 15 percent of all employers, concentrated in the retail sales, banking, and food service industries, and that over 2.5 million tests are given by over 5,000 employers each year.

Although the individual tests differed in a number of specifics, there were a number of features common to virtually all integrity tests. In particular, integrity tests usually include items that refer to one or more of the following areas: (a) direct admissions of illegal or questionable activities, (b) opinions regarding illegal or questionable behavior, (c) general personality traits and thought patterns thought to be related to dishonesty (e.g., the tendency to think constantly about illegal activities), and (d) reactions to hypothetical situations that may or may not feature dishonest behavior.

A distinction is usually drawn between tests that enquire directly about integrity, asking for admissions of past theft or asking about the degree to which the examinee approves of dishonest behaviors, and tests that indirectly infer integrity on the basis of responses to questions that are not obviously integrity related (Sackett, Burris & Callahan, 1989). Examples of tests usually classified as either clear purpose or veiled purpose integrity tests, together with descriptions of dimensions measured by the tests (in some cases, these refer merely to the labels attached to scale scores reported) are presented in Table 18-4; detailed descriptions of the dimensions measured by 43 integrity tests are presented in O'Bannon, Goldinger, and Appleby (1989).

Validity of Integrity Tests

Sackett and his colleagues have conducted several reviews of research on the reliability, validity, and usefulness of integrity tests (Sackett & Decker, 1979; Sackett & Harris, 1984, 1985; Sackett, Burris & Callahan, 1989); Ones, Viswesvaran, and Schmidt (In press) and McDaniel and Jones (1988) have subjected some of the same studies to meta-analyses that are designed to quantitatively summarize the outcomes of multiple validity studies. O'Bannon and his colleagues (1989) have also reviewed this research and, additionally, have given attention to a variety of practical issues that surround the administration and use of integrity tests. Although each review raises different concerns, and most reviews lament the shortcomings of research on the validity of integrity tests, the general conclusion of the more recent reviews is positive. Earlier reviews of research on integrity tests were sharply critical, but it appears that both the research and the tests themselves have improved, partly as a result of the earlier criticism. There is now a reasonable body of evidence showing that integrity tests have *some* validity for predicting a variety of criteria that are relevant to organizations. This research does *not* say that tests of this sort will eliminate theft or dishonesty at work, but it does suggest that individuals who receive poor scores on these tests *tend* to be less desirable employees.

Although the results of recent validity studies are generally positive, this has not quieted the controversy over integrity testing. In response to the continuing debate over the use of tests to infer honesty, dependability, and trustworthiness, there have been two major recent assessments of integrity testing, one conducted by a special task force of the American Psychological Association (APA Task Force, 1991), and the other conducted by the U.S. Congress Office of Technology Assessment (OTA) (Office of Technology Assessment, 1990).

Both reviews reached similar conclusions in at least three important areas. First, it is exceedingly difficult to define honesty, integrity, or whatever attribute these tests are

TABLE 18-4   EXAMPLES OF CLEAR PURPOSE AND VEILED PURPOSE INTEGRITY TESTS

Clear purpose	Dimensions measured or scores reported
Reid Report	Honesty Attitude, Social Behavior, Substance Abuse, Personal Achievements, Service Orientation, Clerical/Math Skills
Stanton Survey	Honesty Attitude, Admissions of Previous Dishonesty
Personnel Selection Inventory (Version 7)	Honesty, Drug Avoidance, Customer Relations, Work Values, Supervision, Employability Index, Validity Scales

Veiled purpose	Dimensions measured or scores reported
Personnel Reaction Blank	Dependability/Conscientiousness
Hogan Reliability Scale	Hostility to Rules, Thrill Seeking, Impulsiveness, Social Insensitivity, Alienation
PDI Employment Inventory	Productive Behavior, Tenure

designed to measure. Different tests seem to focus on very different attitudes, beliefs, or behaviors. For example, there are a number of definitions of employee theft. Researchers often distinguish between trivial and nontrivial theft; conclusions about the extent of theft depended largely on whether taking articles of little value (e.g., pencils, paper, supplies) was included in one's definition of theft. Goldbricking, taking long lunch breaks, using company time to carry out personal business, and similar activities are sometimes labelled time theft.

Both reviews raise a related issue that has been a source of controversy since the time of Hartshorne and May (1928)—the question of whether honesty is a distinct trait. Most researchers believe that situational factors have a very strong impact on the tendency to engage in honest versus dishonest behaviors (Saxe, 1990), and that labelling a person as honest or dishonest is a serious oversimplification. Both reviews lead to the conclusion that we do not really know what integrity tests measure, but whatever it is, it is not quite the same thing as "honesty."

Second, informed consent is a potentially serious issue in integrity testing. The OTA review notes that integrity test publishers advise *against* informing examinees of their test scores. This implies that if an individual is denied employment on the basis of a score on an integrity test, he or she should not be so informed. The *Standards for Educational and Psychological Testing* and the *Ethical Principles of Psychologists* make it clear that psychologists involved in integrity testing are obliged to inform examinees of the risks and consequences of taking the test versus refusing to take the test, the purpose and nature of the test, and the way in which test scores will be used (Lowman, 1989). The ethical standards described in these documents do *not* imply that examinees need to know their final test scores, but they do seem to imply that examinees receive a good deal more information about the tests and their use than is typical in actual testing situations.

Third, there are serious concerns over the way in which integrity tests are scored and in which scores are reported. Despite the claims of some test publishers, it is common to use some sort of dichotomous scoring (e.g., pass-fail) in integrity testing. More sophisticated tests sometimes report test scores in terms of a small number of "zones": high danger, moderate danger, average danger, or low danger of theft, substance abuse, and so on. There is an extensive literature dealing with the highly complex psychometric and legal issues involved in setting cutting scores (see Cascio, Alexander & Barrett, 1988, for a review), but it is not clear whether any of this literature is taken into account by some test publishers. Test scores that are reported on a pass-fail basis are inherently suspect because they blur potentially meaningful differences between individuals in each of the two categories (e.g., it is unlikely that all individuals who fail present the same risks).

One difference between the two reviews is the attention given to the actual use of integrity tests in the field. The APA review has a good deal more to say about the integrity test industry, and much of it is strongly critical. Although the APA review notes that some integrity test publishers are highly responsible in their approach, it also notes that many test publishers fail to live up to both the technical and the ethical requirements in the *Standards for Educational and Psychological Testing*. Some test publishers fail to carry out or adequately report research on the validity of their tests, whereas others resist any independent scrutiny of their instruments. The psychometric quality of some tests is either unknown or so poor that the test publishers are acting irresponsible in distributing them.

The marketing of integrity tests is, in many cases, a disgrace. The APA report notes that the claims made for some of these tests are so excessive and overblown as to be fraudulent. Indeed, if you want to see examples of dishonesty in the workplace, you do not need to look much farther than the marketing brochures for some integrity tests.

Trends in integrity testing.   O'Bannon, Goldinger, and Appleby (1989) cite a number of trends in integrity testing. First, these tests are becoming increasingly broad. Many integrity tests now include subscales that are designed to make inferences about turnover, drug use, emotional instability, and potential for violence. While the development of broader tests is probably a good thing, caution must be observed in interpreting these subscale scores literally. To date, the evidence of the criterion-related validity of integrity tests has focused largely on the integrity scales themselves, and there is not yet clear evidence that a high score on a scale labelled drug use, for example, will in fact indicate a high probability of actual drug use.

A second trend in integrity testing is increased attention to privacy rights and to potential violations of civil rights. In general, the evidence suggests that different subgroups in the population (e.g., male, female, old, young, white, minority) receive roughly similar scores on many tests, which implies that the tests might not systematically discriminate against specific groups. Nevertheless, individual rights to privacy and to fair treatment might be compromised by some integrity tests, and both test publishers and test users are showing increasing concern over these issues.

Integrity Interviews

A number of interview protocols have been developed that are designed to obtain information about an individual's integrity (Buckley, 1989). Although not as standardized as written tests, in many ways these interviews resemble overt or clear-purpose integrity tests. That is, they involve frank discussions of past misdeeds, thefts, and other wrongdoings.

Like all interviews, the validity of this method probably rests as much on the interviewer as on the interview protocol itself (Landy, 1985). That is, some interviewers are probably better than others at putting the respondent at ease and in building up an atmosphere in which he or she will be honest about past behavior. It is therefore difficult to make a meaningful statement about the reliability or validity of integrity interviews. In the hands of a well-trained, skilled interviewer, a carefully constructed interview protocol can probably yield valid information about integrity. On the other hand, the number of qualifications in the preceding sentence suggest a number of ways in which the process could go wrong. Poor training, lack of interpersonal skills, poorly chosen questions, or any combination of these factors could seriously compromise the validity of this technique.

The similarity of integrity interviews and overt integrity tests is both a blessing and a curse. For example, if the questions used in such an interview were similar to those used in a well-validated test, this might provide indirect evidence for the validity of the interview. On the other hand, if the interview were sufficiently similar to the test, you might wonder why you should bother with the interview at all. Written tests are cheaper and simpler to administer, and they are not subject to the large number of biases that are thought to plague most interviews (Arvey & Faley, 1988).

THE VALIDITY OF PERSONNEL TESTS

Most reviews of research on the validity of selection tests suggest that test scores do not provide a basis for completely accurate predictions of job performance. Validity coefficients for tests of abilities and skills known to be necessary for successful job performance are typically close to .30, and rarely exceed .50. Thus, test scores generally account for no more than approximately 10 percent of the variance in job performance, and rarely account for as much as 25 percent of this variance. While it is true that the utility of testing can be substantial even when the validity coefficient is small (see Chapter 8), one of the principal explanations for the rather sporadic use of tests in the private sector is the apparently limited validity of available tests.

Although the low level of validity achieved by most personnel tests is certainly a problem, a far more serious problem is the apparent variability in validity coefficients from job to job and from organization to organization. Ghiselli's (1955) review suggested that tests that showed significant validity coefficients in one job often showed little evidence of validity for predicting performance in other, similar jobs. Furthermore, tests that were shown to be valid predictors of performance in one organization were not necessarily valid predictors of performance in apparently identical jobs in other organizations. The extensive variability in validity coefficients has been confirmed by Ghiselli's later reviews (1966, 1970) and also by Albright, Glennon, and Smith (1963) and Guion (1965a). The extensive variability in test validities suggest that it is difficult, if not impossible, to predict whether a test that is known to be a valid predictor of performance in one job or organization will show comparable levels of validity in another setting.

Validity Generalization

In a series of papers, Schmidt, Hunter, and their colleagues challenge the assumption that validities are typically low and that they are highly variable from job to job and from organization to organization. They note that the size of the validity coefficient obtained in any particular study is affected by statistical artifacts, such as sampling error, range restriction, and unreliability, and that failure to take these statistical artifacts into account has led to an overestimation of the *true* variability of test validities.

Schmidt and Hunter (1977) note that the variability in validity coefficients from job to job or from organization to organization can be broken down into two components:

1. *True differences* in validity: The validity of a test of mechanical comprehension may be truly higher for predicting the performance of mechanics than for predicting the performance of typists.
2. Variability due to *statistical artifacts:* Sampling error, range restriction, and unreliability all affect the size of the validity coefficient. Variability in validity coefficients that is due to these statistical artifacts represents, not true score, but *error variance.* That is, differences in validity coefficients that are caused by these artifacts do not reflect true differences in the validities of tests.

Schmidt and Hunter have developed a validity generalization model that estimates the effects of statistical artifacts upon the variability of test validities. By subtracting the variability due to artifacts (error variance) from the total variability in validity coefficients, it is possible to estimate the *true* variability in the validity of a test in predicting performance in different jobs, organizations, and so forth.

The Schmidt-Hunter validity generalization model has been applied to estimate the validity of predictor tests in clerical occupations (Pearlman, Schmidt & Hunter, 1980); in the petroleum industry (Schmidt, Hunter & Caplan, 1981); for computer programming (Schmidt, Gast-Rosenberg & Hunter, 1980); and in the life insurance industry (Brown, 1981), and it has been the focus for considerable research and debate (Callender & Osburn, 1980, 1981, 1982; Hunter, Schmidt & Pearlman, 1982; Osburn, Callender, Greener & Ashworth, 1983; Schmidt, Hunter & Pearlman, 1982; Schmidt, Hunter, Pearlman & Shane, 1979). Although there is some inconsistency in the results obtained when different sets of validity generalization equations are applied, the general trend suggested by the model is unmistakably clear. The Schmidt-Hunter validity generalization model suggests that in almost every case, *true validities* are (a) substantially *larger* and (b) much *less variable* than psychologists have traditionally believed.

Results presented in Pearlman, Schmidt, and Hunter (1980) help to illustrate the validity generalization process. In their research, data were collected from hundreds of validity studies to test the hypothesis that variability in validity coefficients could be explained primarily by the existence of statistical artifacts. Data bearing on the validity of quantitative ability tests, reasoning tests, and spatial and mechanical ability tests for predicting performance in production and stock clerk jobs are illustrated in Figure 18-2.

As can be seen, the observed validity coefficients were not particularly large (none larger than .30). However, the validity generalization model assumes that range restriction and low levels of reliability for both the test and the criterion serve to artificially depress test validities.[6] Upon correcting for these statistical artifacts, the average validities increase dramatically, ranging from .31 to .60.

Statistical artifacts serve as sources of error variance; the validity generalization model allows an estimation of the true variability in validities by removing the probable effects of error. Figure 18-2 also illustrates the effects of statistical artifacts upon the *mean* of validity coefficients—the cumulative effect of correcting for these statistical artifacts is apparent. When statistical artifacts are taken into account, it appears likely that the validity of employment tests is fairly substantial, and further, is fairly constant from job to job or organization to organization.

The debate over validity generalization and its meaning has been extensively documented. (See Hartigan & Wigdor, 1989; James, Demaree & Mulaik, 1986; Kemery, Mossholder & Roth, 1987; Schmidt, Hunter & Pearlman, 1982; Schmidt, Hunter, Pearlman, Hirsch, Sackett, Schmitt, Tenopyr, Kehoe & Zedeck, 1985; and Thomas, 1988, for a sample of this literature.) Although controversies over specific technical features of validity generalization remain, the general findings of validity generalization research are now well accepted (Hartigan & Wigdor, 1989). See Hunter and Schmidt (1990) for a recent overview of validity generalization methods.

---

[6]Corrections for range restriction and attenuation due to less-than-perfect reliability are discussed in Chapter 8.

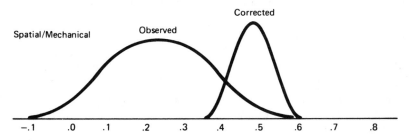

Figure 18-2 Distributions of Validity Coefficients before and after Correcting for Statistical Artifacts

At one time validity generalization research appeared to show that virtually all ability tests were valid in all occupations, which implied that validation studies were not really necessary. Critiques and refinements of the validity generalization model have indirectly led to an *increasing* interest in validity studies, particularly studies that over-come shortcomings of earlier validation research (e.g., small samples, unreliable criteria, range restriction). A series of *Test Validity Yearbooks* (Landy, 1989) was launched to encourage and catalog research on the validity of tests that are used to make decisions in a variety of contexts. It is too soon to tell whether new validity studies that are free of the shortcomings of earlier studies will support the claim that all cognitive ability tests are valid in all jobs, or whether these studies will uncover systematic moderators of test validity. In any case, the combination of validity generalization methods and better validity research should contribute substantially to our understanding of the validity of personnel selection tests.

THE SOCIAL AND LEGAL CONTEXT OF EMPLOYMENT TESTING

Prior to 1964, employment testing was of concern to a relatively small number of testing specialists and business people who used tests in personnel selection and placement. The civil rights movement, together with the Civil Rights Act of 1964, served to focus the attention of society and the legal system on the political and economic consequences of widespread discrimination against minorities. Discriminatory employment practices were seen as both an immediate cause of economic deprivation suffered by minorities and as a symptom of the broader problem, the denial of civil rights to minorities in America. Attempts by the Congress, the courts, and society at large to define, detect, and remove discriminatory employment practices, as well as to partially undo the effects of past discrimination, have changed greatly both the nature and the practice of employment testing. For example, many companies, worried about the possibility of lawsuits, have stopped employment testing altogether (Arvey, 1979; Hale, 1982). Other companies have struggled to develop nondiscriminatory hiring practices or to demonstrate that their current practices do not discriminate. Still other organizations have attempted to repair the damage done by past discrimination, sometimes to the disadvantage of applicants from groups who had traditionally benefited from prejudice against minorities.

The Law and Personnel Testing

The Civil Rights Act of 1964 is the major piece of federal legislation dealing with fair employment practices.[7] The Civil Rights Act is divided into several sections, or "titles," forbidding discrimination in voting, housing, public education, and the like; Title VII of the Civil Rights Act deals with employment practices. Basically, the act as amended states that

> it shall be an unlawful employment practice . . . to hire or to refuse to hire or to discharge an individual or to discriminate against any individual with respect to his compensation, terms, conditions, or privileges of employment, because of such individual's race, color, religion, sex, or national origin.

The interpretation and enforcement of the Civil Rights Act is a complex endeavor. At the heart of the problem is the fact that the act does not forbid employers from using a selection procedure that validly identifies good and poor performers, even if that procedure has the unintended consequence of discriminating against women, minorities, or members of specific ethnic groups. In other words, if an employer can demonstrate the

---

[7]A series of Supreme Court decisions in the 1980s appeared to weaken the Civil Rights Act of 1964. These decisions were reversed with passage of the Civil Rights Act of 1991.

"business necessity" of using a specific selection procedure, that procedure is deemed lawful.

The Equal Employment Opportunity Commission (EEOC), which is charged with enforcing the Civil Rights Act, has a substantial responsibility for determining the standards to be used in evaluating the validity and the business necessity of a specific employment procedure. The EEOC Guidelines provide an indication of the principles and procedures used by the EEOC to determine whether a specific procedure meets with requirements implicit in the commission's interpretation of the act, and of relevant case law. Since the EEOC is empowered to bring suits in federal court to enforce antidiscrimination laws, the guidelines issued by the EEOC are viewed by many as defining the legally acceptable standards for most tests (Arvey, 1979).

In evaluating the EEOC Guidelines, it is important to consider the conflict between the rights of the employer and the rights of applicants. The use of tests in selection (or promotion, transfer, etc.) often results in different selection rates for whites and minorities, or for males and females. If these differences in selection rate are the result of real differences in ability to perform the job, the employer has the right to use the test. For example, in a job that requires frequent use of substantial upper-body strength, such as a center in professional football, the use of a physical strength test that discriminated against women might nevertheless be entirely legal. On the other hand, if differences in test scores have nothing to do with ability to perform the job, the employer who uses the test arbitrarily violates the civil rights of applicants with low test scores. If the same physical strength test described above were used in selecting computer programmers, the test would unfairly discriminate against women and would be illegal. The EEOC Guidelines are used in an effort to determine whether a test that has adverse impact is in fact related to ability to perform the job.

The Search for Equal Employment Opportunity

In the early debates on the Civil Rights Act of 1964, many people assumed that the removal of explicitly discriminatory employment practices would bring about an end to the economic and occupational stratification of our society. It soon became clear that a policy that simply banned overt discrimination would not achieve significant results within the foreseeable future. Attempts to increase the representativeness of the workforce have taken a number of directions, ranging from attempts to recruit and train qualified minorities to the use of selection systems that impose different selection criteria on whites and minorities, or on males and females.

Affirmative action represents one of the most straightforward and one of the most misunderstood efforts to achieve equal employment opportunity. The basic premise of affirmative action is that a person's right to be considered for a job should be limited only by his or her ability to perform that job. Affirmative action involves a voluntary effort on the part of the employer to ensure that all qualified applicants are considered for the job. Affirmative action programs represent a series of activities including recruitment, workforce analyses, efforts to redesign jobs to provide more opportunities for entry-level workers, and efforts to retrain workers in dead-end jobs.

Although affirmative action activities are themselves voluntary, organizations doing business with the federal government are required to file affirmative action plans, goals, and timetables that describe in some detail the steps they plan to take in order to attract qualified applicants from protected groups.

Many analysts have suggested that the policies of the EEOC represent an alternative—some would say covert—strategy for achieving a representative workforce (Wigdor & Garner, 1982). Wigdor (1982) notes that although the EEOC Guidelines go into great detail regarding the technical standards for validating tests, the EEOC appears to have no intrinsic interest in test validity; rather, its mission is to increase the representativeness of the workforce. By choosing a very broad definition for the term "test" and by setting stringent standards for labelling a test valid, the EEOC has nearly outlawed tests, or at least has outlawed those for which minorities, women, or other protected groups receive lower scores. While this strategy of covertly banning tests may increase the representativeness of the workforce, it may do so at considerable cost, especially since it is not necessary to abandon tests altogether to increase the proportion of minorities or women who are hired.

Ethical Problems in Personnel Testing

The psychologist in industry rarely has complete autonomy regarding the use of tests and test scores; he or she is likely to serve in either a staff position or in the role of a consultant and is not likely to have final say regarding the organization's testing policies. However, this reduced role does not absolve the psychologist of his or her ethical responsibilities with regard to testing. For example, a psychologist in industry has the same responsibility to protect applicants against unreasonable invasions of privacy as does a psychologist in private practice. Thus, the use of certain personality tests might constitute an unwarranted invasion of privacy unless the validity of the tests can be firmly established. In this case, use of such tests might be unwarranted if less threatening alternatives were available.

Psychologists' obligations to applicants also include enforcement of appropriate guarantees of confidentiality and of informed consent. The psychologist working in industry also has several obligations to the employer, including the obligation to obtain the most valid tests and the least-contaminated test data available, as well as maintaining the employer's proprietary rights (London & Bray, 1980).

The most pressing ethical requirement in personnel testing is probably the requirement that test users be advised carefully regarding the proper use of tests and the consequences of using tests in specific ways. It is a sad commentary on the state of the field that many psychologists and managerial consultants offer poorly constructed tests as sure-fire cures for personnel problems. The manager is not to be blamed for being receptive to a quick-fix guarantee of success; psychologists in industry are obliged to provide realistic information about what can and cannot be accomplished using tests and about the consequences of adopting particular testing programs.

Interviews—a case in point.   Evidence of the limited validity of the employment interview was discussed earlier in this chapter. The interview not only lacks validity but is prone to several sources of bias (Arvey, 1979). For example, interviewer ratings are likely to be biased in favor of attractive applicants and against minority applicants. Women receive systematically lower ratings than men in some jobs, but not in others. Although it is unlikely that psychologists will ever convince most companies to abandon the interview, it is clearly the responsibility of psychologists to inform organizations of the known limits of the interview as a selection device.

The fact that the interview is prone to a number of somewhat predictable biases suggests that psychologists should investigate actively the extent to which interviews conducted in their own organizations are biased, both in the ratings obtained in the interviews and in the predictive validity of those ratings. Data of this sort would be useful in limiting the potential damage that may be done when a biased instrument of limited validity is used in making personnel decisions.

CRITICAL DISCUSSION:
Personnel Selection from the Applicant's Point of View

We usually think of personnel selection from the organization's point of view, and we focus on the validity and cost-effectiveness of various tests and assessment methods. It is useful to consider personnel selection from the applicant's point of view, since applicants are likely to be concerned with different issues than those that concern organizations. We comment briefly on three of these issues: local accuracy, deception, and the impact of selection procedures on applicant decisions.

Local accuracy. From the organization's point of view, the validity coefficient provides a measure of the test's worth. The applicant is more likely to be concerned with the accuracy of the test at or around the cutting score (i.e., the lowest score needed to get the job). We refer to this type of accuracy as local accuracy. Assume, for example, that an applicant needs a score of 50 to be hired. Applicants whose scores are near 50 will be concerned most with their placement relative to the cutting score, less with the overall accuracy of the test. A test might be highly valid if those with very high scores (e.g., over 80) perform better than those with very low scores (e.g., below 10), yet it might yield essentially random decisions for the majority of the applicants if the cutting score is near the test mean.

Deception. Some tests are straightforward (e.g., mechanical ability tests), but others disguise their purpose. The Personal Outlook Inventory is an example of such a test. This inventory asks a series of innocuous questions such as, "What are your goals in life?" and "How often are you sick?" and purports to yield scores that predict employee theft. Deceptive tests are regarded by some as an invasion of privacy (Hoffman, 1962). Even if job applicants waive their right to privacy, the use of deceptive tests effectively destroys the principle of informed consent (Adair, 1973), for if the applicant is not informed about the purpose of testing, he or she will have no meaningful protection against unreasonable invasions of privacy. Concerns over deception in testing are particularly serious in the area of honesty testing.

Applicant decisions. Once an organization has made its selection decisions, applicants who receive job offers must make decisions about organizations. It is at this point that many organizations lose their top prospects, which can be very costly (Murphy, 1986). There is evidence that the selection process itself can affect applicants' decisions

(Rynes, Heneman & Schwab, 1980; Schmitt & Coyle, 1976). Organizations that employ tedious or arduous selection procedures may alienate applicants and may eventually do themselves more harm than good.

Some selection procedures *look* offensive; routine drug tests in jobs where the likelihood of drug-related problems is low and polygraph examinations are examples.[8] Other procedures are inoffensive in themselves but convey such a negative image of the organization that they may repel qualified applicants; a long, rambling interview with a prospective boss might convince an applicant to take a job elsewhere. Applicants use selection procedures as one means of gaining information about the organization. Failure to consider this fact and to take steps to ensure that the organization is viewed by the applicant in the most favorable light possible can cost organizations dearly.

SUMMARY

A variety of methods are used to predict job performance, ranging from interviews and work samples to standardized tests designed to measure ability and personality characteristics. Paper-and-pencil testing is widespread, and there is consistent evidence that both general ability tests and more specialized tests (e.g., measures of clerical speed and accuracy, or mechanical comprehension) are valid predictors of performance. Contrary to the beliefs of many personnel managers, standardized tests are probably the *best* predictors, especially when both psychometric and practicality criteria are considered.

The biographical and demographic data that is typically collected on application blanks can be used to predict performance, absenteeism, job tenure, and so on. In recent years considerable progress has been made over the blind empirical methods that dominated biodata research in the past. Researchers have attempted to document the constructs that are potentially measureable in terms of biographical data and have constructed detailed theories to link biographical data to job performance.

The employment interview is a source of continuing frustration to industrial psychologists. This technique is probably the most widely used *and* the worst predictor of performance. Interviews *can* be valid predictors, especially if they are structured, with a strong emphasis on behavioral information. In most cases, however, organizations seem to rely on unstructured interviews, which are known to show low levels of reliability or validity.

Work samples are used in both blue-collar and white-collar jobs. In blue-collar jobs, work samples often involve carrying out actual job tasks under controlled conditions (e.g., typing tests). Managerial work samples often represent simulations of key aspects of the manager's job. Both types have shown relatively consistent evidence of validity. Managerial work samples are a frequent component of assessment centers, which represent a strategy for collecting and integrating multiple sources of information about an individual's strengths, weaknesses, present performance, and future potential.

With the demise of the polygraph as a means of inferring honesty at work, paper-

---

[8]The routine use of the polygraph in employment testing is now illegal, although it may still be used in some jobs (e.g., security-related jobs) and in some circumstances (e.g., where there is specific evidence of wrongdoing).

and-pencil integrity tests have become increasingly common. Although they are the focus of considerable controversy, there is some consensus that they can be valid in predicting criteria such as workplace theft, and perhaps overall job performance.

Psychological tests are an important component of the process of personnel selection and classification. Because of their potential impact on members of minority groups (see Chapter 15 for a more extended discussion of this issue), tests have become the center of legal and ethical debates. Although significant controversy over the proper use of psychological tests in personnel selection remains, most reviews suggest that well-developed tests are more valid and more fair than other methods, such as unstructured interviews, that might be used in their place.

CHAPTER 19

PSYCHOLOGICAL MEASUREMENT
IN INDUSTRY:
CRITERION MEASUREMENT

From the organization's point of view, the successful measurement of present and past job performance may be just as critical as the successful prediction of future performance. For one thing, performance measures are typically the primary, if not the sole, criterion for determining the validity of selection tests. At a more fundamental level, performance measures are crucial in assessing and improving organizational effectiveness. An organization that does not have any information regarding the performance of individuals or groups of workers is severely hampered in diagnosing the strengths and correcting the weaknesses of their current operation. Performance measures are also used in providing feedback to employees, in assessing training needs, and in determining salary and promotions. The validity of these measures is therefore a matter of considerable importance.

CRITERION MEASURES

Three general classes of data might be used, singly or in combination, to measure the performance of an individual worker. First, and most obvious, are data arising from some sort of *production count*. It might be possible to count the number of bricks laid by a mason, the number of calls answered by an operator, the number of parts produced by a machinist, or the number of arrests carried out by a policeman and to use this production count to measure job performance. A second type of data that might be used in measuring performance is *personnel data*. It can be argued that workers who are frequently late or absent or who frequently lose time due to accidents produce at a significantly lower level than workers who put in eight hours every day. Finally, it is possible to use *judgmental methods,* such as supervisory performance ratings or rankings, or peer nominations, which depend upon the judgment of a specific person or set of persons, to measure an individual worker's performance.

Of the three, judgmental methods are by far the most widely used; over 80 percent of studies published in the last 25 years have used judgmental ratings or rankings as the primary, if not the sole, method of measuring job performance. When you consider that both production counts and personnel data are "objective," whereas judgmental methods are necessarily subjective, the overwhelming predominance of judgmental methods may come as a surprise.[1] However, close examination of production counts and personnel data suggest that there are serious limitations to these types of measures, and that judgmental methods are often the only practical methods of measuring job performance.

Difficulties in the Objective Measurement of Job Performance

At first glance, production counts appear to be ideal objective measures of job performance. In fact, these measures pose several problems that greatly limit their applicability (Borman, 1991; Guion, 1965a).

First, production counts are not applicable in many jobs, particularly professional and managerial ones. It is not clear what types of units one should count to obtain an objective measure of the performance of a night-shift manager, a judge, or a dentist. Although almost every job involves producing some concrete, quantifiable objects (e.g., widgets, memos, records), a simple count of these objects often fails to capture the essence of the job; a dentist who drills hundreds of cavities is not necessarily a good dentist.

Advances in technology have led to an increasing reliance on computerized monitoring of work performance; a report issued by the federal Office of Technology Assessment (1987) estimated that over 6 million workers were being monitored by computers and that computerized performance monitoring was growing; federal laws have been proposed to limit computerized monitoring in some circumstances. Although computerized monitoring may help solve some of the problems found in using typical objective measures of performance, this method is not without its own problems. Most notably, the presence of a computerized monitoring system probably changes the behaviors of workers, and not necessarily in a positive way. For example, a salesperson whose calls are counted by computer is likely to make many short calls, even though longer discussions with promising customers might, in fact, be more effective. In addition, computerized monitoring may lead to stress, dissatisfaction, and, eventually, to lower performance.

Second, there are many jobs that do result in concrete, countable products, but in which the rate of production is not under the control of the worker whose performance is to be evaluated. For example, it might be possible to measure the performance of an assembly line worker in terms of the number of parts he or she successfully bolted on to passing cars. The problem with this approach is that "performance" is determined almost

---

[1]We use the term "objective" here in the same sense as do Landy and Farr (1983). Objective data are perceptible to persons other than the evaluator, whereas subjective data are unique to the single evaluator.

entirely by the speed of the assembly line. Since the number of cars that come by each hour tends to be constant, there are very strict limits on the potential variability of this performance measure. If there is no variability in the performance measure, it cannot be a valid measure of individual differences in performance.

Data obtained from personnel files are often used as objective measures of performance. Absenteeism, which represents one of the most widely studied criterion measures in organizational research, illustrates many of the problems encountered in using personnel data to measure job performance. First and foremost is the difficulty in arriving at an operational definition of absenteeism. Absenteeism can be defined in any number of ways—as frequency of absences, duration of absences, total time lost due to absences, voluntary absences (e.g., taking a day off to go to a ball game), or involuntary absences (e.g., sick days) (Chadwick-Jones, Brown, Nicholson & Sheppard, 1971; Landy & Farr, 1983; Steers & Rhodes, 1978). Landy and Farr (1983) and Gaudet (1963) describe over 40 separate indices that have been used to measure absenteeism in organizations. The choice of a particular index is by no means unimportant; a worker who is out for two weeks with a medical excuse might receive a high "score" on some absenteeism indices (e.g., duration of involuntary absence) and a very low "score" on other indices (e.g., frequency measures). Since different measures of absenteeism are frequently unrelated (Landy & Farr, 1983), the choice of one index over another could have profound impact on the evaluation of a particular worker's performance.

A second major problem with absenteeism as a measure of job performance has to do with the distribution of absenteeism in the workplace. No matter how it is measured, most people have very low levels of absenteeism, while a few people are absent quite a lot (Hammer & Landau, 1981). The distribution of absenteeism raises some serious statistical problems, but it also suggests a serious conceptual problem. The great majority of workers typically have zero, one, or two absences per year and thus receive nearly identical scores on this measure of performance, yet it is unlikely that all these workers are performing at the same level.

Similar problems emerge when accidents are used to measure performance. Very few people have *any* accidents over the course of a normal year, yet it is unlikely that everyone who did not have an accident performs at the same level, or that everyone who *did* have an accident performs at a lower level than everyone who did not.

The final problem with using personnel data to measure job performance lies in the low levels of reliability of personnel data. For example, Latham and Pursell (1975), Chadwick-Jones and others (1971), Ilgen and Hollenback (1977), and Hammer and Landau (1981) report reliability coefficients of approximately .30 for a variety of absence measures over time spans ranging from 12 weeks to 30 months. Similarly low levels of test-retest reliability have been noted for many other indices that are based on personnel data. The lack of reliability places some rather obvious limits on the value of personnel measures as indicators of job performance.

One interesting finding in research on objective versus subjective measures of job performance is that the validity of tests and other selection measures is typically *higher* when objective criteria are used than when subjective ratings are used to measure performance (Schmitt, Gooding, Noe & Kirsh, 1984). This is important because it suggests that validation research that relies on subjective criteria (this would include the great majority of studies) will probably produce a conservative estimate of the validity of selection tests. Thus, methods that are valid for predicting well-developed subjective measures of performance may be even more valid for predicting objective indices of performance.

Work Samples as Performance Measures

One technique that has shown promise for developing relatively objective measures of job performance has been to use work samples as *measures* of performance. In Chapter 18 we noted that work samples can be valid *predictors* of performance. The experience of the armed services in using similar techniques to assess present performance (rather than predict future levels of performance) suggests that it may be possible to develop measures of several aspects of job performance in which the role of subjective judgment is minimized.

In 1980 the armed services initiated the Joint-Service Job Performance Measurement/ Enlisted Standards (JPM) Project, which represented a large-scale effort to develop robust measures of performance in entry-level military jobs and to link enlistment standards, particularly scores on the ASVAB needed for enlistment and assignment to various specialties, to actual job performance. In JPM, hands-on performance tests were selected as benchmark measures of job performance. A conscious decision was made to assess what the person *can* do, rather than what he or she *will* do on the job (i.e., measures of maximal rather than typical performance were used), an approach criticized as overly narrow (Murphy, 1989a). Nevertheless, the accomplishments of JPM researchers suggest that the particular aspects of performance measured by these tests and methods can be assessed with some precision.

The various divisions of the armed services experimented with several methods of assessing job knowledge and skill; some of these are outlined in Table 19-1. They ranged from simple demonstrations of factual and procedural knowledge to very lifelike simulations of critical tasks involved in the job. In evaluating these measures, JPM researchers used sophisticated applications of generalizability theory, systematic assessments of task sampling adequacy, and investigations of several aspects of construct validity (Wigdor & Green, 1991). Although the use of work samples as performance measures poses a number of technical problems (Smith, 1991) and excludes a number of relevant behaviors from the definition of performance (Murphy, 1989a), evidence from the extensive body of JPM research indicates that work samples can provide valuable measures of performance, particularly when coupled with other methods of measuring job performance.

TABLE 19-1   PERFORMANCE MEASUREMENT STRATEGIES INCLUDED IN JOINT-SERVICE PROJECT

Service	Strategy	Description
Air Force	Walk-through Testing	Combination of hands-on demonstration and verbal descriptions of how person would do certain tasks
Navy	Simulation	Variety of realistic and abstract simulations of tasks sampled from actual job
Marines	Job Knowledge Testing	Multiple-choice tests of factual and procedural knowledge needed to perform tasks

JUDGMENTAL MEASURES

There are two general types of judgments that might be used in measuring performance: *rankings,* which involve comparing workers with one another; and *ratings,* which involve comparing each worker to some standard. There is reason to believe that rating and ranking involve different psychological processes, and that ratings and rankings may not always be comparable (Landy & Farr, 1980). Of the two methods, ratings are used more widely, although both methods have advantages and disadvantages.

Ranking Techniques

Suppose a manager supervises the work of eight construction electricians. The simplest method of evaluating their performance might be to rank-order the employees in terms of their overall effectiveness. There is no doubt that some employees are more effective than others; a ranking is merely a systematic recognition of this fact.

Several different ranking methods exist, ranging from those which provide a crude, partial rank-order to those that provide very exact data on the relative (perceived) effectiveness of each employee. One of the simplest of the partial ranking methods is the *forced distribution.* This ranking method is designed to deal with a very common problem in judgmental performance evaluations: the tendency of most supervisors to rate almost all their employees in the top 5 to 10 percent and to describe the worst employees as merely "above average."[2] A forced distribution scale requires the supervisor to designate a fixed number of workers as belonging to the lowest category, a fixed number as belonging to the highest category, and the rest as belonging to a middle category. It is, of course, possible to employ more than three categories if necessary.

An example of a forced distribution scale is shown in Table 19-2. In the table, eight workers have been sorted into three ordered categories, top, middle, and bottom. It might be more informative to obtain a *full ranking,* which involves determining the rank-order of each of the eight workers and, in effect, sorts the workers into eight ordered categories. Thus, the principal difference between a forced distribution and a full ranking is that in the latter, the number of categories is equal to the number of workers, whereas in a forced distribution, the number of categories may be considerably smaller than the number of workers.

A third method of ranking is the pair-comparison method. An example of a pair-comparison involving four workers is shown in Table 19-3. As is evident from the table, a pair-comparison task involves an extremely simple judgment: For each pair of subordinates, the supervisor must judge which worker is more effective. Although the judgment required is very simple and seemingly crude, the pair-comparison method allows for very exact scaling of the relative effectiveness of each worker. Application of scaling techniques allows one to transform the ordinal data that arise out of pair-comparisons to interval-level measures of effectiveness (Thurstone, 1927; Torgerson, 1958). This precision in measuring the effectiveness of each employee is made possible by the fact that a

---

[2]This tendency is referred to as leniency.

TABLE 19-2   A TYPICAL FORCED-DISTRIBUTION SCALE

Top 25% A	Middle 50% B	Bottom C

Total Number of Subordinates: 8
Your top 2 subordinates belong in catogory "A"
Your bottom 2 subordinates belong in category "C"
Your remaining subordinates belong in category "B"

Subordinates	Category
1. Small, M.	————
2. O'Reilly, J.	————
3. Stetson, K.	————
4. Witherspoon, R.	————
5. Dobson, T.	————
6. Murchinson, A.	————
7. Archer, S.	————
8. Houston, J.	————

relatively large number of comparisons must be obtained in the course of a pair-comparison task. A total of $[n(n-1)/2]$ comparisons are necessary when comparing n employees. Thus, with four employees, six comparisons are necessary $[(4 \times 3)/2 = 6]$; in comparing ten employees, 45 separate pair-comparisons must be made.

Chiu and Allinger (1990) proposed a method that combines aspects of ranking and rating. Using this method, raters must place each individual they evaluate in different ordered categories, but the spread between people can be used to indicate relatively large or relatively small differences between individuals. Suppose, for example, that you thought that Joe and Mary were both poor workers (although Mary was slightly better), and that Sue and Kathleen were both quite good (and that Kathleen was slightly better). You might assign scores of 1, 2, 6, and 7 (on a 7-point scale) to Joe, Mary, Sue, and Kathleen, respectively.

In practice, the method suggested by Chiu and Allinger (1990) is likely to be more similar to a rating scale than to a ranking method. It does, however, force raters to make distinctions between individuals, and it might be useful in settings where it is necessary to rank everyone.

Comparison of ranking methods.   In choosing among ranking techniques, a trade-off must be made between the effort involved in ranking and the precision of the information that will result. A forced distribution provides a relatively crude measure—workers in the top category are judged to be more effective than those in the bottom category. A full ranking provides a more exact comparison of individual workers, but at the price of considerable effort. A pair-comparison procedure provides an interval-level measure of relative effectiveness, but it does so at the price of requiring a large number of comparisons.

In part, the choice of a technique depends on the way in which rankings will be used. For certain promotion decisions, or for allocating cutbacks, a forced-distribution ranking

TABLE 19-3   A TYPICAL PAIR-COMPARISON TASK

Worker to be compared:	Wallsten, A.
	Block, S.
	Barrow, K.
	Carr, M.

Which worker is performing better? Circle one.
   Wallsten or Block?
   Wallsten or Barrow?
   Wallsten or Carr?
   Block or Barrow?
   Block or Carr?
   Barrow or Carr?

may be appropriate. On the other hand, for evaluating the extent to which employees differ in their levels of performance, a pair-comparison ranking might be necessary.

Rating Scales

Rating scales represent the single most common measure of job performance (Landy & Farr, 1980, 1983). As opposed to ranking techniques, which call for comparisons between persons, rating scales require the supervisor to evaluate each worker with regard to a particular standard, that may be vaguely described (e.g., good, average, poor), or that may be described in concrete behavioral terms (e.g., "This teacher could be expected to miss class frequently"). Whereas ranking methods require supervisors to decide on a relative basis which of two workers is a better performer, rating scales require supervisors to evaluate and describe the level of each individual worker's performance.

There are a variety of rating scale formats, ranging from scales that are quite simple and straightforward to those that involve complex scoring rules or extremely concrete behavioral anchors. Two types of rating scales that are widely used and that have been the object of considerable research are graphic rating scales and behavior-based scales.

Graphic rating scales.   The most common, and the simplest form of rating instrument, is the graphic rating scale. This format asks the rater to make a direct judgment about the quality of each worker's performance and to indicate this judgment on a specific response scale. Examples of several different types of graphic rating scales are presented in Table 19-4. Response scale (a) requires the rater to mark, on a 21 centimeter line, the point that corresponds to his or her evaluation of a particular employee. A numeric rating can be obtained by measuring the distance between the lower end of the scale and the supervisor's checkmark. In this case, worker A received a rating of 18, whereas worker B received a rating of 1.

Rating scales (b) and (c) are verbally anchored scales that are divided into a small number of discrete categories. The supervisor's checkmark can be translated into a numeric rating by assigning values to each category. For example, scale (c) can be numbered from 1 to 5, where 1 indicates "Consistently Unsatisfactory" and 5 indicates "Consistently Satisfactory." A worker who was rated "Below Average" would receive a score of 2.

TABLE 19-4   EXAMPLES OF GRAPHIC RATING SCALES MEASURING THE QUALITY OF WORK

(a)	Continuous Scales	

Worker A

		✓
poor		excellent

Worker B

✓		
poor		excellent

(b)   Verbally Anchored Scale

poor	+	+	+	+ excellent

(c)   More Complete Verbally Anchored Scale

Consistently Unsatisfactory	Below Average	Average	Above Average	Consistently Superior

(d)   Numeric Scale
Poor = 1–6;   Average = 7–15;   Good = 16–20
Rating <u>14</u>

(e)   Scale with Explicit Anchors

Errors are very frequent	Work is passable: frequent checks needed	Work sometimes needs to be checked	Work seldom needs to be checked	Work never needs to be checked

Rating scale (d) is an example of a numeric scale. A rater using this scale could indicate with some apparent precision his or her evaluation of each applicant. Thus, if a worker received a rating of 14, as in the table, this would indicate performance that was somewhat better than average but was lower than the level typically described as "good."

The obvious advantage of a graphic scale is its simplicity. Once it is decided what is to be measured, the construction of a graphic scale is quite simple. There are three general principles that should be followed in constructing a graphic rating scale, but within the confines of these principles it probably does not matter what type of scale one decides to construct. First, the number of responses probably should be somewhere between 5 and 9. Second, to whatever degree possible, scale anchors should be fairly explicit. Scale (e) in the table is an example of a scale that meets these two requirements. The third requirement is that the behaviors or traits being measured be defined explicitly.

Unfortunately, the simplicity of a graphic rating scale is also the source of considerable ambiguity. First, there is a good deal of ambiguity with regard to the precise meaning of the performance dimensions being rated. Graphic scales are typically used to measure somewhat broad dimensions of performance, such as "Quality of Work," "Oral Communication," or "Planning." It is never clear precisely what behaviors are included in a dimension such as "Quality," and it is therefore likely that different raters will have different ideas regarding the aspects of employee performance they should consider when rating the "Quality" of each employee's work.

Second, there is often a good deal of ambiguity in the interpretation of the scale anchors. Supervisors almost certainly have different interpretations of what is meant by good or average performance, and in most cases scale anchors do not really provide a concrete, detailed description of the behavior that best represents good, average, or poor performance. Behavior-based scales—a category that includes mixed standard scales, behaviorally anchored rating scales, and behavioral observation scales—were developed in an attempt to remove several sources of ambiguity in rating.

Behavior-based scales.   A mixed standard scale (MSS) is one that presents the rater with concrete behavioral examples of good, average, and poor performance (Blanz & Ghiselli, 1972). Rather than providing a vaguely anchored, absolute evaluation of the ratee's performance (e.g., "slightly better than average"), a supervisor using this type of scale is asked to indicate whether the person being evaluated typically exhibits performance that is better than (+), about equal to (0), or worse than (−) the level of performance exhibited in the behavioral example.

An example of a mixed standard scale used in evaluating police patrol officers is presented in Table 19-5. The scale is used to measure three dimensions of police performance: Judgment, Job Knowledge, and Relations with Others. Each performance dimension is represented by three behavioral examples of good performance, average perform-

TABLE 19-5   A MIXED STANDARD SCALE FOR POLICE PATROL OFFICERS

Dimension	Level			Rating
K	P	1.	The officer could be expected to misinform the public on legal matters through lack of knowledge.	+
R	G	2.	The officer could be expected to take the time to carefully answer a rookie's question.	0
K	G	3.	This patrol officer never has to ask others about points of law.	−
J	G	4.	The officer could be expected to refrain from writing tickets for traffic violations that occur at a particular intersection that is unusually confusing to motorists.	+
J	A	5.	The patrol officer could be expected to call for assistance and clear the area of bystanders before confronting a barricaded, heavily armed suspect.	+
R	P	6.	The officer could be expected to use racially toned language in front of minority-group members.	+
K	A	7.	This officer follows correct procedures for evidence preservation at the scene of a crime.	0
J	P	8.	The patrol officer could be expected to continue to write a traffic violation in spite of hearing a report of a nearby robbery in progress.	+
R	A	9.	This officer is considered friendly by the other officers on the shift.	+

Dimensions*	Performance levels*
J—Judgment	G—Good
R—Relations with Others	A—Average
K—Knowledge	P—Poor

*Note: These labels are *not* provided on an actual mixed standard sclae.

Source: From *Psychology of Work Behavior*, 4th ed., by F. J. Landy. Copyright © 1989 by Wadsworth, Inc. Reprinted by permission of Brooks/Cole Publishing Company, Pacific Grove, CA 93950.

ance, and poor performance. The examples are intermixed randomly, and the supervisor responds to all the examples. Thus, the supervisor must indicate whether the ratee's performance is better than, about equal to, or worse than the examples of good, average, and poor performance for each dimension.

It is possible to use the ratings of the three behavioral examples to derive a numeric rating of each performance dimension, using a scoring system similar to the one shown in Table 19-6. A worker who was rated worse than good, worse than average, and worse than poor is assumed to be a very poor worker and receives a score of 1 for that particular dimension. A worker who is better than poor, better than average, but worse than good is clearly a better worker but may not exhibit the highest possible level of performance; on a scale from 1 to 7, this worker would receive a rating of 5. Thus, the police officer whose ratings are illustrated in Table 19-5 received a rating of 7 on Judgment, a rating of 4 on Job Knowledge, and a rating of 6 on Relations with Others.

TABLE 19-6 SCORING SYSTEM FOR MIXED STANDARD SCALES

	Behavioral examples			Derived rating
	Good	**Average**	**Poor**	
	+	+	+	7
	0	+	+	6
Ratings	−	+	+	5
Given by	−	0	+	4
Supervisor	−	−	+	3
	−	−	0	2
	−	−	−	1

Note: + the ratee's performance is better than that in the example
  0 the ratee's performance is about equal to that in the example
  − the ratee's performance is worse than that in the example

Mixed standard scales have two appealing features. First, they present concrete, behavioral standards for evaluating good, average, and poor performance. Second, they seem to require relatively simple judgments on the part of the rater—is the ratee's performance as good as, better than, or worse than the level described in the behavioral example? However, there are problems with the use of these scales, the most serious of which is that raters are inconsistent. Thus, it is possible to find a worker who is rated as better than good but worse than average on the same dimension. Scoring schemes have been proposed that take into account inconsistent responses (Saal, 1979), but these methods are not applied or accepted widely.

One of the most heavily researched rating scale formats, behaviorally anchored rating scales (BARS)[3] were developed to deal with the two principal sources of ambiguity that plague graphic rating scales: (a) ambiguity in the dimensions being rated and (b) ambiguity in the scale anchors. BARS provide concrete behavioral statements that are used to identify particular levels of performance and that, taken together, provide a series of clear behavioral exemplars of the performance dimension under consideration

[3]These scales are sometimes referred to as behavior expectation scales (BES).

(Smith & Kendall, 1963). An example of a behaviorally anchored rating scale used to measure the job knowledge of police patrol officers is presented in Table 19-7.

The development of behaviorally anchored rating scales typically involved extensive input from the supervisors and workers who use the scale (Landy, 1985). The goal of this input is to develop behavioral anchors that have three properties. First, they should be relevant to the work setting. Second, they should provide good illustrations of the *dimension* being measured. Thus, a police officer who was not sure exactly what is meant by "job knowledge" could consult the scale shown in the table for behavioral examples. Third, they should provide a good illustration of a particular *level* of performance. Thus, an officer who consults the scale shown in the table should have a good idea of what is meant by good, average, and poor performance.

Various aspects of the voluminous literature on behaviorally anchored rating scales have been reviewed by Bernardin and Smith (1981), Jacobs, Kafry, and Zedeck (1980), Landy and Farr (1980), Kingstrom and Bass (1981), and Schwab, Heneman, and DeCotiis (1975). There is general agreement that BARS have not lived up to their promise; ratings obtained using BARS do not appear to be substantially more accurate or

TABLE 19-7   BEHAVIORALLY ANCHORED RATING SCALE FOR POLICE PATROL OFFICERS. JOB KNOWLEDGE: AWARENESS OF PROCEDURES, LAWS, AND COURT RULINGS AND CHANGES IN THEM

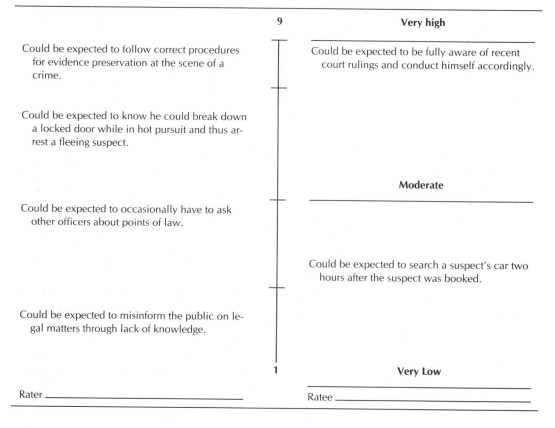

	9	**Very high**
Could be expected to follow correct procedures for evidence preservation at the scene of a crime.		Could be expected to be fully aware of recent court rulings and conduct himself accordingly.
Could be expected to know he could break down a locked door while in hot pursuit and thus arrest a fleeing suspect.		
		Moderate
Could be expected to occasionally have to ask other officers about points of law.		
		Could be expected to search a suspect's car two hours after the suspect was booked.
Could be expected to misinform the public on legal matters through lack of knowledge.		
	1	**Very Low**

Rater _____   Ratee _____

less prone to bias than ratings obtained using simpler graphic scales (Borman, 1991). However, the process of developing BARS may itself be highly beneficial to an organization, and it may very well justify the investment of the organization's time and resources.

First, as the result of developing BARS, the organization arrives at fairly precise, agreed-upon behavioral definitions of performance in specific aspects of the job (Landy & Farr, 1980). This outcome contrasts sharply with that achieved by organizations that employ graphic rating scales, in which every supervisor might have a unique definition of average performance. Second, the process of scale development involves many members of the organization (Borman & Vallon, 1974). There is a good deal of evidence that participation in the scale development process itself contributes to the acceptance of performance appraisal systems and to the perception that these systems are fair and accurate (Dipboye & de Pontbriand, 1981; Landy & Farr, 1980).

Latham and Wexley (1977) have criticized both graphic rating scales and behaviorally anchored scales; they note that the former require raters to make vague, unanchored judgments, whereas the latter require raters to indicate what sort of behaviors they would expect, even though in many cases none of the behavioral anchors included in the scale have been observed. They suggest a simpler alternative, the behavioral observation scale (BOS). A BOS is made up of a list of behaviors believed to be critical for effective job performance. An example of a BOS used in measuring the performance of teachers is presented in Table 19-8.

The rater who uses a BOS is asked to indicate how frequently each of the critical incidents on the scale has occurred over a specific period of time (Latham, Fay & Saari, 1979). Items that depict ineffective performance, such as items 3, 4, 8, 9, or 12 in the table, are rescaled so that large scale values indicate low frequency of occurrence, and scores are obtained by summing the frequency ratings assigned to each item. Thus, a worker who frequently performs effective critical behaviors and who very rarely per-

TABLE 19-8 A BEHAVIORAL OBSERVATION SCALE FOR TEACHERS

Rate the frequency with which each of the following behaviors has occurred this month. Use the following scale to rate frequency.

1	2	3	4	5	6	7
Never	Almost never	A few times	About half of the time	Often	Most of the time	All of the time

1. Examples were presented which were clearly related to the central topic. _____
2. Lecturer used purposeful nonverbal behaviors (smiles, points) to emphasize points. _____
3. Lecturer stops in mid sentence. _____
4. Lecturer is hesitant, says "uh" or "um." _____
5. Lecturer establishes eye contact with audience. _____
6. Lecturer provides facts or evidence to support broad generalizations. _____
7. Lecturer speaks clearly. _____
8. Lecturer acts nervous. _____
9. Lecturer speaks in a monotone for a sustained period. _____
10. Lecturer gives clear answers to questions. _____
11. Lecturer varies his or her facial expression. _____
12. Lecturer appears unsure of what he or she is saying. _____

forms ineffective behaviors receives a high rating, while a worker who frequently performs ineffective behaviors receives a low rating.

One of the principal advantages of the BOS technique is its apparent simplicity. Rather than asking supervisors to make complex, unreliable judgments about workers, this type of rating scale merely asks raters to report how frequently different behaviors have occurred; the psychological process involved in completing a BOS therefore seems considerably simpler and more straightforward (less prone to error) than with other types of scales (Latham, Saari & Fay, 1980). However, several investigators have suggested that the processes involved in filling out a BOS are neither simple nor straightforward but, rather, may depend upon the same general impressions and vague judgments that affect ratings obtained using other types of scales. Murphy, Martin, and Garcia (1982) suggest that supervisors cannot recall the frequency of critical behaviors over extended periods of time; rather, they infer the frequency with which effective behaviors have occurred on the basis of their general impressions of each worker. Murphy and Balzer (1981, 1986) have gone further, suggesting that behavioral observation scales are, in fact, trait-rating scales in disguise. Supervisors infer that workers they perceive as good *must have* carried out many effective work behaviors, rather than inferring that a worker is good *because* he or she carried out the specific behaviors included in the BOS.

Comparing Performance Appraisal Scales

Landy and Farr (1980) suggest that 30 years of research on scale formats has failed to produce an alternative that is demonstrably more efficient or more psychometrically sound than simple graphic rating scales. On this basis, they called for a moratorium on format-related research. While this recommendation may represent a somewhat extreme reaction, their review does bring into focus the relatively minor impact of rating scale formats on the outcomes of rating. A good graphic scale is probably adequate for measuring the performance of one's workers, and the use of a complex behavioral format is unlikely to improve the quality of rating data.

Although rating scales have little effect on the outcomes of rating, they may dramatically affect the *process* of rating. As Table 19-9 suggests, the psychological processes implied by graphic rating scales, mixed standard scales, behaviorally anchored rating scales, and behavioral observation scales are quite different. Although research on rating scale formats has failed in its original mission—to develop the one best scale for rating

TABLE 19-9   PSYCHOLOGICAL PROCESSES PRESUMABLY INVOLVED WHEN USING DIFFERENT RATING SCALES

Scale	Processes involved
Graphic Rating Scale	Unanchored judgment
Mixed Standard Scale	Discrete better-than/worse-than comparison
Behaviorally Anchored Rating Scale	Continuous comparison that involves matching performance levels to behavioral anchors
Behavioral Observation Scale	Observation and recall of behavior frequency

job performance—future research on rating scale formats may shed light on the judgment processes involved in performance evaluation (Murphy & Constans, 1987, 1988).

Research on performance appraisal has been increasingly directed at an evaluation of the cognitive processes that seem to underlie rating (Cooper, 1981; DeNisi & Williams, 1988; Feldman, 1981; Landy & Farr, 1980). It is possible that once the rating process is better understood, rating formats and rater training programs will be designed to capitalize on those aspects of the rating task that are most easily or most readily carried out, thereby avoiding asking supervisors to perform tasks that are beyond their cognitive capacity (e.g., remember the frequency of specific behavior over the span of a year). Thus, the development of better rating formats is not necessarily a hopeless task; rather, it awaits progress in understanding the rating process (Banks & Murphy, 1985).

The question of *who* evaluates your performance may be more important than the question of what type of scale is used. Many organizations have experimented with the use of peer ratings (i.e., evaluations obtained from co-workers rather than supervisors) and even self-ratings as supplements to supervisory ratings. There is clear evidence that (a) self-ratings are consistently higher than peer or supervisory ratings and (b) peers and supervisors agree more closely with one another than either agrees with self-ratings (Harris & Schaubroeck, 1988). A number of explanations for these differences have been suggested (Murphy & Cleveland, 1991), but the implications of this research are clear—if you want high ratings, do them yourself!

The Validity of Criterion Measures

In the introduction to this chapter, it was noted that most applications of psychological testing in industry are concerned, in one way or another, with the construct of job performance. Selection tests are used to *predict* future job performance; therefore, the validity of those predictions is of major importance in assessing the overall worth of the test. The second broad class of measures frequently encountered in personnel administration is the set of indices used to *measure* job performance. Except in a limited number of cases in which meaningful production counts can be obtained, judgmental methods (i.e., ratings or rankings) are used to measure the performance of workers. The validity of these measures is the central concern of this section.

There is no simple way to determine or to demonstrate the validity of most measures of job performance. Consider, for example, supervisory performance ratings. Ideally, the validity of ratings might be determined by correlating these ratings with other measures of job performance (Kavanaugh, 1971). The problem with this approach is that ratings are often the *only* available measure of the worker's performance; there is rarely any other acceptable standard against which ratings can be compared.[4] In short, there are rarely ''criteria for criteria''; it is rarely possible to demonstrate convincingly that a particular measure of job performance is, in fact, a valid measure of the performance of individual workers. Because there are typically no standards against which most criterion

---

[4]There are a few studies that demonstrate that ratings are positively correlated with objective measures of performance (e.g., Bass and Turner, 1973; Ross, 1966). However, there are so few studies of this sort that it is difficult to rely exclusively on these studies to determine the validity of subjective measures.

measures can be compared, it is difficult to use the predictive or concurrent validity strategies in assessing the validity of criteria.

Recognizing that the strategy of determining the validity of a criterion measure directly by comparing that measure to some standard is often impossible, a number of authors have suggested indirect strategies for assessing the validity of criterion measures. For example, it is often possible to determine the extent to which raters discriminate among individuals, or differentiate among performance dimensions in their ratings of job performance (Kavanaugh, MacKinney & Wolins, 1971; Saal, Downey & Lahey, 1980; Stanley, 1961). It is assumed that raters who are sensitive to differences in their subordinates' levels of performance are more accurate than those who give everyone similar ratings. Other authors suggest that inter-rater agreement be used as an indirect indicator of the validity of ratings (Bernardin, Alveres & Cranny, 1976; Lawler, 1967). Although it is true that valid ratings also should be reliable, several authors have noted that reliability does not necessarily imply validity, and on this basis have questioned the use of inter-rater agreement as an indicator of valid ratings (Buckner, 1959; Freeberg, 1959; Wherry & Bartlett, 1982).

Finally, James (1973) has proposed the most comprehensive approach to assessing the validity of criterion measures—the construct validity approach. He notes that performance can be thought of as a construct, and that the relationships between a measure of performance and a number of other observable behaviors could be compared to the pattern of relationships implied by the theoretical network in which the construct "performance" is embedded to assess the validity of a criterion measure.

Research on the construct validity of performance ratings has progressed significantly in recent years. For example, the research teams involved in U.S. Armed Forces Project A relied on careful explications of the construct domain of job performance to develop concrete performance measures (see *Personnel Psychology,* Vol. 43, No. 2, for a detailed description of this project). Kraiger and Teachout (1990) illustrated ways in which analyses of the generalizability of ratings (see Chapter 5 for an overview of generalizability theory) could be used to assess construct validity. Other authors (e.g., Lance, Teachout & Donnelly, 1992; Murphy, 1989a) have suggested methods for identifying dimensions that underlie the performance domain.

Rater errors.   Research in organizations suggests that supervisors fall prey to several errors in evaluating the performance of subordinates. Some raters fail to discriminate good performers from bad ones; others fail to identify the strengths and weaknesses of individual workers. A number of indices have been proposed to measure raters' tendencies to commit these errors; these so-called rater error measures represent the most common criteria for evaluating performance ratings. Rater error measures are used by some researchers as indirect measures of rating accuracy, in that ratings that show little or no evidence of specific rater errors are assumed to be more accurate then ratings that show strong evidence of such errors (Jacobs, Kafry & Zedeck, 1980).

Rater errors fall into three categories:

1. *halo errors,* which represent a failure to identify employee strengths and weaknesses

2. *leniency errors,* which represent a tendency to assign ratings that are either unduly lenient or unduly harsh

3. *range restriction errors,* which represent a failure to discriminate among workers in terms of their overall level of performance

Halo errors are thought to reflect raters' tendencies to allow their overall evaluation of each worker to affect their evaluation of each specific aspect of that person's performance (Cooper, 1981; Thorndike, 1920). Thus, a worker who receives a favorable overall rating might also receive high marks for all specific aspects of performance on which he or she is rated; a worker who receives a poor overall rating might also receive poor ratings on every specific performance dimension. In fact, it is unlikely that many workers are either very good, very bad, or even average in *all* aspects of their work. It is therefore likely that the supervisor who rates individual workers as uniformly good or uniformly poor is not providing accurate ratings, at least on some dimensions.

Halo error is most clearly manifest in the correlations between ratings of different performance dimensions. When raters commit halo error, ratings of apparently unrelated performance dimensions show substantial positive correlations. The correlation between different performance dimensions is therefore used as a measure of halo error (Saal, Downey & Lahey, 1980). The higher the correlation between ratings of different performance dimensions, the greater the likelihood that halo error is present.

Leniency errors are thought to reflect an inappropriate judgmental standard on the part of the rater. When a supervisor indicates that all of his or her workers are top performers or, conversely, that all workers are extremely poor performers, it is likely that the ratings tell us more about the rater than they do about the people being rated. Leniency errors are thought to be most clearly indicated by the mean rating; it is assumed that when the average rating is 9.5 on a 10-point scale, the rater is unduly lenient.[5] Conversely, when the average rating is 2 on a 10-point scale, it is assumed that the rater is unduly severe.

Range restriction errors are thought to reflect supervisors' inability or unwillingness to discriminate good from poor workers. For example, some supervisors rate most or all workers as average, and they seem to be unwilling to go out on a limb in describing specific workers as either good or poor. Range restriction error is most clearly manifest in measures of the variability in ratings, such as the standard deviation. If the range, or the standard deviation, of the ratings assigned by a specific supervisor to a group of workers is very near zero, it is probably safe to assume that range restriction error is present.

Rater error measures have been used widely in evaluating performance appraisal scales (Landy & Farr, 1980) and rater training programs (Spool, 1978). Nevertheless, these measures have been the focus of considerable criticism. First, there is a great deal of inconsistency in the operational definitions of these measures (Balzer & Sulsky, 1992; Murphy, 1982; Murphy & Balzer, 1981; Saal, Downey & Lahey, 1980). Alternate measures of halo, leniency, or range restriction are rarely equivalent, and sometimes are unrelated. Second, the assumptions underlying rater error measures often are inappropriate. Finally, and most important, there is little empirical or theoretical support for the

[5]A similar assumption underlies the perennial debate over grade inflation.

position that rater errors are related to rating accuracy (Borman, 1977; Cooper, 1981; Murphy & Balzer, 1989). As a result, the use of rater error measures as criteria for evaluating ratings is becoming increasingly rare (Balzer & Sulsky, 1990, 1992).

Rating accuracy.   Borman (1977) has noted that in order to evaluate the accuracy of the rating assigned to a specific worker, ratings must be compared with a "true score" measure of the worker's performance. In real work settings, it is generally impossible to obtain measures against which performance ratings can be directly evaluated, and, as a result, indirect measures such as rater error measures must be used. However, in laboratory experiments in which performance is preserved on videotape, it is possible to develop direct measures of rating accuracy. Methods of measuring the accuracy of ratings of videotaped performance have been developed and applied by Borman (1977, 1978) and others (Murphy, Balzer, Kellam & Armstrong, 1984; Murphy, Garcia, Kerkar, Martin & Balzer, 1982; Penn & Bowser, 1977).

To date, much of the research on rating accuracy has examined aspects of the rating process that contribute to accuracy in evaluating performance. For example, Murphy, Garcia and their colleagues (1982) showed that accuracy in observing behavior is related to accuracy in rating performance, although this relationship is not a simple one, owing to the multiple definitions of rating accuracy (Cronbach, 1955; Wiggins, 1973).

Other researchers have examined the relationship between memory and rating accuracy. Research in social cognition has shown that there are systematic distortions in memory of behavior; these distortions are thought by many to significantly affect the accuracy of memory-based performance ratings (Feldman, 1981; Hastie et al., 1980; Murphy & Balzer, 1986; Murphy, Martin & Garcia, 1982; Shweder & D'Andrade, 1980).

Finally, Landy and Farr (1980) have suggested that a number of contextual variables, such as the timing, format, and purpose of rating, affect the accuracy of performance evaluations. For example, several studies have suggested that ratings collected for the purpose of making administrative decisions (i.e., salary and promotion decisions) are systematically more lenient than ratings collected for research purposes. However, other research casts some doubts upon the relationship between the purpose of rating and the accuracy of ratings (Murphy et al., 1984; Murphy, Philbin & Adams, 1989).

Research on rating accuracy suggests that under optimal conditions raters are capable of achieving high levels of accuracy in evaluating the performance of others. Thus, the central issue in current research on rating accuracy is not whether raters are capable of accuracy but, rather, under what conditions they will achieve accuracy. For example, Mohrman and Lawler (1983) suggest that supervisors are rarely motivated to provide accurate ratings, and in several instances may actually be motivated to provide *inaccurate* ratings. Since organizations rarely reward supervisors for accuracy in assessing their workers' performance, the supervisor often has nothing to gain—and quite a bit to lose— if he or she gives a poor evaluation to a worker (Murphy & Cleveland, 1991).

Other researchers suggest that the accuracy of ratings is affected by characteristics of the rater, characteristics of the worker, the variability of performance, the use of memory aids, such as behavior diaries, and the broader social context in which rating occurs (Bernardin & Walter, 1977; Landy & Farr, 1980, 1983; Lerner, 1983; Locke, 1983; Murphy & Cleveland, 1990; Wherry & Bartlett, 1982). More research is needed before the circumstances under which ratings provide an accurate measure of an individual worker's performance can be described clearly.

The Appraisal Process and Criterion Validity

Research in the 1950s through the early 1980s attempted to identify refinements in rating scales that might lead to more accurate or valid ratings. It is now clear that the influence of the rating scale on the quality of rating data is very limited (Landy & Farr, 1980). It also seems likely that other traditional strategies, such as rater training, are limited in their usefulness (Bernardin & Beatty, 1984; Murphy & Cleveland, 1991). A more promising avenue for increasing the validity and accuracy of performance ratings collected in industry is to focus on the rating process. For example, much of the recent appraisal research has examined cognitive processes in rating, and this research has shown how cognitive limitations can affect performance rating outcomes (DeNisi & Williams, 1988). Other researchers have examined the conditions that motivate raters to render either accurate or inaccurate ratings (Mohrman & Lawler, 1983; Murphy & Cleveland, 1991).

Many of the controversies in performance appraisal are the result of disagreements over how rating is done rather than over the quality of measurement. This is particularly true in the public sector, where there are a large number of constituencies (e.g., supervisors, subordinates, and taxpayers) who have valid concerns about the evaluation of job performance. One approach to this problem is to develop specific standards that govern the process of appraisal, by specifying who should appraise employees, what factors they should consider, and so forth. This is exactly the strategy behind the *Performance Evaluation Standards* developed by the Joint Committee on Standards for Educational Evaluation. These standards provide guidelines for evaluating the performance of educators at all levels in educational systems (i.e., primary school through university levels). This volume contains 21 standards that define the propriety, utility, feasibility, and accuracy requirements of performance appraisal systems in educational settings. While guidelines such as these cannot resolve all controversies in performance evaluation, they do represent a substantial step forward in the practice of performance appraisal.

It is not clear whether increased attention to the process of developing and applying performance appraisal systems will lead to more valid and accurate measures of job performance. Regardless of whether this approach eventually leads to better measurement, we think it will be worthwhile for the simple reason that it encourages us to think of validity as a property of the outcomes of a complex system (i.e., the ratings themselves) rather than simply a property of the rating scales.

CAN WE MEASURE THE VALUE OF PERFORMANCE?

Everyone agrees that effective employees are more valuable to an organization than ineffective employees. Indeed, this is the ultimate rationale for investing time, energy, and money in personnel selection, training, incentive programs, and in other programs aimed at increasing productivity. The question addressed in this section is whether the *value* of job performance can be measured. More specifically, is it possible to measure the dollar value

of performance on the job and to compare the value of an average worker's job performance to the value associated with a superior worker's job performance?

In some jobs, it is quite easy to measure the value of a person's work simply by
counting some relevant unit. For example, it is possible to count the dollar value of the
goods sold by an appliance salesman, deduct wholesale prices and overhead, and compute the profit generated by that salesman. In other jobs, such as manager, electrician, or
librarian, such counting methods will not work. Note that the problem here is the same as
that raised earlier in our discussion of output measures—in most jobs, there are no
particular output measures that adequately represent the employee's level of job performance. Therefore, the strategy of counting all dollar values of the goods produced by an
employee will not reflect adequately the value of that employee's job performance.

Schmidt, Hunter, McKenzie, and Muldrow (1979) devised an alternative method of
measuring the value of performance that is applicable to many, if not all, jobs. These
researchers were concerned with measuring the *variability* in the value of performance.
For example, their method assesses the difference between the value of an average
worker's performance (i.e., a worker in the fiftieth percentile) and the value of a highly
superior worker's performance (i.e., a worker in the eighty-fifth percentile). They note
that in a normal distribution, this difference would be approximately the same size as the
standard deviation of the performance distribution, and that measures of this difference
can be used to estimate the *standard deviation of performance, measured in terms of
dollar value.*

The methods developed by Schmidt and his associates (1979) require a series of
judgments from several supervisors who are familiar with the job. Considerable evidence
indicates that these methods yield reliable and valid estimates of the value of performance (Bobko, Karren & Parkington, 1983; Schmidt & Hunter, 1983; Schmidt, Hunter,
McKenzie & Muldrow, 1979; Schmidt, Hunter & Pearlman, 1982). Furthermore, there is
evidence that the standard deviation of performance is closely related to the salary level
of the job in question; in most jobs, the standard deviation of performance is approximately 40 percent as large as the salary level. More recent research suggests that the
percentage may be even higher (Becker & Huselid, 1992; Judiesch, Schmidt & Mount,
1992).

In concrete terms, a standard deviation that is equal to 40 percent of salary means
that the difference between the level of performance shown by an average worker and
the level of performance shown by a highly superior worker (i.e., eighty-fifth percentile)
in a job with a salary of $20,000 has an annual value of approximately $8,000 (i.e, one
standard deviation). In a higher-level job in which the salary is $50,000, this same
difference has an annual value to the organization of $20,000.

The consistent relationship between salary level and value of performance is both a
strength and a weakness of this method. On the one hand, it is possible to estimate the
value of performance for any given job without studying that job in depth, simply by
multiplying the salary level by .4. On the other hand, a consistent finding that judgments
about the value of performance are related to salary level suggests a potential problem:
Across several studies and many different jobs, it has been shown that the higher the
salary, the higher the judged value of performance. The simplest way to account for this
finding is to assume that judgments about the value of performance are directly affected
by salary levels. That is, supervisors tend to assume that a highly paid person's perform-

ance must be valuable to the organization. Indeed, there is evidence that supervisors base their judgments in part upon the salary level of the job they are evaluating (Bobko et al., 1983).

A variety of methods now exist for estimating the value of an individual's job performance, ranging from those that involve simple global judgments to those that require careful behavioral analysis (e.g., Cascio & Ramos, 1986). The results of these methods usually converge, although in different circumstances one method might provide more reliable and valid estimates than another (Burke & Frederick, 1986). The most important outcome of research on various methods of estimating the value of an individual's performance is not the development of one method that is best in all circumstances but, rather, the demonstration that this aspect of job performance *can* be reliably measured and that information about the value of job performance can be integrated in evaluating programs, such as personnel selection and training, which are designed to increase the value of human resources in organizations (Boudreau, 1991).

Value of Performance and Selection Utility

As noted in Chapter 8, utility theory provides a means to determine the impact of valid tests on the quality of selection decisions. In general, the better the test, the more likely that the best candidates will be hired—that is, those candidates who subsequently perform at a high level (see, however, Murphy, 1986). Since it is possible to measure the value of a superior worker's performance as compared to an average worker's performance, it also will be possible to measure the economic impact of selection testing; as discussed in Chapter 8, this impact is often substantial. For example, Hunter and Hunter (1984) estimated that the use of valid selection tests on a nationwide basis would lead to an increase in productivity worth more than $15 billion per year. More recent analyses carried out by the National Academy of Sciences (Hartigan & Wigdor, 1989) suggest that the effects of testing on productivity are much smaller than this figure but are still substantial.

In general, selection tests lead to the greatest gain when the value of performance varies from worker to worker. In this situation a superior worker produces goods and services that are clearly more valuable than those produced by an average worker, and substantially more valuable than those produced by a below-average worker, in the same amount of time. In this situation a valid test that successfully discriminates superior workers from average and below-average workers could have a substantial impact on workforce productivity.

On the other hand, if there is little variability in the value of performance, tests will have little impact, since the best workers must be producing goods and services that are not much more valuable than those produced by the worst workers. In this case, even if a test successfully discriminates the best candidates from the worst candidates, it will make little difference, in terms of the value of performance, who is hired. It is for this reason that attention has been increasingly focused on estimating the standard deviation of performance. No matter how good a test is, it will not have much impact on the bottom line if there is no variability in performance. An organization has the most to gain by focusing its efforts in selection and placement on those jobs where the value of the goods and services produced varies the most.

CRITICAL DISCUSSION:
The Ethics of Evaluation—Telling More Than You Know

Put yourself in the place of a sales manager who is asked to evaluate several salespeople on the following dimensions: use of time, oral communication skills, customer contact, and accuracy in following procedures. Because your customers are scattered over a wide area, you never actually *see* your sales force in action in the field. Thus, the only way you find out anything about your salespeople's performance is through their sales figures, or through rare compliments or complaints from customers. Thus, you really have no idea how your salespeople performed in most of the areas listed on the performance appraisal form. What should you do when performance appraisal time rolls around?

Performance appraisal often requires supervisors to "tell more than they know."[6] Does this present an ethical problem? A psychologist who provided assessments that had no basis in terms of the behaviors observed or reported would certainly violate professional ethics. In the case of the sales manager, however, the picture is not so clear. First, professional ethics apply only to professionals; managers are not bound by the same set of rules. On the contrary, managers are expected to make evaluations on the basis of whatever information is available. Thus, if a manager knows nothing about the way in which a salesman uses his time, the manager is likely to base ratings in this area on his or her general impression of the salesman.

The best solution to the problem described above is probably in the design of performance appraisal systems. Explicit attention should be given to the question of whether raters have the information necessary to evaluate ratees accurately. If supervisors do not have the opportunity to observe relevant behaviors or to provide relevant feedback to workers, they should not be asked to evaluate the effectiveness of that aspect of the person's performance.

SUMMARY

A variety of measures are available to measure job performance, including both objective methods, in which little or no judgment is required to obtain adequate measures, and subjective methods, which rely on the judgments of one or more evaluators to "measure" job performance. Given all the potential problems associated with subjective methods, their popularity is at first difficult to understand. However, in many jobs, it is essentially impossible to obtain objective measures that adequately represent the performance of the individuals being assessed, which means that subjective measures are the only practical choice.

Judgmental measures might require ranking (i.e., comparisons of persons to one another) or rating (i.e., comparisons of persons to some standard). On the whole, rating methods are more common, and a great deal of research has been devoted to developing the best possible rating scales. A number of scale formats have been developed that use behavioral examples to define or measure levels of performance, but while behavior-

---

[6]See Nisbett and Wilson (1977) for examples of similar problems in cognitive research.

based scales are popular, there is little evidence that the rating scale format makes much of a difference in the psychometric quality of the ratings.

Three general methods have been used to evaluate the validity of ratings. First, an increasing number of researchers have applied construct validation methods to the analysis of performance ratings, and there is some consensus that supervisors in organizations are capable of providing reasonably valid measures of their subordinates' performance (Milkovich & Wigdor, 1991). Second, researchers have developed a number of rater-error measures, which are designed to reflect specific types of judgment errors (e.g., excessive leniency in rating subordinates). Although these measures are still somewhat popular, there is an increasing body of research demonstrating their shortcomings. Finally, methods have been developed to directly measure the accuracy of ratings. Unfortunately, these measures are limited to laboratory experiments and other artificial settings, and they have had relatively little applicability to field settings.

In Chapter 8 we discussed utility analysis. One cornerstone of this type of analysis is determining the value of job performance. Validity studies might be used to determine how much of an increase in performance is expected given certain interventions (e.g., better tests, better training), but unless a specific value can be attached to that increase, it is difficult to evaluate different personnel programs. Utility reserachers have developed a number of methods of determining the value of job performance, and their results suggest that programs such as selection testing often have substantial payoffs for organizations.

CHAPTER 20

PERSONALITY TESTING IN CLINICAL SETTINGS

This chapter opens our discussion of the psychological tests and measurement techniques that are used most frequently by clinical psychologists. A greater number and wider variety of tests are discussed in this section than in the preceding ones, largely because a broader range of decisions is necessary in clinical settings than in industrial or educational settings. In personnel selection, educational admissions, and similar applications, the examiner usually has a clear understanding of the goal of testing (e.g., to select aircraft mechanics) and of the type of information needed to make decisions about individuals (e.g., information about mechanical aptitude, spatial visualization ability). In these settings, the situation dictates the goal and purpose of testing. In clinical settings, the individual client defines the goals and purpose of testing. The tests that are most appropriate for one client may be inappropriate for the next. Thus, a clinician may need a broader and more varied arsenal of tests than would a psychologist employed in industry or in a school.

In this chapter we discuss some of the most widely used measures of personality, along with several of the recurring issues in personality measurement. Although the tests described here vary considerably in content and in methods of administration and scoring, they all are designed to provide a general description of the person being tested along one or several dimensions that are thought to be relevant for understanding that person's behavior in everyday situations.

In the next chapter we discuss tests and measurement techniques that are geared toward the assessment of psychopathology. These tests are not so informative in describing most individuals, but they are very useful in understanding and diagnosing abnormal behavior.

In the final chapter we discuss methods used by clinicians to integrate information from several tests into their assessments of individual clients. That chapter also considers the effects of human judgment on psychological measurement and assessment in clinical settings.

DEVELOPMENT OF PERSONALITY TESTING

Chapter 12 contained a brief review of the history of personality testing. It is useful once again to consider the major trends in personality testing, since the diversity of personality tests still reflects the variety of approaches to personality measurement developed in the early part of this century.

Historically, the first attempt to measure personality or character traits through the use of a test is usually accorded to Fernald. His work involved writing items reflecting his theories about personality, then organizing them into a test of personality. While much of this early work was done at the turn of the century, the next milestone in personality measurement occurred during World War I. The need to select personnel for the military led to the development of instruments designed to predict whether a new recruit would make a satisfactory adjustment to the military. Basically, these early tests were collections of items based on clinical literature describing normal patterns of behavior. They generally attempted to assess only one facet of personality, such as submission to authority, adjustment to the military, or degree of comfort when associating with others.

The most notable improvement in personality measurement during the next two decades was the appearance of multiscaled tests. Typically, personality tests introduced in this era measured such things as anxiety, assertiveness, home adjustment, general health, impulsiveness, and interest in masculine or feminine activities. Some attempt at assessing defensiveness or conscious concealment on the test was also included, although these early scales were often quite primitive and obtrusive. For example, a typical item designed to measure defensiveness might ask the examinee to indicate the number of friends he or she had. The multiple-choice responses available would be "none," "few," or "hundreds." The first choice was judged to measure maladjustment, while the third choice was thought to indicate defensiveness.

During the 1930s and 1940s, two new developments in the measurement of personality appeared: empirically derived methods of testing and projective tests. Empirically derived tests represented a change from theoretically based item selection to mathematically based selection. Instead of relying on various personality theories to determine which dimensions of personality should be measured, the basis of decision making shifted to the inherent mathematical relationships that existed among test items. Empirically based personality tests essentially branched out into two major groups, factor analytically derived tests and criterion-referenced tests.

Projective testing also began to blossom during this period. The work of Murray and his associates on the Thematic Apperception Test and Rorschach on his inkblot test became the pioneering efforts in projective testing. The development of this approach to personality measurement represented a shift from the use of clear, unambiguous tasks to unstructured, less-defined activities. Proponents of projective testing were interested in developing measures of personality that were more global, less subject to distortion and defensiveness, and more directed at the hidden or unconscious facets of personality.

The decades since the 1940s have seen few significant new trends in personality testing. The emphasis has been much more on researching the established tests and modifying them in an attempt to alleviate their shortcomings. While new instruments have emerged, they all have tended to be variants of earlier themes and have employed similar methods of construction. Later in this chapter we survey several tests that reflect these major strategies of construction.

OBJECTIVE MEASURES OF PERSONALITY

Tests of personality are often classified as either objective or projective, depending on the structure and clarity of the task required of examinees. According to this classification scheme, objective tests are seen as containing highly structured, clear, unambiguous test items that are objectively scored. Projective tests, on the other hand, are seen as having unstructured, ambiguous items that encourage examinees to *project* their personality into the tasks utilizing hidden wishes, attitudes, and needs in responding to the stimuli presented. While this has proven to be a useful distinction for classification purposes, there has been some controversy about the value of this classification system (Lichtenburg, 1985). Nevertheless, we believe that although this historical distinction may be somewhat arbitrary, it is useful in referring to and categorizing the many personality tests in use today.

In surveying the field of objective personality measurement, we examine four instruments that illustrate key developments in personality testing. The California Personality Inventory provides an example of one of the better, frequently used personality tests, measuring common elements of interpersonal functioning. The Personality Research Form represents one of the newest and more promising instruments. The Edwards Personal Preference Schedule shows the application of a forced-choice, ipsative format to the problem of personality measurement, and the Sixteen Personality Factors Test demonstrates the application of factor analysis in the development of a personality inventory.

California Psychological Inventory

The California Psychological Inventory (CPI) was initially developed and first published by Harrison Gough in 1957. Thirty years later Gough revised his inventory by adding several new scales and revamping or eliminating a number of dated, sexist, or difficult to read items. The current version of the CPI (Gough, 1987) contains 462 true-false items designed to measure various facets of the normal personality. It is intended to be used with both adolescents and adults to predict how individuals will behave and react in a variety of interpersonal situations.

The items are grouped into 20 scales designed to measure attributes of personality involved in interpersonal behavior and social interaction. These scaled variables were chosen by Gough because he believed they were important and meaningful personality attributes in all cultures and societies, were readily understandable and interpretable to the test user, and were valid predictors of future behavior in similar social contexts. In addition, three of the scales also provide measures of test-taking attitudes and response sets that, if operable, could reduce the usefulness of the test results. A list of the 20 scales and a brief description of their operation is presented in Table 20-1.

The CPI was constructed primarily of empirically built scales. The general scheme followed was to select two groups of people who differed with respect to a particular psychological trait (e.g., people rated as high or low dominant) and have them complete the inventory. Next, Gough searched for items that significantly differentiated the two groups and combined them into a scale reflecting that personality attribute. Thirteen of the scales were built using this technique. Four of the scales were constructed to be internally consistent by selecting items that appeared to measure the desired trait and then intercorrelating them to refine the measure. The remaining three scales were formed by a mixture of the two above scale-construction approaches.

In addition to the 20 basic personality scales, Gough has recently identified three major vectors that underlie personality functioning. He sees these vectors as forming a three-dimensional construct of personality. Utilizing special scoring instructions, users of the CPI are able to identify an individual's relative position along these three structural components of personality (i.e., interpersonal orientation, normative perspective, and level of realization).

Administration and scoring of the CPI is rather quick and easy. It can be administered individually or in a group setting, usually in about an hour. Scoring consists of counting the number of items endorsed on each scale and plotting the raw scores on a profile. This can be done either by hand or machine. In either case the scored profile readily converts raw scores to T scores for ease of interpretation.

Gough maintains that the CPI is most appropriate for evaluating an individual's behavior in and attitude toward interpersonal situations. He states that while the original intent of the scales is relatively clear, the diagnostic implications of certain combinations of scales is less self-evident and requires a trained person to interpret all the nuances inherent in various profile configurations.

As an example of a CPI and its interpretation, consider the case of Marianne. At one point in her early academic career, she was undecided about her future career plans. She was uncertain if she possessed sufficient social skills to be successful in an occupation requiring considerable people contact. As part of career counseling at that time, she completed a CPI. Figure 20-1 presents her score profile.

The interpretation process begins with a check on the three validity scales (Wb, Gi, Cm). Her responses on the test indicate that she was feeling quite buoyant, optimistic, and free of stress at the time the test was taken. Her self-image was positive, and she generally presents herself in a well-adjusted manner. The responses she gave on the test are consistent with those given by people who conscientiously completed the inventory. This suggests that her profile is likely to present an accurate reflection of her opinions, beliefs, and behavior patterns.

Marianne's profile also reveals that she is quite similar to dominant people who easily manage positions of authority and leadership. She indicates significantly above-average interpersonal attitudes and social behaviors. In unfamiliar social settings, Marianne probably initiates social contacts. In the area of achievement orientation, her results

TABLE 20-1   CALIFORNIA PSYCHOLOGICAL INVENTORY SCALES AND DESCRIPTIONS

	Low scorers	High scorers
Do (Dominance)	unassuming; not forceful	confident; assertive, dominant, task-oriented
Cs (Capacity for Status)	unsure of self; dislikes direct competition	ambitious; wants to be a success; independent
Sy (Sociability)	shy; feels uneasy in social situations; prefers to keep in the background	sociable; likes to be with people; friendly
Sp (Social Presence)	cautious; hesitant to assert own views or opinions; not sarcastic	self-assured; spontaneous; a good talker; not easily embarrassed
Sa (Self-acceptance)	self-doubting; readily assumes blame when things go wrong; often thinks others are better	has good opinion of self; sees self as talented, and as personally attractive
In (Independence)	lacks self-confidence; seeks support from others	self-sufficient; resourceful; detached
Em (Empathy)	ill at ease in many situations; unempathic	comfortable with self and well accepted by others; understands the feelings of others
Re (Responsibility)	not overly concerned about duties and obligations; may be careless or lazy	responsible; reasonable; takes duties seriously
So (Socialization)	resists rules and regulations; finds it hard to conform; not conventional	comfortably accepts ordinary rules and regulations; finds it easy to conform
Sc (Self-control)	has strong feelings and emotions, and makes little attempt to hide them; speaks out when angry or annoyed	tries to control emotion and temper; takes pride in being self-disciplined
Gi (Good Impression)	insists on being himself or herself, even if this causes friction or problems	wants to make a good impression; tries to do what will please others
Cm (Communality)	sees self as different from others; does not have the same ideas, preferences, as others	fits in easily; sees self as a quite average person
Wb (Well-Being)	concerned about health and personal problems; worried about the future	feels in good physical and emotional health; optimistic about the future
To (Tolerance)	not tolerant of others; skeptical about what they say	is tolerant of others' beliefs and values, even when different from or counter to own beliefs
Ac (Achievement via Conformance)	has difficulty in doing best work in situations with strict rules and expectations	has strong drive to do well; likes to work in setting where tasks and expectations are clearly defined

TABLE 20-1   continued

	Low scorers	High scorers
Ai (Achievement via Independence)	has difficulty in doing best work in situations that are vague, poorly defined, and lacking in clear-cut methods and standards	has strong drive to work well; likes to work in settings that encourage freedom and individual initiative
Ie (Intellectual Efficiency)	has a hard time getting started on things, and seeing them through to completion	efficient in use of intellectual abilities; can keep on at a task where others might get bored or discouraged
Py (Psychological-mindedness)	more interested in the practical and concrete than the abstract; looks more at what people do than what they feel or think	more interested in why people do what they do than in what they do; good judge of how people feel and what they think about things
Fx (Flexibility)	not changeable; likes a steady pace and well-organized life; may be stubborn and even rigid	flexible; likes change and variety; easily bored by routine life and everyday experience; may be impatient, and even erratic
F/M (Femininity/Masculinity)	decisive, action-oriented; takes the initiative; not easily subdued; rather unsentimental	sympathetic, helpful; sensitive to criticism; tends to interpret events from a personal point of view; often feels vulnerable

Source: From the *Manual for the California Psychological Inventory.* Copyright © 1957, 1960, 1964, 1969, 1987 by Harrison Gough. Reprinted by permission.

reveal that she performs equally well in both structured and unstructured situations. She reports few complaints that interfere with her ability to concentrate and be intellectually productive. Her intrapersonal controls over internal impulses are well within normal limits, as are her attitudes and feelings about societal roles and mores. She also indicates a tolerant attitude toward those holding beliefs and values different from her own. Overall, Marianne appears to be a well-adjusted, interpersonally adept, and socialized woman. There are no indications from her profile that she would be unsuccessful in a career requiring extensive social interaction and interpersonal skill.

Research on the CPI (Megargee, 1972) has established that it is extremely useful in predicting underachievement in academic settings and potential delinquency. The personality dynamics underlying these two behavioral patterns are apparently well assessed by this test. There is also evidence that the CPI predicts job performance in a number of careers, as well as performance in school. Factor analyses of the CPI have suggested that its scales are not independent but, rather, show considerable overlap. This scale overlap is consistent with the goal of the inventory, however, to assess common areas of personality functioning that are hypothesized to be related in the "real" world. Two studies on the original version of the CPI (Crites, Bechtoldt, Goodstein & Heilbrun, 1961; Mitchell & Pierce-Jones, 1960) reported that five or six basic factors accounted for most of the variance on the test. Recent factor analysis of the revised CPI (Gough, 1987) showed that

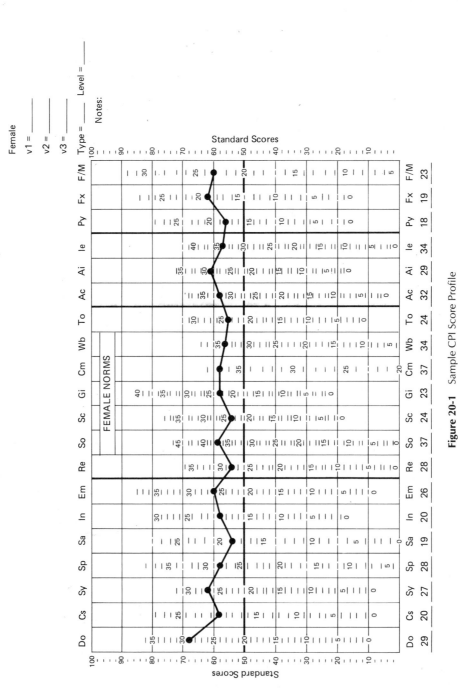

Figure 20-1 Sample CPI Score Profile

Source: Copyright © 1957, 1960, 1964, 1969, 1987 by Harrison Gough and published by Consulting Psychologists Press. Reprinted by permission.

the 20 scales could be reduced to four primary factors (i.e., extraversion, control, flexibility, and consensuality).

While the CPI has been severely criticized for its psychometric shortcomings, its proponents point out that clinicians with sufficient interpretive experience can predict behavior accurately in many social contexts. It remains one of the better researched and more frequently used measures of normal personality (Piotrowski & Keller, 1984).

Personality Research Form

The Personality Research Form (PRF) was developed and published by Douglas Jackson in 1967. It represents a relatively sophisticated attempt to measure dimensions of the normal personality. It is based on the variables of personality originally defined by Henry Murray and his colleagues at the Harvard Psychological Clinic (Murray, 1938). This test is available in several forms that differ in length and in the number of Murray's variables assessed. The characteristics chosen for assessment on the PRF were those judged to be the most important or most relevant for assessing a wide area of personal living and functioning.

Initially, the PRF appeared in two sets of parallel forms, differing in item length and number of scales. The shorter forms (A and B) contained 300 items divided into 14 personality scales and a validity indicator designed to detect possible scoring errors and careless test-taking attitudes, such as random responding. The longer forms (AA and BB) contained 440 items comprising 20 personality dimensions and two validity scales. The second validity scale, added to the longer forms, was intended to measure the tendency to give socially desirable responses. Both sets of parallel forms have been used primarily with college students. This necessitated the development of a newer form (E) of the PRF (Jackson, 1984) that permitted its extension to other populations. Since it was developed later, it was possible to use modified item selection techniques that permitted including all 22 scales of the older, longer forms in a shortened 352-item test.

A list of all 22 scales appearing on the PRF is given in Table 20-2, along with a brief description of each personality dimension being assessed. Jackson designed his scales to be bipolar in nature, meaning that a low score on any scale signifies not just the absence of the trait but also the presence of its opposite. For example, if many items were endorsed on the exhibition scale, it would mean that the respondent has a positive need to be conspicuous, dramatic, and colorful in social situations. A low score on the exhibition scale would be interpreted as indicating a fear of group activities and the active avoidance of them.

The PRF scales were constructed by first carefully studying each of the personality constructs outlined by Murray. Then, over 100 items for each scale were written to measure the hypothesized trait or personality dimension in question. Next, these items were reviewed by editors to eliminate redundancy and unclearly worded items. The provisional scales were then administered to large numbers of college subjects. Their responses were used to reduce the scales to a smaller number of internally consistent items, that is, items showing greater correlations with other items in their own scale than to other scales. All items showing extreme endorsement frequencies—above 95 percent and less than 5 percent of the samples tested—were eliminated from consideration, since such items generally add little new information that differentiates one respondent from

TABLE 20-2 PERSONALITY RESEARCH FORM SCALES AND DESCRIPTIONS

Abasement—Shows a high degree of humility; accepts blame and criticism, even when not deserved, self-effacing.

Achievement—Aspires to accomplish difficult tasks; maintains high standards and works toward distant goals; enjoys competition

Affiliation—Enjoys being with friends and people in general; very accepting of others; establishes and keeps relationships with friends.

Aggression—Enjoys combat and argument; easily annoyed; may seek to retaliate with people perceived as causing harm; willing to offend to get own way.

Autonomy—Tries to break away from restraints, confinement, or restrictions of any kind; enjoys being free and unattached.

Change—Likes new and different experiences; dislikes routine and avoids it; adapts readily to changes in environment.

Cognitive Structure—Dislikes ambiguity in information; desires to make decisions based upon definite knowledge rather than probabilities.

Defendence—Ready to defend self against real or imagined harm from others; takes offense easily; does not accept criticism readily.

Dominance—Attempts to control environment and to influence or direct others; enjoys the role of leader.

Endurance—Willing to work long hours; doesn't give up quickly; persevering even in the face of problems.

Exhibition—Enjoys being the center of attention; may enjoy being dramatic or witty; likes an audience.

Harm avoidance—Dislikes exciting activities, especially if danger is involved; avoids risk of bodily harm.

Impulsivity—Tends to act on the "spur of the moment" without deliberation; gives vent readily to feelings and wishes; speaks freely.

Nurturance—Gives sympathy and comfort, assists others whenever possible; readily performs favors for others; likes caring for others.

Order—Concerned with keeping personal effects and surroundings neat and organized; dislikes clutter, confusion, and disorganization.

Play—Does many things "just for fun"; enjoys jokes and funny stories; maintains an easy-going, light-hearted attitude toward life.

Sentience—Notices smells, sounds, sights, tastes, and the way things feel; remembers the sensations and believes that they are important.

Social Recognition—Desires to be held in high esteem by acquaintances; concerned about reputation and what others think; works for approval.

Succorance—frequently seeks the sympathy, protection, love, advice, and reassurance of others; may feel insecure or helpless without support.

Understanding—Values synthesis of ideas, logical thought, and verifiable generalizations.

Desirability—Describes self in terms judged as desirable; presents favorable picture of self.

Infrequency—Responds in implausible or pseudo-random manner due to carelessness, confusion, etc.

Source: From Manual for the Personality Research Form. Copyright © 1967, 1974, 1984 by Douglas N. Jackson. Reprinted by permission of Sigma Assessment Systems, Inc., 1110 Military Street, P.O. Box 984, Port Huron, MI 48061-0984.

another. The end result was the production of a set of scales that are highly reliable, reasonably free of response set bias, and capable of discriminating examinees along a continuum of personality characteristics.

Jackson had two goals in mind for the PRF. First, he wanted to design a useful tool for personality research. Second, he intended to develop an instrument for assessing general personality dimensions assumed to be of importance in such environments as schools, guidance clinics, and industry. While the PRF has enjoyed fairly widespread use in a number of different research applications ranging from the study of group differences and sociometric studies to investigations of academic achievement and creativity, it has also been increasingly applied in clinical settings. With the publishing of the more versatile Form E, the PRF has been used with junior and senior high-school students, in vocational counseling for noncollege populations, in mental health centers, with older populations, and in personnel selection and placement.

Several studies (Kusyszyn, 1968; Jackson & Guthrie, 1968; Ostendorf, Angleitner & Ruch, 1983) have provided validational data on the PRF. The general strategy of these studies has been to have close acquaintances of the subjects rate them on a number of personality traits and then correlate these criterion ratings with the appropriate PRF scores. The results of these studies have generally substantiated the validity of the PRF scales. Consequently, although the PRF is a relatively new test, it appears to be well constructed, have good psychometric characteristics, and offers the promise of becoming one of the more useful measures of important dimensions of the normal personality.

Sixteen Personality Factors Test

Better known as the 16 PF, the Sixteen Personality Factors Test was first published commercially in 1949 and later revised in 1982 by the Institute for Personality and Ability Testing under the authorship of Raymond Cattell. He and his associates believed that a personality test should measure the most fundamental dimensions of normal personality and comprise all the characteristics and attributes found in adults.

In order to develop so comprehensive an instrument, Cattell and his associates decided to survey all the words in the English language that described personal characteristics. Other researchers (Allport & Odbert, 1936) had searched through dictionaries and found approximately 4,000 English adjectives that described personality characteristics. Cattell and his co-workers began with this large group of adjectives, intending to factor analyze them to extract a smaller number of more basic adjectives. Because of the limitations of factor analysis at that time, they were forced to categorize the words into 45 groups, based primarily upon an inspection of their linguistic similarities. Once they had obtained the 45 categories, they were able to factor analyze this more manageable group into approximately 15 factors, which were simply labeled A through O. The most important factor, accounting for the greatest amount of variance among the 45 characteristics, was assigned the letter A. Each subsequent letter appeared to be less important and was sequentially assigned a lower alphabetic label. Some of these factors were not easily replicable in adults, however, and so they were dropped from consideration.

Other factors that were identified from factor analyses of other personality questionnaires were found to be quite important in describing behavior, so they were included on the test. The latter factors were given the designations Q_1, Q_2, Q_3, and Q_4 to identify their questionnaire origin. The end result was a personality test built by factor analytic methods that contained 16 factors generally independent of one another and potentially able to describe all aspects of normal personality function when taken together collectively.

Currently the 16 PF is available in a number of forms, extending its use from adults and adolescents with a high school education to less literate groups. It also is combined with a set of 12 dimensions of pathology to form the *Clinical Analysis Questionnaire,* designed to measure simultaneously normal and pathological personality characteristics. It can therefore be used in working with emotionally disturbed populations. The commonly used form of the 16 PF consists of 187 items responded to along a 3-point Likert scale. Because of its factor-analytic method of construction, the scales have been designed to be as independent as possible, with no item contributing to the score of more than one scale.

Nevertheless, because of the nature of personality, there are some interrelationships that exist among the scales, some of which are identified as second-order factors on the test. These factors are postulated to be more broadly operative dimensions of personality. The 16 first-order factors and four second-order factors are listed in Table 20-3.

Administering and scoring the 16 PF requires little special training. Each item response is assigned a unit weight of 0, 1, or 2 points, except for the items on scale B, intelligence, which are either 0 or 1, depending on whether the response is correct or incorrect. Summations of the item weights produce a raw score which, when compared with one of the norming tables provided in the manual, translates the raw score to a type of standard score called a "sten," or standard ten scale. The sten is then profiled on a chart that shows graphically where the individual stands in reference to the norm group used for comparison. Scoring of the second-order scales is a bit more complicated. A special scoring formula is needed, provided both in the manual and the handbook for combining the necessary part scores to arrive at the second order scores.

Figure 20-2 shows the profile used with the 16 PF. Note that the average area is clearly outlined, while the percentage of people scoring like the examinee are shown below. For ease of interpretation, the profile provides a shaded area that outlines the normal range of scores for the standardization population. At the bottom of the profile, the percentages of the normal population scoring at each of the ten score divisions is also given as an aid in translating stens into a normal score distribution. While some find the sten system very easy to use when interpreting test results, others find it somewhat cumbersome to explain and much prefer the T-score system of reporting results employed by the majority of personality tests.

Clinically, the 16 PF has been used in a wide variety of settings. It has well-developed norms based on more than 15,000 individuals, including high school, college, and adult populations. It has been employed in vocational psychology to determine the personality profiles of various occupational groups. Personnel selection and placement have been undertaken using scores from the 16 PF as important data in the decision-making process. Counseling and mental health centers also have used this test as a diagnostic, screening, and treatment evaluation tool. Perhaps it is because scale names are unfamiliar and difficult to relate to everyday behavior that the 16 PF has not enjoyed the extensive usage its excellent psychometric characteristics might indicate. Clinicians have apparently not felt as comfortable interpreting it to their clients as they have other instruments, even though the others may be inferior from a technical standpoint. Its

TABLE 20-3   PERSONALITY CHARACTERISTICS MEASURED BY THE SIXTEEN PF

First-order factors		Second-order factors
Warmth	Suspiciousness	Extraversion
Intelligence	Imagination	Anxiety
Ego Strength	Shrewdness	Tough Poise
Dominance	Guilt Proneness	Independence
Impulsivity	Rebelliousness	
Group Conformity	Self-sufficiency	
Boldness	Compulsivity	
Tender-Mindedness	Free-floating Anxiety	

Factor	Meaning of Score on Left	Meaning of Score on Right
A	Cool, Reserved, Impersonal, Detached, Formal, Aloof	Warm, Outgoing, Kindly, Easy-going, Participating, Likes People
B	Concrete-thinking, Less Intelligent	Abstract-thinking, More Intelligent, Bright
C	Affected by Feelings, Emotionally Less Stable, Easily Annoyed	Emotionally Stable, Mature, Faces Reality, Calm
E	Submissive, Humble, Mild, Easily Led, Accommodating	Dominant, Assertive, Aggressive, Stubborn, Competitive, Bossy
F	Sober, Restrained, Prudent, Taciturn, Serious	Enthusiastic, Impulsive, Heedless, Expressive, Cheerful
G	Expedient, Disregards Rules, Self-indulgent	Conscientious, Persistent, Moralistic, Staid, Rule-bound
H	Shy, Threat-sensitive, Timid, Hesitant, Intimidated	Bold, Venturesome, Uninhibited, Can Take Stress
I	Tough-minded, Self-reliant, No-nonsense, Rough, Realistic	Tender-minded, Sensitive, Over-protected, Intuitive, Refined
L	Trusting, Accepting Conditions, Easy to Get on with	Suspicious, Hard to Fool, Distrustful, Skeptical
M	Practical, Concerned with "Down to Earth" Issues, Steady	Imaginative, Absent-minded, Absorbed in Thought, Impractical
N	Forthright, Unpretentious, Open, Genuine, Artless	Shrewd, Polished, Socially Aware, Diplomatic, Calculating
O	Self-assured, Secure, Feels Free of Guilt, Untroubled, Self-satisfied	Apprehensive, Self-blaming, Guilt-prone, Insecure, Worrying
Q_1	Conservative, Respecting Traditional Ideas	Experimenting, Liberal, Critical, Open to Change
Q_2	Group-oriented, A "Joiner" and Sound Follower, Listens to Others	Self-sufficient, Resourceful, Prefers Own Decisions
Q_3	Undisciplined Self-conflict, Lax, Careless of Social Rules	Controlled, Self-respecting, Socially Precise, Compulsive
Q_4	Relaxed, Tranquil, Composed, Has Low Drive, Unfrustrated	Tense, Frustrated, Overwrought, Has High Drive

A sten of 1, 2, 3, 4, 5, 6, 7, 8, 9, 10 is obtained by about 2.3% 4.4% 9.2% 15.0% 19.1% 19.1% 15.0% 9.2% 4.4% 2.3% of adults

Figure 20-2 16 PF Profile

Source: Copyright © 1956, 1973, 1982 by the Institute for Personality and Ability Testing. Reprinted by permission.

potential as a research tool has, however, led to the 16 PF being selected as the instrument of choice in many studies of personality and therapeutic outcome. Until clinicians become more attuned to the 16 PF, it will probably continue to find its greatest use in research.

Edwards Personal Preference Schedule

Developed by Allen Edwards and first published in 1954, the Edwards Personal Preference Schedule (EPPS) represented a novel attempt to reduce the effects of social desirability in personality assessment. Edwards began by operationally defining 15 latent personality needs outlined earlier by Murray and his associates at the Harvard Psychological Clinic (Murray, 1938). After generating a pool of items to reflect these needs, he administered them to various groups of college students with instructions to rate each item according to its social desirability. Once these ratings were determined, Edwards was able to pair items measuring different needs that had equal social desirability ratings. This procedure yielded an ipsative test designed to eliminate the effects of social desirability, while providing a measure of the relative strengths of competing latent personality characteristics.

The 15 latent needs assessed by the EPPS are outlined in Table 20-4. Each need is paired with the other 14 needs twice on the test. Scoring consists of a summation of the number of times a need is chosen out of 28 possible pairs. Raw scores are converted to percentile equivalents, with the use of various norm tables representing both college and general adult populations. One additional scale, a measure of response consistency, provides a check on random responding. It is composed of 15 repeated items. Respondents who carefully complete the EPPS generally answer at least nine or more of the 15 items consistently. Lower scores are indicative of potential interpretive problems.

The strength of the EPPS in clinical use is that it measures dimensions of personality that are nonthreatening to the client. Open discussion of test results often provides an important stimulus for further self-exploration. Sharing the definitional statements that give meaning to the manifest need variables measured with counselees also tends to demystify testing and hence reduce defensiveness on the part of the client.

Unfortunately, the weaknesses of the EPPS outweigh its advantages. Research (Corah, Feldman, Cohen, Gruen, Meadow & Ringwall, 1958; Feldman & Corah, 1960) has shown that the effects of social desirability on the test have not been eliminated, or even satisfactorily controlled as Edwards had contended. The additional psychometric problems and limitations that accompany the use of an ipsative, forced-choice item format seems to be a poor trade-off if no benefit of social desirability control is obtained.

TABLE 20-4   EDWARDS PERSONAL PREFERENCE SCHEDULE SCALES AND DESCRIPTIONS

Achievement—To be successful, to solve difficult puzzles and problems, to be able to do things better than others.

Deference—To get suggestions from others, to find out what others think, to follow instructions.

Order—To have written work neat and organized, to make plans before starting on a difficult job or task.

Exhibition—To say witty and clever things, to tell amusing jokes and stories, to have others notice you.

Autonomy—To be able to come and go as desired, to say what you want; to do things that are unconventional.

Affiliation—To be loyal to friends, to participate in friendly groups, to do things for friends.

Intraception—To analyze your motives and feelings, to observe others, to analyze the behavior of others.

Succorance—To have others provide help when in trouble, to seek encouragement from others, to gain sympathy.

Dominance—To argue for your point of view, to be a leader, to persuade and influence others.

Abasement—To feel guilty when you do something wrong, to accept blame when things do not go right.

Nurturance—To help friends when they are in trouble, to assist others less fortunate, to treat others kindly.

Change—To do new and different things, to travel, to experience novelty, to experiment with new jobs.

Endurance—To keep at a job until it is finished, to complete any job undertaken, to work hard at a task.

Heterosexuality—To go out with members of the opposite sex, to engage in social activities with the opposite sex.

Aggression—To attack contrary points of view, to tell others what you think about them, to criticize others.

Consistency—To determine if the responses given on matching pairs are identical and show consistency.

Source: From the Manual of the Edwards Personal Preference Schedule. Copyright © 1954, 1959 by The Psychological Corporation. Reproduced by permission. All rights reserved.

Since its publication, there has not been much research supporting its validity other than that initially reported in the manual. It is quite doubtful that it measures any latent needs, but rather provides a picture of how clients see themselves when tested.

Despite the paucity of research data supporting its validity and the apparent problems of its ipsative format, the EPPS still is employed rather widely in guidance centers, vocational counseling, school settings, and employment situations. In a study assessing how frequently various psychological tests were used by clinicians in counseling agencies (Zytowski & Warman, 1982), the results showed that the EPPS was ranked third in overall usage behind the SII and the Kuder OIS. While it represents an ingenious attempt to improve the art of personality test construction and is rather frequently used, it does not fulfill the requirements of a well-validated and psychometrically sound instrument.

PROJECTIVE TESTS OF PERSONALITY

All projective tests share in common the utilization of ambiguous stimuli or tasks designed to provide a wide range of responses from examinees. These tests are especially sensitive in detecting unconscious or covert personality characteristics. They are based on the assumption that the use of ambiguous stimuli eliminates or greatly reduces defensiveness and other conscious attempts to distort test results. Proponents believe that examinees project themselves into the task and respond both to the meaning they impart to the stimuli and to the feelings they experience while responding. Interpretation of projective tests is dependent on the total analysis of examinees' responses, without regard to any preconceived notions about the correctness of any response given on the test.

The history of projective testing dates back to the late nineteenth century. Early attempts with inkblots were aimed at measuring imagination and intelligence. With the publishing of his inkblot test in 1921, Hermann Rorschach really began the modern era of projective assessment. His use of inkblots to measure personality characteristics was largely an empirical effort at test construction. Henry Murray, however, was more interested in developing a comprehensive theory of personality and an instrument for its measurement. The result was the Thematic Apperception Test, published in 1943. These two tests have provided a major impetus in the area of projective testing. They have profoundly affected the practice of psychology and psychiatry, have led to an enormous amount of published research, and have been the stimuli for several later-generation projective instruments.

Rorschach Inkblot Test

The Rorschach consists of a series of ten bilaterally symmetrical inkblots placed on individual 5½ by 9½-inch cards. Five of the cards are in black and white only, two cards are basically red and gray, and three are multicolored. Figure 20-3 depicts a typical blot from the test. The cards are presented to the examinee in a predetermined sequential order. Respondents are asked to view each card and relate everything they see, or to hand it back when they are finished describing as much as they can. Examinees are allowed to turn the cards any way they wish. Examiners attempt to divulge as little as possible about the task and permit as many responses to be given as the examinee wishes.

Figure 20-3 Typical Blot from Rorschach

Source: From Rorschach, H., *Psychodiagnostics* [*Psychodiagnostik*]. Copyright © 1921 by Verlag Hans Huber, Bern (renewed 1948). Reproduced by permission.

After all ten cards have been responded to, the examiner goes back over all of the cards with the examinee during the "inquiry" phase of testing. The examiner records on a special miniature reproduction of each blot the areas or portion of each blot used as the basis of the examinee's response. Considerable skill is required to conduct the inquiry so as to extract clarification about their responses and permit examinees the opportunity to give additional information about each card while not influencing their experiences of the inkblots.

Some Rorschach users add a third phase to the testing during which they test the limits of responding by probing for more examinee responses. This technique is especially useful if earlier responses of the examinee are noticeably lacking in some form of responding commonly found in Rorschach protocols. There is some debate among examiners about the wisdom of this technique, however, because it may have a detrimental effect on any future testing using the Rorschach.

Scoring the Rorschach is a complex process requiring a classification of the responses given into three major categories: location, determinants, and content. Location has reference to the area of the blot used by the examinee in determining his or her responses. Some of the possibilities included in scoring are the whole blot, a part of it, and the white space on which the blot is printed. The category of determinants has reference to what qualitative characteristics were perceived on the card that determined the responses. The scored characteristics in this group are the form or shape of the blot, movement inferred to be going on, and the use of color. Content refers to what is reported as actually seen in the blot and is treated as the least important variable scored on the Rorschach. A subcategory here looks at the frequency with which the response in question is given by others.

Unfortunately, there is not universal agreement among Rorschach users or experts as to which type of responses should be scored or how much emphasis should be placed on them. Various scoring systems have been developed to try and remedy this problem, but there are discrepancies among them. A part of the problem stems from the fact that some of the current subcategories of responses were not recognized by Rorschach himself, and consequently they are not accepted universally as necessary or meaningful.

Interpreting the results of a Rorschach consists of examining the relationships that exist among the responses given by examinees. The numbers of responses given in each category and various ratios among them are used to develop an interpretive picture of the individual. One obviously important source of variance on the test, therefore, involves the total number of responses given by the subject. The greater the number of responses given, the larger the amount of data from which to draw interpretive conclusions. Hersen and Greaves (1971) have reported that simply saying "good" after each response often increased the total number of responses given by as much as 50 percent. An attempt to control for this weakness in the Rorschach has been offered by Holtzman, who developed an analogous set of inkblots but expanded the number of cards to 45 and limited the number of responses to one per card.

In analyzing the relationships that exist among responses given by an examinee, certain diagnostic patterns have been formulated. These include such things as the use of color, indicating the presence of emotionality; movement, indicating imagination; the ratio of total responses to movement responses, suggesting over- or underachievement; and time required to respond, being an indicator of anxiety. Certain combinations of categories are also used to diagnose emotional disorders such as neuroses, psychoses, and brain damage.

Psychometrically, the Rorschach has continually been shown to be woefully inadequate (Gleser, 1963; Zubin, Eron & Schumer, 1965). The reliability and validity data on the test do not meet the accepted values established for objective measures of personality. Nevertheless, it is used widely by clinicians (Wade & Baker, 1977) and enjoys a position of prominence among the diagnostic tools utilized in daily clinical practice.

Modifications of the Rorschach technique.

The Rorschach is not a test, in the ordinary sense of the word, but represents a relatively unstructured technique for personality measurement and assessment. It is not clear whether the psychometric deficiencies of the Rorschach represent problems with the inkblots themselves, the various scoring systems in use, or the clinicians who use the test. Several attempts have been made to improve the Rorschach technique, and some of these have increased the psychometric adequacy of the Rorschach substantially. Two of the most notable efforts in this direction have been undertaken by Exner (1974, 1978) and Holtzman (1968).

One of the most serious problems with the Rorschach technique has been the lack of standardization in its administration, scoring, and interpretation. The Exner system was designed to meet these needs. Although it has not been adopted uniformly, the Exner system is sufficiently widespread to provide a reasonable normative base and to provide evidence about the potential reliability and validity of Rorschach scores. In general, Exner's studies suggest that the Rorschach can be reliably scored and that scores can be interpreted along several dimensions. This research has not yet demonstrated the usefulness of the Rorschach in making clinical decisions, but it does provide some hope for this technique.

The Holtzman inkblot technique represents a psychometrically sophisticated adaptation of Rorschach's basic approach. The Holtzman comprises a set of 45 inkblots, empirically selected to maximize scorer reliability, as well as validity for clinical classification. Unlike the Rorschach, the Holtzman allows one response per card; standardized procedures exist for scoring this set of 45 responses on many of the major Rorschach dimensions.

Several reviews (Forer, 1965; Thetford, 1965) of the Holtzman suggest that scores on this test show acceptable levels of both internal consistency and temporal stability.

Validity data are less conclusive but generally suggest that Holtzman scores are more useful than Rorschach scores, particularly when unstandardized or informal scoring systems are used for the Rorschach.

CRITICAL DISCUSSION:
Reliability and Validity of Projective Tests, Personality
Inventories, and Intelligence Tests

The sheer volume of research on popular psychological tests makes it difficult to establish with any precision the psychometric characteristics of these tests. For example, the number of studies prior to 1980 on the Minnesota Multiphasic Personality Inventory (MMPI) and the Rorschach alone exceeded 10,000 and probably far exceeds this figure by now. The recent growth of meta-analysis (see Hedges & Olkin, 1985; Hunter, Schmidt & Jackson, 1982), which represents a group of statistical techniques for summarizing the results of large numbers of studies, provides one way of potentially keeping up with the voluminous literature on specific psychological tests.

    Parker, Hanson, and Hunsley (1988) applied meta-analysis to research on the MMPI, the Rorschach, and the Wechsler Adult Intelligence Scale (WAIS); this study provides a unique opportunity to compare the psychometric qualities of widely different types of tests. Their study summarized findings from 411 studies published between 1970 and 1981 in two leading journals. They found that all three tests were highly reliable, and that all three were correlated with criteria of interest. Their most interesting findings, however, involved comparisons of the three tests. The WAIS was selected as a point of comparison because it is widely acknowledged as a psychometrically superior test. However, measures of reliability and temporal stability of the three tests were comparable; this result runs counter to the widely held belief that personality inventories and projective tests are necessarily less reliable than tests of intelligence. The WAIS showed higher levels of validity for predicting theoretically relevant criteria (e.g., academic success), but the other two tests also showed very respectable levels of validity.

    The Parker, Hanson, and Hunsley (1988) study illustrates both the strengths and weaknesses of meta-analysis. On the one hand, this technique provides a means for dealing with long-standing controversies, such as the reliability and validity of different types of tests. On the other hand, a meta-analysis is only as good as the data that are incorporated into the analysis. For example, Parker and his colleagues (1988) note that all their data on the Rorschach were obtained from a single journal with a long history of association with the Rorschach and so there might be editorial bias in favor of that test. Because of the potential problems in interpreting meta-analyses, it is not yet clear whether Parker and his associates' results are accurate. However, they do suggest that a variety of types of tests can show high levels of reliability and validity.

Thematic Apperception Test

Henry Murray (1943) developed another major projective instrument by using pictures rather than inkblots. In Murray's Thematic Apperception Test (TAT), examinees tell a story about each picture shown to them. The story is to consist of a beginning, a middle, and an end. One of the cards shown to examinees is totally blank, providing a maximally ambiguous stimulus. Murray postulated that respondents would project into their stories information concerning their needs, emotions, conflicts, attitudes, and emotional difficulties. Particular attention is paid to the protagonist of each story, and the environmental stresses that impinge upon him or her. The hero is presumed to represent the examinee. Scoring involves subjectively analyzing all story content and evaluating it for various themes. Particular themes that emerge are seen as indicative of various personality dynamics.

Figure 20-4 illlustrates a typical card from the TAT. Interpretations of the narratives that are provided for each card are combined to establish themes suggestive of hypotheses about the personality dynamics of the individual. Some themes occur sufficiently frequently in disturbed examinees to be indicative of pathology. Examples of some commonly occurring themes include extreme attention to detail, suggesting an obsessive-compulsive personality; violent stories, suggesting impulse-control difficulties; and delays in responding, reflecting possible depression.

As with the Rorschach, the psychometric characteristics of the TAT have not been shown to be very impressive (Zubin, Eron & Schumer, 1965). Various scoring systems that improve its reliability have been adopted, but the validity of the TAT as yet remains unsubstantiated. Nevertheless, many clinicians use it as a diagnostic tool, believing it adds a rich source of data in formulating conceptualizations about clients.

Rotter Incomplete Sentences Blank

The incomplete-sentence method of assessing personality has its roots in the work of Ebbinghaus around the beginning of the twentieth century. Many different sentence-completion instruments have been developed, but the work of Julian Rotter and his

Figure 20-4 Typical Card from TAT

Source: From Murray, H., *Thematic Apperception Test*. Cambridge, MA: Harvard University Press. Copyright © 1943 by the President and Fellows of Harvard College, © 1971 by Henry A. Murray. Reprinted by permission of the publishers.

associates has led to the development of the best standardized, most objectively scored, and most rigorous of all such instruments. His original work began with the Army (Rotter & Willerman, 1947) but later led to the construction of the Rotter Incomplete Sentences Blank (RISB) for college students (Rotter & Rafferty, 1950). It was later expanded for use with noncollege adults and adolescents of high school age. As a result, this test has enjoyed greater usage than other sentence-completion methods that have emerged in the field of personality assessment.

The RISB is generally considered to be a semi-structured, projective test, because the items consist of sentence stems that must be woven into a complete thought by the examinee. As is the case with other projective methods of personality assessment, the underlying assumption is that examinees project their wishes, desires, fears, and attitudes into the sentences they create. It differs from other projective tests, however, in several respects.

While examinees responding to tests like the Rorschach and TAT are rarely aware of what they are revealing about themselves, due in part to the ambiguous nature of the test items, examinees responding to the RISB are generally more aware of the feelings, attitudes, and fears they are disclosing because the task is more structured. A second difference concerns the purpose of testing. Other projective instruments have been designed to reveal information about the inner, deeper dimensions of personality, while the RISB and other sentence-completion methods have been designed principally to screen for emotional maladjustment.

The RISB consists of 40 items, each containing a sentence stem that the examinee uses to create a complete sentence dealing with the content of the item. Several examples from the test are shown in Table 20-5. An interesting feature of the RISB is its ease of administration. It can be given either individually or in a group setting and requires no special training to administer. Unlike many of its projective counterparts, the RISB has a rigorous and systematic scoring system that research has shown yields extremely high inter-scorer reliability (Rotter, Rafferty & Schachtitz, 1949; Rotter, Rafferty & Lotsof, 1954).

Scoring consists of assigning a weight to each item ranging from 0 to 6, depending on the content of the sentence formed. Responses are scored as to the degree of conflict expressed, the amount of optimism shown, the presence of qualifying statements, the length of responses, and omissions. The manual provides a number of sample responses and indicates the appropriate item weights to be assigned to each. Since it is impossible to include an example for all possible responses, guidelines are given to aid in scoring responses not found in the manual. A total score is summed over all items, which provides a measure of general emotional adjustment. Many clinicians go beyond this

---

TABLE 20-5   SAMPLE RISB ITEMS

1. The happiest time _____
2. I want to know _____

Source: From the Rotter Incomplete Sentences Blank. Copyright © 1950, renewed 1978 by The Psychological Corporation. Reprinted by permission. All rights reserved.

score, however, and examine the content of the responses for particular insights into major areas of difficulty for the individual.

The positive psychometric properties of the RISB as reported in the manual have generally been sustained by later research (Goldberg, 1965). Research has shown it to be a rather sensitive measure of emotional maladjustment among college students and adults. Its psychometric advantage over other projective tests, however, has not affected its lower frequency of use by clinicians, who are critical of its failure to examine more dynamic, deeper levels of personality functioning. Some of its proponents do attempt such analyses through examining the content of the sentences generated on the RISB, but there has been little research support for this method of interpretation (Goldberg, 1965). Nevertheless, the RISB continues to offer the clinician the advantages of group administration, quick administration and scoring capability, acceptable reliability and validity estimates, and an objective scoring system, all of which are absent in the more popular projective tests.

Draw-a-Person Test

The Draw-a-Person Test (DAP) grew out of the work of Karen Machover (1949). The basic hypothesis underlying the development of the DAP was that examinees project themselves into the human figures they are asked to draw. These reproductions are believed to reveal the examinee's impulses, anxieties, and other internal emotional states.

The DAP consists of having examinees draw two human figures. First they are instructed to simply draw a person and, following completion of that task, are told to draw a person of the opposite sex from that of the first drawing. While the examinee goes about these tasks, the clinician observes such things as the sequence of body parts drawn, verbalizations made by the examinee, and other factors associated with the actual drawing process. Occasionally, a period of questioning occurs after both drawings have been completed. During this inquiry information is elicited about the figures, such as age, occupation, and family relationship.

Scoring and interpreting the DAP is a complex, subjective task. Machover outlined a number of structural and formal aspects of the drawings that are important in the interpretation process. These include such aspects as the size and placement of the figures on the paper, the amount of action depicted in the drawings, the systematization followed in doing the task, erasures, shading, and differential treatment of male and female figures. Attention is also given to specific body parts. A partial list of these structures along with their hypothesized significance is summarized in Table 20-6.

The research evidence summarized by Swensen (1957, 1968) and Roback (1968) on the DAP has not supported many of the theoretical relationships hypothesized by Machover concerning particular diagnostic signs and emotional disturbance. There have been indications that there may be some validity to interpreting the significance of overall patterns of signs rather than the individual signs themselves as indications of general adjustment level. The relationships that have been shown are not sufficiently impressive, however, to warrant the use of the DAP over most other personality measures. Quantitative scoring systems have been developed for the DAP, which may help to reduce unreliability due to subjectivity in scoring (Naglieri, 1988). However, the *validity* of the scores

TABLE 20-6   SIGNIFICANCE OF BODY PARTS EMPHASIZED ON THE DRAW-A-PERSON TEST

Body part	Psychological significance
Head Size	Perceived intellectual ability, impulse control, narcissism
Facial Expression	Fear, hate, aggression, meekness
Emphasis on Mouth	Eating problems, alcoholism, gastric distress
Eyes	Self-concept, social problems, paranoia
Hair	Sign of virility, potential sexual dysfunction
Arms and Hands	Degree of contact with the environment, openness to others
Fingers	Ability to manipulate and experience others
Legs and Feet	Amount of support, sexual concerns, aggression
Emphasis on Breasts	Sexual immaturity, preoccupation, and neurosis

obtained from the DAP, even with objective scoring, remain in doubt. Nevertheless, the DAP ranks among the ten most frequently used assessment devices by clinicians (Lubin, Larsen & Matarazzo, 1984).

CRITICAL DISCUSSION:
Are Scales on Personality Tests Interpreted Independently?

In studying several personality test profiles and examining what they reveal about the people who complete them, the interpretation process would probably appear to be fairly straightforward and uncomplicated. Interpretation might seem to be nothing more than a collection of statements made about each scale individually, with no provision for interactions between or among the scales. Things are not so simple.

In interpreting a personality test, three major characteristics of the test profile need to be taken into consideration. First, the average score of all scales on the test needs to be noted. A second characteristic of personality test profiles involves the degree of scatter among the scales. The focus here is on the amount of variability among the scores (i.e., Are all scores relatively at the same level, or is there great variation among the scales?). Finally, the shape of the profile must be taken into consideration (i.e., Which scales are elevated? Which are depressed?). It is particularly this last feature of test profiles that has led to the study of scale interactions.

The pattern of scores on a personality test must be taken into account when interpreting the test profile. Scales often interact with each other such that the resulting combination of two scales yields a different interpretation of the individual than either scale would indicate if considered alone. To illustrate this point, let us focus our attention on the CPI.

Heilbrun, Daniel, Goodstein, Stephenson, and Crites (1962) have studied several scale interactions on the original CPI and have presented clear evidence of scale blending. It is as if the characteristic measured by one scale is moderated or slightly changed by the influence of another personality characteristic. For example, these researchers found that when scores on the Responsibility (Re) and the Capacity for Status (Cs) scales were both significantly above average on a profile, the individual was described as efficient, forceful, persevering, poised, resourceful. When the Re score was above average, but the Cs score was below average, however, the individual was described as sincere, conscientious, mild, patient, and unassuming. A different clinical picture was generated when the Re score was below average and the Cs score was above average. In this case, the individual was usually described as aggressive, manipulative, self-centered, skeptical, and opportunistic. Finally, when both Re and Cs were below average on a profile, the adjectives used to describe such an individual were apathetic, awkward, distrustful, indifferent, and undependable.

In their work with the CPI, Heilbrun and his colleagues studied several additional pairs of scales and found similar patterns of scale interactions between them. This type of research clearly illustrates the complexity of profile analysis and suggests that scores on any one personality scale cannot be interpreted in isolation.

SUMMARY

The history of personality measurement has progressed through several relatively distinct stages. Initially, testing was deeply rooted in personality theory. Test developers drew heavily on personality theory to direct the writing of items and the determination of what constituted the dimensions of personality. These early instruments were subject to much distortion but provided easily interpretable data. Next came the emergence of empirically derived tests. The basis for item selection shifted from the author's theory about personality to empirically observed relationships between item endorsement and criterion-group differences. While this method yielded tests with high criterion-related validity, it did not produce theoretically meaningful scores that could easily be related to established personality theory. During this same period projective testing also became prominent. The content of projective test items was designed to provide less-structured, more ambiguous stimuli to assess the deeper aspects of personality.

With the development of advanced statistical procedures and computer technology, test constructors turned to factor analysis as the basis for item selection. A more recent development in the field of testing is to combine both rational and empirical approaches in order to select theoretically meaningful items that clearly distinguish various criterion groups.

The field of projective testing has seen the development of strongly theoretically based, yet poorly validated, instruments. The two most widely used tests, the Rorschach inkblot test and the Thematic Apperception Test, were developed initially during the 1920s. Little attention was paid to established practices of test development; consequently, issues such as reliability and validity were not addressed adequately. The years since their initial appearance have been marked by countless attempts to modify or standardize the administration and scoring of these tests to attain desirable psychometric characteristics. Despite these efforts, there has been little success.

The Rotter Incomplete Sentences Blank provides an example of a projective test designed to have acceptable psychometric properties, but it unfortunately does not enjoy the extensive use of its less well constructed counterparts. The Draw-a-Person Test, while fascinating in its speculation about the relationships between certain features of human drawings and personality dynamics, has little data to substantiate its claims. Nevertheless, it ranks among the top ten tests in total overall use among clinicians.

The appeal of projective tests would appear to be their rich source of exploratory hypotheses about the inner dynamics of the individual. However, their importance and widespread use in personality measurement cannot be justified on the basis of current research data.

CHAPTER 21

DIAGNOSTIC TESTING: CLINICAL APPLICATIONS

In the previous chapter, we considered several personality tests that are used widely in clinical settings. While these tests may be used in the diagnosis of psychopathology, their primary purpose is somewhat broader—to provide a multifaceted measure of the personality of the individual taking the test. This chapter considers a set of tests and measurement techniques that are geared toward a more limited purpose, the differential diagnosis of psychopathology.

First, we discuss two of the most widely used diagnostic tests, the Minnesota Multiphasic Personality Inventory (MMPI) and the Bender-Gestalt test. Both tests are thought to be useful in diagnosing a wide array of problems the clinician might encounter. Second, we consider the diagnostic use of intelligence test scores. There is some reason to believe that patterns of subtest scores on tests of general intelligence convey information that is not conveyed by an overall test score (i.e., IQ). Finally, we describe the classification system most commonly used in clinical diagnosis.

The chapter closes with a discussion of the value—or lack of value—of clinical diagnosis. For too long psychodiagnosis has seemed to be an end in itself rather than a means for directing therapy and treatment. It is important to determine whether accurate diagnosis does in fact contribute to the progress of treatment or to the determination of the client's prognosis. It if does not, clinical diagnosis may not be worth the considerable time and effort devoted to it.

THE MINNESOTA MULTIPHASIC PERSONALITY INVENTORY

The Minnesota Multiphasic Personality Inventory, first published in 1943, represents one of the most widely used and most widely researched psychological tests in existence. It is estimated that there are well over 10,000 published articles and reports dealing with the MMPI; by the time you read this, the total will no doubt be substantially higher.[1] Although the MMPI has been the focus of a great deal of debate and criticism (Butcher, 1972; Newmark, 1979), it nevertheless is recognized as one of the most broadly useful diagnostic tests currently available. According to King (1978), "The MMPI remains matchless as the objective instrument for the assessment of psychopathology" (p. 616).

The test itself is made of 550 affirmative statements, similar to those listed below:

I was often in trouble at school.

Most of the time I feel happy.

Someone is controlling my thoughts.

When I play cards or games, it is important that I win.

A person taking the test responds to each item by indicating "true," "false," or "cannot say." As typically administered, the MMPI yields scores on ten "clinical" scales:[2]

1. *Hypochondriasis* (Hs)—a neurotic pattern characterized by extreme concern for health and bodily functions
2. *Depression* (D)—an affective disorder usually characterized by sadness, feelings of lack of worth, loss of energy and interest
3. *Hysteria* (Hy)—a neurotic condition in which physical symptoms are used to avoid or solve conflicts, and to avoid responsibilities
4. *Psychopathic Deviate* (Pd)—a personality disorder characterized by an extreme and flagrant disregard for social and moral norms
5. *Masculine-Feminine* (Mf)—the extent to which the respondent accepts extreme, stereotypic sex roles
6. *Paranoia* (Pa)—delusions of reference, influence, grandeur, persecution
7. *Psychasthenia* (Pt)—obsessive-compulsive behavior or thought patterns
8. *Schizophrenia* (Sc)—a disorder characterized by a lack of connection between affect and cognition
9. *Hypomania* (Ma)—a disorder characterized by overactivity, flight of ideas, emotional excitement
10. *Social Introversion* (Si)—a disorder characterized by a withdrawal, avoidance of social contact

---

[1]Research on the MMPI prior to 1975 is reviewed extensively in a two-volume MMPI handbook (Dahlstrom, Welsh & Dahlstrom, 1972, 1975).

[2]Originally there were eight clinical scales. Masculine-Feminine and Social Introversion were added later.

Self-report measures are believed to be influenced by a number of conscious and unconscious response sets. A measure that asks many sensitive questions might be especially prone to conscious faking. To aid in the interpretation of MMPI scores, scores on three administrative scales are typically reported.

1. *Lie Score* (L)—a scale made up of items that are quite unlikely to be true and that put the respondent in a very favorable light (e.g., "I never do anything bad"). A high score may indicate an attempt to distort one's responses.
2. *Validity Score* (F)—a scale made up of a set of extremely infrequent responses. A high score may indicate a careless or random response pattern.
3. *Correction Score* (K)—a measure of psychological defensiveness that can indicate a tendency to "fake good" (high score) or "fake bad" (low score). Scores are used to correct certain clinical scales for artificially low scores that might result from defensiveness in responding to the MMPI.

The total set of clinical scores, together with the administrative indices, are typically displayed on a score profile such as the one shown in Figure 21-1. Scores on each of the clinical scales are reported on a T-score scale with a mean of 50 and a standard deviation of 10; norms for T-score conversion were obtained from the group of normal control subjects used in constructing the clinical scales (see below). Scores of 70 or higher (two standard deviations above the mean) are considered to have possible clinical significance; scores within two standard deviations of the mean are regarded as within the normal range.

Development of the MMPI

The MMPI is an outstanding example of the *empirical* or *criterion-keying* approach to test development. The original clinical scales were developed by contrasting the responses of groups of psychiatric patients diagnosed as exhibiting hypochondriasis, depression, paranoia, and other disorders, with the responses of normal subjects, a group primarily comprised of approximately 700 visitors to the University of Minnesota hospital. Statements were included in a particular clinical scale if the responses of psychiatric patients exhibiting that particular condition were reliably different from the responses of normal subjects and of patients exhibiting other psychiatric syndromes. The Masculinity-Femininity scale is made up of items that are answered differently by apparently normal males and females. The Social Introversion scale is made up of items that discriminate persons involved in a large number of social activities from those involved in a few.

Over the years, over 500 additional scales have been developed from the pool of 550 MMPI items (Dahlstrom et al., 1975; Faschingbauer, 1979); in theory it would be possible to obtain more scale scores than items on the test. Examples include scales measuring Ego Strength, Prejudice, Social Status, and Dominance. More exotic special scales, such as one predicting "Success in Baseball," have also been developed (Clopton, 1979). In principal there is no limit to the number of additional scales that might be developed—if the responses of tall people were reliably different from those of people in general, one could develop an MMPI scale labelled "Height." Thus, in a sense, it is

CLINICAL PROFILE

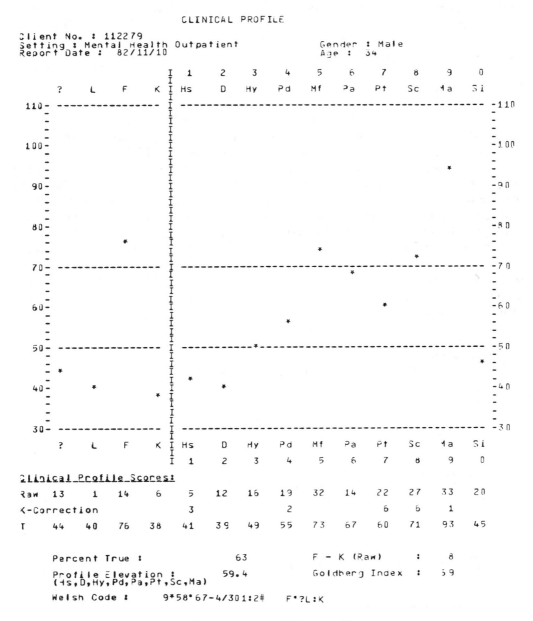

Client No. : 112279
Setting : Mental Health Outpatient   Gender : Male
Report Date :   82/11/10   Age :   34

Figure 21-1 An MMPI Score Profile

Source: Minnesota Multiphasic Personality Inventory. Copyright © 1943, renewed 1970 (form 1982).

difficult to describe or evaluate the MMPI itself. The MMPI is not so much a test as a set of responses from which any number of scales might be devised. Nevertheless, most applications rely on the ten clinical scales and the three administrative scales; hence, for the most part our descriptions and evaluations of the MMPI refer to this standard set of scores.

Interpretation of MMPI Scores

Although as a general rule scores above 70 on any of the clinical scales are considered potentially significant, scores on individual scales do not yield a simple interpretation. For example, a score of 75 on the depression scale does not lead automatically to a diagnosis of clinical depression. Rather, patterns or configurations of test scores are considered in the diagnostic use of the MMPI (Webb & McNamara, 1979). For example, Graham (1977) described a number of *two-point code* types, based upon profiles grouped according to their two highest clinical scales. Figure 21-2 depicts hypothetical MMPI profiles that illustrate the two-point code types 12 and 18, together with a brief description of the modal pattern associated with that code. Although both of these profiles show elevated scores on the Hypochondriasis scale, the combination of a high score on this scale with a high score on Depression (code 12) produces a very different diagnosis than a high score on Hypochondriasis coupled with a high score on Hypomania (code 18).

Two-Point Code: 1 2

Description - characterized by semantic discomfort and pain, with no evidence of organic basis; individuals are anxious, self-conscious, may be prone to excessive use of alcohol

Two-Point Code: 1 8

Description - individuals harbor feelings of hostility and aggression but cannot express these in an adaptive manner; feel socially inadequate, especially with the opposite sex; may present intense somatic concerns (e.g., severe headaches).

Figure 21-2 Hypothetical MMPI Profiles Illustrating Different Two-Point Code Types

The two-point code represents the simplest configural interpretations of the MMPI. More complex configural interpretations are suggested in several atlases (Dahlstrom, Welsh & Dahlstrom, 1972) and actuarial code books (Gilberstadt & Druker, 1965; Marks & Seeman, 1963; Marks, Seeman & Haller, 1974). However, there is little evidence that the complex scoring codes are significantly more valid or more useful than the simpler two-point codes (Graham, 1977; Marks et al., 1974). In addition, complex scoring rules are more difficult to apply consistently than the two-point scoring method. As a result, although the interpretation of the MMPI is essentially configural, very simple rules for identifying a small number of possible configurations typically are applied.

A number of computerized MMPI scoring and interpretation services are available in the United States (Fowler, 1979; Graham, 1977; Matarazzo, 1986). These range from relatively simple machine-scoring systems that provide scores on the clinical scales and several special scales to systems that provide various types of reports, depending on the expertise of the user, and that provide computer-generated narrative reports in addition to scale scores.

There are three obvious advantages of computerized interpretation of the MMPI. First, computerized systems allow complex scoring rules to be applied in a completely reliable fashion. As long as a set of scoring rules can be translated into a computer program, it is possible to apply those rules consistently to every test processed. Furthermore, it is no more difficult to apply extremely complex scoring rules than it is to apply simple ones. Thus, computerized interpretation services might allow users to obtain the maximum benefit from the configural interpretation of the MMPI.

Second, computerized scoring systems provide a workable means for integrating the vast accumulation of data on the MMPI in interpreting an individual's test scores. For example, Fowler (1979) notes that there is evidence that the optimal interpretation of test scores may depend on the age, sex, or other demographic characteristics of the respondent. It is unlikely that the individual clinician will be able to take all the relevant demographic variables into account when interpreting each test profile.

Finally, computerized interpretation can be substantially less expensive than individual clinical interpretation. If individual clinical interpretation were the only method available, it is likely that many patients would, for economic reasons, receive no psychological or psychiatric screening (Fowler, 1979).

Most reviews conclude that computerized interpretation of the MMPI is useful, but that it is not an adequate substitute for professional clinical judgment (Graham, 1977; Matarazzo, 1986; see, however, Murphy, 1987a). First, in most clinical applications, the MMPI is not the only test or assessment device employed. Thus, computerized MMPI interpretations do not take into account a good deal of information that is available to the clinician. Second, the validity of the narrative descriptions that form a major part of most computerized MMPI reports is not always well established (Layon, 1984; Meehl, 1972). Since many people overestimate the accuracy of computer-generated reports, it is particularly important to demonstrate the validity of these interpretations. There is at present a good possibility that some test users will disregard potentially valid and important information that is at variance with the computer summary. Nevertheless, if proper caution is observed in the use of the reports, computerized MMPI interpretations may be a quite useful addition to the clinician's arsenal.

Evaluation of the MMPI

One of the most striking features of the MMPI is the amount of data that is available for interpreting and evaluating test scores. The archive of empirical data on the MMPI probably exceeds that available for any other test. For example, Swenson, Pearson, and Osborne (1973) were able to establish norms for medical (nonpsychiatric) outpatients on a sample of 50,000 completed MMPIs.

Given the widespread use of the MMPI and the veritable mountain of data that is available regarding this test, the test itself is a bit disappointing. As we note below, a recent revision of the MMPI may help to overcome many of the shortcomings of the original instrument. However, the transition between the original and revised MMPI is likely to be long and difficult, and many of the criticisms of the original MMPI raised here will continue to be relevant for a long time to come.

First, the MMPI clinical scales are based on an outmoded set of diagnostic categories; most psychologists refer to the clinical scales by number rather than by name, in part out of recognition of the dubious value of the diagnostic labels attached to each scale (Faschingbauer, 1979; Graham, 1977). Second, the norms that are used to convert raw scores to T scores are widely viewed as unrepresentative. Thus, a T score of 70 indicates a raw score that is two standard deviations above the mean. It is not entirely clear, however, whether the mean (or the standard deviation) of the normative sample is in any way representative of the mean one would expect from the population of people who are now likely to take the test.

There are related concerns regarding the samples of psychiatric patients employed in constructing the original clinical scales, for as few as 50 patients in the psychiatric group were employed in constructing the scales. Updated norms, using larger and more representative groups, have been developed (Colligan, Osborne, Swenson & Offord, 1983), but to date these new norms have not had any major impact on the interpretation of the MMPI.

Evaluations of the measurement properties of the test are not altogether encouraging. As is frequently the case for tests that yield scores on many different scales, the reliability of scores on individual clinical scales is disappointingly low. This problem is offset partially by the use of conservative decision rules in interpreting test scores; for example, scores within two standard deviations of the mean, which represent the great majority of test scores, are not considered clinically significant. Nevertheless, the lack of reliability detracts from the potential value of individual scale scores. In addition, scale scores tend to be positively intercorrelated. As a result, persons with high scores on any one scale are likely to show high scores on many, if not most, of the other scales. The fact that the clinical scales tend to be positively correlated severaly restricts the usefulness of any configural interpretation of the MMPI.

Meehl (1972) reminds us that it is difficult to evaluate the MMPI itself, independent of the way in which the MMPI is scored or used. Thus, a defect in a particular clinical or research scale is not necessarily a defect in the MMPI itself; the particular scores that are typically obtained using the MMPI are not necessarily the optimal scores for any particular purpose. Thus, deficiencies in interpretation or in the decisions that are made on the basis of the test may reflect an inappropriate choice of scales or scoring strategy, rather than a shortcoming of the test itself.

Meehl notes that the MMPI seldom is used as well as it could be used. For example, a combination of clinical judgment and computerized scoring would probably yield more valid results than are typically obtained using either clinical judgment without the aid of computers or computers without the aid of clinical judgment. Thus, the question of whether the MMPI is a good or useful test depends as much on the test user's ability to glean relevant information out of the test responses as on the content or form of the test itself.

MMPI-2

In 1990 the first major revision of the MMPI was completed. This revision, the MMPI-2, represents the culmination of a long and difficult process of research and test development. (See Campbell, 1972; Hathaway, 1972; Holden, 1986, for discussions of the difficulties in revising a test like the MMPI.) It goes a long way toward solving many of the technical problems noted above for MMPI. MMPI-2 retains the same basic test format as MMPI, and it reports scores on the same basic scales, together with additional validity scales, new clinical scales, and measures of gender roles.

There are four major features to the revision of MMPI. First, new items have been written, duplicate items and items with objectionable content have been removed, and the total number of items has been increased to 567. Items have been rearranged so that it is possible to score all of the basic scales from the first 370 items, greatly facilitating abbreviated testing sessions. Second, new norms have been developed from larger samples (the total n exceeds 2,500) that are much more representative of the U.S. population than previous normative samples. Third, T scores on the clinical scales have been standardized in a way that makes it easier to validly compare scores across scales. Fourth, content-oriented scales (e.g., scales indicating levels of anxiety, obsessiveness, social discomfort, and family problems) have been added (Butcher, Graham, Williams & Ben-Porath, 1990). In contrast to the original MMPI, in which scales were developed solely on an empirical basis, these content-oriented scales were developed on a rational basis, to provide interpretable measures of constructs judged to be important in assessing personality and clinical disorders.

Although MMPI-2 is clearly technically superior to MMPI, the process of changing from the original test to the revised test may be a slow one. Clinicians and other test users may be reluctant to abandon the wealth of data, clinical lore, and experience associated with the original MMPI. Thus, it is possible that the new MMPI will be technically superior to the original but will not be used as widely until a new generation of clinicians is trained in its use. To help ease the transition from MMPI to MMPI-2, efforts have been made to ensure that most of the items and many of the special scales developed for the original MMPI survive intact in MMPI-2, and that score profiles from the two instruments will be comparable (Levitt, 1990; Munley & Zarantonello, 1990). In addition, several handbooks have been developed for applying MMPI-2, and most of these refer extensively to comparisons between MMPI and MMPI-2 (Butcher, 1990; Graham, 1990; Greene, 1991).

THE BENDER-GESTALT

The Bender Visual-Motor Gestalt Test is a deceptively simple measure that is useful in the differential diagnosis of perceptual disorders and organic brain damage, as well as a diagnosis of many types of psychopathology (e.g., schizophrenia, depression). In its simplest form, the Bender-Gestalt is a picture-copying task in which the respondent is required to copy geometric forms similar to those shown in Figure 21-3. In the process of copying the figures, subjects make errors that (it is assumed) are not simply a function of a lack of artistic skill, and these distortions form the basis of the clinical interpretation of the Bender-Gestalt. An example of a Bender-Gestalt protocol produced by a patient suffering from organic brain damage is presented in Figure 21-4.

    In developing this test, Bender (1938) applied the principles of Gestalt psychology to the selection of stimulus figures and to the interpretation of distortions made when persons taking the test reproduced the figures. According to Bender, "The final product is a visual motor pattern which reveals modifications in the original pattern by the integrating mechanisms of the individual who has experienced it" (p. 3). More modern interpretations of the Bender-Gestalt have placed less emphasis on the principles of

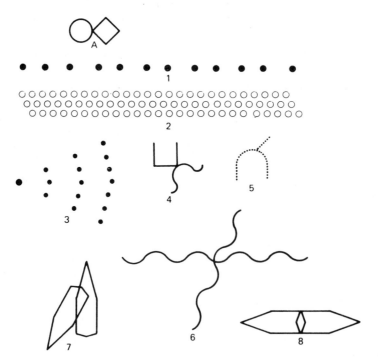

Figure 21-3   The Bender-Gestalt Test

Source: From Bender Visual-Motor Gestalt Test, published by American Orthopsychiatric Association, 1938.

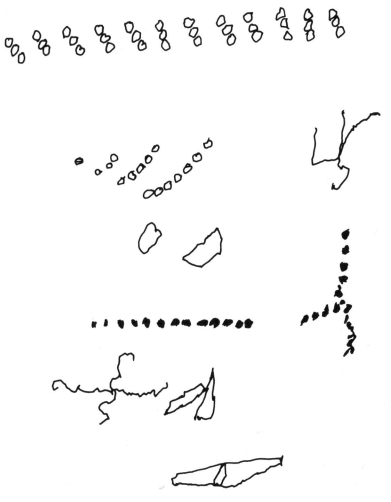

Figure 21-4 Bender-Gestalt Protocols from Patient Suffering from Organic Brain Damage

Source: From Lacks, 1984, p. 34. Copyright © 1984 by John Wiley & Sons. Reprinted by permission.

Gestalt psychology and more emphasis on the systematic differences in response as a function of organic brain damage or of psychopathology.[3]

Interpretation of the Bender-Gestalt

A variety of methods for scoring and interpreting the Bender-Gestalt have been proposed. For example, Spraings (1966) and Labrentz, Linkenhoker, and Aaron (1976) have

[3]Several explanations, other than those implied by Gestalt principles, have been offered for the diagnostic power of the Bender-Gestalt. For example, Pascal and Suttell (1951) claim that the test measures, among other things, "attitude toward reality," or the degree to which one is in contact with external reality.

developed multiple-choice scoring formats. Probably the most widely researched scoring method is referred to as the Hutt adaptation of the Bender-Gestalt (Hutt, 1977). This adaptation treats the Bender-Gestalt as a projective test. It is assumed that in the process of generating, elaborating, and describing his or her drawings, the respondent projects important needs or conflicts.

The Hutt adaptation consists of three separate phases:

1. the *Copy Phase,* in which the respondent is shown the standard set of Bender-Gestalt figures and is asked to copy them freehand
2. the *Elaboration Phase,* in which the subject is given both his or her drawings and the original figures and is asked to modify or change the drawings in any way he or she wishes to make them "better" or "more pleasing"
3. the *Association Phase,* in which the respondent looks at both the stimulus card and the elaborated drawings and tells the examiner what each figure calls to mind

The interpretation of the respondent's test protocol takes into account the features of the drawings themselves, the types of elaborations done to make the original drawings "better" or "more pleasing," and the associations they evoke. Table 21-1 lists several of the 26 features of the drawings that are considered in scoring Bender-Gestalt protocols.

Evaluation of the Bender-Gestalt

As was the case with the MMPI, the Bender-Gestalt is regarded as useful in the diagnosis of a wide variety of disorders. For example, Bender's (1938) original manuscript discussed response patterns associated with sensory aphasia, organic brain disease, schizophrenia, manic-depressive psychosis, mental retardation, and psychoneuroses. More recent research suggests that the Bender-Gestalt may be useful in diagnosing depression, anxiety states, and a variety of adjustment problems and learning disorders (Tolor & Brannigan, 1980). As might be expected, given the perceptual-motor emphasis of the test, the Bender-Gestalt is most useful in diagnosing brain damage and other forms of organic dysfunction (Tolor & Brannigan, 1980). Marley (1982) has presented evidence that suggests that the Bender-Gestalt may be used to localize some types of brain pathology and provide information useful in estimating prognosis under different forms of therapy.

Evidence for the validity of the Bender-Gestalt in the differential diagnosis of nonorganic pathologies is not so well established, although there is evidence that in psychotic patients, the degree of distortion in Bender-Gestalt drawings is related to the degree of pathology.

TABLE 21-1   SOME OF THE FEATURES CONSIDERED IN SCORING
THE HUTT ADAPTATION OF THE BENDER-GESTALT TEST

1. Sequence of drawings	5. Use of margin
2. Position of first drawing	6. Closure difficulty
3. Use of space	7. Simplification
4. Collision	8. Consistency in direction of movement

As with the MMPI, the Bender-Gestalt is not so much a single, well-defined test as a general technique for diagnosis. The validity of diagnoses based upon the Bender-Gestalt depends upon a number of factors, such as the particular scoring system chosen and the clinician's skill and reliability in applying that system. The reliability and validity of Bender-Gestalt diagnoses also depend on the type of condition being diagnosed and on the level of specificity of the diagnosis. The test is likely to be more successful in diagnosing brain dysfunction than schizophrenia, and more useful in making gross diagnoses than in making highly localized diagnoses of lesions or brain damage.

The essential strategy behind most Bender-Gestalt scoring systems is similar to that employed by the MMPI. With some exceptions, Bender-Gestalt systems are the product not of well-developed theories of psychopathology but, rather, of systematic differences in test responses as a function of type and severity of psychopathology. However, with the exception of multiple-choice versions of the test (e.g., Spraings, 1966), the scoring of the Bender-Gestalt is more subjective than objective. Thus, it is not as easy to apply the empirical criterion-keying strategy to the Bender-Gestalt as is the case with the MMPI. It is therefore even more difficult to determine whether the Bender-Gestalt test is as useful as it could be in diagnosing organic and nonorganic pathologies. Although the Bender-Gestalt is one of the most widely used psychological tests, a Bender-Gestalt data base comparable to that which exists for the MMPI is simply not feasible.

Neurological Assessment

Brain damage often affects a person's cognitive, emotional, and psychomotor functioning. Furthermore, damage to specific portions of the brain can affect highly specific functions. It should be possible, therefore, to use performance on a variety of psychological tests to assist in the diagnosis of several types of brain damage and dysfunction. This is exactly what is done by clinical neuropsychologists. Tests such as the Bender-Gestalt, discussed in the previous section, are often useful in such assessments. Test batteries, such as the Halstead-Reitan Neuropsychological Battery and the Luria-Nebraska Neuropsychological Battery, were developed for this specific purpose and have shown consistent evidence of their validity and usefulness (Kane, 1986).

Spreen and Strauss (1991) describe a wide variety of tests used in neuropsychological assessment; descriptions of five categories of tests are presented in Table 21-2. They note that many of the tests used by practicing neuropsychologists are experimental in nature or are developed by in-house research teams, so that information about the

TABLE 21-2   TYPES OF TESTS USED IN NEUROPSYCHOLOGICAL ASSESSMENT

Test type	Description
Attention and Memory	visual presentation of simple stimulus, followed by recall or recognition test
Language	comprehension of simple passages, ability to name objects
Visual and Visuomotor	assessment of spatial orientation, usually using geometric figures or abstract drawing
Tactile	assessment of tactile sensitivity, recognition of unseen objects by touch
Motor	assessment of coordination and movement

norms and psychometric characteristics of these tests is often unavailable. The Wechsler Memory Scale is an important exception.

The Wechsler Memory Scale–Revised (Wechsler, 1987) contains a variety of subtests designed to tap different aspects of short-term memory, including (a) Mental Control—ability to correctly say a series of letters or numbers, (b) Figural Memory—recognition memory for abstract designs, (c) Logical Memory—ability to recall ideas in stories presented verbally, (d) Visual Paired Associates—ability to learn simple associations, (e) Visual Reproduction—ability to draw geometric designs after brief exposure, (f) Digit Span—ability to repeat set of digits either forwards or backwards, and (g) Visual Memory Span—ability to duplicate the sequence of colors touched by the examiner. The Wechsler Memory Test–Revised has shown evidence of both reliability (test-retest reliabilities in the .70s, inter-scorer reliabilities in the .90s) and construct validity. The test manual also provides unusually good normative information, making the Wechsler Memory Scale–Revised one of the most psychometrically sophisticated instruments commonly used for neuropsychological assessment (Butler, Retzlaff & Vanderploeg, 1991).

The tasks included on the Wechsler Memory Scale–Revised and on other neuropsychological test batteries are usually quite simple in the sense that individuals with no impairment do very well on most of these tasks. Neuropsychological assessment is often reserved for individuals who show some evidence of severe impairment on one or more cognitive or behavioral functions, especially where there are reasons to suspect organic brain damage (e.g., in cases of severe cognitive deficits that emerge after exposure to toxic substances). Despite the proven validity of some neuropsychological tests, the results of neuropsychological assessments are not always viewed as reliable. In particular, several court cases in the last few years have involved the use of neuropsychological assessments as evidence of brain damage in lawsuits over industrial accidents, exposure to toxins, and the like. In most cases the courts have been reluctant to admit the testimony of psychologists regarding diagnoses of brain damage or dysfunction, largely on the basis of the nonmedical nature of the diagnoses. Whereas the courts are likely to admit the testimony of neurologists, especially if their opinions are based on standard medical tests, they often question psychologists' ability and expertise in diagnosing brain damage.

Unfortunately, there are some good reasons for concern over the quality of some neuropsychological assessments. The survey of neuropsychological test usage made by Butler and his colleagues (1991) suggests that the most common assessment instrument used by neuropsychologists is the Wechsler Adult Intelligence Scale–Revised (WAIS-R) (see Chapter 13). The WAIS-R is a fine test, but its use in neuropsychological assessment often involves an analysis of differences in performance on different parts of the test; that is, it involves scatter analysis. As you will see in the section that follows, the assessment of scatter can create a variety of problems and can lead to highly questionable assessments.

SCATTER ANALYSIS

Intelligence tests are widely viewed as useful components of a total diagnostic testing package. Tests such as the Wechsler Intelligence Scale for Children (WISC) or the WAIS, which provide scores on individual scales and subtests, are regarded as especially useful, since they provide information not only about general levels of mental ability but also about *patterns* of strengths and weaknesses in relatively specific areas of cognitive functioning (Rapaport, Gill & Schafer, 1968; Robb, Bernardoni & Johnson, 1972). These patterns of performance, in turn, are believed to have diagnostic significance. For example, both McFie (1960) and Meyer and Jones (1957) claimed that patterns of performance on the WAIS and the WISC, particularly comparisons of verbal and performance scores, could be useful in diagnosing and locating specific types of brain lesions; more recent research supporting these claims is reviewed by Matarazzo and Herman (1985) and Zimmerman and Woo-Sam (1985).

Rapaport, Gill, and Schafer (1968) suggest that comparisons of individual subtest scores can be revealing. For example, a subject who takes the WAIS and receives high scores on the vocabulary and information subtests but a low score on the comprehension subtest is likely to give inappropriate responses to questions as a result of impaired judgment rather than a lack of knowledge.

The most extensive literature dealing with pattern interpretation of scores on intelligence tests examines the diagnostic significance of differences between verbal and performance IQ scores (Kaufman, 1979; Rapaport, Gill & Schafer, 1968). The existence of sizable differences in verbal and performance scale scores on tests such as the WAIS or the WISC is believed by many to be significant in the diagnosis of a variety of cognitive, affective, and behavioral disorders. However, reviews of the research on verbal-performance differences suggest considerable inconsistency in the apparent effects of these differences (Matarazzo, 1972; Zimmerman & Woo-Sam, 1972).

One reason for the inconsistency in the apparent effects of verbal-performance differences is the tendency of some researchers to attempt to interpret relatively trivial differences in scale scores as an indication of clinically significant discrepancies in performance. In fact, examination of the confidence intervals around scores on the WAIS or the WISC suggests that verbal-performance IQ differences of as much as 15 points could be attributed to chance (Kaufman, 1979). A second reason for the inconsistency of the research dealing with verbal-performance difference is the inherent unreliability of difference scores (see Chapter 6). There is some degree of error in the measurement of verbal and performance IQs; a score that represents the difference between these two IQ measures necessarily will be less reliabile than *either* measure.[4]

Limited reliability poses problems when comparing verbal and performance IQ scores, although some investigators question the seriousness of these problems (Matarazzo & Herman, 1985). Such problems probably are most severe when scores on individual subtests are compared. For example, Rapaport, Gill, and Schafer (1968) discuss the clinical significance of "vocabulary scatter," defined as the difference between the scale score on the WAIS vocabulary subtest and the score on any other subtest. It is quite likely however, that substantial differences between subtest scores arise through chance alone, since individual subtests show comparatively low levels of reliability (Conger & Conger, 1975). For example, Kaufman (1979) notes that two thirds of all normal children who are tested using the WISC have scale score ranges (difference between highest and lowest

---

[4]Recall from Chapter 6 that the correlation between two tests also affects the reliability of difference scores. Verbal and performance IQ scores are positively correlated, which serves to *lower* the reliability of their differences.

subtest score) of 7 ± 2. The maximum possible scale score range is 18, and ranges of 5 points or more often are regarded as significant. Unless we assume that two thirds of all apparently normal children exhibit clinically significant abnormalities in their cognitive functioning, the relatively high frequency of substantial scatter in subtest scores would seem to argue against giving such patterns substantial weight in clinical predictions.

The most likely explanation for the widespread scatter in subtest scores is the low level of reliability exhibited by many subtests. A good deal of scatter may be attributed to measurement error rather than to clinically significant differences in specific mental abilities. Although the research evidence clearly indicates that large degrees of scatter are common, and that simple measures of scatter are *not* related in any consistent way to brain damage or to mental dysfunction (Golden, 1990; Kamphaus & Reynolds, 1987; Ryan, Paolo & Smith, 1992), many test users still view scatter as a useful evidence in forming a diagnosis (Kramer, Henning-Stout, Ullman & Schellenberg, 1987). In clinical diagnosis it is not uncommon for personal experience, clinical tradition, and personal beliefs about the effectiveness of specific tests or diagnostic techniques to outweigh negative research results (e.g., tests with doubtful validity, such as the Draw-a-Person Test, are quite popular). However, clinicians are not alone in ignoring evidence that contradicts their preferred methods of practice. As Dawes (1979, 1980) notes, although many psychologists are well aware of the doubtful validity of interviews and of subjective methods of judging candidates, they still use them in selecting faculty and students (see Chapter 22 for further discussion of this issue).

The bandwidth-fidelity dilemma described in Chapter 6 has serious implications for the clinical interpretations of patterns of test scores. Basically, there are two choices when the amount of testing time is limited: (a) measure a few variables with a high degree of accuracy or (b) measure many variables with very little accuracy. In the context of clinical testing, this dilemma suggests that attempts to measure many different variables (e.g., multiple subtest scores) with a limited number of items, observations, and so on, will often lead to limited reliability in each test score—the more subtests, the lower the reliability of each. Furthermore, the more subtests considered, the more likely that scores on at least two tests will differ substantially. Thus, increasing the number of subtests to be considered in a search for clinically significant patterns (defined by differences between subtest scores) creates a "snowball" effect: The more tests, the lower the reliability; the lower the reliability, the greater the likelihood that two test scores will differ greatly due to measurement error (chance); and the more unreliable tests compared, the greater the likelihood that an individual will exhibit a substantial range of test scores and the greater the likelihood of a "clinically significant" scatter pattern.

Although reliability considerations limit the usefulness of diagnostic strategies that depend upon patterns or configurations of test scores, these strategies are by no means useless. Rather, their application should be limited to specific situations in which several conditions are met.

First, there should be clear evidence that a pattern of test scores has some validity as a predictor of important clinical criteria. Furthermore, consideration of the pattern of test scores must improve the validity of the predictions that could be made on the basis of average test scores alone (Nystedt & Murphy, 1979).

Second, the reliability of individual tests must be considered in determining the significance of apparent patterns obtained in a single test administration. The use of confidence intervals would help discourage the natural tendency to overinterpret patterns that in fact may be due to measurement error rather than to real differences in the abilities and traits being compared.

Finally, the number of tests being compared and the number of possible patterns under consideration should be as small as possible. If the results of ten different tests are compared to 45 different diagnostic patterns, the likelihood of a misdiagnosis is considerable. When a smaller number of tests and patterns is considered, the likelihood that test scores will, by chance, match any present pattern is significantly reduced.

DIAGNOSTIC CLASSIFICATION SYSTEM

Clinical assessment typically results in a classification of the individuals being assessed. For example, a patient at a mental institution may be diagnosed as schizophrenic, or as psychotic without signs of schizophrenia. A school psychologist may determine that certain children suffer from specific learning disabilities and on this basis may assign them to special education programs. An industrial psychologist may help in determining which management trainees represent fast-track employees and hence should be given challenging assignments as soon as possible. In each case the individual being assessed is classified as a member of a specific category of persons who exhibit similar behavior in specific situations and who are demonstrably different from other categories of persons.

In some contexts, classification involves the use of few categories (e.g., learning disabled versus not disabled) that may be poorly defined (e.g., fast-track employees at one company may fail at another). However, in the practice of clinical psychology and psychiatry a complex, standard set of categories is used to classify or diagnose mental disturbances. The classification system used in the diagnosis of mental illness is described in the American Psychiatric Association's *Diagnostic and Statistical Manual of Mental Disorders* (third edition-revised), commonly referred to as DSM-III-R.

DSM-III

The *Diagnostic and Statistical Manual of Mental Disorders* is designed to provide clear descriptions of diagnostic categories that enable clinicians to diagnose, treat, study, and communicate about mental disorders (Spitzer, Williams & Skodol, 1980). The manual (DSM-III) was revised a few years after its release, and in its current form it is referred to as DSM-III-R. Because DSM-III and DSM-III-R are so highly similar, we will generally use the term "DSM-III" to refer to both diagnostic manuals and will use "DSM-III-R" to refer specifically to the current revision.

The manual describes over 230 diagnostic categories and calls for *multiaxical classification,* which entails the use of a number of different facets, or axes, in the assessment and diagnosis of an individual patient. The five axes described in the DSM-III-R include

Axis I   Clinical Syndromes
Axis II   Developmental Disorders and Personality Disorders
Axis III   Physical Disorders and Conditions

Axis IV   Severity of Psychosocial Stressors

Axis V   Global Assessment of Functioning

Axes I and II comprise the primary classification of mental disorders; Axis II was included to direct the clinician's attention to long-term disorders that may be missed if attention is focused exclusively on the patient's current situation. The possible behavioral effects of physical disorders are recognized in Axis III. Axis IV represents the clinician's assessment of the severity of occupational, financial, legal, familial, and other psychosocial stressors affecting the individual. Finally, Axis V represents the clinician's assessment of how well the individual has adapted to the demands of everyday life.

Some of the axes of DSM-III-R require the clinician to identify specific disorders or conditions (e.g., Axes I, II, and III), whereas others require ratings on a continuum. For example, assessments of Axis IV (Severity of Psychosocial Stressors) requires a rating from 1 to 6 (a rating of 0 is assigned if the clinician does not have sufficient information to make a judgment) on the scale illustrated in Table 21-3. Presumably the behavior of an individual who has experienced acute or chronic conditions at the high end of the scale (e.g., those indicating severe or catastrophic stress) will be interpreted differently from that of an individual who has experienced no identifiable stressors.

TABLE 21-3   RATING SCALE USED TO DESCRIBE SEVERITY OF PSYCHOSOCIAL STRESSORS

		Examples of stressors	
Rating	Term	Acute events	Enduring circumstances
1	None	no relevant event	no relevant enduring circumstance
2	Mild	broke up with boyfriend/girlfriend	family arguments, job dissatisfaction
3	Moderate	marriage, retirement	marital discord, serious financial problems
4	Severe	divorce, birth of first child	unemployment, poverty
5	Extreme	death of spouse, rape	serious chronic illness of self or child
6	Catastrophic	death of child, suicide of spouse	captivity as a hostage, concentration camp experience

DSM-III is esentially a medical taxonomy that attempts to classify mental disorders in the same way that other medical taxonomies classify physical diseases. This taxonomy pays little attention to the effects of social and environmental variables; rather, it is built around the assumption that mental disorders are the result of variables within the person, much in the same way that physical diseases can be traced to bacteria, viruses, or malfunctions of internal organs (Schact & Nathan, 1977). Thus, the unit of analysis for DSM-III is the mental disorder, defined as a clinically significant behavioral or psychological pattern that is associated with distress, impairment, or risk. (See McReynolds, 1989, for a discussion of definitional issues.)

While psychologists generally acknowledge that in many ways DSM-III is superior to its predecessors, DSM and DSM-II,[5] many psychologists object strenuously to the use

---

[5]Major differences between DSM-III and its immediate predecessor, DSM-II, include the use of multiaxial diagnoses and the decision to discontinue the use of the term "neurosis" in classifying mental disorders.

of this taxonomy in classifying mental disorders. The most widespread objection to this DSM-III involves the questionable relevance of the medical model (McReynolds, 1979; Smith & Kraft, 1983). The DSM-III classifies a wide variety of behavioral problems, ranging from loneliness to paranoia, as medical diseases. While some behavioral disorders *are* medical in nature, it is not clear whether the concept of disease is appropriate for describing a number of problems of everyday living.

Other psychologists complain that by focusing on factors within the individual, the DSM-III ignores social and interpersonal factors that affect mental well-being (McLemore & Benjamin, 1979). Thus, the DSM-III fails to consider factors that most psychologists consider critical determinants of both normal and abnormal behavior. Still other psychologists complain that DSM-III is irrelevant to the understanding of human behavior (Miller, Bergstrom, Cross & Grube, 1981), that it is too narrowly descriptive (Frances & Cooper, 1981), or that it is biased against women (Kaplan, 1983). Miller, Bergstrom, Cross, and Grube (1981) note that many psychologists use the DSM-III diagnostic system *solely* because they are required to do so by third-party payers (i.e., medical insurance plans). Indeed, Eysenck, Wakefield, and Friedman (1983) note that the DSM-III is so lacking in scientific basis that the primary justification for its use is probably administrative. The revision of DSM-III did little to address these problems (McReynolds, 1989).

The most important criticism of DSM-III, in our opinion, is its lack of a scientific basis. In a comment that is typical of many of the critiques of this diagnostic system, Eysenck (1986) refers to it as the "scientifically disastrous DSM-III" (p. 74). Several authors are already looking forward to the next revision (DSM-IV), and there is some hope that the next diagnostic system will reflect scientific consensus rather than political compromise between different power groups and lobbies within the psychological and psychiatric communities. Volumes edited by Last and Hersen (1987) and by Millon and Klerman (1986) provide a variety of viewpoints on the strengths and weaknesses of DSM-III.

The ultimate criterion that should be used in evaluating a diagnostic system such as the DSM-III is the usefulness of the diagnostic classifications for forecasting prognoses, specifying appropriate treatments, or predicting future behavior. After all, diagnosis is not an end in itself; a diagnosis is useful only to the extent that it contributes to the understanding and treatment of mental or behavioral disorders.

Unfortunately, evidence for the usefulness of DSM-III diagnoses is equivocal (Begelman, 1976; McReynolds, 1979, 1989). Although there is wide agreement that the use of DSM-III may improve the *reliability* of diagnoses, as compared to diagnoses using DSM-II, as yet there is no clear evidence that the use of DSM-III contributes to the *validity* of clinical diagnoses. In particular, at present there is little evidence that the use of DSM-III contributes significantly to the quality of clinical decisions (e.g., the choice of therapies). However, as Hayes, Nelson, and Jarrett (1987) note, it is difficult to do research on the utility of any assessment device or system. It may therefore be many years before definitive conclusions can be reached regarding the contribution of DSM-III and DSM-III-R to clinical diagnosis and treatment. Many practicing clinicians have complained that neither DSM-III nor DSM-III-R is useful, and they have ignored these diagnostic taxonomies except when required by regulation (or by insurance company reimbursement policies) to record DSM diagnoses (Morey & Ochoa, 1989). Both versions of DSM-III employ criteria that are inconsistent with internationally recognized diagnostic systems (although DSM-III appears to be more widely used than competing systems; Maser,

Kaebler & Weise, 1991). If current plans for further revision to the diagnostic taxonomy used by American psychologists and psychiatrists go on as planned, perhaps the question of the validity and utility of DSM-III and DSM-III-R will become moot.

DSM-IV. The process by which DSM-III and DSM-III-R were produced has been criticized on a number of grounds, in particular the relative lack of scientific bases for many of the decisions made in producing both manuals (Widiger & Trull, 1991). Shortly after the completion of DSM-III-R, work was begun on a fourth version of the *Diagnostic and Statistical Manual of Mental Disorders* (i.e., DSM-IV). Scheduled for completion in 1993, DSM-IV is designed to provide closer correspondence to the *International Classification of Diseases and Related Health Problems (*ICD-10) (Kendell, 1991).

A key goal in the development of DSM-IV is to provide a stronger empirical base for diagnostic categories than in previous editions. A special issue of the *Journal of Abnormal Psychology* (1991) describes in detail some of the methods that will be used to accomplish that goal. While the general goals of DSM-IV are admired, this most recent revision has been criticized. First, skepticism has been expressed regarding the *real* reason for the frequent revision of DSM (Zimmerman, 1990; Zimmerman, Jampala, Sierles, & Taylor, 1991); economic factors like the profits from the sale of DSM or the reimbursement policies of major insurers seem as important as scientific ones in the decisions to issue DSM-III-R and DSM-IV. Second, there is pressure (as was the case with DSM-III-R) to include potentially questionable diagnostic categories in DSM-IV (Widiger & Trull, 1991). Finally, there is a continuing failure to define exactly what the DSM refers to. In particular, there is still no clear consensus about what is meant by a mental disorder, illness, or disease (Frances et al., 1991; Widiger & Trull, 1991). Thus, there is no good way of distinguishing between conditions that are most appropriate for medical, psychiatric, or psychological treatment, or for distinguishing mental disorders from a wide variety of minor problems of adjustment that are experienced by virtually everyone.

In our judgment, DSM-IV is likely to be an improvement on the previous versions of DSM, but it is unlikely to fully meet the important goal of scientific respectability. The process of developing a diagnostic taxonomy is so strongly affected by political and economic factors that have little to do with good diagnosis that it is difficult to imagine that the scientists will win all their arguments with the accountants and bureaucrats. Even more important, it is not really clear whether a good diagnostic taxonomy contributes in a meaningful way to the usefulness of clinical diagnosis.

Is clinical diagnosis useful? The debate over the relative merits and demerits of DSM-III is part of a larger debate over the relative merits of psychological diagnosis itself. In medical settings, diagnosis is clearly important, since different medical treatments are necessary for different diseases. For example, a patient suffering from chronic high blood pressure should receive different treatment from a patient with leukemia. However, in the case of psychological disturbances, it is not always clear whether accurate diagnosis is necessary, or even helpful, for the choice of appropriate therapies or treatments.

There are two conditions that must be met in order to demonstrate the usefulness of psychological diagnoses. First, different treatments (e.g., psychotherapy, hospitalization, shock therapy, no treatment) must be indicated for individuals who receive different diagnoses. Second, the treatments must be differentially valid for people with different diagnoses.[6] In other words, if different treatments are chosen for individuals who receive different diagnoses, it must be demonstrated that it makes a difference which persons are assigned to which treatments. Differential diagnosis of psychopathology would clearly not be useful if everyone received the same therapy, regardless of their diagnosis, or if the success of a particular course of therapy did not depend in any way on the diagnosis.

There is some evidence that gross differences in diagnosis have value in choosing treatments. The course of treatment that is most likely to alleviate depressive symptoms is different from the treatment that would be chosen in cases of mental retardation, phobia, or sociopathic personality disorder. In some cases, more detailed diagnoses may have clear treatment implications (Rahman & Eysenck, 1978). However, there is little evidence that the hundreds of diagnostic categories that make up the DSM-III all have different implications for treatment (Miller & Berman, 1983; Smith & Glass, 1977). Thus, the value of distinguishing among hundreds of different types of pathology, as opposed to a very small number of major syndromes, is in doubt. For example, in the DSM-III there are six different categories for disorders of impulse control and three major categories of affective disorders. Little evidence has been presented to date to suggest that all these different categories of psychopathology would call for different types of treatment. As a result, the usefulness of fine-grained psychological diagnoses such as those suggested by DSM-III is questionable.

Eysenck, Wakefield, and Friedman (1983) note that psychological problems are generally not analogous to medical diseases in that psychological problems are often extreme examples of behavior that is exhibited by "normal" persons every day, whereas many medical problems represent separate categories that often can be traced to a single pathogen. As long as the diagnostic classification systems in use are drawn up by psychiatrists, the medical tradition of categorical diagnosis is likely to persist. It is likely, though, that the most useful diagnostic systems eventually will adopt a dimensional rather than a categorical approach (Eysenck, Wakefield & Friedman, 1983; Lang, 1978). That is, rather than assigning each individual being assessed to a discrete diagnostic category (e.g., a typical paranoid disorder), it might be useful to describe each individual along several psychologically meaningful and adequately measured dimensions. Examples include intelligence, extraversion, psychoticism, and neuroticism (Eysenck, 1976, 1981). Thus, rather than saying that a patient is suffering from a borderline conversion disorder, it might be more useful to describe the individual's functioning in terms of a relevant set of cognitive, emotional, and behaviorial dimensions.

The debate over the utility of clinical diagnosis is related to a somewhat more narrow debate over the contribution of psychological tests and assessment devices to the treatment of psychological and behavioral disorders. Hayes and his associates (1987) note that, despite the long history of the clinical application of psychological assessment, "clinical assessment has not yet proven its value in fostering favorable treatment outcomes." (p. 963). They identified several problems with current research on the utility of psychological assessment for diagnosis and the selection of treatments and proposed an integrated framework for designing, conducting, and evaluating research on this critical

---

[6]Cronbach and Snow (1977) make a similar argument in evaluating educational programs.

topic. We agree that there is a substantial need for more and better research on the contribution of psychological assessment to clinical practice, but we are pessimistic about the possibility of this happening at least in the short run. Throughout the long history of clinical assessment and treatment, research on validity and utility has been a very low priority, and the research that *has* been carried out is often ignored by practitioners.[7] It seems likely that clinical lore and subjective judgments will continue to play a dominant role in assessments of the extent to which psychological tests and assessment devices contribute to treatment outcomes.

CRITICAL DISCUSSION:
Politics, Economics, and Diagnosis

In 1980 the American Psychiatric Association published the third version of its *Diagnostic and Statistical Manual of Mental Disorders* (DSM-III), which was subsequently revised and is now distributed as DSM-III-R. This manual, which provides a standard set of diagnostic categories and criteria for the diagnosis of psychopathology, has been the focus of a great deal of controversy. The technical evaluations of DSM-III and DSM-III-R have generally been favorable, although significant reservations have been expressed (McReynolds, 1989). The controversy over this manual is not over its technical merits but, rather, over the extent to which political and economic considerations have influenced the choice and description of diagnostic categories (McReynolds, 1989; Schacht, 1985a, 1985b; Spitzer, 1985).

An example of a political issue playing a role in the development of DSM-III is the decision of whether or not to include homosexuality as a diagnostic category (it was included in earlier versions of DSM, but not in DSM-III). An example of the influence of economic considerations is seen in the decision to drop the category "chronic minor affective disorders" largely on the grounds that insurance companies would not reimburse psychologists or psychiatrists for treatments of disorders in this category (Schacht, 1985a).

When you consider that DSM-III diagnoses will be applied to very large numbers of people (the number of Americans likely to seek treatment for mental health problems is in the millions) and that DSM-III categories affect the reimbursements that providers of mental health care receive, it is unrealistic to expect that DSM-III will *not* be affected by political and economic concerns. The question, then, is whether the influence of politics and economics on this document is so pervasive as to destroy the credibility and usefulness of DSM-III and DSM-III-R. Most commentators agree that even given its biases (political and economic, as well as a bias toward a "disease" model of psychopathology), the DSM-III-R is useful and represents a definite advance over previous diagnostic manuals. Preliminary indications suggest that DSM-IV will represent yet another advance.

SUMMARY

A wide variety of tests are used for diagnostic purposes in clinical settings; this chapter has discussed only a handful of the available tests. The Minnesota Multiphasic Personality Inventory (MMPI) is one of the most widely researched psychological tests, and it

---

[7]Despite years of research demonstrating their lack of validity, complex interpretations of tests such as the Draw-a-Person Test are still common among practicing clinicians.

continues to be used in contexts ranging from clinical diagnosis to personnel selection (although the validity of this instrument for that purpose is doubtful; Lowman, 1989). The release of the MMPI-2 represents an advance along several fronts. First, the test now incorporates both empirical and rational test-development strategies (see Chapter 10). The continued use of the empirically developed scales maximized the comparability of MMPI and MMPI-2, while the addition of content-oriented scales addresses one of the most frequent criticisms of this inventory. Second, better norms, scoring procedures, and validity research make the interpretation of MMPI-2 considerably simpler than was true for MMPI.

The Bender Visual-Motor Gestalt Test is used for a variety of purposes, from neuropsychological assessment to psychiatric diagnosis. A variety of other tests used in neuropsychological assessment were also discussed. One common practice in neuro-psychological assessment, the use of scatter (i.e., differences among subtest scores) in diagnosing brain damage and learning disabilities, presents some serious problems. Differences among test scores can arise for a number of reasons, and many instances of "clinically significant" scatter appear to represent nothing more than measurement error.

The diagnostic classification system embodied in DSM-III-R (and soon in DSM-IV) was discussed. There are several appealing features to this system, including the use of multiaxial diagnosis and attempts to increase the scientific credibility of the diagnostic categories and rules in DSM-IV. However, a close examination of the process by which DSM-III and DSM-III-R were developed leaves considerable room for skepticism. It is often unclear what role science, politics, and economics played in the development of DSM-III and DSM-III-R, and it is naive to think that the same set of problems will not plague DSM-IV. More generally, the contribution of a well-defined diagnostic classification scheme is not as clear for psychological and psychiatric complaints as for some purely medical ones. Although DSM-IV will probably contribute to the reliability of diagnoses, it is not clear whether it will make a large contribution to the usefulness of those diagnoses.

CHAPTER 22

CLINICAL
ASSESSMENT

Intelligence tests, personality tests, behavioral assessments, and clinical interviews all yield potentially important information about the person being tested, but none of these techniques provides an overall assessment of the examinee's level of functioning. In other words, no individual test provides a complete picture of the individual; it provides only a specific piece of information about that person. One of the major tasks of psychologists involved in assessment is to evaluate information provided by many tests, interviews, and observations and to combine this information to make complex and important judgments about individuals. For example, when an individual shows evidence of difficulty in adjusting to the demands of daily life, a clinician must decide whether therapy would be helpful and, if so, what type of therapy would be most appropriate.

Psychologists also are called upon to assess individuals in a variety of nonclinical settings. For example, school psychologists might consider information about a child's intellectual performance, social skills, and home environment in recommending placement in special education programs. Industrial psychologists might be asked to evaluate management trainees who participate in a series of assessment exercises. In each case it is assumed that the assessment is more than a simple combination of test scores—it is a judgment on the part of a trained professional.

Although expert judgment plays a part in each form of psychological measurement, the practice of clinical assessment—broadly defined as the integration of multiple pieces of information into an overall evaluation of the present state of the individual being assessed—is somewhat unique in that human judgment is an *integral* component of the process. This chapter deals principally with the individual assessor's contribution to the reliability and validity of psychological measurement in a variety of clinical and non-clinical settings. In particular, this chapter examines the impact of the clinician's judgment on the quality of psychological measurement and clinical decisions.

First we discuss the general nature of clinical assessment, together with a brief consideration of the tests that are used most often in assessment. Next we describe several methods of studying expert clinical judgment. A number of influential reviews have suggested that clinical judgments often can be duplicated, and perhaps even improved, through the use of mechanical or statistical methods of prediction. Here we compare some of the clinical and statistical methods of combining information from many sources to form an overall assessment of an individual. Finally, we describe several structured programs of psychological assessment. Many of the functions carried out by individual clinicians in a relatively unstructured way are also carried out by groups of psychologists in large-scale assessment programs.

THE NATURE OF CLINICAL ASSESSMENT

Korchin and Schuldberg (1981) define psychodiagnosis as a process that

> (a) uses a number of procedures, (b) intended to tap various areas of psychological functions, (c) both at a conscious and unconscious level, (d) using projective techniques as well as more objective and standardized tests, (e) in both cases, interpretation may rest on symbolic signs as well as scorable responses, (f) with the goal of describing individuals in personological rather than normative terms. (p. 1147)

Korchin and Schuldberg's definition of psychodiagnosis might be applied more aptly to the neutral term "clinical assessment." The central difference between clinical assessment and other testing applications is that the clinician, rather than the test, is at the center of the assessment process. Indeed, as Wiggins (1973) notes, the clinician has two distinct functions, both of which are essential to the assessment process. First, the clinician must *gather* data. Although standardized tests are used in clinical assessment, projective tests, interviews and behavioral observations represent the clinician's most important measurement tools (Korchin & Schuldberg, 1981; McReynolds, 1968; Wade & Baker, 1977). Second, the clinician must *integrate* data from various tests, interviews, and observations in order to form an overall assessment of the individual.

The data-gathering function has clear implications for the quality of psychological measurement. A clinician who makes inaccurate observations, conducts poorly structured interviews, or misinterprets or misrecords responses to open-ended questions or ambiguous stimuli (e.g., responses to Rorschach cards) is not likely to produce valid assessments. The clinician often functions as a measurement instrument, and it is important to assess the reliability and validity of the clinical data he or she gathers.

Although it may not be immediately obvious, the clinician's second function—the integration of clinical data—also affects the quality of psychological measurement in clinical settings. Assessment represents an attempt to arrive at a valid classification of each individual patient or client. In some cases, clinicians may be called upon to diagnose or assist in the diagnosis of mental or behavioral disorders. In others, the clinician must make recommendations regarding the placement of children or adults in remedial education or in therapeutic programs. In any case, the classification of individuals represents a fundamental type of measurement (see Chapter 1), and the clinician's skill in integrating diverse sources of data may be a critical factor in determining the validity of his or her classifications and assessments of individuals.

Testing, Assessment, and Clinical Practice

At one time psychological testing represented one of the most important activities of clinical psychologists (Korchin & Schuldberg, 1981; McReynolds, 1968; Rabin, 1981). Since the early 1980s the practice of clinical psychologists has shifted steadily from an emphasis on assessment and diagnosis to an emphasis on psychotherapy and adjustment (Matarazzo, 1992; Rabin, 1981). Predictions about the future of clinical psychology (e.g., Matarazzo, 1992) suggest that testing will remain an important activity and that many of the tests now widely used (e.g., standardized measures of intelligence, the Minnesota Multiphasic Personality Inventory–2, or MMPI-2) will remain popular but will be supplemented by new testing technologies.

Although clinicians do not appear to devote as much of their time to testing as in the past, psychological testing still represents an important activity for practicing clinicians. Wade and Baker's (1977) survey suggested that over 85 percent of practicing clinical psychologists use tests, and that over one third of their therapy time is devoted to test administration and evaluation. Furthermore, patterns of test use have been quite stable over the past 20 years (Lubin, Larsen & Matarazzo, 1984; Pietrowski & Keller, 1989a, 1989b) and probably will remain so for the foreseeable future. Finally, testing appears to be a common activity, regardless of the psychologist's therapeutic orientation (e.g., behavioral, Freudian).

The most widely used clinical tests can be divided into three types: (a) individual tests of general mental ability, (b) personality tests, and (c) neurological tests. The Wechsler Intelligence Scales (WISC-III and WAIS-R) and the Stanford-Binet represent the most popular tests of general mental ability (Korchin & Schuldberg, 1981). These tests serve a dual function in forming assessments of individuals. First, an evaluation of general mental ability often is crucial for understanding an individual's behavior, since many behavioral problems are linked to intellectual deficits. Second, individual intelligence tests present an opportunity to observe the examinee's behavior in response to several intellectually demanding tasks, and thus they provide data regarding the subject's persistence, maturity, problem-solving styles, and other characteristics.

The Rorschach, the Thematic Apperception Test (TAT), and the Minnesota Multiphasic Personality Inventory (MMPI) represent three of the most popular personality tests. Of the three, the MMPI is most closely associated with the diagnosis of psychopathology, while the TAT is most closely associated with the assessment of motives and drives. The Rorschach may be used for a variety of purposes, ranging from the assessment of specific personality traits to the diagnosis of perceptual disorders, depending on the scoring system used.

The Bender-Gestalt and the Luria-Nebraska Battery are used widely in the diagnosis of neurological disorders. The Bender-Gestalt is used in the assessment of perceptual disorders and of organic dysfunctions, although, as noted in the previous chapter, it may be used for a wide range of diagnostic purposes, whereas the Luria-Nebraska Battery provides a wide-ranging assessment of perceptual, motor, and intellectual functions that might be affected by damage to specific portions of the brain.

The clinical interview.   Most clinical tests (e.g., the WAIS, the Rorschach) represent structured interactions between the clinician and the individual being examined. In other words, most clinical tests require the examinee to respond to specific, standardized stimuli (e.g., an inkblot) presented by the examiner, and the clinician must record and interpret the individual's responses. These structured interactions between the examiner and the examinee represent one of the major sources of information to be used in assessing the examinee.

The clinical interview, which represents a less-structured interaction between the examiner and the examinee, is the second major source of information used in assessing individuals (Sundberg, 1977). In many ways the clinical interview is similar to the employment interview (see Chapter 18). In both cases the interview represents an opportunity to obtain information about an individual that is not obtained readily from written tests. In addition, the interviewer is likely in both cases to pay attention to the content of the examinee's responses and to the examinee's behavior in responding to (or avoiding) questions.

Despite the similarity between employment interviews and clinical interviews, there is a critical difference between the two that has important implications for the quality of the clinical interview as a measurement tool. The goal of an employment interview is known beforehand—the interviewer's task is to select applicants who best fill the demands of a particular job or set of jobs. As a result, employment interviews often are fairly structured and may be directed toward obtaining a few relatively concrete types of information. In contrast, clinical interviews are almost certain to be unstructured. Although most clinical interviews strive to fulfill the same general goal (e.g., obtain important information about examinees), the specific goal of a particular clinical interview depends almost entirely on the needs and the conditions of the particular individual being interviewed. As a result, the specific goals of a clinical interview may be quite difficult to determine in advance. For example, in theory there is a clear distinction between a therapeutic interview, which entails both an attempt to obtain information and an attempt to alleviate the client's problem, and a research interview, which is aimed strictly at obtaining specific information.

Research interviews can be broken down further into types, the case history and the intake or pinpointing interview (Nay, 1979). In practice, the distinction between information gathering and therapeutic intervention is not always so sharp. For example, in gathering information, it may not be clear what questions the clinician should ask, or which topics should be pursued, until the interview gets under way. Nor will it be clear whether all of the relevant information has been obtained until well after the conclusion of the initial interview. Furthermore, the process of gathering information may itself have therapeutic value, and the clinician may intersperse attempts to elicit factual information with attempts to resolve problems which are uncovered during the interview.

Because the clinical interview is a relatively unstructured search for relevant information, it is important to consider factors that may affect the accuracy and comprehensiveness of this search. Research on *hypothesis confirmation bias* (Darley & Fazio, 1980) suggests that it may be difficult to conduct a search for unbiased and comprehensive information in an unstructured setting such as the clinical interview. This research suggests that decision makers form hypotheses to explain the behavior of others and then actively search for information that confirms their hypotheses. More important, decision makers typically ignore, or actively discount, information that runs counter to their hypotheses. In the context of the clinical interview, this research suggests that clinicians are likely to conduct biased searches for information that confirms their early impressions of each examinee. Information that is ambiguous tends to be interpreted to support first impressions; information that contradicts the initial hypotheses may receive little weight.

Research on *self-fulfilling prophecies* (Dipboye, 1982) suggests a second factor that may limit the validity of interviews in general and may be especially problematic in unstructured clinical interviews. This research suggests that the interviewer's expectations affect the behavior of the person being interviewed and that interviewees may change their behavior to match the interviewer's expectations. For example, a clinician may develop the hypothesis that family problems are the root cause of the client's problems and therefore may focus on familial issues during the interview. The interviewer's persistence in examining this topic may, in turn, lead the client to believe that family problems *are* responsible for his or her troubles, and as a result that client may present or emphasize information that tends to confirm the clinician's hypothesis.

Research on confirmatory biases and self-fulfilling prophecies suggests that early impressions could have a decisive impact on the scope and conduct of the interview. If the clinician's early hypotheses are largely correct, the interview may serve as a valuable source of valid information. However, if early hypotheses are incorrect, it may be difficult for the clinician (or the client) to recognize the problem and to redirect the search for relevant information.

Clinicians typically regard the interview as a highly useful source of information and often place more weight on the interview than on written tests in their assessments of individuals (Korchin & Schuldberg, 1981; Wiggins, 1973). Unfortunately, empirical evidence regarding the validity of the clinical interview is spotty at best (Wiggins, 1973). As was the case with the employment interview, research suggesting that clinical interviews are limited in their validity has not had a major impact on their popularity or their perceived worth. Possible reasons for the continuing popularity of the clinical interview were cited by Arvey and Campion (1982). First, there is a widespread belief that clinical interviews *should* work; clinicians are highly trained in observing and interpreting behavior, and if *anyone* is able to gather valid information using highly unstructured techniques, clinical psychologists and psychiatrists certainly are the most likely candidates. Second, there is a pervasive tendency to overestimate the accuracy of one's judgments, and clinicians do not seem to be immune from this tendency (Nisbett & Ross, 1980). Thus, individual clinicians are likely to believe that *they* are accurate interviewers, even if the research evidence suggests that most of their colleagues are not. Finally, clinicians rely heavily upon the interview because it may provide important information about individuals that tests alone cannot provide. The validity of this information is open to doubt; but practicing clinicians argue that if they are confined to the role of passively intepreting test scores, they will be severely handicapped in their efforts to understand the individuals they are asked to assess (Holt, 1969).

There have been several recent efforts to provide more structure for clinical interviews, thereby (hopefully) increasing their reliability and validity (McReynolds, 1989; Robins & Helzer, 1986). A variety of interview schedules, including the Structured Clinical Interview for DSM-III-R (SCID), Schedule of Affective Disorders and Schizophrenia (SADS), and Personality Disorder Examination (PDE), have been developed to provide structure for either wide-ranging clinical interviews (e.g., the SCID) or interviews that are more narrowly focused (e.g., the SADS). These interview schedules typically include a mix of objective and open-ended questions and often call for clinical judgments at various branching points in the interview (i.e., at points where the next line of inquiry depends on your interpretation of what has been said so far). These structured interview schedules are likely to increase the reliability of clinical interviews; it is still not clear whether they lead to increased validity (McReynolds, 1989).

STUDYING CLINICAL JUDGMENT

There are a variety of methods that might be used to study clinical judgment. For example, Kleinmuntz (1968, 1970) described several applications of the think-aloud technique, in which the clinician attempts to describe the different steps he or she follows while evaluating individual examinees or case reports. These methods are useful in that they shed light on the *processes* involved in clinical judgment. The implications of this type of research for the accuracy of clinical judgments, however, are not entirely clear.

Other methods focus on the *outcomes* of clinical judgments; research of this type seems more directly relevant for determining the factors that affect the accuracy of clinical inference. In particular, applications of Brunswick's Lens Model seem especially useful in understanding features of the clinician's judgment that may contribute to, or detract from, the accuracy of assessments (Brunswick, 1956; Hammond, 1955, 1966; Hoffman, 1960).

The Lens Model describes the relationship between the individual being assessed, the information used in assessing that individual, and the judgment of the clinician, as portrayed in Figure 22-1. The model suggests that in order to understand the factors affecting the accuracy of clinical judgments, we must examine two factors: (a) the validity of the information provided by tests, observations, interviews, and the like; and (b) the way in which the clinician uses this information. For example, the model suggests that the accuracy of clinical judgments is limited by the validity of the information available to the clinician. If the tests that are chosen provide little information about the status of the individual being assessed, it is unreasonable to expect the clinician to make accurate judgments. On the other hand, if the information provided by tests *is* highly valid, there is still no guarantee that the clinician's judgments will be accurate. The accuracy of these judgments also depends upon the way in which the clinician uses the available information.

Correlational methods have typically been used to study the accuracy of judgments, the validity of information, and the use of that information. In this setting, accuracy can be defined by the correlation between the clinician's judgments regarding an individual and the actual status of that individual. Validity can be defined in terms of the relationship between the available information (e.g., test scores) and the status of the individual. The clinician's use of the available information in part can be described in terms of the

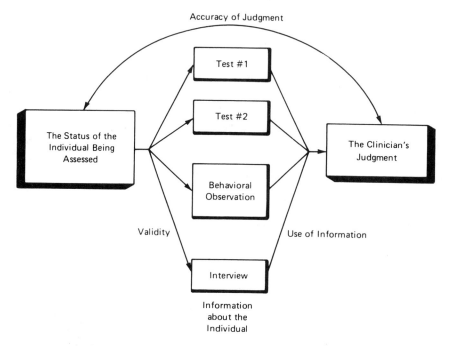

Figure 22-1   The Lens Model Applied to Clinical Judgment

relationships between different pieces of information and the clinician's final judgment (Beach, 1967; Castellan, 1992; Christal, 1968; Goldberg, 1968; Slovic & Lichtenstein, 1971).

Clinical versus Statistical Prediction

The Lens Model suggests two different ways that information might be used to predict or assess the status of a particular individual. First, that information could be used indirectly. That is, test scores and measures obtained from interviews and observations could be given to a clinician, who would then make judgments about the individual being assessed. This method is referred to as *clinical prediction*. A second, simpler alternative would be to use the information directly in making predictions about the individual. Statistical techniques such as multiple regression analysis are designed to predict "scores" on one variable (e.g., the status of the individual) on the basis of information provided by other variables (e.g., test scores). Using these techniques, it would be possible to bypass the clinician altogether and make predictions solely on the basis of test scores. This method is referred to as *statistical prediction*.

As stated at the beginning of this chapter, of central concern in clinical assessment is the effect of human judgment on the accuracy of clinical assessments and decisions. Comparisons between the accuracy of clinical prediction and the accuracy of statistical predictions would seem to shed considerable light on this issue. A statistical system of prediction represents a simple, mechanical method of combining information to arrive at an overall assessment of an individual.[1] It is useful to determine whether a clinician, given the same information, arrives at judgments that are more accurate or less accurate than the predictions obtained using statistical techniques. On the one hand, one might expect a trained, experienced professional to make better decisions than can be made on the basis of some statistical combination of test scores. On the other hand, human judgment is not perfectly valid or reliable, and it is possible that errors in human judgment lead to predictions or assessments that are *less* accurate than those obtained using statistical techniques.

The accuracy of clinical and statistical predictions has been extensively studied. A typical method is to obtain information from the files of a number of patients whose diagnoses are known and to present that information to clinicians in a form such as that shown in Table 22-1. The clinician's task is to read each case description and to make a diagnosis. Since the actual diagnosis for each case is known in advance, it is possible to directly assess the clinician's accuracy. Similarly, the scores on the different tests can be combined using a statistical technique such as multiple regression, and the predicted diagnosis can be compared with the actual diagnosis to assess the accuracy of the statistical prediction.

In a highly influential review, Meehl (1954) examined 20 studies comparing the accuracy of clinical and statistical predictions. He concluded that in almost every case statistical methods produced predictions that were at least as accurate as clinical predictions, and they were often more accurate than the judgments of trained professionals. Later reviews by Meehl (1957, 1965) reached essentially similar conclusions. These reviews seemed to suggest that clinicians did not make more accurate assessments than could be achieved using simple statistical procedures for combining the available information and that clinicians might, in fact, do *worse* than statistical methods in predicting the status of individuals.

Some years after Meehl's reviews, research in judgment and decision making dealt a second blow to the proponents of clinical prediction. Several researchers used statistical techniques to predict, or model, the clinicians' decisions, rather than predicting the actual diagnoses. This process is referred to as *bootstrapping*. It was found that, in general, the statistical models were highly accurate in predicting the clinician's behavior (Dawes & Corrigan, 1974). More important, these statistical models were often *more accurate* in predicting the actual diagnoses than were the clinicians whose decision behavior was being modeled (Dawes, 1971; Dawes & Corrigan, 1974; Goldberg, 1970).

Meehl's reviews, together with research on bootstrapping, seem to suggest that (a) clinicians very rarely make better predictions than can be made using simple statistical methods, (b) statistical methods are in many cases more accurate in predicting relevant criteria than are highly trained clinicians, and (c) clinical judgment should therefore be replaced, wherever possible, by simple statistical methods of integrating the information used in forming assessments. As one might imagine, these sorts of conclusions do not always sit well with clinical psychologists.

---

[1]The simplest statistical method is to take the average of all test scores and to predict one outcome for people who receive high averages, another outcome for people who receive low averages. Regression equations produce a *weighted* average rather than a simple unweighted average.

TABLE 22-1   A HYPOTHETICAL CASE REPORT USED TO STUDY CLINICAL VERSUS STATISTICAL PREDICTION

Case #122			
Edwards Personal Preference Schedule— Percentiles		**WAIS-R Scores**	
Achievement	55	Full	118
Deference	42	Verbal	123
Order	78	Performance	113
Exhibition	35		
Autonomy	40	*Health and adjustment:* Client complains of stomach disorders, with no diagnosed causes. Shows no clear signs of maladjustment, but is occasionally undependable.	
Affiliation	55		
Intraception	62		
Succorance	35		
Dominance	44		
Abasement	67	*DSM-III-R Diagnosis*	
Nurturance	32	Axis I—	
Change	25	Axis II—	
Endurance	50	Axis III—	
Heterosexuality	38	Axis IV—	
Aggression	60	Axis V—	

Arguments against statistical prediction.   Meehl's reviews, and the research on statistical prediction that followed, stimulated several papers questioning the relevance of studies comparing clinical and statistical prediction and disputing the supremacy of statistical techniques. For example, both Holt (1958) and McArthur (1968) suggested that the comparison between clinical and statistical prediction in most studies was essentially unfair and that most studies were biased strongly in favor of statistical models.

First, they noted that the clinician's task in these studies was quite different from the clinician's task in his or her day-to-day practice. Clinicians do not merely read a set of test scores or brief descriptions of clients and then make snap diagnoses; rather, they interact with clients for a substantial period of time before making their diagnoses. Thus, the task that clinicians typically performed in studies of clinical prediction was not really a clinical judgment task but a simulation for which clinicians did not have access to the type of direct observational data they would normally use in forming their assessments.

Second, the criterion used to evaluate both clinical and statistical predictions is the correlation between predicted and actual judgments. Statistical models are designed explicitly to maximize this correlation; the clinician *cannot* beat the statistical model unless he or she has access to information that is not readily integrated into statistical models (e.g., observations of the client) or can validly recognize cases in which statistical methods will err. Neither of these conditions is likely to occur in the typical study of clinical versus statistical prediction (Nystedt & Murphy, 1979).

Sawyer (1966) noted a second shortcoming in studies on clinical versus statistical prediction—the failure to separate the clinician's role in data collection from his or her role in integrating the available information to form an overall assessment. In most studies, the clinician was put in a relatively passive role and asked to make a decision solely on the basis of numerical information presented in a case report. Sawyer noted that in actual clinical settings, *both* clinical and mechanical (e.g., objective tests) methods are used to collect data that may contain important information about the person being assessed. Similarly, both clinical (judgmental) and statistical methods often are used to integrate the data obtained from tests and judgments. Most of the studies cited by Meehl and others concentrated exclusively on the relative accuracy of clinical and statistical methods of data integration and paid no attention to clinical methods of data collection or to the interaction between data collection and data integration methods.

Sawyer suggested that the debate over clinical versus statistical is somewhat artificial. The critical issue is the accuracy of clinical predictions, not the method by which those predictions are made. Hence, rather than trying to decide which method is best, we should try to determine how best to use *each* method to improve the accuracy of clinical predictions and decisions. Clinicians may be uniquely qualified to collect certain types of data via interviews and behavioral observation, whereas objective tests may be optimal for predicting specific psychopathologies or other diagnostic or treatment criteria. Clinical judgment is important in deciding which tests or pieces of information are relevant, whereas statistical methods, such as computing a weighted average of a person's test scores, may be optimal for summarizing trends in the data collected from that individual. Indeed, Sawyer's review suggested that clinical predictions were most accurate when (a) both clinical and mechanical (i.e., objective) methods of data collection were used and (b) mechanical or statistical methods were used to combine the data collected.

What have we learned from the clinical versus statistical debate?

For many years the debate over the supremacy of clinical or of statistical methods obscured the more important (and more illuminating) question of why simple statistical methods performed so well. To put this another way, why is it that a clerk with an adding machine could often make better predictions than those made by highly trained, experienced clinicians? The answer to this question sheds light on several of the most pressing measurement issues in the context of clinical assessment.

One secret to the success of statistical models is their reliability (Dawes & Corrigan, 1974). If the same numbers are fed into a particular regression equation today, tomorrow, and next week, the prediction will always be the same. This is not true of clinical prediction. Clinicians, being human, are not perfectly reliable; if confronted with identical, or essentially identical, information about a case on two different occasions, they may make different predictions. This lack of perfect reliability puts the clinician at a considerable disadvantage when competing with statistical techniques. When a clinician makes two different predictions based upon the same set of test scores, at least one of those predictions must be in error. If the clinician used the same strategy as is implied by the statistical approach (i.e., "take the average of all test scores, and predict from that"), the unreliable clinician, in the long run, always would perform worse than the perfectly reliable statistical model. Thus, in order for a clinician to produce more accurate predictions than those produced using statistical models, he or she must devise a strategy for combining information that is more valid than the simple strategy implied by the statistical model.

The second secret to the success of statistical predictions lies in the *robust* nature of the statistical models employed (Dawes, 1979; Dawes & Corrigan, 1974). Simple statistical methods, such as using the average of many test scores to predict a specific outcome, are often highly accurate and may be nearly as accurate as the best possible strategy. Furthermore, the decision to employ statistical techniques that either give all tests equal weight or give some tests more weight than others has little effect on the accuracy of the model's predictions (Einhorn & Hogarth, 1975; Wainer, 1976). Thus, in many clinical judgment situations a wide variety of simple statistical strategies could be applied that would be equally (or highly) accurate in predicting relevant clinical criteria. Although complex clinical strategies may exist that, in theory, are more accurate than statistical strategies, the robust nature of the type of statistical models typically employed in studying clinical judgment guarantees that the difference between the accuracy of a statistical prediction and the accuracy attained by the best clinical strategy will generally be small.

A third secret is that statistical models avoid the all-too-human tendency to "see" relationships that do not, in fact, exist and to "identify" individual exceptions to general actuarial trends that do not, in fact, apply (Dawes, Faust & Meehl, 1989). Well-trained clinicians are no more immune than anyone else to the tendency to ignore relevant background information (e.g., base rates) and to treat each case as a unique individual, for whom general trends that exist in the population do not apply. This issue surfaced in the debate over computerized versus clinical interpretations of psychological tests. Matarazzo (1986) complained that computerized interpretations were "all mean and no sigma," meaning that they reflected actuarial trends in the data but did not consider the individual characteristics of the respondent in the same way as a clinician would. Murphy (1987a) retorted that clinical judgments often incorporate too much irrelevant information; clinical judgments might be characterized as too much sigma and not enough mean (i.e., they incorporate information about irrelevant differences but ignore information about general trends in the population).

The most valuable outcome of the clinical-versus-statistical debate is the recognition that the clinical judgment process can be broken down into several subtasks (e.g., data collection, integration of information) and that some of these tasks are done most efficiently using statistical techniques. Rather than regarding statistical techniques as a replacement for clinical judgments, these methods should be regarded as tools that clinicians can use to enhance the accuracy of their predictions. Statistical methods are superior to human judgment when it comes to very specific tasks, such as determining the average or the trend in responses to several tasks. However, in the long run the automation of clinical prediction would limit the accuracy of clinical decisions, since it would preclude the use of behavioral observation data or the selection of appropriate tests to optimally assess the status of each individual client. The combination of clinical *and* statistical prediction in most cases is preferable to the use of purely clinical or purely statistical methods of prediction.

Patterns, Configurations, and Clinical Judgment

Experiments designed to obtain statistical representations of clinical judgment have shown consistently that a simple model, in which the average of all test scores for an individual are used to predict his or her status, is highly accurate in predicting the assessments reached by clinicians (Wiggins, 1973). This finding led several investigators to conclude that this simple model provided a fairly good representation of the clinician's decision-making strategy (Christal, 1968; Hursch, Hammond & Hursch, 1964). Clinicians, however, insist that they do more than simply add test scores together when they access individuals—they also try to pay attention to *patterns* or *configurations* of test scores.

Table 22-2 presents a simple example that illustrates the distinction between the average test score and the pattern of test scores. Although the average scores for the three individuals depicted in the table are identical, the patterns are very different. Individual A received average scores on all three tests, individual B is highly immature and very concerned with health, and individual C shows evidence of paranoia, together with little concern for his health. Clinicians maintain that patterns of scores on tests, interviews, and the like reveal important information that is not revealed by average test scores. Experimental studies of clinical judgments frequently demonstrate that clinicians consider patterns or configurations of test scores in their assessment of individuals (Dana, Cocking & Dana, 1970; Goldberg, 1965; Hoffman, 1960; Wiggins & Kohen, 1971). The question of whether efforts to consider patterns of test scores as well as average test scores contribute to the accuracy of clinical predictions is exceedingly complex. For example, one aspect of this question concerns the validity of clinicians' interpretations of specific patterns. Granted, a high score on a paranoia scale coupled with a low score on a depression scale may mean something different than a medium score on both. It is not always clear, however, precisely *what* that specific pattern may indicate. A second aspect of this question involves the way in which patterns are defined. Consider, for example a diagnostic system that includes the following as indicators of the hypothetical mental disorder called *Brunswick's Egonia:*

1. Lower-than-average full-scale IQ (less than 100)
2. Performance IQ higher than verbal IQ
3. Verbal IQ not less than 70

In Table 22-3, each of the cases appears to fit the pattern for *Brunswick's Egonia,* but in some cases, the data more clearly fit the pattern than in others. For example, individual A clearly appears to meet all three diagnostic criteria. Individuals B and C also meet the criteria, but there is reason to doubt that they *really* exhibit the pattern the diagnostic manual describes. For example, one might question whether individual A's performance IQ *really* exceeds his or her verbal IQ, and whether the verbal score really exceeds the

TABLE 22-2 TEST SCORES THAT DIFFER IN PATTERN, BUT NOT IN AVERAGE

Individual	Maturity* scale	Paranoid thought scale	Health concern scale	Average score
A	5	5	5	5
B	2	4	9	5
C	6	8	1	5

*Note: All three indices employ a 10-point scale, where 1 = low, 5 = average, 10 = high

TABLE 22-3   CASES THAT APPEAR TO FIT THE DIAGNOSTIC PATTERN
FOR BRUNSWICK'S EGONIA

	Criteria		
	(a) Full IQ is less than 100 (b) Performance IQ is higher than verbal IQ (c) Verbal IQ is not less than 70		
Case	**Full IQ**	**Verbal IQ**	**Performance IQ**
A	86	80	95
B	70	70	71
C	99	85	113

cutoff suggested by the third diagnostic criterion. Similarly, one might question whether individual C, who has a reported IQ of 99, should really be regarded as "below average" in intelligence. In both cases, the limited reliability of psychological tests leaves room for doubt regarding the degree of fit between the characteristics of the individual and the characteristics of the specific pattern of scores used to predict *Brunswick's Egonia*. For example, if individual B were to be retested, it is not at all unlikely that she would receive an IQ of 100 or more. Of course, it is possible that each individual would receive the same scores on their second testing. It is more likely, however, that scores would vary somewhat, and that *all* trivial differences between test scores observed in the first testing (e.g., the difference between the performance and verbal scores of individual B) will not recur in the second.

The limited reliability of psychological tests has important implications for clinical assessment strategies that involve examining patterns or configurations of test scores. The reliability of psychological tests is not, however, the only issue in assessing the clinician's ability to react to patterns or configurations of test scores. Rather, in examining the clinician's use of score configurations, it may also be important to consider the *clinician's* reliability in applying complex diagnostic rules. As has been discussed, one major advantage of statistical, as opposed to clinical methods of prediction is that the former are highly reliable, while the latter are not. There are good reasons to believe that judges will be less reliable in applying complex diagnostic strategies than they will be in applying a relatively straightforward, simple one (Murphy, 1979). Thus, attempts to develop complex clinical prediction strategies designed to outperform simple statistical prediction methods may actually *reduce* rather than increase the accuracy of clinical predictions.

Can We Improve Clinical Judgment?

If your goal is to improve the reliability and validity of clinical judgment, two strategies seem reasonable. First, you might try to improve the judges, perhaps through better training. Second, you might try to improve the judgment process, perhaps through the use of statistical methods for the integration of data. We have already reviewed evidence suggesting that the second strategy can be effective. Less is known about whether the first strategy (improving the judges) will work.

One way to determine whether new and better methods of training clinicians will improve clinical judgment is to look at the impact of the training (both formal and on-the-job) that clinicians currently receive on the validity of their judgments. Garb (1989) reviewed the results of 55 studies on the effects of clinical training and professional experience on the validity of clinical judgments. These studies compared the clinical judgments of experienced and less-experienced clinicians, of clinicians and graduate students, of advanced and beginning graduate students, and of clinicians (including graduate students) and laypersons. The results of these studies were fairly clear—on-the-job experience is not related to the validity of clinical judgments, and training is only weakly related to validity. In other words, an experienced Ph.D. makes clinical judgments that are not substantially better than those made by someone with essentially no training or experience. Garb notes that similar findings have been reported in medicine. High-school graduates, given a few weeks of training and explicit protocols for diagnosis and treatment, are as effective as fully trained physicians in treating a limited range of problems (Shortliffe, Buchanan & Feignbaum, 1979).

Clinicians typically receive several years of post-graduate experience and deal with large numbers of clients each month. Since this level of training and experience has so little effect on the validity of clinical judgment, it seems unlikely that a little more training or experience will really make a difference. Unfortunately, research on the effects of training and experience on clinical judgment has had little to offer in the way of concrete suggestions for improving the ability of clinicians to make these critical judgments. Garb (1989) suggests that clinicians must rely more heavily on relevant research in making judgments (and less on intuition and experience), and that automated decision-making aids might help.

Rapid developments in technology make it likely that the strategy of improving the judgment process (rather than improving the judge) will dominate efforts to increase the validity of clinical judgments. In the early years of the clinical-versus-statistical-prediction debate (i.e., the 1950s and 1960s), the issue was somewhat academic because individual clinicians rarely had access to computers capable of carrying out complex statistical integration tasks. Now, the most complex clinical integration tasks are easily handled by computers that in terms of cost and ease of use are accessible to virtually any clinician. In addition, software for performing statistical integration or for assessing normative databases is widely available and easy to use. Finally, computerized test interpretation services are available; several issues in computerized assessment were discussed in Chapter 11. While these will not and should not replace the individual clinician (Matarazzo, 1986), they can provide a valuable tool for increasing the reliability and validity of clinical judgments.

STRUCTURED ASSESSMENT PROGRAMS

Up to this point we have concentrated on applications of clinical assessment in which an individual clinician gathers and integrates various types of information in forming an integrated diagnosis of an individual client's current status and future prognosis. The same sorts of activities that are carried out by individual clinicians on a case-by-case basis are also carried out on a larger scale as part of a number of structured assessment programs. One of the most notable examples of a structured assessment program was the one carried out by the Office of Strategic Services (OSS) in selecting intelligence agents during World War II. This program, which is described in the section that follows, was the forerunner of a number of large-scale assessment programs carried out today by both the government and private industry.

The most obvious difference between individual clinician assessment and structured programs of assessment is that of scale. For example, the OSS program assessed over 5,000 recruits over a period of approximately three years. Other differences, which may not be so obvious, are even more important for understanding the similarities and differences between individual assessment and structured programs of assessment.

First, in structured assessment the goal of the program is likely to be fairly well defined. The OSS program was designed to select effective intelligence agents; similar assessment programs are used widely in business to identify and develop promising candidates for higher levels of management. Although it may be difficult to specify exactly what one is looking for in a secret agent or in a manager, structured programs nevertheless typically have clearer goals than the individual clinician whose goals are in part shaped by the clients' problems.

Second, structured programs often, though not always, are standardized in such a way that the assessment activities do not vary as a function of the behavior of the person or persons being assessed. Individual assessment, by contrast, is typically adaptive rather than fixed (Cronbach & Gleser, 1965). Rather than using the same set of tests, interviews, and observations with every client, individual clinicians must tailor their assessment activities to fit the client's apparent status.

Third, structured assessment programs very frequently involve multiple assessors (e.g., psychologists, psychiatrists, physicians, and managers). Research on group decision making is therefore relevant to understanding the outcomes of structured assessment programs.

Finally, large-scale assessment programs are typically concerned with individual differences within the wide range of behavior we typically label as normal, and they are likely to be less concerned with psychopathology. Thus, the goal of structured assessment is rarely to understand and alleviate psychological or behavioral problems experienced by the individuals being assessed. There are, however, exceptions; later in this chapter we discuss a structured assessment program used in assessing and designing treatment for learning-disabled children.

The OSS Assessment Program

The Office of Strategic Services, forerunner of the CIA, was created shortly after the United States entered World War II. Among the functions of the OSS was the selection and training of agents to work, often behind enemy lines, in gathering intelligence, conducting sabotage and propaganda campaigns, and assisting resistance movements. In many respects, the task facing the OSS during World War II was reminiscent of that facing the U.S. Army in World War I. That is, they were charged with developing a large and effective force of agents in a short period of time, starting pretty much from scratch. In World War I, group-administered tests of general intelligence (i.e., Army Alpha and Army Beta) had provided a partial solution to the army's problem of identifying officer candidates. The task facing the OSS in World War II was much more complex, however. The OSS had to select agents from a very heterogeneous group of recruits, under conditions that precluded testing for specific, assignment-related skills, for a wide variety of ill-defined jobs and missions (OSS Staff, 1948). Psychologists and staff members affiliated with the OSS developed a complex "multiform organismic system of assessment" to cope with this task.

The system of assessment employed by the OSS had its roots in the methods employed by both British and German military psychologists, as well as those employed by Murray at the Harvard Psychological Clinic (Wiggins, 1973). The cornerstone of the assessment technique employed by OSS was the use of several different types of procedures, and several procedures of each type, to assess each recruit's standing in several different dimensions. These dimensions are listed in Table 22-4. For example, each candidate would receive a rating on the dimension Social Relations, based on information obtained from (a) interviews, (b) informal observation, (c) individual situational tests, (d) group situational tests, (e) projective tests, and (f) sociometric questionnaires. The situational tests were an especially important part of the assessment procedures developed by OSS. Each of these tests put the recruit in a lifelike situation that was designed to illustrate specific aspects of the recruit's behavior in difficult or demanding situations. For example, three individual situational tests were used in assessing the recruits' skill in Social Relations:

1. *Construction test*—the recruit was asked to build a simple structure with the help of two assistants. The assistants were, in fact, confederates of the assessment staff and were consistently uncooperative, argumentative, and ineffective; their "assistance" made it nearly impossible to complete the structure.

2. *Recruitment test*—the person being assessed played the role of a recruiter, interviewing an applicant. The applicant was, once again, a confederate of the assessment staff.

3. *Improvisation*—a role-playing test in which the recruits were given a description of a situation and were required to interact in the roles of the characters in that situation.

Typical OSS assessments involved a group of 18 recruits who were studied extensively over a three-day period. Over these three days each recruit would complete a number of tests, interviews, and exercises, be observed and rated by his peers and by a number of psychologists on the assessment staff, and participate in the evaluation of other recruits. At the end of this period the assessment staff was responsible for pulling

TABLE 22-4   AREAS RATED IN OSS ASSESSMENTS

1. Motivation for assignment	6. Leadership
2. Energy and initiative	7. Security
3. Effective intelligence	8. Physical ability
4. Emotional stability	9. Observing and reporting
5. Social relations	10. Propaganda skills

together all the available information to form an overall assessment of each recruit's suitability for assignment in the OSS. This information would be combined in assessment staff conferences in order to reach a consensus on a coherent, comprehensive description of each recruit's strengths and weaknesses. One of the most important products of the assessments was a written personality sketch of each assessee that attempted to "predictively describe him as a functioning member of the organization" (OSS Staff, 1948, p. 53).

There are several features of the OSS assessment program that distinguish it from other methods that might have been used in evaluating recruits. First, the program represented an attempt to carry out assessment in a natural social setting. Recruits spent three days living, eating, and drinking with the assessment staff in a remote location; observation of the recruits' behavior in non-test situations was thought to provide especially useful information. Second, assessment included a number of lifelike tasks. Rather than relying on tests of specific skills, abilities, or traits, the assessment staff used behavior in natural settings to predict future behavior in similar settings. Third, the assessment included multiple, overlapping procedures. Thus, each important variable was measured using a number of distinct methods. Finally, there was an attempt to arrive at agreement regarding each recruit's personality. Rather than attempting to assess several specific abilities, aptitudes, and skills, the OSS assessment procedure was designed to reach a coherent impression of each recruit as a person.

The OSS assessment program has set the pattern for many large-scale assessment exercises. Several of its features have been carried over to the assessment centers that have become increasingly popular for assessing managers and executives (see Chapter 18). In the early 1960s, an assessment program was developed by the Peace Corps that drew upon, and in many ways improved, the assessment techniques developed and applied by the OSS.

Assessment in the Peace Corps

The Peace Corps was established in 1961 to provide a wide range of medical, educational, and technical assistance to developing countries. Volunteers typically spent two years in the host country, often living under conditions of considerable hardship. The assessment problem facing the Peace Corps was strikingly similar to that facing the OSS some years earlier. A large number of volunteers were available for difficult, ill-defined missions that varied tremendously from country to country and also varied over time (Henry, 1965). In addition, many Peace Corps volunteers were young and inexperienced (Hobbs, 1963). Thus, there often was little in the volunteers' background that could give firm indications of success or failure overseas.

The assessment procedure developed by the Peace Corps in the 1960s consisted of two separate stages: suitability screening and field selection.

Suitability screening.   Peace Corps training was both expensive and arduous. Rather than admitting all applicants to training, the Peace Corps developed a method of screening out applicants who were unlikely to succeed in their assignments, before they entered training. Each applicant would fill out a questionnaire assessing his or her training, experience and technical qualifications; take written placement tests, which included measures of language aptitude; and provide academic transcripts and references.[2] On the basis of this information, a number of applicants were invited to training. Those applicants who accepted training were then subject to a civil service background examination and a strict medical exam. Those applicants who cleared these final hurdles were admitted to the training program. The Peace Corps's suitability screening process is diagrammed in Figure 22-2.

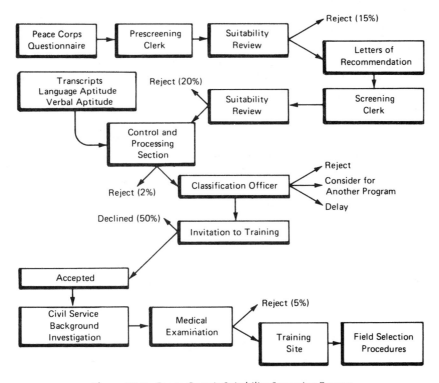

Figure 22-2 Peace Corps's Suitability Screening Process

Source: Adapted from Wiggins, 1973, p. 587. Copyright © 1972 by Newbery Award Records, Inc., and Random House, Inc. Reproduced by permission.

Several features of the suitability screening process are noteworthy. First, the process was quite intensive—approximately one applicant out of six passed this initial screening and reached the training site. However, as the figure shows, the majority of the screening decisions were made by individual applicants, rather than by the Peace Corps itself; approximately half of the applicants invited to training decided not to accept. Second, despite intensive pressure to conduct personal interviews with each applicant, the entire suitability screening process was accomplished without any personal contact with the applicants (Hobbs, 1963; Wiggins, 1973). Thus, the screening procedure developed by the Peace Corps represents one of the few large-scale assessment programs that

[2]As many as 22 letters of reference were solicited for any given candidate.

appear to corroborate the large body of research demonstrating the questionable validity of interviews. However, note that this was only the first step in a complex selection program.

Field selection.   Peace Corps training typically lasted two to three months. This period provided extensive opportunities to observe each volunteer's behavior in the context of an intense, demanding training program. Final selection decisions were made at the training sites, based largely upon the recommendations of Advisory Selection Boards. The selection strategy employed at the training site is diagrammed in Figure 22-3.

Approximately halfway through training, each candidate would be assessed by an Intermediate Advisory Selection Board made up of psychologists, psychiatrists, physicians, training staff, representatives familiar with overseas conditions, and experienced Peace Corps volunteers. This board had access to all of the information collected during

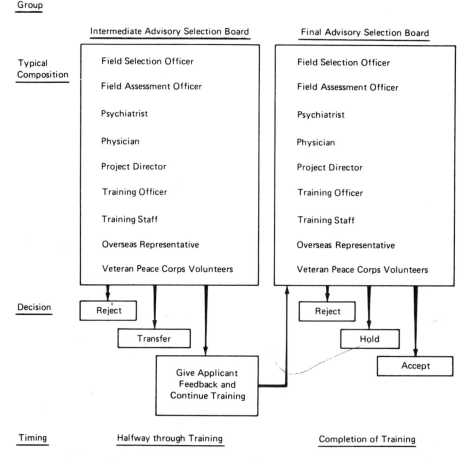

Figure 22-3   Peace Corps's Field Selection Strategy

the training. For example, they would have access to interviewer ratings, scores on psychological tests (e.g., MMPI), peer ratings, training course grades, medical records, staff ratings, and behavior observations. The board's task was to collect and integrate relevant data and to present recommendations to the Field Selection Officer, who was responsible for making decisions regarding each candidate. At this stage, candidates could be rejected, transferred to another program or site, or retained for further training. Those candidates who were retrained received extensive feedback regarding their strengths and weaknesses, with special attention given to shortcomings that could be corrected during the remainder of the training period.

At the end of training, the Final Advisory Selection Board met to consider the total information available for each remaining candidate. At this point the Field Selection Officer made a decision, based upon information provided by the board, to accept, reject, or hold the candidate for another project or assignment. Approximately 70 percent of the candidates who began training were eventually accepted for assignment overseas.

Comparison of OSS and Peace Corps Programs

The assessment programs developed by the OSS and the Peace Corps were similar in many ways. Both employed multiple methods of measurement and both relied on the "diagnostic council," a meeting of assessors that attempted to forge a coherent picture of each volunteer as a potential member of the organization. Yet there are several important differences that suggest that the Peace Corps program had a greater potential for producing valid, useful assessments. First, the Peace Corps employed a largely objective screening system that eliminated a large number of unsuitable candidates. Admittedly, much of the screening involved self-selection, and some of those who were eliminated at the screening stage might have performed successfully overseas. Nevertheless, the use of a multistage assessment procedure was definitely an advance, particularly in light of the fact that the selection ratio (number of assignments/number of applicants) was known to be low. Second, the Peace Corps program formally separated the roles of data collection (e.g., by physicians, training staff), data integration (e.g., by field assessment officer), and decision making (e.g., by field selection officer) (Wiggins, 1973). In contrast, members of the OSS assessment staff carried out all three activities on an ongoing basis. Third, each decision made in the Peace Corps program was made on the basis of the cumulative weight of evidence. While there is a good possibility that previous evaluations of a candidate can bias later evaluations of that same candidate (Murphy, Balzer, Lockhart & Eisenman, 1985), nevertheless this procedure made it possible to test and reevaluate early impressions of the candidate.

Because of difficulties in obtaining useful criterion measures (especially in the case of the OSS program), it is difficult to determine which program was, in fact, more successful. The OSS staff concluded that there was little definitive evidence for the predictive validity of their assessments (OSS Staff, 1948). However, later analyses of data presented by the OSS (Wiggins, 1973) suggest that the use of psychological assessment resulted in at least a modest increase in the number of correct decisions made by the OSS.

Several sorts of data are available for evaluating the accuracy of the Peace Corps's selection decisions. Of particular interest are statistics regarding the number of volunteers who were unable to complete their two-year tour of duty due to emotional or physical illness, adjustment problems, or situations at home necessitating their return. In the early years of the Peace Corps it was assumed that between 20 percent and 50 percent of all volunteers would be unable to complete their tours (Hobbs, 1963). It is worth noting that between 10 percent and 15 percent of the age cohort from which most volunteers were drawn, *under normal circumstances,* will suffer clinical impairment due to emotional illness at some point in their lives. However, through 1964 only approximately 8 percent of the volunteers sent overseas had returned prematurely, and fewer than 1 percent returned for psychiatric reasons (Menninger & English, 1965). It has been estimated that 95 percent of those selected for overseas assignment represented true-positive decisions (i.e., were correctly sent overseas) (Wiggins, 1973).[3]

Behavioral Assessment in Mental Retardation

The final structured assessment program to be discussed is not a program per se, at least not in the sense of the large-scale programs of the OSS and the Peace Corps. Rather, it is a structured set of measurement activities used to assess severe learning disabilities in children and to design training programs tailored to the individual child's weaknesses and capabilities. The core of this assessment program is the Learning Potential Assessment Device (LPAD), developed by Feuerstein (1970) and his colleagues (cf. Haywood, Filler, Shifman & Chatelant, 1975).

In a sense, the LPAD integrates the functions of training and assessment. Using the LPAD, a psychologist asks a child to perform a number of tasks, some of which are quite novel and complex. The amount and type of training that is necessary to achieve successful performance on each task is a critical aspect of the clinician's assessment. Thus, LPAD assesses a child's level of functioning in part by examining the extent and the means necessary to modify his or her performance. It is assumed that functions that are easily modifiable show less impairment than those that require extensive training to modify.

The LPAD is made up of four distinct tests:

1. *Organization of Dots.* The child is required to detect geometric patterns in a cloud of dots and to construct them by connecting the dots. Successful performance is a function of ability to plan and delay responses, analytic ability, and ability to learn new performance strategies as the patterns become more complex.
2. *Plateau Test.* The test materials consist of four plates, each with nine buttons on its surface. One or more of the buttons is fixed in place. The child's task is to locate a fixed button and remember its location as the plates are stacked, rotated, or represented in a drawing. This task taps associative learning, memory, and spatial transformation ability.
3. *LPAD Matrices Test.* Essentially similar to Raven's Progressive Matrices, this test taps reasoning ability and ability to discriminate relevant from irrelevant dimensions.

---

[3]However, because over 85 percent of those who applied were not accepted for overseas assignment, a larger number of false-negative errors were almost certainly made.

4. *Representational Stencil Design Test.* The test consists of 20 stencils, each of which has a unique design. The child is shown models, which are constructed by overlaying two or more stencils, and must pick out the stencils needed to reproduce the design and indicate their order of placement. This test taps color, form, and size discrimination; mental manipulation; and ability to integrate feedback from earlier solutions.

Each of the tests that make up the LPAD can be varied independently on three different dimensions: (a) the novelty or complexity of the task, (b) the modality of presentation, and (c) the cognitive operations required for successful task performance. The clinician can systematically manipulate these dimensions in any or all of the LPAD test to probe the child's capabilities and limits. Thus, the LPAD is at the same time a structured, multitest program and an assessment method which can be tailored to the performance levels exhibited by the child being assessed.

The LPAD is clearly different in its structure and its goals from the large-scale structured programs described earlier. Nevertheless, this assessment technique shares several essential features with the methods employed by the OSS and the Peace Corps. First, LPAD employs multiple tests, which assess, in part, overlapping functions. Second, LPAD incorporates performance tests. While these are not as naturalistic or complex as some of the situational tests employed by the OSS, they nevertheless require the child to actively solve problems, rather than simply answer the clinician's question. Finally, this technique requires the clinician to integrate information from a variety of different sources (e.g., test, effects of manipulating novelty of the material presented, mode presentation, cognitive demands) to form an overall assessment of the child's level of functioning.

LPAD is one of several methods of dynamic assessment, which relies heavily on the observation of performance in novel or complex tasks for evaluating cognitive abilities and skills. While these assessment methods in general, and LPAD in particular, have attracted favorable reviews (e.g., Hamilton, 1983), other researchers have expressed concerns. Research on both the reliability and the construct and criterion-related validity of LPAD suggests that this method does not meet the same psychometric standards as more traditional paper-and-pencil devices (Glutting & McDermott, 1990; Hamilton, 1983).

Evaluating Structured Assessment Programs

Structured assessment programs typically incorporate many features that are consistent with the general principles of measurement discussed in Chapters 5 through 9. For example, they employ multiple observations and often multiple assessors. This should help to increase the reliability, and possibly the validity, of assessments, and reduce their susceptibility to bias. On the other hand, the frequent reliance on clinical (judgmental) methods of integrating data seems justified more on the basis of tradition than on the basis of empirical evidence. Despite a significant body of research showing that mechanical methods are generally preferable to judgmental methods of combining information from multiple sources (e.g., Dawes, 1979; 1980; Wiggins, 1973), assessment programs stubbornly cling to some version of the "diagnostic council," in which an individual clinician or a group of clinicians attempts to form a unified, coherent impression of the mass of data collected in assessment.

Sawyer (1966) noted that predictions seemed to be most accurate when objective and judgmental methods were used to *collect* data, while mechanical methods were used to *integrate* data. Even departments of psychology are reluctant to rely solely on statistical methods to make final decisions (Dawes, 1979). It may be unrealistic, therefore, to expect assessment programs to adopt the statistical method. As currently conducted, structured assessment programs often lead to better decisions than simpler methods of prediction (e.g., written tests), although the increase in accuracy may not always offset the high cost of assessment. However, considering their *potential* level of accuracy (if optimal measurement and prediction strategies were adopted), structured assessment programs, as currently designed, are not all that impressive. In other words, structured assessment may be better than simpler testing methods, but the structured assessment approach is probably not as useful as it could be if better use were made of statistical prediction models and other automated data-integration aids.

There is an extensive body of research on the use of assessment centers for predicting and developing managerial performance (cf. Thornton, 1992; Thornton & Byham, 1982). This literature illustrates several of the issues that are relevant for evaluating assessment programs in general. As was discussed in Chapter 18, assessment centers involve the use of multiple methods and multiple evaluators to assess managerial candidates on dimensions such as verbal ability, leadership, delegation of authority, and planning ability. Data from several distinct exercises and testing techniques are combined and a consensus is reached as to each candidate's overall assessment.

Research on assessment centers suggests several conclusions that may apply quite broadly to other assessment programs. First, it is not easy to evaluate the validity of assessment centers, largely as the result of problems in developing adequate criteria. In order to evaluate the validity of any assessment program, assessment outcomes must be compared against some external criterion, and many of the criterion measures employed are of questionable reliability and validity, or, worse yet, are directly biased by assessment outcomes (Klimoski & Strickland, 1977). Structured assessment programs are likely to be used to make complex predictions (e.g., predicting managerial success, success of remedial training programs), and these predictions are difficult to validate.

Second, there is little support for the continued use of judgmental rather than statistical methods of aggregating assessment data (Borman, 1982; Borman, Eaton, Bryan & Rosse, 1983; Sackett & Wilson, 1982). Each assessment exercise typically yields a set of scores for each assessee; the research cited above consistently showed that a simple sum of all these ratings was as good as, and often better than, assessment reached by consensus in terms of its ability to predict relevant criteria. Sackett and Wilson (1982) suggest that "diagnostic councils" rarely need to meet, and that statistical methods of combining assessment data would be more practical and more valid than the judgmental methods currently employed.

Assessment programs typically are designed to measure several attributes, in much the same way that multiple aptitude test batteries are designed to measure several distinct abilities and skills. For example, the managerial assessment centers of American Telephone and Telegraph (AT&T) include ratings on 25 or more separate characteristics, ranging from passivity to work motivation. As noted in Chapter 14, the measurement of several distinct attributes is difficult, and not always successful. Research on assessment centers suggests that similar difficulties may be encountered when several distinct methods are used to measure multiple attributes of the persons being assessed. Sackett and Dreher (1982) suggest that various assessment exercises provide valid measures of a person's overall performance but do not provide valid measures of several distinct attributes. In part, this is a result of the strong reliance on individual and group assessment techniques that rely on assessors' judgments (e.g., interviews, behavior observations). Human judges are notorious for exhibiting general evaluative bias and have difficulty assessing individual attributes in a way that is not affected by their overall evaluation of the assessee (Murphy, 1982).

In general, structured assessment programs have shown consistent evidence of reliability and criterion-related validity (Thornton, 1992; Thornton & Byham, 1982), although there is still some uncertainty about *why* assessment center predictions are valid (Klimoski & Bickner, 1987). Evidence regarding their content and construct validity is somewhat less consistent. In part, this is a reflection of too much optimism in the design of assessment programs. Returning to an earlier example, managerial assessment centers used by AT&T attempt to evaluate 25 separate dimensions. There are reasons to doubt that there *are* that many discriminably different dimensions or, if that many dimensions really do exist, that *any* assessment technique could yield valid information about all of them. Thus, the failure of assessors to discriminate among this large set of dimensions may tell us more about the domain being measured than about the shortcomings of the assessment technique.

Structured assessment programs present many appealing features, especially their reliance on multiple testing techniques. Clearly, there is still room for improvement in most assessment programs, but these programs could potentially represent the most comprehensive and the most valid method of measuring the attributes of individuals. In evaluating these programs, it may be necessary to move away from the traditional criteria used to evaluate individual tests (e.g., reliability, validity) and focus attention on the one criterion that has been emphasized throughout this book: A method is useful only if it results in better decisions. On the whole, multiple assessment techniques do seem to help in making fair and accurate decisions. The full potential of this approach has probably not been exploited, but it seems clear that the use of a single test score in making important decisions has become a thing of the past. It is therefore likely that research on the best (i.e., most accurate and most practical) methods of combining information from multiple assessment devices will become an increasingly important aspect of the application of the principles of psychological measurement to decision making.

CRITICAL DISCUSSION:
Psychological Assessment in the Courtroom

There is a strange link between the nation's first and its most recent presidential assassination attempts: the successful use of insanity as a legal defense. The first known assassination attempt was made against President Andrew Jackson by Richard Lawrence. Lawrence's defense was one of the first in this nation to be based successfully on a plea of insanity (Zonana, 1984). When John Hinkley attempted to assassinate President Reagan, his successful insanity defense touched off a legal and psychiatric controversy that continues today.

Psychological assessment in criminal trials must often deal with two separate issues: the defendant's competence to stand trial and the defendant's sanity at the time the crime was committed. Although questions of sanity have received considerable attention in the press, the issue of competence has greater impact on the conduct and dispensation of legal proceedings. It is much more likely that a disturbed defendant will be found incompetent to stand trial than not guilty by reason of insanity.

Competence refers to the defendant's present state of mind. A defendant is ruled not competent to stand trial if, because of some mental disorder, he or she is unable to understand the charges and/or is unable to participate in his or her own defense. Insanity refers to the defendant's state of mind at the time the crime was committed. The American Law Institute's definition of insanity states:

> A person is not responsible for criminal conduct if at the time of such conduct, as a result of mental disease of defect, he lacks substantial capacity either to appreciate the wrongfulness of his conduct or to conform his conduct to the requirements of the law. (Zonana, 1984, p. 311)

There is no standard procedure for assessing competency or sanity. It is common, however, to use psychological tests such as the MMPI as evidence. More specific diagnostic tools, such as the Schedule of Affective Disorders and Schizophrenia or the Competency Screening Test (Nicholson & Kugler, 1991; Nicholson, Robertson, Johnson & Jensen, 1988; Rogers, Thatcher & Cavanaugh, 1984). The use of interviews and self-report measures in assessment has probably contributed to juries' skepticism when evaluating insanity pleas. As a result, successful insanity pleas are much less frequent than one might think. For example, in 1980 there were 259 successful insanity pleas out of over 50,000 defendants tried in California. More recent surveys suggest that the insanity plea frees defendants in about three of every 1,000 criminal cases tried and that the plea is even less successful in serious cases (e.g., murder trials). The insanity plea is not an easy way out.

In general, assessments of sanity are more difficult and more controversial than assessments of competence. First, it is difficult to obtain reliable information about a defendant's past behavior (i.e., at the time of the crime); in assessing competence, past behavior is irrelevant. Second, there is not as much incentive to fake incompetence as there might be to fake insanity. If a defendant is found incompetent to stand trial, the judge may simply defer the charges and commit the defendant to a mental institution until he or she is ready to stand trial. (Note, however, that indefinite commitment may be unconstitutional, since it infringes on the defendant's right to a speedy trial.) A defendant who is found not guilty by reason of insanity might also be committed to a mental institution, but he or she must be freed and cannot be retried if "cured."

Significant scientific and professional criticisms have come to surround the practice of forensic psychology. Several studies and reviews of the literature seem to show that psychologists do a poor job of predicting the future behavior of violent individuals or of evaluating the sanity of defendants (Dawes, 1989; Faust, 1989; Faust & Ziskin, 1988). On the whole, this research suggests that mental health professionals do not have any special skill, in the sense that their judgments are not demonstrably better than those of laypersons, in evaluating sanity or competency to stand trial. Like laypersons, psychologists and other professionals in related fields make a substantial number of errors in these judgments. Although detailed ethical guidelines have been drawn up to regulate the practice of psychology as it relates to the legal system (Committee on Ethical Guidelines for Forensic Psychologists, 1991), strong doubts have been expressed about the usefulness of the testimony of forensic psychologists. Like Nicholson and Kugler (1991), we believe that part of the answer to improving the quality of practice in forensic psychology is the development of well-validated, objective screening instruments that can replace the often bewildering array of techniques now used in the assessment of competency and sanity.

Summary

Clinical assessment is one of several methods of psychological measurement in which subjective judgment is an integral part of the process of measurement and evaluation (other examples include employment interviews and performance appraisals). Clinical assessments usually involve psychological tests, and thus they can be thought of as a second level of psychological measurement. That is, psychological tests provide many sorts of information about individuals, information that is integrated, together with clinical interviews, observations, life history data, and other information to form an overall assessment or diagnosis. The use of tests with consistent evidence of reliability and validity contributes to, but does not guarantee, the validity of these assessments.

Research on clinical judgment suggests that it is very difficult to reliably apply complex judgment strategies in assessing individuals. The task of integrating information from multiple tests can often be done with a calculator; the average of several test scores often provides a more valid assessment than does the unaided judgment of a well-trained clinician. Clinical skills and experience are probably useful for *collecting and interpreting* data on individuals, but the task of integrating scores on several tests is not one that should be done via subjective judgment.

Three structured assessment programs or systems were discussed. The OSS assessment program established the "ground rules" for several types of behavioral assessment, including the assessment centers that are widely used to evaluate managers and job applicants in industry. The assessment program developed by the Peace Corps was a clear success, and it suggests that clinical assessment *can* be done with a high level of reliability and validity. On the other hand, assessment systems such as LPAD illustrate some of the difficulties in clinical assessment.

Chapters 5–9 of this book were largely devoted to evaluating psychological tests. As we note here, it can be more difficult to evaluate assessment programs. The best programs incorporate many of the suggestions that come out of psychometric theory (e.g., they use multiple tests and multiple methods of measurement), but they also often incorporate features, such as clinical rather than statistical integration, that have been widely criticized in the technical literature. Nevertheless, the research on assessment suggests that the use of subjective judgment as part of the measurement process does *not* mean that the resulting assessments will be unreliable or invalid. If they are carefully carried out, clinical assessments can show high levels of reliability and validity.

APPENDIX A

FORTY
REPRESENTATIVE
TESTS

INTELLIGENCE AND SCHOLASTIC APTITUDE

Group Tests

College Board Scholastic Aptitude Test
Culture-Fair Intelligence Test
Graduate Record Examinations
Lorge-Thorndike Intelligence Tests, Multi-level Edition
Multidimensional Aptitude Battery

Individual Tests

Kaufman Assessment Battery for Children
Stanford-Binet Intelligence Scale
System of Multicultural Pluralistic Assessment
Wechsler Adult Intelligence Scale–Revised
Wechsler Intelligence scale for Children–Revised

MULTIPLE APTITUDE BATTERIES

Armed Services Vocational Aptitude Battery
Differential Aptitude Tests

USES General Aptitude Test Battery
USES Nonreading Aptitude Test Battery

NEUROPSYCHOLOGICAL

Halstead-Reitan Neuropsychological Test Battery
Luria-Nebraska Neuropsychological Test Battery
Wechsler Memory Test

PERSONALITY

Bem Sex-Role Inventory
Edward Personal Preference Schedule
The Holtzman Inkblot Technique
Millon Adolescent Personality Inventory
Minnesota Multiphasic Personality Inventory
Myer-Briggs Type Indicator
Personality Research Form
Rorschach Inkblot Technique
Sixteen Personality Factor Questionnaire
State-Trait Anxiety Inventory

Tennessee Self-Concept Scale
Thematic Apperception Test

SENSORY-MOTOR

Bender-Gestalt Test
Fine Dexterity Test
Peabody Developmental Motor Scales

VOCATIONAL

Interest

Jackson Vocational Interest Survey
Occupational Interest Inventories

Strong Interest Inventory
Vocational Preference Inventory

Aptitude and Skills

Minnesota Clerical Tests
NOCTI Student Occupational Competency
  Tests
The Short Employment Tests
Wonderlic Personnel Test

A P P E N D I X   B

ETHICAL PRINCIPLES OF PSYCHOLOGISTS AND CODE OF CONDUCT*

INTRODUCTION

The American Psychological Association's (APA's) Ethical Principles of Psychologists and Code of Conduct (hereinafter referred to as the Ethics Code) consists of an Introduction, a Preamble, six General Principles (A–F), and specific Ethical Standards. The Introduction discusses the intent, organization, procedural considerations, and scope of application of the Ethics Code. The Preamble and General Principles are *aspirational* goals to guide psychologists toward the highest ideals of psychology. Although the Preamble and General Principles are not themselves enforceable rules, they should be considered by psychologists in arriving at an ethical course of action and may be considered by ethics bodies

*These principles were adopted by the American Psychological Association's Council of Representatives during its meeting, August 13 and 16, 1992, and are effective beginning December 1, 1992. Reprinted with the permission of the American Psychological Association.

in interpreting the Ethical Standards. The Ethical Standards set forth *enforceable* rules for conduct as psychologists. Most of the Ethical Standards are written broadly, in order to apply to psychologists in varied roles, although the application of an Ethical Standard may vary depending on the context. The Ethical Standards are not exhaustive. The fact that a given conduct is not specifically addressed by the Ethics Code does not mean that it is necessarily either ethical or unethical.

Membership in the APA commits members to adhere to the APA Ethics Code and to the rules and procedures used to implement it. Psychologists and students, whether or not they are APA members, should be aware that the Ethics Code may be applied to them by state psychology boards, courts, or other public bodies.

This Ethics Code applies only to psychologists' work-related activities, that is, activities that are part of the psychologists' scientific and professional functions or that are psychological in nature. It includes the clinical or counseling practice of psychology, research, teaching, supervision of trainees, development of assessment instruments, conducting assessments, educational counseling, organizational consulting, social intervention, administration, and other activities as well. These work-related activities can be distinguished from the purely private conduct of a psychologist, which ordinarily is not within the purview of the Ethics Code.

The Ethics Code is intended to provide standards of professional conduct that can be applied by the APA and by other bodies that choose to adopt them. Whether or not a psychologist has violated the Ethics Code does not by itself determine whether he or she is legally liable in a court action, whether a contract is enforceable, or whether other legal consequences occur. These results are based on legal rather than ethical rules. However, compliance with or violation of the Ethics Code may be admissible as evidence in some legal proceedings, depending on the circumstances.

In the process of making decisions regarding their professional behavior, psychologists must consider this Ethics Code, in addition to applicable laws and psychology board regulations. If the Ethics Code establishes a higher standard of conduct than is required by law, psychologists must meet the higher ethical standard. If the Ethics Code standard appears to conflict with the requirements of law, then psychologists make known their commitment to the Ethics Code and take steps to resolve the conflict in a responsible matter. If neither law nor the Ethics Code resolves an issue, psychologists should consider other professional materials[1] and the dictates of their own conscience, as well as seek consultation with others within the field when this is practical.

The procedures for filing, investigating,

and resolving complaints of unethical conduct are described in the current Rules and Procedures of the APA Ethics Committee. The actions that APA may take for violations of the Ethics Code include actions such as reprimand, censure, termination of APA membership, and referral of the matter to other bodies. Complainants who seek remedies such as monetary damages in alleging ethical violations by a psychologist must resort to private negotiation, administrative bodies, or the courts. Actions that violate the Ethics Code may lead to the imposition of sanctions on a psychologist by bodies other than APA, including state psychological associations, other professional groups, psychology boards, other state or federal agencies, and payors for health services. In addition to actions for violation of the Ethics Code, the APA Bylaws provide that APA may take action against a member after his or her conviction of a felony, expulsion or suspension from an affiliated state psychological association, or suspension or loss of licensure.

PREAMBLE

Psychologists work to develop a valid and reliable body of scientific knowledge based on research. They may apply that knowledge to human behavior in a variety of contexts. In doing so, they perform many roles, such as researcher, educator, diagnostician, therapist, supervisor, consultant, administrator, social interventionist, and expert witness. Their goal is to broaden knowledge of behavior and, where appropriate, to apply it pragmatically to improve the condition of both the individ-

---

[1]Professional materials that are most helpful in this regard are guidelines and standards that have been adopted or endorsed by professional psychological organizations. Such guidelines and standards, whether adopted by the American Psychological Association (APA) or its Divisions, are not enforceable as such by this Ethics Code, but are of educative value to psychologists, courts, and professional bodies. Such materials include, but are not limited to, the APA's *General Guidelines for Providers of Psychological Services* (1987), *Specialty Guidelines for the Delivery of Services by Clinical Psychologists, Counseling Psychologists, Industrial/ Organizational Psychologists, and School Psycholo-*

gists (1981), *Guidelines for Computer Based Tests and Interpretations* (1987), *Standards for Educational and Psychological Testing* (1985), *Ethical Principles in the Conduct of Research With Human Participants* (1982), *Guidelines for Ethical Conduct in the Care and Use of Animals* (1986), *Guidelines for Providers of Psychological Services to Ethnic, Linguistic, and Culturally Diverse Populations* (1990), and *Publication Manual of the American Psychological Association* (3rd ed., 1983). Materials not adopted by APA as a whole include the APA Division 41 (Forensic Psychology)/American Psychology–Law Society's *Specialty Guidelines for Forensic Psychologists* (1991).

ual and society. Psychologists respect the central importance of freedom of inquiry and expression in research, teaching, and publication. They also strive to help the public in developing informed judgments and choices concerning human behavior. This Ethics Code provides a common set of values upon which psychologists build their professional and scientific work.

This Code is intended to provide both the general principles and the decision rules to cover most situations encountered by psychologists. It has as its primary goal the welfare and protection of the individuals and groups with whom psychologists work. It is the individual responsibility of each psychologist to aspire to the highest possible standards of conduct. Psychologists respect and protect human and civil rights, and do not knowingly participate in or condone unfair discriminatory practices.

The development of a dynamic set of ethical standards for a psychologist's work-related conduct requires a personal commitment to a lifelong effort to act ethically; to encourage ethical behavior by students, supervisees, employees, and colleagues, as appropriate; and to consult with others, as needed, concerning ethical problems. Each psychologist supplements, but does not violate, the Ethics Code's values and rules on the basis of guidance drawn from personal values, culture, and experience.

General Principles

PRINCIPLE A: COMPETENCE

Psychologists strive to maintain high standards of competence in their work. They recognize the boundaries of their particular competencies and the limitations of their expertise. They provide only those services and use only those techniques for which they are qualified by education, training, or experience. Psychologists are cognizant of the fact that the competencies required in serving, teaching, and/or studying groups of people vary with the distinctive characteristics of those groups. In those areas in which recognized professional standards do not yet exist, psychologists exercise careful judgment and take appropriate precautions to protect the welfare of those with whom they work. They

maintain knowledge of relevant scientific and professional information related to the services they render, and they recognize the need for ongoing education. Psychologists make appropriate use of scientific, professional, technical, and administrative resources.

PRINCIPLE B: INTEGRITY

Psychologists seek to promote integrity in the science, teaching, and practice of psychology. In these activities psychologists are honest, fair, and respectful of others. In describing or reporting their qualifications, services, products, fees, research, or teaching, they do not make statements that are false, misleading, or deceptive. Psychologists strive to be aware of their own belief systems, values, needs, and limitations and the effect of these on their work. To the extent feasible, they attempt to clarify for relevant parties the roles they are performing and to function appropriately in accordance with those roles. Psychologists avoid improper and potentially harmful dual relationships.

PRINCIPLE C: PROFESSIONAL AND SCIENTIFIC RESPONSIBILITY

Psychologists uphold professional standards of conduct, clarify their professional roles and obligations, accept appropriate responsibility for their behavior, and adapt their methods to the needs of different populations. Psychologists consult with, refer to, or cooperate with other professionals and institutions to the extent needed to serve the best interests of their patients, clients, or other recipients of their services. Psychologists' moral standards and conduct are personal matters to the same degree as is true for any other person, except as psychologists' conduct may compromise their professional responsibilities or reduce the public's trust in psychology and psychologists. Psychologists are concerned about the ethical compliance of their colleagues' scientific and professional conduct. When appropriate, they consult with colleagues in order to prevent or avoid unethical conduct.

PRINCIPLE D: RESPECT FOR PEOPLE'S RIGHTS AND DIGNITY

Psychologists accord appropriate respect to the fundamental rights, dignity, and worth of all people. They respect the rights of individuals to privacy, confidentiality, self-determination, and autonomy, mindful that legal and other obligations may lead to inconsistency and conflict with the exercise of these rights. Psychologists are aware of cultural, individual, and role differences, including those due to age, gender, race, ethnicity, national origin, religion, sexual orientation, disability, language, and socioeconomic status. Psychologists try to eliminate the effect on their work of biases based on those factors, and they do not knowingly participate in or condone unfair discriminatory practices.

PRINCIPLE E: CONCERN FOR OTHERS' WELFARE

Psychologists seek to contribute to the welfare of those with whom they interact professionally. In their professional actions, psychologists weigh the welfare and rights of their patients or clients, students, supervisees, human research participants, and other affected persons, and the welfare of animal subjects of research. When conflicts occur among psychologists' obligations or concerns, they attempt to resolve these conflicts and to perform their roles in a responsible fashion that avoids or minimizes harm. Psychologists are sensitive to real and ascribed differences in power between themselves and others, and they do not exploit or mislead other people during or after professional relationships.

PRINCIPLE F: SOCIAL RESPONSIBILITY

Psychologists are aware of their professional and scientific responsibilities to the community and the society in which they work and live. They apply and make public their knowledge of psychology in order to contribute to human welfare. Psychologists are concerned about and work to mitigate the causes of human suffering. When undertaking research, they strive to advance human welfare and the science of psychology. Psychologists try to avoid misuse of their work. Psychologists comply with the law and encourage the development of law and social policy that serve the interests of their patients and clients and the public. They are encouraged to contribute a portion of their professional time for little or no personal advantage.

ETHICAL STANDARDS

1. GENERAL STANDARDS

These General Standards are potentially applicable to the professional and scientific activities of all psychologists.

1.01 Applicability of the Ethics Code
The activity of a psychologist subject to the Ethics Code may be reviewed under these Ethical Standards only if the activity is part of his or her work-related functions or the activity is psychological in nature. Personal activities having no connection to or effect on psychological roles are not subject to the Ethics Code.

1.02 Relationship of Ethics and Law
If psychologists' ethical responsibilities conflict with law, psychologists make known their commitment to the Ethics Code and take steps to resolve the conflict in a responsible manner.

1.03 Professional and Scientific Relationship
Psychologists provide diagnostic, therapeutic, teaching, research, supervisory, consultative, or other psychological services only in the context of a defined professional or scientific relationship or role. (See also Standards 2.01, Evaluation, Diagnosis, and Interventions in Professional Context, and 7.02, Forensic Assessments.)

1.04 Boundaries of Competence
(a) Psychologists provide services, teach, and conduct research only within the boundaries of their competence, based on their education, training, supervised experience, or appropriate professional experience.

(b) Psychologists provide services, teach, or conduct research in new areas or involving new techniques only after first undertaking appropriate study, training, supervision, and/or consultation from persons who are competent in those areas or techniques.

(c) In those emerging areas in which generally recognized standards for preparatory training do not yet exist, psychologists nevertheless take reasonable steps to ensure the competence of their work and to protect patients, clients, students, research participants, and others from harm.

1.05 Maintaining Expertise
Psychologists who engage in assessment, therapy, teaching, research, organizational

consulting, or other professional activities maintain a reasonable level of awareness of current scientific and professional information in their fields of activity, and undertake ongoing efforts to maintain competence in the skills they use.

1.06 Basis for Scientific and Professional Judgments

Psychologists rely on scientifically and professionally derived knowledge when making scientific or professional judgments or when engaging in scholarly or professional endeavors.

1.07 Describing the Nature and Results of Psychological Services

(a) When psychologists provide assessment, evaluation, treatment, counseling, supervision, teaching, consultation, research, or other psychological services to an individual, a group, or an organization, they provide, using language that is reasonably understandable to the recipient of those services, appropriate information beforehand about the nature of such services and appropriate information later about results and conclusions. (See also Standard 2.09, Explaining Assessment Results.)

(b) If psychologists will be precluded by law or by organizational roles from providing such information to particular individuals or groups, they so inform those individuals or groups at the outset of the service.

1.08 Human Differences

Where differences of age, gender, race, ethnicity, national origin, religion, sexual orientation, disability, language, or socioeconomic status significantly affect psychologists' work concerning particular individuals or groups, psychologists obtain the training, experience, consultation, or supervision necessary to ensure the competence of their services, or they make appropriate referrals.

1.09 Respecting Others

In their work-related activities, psychologists respect the rights of others to hold values, attitudes, and opinions that differ from their own.

1.10 Nondiscrimination

In their work-related activities, psychologists do not engage in unfair discrimination based on age, gender, race, ethnicity, national origin, religion, sexual orientation, disability,

socioeconomic status, or any basis proscribed by law.

1.11 Sexual Harassment

(a) Psychologists do not engage in sexual harassment. Sexual harassment is sexual solicitation, physical advances, or verbal or nonverbal conduct that is sexual in nature, that occurs in connection with the psychologist's activities or roles as a psychologist, and that either: (1) is unwelcome, is offensive, or creates a hostile workplace environment, and the psychologist knows or is told this; or (2) is sufficiently severe or intense to be abusive to a reasonable person in the context. Sexual harassment can consist of a single intense or severe act or of multiple persistent or pervasive acts.

(b) Psychologists accord sexual-harassment complainants and respondents dignity and respect. Psychologists do not participate in denying a person academic admittance or advancement, employment, tenure, or promotion, based solely upon their having made, or their being the subject of, sexual-harassment charges. This does not preclude taking action based upon the outcome of such proceedings or consideration of other appropriate information.

1.12 Other Harassment

Psychologists do not knowingly engage in behavior that is harassing or demeaning to persons with whom they interact in their work based on factors such as those persons' age, gender, race, ethnicity, national origin, religion, sexual orientation, disability, language, or socioeconomic status.

1.13 Personal Problems and Conflicts

(a) Psychologists recognize that their personal problems and conflicts may interfere with their effectiveness. Accordingly, they refrain from undertaking an activity when they know or should know that their personal problems are likely to lead to harm to a patient, client, colleague, student, research participant, or other person to whom they may owe a professional or scientific obligation.

(b) In addition, psychologists have an obligation to be alert to signs of, and to obtain assistance for, their personal problems at an early stage, in order to prevent significantly impaired performance.

(c) When psychologists become aware of personal problems that may interfere with their performing work-related duties adequately, they take appropriate measures, such as obtaining professional consultation or assistance, and determine whether they should limit, suspend, or terminate their work-related duties.

1.14 Avoiding Harm

Psychologists take reasonable steps to avoid harming their patients or clients, research participants, students, and others with whom they work, and to minimize harm where it is foreseeable and unavoidable.

1.15 Misuse of Psychologists' Influence

Because psychologists' scientific and professional judgments and actions may affect the lives of others, they are alert to and guard against personal, financial, social, organizational, or political factors that might lead to misuse of their influence.

1.16 Misuse of Psychologists' Work

(a) Psychologists do not participate in activities in which it appears likely that their skills or data will be misused by others, unless corrective mechanisms are available. (See also Standard 7.04, Truthfulness and Candor).

(b) If psychologists learn of misuse or misrepresentation of their work, they take reasonable steps to correct or minimize the misuse or misrepresentation.

1.17 Multiple Relationships

(a) In many communities and situations, it may not be feasible or reasonable for psychologists to avoid social or other nonprofessional contacts with persons such as patients, clients, students, supervisees, or research participants. Psychologists must always be sensitive to the potential harmful effects of other contacts on their work and on those persons with whom they deal. A psychologist refrains from entering into or promising another personal, scientific, professional, financial, or other relationship with such persons if it appears likely that such a relationship reasonably might impair the psychologist's objectivity or otherwise interfere with the psychologist's effectively performing his or her functions as a psychologist, or might harm or exploit the other party.

(b) Likewise, whenever feasible, a psychologist refrains from taking on professional or scientific obligations when preexisting relationships would create a risk of such harm.

(c) If a psychologist finds that, due to unforeseen factors, a potentially harmful multiple relationship has arisen, the psychologist

attempts to resolve it with due regard for the best interests of the affected person and maximal compliance with the Ethics Code.

1.18 Barter (with Patients or Clients)

Psychologists ordinarily refrain from accepting goods, services, or other nonmonetary remuneration from patients or clients in return for psychological services because such arrangements create inherent potential for conflicts, exploitation, and distortion of the professional relationship. A psychologist may participate in bartering *only* if (1) it is not clinically contraindicated, *and* (2) the relationship is not exploitative. (See also Standards 1.17, Multiple Relationships, and 1.25, Fees and Financial Arrangements.)

1.19 Exploitative Relationships

(a) Psychologists do not exploit persons over whom they have supervisory, evaluative, or other authority such as students, supervisees, employees, research participants, and clients or patients. (See also Standards 4.05–4.07 regarding sexual involvement with clients or patients.)

(b) Psychologists do not engage in sexual relationships with students or supervisees in training over whom the psychologist has evaluative or direct authority, because such relationships are so likely to impair judgment or be exploitative.

1.20 Consultations and Referrals

(a) Psychologists arrange for appropriate consultations and referrals based principally on the best interests of their patients or clients, with appropriate consent, and subject to other relevant considerations, including applicable law and contractual obligations. (See also Standards 5.01, Discussing the Limits of Confidentiality, and 5.06, Consultations.)

(b) When indicated and professionally appropriate, psychologists cooperate with other professionals in order to serve their patients or clients effectively and appropriately.

(c) Psychologists' referral practices are consistent with law.

1.21 Third-Party Requests for Services

(a) When a psychologist agrees to provide services to a person or entity at the request of a third party, the psychologist clarifies to the extent feasible, at the outset of the service, the nature of the relationship with each party. This clarification includes the role of the psychologist (such as therapist, organizational consultant, diagnostician, or expert witness), the probable uses of the services provided or the information obtained, and the fact that there may be limits to confidentiality.

(b) If there is a foreseeable risk of the psychologist's being called upon to perform conflicting roles because of the involvement of a third party, the psychologist clarifies the nature and direction of his or her responsibilities, keeps all parties appropriately informed as matters develop, and resolves the situation in accordance with this Ethics Code.

1.22 Delegation to and Supervision of Subordinates

(a) Psychologists delegate to their employees, supervisees, and research assistants only those responsibilities that such persons can reasonably be expected to perform competently, on the basis of their education, training, or experience, either independently or with the level of supervision being provided.

(b) Psychologists provide proper training and supervision to their employees or supervisees and take reasonable steps to see that such persons perform services responsibly, competently, and ethically.

(c) If institutional policies, procedures, or practices prevent fulfillment of this obligation, psychologists attempt to modify their role or to correct the situation to the extent feasible.

1.23 Documentation of Professional and Scientific Work

(a) Psychologists appropriately document their professional and scientific work in order to facilitate provision of services later by them or by other professionals, to ensure accountability, and to meet other requirements of institutions or the law.

(b) When psychologists have reason to believe that records of their professional services will be used in legal proceedings involving recipients of or participants in their work, they have a responsibility to create and maintain documentation in the kind of detail and quality that would be consistent with reasonable scrutiny in an adjudicative forum. (See also Standard 7.01, Professionalism, under Forensic Activities.)

1.24 Records and Data

Psychologists create, maintain, disseminate, store, retain, and dispose of records and data relating to their research, practice, and other work in accordance with law and in a manner that permits compliance with the requirements of this Ethics Code. (See also Standard 5.04, Maintenance of Records.)

1.25 Fees and Financial Arrangements

(a) As early as is feasible in a professional or scientific relationship, the psychologist and the patient, client, or other appropriate recipient of psychological services reach an agreement specifying the compensation and the billing arrangements.

(b) Psychologists do not exploit recipients of services or payors with respect to fees.

(c) Psychologists' fee practices are consistent with law.

(d) Psychologists do not misrepresent their fees.

(e) If limitations to services can be anticipated because of limitations in financing, this is discussed with the patient, client, or other appropriate recipient of services as early as is feasible. (See also Standard 4.08, Interruption of Services.)

(f) If the patient, client, or other recipient of services does not pay for services as agreed, and if the psychologist wishes to use collection agencies or legal measures to collect the fees, the psychologist first informs the person that such measures will be taken and provides that person an opportunity to make prompt payment. (See also Standard 5.11, Withholding Records for Nonpayment.)

1.26 Accuracy in Reports to Payors and Funding Sources

In their reports to payors for services or sources of research funding, psychologists accurately state the nature of the research or service provided, the fees or charges, and where applicable, the identity of the provider, the findings, and the diagnosis. (See also Standard 5.05, Disclosures.)

1.27 Referrals and Fees

When a psychologist pays, receives payment from, or divides fees with another professional other than in an employer-employee relationship, the payment to each is based on the services (clinical, consultative, administrative, or other) provided and is not based on the referral itself.

2. EVALUATION, ASSESSMENT, OR INTERVENTION

2.01 Evaluation, Diagnosis, and Interventions in Professional Context

(a) Psychologists perform evaluations, diagnostic services, or interventions only within the context of a defined professional relationship. (See also Standard 1.03, Professional and Scientific Relationship.)

(b) Psychologists' assessments, recommendations, reports, and psychological diagnostic or evaluative statements are based on information and techniques (including personal interviews of the individual when appropriate) sufficient to provide appropriate substantiation for their findings. (See also Standard 7.02, Forensic Assessments.)

2.02 Competence and Appropriate Use of Assessments and Interventions

(a) Psychologists who develop, administer, score, interpret, or use psychological assessment techniques, interviews, tests, or instruments do so in a manner and for purposes that are appropriate in light of the research on or evidence of the usefulness and proper application of the techniques.

(b) Psychologists refrain from misuse of assessment techniques, interventions, results, and interpretations and take reasonable steps to prevent others from misusing the information these techniques provide. This includes refraining from releasing raw test results or raw data to persons, other than to patients or clients as appropriate, who are not qualified to use such information. (See also Standards 1.02, Relationship of Ethics and Law, and 1.04, Boundaries of Competence.)

2.03 Test Construction

Psychologists who develop and conduct research with tests and other assessment techniques use scientific procedures and current professional knowledge for test design, standardization, validation, reduction or elimination of bias, and recommendations for use.

2.04 Use of Assessment in General and with Special Populations

(a) Psychologists who perform interventions or administer, score, interpret, or use assessment techniques are familiar with the reliability, validation, and related standardization or outcome studies of, and proper applications and uses of, the techniques they use.

(b) Psychologists recognize limits to the certainty with which diagnoses, judgments, or predictions can be made about individuals.

(c) Psychologists attempt to identify situations in which particular interventions or assessment techniques or norms may not be applicable or may require adjustment in administration or interpretation because of factors such as individuals' gender, age, race, ethnicity, national origin, religion, sexual orientation, disability, language, or socioeconomic status.

2.05 Interpreting Assessment Results

When interpreting assessment results, including automated interpretations, psychologists take into account the various test factors and characteristics of the person being assessed that might affect psychologists' judgments or reduce the accuracy of their interpretations. They indicate any significant reservations they have about the accuracy or limitations of their interpretations.

2.06 Unqualified Persons

Psychologists do not promote the use of psychological assessment techniques by unqualified persons. (See also Standard 1.22, Delegation to and Supervision of Subordinates.)

2.07 Obsolete Tests and Outdated Test Results

(a) Psychologists do not base their assessment or intervention decisions or recommendations on data or test results that are outdated for the current purpose.

(b) Similarly, psychologists do not base such decisions or recommendations on tests and measures that are obsolete and not useful for the current purpose.

2.08 Test Scoring and Interpretation Services

(a) Psychologists who offer assessment or scoring procedures to other professionals accurately describe the purpose, norms, validity, reliability, and applications of the procedures and any special qualifications applicable to their use.

(b) Psychologists select scoring and interpretation services (including automated services) on the basis of evidence of the validity of the program and procedures as well as on other appropriate considerations.

(c) Psychologists retain appropriate responsibility for the appropriate application, interpretation, and use of assessment instruments, whether they score and interpret such tests themselves or use automated or other services.

2.09 Explaining Assessment Results

Unless the nature of the relationship is clearly explained to the person being assessed in advance and precludes provision of an explanation of results (such as in some organizational consulting, preemployment or security screenings, and forensic evaluations), psychologists ensure that an explanation of the results is provided using language that is reasonably understandable to the person assessed or to another legally authorized person on behalf of the client. Regardless of whether the scoring and interpretation are done by the psychologist, by assistants, or by automated or other outside services, psychologists take reasonable steps to ensure that appropriate explanations of results are given.

2.10 Maintaining Test Security

Psychologists make reasonable efforts to maintain the integrity and security of tests and other assessment techniques consistent with law, contractual obligations, and in a manner that permits compliance with the requirements of this Ethics Code. (See also Standard 1.02, Relationship of Ethics and Law.)

3. ADVERTISING AND OTHER PUBLIC STATEMENTS

3.01 Definition of Public Statements

Psychologists comply with this Ethics Code in public statements relating to their professional services, products, or publications or to the field of psychology. Public statements include but are not limited to paid or unpaid advertising, brochures, printed matter, directory listings, personal resumes or curricula vitae, interviews or comments for use in media, statements in legal proceedings, lectures and public oral presentations, and published materials.

3.02 Statements by Others

(a) Psychologists who engage others to create or place public statements that promote their professional practice, products, or activities retain professional responsibility for such statements.

(b) In addition, psychologists make reasonable efforts to prevent others whom they do not control (such as employers, publishers, sponsors, organizational clients, and representatives of the print or broadcast media) from making deceptive statements concerning psychologists' practice or professional or scientific activities.

(c) If psychologists learn of deceptive statements about their work made by others, psychologists make reasonable efforts to correct such statements.

(d) Psychologists do not compensate employees of press, radio, television, or other communication media in return for publicity in a news item.

(e) A paid advertisement relating to the psychologist's activities must be identified as such, unless it is already apparent from the context.

3.03 Avoidance of False or Deceptive Statements

(a) Psychologists do not make public statements that are false, deceptive, misleading, or fraudulent, either because of what they state, convey, or suggest or because of what they omit, concerning their research, practice, or other work activities or those of persons or organizations with which they are affiliated. As examples (and not in limitation) of this standard, psychologists do not make false or deceptive statements concerning (1) their training, experience, or competence; (2) their academic degrees; (3) their credentials; (4) their institutional or association affiliations; (5) their services; (6) the scientific or clinical basis for, or results or degree of success of, their services; (7) their fees; or (8) their publications or research findings. (See also Standards 6.15, Deception in Research, and 6.18, Providing Participants With Information About the Study.)

(b) Psychologists claim as credentials for their psychological work, only degrees that (1) were earned from a regionally accredited educational institution or (2) were the basis for psychology licensure by the state in which they practice.

3.04 Media Presentations

When psychologists provide advice or comment by means of public lectures, demonstrations, radio or television programs, prerecorded tapes, printed articles, mailed material, or other media, they take reasonable precautions to ensure that (1) the statements are based on appropriate psychological literature and practice, (2) the statements are otherwise consistent with this Ethics Code, and (3) the recipients of the information are not encouraged to infer that a relationship has been established with them personally.

3.05 Testimonials

Psychologists do not solicit testimonials from current psychotherapy clients or patients or other persons who because of their particular circumstances are vulnerable to undue influence.

3.06 In-Person Solicitation

Psychologists do not engage, directly or through agents, in uninvited in-person solicitation of business from actual or potential psychotherapy patients or clients or other persons who because of their particular circumstances are vulnerable to undue influence. However, this does not preclude attempting to implement appropriate collateral contacts with significant others for the purpose of benefiting an already engaged therapy patient.

4. THERAPY

4.01 Structuring the Relationship

(a) Psychologists discuss with clients or patients as early as is feasible in the therapeutic relationship appropriate issues, such as the nature and anticipated course of therapy, fees, and confidentiality. (See also Standards 1.25, Fees and Financial Arrangements, and 5.01, Discussing the Limits of Confidentiality.)

(b) When the psychologist's work with clients or patients will be supervised, the above discussion includes that fact, and the name of the supervisor, when the supervisor has legal responsibility for the case.

(c) When the therapist is a student intern, the client or patient is informed of that fact.

(d) Psychologists make reasonable efforts to answer patients' questions and to avoid apparent misunderstandings about therapy. Whenever possible, psychologists provide oral and/or written information, using language that is reasonably understandable to the patient or client.

4.02 Informed Consent to Therapy

(a) Psychologists obtain appropriate informed consent to therapy or related procedures, using language that is reasonably understandable to participants. The content of informed consent will vary depending on many circumstances; however, informed consent generally implies that the person (1) has the capacity to consent, (2) has been informed of significant information concerning the procedure, (3) has freely and without undue influence expressed consent, and (4) consent has been appropriately documented.

(b) When persons are legally incapable of giving informed consent, psychologists obtain informed permission from a legally authorized person, if such substitute consent is permitted by law.

(c) In addition, psychologists (1) inform those persons who are legally incapable of giving informed consent about the proposed interventions in a manner commensurate with the persons' psychological capacities, (2) seek their assent to those interventions, and (3) consider such persons' preferences and best interests.

4.03 Couple and Family Relationships

(a) When a psychologist agrees to provide services to several persons who have a relationship (such as husband and wife or parents and children), the psychologist attempts to clarify at the outset (1) which of the individuals are patients or clients and (2) the relationship the psychologist will have with each person. This clarification includes the role of the psychologist and the probable uses of the services provided or the information obtained. (See also Standard 5.01, Discussing the Limits of Confidentiality.)

(b) As soon as it becomes apparent that the psychologist may be called on to perform potentially conflicting roles (such as marital counselor to husband and wife, and then witness for one party in a divorce proceeding), the psychologist attempts to clarify and adjust, or withdraw from, roles appropriately. (See also Standard 7.03, Clarification of Role, under Forensic Activities.)

4.04 Providing Mental Health Services to Those Served by Others

In deciding whether to offer or provide services to those already receiving mental health services elsewhere, psychologists carefully consider the treatment issues and the potential patient's or client's welfare. The psychologist discusses these issues with the patient or client, or another legally authorized person on behalf of the client, in order to minimize the risk of confusion and conflict, consults with the other service providers when appropriate, and proceeds with caution and sensitivity to the therapeutic issues.

4.05 Sexual Intimacies with Current Patients or Clients

Psychologists do not engage in sexual intimacies with current patients or clients.

4.06 Therapy with Former Sexual Partners

Psychologists do not accept as therapy patients or clients persons with whom they have engaged in sexual intimacies.

4.07 Sexual Intimacies with Former Therapy Patients

(a) Psychologists do not engage in sexual intimacies with a former therapy patient or client for at least two years after cessation or termination of professional services.

(b) Because sexual intimacies with a former therapy patient or client are so frequently harmful to the patient or client, and because such intimacies undermine public confidence in the psychology profession and thereby deter the public's use of needed services, psychologists do not engage in sexual intimacies with former therapy patients and clients even after a two-year interval except in the most unusual circumstances. The psychologist who engages in such activity after the two years following cessation or termination of treatment bears the burden of demonstrating that there has been no exploitation, in light of all relevant factors, including (1) the amount of time that has passed since therapy terminated, (2) the nature and duration of the therapy, (3) the circumstances of termination, (4) the patient's or client's personal history, (5) the patient's or client's current mental status, (6) the likelihood of adverse impact on the patient or client and others, and (7) any statements or actions made by the therapist during the course of therapy suggesting or inviting the possibility of a posttermination sexual or romantic relationship with the patient or client. (See also Standard 1.17, Multiple Relationships.)

4.08 Interruption of Services

(a) Psychologists make reasonable efforts to plan for facilitating care in the event that psychological services are interrupted by factors such as the psychologist's illness, death, unavailability, or relocation or by the client's relocation or financial limitations. (See also Standard 5.09, Preserving Records and Data.)

(b) When entering into employment or contractual relationships, psychologists provide for orderly and appropriate resolution of responsibility for patient or client care in the event that the employment or contractual relationship ends, with paramount consideration given to the welfare of the patient or client.

4.09 Terminating the Professional Relationship

(a) Psychologists do not abandon patients or clients. (See also Standard 1.25e, under Fees and Financial Arrangements.)

(b) Psychologists terminate a professional relationship when it becomes reasonably clear that the patient or client no longer needs the service, is not benefiting, or is being harmed by continued service.

(c) Prior to termination for whatever reason, except where precluded by the patient's or client's conduct, the psychologist discusses the patient's or client's views and needs, provides appropriate pretermination counseling, suggests alternative service providers as appropriate, and takes other reasonable steps to facilitate transfer of responsibility to another provider if the patient or client needs one immediately.

5. PRIVACY AND CONFIDENTIALITY

These Standards are potentially applicable to the professional and scientific activities of all psychologists.

5.01 Discussing the Limits of Confidentiality

(a) Psychologists discuss with persons and organizations with whom they establish a scientific or professional relationship (including, to the extent feasible, minors and their legal representatives) (1) the relevant limitations on confidentiality, including limitations where applicable in group, marital, and family therapy or in organizational consulting, and (2) the foreseeable uses of the information generated through their services.

(b) Unless it is not feasible or is contraindicated, the discussion of confidentiality occurs at the outset of the relationship and thereafter as new circumstances may warrant.

(c) Permission for electronic recording of interviews is secured from clients and patients.

5.02 Maintaining Confidentiality

Psychologists have a primary obligation and take reasonable precautions to respect the confidentiality rights of those with whom they work or consult, recognizing that confidentiality may be established by law, institutional rules, or professional or scientific relationships. (See also Standard 6.26, Professional Reviewers.)

5.03 Minimizing Intrusions on Privacy

(a) In order to minimize intrusions on privacy, psychologists include in written and oral reports, consultations, and the like, only information germane to the purpose for which the communication is made.

(b) Psychologists discuss confidential information obtained in clinical or consulting relationships, or evaluative data concerning patients, individual or organizational clients, students, research participants, supervisees, and employees, only for appropriate scientific or professional purposes and only with persons clearly concerned with such matters.

5.04 Maintenance of Records

Psychologists maintain appropriate confidentiality in creating, storing, accessing, transferring, and disposing of records under their control, whether these are written, automated, or in any other medium. Psychologists maintain and dispose of records in accordance with law and in a manner that permits compliance with the requirements of this Ethics Code.

5.05 Disclosures

(a) Psychologists disclose confidential information without the consent of the individual only as mandated by law, or where permitted by law for a valid purpose, such as (1) to provide needed professional services to the patient or the individual or organizational client, (2) to obtain appropriate professional consultations, (3) to protect the patient or client or others from harm, or (4) to obtain payment for services, in which instance disclosure is limited to the minimum that is necessary to achieve the purpose.

(b) Psychologists also may disclose confidential information with the appropriate consent of the patient or the individual or organizational client (or of another legally authorized person on behalf of the patient or client), unless prohibited by law.

5.06 Consultations

When consulting with colleagues, (1) psychologists do not share confidential information that reasonably could lead to the identification of a patient, client, research participant, or other person or organization with whom they have a confidential relationship unless they have obtained the prior consent of the person or organization or the disclosure cannot be avoided, and (2) they share information only to the extent necessary to achieve the purposes of the consultation. (See also Standard 5.02, Maintaining Confidentiality.)

5.07 Confidential Information in Databases

(a) If confidential information concerning recipients of psychological services is to be entered into databases or systems of records

available to persons whose access has not been consented to by the recipient, then psychologists use coding or other techniques to avoid the inclusion of personal identifiers.

(b) If a research protocol approved by an institutional review board or similar body requires the inclusion of personal identifiers, such identifiers are deleted before the information is made accessible to persons other than those of whom the subject was advised.

(c) If such deletion is not feasible, then before psychologists transfer such data to others or review such data collected by others, they take reasonable steps to determine that appropriate consent of personally identifiable individuals has been obtained.

5.08 Use of Confidential Information for Didactic or Other Purposes

(a) Psychologists do not disclose in their writings, lectures, or other public media, confidential, personally identifiable information concerning their patients, individual or organizational clients, students, research participants, or other recipients of their services that they obtained during the course of their work, unless the person or organization has consented in writing or unless there is other ethical or legal authorization for doing so.

(b) Ordinarily, in such scientific and professional presentations, psychologists disguise confidential information concerning such persons or organizations so that they are not individually identifiable to others and so that discussions do not cause harm to subjects who might identify themselves.

5.09 Preserving Records and Data

A psychologist makes plans in advance so that confidentiality of records and data is protected in the event of the psychologist's death, incapacity, or withdrawal from the position or practice.

5.10 Ownership of Records and Data

Recognizing that ownership of records and data is governed by legal principles, psychologists take reasonable and lawful steps so that records and data remain available to the extent needed to serve the best interests of patients, individual or organizational clients, research participants, or appropriate others.

5.11 Withholding Records for Nonpayment

Psychologists may not withhold records under their control that are requested and imminently needed for a patient's or client's treatment solely because payment has not been received, except as otherwise provided by law.

6. TEACHING, TRAINING SUPERVISION, RESEARCH, AND PUBLISHING

6.01 Design of Education and Training Programs

Psychologists who are responsible for education and training programs seek to ensure that the programs are competently designed, provide the proper experiences, and meet the requirements for licensure, certification, or other goals for which claims are made by the program.

6.02 Descriptions of Education and Training Programs

(a) Psychologists responsible for education and training programs seek to ensure that there is a current and accurate description of the program content, training goals and objectives, and requirements that must be met for satisfactory completion of the program. This information must be made readily available to all interested parties.

(b) Psychologists seek to ensure that statements concerning their course outlines are accurate and not misleading, particularly regarding the subject matter to be covered, bases for evaluating progress, and the nature of course experiences. (See also Standard 3.03, Avoidance of False or Deceptive Statements.)

(c) To the degree to which they exercise control, psychologists responsible for announcements, catalogs, brochures, or advertisements describing workshops, seminars, or other non-degree-granting educational programs ensure that they accurately describe the audience for which the program is intended, the educational objectives, the presenters, and the fees involved.

6.03 Accuracy and Objectivity in Teaching

(a) When engaged in teaching or training, psychologists present psychological information accurately and with a reasonable degree of objectivity.

(b) When engaged in teaching or training, psychologists recognize the power they hold over students or supervisees and therefore make reasonable efforts to avoid engaging in conduct that is personally demeaning to students or supervisees. (See also Standards

1.09, Respecting Others, and 1.12, Other Harassment.)

6.04 Limitation on Teaching

Psychologists do not teach the use of techniques or procedures that require specialized training, licensure, or expertise, including but not limited to hypnosis, biofeedback, and projective techniques, to individuals who lack the prerequisite training, legal scope of practice, or expertise.

6.05 Assessing Student and Supervisee Performance

(a) In academic and supervisory relationships, psychologists establish an appropriate process for providing feedback to students and supervisees.

(b) Psychologists evaluate students and supervisees on the basis of their actual performance on relevant and established program requirements.

6.06 Planning Research

(a) Psychologists design, conduct, and report research in accordance with recognized standards of scientific competence and ethical research.

(b) Psychologists plan their research so as to minimize the possibility that results will be misleading.

(c) In planning research, psychologists consider its ethical acceptability under the Ethics Code. If an ethical issue is unclear, psychologists seek to resolve the issue through consultation with institutional review boards, animal care and use committees, peer consultations, or other proper mechanisms.

(d) Psychologists take reasonable steps to implement appropriate protections for the rights and welfare of human participants, other persons affected by the research, and the welfare of animal subjects.

6.07 Responsibility

(a) Psychologists conduct research competently and with due concern for the dignity and welfare of the participants.

(b) Psychologists are responsible for the ethical conduct of research conducted by them or by others under their supervision or control.

(c) Researchers and assistants are permitted to perform only those tasks for which they are appropriately trained and prepared.

(d) As part of the process of development and implementation of research projects, psychologists consult those with expertise concerning any special population under investigation or most likely to be affected.

6.08 Compliance with Law and Standards

Psychologists plan and conduct research in a manner consistent with federal and state law and regulations, as well as professional standards governing the conduct of research, and particularly those standards governing research with human participants and animal subjects.

6.09 Institutional Approval

Psychologists obtain from host institutions or organizations appropriate approval prior to conducting research, and they provide accurate information about their research proposals. They conduct the research in accordance with the approved research protocol.

6.10 Research Responsibilities

Prior to conducting research (except research involving only anonymous surveys, naturalistic observations, or similar research), psychologists enter into an agreement with participants that clarifies the nature of the research and the responsibilities of each party.

6.11 Informed Consent to Research

(a) Psychologists use language that is reasonably understandable to research participants in obtaining their appropriate informed consent (except as provided in Standard 6.12, Dispensing With Informed Consent). Such informed consent is appropriately documented.

(b) Using language that is reasonably understandable to participants, psychologists inform participants of the nature of the research; they inform participants that they are free to participate or to decline to participate or to withdraw from the research; they explain the foreseeable consequences of declining or withdrawing; they inform participants of significant factors that may be expected to influence their willingness to participate (such as risks, discomfort, adverse effects, or limitations on confidentiality, except as provided in Standard 6.15, Deception in Research); and they explain other aspects about which the prospective participants inquire.

(c) When psychologists conduct research with individuals such as students or subordinates, psychologists take special care to protect the prospective participants from adverse consequences of declining or withdrawing from participation.

(d) When research participation is a course requirement or opportunity for extra credit, the prospective participant is given the choice of equitable alternative activities.

(e) For persons who are legally incapable of giving informed consent, psychologists nevertheless (1) provide an appropriate explanation, (2) obtain the participant's assent, and (3) obtain appropriate permission from a legally authorized person, if such substitute consent is permitted by law.

6.12 Dispensing with Informed Consent

Before determining that planned research (such as research involving only anonymous questionnaires, naturalistic observations, or certain kinds of archival research) does not require the informed consent of research participants, psychologists consider applicable regulations and institutional review board requirements, and they consult with colleagues as appropriate.

6.13 Informed Consent in Research Filming or Recording

Psychologists obtain informed consent from research participants prior to filming or recording them in any form, unless the research involves simply naturalistic observations in public places and it is not anticipated that the recording will be used in a manner that could cause personal identification or harm.

6.14 Offering Inducements for Research Participants

(a) In offering professional services as an inducement to obtain research participants, psychologists make clear the nature of the services, as well as the risks, obligations, and limitations. (See also Standard 1.18, Barter [With Patients or Clients].)

(b) Psychologists do not offer excessive or inappropriate financial or other inducements to obtain research participants, particularly when it might tend to coerce participation.

6.15 Deception in Research

(a) Psychologists do not conduct a study involving deception unless they have determined that the use of deceptive techniques is justified by the study's prospective scientific, educational, or applied value and that equally effective alternative procedures that do not use deception are not feasible.

(b) Psychologists never deceive research participants about significant aspects that would affect their willingness to participate, such as physical risks, discomfort, or unpleasant emotional experiences.

(c) Any other deception that is an integral feature of the design and conduct of an experiment must be explained to participants as early as is feasible, preferably at the conclusion of their participation, but no later than at the conclusion of the research. (See also Standard 6.18, Providing Participants With Information About the Study.)

6.16 Sharing and Utilizing Data

Psychologists inform research participants of their anticipated sharing or further use of personally identifiable research data and of the possibility of unanticipated future uses.

6.17 Minimizing Invasiveness

In conducting research, psychologists interfere with the participants or milieu from which data are collected only in a manner that is warranted by an appropriate research design and that is consistent with psychologists' roles as scientific investigators.

6.18 Providing Participants with Information About the Study

(a) Psychologists provide a prompt opportunity for participants to obtain appropriate information about the nature, results, and conclusions of the research, and psychologists attempt to correct any misconceptions that participants may have.

(b) If scientific or humane values justify delaying or withholding this information, psychologists take reasonable measures to reduce the risk of harm.

6.19 Honoring Commitments

Psychologists take reasonable measures to honor all commitments they have made to research participants.

6.20 Care and Use of Animals in Research

(a) Psychologists who conduct research involving animals treat them humanely.

(b) Psychologists acquire, care for, use, and dispose of animals in compliance with current federal, state, and local laws and regulations, and with professional standards.

(c) Psychologists trained in research methods and experienced in the care of laboratory animals supervise all procedures involving animals and are responsible for ensuring appropriate consideration of their comfort, health, and humane treatment.

(d) Psychologists ensure that all individuals using animals under their supervision have received instruction in research methods and in the care, maintenance, and handling of the species being used, to the extent appropriate to their role.

(e) Responsibilities and activities of individuals assisting in a research project are consistent with their respective competencies.

(f) Psychologists make reasonable efforts to minimize the discomfort, infection, illness, and pain of animal subjects.

(g) A procedure subjecting animals to pain, stress, or privation is used only when an alternative procedure is unavailable and the goal is justified by its prospective scientific, educational, or applied value.

(h) Surgical procedures are performed under appropriate anesthesia; techniques to avoid infection and minimize pain are followed during and after surgery.

(i) When it is appropriate that the animal's life be terminated, it is done rapidly, with an effort to minimize pain, and in accordance with accepted procedures.

6.21 Reporting of Results

(a) Psychologists do not fabricate data or falsify results in their publications.

(b) If psychologists discover significant errors in their published data, they take reasonable steps to correct such errors in a correction, retraction, erratum, or other appropriate publication means.

6.22 Plagiarism

Psychologists do not present substantial portions or elements of another's work or data as their own, even if the other work or data source is cited occasionally.

6.23 Publication Credit

(a) Psychologists take responsibility and credit, including authorship credit, only for work they have actually performed or to which they have contributed.

(b) Principal authorship and other publication credits accurately reflect the relative scientific or professional contributions of the individuals involved, regardless of their relative status. Mere possession of an institutional position, such as Department Chair, does not justify authorship credit. Minor contributions to the research or to the writing for publications are appropriately acknowledged, such as in footnotes or in an introductory statement.

(c) A student is usually listed as principal

author on any multiple-authored article that is substantially based on the student's dissertation or thesis.

6.24 Duplicate Publication of Data

Psychologists do not publish, as original data, data that have been previously published. This does not preclude republishing data when they are accompanied by proper acknowledgment.

6.25 Sharing Data

After research results are published, psychologists do not withhold the data on which their conclusions are based from other competent professionals who seek to verify the substantive claims through reanalysis and who intend to use such data only for that purpose, provided that the confidentiality of the participants can be protected and unless legal rights concerning proprietary data preclude their release.

6.26 Professional Reviewers

Psychologists who review material submitted for publication, grant, or other research proposal review respect the confidentiality of and the proprietary rights in such information of those who submitted it.

7. FORENSIC ACTIVITIES

7.01 Professionalism

Psychologists who perform forensic functions, such as assessments, interviews, consultations, reports, or expert testimony, must comply with all other provisions of this Ethics Code to the extent that they apply to such activities. In addition, psychologists base their forensic work on appropriate knowledge of and competence in the areas underlying such work, including specialized knowledge concerning special populations. (See also Standards 1.06, Basis for Scientific and Professional Judgments; 1.08, Human Differences; 1.15, Misuse of Psychologists' Influence; and 1.23, Documentation of Professional and Scientific Work.)

7.02 Forensic Assessments

(a) Psychologists' forensic assessments, recommendations, and reports are based on information and techniques (including personal interviews of the individual, when appropriate) sufficient to provide appropriate substantiation for their findings. (See also Standards 1.03, Professional and Scientific Relationship;

1.23, Documentation of Professional and Scientific Work; 2.01, Evaluation, Diagnosis, and Interventions in Professional Context; and 2.05, Interpreting Assessment Results.)

(b) Except as noted in (c), below, psychologists provide written or oral forensic reports or testimony of the psychological characteristics of an individual only after they have conducted an examination of the individual adequate to support their statements or conclusions.

(c) When, despite reasonable efforts, such an examination is not feasible, psychologists clarify the impact of their limited information on the reliability and validity of their reports and testimony, and they appropriately limit the nature and extent of their conclusions or recommendations.

7.03 Clarification of Role

In most circumstances, psychologists avoid performing multiple and potentially conflicting roles in forensic matters. When psychologists may be called on to serve in more than one role in a legal proceeding—for example, as consultant or expert for one party or for the court and as a fact witness—they clarify role expectations and the extent of confidentiality in advance to the extent feasible, and thereafter as changes occur, in order to avoid compromising their professional judgment and objectivity and in order to avoid misleading others regarding their role.

7.04 Truthfulness and Candor

(a) In forensic testimony and reports, psychologists testify truthfully, honestly, and candidly and, consistent with applicable legal procedures, describe fairly the bases for their testimony and conclusions.

(b) Whenever necessary to avoid misleading, psychologists acknowledge the limits of their data or conclusions.

7.05 Prior Relationships

A prior professional relationship with a party does not preclude psychologists from testifying as fact witnesses or from testifying to their services to the extent permitted by applicable law. Psychologists appropriately take into account ways in which the prior relationship might affect their professional objectivity or opinions and disclose the potential conflict to the relevant parties.

7.06 Compliance with Law and Rules

In performing forensic roles, psychologists are reasonably familiar with the rules governing their roles. Psychologists are aware of the occasionally competing demands placed upon them by these principles and the requirements of the court system, and attempt to resolve these conflicts by making known their commitment to this Ethics Code and taking steps to resolve the conflict in a responsible manner. (See also Standard 1.02, Relationship of Ethics and Law.)

8. RESOLVING ETHICAL ISSUES

8.01 Familiarity with Ethics Code

Psychologists have an obligation to be familiar with this Ethics Code, other applicable ethics codes, and their application to psychologists' work. Lack of awareness or misunderstanding of an ethical standard is not itself a defense to a charge of unethical conduct.

8.02 Confronting Ethical Issues

When a psychologist is uncertain whether a particular situation or course of action would violate this Ethics Code, the psychologist ordinarily consults with other psychologists knowledgeable about ethical issues, with state or national psychology ethics committees, or with other appropriate authorities in order to choose a proper response.

8.03 Conflicts Between Ethics and Organizational Demands

If the demands of an organization with which psychologists are affiliated conflict with this Ethics Code, psychologists clarify the nature of the conflict, make known their commitment to the Ethics Code, and to the extent feasible, seek to resolve the conflict in a way that permits the fullest adherence to the Ethics Code.

8.04 Informal Resolution of Ethical Violations

When psychologists believe that there may have been an ethical violation by another psychologist, they attempt to resolve the issue by bringing it to the attention of that individual if an informal resolution appears appropriate and the intervention does not violate any confidentiality rights that may be involved.

8.05 Reporting Ethical Violations

If an apparent ethical violation is not appropriate for informal resolution under Standard 8.04 or is not resolved properly in that fashion, psychologists take further action appropriate to the situation, unless such action conflicts with confidentiality rights in ways that cannot be resolved. Such action might include referral to state or national committees on professional ethics or to state licensing boards.

8.06 Cooperating with Ethics Committees

Psychologists cooperate in ethics investigations, proceedings, and resulting requirements of the APA or any affiliated state psychological association to which they belong. In doing so, they make reasonable efforts to resolve any issues as to confidentiality. Failure to cooperate is itself an ethics violation.

8.07 Improper Complaints

Psychologists do not file or encourage the filing of ethics complaints that are frivolous and are intended to harm the respondent rather than to protect the public.

APPENDIX C

CODE OF FAIR TESTING PRACTICES IN EDUCATION

PREPARED BY THE JOINT COMMITTEE ON TESTING PRACTICES

The Code of Fair Testing Practices in Education states the major obligations to test takers of professionals who develop or use educational tests. The Code is meant to apply broadly to the use of tests in education (admissions, educational assessment, educational diagnosis, and student placement). The Code is not designed to cover employment testing, licensure or certification testing, or other types of testing. Although the Code has relevance to many types of educational tests, it is directed primarily at professionally developed tests such as those sold by commercial test publishers or used in formally administered testing programs. The Code is not intended to cover tests made by individual teachers for use in their own classrooms.

The Code addresses the roles of test developers and test users separately. Test users are people who select tests, commission test development services, or make decisions on the basis of test scores. Test developers are people who actually construct tests as well as those who set policies for particular testing programs. The roles may, of course, overlap as when a state education agency commissions test development services, sets policies that control the test development process, and makes decisions on the basis of the test scores.

The Code presents standards for educational test developers and users in four areas:

  A. Developing/Selecting Tests

  B. Interpreting Scores

  C. Striving for Fairness

  D. Informing Test Takers

Organizations, institutions, and individual professionals who endorse the Code commit themselves to safeguarding the rights of test takers by following the principles listed. The Code is intended to be consistent with the relevant parts of the *Standards for Educational and Psychological Testing* (AERA, APA, NCME, 1985). However, the Code differs from the Standards in both audience and purpose. The Code is meant to be understood by the general public; it is limited to educational tests; and the primary focus is on those issues that affect the proper use of tests. The Code is not meant to add new principles over and above those in the Standards or to change the meaning of the Standards. The goal is rather to represent the spirit of a selected portion of the Standards in a way that is meaningful to test takers and/or their parents or guardians. It is the hope of the Joint Committee that the Code will also be judged to be consistent with existing codes of conduct and standards of other professional groups who use educational tests.

    The Code has been developed by the Joint Committee on Testing Practices, a cooperative effort of several professional organizations, that has as its aim the advancement, in the public interest, of the quality of testing practices. The Joint Committee was initiated by the American Educational Research Association, the American Psychological Association, and the National Council on Measurement in Education. In addition to these three groups, the American Association for Counseling and Development/Association for Measurement and Evaluation in Counseling and Development, and the American Speech-Language-Hearing Association are now also sponsors of the Joint Committee.

    This is not copyrighted material. Reproduction and dissemination are encouraged. Please cite this document as follows:

    Code of Fair Testing Practices in Education.   (1988) Washington, D.C.: Joint Committee on Testing Practices. (Mailing Address: Joint Committee on Testing Practices, American Psychological Association, 1200 17th Street, NW, Washington, D.C. 20036.)

A. DEVELOPING/SELECTING APPROPRIATE TESTS

TEST DEVELOPERS SHOULD:	**TEST USERS SHOULD:**
1. Define what each test measures and what the test should be used for. Describe the population(s) for which the test is appropriate.	**1.** First define the purpose for testing and the population to be tested. Then, select a test for that purpose and that population based on a thorough review of the available information.
2. Accurately represent the characteristics, usefulness, and limitations of tests for their intended purposes.	**2.** Investigate potentially useful sources of information, in addition to test scores, to corroborate the information provided by tests.

TEST DEVELOPERS SHOULD:

3. Explain relevant measurement concepts as necessary for clarity at the level of detail that is appropriate for the intended audience(s).

4. Describe the process of test development. Explain how the content and skills to be tested were selected.

5. Provide evidence that the test meets its intended purpose(s).

6. Provide either representative samples or complete copies of test questions, directions, answer sheets, manuals, and score reports to qualified users.

7. Indicate the nature of the evidence obtained concerning the appropriateness of each test for groups of different racial, ethnic, or linguistic backgrounds who are likely to be tested.

8. Identify and publish any specialized skills needed to administer each test and to interpret scores correctly.

TEST USERS SHOULD:

3. Read the materials provided by test developers and avoid using tests for which unclear or incomplete information is provided.

4. Become familiar with how and when the test was developed and tried out.

5. Read independent evaluations of a test and of possible alternative measures. Look for evidence required to support the claims of test developers.

6. Examine specimen sets, disclosed tests or samples of questions, directions, answer sheets, manuals, and score reports before selecting a test.

7. Ascertain whether the test content and norms group(s) or comparison group(s) are appropriate for the intended test takers.

8. Select and use only those tests for which the skills needed to administer the test and interpret scores correctly are available.

B. INTERPRETING SCORES

TEST DEVELOPERS SHOULD:

9. Provide timely and easily understood score reports that describe test performance clearly and accurately. Also explain the meaning and limitations of reported scores.

10. Describe the population(s) represented by any norms or comparison group(s), the dates the data were gathered, and the process used to select the samples of test takers.

11. Warn users to avoid specific, reasonably anticipated misuses of test scores.

TEST USERS SHOULD:

9. Obtain information about the scale used for reporting scores, the characteristics of any norms or comparison group(s), and the limitations of the scores.

10. Interpret scores taking into account any major differences between the norms or comparison groups and the actual test takers. Also take into account any differences in test administration practices or familiarity with the specific questions in the test.

11. Avoid using tests for purposes not specifically recommended by the test developer unless evidence is obtained to support the intended use.

TEST DEVELOPERS SHOULD:	**TEST USERS SHOULD:**

12. Provide information that will help users follow reasonable procedures for setting passing scores when it is appropriate to use such scores with the test.

12. Explain how any passing scores were set and gather evidence to support the appropriateness of the scores.

13. Provide information that will help users gather evidence to show that the test is meeting its intended purpose(s).

13. Obtain evidence to help show that the test is meeting its intended purpose(s).

C. Striving for Fairness

TEST DEVELOPERS SHOULD:

TEST USERS SHOULD:

14. Review and revise test questions and related materials to avoid potentially insensitive content or language.

14. Evaluate the procedures used by test developers to avoid potentially insensitive content or language.

15. Investigate the performance of test takers of different races, gender, and ethnic backgrounds when samples of sufficient size are available. Enact procedures that help to ensure that differences in performance are related primarily to the skills under assessment rather than to irrelevant factors.

15. Review the performance of test takers of different races, gender, and ethnic backgrounds when samples of sufficient size are available. Evaluate the extent to which performance differences may have been caused by inappropriate characteristics of the test.

16. When feasible, make appropriately modified forms of tests or administration procedures available for test takers with handicapping conditions. Warn test users of potential problems in using standard norms with modified tests or administration procedures that result in non-comparable scores.

16. When necessary and feasible, use appropriately modified forms of tests or administration procedures for test takers with handicapping conditions. Interpret standard norms with care in the light of the modifications that were made.

D. Informing Test Takers

TEST DEVELOPERS OR TEST USERS SHOULD:

17. When a test is optional, provide test takers or their parents/guardians with information to help them judge whether the test should be taken, or if an available alternative to the test should be used.

18. Provide test takers the information they need to be familiar with the coverage of the test, the types of question formats, the directions, and appropriate test-taking strategies. Strive to make such information equally available to all test takers.

19. Provide test takers or their parents/guardians with information about rights test takers may have to obtain copies of tests and completed answer sheets, retake tests, have tests rescored, or cancel scores.

20. Tell test takers or their parents/guardians how long scores will be kept on file and indicate to whom and under what circumstances test scores will or will not be released.

21. Describe the procedures that test takers or their parents/guardians may use to register complaints and have problems resolved.

APPENDIX D

REVIEW
OF BASIC STATISTICS*

GRAPHIC PRESENTATIONS

Data can be organized in several ways. One of the most useful methods of presenting data is the graphic method. A graph provides a picture which summarizes many important features of the data. For most measurement applications, two methods seem most popular—frequency polygons and histograms. To illustrate these two approaches, data from Table A-1 are used. Both a frequency polygon and histogram are shown on the same graph, which is displayed in Figure A-1. Note that the frequency polygon is a closed diagram, where points are raised to a height equal to the frequency and are plotted at the midpoints. On the other hand, the histogram has vertical bars which surround a score interval from the lower to the upper limit, and the vertical bars are at a height equal to the frequency.

Although the mechanics are somewhat different in the construction of the two graphs, both indicate the same basic pattern of scores—a somewhat bimodal distribution, where there are two general areas on the score scale at which the frequencies concentrate.

CENTRAL TENDENCY INDICATORS

After having organized a set of measurement data, it is then necessary to summarize specific statistical characteristics of the distribution. First, an indication would be ob-

*This appendix was contributed by Dennis Roberts. We gratefully acknowledge his efforts.

TABLE A-1 DISTRIBUTION OF SCORES ON A VOCABULARY TEST

Score	Number of persons receiving that score
12	2
14	3
16	5
18	11
20	2
22	7
24	6
26	4
	N = 40

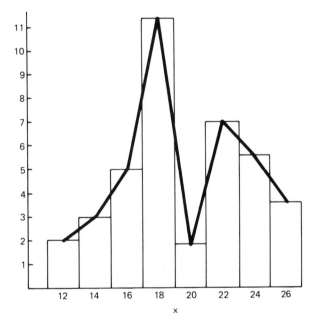

Figure A-1 Frequency Polygon and Histogram for Data in Table A-1

tained of the typical score value in the distribution (i.e., a measure of central tendency). The most common measures of central tendency are the mode, median, and mean; each are discussed briefly.

Mode

The mode is a measure that indicates which score occurred most frequently in the distribution. In Figure A-1, that score is 18. The mode is a very simple measure of central tendency; unfortunately, its simplicity is overshadowed by certain technical problems. The most serious of these is that a slight shifting of frequencies could alter the modal value radically. If three of the students who received scores of 18 had received scores of 22 instead, the mode would shift from 18 to 22.

Median

The median is the score that divides the distribution into two equal parts, so that 50 percent of the scores (frequencies) are above and below the median point. In very simple distributions, the median may be simply the score in the middle position on the score scale. However, this is not always the case. Since most distributions have some degrees of skew, the median usually tends to be somewhat higher or lower than the middle value.

The first step in finding the median is to construct a frequency distribution. Then, from the bottom, start counting up the frequencies of the various test scores until the sum of the frequencies is equal to N/2. In most cases, in counting up the frequencies, the N/2 value will not be reached exactly. More likely, at the bottom of one score interval (remember, a score has an interval from a lower to an upper limit), the accumulated frequencies are not enough to equal N/2. However, going to the top of the same interval results in having more than N/2 frequencies. When working in frequency distributions where this happens, it may be necessary to use an interpolation procedure to find the median. When interpolation is used, the assumption is made that the frequencies within the score interval spread out evenly throughout the interval.

Mean

The measure of central tendency used most often is the mean ($\bar{X}$). The mean is what we generally think of as the average. In this case, the mean has the characteristic of being a balance or fulcrum point in the distribution in terms of deviations (differences between each X score and $\bar{X}$) around the $\bar{X}$ value. That is, the deviations above $\bar{X}$ are equal in algebraic sum to the deviations below $\bar{X}$, or that the overall algebraic sum of the deviations around $\bar{X}$ equals zero. The formula for $\bar{X}$ is

$$\bar{X} = \frac{\Sigma X}{N} \qquad\qquad \text{[A-1]}$$

where

$$\Sigma X = \text{sum of all scores}$$
$$N = \text{number of scores}$$

From Table A-1, $\Sigma X = 796$ and $N = 40$. Therefore,

$$\bar{X} = \frac{796}{40}$$
$$\bar{X} = 19.9$$

Differences in Values

One of the things that is obvious when finding the numerical values for the mode, median, and mean is that the values tend to be different even for the same set of data. In examining this problem more closely, we find that the degree to which a distribution is

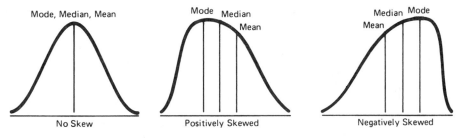

Figure A-2   Effect of Skew on the Positions of the Mode, the Median, and the Mean

symmetrical (0 skew) or asymmetrical (± skew) determines whether the three central tendency values are the same or different. In symmetrical, unimodal distributions, all three central tendency measures fall at the center point. However, in skewed distributions, the central tendency measures are different and the amount of differences depends on the amount of skew. In only slightly skewed data sets, the mode, median and mean will be quite similar. In more seriously skewed distributions, the differences could be substantial. Figure A-2 shows the relative positions of the three central tendency measures, depending on whether the distribution has a 0 or ± skew. As you can see, the mode is always located at the high frequency point, but the location of the mean and the median depends on the skew. If there is no skew, the three values are identical. If there is positive skew, the mean will be higher than the median, which is higher than the mode. If there is negative skew, this pattern will be reversed.

POSITION INDICATORS

Another type of useful descriptive statistical procedure involves indicators of the relative positions of scores within data distributions. At a very rough level of description, one could simply say that a score was above or below the mean. However, such an indication is generally not precise enough. Three measures that are used frequently are ranks, percentile ranks and z scores. Each will be discussed briefly below.

Ranks

In a frequency distribution, the simplest way to indicate relative position is to assign each score a numerical rank according to its distance from the top value. The top value is generally given a rank of 1, second highest score a rank of 2, and so on, until the last value at the bottom receives a rank value equal to N. In a distribution with $N = 55$, a person located in the twelfth position from the top has a rank of 12.

Unfortunately, as seems to happen with every simple procedure, there are problems. First, in many distributions there are multiple scores of the same value. This creates a slight difficulty in the ranking process, since the ranks assigned to the tied scores need to be averaged. However, the more serious problem is that converting raw scores to ranks tends to create a loss in information in the same way as grouping tends to force a loss of the identity of the individual data points. For example, the scores of 22, 16, 15, and 11 would receive the ranks of 1, 2, 3, and 4, respectively. However, the *difference* in the ranks does not necessarily reflect the differences in the raw scores. The difference in raw score points for ranks of 1 and 2 is 6, but the same difference in ranks between 2 and 3 is 1 score point. Ranking usually masks the differences along the underlying score scale. In general, ranks are not completely adequate measures of position.

Percentile Ranks

Another way of indicating position is to calculate the percentage of scores (i.e., frequencies) falling below a particular score point. Such a statistic is called a percentile rank. Percentile ranks are perhaps the most widely used measure of position, primarily because they are very easy to understand. Actually, one of the percentile ranks already has been discussed—the median, which happens to have a percentile rank of 50.

To illustrate how percentile ranks are calculated, data from the distribution in Table A-1 are used. For example, 75 percent of the scores (i.e., 30/40) are greater than 16. Therefore, 16 represents the twenty-fifth percentile in this distribution, in that 25 percent of the individuals have scores of 16 or lower. A score of 24 represents the ninetieth percentile.

Several comments should be made about percentile ranks. First, although percentile ranks are relatively easy to interpret, they are sometimes confused with percentage-correct scores on tests. However, rarely would the percentage of correct answers also equal the percentage of people obtaining scores less than that. Percentile ranks represent percentages of *people* below a score point, not a percentage of items responded to correctly. Second, although percentile ranks are based on a simple 100-point scale (centiles), and equal differences along that scale have equal frequencies (between percentile ranks of 30 and 40 there are 10 percent of the scores, just as there are 10 percent between 70 and 80), that is not necessarily true for the underlying score scale. For a rectangular or flat distribution, equal percentile rank differences would be accompanied by equal raw score differences. However, that is not necessarily true in a seriously skewed distribution. For example, in a positively skewed distribution, since most of the frequencies concentrate at the low end of the score scale, changing 10 percentile rank points along the percentile scale might only represent a short distance on the raw-score scale. However, changing the same 10 percentile rank points at the upper end of the score scale would require a greater score scale distance, because there are very few frequencies located at the upper end.

Finally, one must remember that percentile ranks only represent relative positions on the score scale and do not necessarily say anything about absolute performance levels. For example, there will be a ninetieth percentile rank point in a test score distribution from a very difficult examination (which may still be poor absolute performance), just as there will be a ninetieth percentile rank point in a distribution based on a very easy test (which may represent a high level of absolute performance).

z Scores.

Another way of indicating position is with z scores. A z score is a technique that utilizes both the mean and standard deviation and indicates the distance a specific score (X) is away from $\bar{X}$ in terms of standard deviation units. In a formula, z scores can be found by

$$z = \frac{X - \bar{X}}{\text{standard deviation of } X} \qquad [A\text{-}2]$$

For example, if $\bar{X} = 20$ and the standard deviation (σ) is 5, then a score of 30 would have a z of 2.00, a score of 20 (that is, $X = \bar{X}$) would have a z of 0, and a score of 17 would have a z of $-.6$.

Several points related to z values should be noted. First, values can be either positive or negative; that simply reflects the fact that scores can be above or below $\bar{X}$. Second, a z value could be 0 if X happened to be equal to $\bar{X}$. Third, it does not matter what the values for X and σ are, any X score one σ unit away from $\bar{X}$ will have a z of 1.00. The same holds true for other positions. A z value always represents the distance from $\bar{X}$ (no matter what $\bar{X}$ is) in terms of σ units (no matter what σ is).

Several additional comments should be made concerning z values. First, z values represent the most precise way of indicating position within a distribution. In addition, since z values are based on deviations from $\bar{X}$, z values are the most useful in a statistical sense. Second, although it does not make statistical sense to compute averages of ranks or percentile ranks, it is perfectly legitimate when using z scores. For example, if a person had a z of 1.50 on a spelling test, and a z of $-.50$ on a mathematics test, the number of standard deviations away from both means, on the average, would be $1.50 + -.5 = 1.00/2 = .5$, or half of one standard deviation above the mean of the X's.

A third characteristic of z scores is that the mean of the z values is always 0 and the standard deviation is always 1. Without having to prove this, it can be visualized in the following way. On the z score scale, any *raw* score of $\bar{X}$ is converted to a z of 0; therefore, $\bar{z}$ must be 0. Also, since any raw score distance of one σ unit (5, 10, 20, etc.) is equal to a z score scale distance of 1 unit, σz must be equal to 1.

Normal Distribution

The last descriptive statistical topic to be reviewed is the normal distribution. A normal curve has a symmetrical unimodal, or bell-shaped, form. Figure A-3 presents the typical shape of a normal or Gaussian curve, with both the z score and percentile rank scales marked off on the baseline along with the approximate percentages of the total area falling between selected z score points. For example, a little more than 34 percent of the

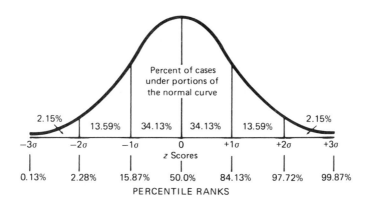

Figure A-3   Areas under the Normal Curve, z Scores, and Cumulative Percentages

area falls between either a z of 0 and z of 1, or a z of 0 and z of -1; a little less than 14 percent falls between z of 1 and z of 2, or z of -1 and z of -2; and finally, a little more than 2 percent falls between a z of 2 and z of 3, or z of -2 and z of -3. These are fixed percentages that do not change, regardless of the raw score X's and σ's. In terms of the cumulative percentages or percentile ranks, less than 1 percent has been accumulated up to a z of -3, a little more than 2 percent up to a z of -2, and almost (but not quite) 100 percent up to a z of 3.

One of the primary applications of the normal curve table in measurement data relates to finding percentile ranks for given raw scores. Figure A-3 could be used with raw scores that just happen to fall on whole number z values, like -2 (percentile rank of 2.28), or 1 (percentile rank of 84.13). Most statistics tests include tables that allow conversion of only z scores into a measure of "area under the normal curve." Actually, these "area" values are percentile ranks. For example, up to a z value of -2.42, there is about 0.78 or 1 percent of the frequencies; therefore, the percentile rank for a score having a $z = -2.42$ is about 0.78 in a normal distribution. For a score having a z of 1.79, the area and percentile rank value is about 96.33 in a normal distribution.

Before leaving the topic of normal distribution, it must be stressed that the Gaussian or normal curve should not be thought of as an ideal curve. There is no particular magic to a normal distribution, nor necessity for building tests or scales that produce normal distributions. However, it does happen that many of the distributions of variables commonly used in psychological measurement situations yield a set of data that is close to being normally distributed. If data sets do tend to conform to such a pattern, then it makes sense to utilize the characteristics of a normal curve for description or problem-solving purposes. As long as the distribution does not depart too much from the symmetrical, unimodal shape, the features of the normal curve should be utilized. However, if the data sets on which one is working are seriously skewed or of a multimodal variety, then forcing an interpretation as if the data were normally distributed makes little sense.

REFERENCES

Abrahams, N. M., Neumann, I., & Githens, W. H. (1968, February). The Strong Vocational Interest Blank in Predicting NROTC officer retention. Part II, Fakability. U.S. Naval Personnel Research Activity, Technical Bulletin STB 68–9.

Ackerman, P. L. (1987). Individual differences in skill learning: An integration of psychometric and information processing perspectives. *Psychological Bulletin, 102,* 3–27.

Ackerman, P. L., & Humphreys, L. G. (1990). Individual differences theory in industrial and organizational psychology. In M. Dunnette & L. Hough (Eds.), *Handbook of industrial and organizational psychology* (2nd ed., Vol. 1), pp. 223–282. Palo Alto, CA: Consulting Psychologists Press.

Adams, K. M., & Brown, G. C. (1986). The role of the computer in neuropsychological assessment. In I. Grant and K. Adams (Eds.), *Neuropsychological assessment of neuropsychiatric disorders.* New York: Oxford University Press.

Adair, J. G. (1973). *The human subject: The social psychology of the psychological experiment.* Boston: Little, Brown.

Adorno, T. W., Frenkel-Brunswik, E., Levinson, D. J., & Sanford, R. N. (1950). *The authoritarian personality.* New York: Harper Bros.

Ahlburg, D. A. (1992). Predicting the job performance of managers: What do the experts know? *International Journal of Forecasting, 7,* 467–472.

Albright, L. E., Glennon, J. R., & Smith, W. J. (1963). *The uses of psychological tests in industry.* Cleveland, OH: Allen.

Allinger, G. M. (1988). Do zero correlations really exist among measures of different intellectual abilities? *Educational and Psychological Measurement, 48,* 275–280.

Allport, G. W., & Odbert, H. S. (1936). Trait names: A psycholexical study. *Psychological Monographs, 47 (1,* Whole No. 211).

Allran, K. D. (1989). *The reliability of a computerized method for assessment of anaerobic power and work capacity using maximal cycle ergometry.* Eugene, OR: Microform Publication, College of Human Development and Performance, University of Oregon.

American College Test Program (1988). *Using the ACT assessment on campus.* Iowa City, IA: American College Test Program.

American Psychiatric Association. (1980). *Diagnostic and statistical manual of mental disorders* (3rd ed.). Washington, DC: Author.

American Psychological Association. (1954). *Technical Recommendations for psychologi-*

cal tests and diagnostic techniques. Washington, DC: Author.

American Psychological Association. (1981). Ethical principles of psychologists. *American Psychologist, 36,* 633–638.

American Psychological Association, Committee on Professional Standards. (1981). Specialty guidelines for the delivery of services by clinical psychologists. *American Psychologist, 36,* 640–651.

American Psychological Association, Committee on Professional Standards. (1981). Specialty guidelines for the delivery of services by counseling psychologists. *American Psychologist, 36,* 652–663.

American Psychological Association, Committee on Professional Standards. (1981). Specialty guidelines for the delivery of services by industrial/organization psychologists. *American Psychologist, 36,* 664–669.

American Psychological Association, Committee on Professional Standards. (1981). Specialty guidelines for the delivery of services by school psychologists. *American Psychologist, 36,* 670–681.

American Psychological Association, Committee on Professional Standards. (1982). Casebook for providers of psychological services. *American Psychologist, 37,* 698–701.

American Psychological Association, Committee on Professional Standards. (1983). Casebook for providers of psychological services. *American Psychologist, 38,* 708–713.

American Psychological Association (1986). *Guidelines for computer-based tests and interpretations.* Washington, DC: Author.

Anastasi, A. (1982). *Psychological testing* (5th ed.). New York: Macmillan.

Andrews, L. W., & Gutkin, T. B. (1991). The effects of human versus computer authorship on consumers' perceptions of psychological reports. *Computers in Human Behavior, 7,* 311–317.

Angoff, W. H. (1971). Scales, norms and equivalent scores. In R. L. Thorndike (Ed.), *Educational measurement* (2nd ed.). Washington, DC: American Council on Education.

Angoff, W. H. (1988). The nature-nurture debate, aptitudes, and group differences. *American Psychologist, 43,* 713–720.

APA Task Force (1991). *Questionnaires used in the prediction of trustworthiness in pre-employment selection decisions: An A.P.A. Task Force Report.* Washington, DC: American Psychological Association.

Arvey, R. D. (1979). *Fairness in selecting employees.* Reading, MA: Addison-Wesley.

Arvey, R. D., & Campion, J. E. (1982). The employment interview: A summary and review of recent research. *Personnel Psychology, 35,* 281–322.

Arvey, R. D. & Faley, R. H. (1988). *Fairness in selecting employees* (2nd ed.). Reading, MA: Addison-Wesley.

Ash, P. (1976). The assessment of honesty in employment. *South African Journal of Psychology, 6,* 68–79.

Asher, J. J. (1972). The biographical item: Can it be improved? *Personnel Psychology, 25,* 251–269.

Asher, J. J., & Sciarrino, J. A. (1974). Realistic work sample tests: A review. *Personnel Psychology, 27,* 519–553.

Ashton, S. G., & Goldberg, L. R. (1973). In response to Jackson's challenge: The comparative validity of personality scales constructed by the external (empirical) strategy and scales developed intuitively by the experts, novices, and laymen. *Journal of Research in Personality, 7,* 1–20.

Ayers, J. D. (1972). Review of the Concept Assessment Kit—Conservation. In O. K. Buros (Ed.). *The eighth mental measurements yearbook.* Highland, NJ: Gryphon Press.

Bachelor, P. A. (1989). Maximum likelihood confirmatory factor-analytic investigation of factors within Guilford's structure of intellect model. *Journal of Applied Psychology, 74,* 797–804.

Baehr, M., & Williams, G. B. (1967). Underlying dimensions of personal background data and their relationship to occupational classification. *Journal of Applied Psychology, 51,* 481–490.

Balzer, W. K., & Sulsky, L. M. (1990). Performance appraisal effectiveness. In K. Murphy & F. Saal (Eds.), *Psychology in organizations: Integrating science and practice.* Hillsdale, NJ: Erlbaum.

Balzer, W. K., & Sulsky, L. M. (1992). Halo and performance appraisal research: A critical examination. *Journal of Applied Psychology.*

Banks, C. G., & Murphy, K. R. (1985). Toward narrowing the research-practice gap in performance appraisal. *Personnel Psychology, 38,* 335–345.

Bannatyne, A. (1974). Diagnosis: A note on the recategorization of the WISC scaled scores. *Journal of Learning Disorders, 7,* 272–273.

Barrett, G. V., Alexander, R. A., Doverspike, D., Cellar, D., & Thomas, J. C. (1982). The development and application of a computerized information-processing test. *Applied Psychological Measurement, 6,* 13–29.

Barrett, G. V., Phillips, J. S., & Alexander, R. A. (1981). Concurrent and predictive validity designs: A critical reanalysis. *Journal of Applied Psychology, 66,* 1–6.

Barrick, M. R., & Mount, M. K. (1991). The Big Five personality dimensions and job performance: A meta analysis. *Personnel Psychology, 44,* 1–26.

Bartlett, C., & O'Leary, B. (1969). A differential prediction model to moderate the effects of heterogeneous groups in personnel selection and classification. *Personnel Psychology, 22,* 1–17.

Bass, A., & Turner, J. (1973). Ethnic group differences in relationships among criterion of job performance. *Journal of Applied Psychology, 57,* 101–109.

Bass, B. M. (1954). The leaderless group discussion. *Psychological Bulletin, 51,* 465–492.

Beach, L. (1967). Multiple regression as a model of human information utilization. *Organizational Behavior and Human Performance, 2,* 276–289.

Becker, B. E., & Huselid, M. A. (1992). Direct estimates of SD_y and the implications for utility analysis. *Journal of Applied Psychology, 77,* 227–233.

Begelman, D. A. (1976). Behavioral classification. In M. Hersen & A. Bellack (Eds.), *Behavioral assessment: A practical handbook.* New York: Pergamon Press.

Bem, D. J., & Funder, D. C. (1978). Predicting more of the people more of the time: Assessing the personality of situations. *Psychological Review, 85,* 485–501.

Bender, L. (1938). *A visual motor gestalt test and its clinical use.* Research monograph, No. 3, American Orthopsychiatric Association.

Bennett, G., Seashore, H., & Wesman, A. (1974). *Fifth edition manual for the Differential Aptitude Tests.* New York: The Psychological Corporation.

Ben-Shakar, G., Bar-Hillel, M., Blum, Y., Ben-Abba, E., & Flug, A. (1986). Can graphology predict occupational success: Two empirical studies and some methodological ruminations. *Journal of Applied Psychology, 71,* 645–653.

Ben-Shakar, G., Lieblich, I., & Bar-Hillel, M. (1982). An evaluation of polygraphers' judgments: A review from a decision theoretic perspective. *Journal of Applied Psychology, 67,* 701–713.

Berk, R. A. (1982). *Handbook for detecting test bias.* Baltimore, MD: Johns Hopkins University Press.

Bernardin, H. J., Alveres, K. M., & Cranny, C. J. (1976). A recomparison of behavioral expectation scales to summated scales. *Journal of Applied Psychology, 61,* 564–570.

Bernardin, H. J., & Beatty, R. W. (1984). *Performance appraisal: Assessing human behavior at work.* Boston: Kent.

Bernardin, H. J., & Smith, P. C. (1981). A clarification of some issues regarding the development and use of behaviorally anchored rating scales (BARS). *Journal of Applied Psychology, 66,* 458–463.

Bernardin, H. J., & Walter, C. S. (1977). Effects of rater training and diary-keeping on psychometric error in ratings. *Journal of Applied Psychology, 62,* 64–69.

Binet, A., & Henri, V. (1895). La psychologie individuelle. *Annee Psychologique, 2,* 411–463.

Binet, A., & Simon, T. (1905). Methodes nouvelles pour le diagnostic du nivau intellectuel des anormaux. *Annee Psychologique, 11,* 191–244.

Binning, J. F., & Barrett, G. V. (1989). Validity of personnel decisions: A conceptual analysis of the inferential and evidential bases. *Journal of Applied Psychology, 74,* 478–494.

Birren, J. E., & Schaie, K. W. (1977). *Handbook of the psychology of aging.* New York: Van Nostrand-Reinhold.

Blanz, F., & Ghiselli, E. (1972). The mixed standard scale: A new rating system. *Personnel Psychology, 25,* 185–199.

Bloom, B. S. (1976). *Human characteristics and school learning.* New York: McGraw-Hill.

Bobko, P., Karren, R., & Parkington, J. (1983). Estimation of standard deviations in utility analyses: An empirical test. *Journal of Applied Psychology, 68,* 170–176.

Boehm, A. E. (1985). Educational applications of intelligence testing. In B. Wolman (Ed.), *Handbook of intelligence: Theories, measurements and applications.* New York: Wiley.

Boehm, V. (1977). Differential prediction: A statistical artifact? *Journal of Applied Psychology, 62,* 146–154.

Borgen, F. H. (1988). Strong-Campbell Interest Inventory. In J. T. Kapes & M. M. Mastic (Eds.), *A counselor's guide to career assessment instruments* (2nd ed.). Alexandria, VA: National Career Development Association.

Borman, W. C. (1977). Consistency of rating accuracy and rating errors in the judgment of human performance. *Organizational Behavior and Human Performance, 20,* 238–252.

Borman, W. C. (1978). Exploring the upper limits of reliability and validity in job performance ratings, *Journal of Applied Psychology, 63,* 135–144.

Borman, W. C. (1982). Validity of behavioral assessment for predicting military recruiter performance. *Journal of Applied Psychology, 67,* 3–9.

Borman, W. C. (1991). Job behavior, performance, and effectiveness. In M. Dunnette & L. Hough (Eds.), *Handbook of industrial and organizational psychology* (2nd ed., vol. 2), pp. 271–326. Palo Alto, CA: Consulting Psychologists Press.

Borman, W. C., Eaton, N. K., Bryan, J. D., & Rosse, R. L. (1983). Between-assessor differences in assessment validity. *Journal of Applied Psychology, 68,* 415–419.

Borman, W. C., & Vallon, W. R. (1974). A view of what can happen when behavioral expectation scales are developed in one setting and used in another. *Journal of Applied Psychology, 59,* 197–201.

Bouchard, T. J., Lykken, D. T., McGue, M., Segal, N. L., et al. (1990, October). Sources of human psychological differences: The Minnesota Study of Twins Reared Apart. *Science, 250,* 223–228.

Bouchard, T. J., & Segal, N. L. (1985). Environment and IQ. In B. Wolman (Ed.), *Handbook of intelligence: Theories, measurements and applications.* New York: Wiley.

Boudreau, J. W. (1991). Utility analysis for decisions in Human Resource Management. In M. Dunnette & L. Hough (Eds.), *Handbook of industrial and organizational psychology* (2nd ed., Vol. 2), pp. 621–745. Palo Alto, CA: Consulting Psychologists Press.

Brandt, J. E., & Hood, A. B. (1968). Effect of personality adjustment on the predictive validity of the Strong Vocational Interest Blank. *Journal of Counseling Psychology, 15,* 547–551.

Brass, D. J., & Oldham, G. R. (1976). Validating an in-basket test using an alternative set of leadership scoring dimensions. *Journal of Applied Psychology, 61,* 652–657.

Braun, H. I., & Holland, P. W. (1982). Observed test-score equating: A mathematical analysis of some ETS equating procedures. In P. W. Holland, and D. B. Rubin (Eds.), *Test equating,* pp. 9–50. New York: Academic Press.

Bray, D. W., Campbell, R. J., & Grant, D. L. (1974). *Formative years in business: A long-term AT&T study of managerial lives.* New York: Wiley.

Bray, D. W., & Grant, D. L. (1966). The assessment center in the measurement of potential for business management of potential for business management. *Psychological Monographs, 80* (Whole Number 17).

Brennan, R. L. (1983). *Elements of generalizability theory.* Iowa City, IA: American College Test Program.

Brown, S. H. (1981). Validity generalization and situational moderation in the life insurance industry. *Journal of Applied Psychology, 66,* 664–670.

Brunswick, E. (1956). *Perception and the representative design of psychological experiments.* Berkeley: University of California Press.

Brush, D. H., & Owens, W. A. (1979). Implementation and evaluation of an assessment classification model for manpower utilization. *Personnel Psychology, 32,* 369–383.

Buckley, J. P. (1989). The integrity interview: Behavioral analysis interviews for job applicants. *The Investigator, 5* (3), 9–12. Chicago: John E. Reid & Associates.

Buckley, M. R., Cote, J. A., & Comstock, S. M. (1990). Measurement errors in the behavioral science: The case of personality/attitude research. *Educational and Psychological Measurement, 50,* 447–474.

Buckner, D. N. (1959). The predictability of ratings as a function of interrater agreement. *Journal of Applied Psychology, 43,* 60–64.

Burke, H. R. (1972). Raven's progressive matrices: Validity, reliability, and norms. *The Journal of Psychology, 82,* 253–257.

Burke, M. J., & Frederick, J. T. (1986). A comparison of economic utility estimates for alternate SD$_y$ estimation procedures. *Journal of Applied Psychology, 71,* 334–339.

Buros, O. K. (1974). *Tests in print II.* Highland Park, NJ: Gryphon Press.

Buros, O. K. (1975a). *Intelligence tests and reviews.* Highland Park, NJ: Gryphon Press.

Buros, O. K. (1975b). *Personality tests and reviews II.* Highland Park, NJ: Gryphon Press.

Buros, O. K. (1975c). *Vocational tests and reviews.* Highland Park, NJ: Gryphon Press.

Buros, O. K. (1978). *The eighth mental measurements yearbook.* Highland Park, NJ: Gryphon Press.

Butcher, J. N. (1972). *Objective personality assessment: Changing perspectives.* New York: Academic Press.

Butcher, J. N. (1987). *Computerized psychological assessment: A practitioner's guide.* New York: Basic Books.

Butcher, J. N. (1990). *MMPI-2 in psychological treatment.* New York: Oxford University Press.

Butcher, J. N., Graham, J. R., Williams, C. L., & Ben-Porath, Y. S. (1990). *Development and use of the MMPI-2 content scales.* Minneapolis: University of Minnesota Press.

Butler, M., Retzlaff, P., & Vanderploeg, R. (1991). Neuropsychological test usage. *Professional Psychology: Research and Practice, 22,* 510–512.

Callender, J. C., & Osburn, H. G. (1980). Development and test of a new model for validity generalization. *Journal of Applied Psychology, 65,* 543–558.

Callender, J. C., & Osburn, H. G. (1981). Testing the constancy of validity with computer-generated sampling distributions of the multiplicative model variance estimate: Results for petroleum industry validation research. *Journal of Applied Psychology, 66,* 274–281.

Callender, J. C., & Osburn, H. G. (1982). Another view of progress in validity generalization. *Journal of Applied Psychology, 67,* 846–852.

Campbell, D. P. (1966). Occupations ten years later of high school seniors with high scores on the SVIB life insurance salesman scale. *Journal of Applied Psychology, 50,* 369–372.

Campbell, D. P. (1971). *Handbook for the Strong Vocational Interest Blank.* Stanford, CA: Stanford University Press.

Campbell, D. P., & Hansen, J. C. (1981). *Manual for the SVIB-SCII* (3rd ed.). Stanford, CA: Stanford University Press.

Campbell, D. T. (1972). The practical problems of revising an established psychological test. In J. Butcher (Ed.), *Objective personality assessment: Changing perspectives.* New York: Academic Press.

Campbell, D. T., & Fiske, D. W. (1959). Convergent and discriminant validation by the multitrait-multimethod matrix. *Psychological Bulletin, 56,* 81–105.

Campion, M. A., Pursell, E. D., & Brown, B. K. (1988). Structured interviewing: Raising the psychometric properties of the employment interview. *Personnel Psychology, 41,* 25–42.

Carrier, M. R., Delessio, A. T., & Brown, S. H. (1990). Correspondence between estimates of content and criterion-related validity values. *Personnel Psychology, 43,* 85–100.

Carroll, J. B., & Maxwell, S. E. (1979). Individual differences in cognitive abilities. *Annual Review of Psychology, 30,* 603–640.

Carson, R. C. (1989). Personality. *Annual Review of Psychology, 40,* 227–248.

Carson, R. C. (1990). Assessment: What role the assessor? *Journal of Personality Assessment, 54,* 435–445.

Carvajal, H., Hardy, K., Smith, K., & Weaver, K. (1988). Relationships between scores on Stanford-Binet IV and Wechsler Preschool and Primary Scale of Intelligence. *Psychology in the Schools, 25,* 129–131.

Carvajal, H., Gerber, J., Hewes, P., & Weaver, K. (1987). Correlations between scores on Stanford-Binet IV and Wechsler Adult Intelligence Scale-Revised. *Psychological Reports, 61,* 83–86.

Carvajal, H., & Weyand, K. (1986). Relationships between scores on Stanford-Binet IV and Wechsler Intelligence Scale for Children-Revised. *Psychological Reports, 59,* 963–966.

Cascio, W. F. (1976). Turnover, biographical data, and fair employment practice. *Journal of Applied Psychology, 61,* 576–580.

Cascio, W. F. (1982). *Applied psychology in personnel management* (2nd ed.). Reston, VA: Reston.

Cascio, W. F., Alexander, R. A., & Barrett, G. V. (1988). Setting cutoff scores: Legal, psychometric, and professional issues and guidelines. *Personnel Psychology, 41,* 1–24.

Cascio, W. F., & Ramos, R. A. (1986). Development and application of a new method for assessing job performance in behavioral/economic terms. *Journal of Applied Psychology, 71,* 20–28.

Castellan, N. J. (1992). Relations between linear models: Implications for the lens model. *Organizational Behavior and Human Decision Processes, 51,* 364–381.

Cattell, J. (1890). Mental tests and measurements. *Mind, 15,* 373–381.

Cattell, R. B. (1940). A culture-free intelligence test: Part I. *Journal of Educational Psychology, 31,* 161–179.

Cattell, R. B. (1957). *Personality and motivation structure and measurement.* Yonkers, NY: World Book.

Cattell, R. B. (1963). Theory of fluid and crystallized intelligence: A critical experiment. *Journal of Educational Psychology, 54,* 1–22.

Chadwick-Jones, J. K., Brown, C. A., Nicholson, N., & Sheppard, C. (1971). Absence measures: Their reliability and stability in an industrial setting. *Personnel Psychology, 24,* 463–470.

Chapman, L. J., & Chapman, J. P. (1969). Illusory correlation as an obstacle to the use of valid psycho-diagnostic signs. *Journal of Abnormal Psychology, 74,* 271–280.

Chiu, K., & Allinger, G. M. (1990). A proposed method to combine ranking and graphic rating in performance appraisal: The quantitative ranking scale. *Educational and Psychological Measurement, 50,* 493–503.

Christal, R. (1968). Selecting a harem—and other applications of the policy capturing model. *Journal of Experimental Education, 36,* 35–41.

Cleary, T., Humphreys, L., Kendrick, S., & Wesman, A. (1975). Educational use of tests with disadvantaged students. *American Psychologist, 30,* 15–41.

Clopton, J. (1979). Development of special MMPI scales. In C. Newmark (Ed.), *MMPI: Clinical and research trends.* New York: Praeger.

Code of fair testing practices in education. (1988). Washington, DC: Joint Committee on Testing Practices.

Coffman, W. E. (1985). Review of Kaufman Assessment Battery for Children. *The ninth mental measurements yearbook.* Lincoln, NE: Buros Institute of Mental Measurement.

Cohen, J. A. (1957a). A factor-analytic based rationale for the Wechsler Adult Intelligence Scale. *Journal of Consulting Psychology, 21,* 451–457.

Cohen, J. A. (1957b). The factorial structure of the WAIS between early childhood and old age. *Journal of Consulting Psychology, 21,* 283–290.

Cohen, J. A. (1959). The factorial structure of the WISC at ages 7–6, 10–6, and 13–6. *Journal of Consulting Psychology, 23,* 285–299.

Cohen, J. A., & Cohen, P. (1983). *Applied multiple regression/correlation analysis for the behavioral sciences* (2nd ed.). Hillsdale, NJ: Erlbaum.

Cole, N. S. (1973). Bias in selection. *Journal of Educational Measurement, 10,* 237–255.

Coleman, J. S., et al. (1966). *Equality of educational opportunity.* Washington, DC: U.S. Office of Education.

College Entrance Examination Board. (1987). *ATP guide for high schools and colleges.* Princeton, NJ: Educational Testing Service.

Colligan, R. C., Osborne, D., Swenson, W. M., & Offord, K. P. (1983). *The MMPI: A contemporary normative study.* New York: Praeger.

Collins, L. M., & Horn, J. L. (1991). *Best methods for the analysis of change.* Washington, DC: American Psychological Association.

Committee on Ethical Guidelines for Forensic Psychologists (1991). Specialty guidelines for forensic psychologists. *Law and Human Behavior, 15,* 655–665.

Committee on Psychological Tests and Assessment. (1988). *Implications for test fairness of the "Golden Rule" company settlement.* Washington, DC: American Psychological Association.

Conger, A. C., & Conger, J. C. (1975). Reliable dimensions from WISC profiles. *Educational and Psychological Measurement, 35,* 847–863.

Conoley, C. W., Plake, B. S., & Kemmerer, B. E. (1991). Issues in computer-based test interpretative systems. *Computers in Human Behavior, 7,* 97–102.

Conoley, J. C., & Kramer, J. J. (1989). *Tenth mental measurements yearbook.* Lincoln, NE: University of Nebraska Press.

Coombs, C. H., Dawes, R. M., & Tversky, A. (1970). *Mathematical psychology: An elementary introduction.* Englewood Cliffs, NJ: Prentice-Hall.

Cooper, D., & Fraboni, M. (1988). Relationship between the Wechsler Adult Intelligence Test–Revised and the Wide Range Achievement Test–Revised in a sample of normal adults. *Educational and Psychological Measurement, 48,* 799–803.

Cooper, W. (1981). Ubiquitous halo. *Psychological Bulletin, 90,* 218–244.

Corah, N. L., Feldman, M. J., Cohen, I. S., Gruen, W., Meadow, A., & Ringwall, E. A. (1958). Social desirability as a variable in the Edwards Personal Preference Schedule. *Journal of Consulting Psychology, 22,* 70–72.

Cortina, J. M. (In press). What is coefficient alpha?: An examination of theory and applications. *Journal of Applied Psychology.*

Costa, P. T., & McCrae, R. R. (1992). Normal personality assessment in clinical practice: The NEO Personality Inventory. *Psychological Assessment, 4,* 5–13.

Crites, J. O., Bechtoldt, H. P., Goodstein, L. D., & Heilbrun, A. B., Jr. (1961). A factor analysis of the California Psychological Inventory. *Journal of Applied Psychology, 45,* 408–414.

Cronbach, L. J. (1951). Coefficient alpha and the internal structure of tests. *Psychometrika, 16,* 297–334.

Cronbach, L. J. (1955). Processes affecting scores on "understanding of others" and "assumed similarity." *Psychological Bulletin, 52,* 177–193.

Cronbach, L. J. (1970). *Essentials of psychological testing* (3rd ed.). New York: Harper & Row.

Cronbach, L. J. (1971). Test validation. In R. L. Thorndike (Ed.), *Educational measurement* (2nd ed.). Washington, DC: American Council of Education.

Cronbach, L. J. (1975). Five decades of public controversy over psychological testing. *American Psychologist, 30,* 1–14.

Cronbach, L. J. (1978). Review of the BITCH Test. In O. K. Buros (Ed.), *The eighth mental measurements yearbook.* Highland Park, NJ: Gryphon Press.

Cronbach, L. J. (1979). The Armed Services Vocational Aptitude Battery—A test battery in transition. *Personnel and Guidance Journal, 57,* 232–237.

Cronbach, L. J. (1988). Five perspectives on the validity argument. In H. Wainer and H. Brown (Eds.), *Test validity.* Hillsdale, NJ: Erlbaum.

Cronbach, L. J. (1989). Construct validation after thirty years. In R. Linn (Ed.), *Intelligence: Measurement, theory, and public policy.* Urbana, IL: University of Illinois Press.

Cronbach, L. J., & Gleser, G. (1965). *Psychological tests and personnel decisions* (2nd ed.). Urbana, IL: University of Illinois Press.

Cronbach, L. J., Gleser, G. C., Nanda, H., & Rajaratnam, N. (1972). *The dependability of behavioral measurements: Theory of generalizability for scores and profiles.* New York: Wiley.

Cronbach, L. J., & Meehl, P. E. (1955). Construct validity in psychological tests. *Psychological Bulletin, 52,* 281–302.

Cronbach, L. J., & Snow, R. E. (1977). *Aptitudes and instructional methods: A handbook for research on interactions.* New York: Halstead Press.

Cronshaw, S. F., & Alexander, R. A. (1985). One answer to the demand for accountability: Selection utility as an investment decision. *Organizational Behavior and Human Decision Processes, 35,* 102–118.

Crouse, J., & Trusheim, D. (1988). *The case against the SAT.* Chicago: University of Chicago Press.

Crow, J. F. (1969). Genetic theories and influences: Comments on the value of diversity. *Harvard Educational Review, 39,* 301–309.

Cudeck, R. (1985). A structural comparison of conventional and adaptive versions of the ASVAB. *Multivariate Behavioral Research, 20,* 305–322.

Cureton, E. E. (1957). The upper and lower twenty-seven percent rule. *Psychometrika, 22,* 293–296.

Dahlstrom, W., Welsh, G., & Dahlstrom, L. (1972). *An MMPI handbook: Vol. I. Clinical interpretation.* Minneapolis, MN: University of Minnesota Press.

Dahlstrom, W., Welsh, G., & Dahlstrom, L. (1975). *An MMPI handbook: Vol. II. Research developments and applications.* Minneapolis, MN: University of Minnesota Press.

Dana, R., Cocking, R., & Dana, J. (1970). The effects of experience and training on accuracy and configural analysis. *Journal of Clinical Psychology, 26,* 28–32.

Dankin, S., & Armstrong, J. S. (1989). Predicting job performance: A comparison of expert opinion and research findings. *International Journal of Forecasting, 5,* 187–194.

Darley, J., & Fazio, R. (1980). Expectancy confirmation processes arising in the social interaction sequence. *American Psychologist, 35,* 867–881.

Darlington, R. B. (1968). Multiple regression in psychological research and practice. *Psychological Bulletin, 69,* 161–182.

Davis, C., & Cowles, M. (1989). Automated psychological testing: Method of administration, need for approval, and measures of anxiety. *Educational and Psychological Measurement, 49,* 311–337.

Dawes, R. (1971). A case study of graduate admissions: Application of three principles of human decision making. *American Psychologist, 26,* 180–188.

Dawes, R. (1979). The robust beauty of improper linear models in decision making. *American Psychologist, 34,* 571–582.

Dawes, R. (1980). Apologia for what works. *American Psychologist, 35,* 678.

Dawes, R. M. (1989). Experience and the validity of clinical judgment: The illusory correlation. *Behavioral Sciences and the Law, 7,* 457–467.

Dawes, R., & Corrigan, B. (1974). Linear models in decision making. *Psychological Bulletin, 81,* 95–106.

Dawes, R. M., Faust, D., & Meehl, P. E. (1989). Clinical versus actuarial judgment. *Science, 243,* 1668–1674.

Delahunty, R. J. (1988). Perspectives on within-group scoring. *Journal of Vocational Behavior, 33,* 463–477.

DeFries, J. C., & Plomin, R. (1978). Behavioral genetics. *Annual Review of Psychology, 29,* 473–515.

DeNisi, A. S., & Williams, K. J. (1988). Cognitive approaches to performance appraisal. In G. Ferris & K. Rowland (Eds.), *Research in personnel and human resources management* (Vol. 6). Greenwich, CT: JAI Press.

De Vries, R., & Kohlberg, L. (1969). The Concept Assessment Kit—Conservation. *Journal of Educational Measurement, 6,* 263–266.

Dickson, D. H., & Kelly, I. W. (1985). The Barnum effect in personality assessment: A review of the literature. *Psychological Reports, 57,* 367–382.

Digman, J. M. (1990). Personality structure: Emergence of the five-factor model. *Annual Review of Psychology, 41,* 417–440.

Dipboye, R. (1982). Self-fulfilling prophecies in the selection-recruitment interview. *Academy of Management Review, 7,* 579–586.

Dipboye, R. L., & de Pontbriand, R. (1981). Correlates of employee reactions to performance appraisals and appraisal systems. *Journal of Applied Psychology, 66,* 248–251.

Dodrill, C. B., & Warner, M. H. (1988). Further studies on the Wonderlic Personnel Test as a brief measure of intelligence. *Journal of Consulting and Clinical Psychology, 56,* 145–147.

Doll, E. E. (1965). *Vineland social maturity scale, condensed. Revised edition. Manual of direction.* Minneapolis, MN: American Guidance Service.

Dolliver, R. H. (1969). Strong Vocational Interest Blank versus expressed occupational interests: A review. *Psychological Bulletin, 72,* 94–107.

Dolliver, R. H., Irvin, J. A., & Bigley, S. E. (1972). Twelve-year follow-up of the Strong Vocational Interest Blank. *Journal of Counseling Psychology, 19,* 212–217.

Doppelt, J. E., & Wallace, W. L. (1955). Standardization of the Wechsler Adult Intelligence Scale for older persons. *Journal of Abnormal and Social Psychology, 51,* 312–330.

Dorans, N. J. (1990). Equating methods and sampling designs. *Applied Measurement in Education, 3,* 3–17.

Drasgow, F., & Guertler, E. (1987). A decision-theoretic approach to the use of appropriateness measurement for detecting invalid test and scale scores. *Journal of Applied Psychology, 72,* 10–18.

Drasgow, F., & Hulin, C. L. (1991). Item response theory. In M. Dunnette & L. Hough (Eds.), *Handbook of industrial and organizational psychology* (2nd ed., Vol. 1), pp. 577–636. Palo Alto, CA: Consulting Psychologists Press.

Drasgow, F., & Kanfer, R. (1985). Equivalence of psychological measurement in heterogeneous populations. *Journal of Applied Psychology, 70,* 662–680.

Dreher, G. F., Ash, R. A., & Hancock, P. (1988). The role of traditional research design in the underestimation of the validity of the employment interview. *Personnel Psychology, 41,* 315–327.

Droege, R. C. (1984). The General Aptitude Test Battery and its international use. *International Review of Applied Psychology, 33,* 413–416.

Dubois, P. H. (1970). *A history of psychological testing.* Boston: Allyn & Bacon.

Eckberg, D. L. (1979). *Intelligence and race: The origins and dimensions of the IQ controversy.* New York: Praeger.

Edwards, A. J. (1964). Social desirability and performance on the MMPI. *Psychometrika, 29,* 295–308.

Edwards, A. J. (1972). *Individual mental testing. Part II, measurement.* San Francisco: Intext Educational Publishers.

Edwards, A. L. (1957). *Techniques of attitude scale construction.* New York: Appleton-Century-Crofts.

Edwards, A. L. (1970). *The measurement of personality traits by scales and inventories.* New York: Holt, Rinehart & Winston.

Edwards, W., & Newman, J. R. (1983). *Multiattribute evaluation.* Beverly Hills, CA: Sage.

Eells, K., et al. (1951). *Intelligence and cultural differences.* Chicago: University of Chicago Press.

Einhorn, H., & Hogarth, R. M. (1975). Unit weighting schemes for decision making. *Organizational Behavior and Human Performance, 13,* 171–192.

Einhorn, H. J., & Hogarth, R. M. (1978). Confidence in judgment: Persistence of the illusion of validity. *Psychological Review, 85,* 395–416.

Elwood, D. L. (1969). Automation of psychological testing. *American Psychologist, 24,* 287–288.

Embertson, S. E. (1985). *Test design: Developments in psychology and psychometrics.* New York: Academic Press.

Engelhart, M. D. (1965). A comparison of several item discrimination indices. *Journal of Educational Measurement, 2,* 69–76.

Epstein, S. (1980). The stability of behavior II. Implications for psychological research. *American Psychologist, 35,* 790–806.

Eysenck, H. J. (1960). *Experiments in personality.* London: Routledge & Kegan Paul.

Eysenck, H. J. (1976). *The measurement of personality.* Baltimore, MD: University Park Press.

Eysenck, H. J. (1979). *The structure and measurement of intelligence.* New York: Springer-Verlag.

Eysenck, H. J. (1981). *A model for personality.* Berlin: Springer.

Eysenck, H. J. (1987). A critique of contemporary classification and diagnosis. In T. Millon & G. L. Klerman (Eds.), *Contemporary directions in psychopathology: Toward DSM-IV.* New York: Guilford Press.

Eysenck, H. J., & Eysenck, S. B. (1969). *Personality structure and measurement.* San Diego, CA: Knapp.

Eysenck, H. J., Wakefield, J., & Friedman, A. (1983). Diagnosis and clinical assessment: The DMS-III. *Annual Review of Psychology, 34,* 167–193.

Exner, J. E. (1974). *The Rorschach: A comprehensive system.* New York: Wiley.

Exner, J. E. (1978). *The Rorschach: A comprehensive system, Vol. 2: Current research and advanced interpretations.* New York: Wiley-Interscience.

Exner, J. E. (1986). *The Rorschach: A comprehensive system* (2nd ed.). New York: Wiley.

Fairbanks, B. A. (1987). The use of presmoothing and postsmoothing to increase the precision of equipercentile equating. *Applied Psychological Measurement, 11,* 245–262.

Farrell, A. D. (1989). Impact of standards for computer-based tests on practice: Consequences of the information gap. *Computers in Human Behavior, 5,* 1–11.

Faschingbauer, T. (1979). The future of the MMPI. In C. Newmark (Ed.), *MMPI: Clinical and research trends.* New York: Praeger.

Faust, D. (1989). Data integration in legal evaluations: Can clinicians deliver on their promises. *Behavioral Sciences and the Law, 7,* 469–483.

Faust, D., & Ziskin, J. (1988, July 1). The expert witness in forensic psychology and psychiatry. *Science, 241,* 31–35.

Feldman, J. (1981). Beyond attribution therapy: Cognitive processes in performance appraisal. *Journal of Applied Psychology, 66,* 127–148.

Feldman, M. J., & Corah, N. L. (1960). Social desirability and the forced choice method. *Journal of Consulting Psychology, 24,* 480–482.

Ferguson, G. (1981). *Statistical analysis in psychology and education.* New York: McGraw-Hill.

Ferguson, R. L., & Novick, M. R. (1973). Implementation of a Bayesian system for decision analysis in a program of individually prescribed instruction. *ACT Research Report,* No. 60.

Feuerstein, R. (1970). A dynamic approach to the causation, prevention, and alleviation of retarded performance. In H. Haywood (Ed.), *Social-cultural aspects of mental retardation.* New York: Appleton-Century-Crofts.

Finkle, R. B. (1976). Managerial assessment centers. In M. Dunnette (Ed.), *Handbook of industrial and organizational psychology.* Chicago: Rand McNally.

Fisher, K. (1986, July). DSM-III-R protest. *APA Monitor, 17*(7), 4.

Fiske, D. W. (1987). Construct invalidity comes from method effects. *Educational and Psychological Measurement, 47,* 285–307.

Flanagan, J. C. (1937). A proposed procedure for increasing the efficiency of objective tests. *Journal of Educational Psychology, 26,* 17–21.

Flanagan, J. C. (1954). The critical incidents technique. *Psychological Bulletin, 51,* 327–358.

Flynn, J. R. (1980). *Race, IQ and Jensen.* London: Routledge & Kegan Paul.

Flynn, J. R. (1984). The mean IQ of Americans: Massive gains 1932 to 1978. *Psychological Bulletin, 95,* 29–51.

Flynn, J. R. (1987). Massive IQ gains in 14 nations: What IQ tests really measure. *Psychological Bulletin, 101,* 171–191.

Folger, R., & Greenberg, J. (1985). Procedural justice: An interpretive analysis of personnel systems. In K. Rowland & J. Ferris (Eds.), *Research in personnel and human resources management* (Vol. 3). Greenwich, CT: JAI Press.

Forer, B. R. (1965). Review of the Holtzman Inkblot Technique. In O. K. Buros (Ed.), *The sixth mental measurements yearbook.* Highland Park, NJ: Gryphon Press.

Fowler, R. (1979). The automated MMPI. In C. Newmark (Ed.), *MMPI: Clinical and research trends.* New York: Praeger.

Frances, A. J., & Cooper, A. (1981). Descriptive and dynamic psychiatry: A perspective on DMS-III. *American Journal of Psychiatry, 138,* 1998–1202.

Frances, A. J., First, M. B., Widiger, T. A., Miele, G. M., Tilly, S. M., Davis, W. W., & Pincus, H. A. (1991). An A to Z guide to DSM-IV conundrums. *Journal of Abnormal Psychology, 100,* 407–412.

Frank, L. K. (1939). Projective methods for the study of personality. *Journal of Psychology, 8,* 389–409.

Fredericksen, N. (1962). Factors in in-basket performance. *Psychological Monographs, 76*(22, Whole No. 541).

Frederickson, N. (1986). Construct validity and construct similarity: Methods for use in test development and test validation. *Multivariate Behavioral Research, 21,* 3–28.

Freeberg, N. E. (1969). Relevance of rater-ratee acquaintance in the validity and reliability of rating. *Journal of Applied Psychology, 53,* 518–524.

Friedman, T., & Williams, E. B. (1982). Current use of tests for employment. In A. Wigdor & W. Garner (Eds.), *Ability testing: Uses, consequences and controversies, Part II: Documentation section.* Washington, DC: National Academy Press.

Furnham, A., & Schofield, S. (1987). Accepting personality test feedback: A review of the Barnum effect. *Current Psychological Research and Reviews, 6,* 162–178.

Gael, S., Grant, D., & Richie, R. (1975). Employment test validation for minority and nonminority clerks and work sample criteria. *Journal of Applied Psychology, 60,* 420–426.

Gaito, J. (1980). Measurement scales and statistics: Resurgence of an old misconception. *Psychological Bulletin, 87,* 564–567.

Gallucci, N. T. (1986). General and specific objections to the MMPI. *Educational and Psychological Measurement, 46,* 985–988.

Galton, F. (1869). *Hereditary genius: An inquiry into its laws and consequences.* London: Macmillan.

Garb, H. N. (1989). Clinical judgment, clinical training, and professional experience. *Psychological Bulletin, 105,* 387–396.

Gardner, H. (1983). *Frames of mind: The theory of multiple intelligences.* New York: Basic Books.

Gaudet, F. J. (1963). *Solving the problems of employee absence.* New York: American Management Association.

Gaugler, B. B., Rosenthal, D. B., Thornton, G. C., & Bentson, B. (1987). Meta-analysis of assessment center validity. *Journal of Applied Psychology, 72,* 493–511.

Geary, D. C., & Whitworth, R. H. (1988). Dimensional structure of the WAIS-R in a simultaneous multi-sample analysis. *Educational and Psychological Measurement, 48,* 945–959.

George, M. S., & Skinner, H. A. (1990). Using response latency to detect inaccurate responses in a computerized lifestyle assessment. *Computers in Human Behavior, 6,* 167–175.

Gesell, A. L. (1948a). *The first five years of life.* New York: Harper & Bros.

Gesell, A. L. (1948b). *Studies in child development.* New York: Harper & Bros.

Gesell, A. L. (1956). *Youth: The years from ten to sixteen.* New York: Harper & Bros.

Ghiselli, E. E. (1955). *The measurement of occupational aptitude.* Berkeley, CA: University of California Press.

Ghiselli, E. E. (1966). *The validity of occupational aptitude tests.* New York: Wiley.

Ghiselli, E. E. (1970). The validity of aptitude tests in personnel selection. *Personnel Psychology, 26,* 461–477.

Gilberstadt, H., & Druker, J. (1965). *A handbook for clinical and actuarial MMPI interpretation.* Philadelphia: Saunders.

Ginton, A., Dail, N., Elaad, E., & Ben-Shakar, G. (1982). A method for evaluating the use of the polygraph in a real-life situation. *Journal of Applied Psychology, 67,* 131–137.

Gleser, G. C. (1963). Projective methodologies. *Annual Review of Psychology, 14,* 391–422.

Glutting, J. J., & McDermott, P. A. (1990). Childhood learning potential as an alternative to traditional ability measures. *Psychological Assessment, 2,* 398–403.

Golden, C. J. (1990). *Clinical interpretation of objective psychological tests.* (2nd Ed.). Boston: Allyn & Bacon.

Goldberg, L. R. (1965). Diagnosticians versus diagnostic signs: The diagnosis of psychosis versus neurosis from the MMPI.

Psychological Monographs, 79(9, Whole No. 602).

Goldberg, L. R. (1968). Simple models or simple processes? Some research on clinical judgments. *American Psychologist, 23,* 483–496.

Goldberg, L. R. (1970). Man versus model of man: A rationale plus evidence for a method of improving clinical inference. *Psychological Bulletin, 73,* 422–432.

Goldberg, L. R., & Slovic, P. (1967). The importance of test item content. An analysis of a corollary of the deviation hypothesis. *Journal of Counseling Psychology, 14,* 462–472.

Goldberg, P. A. (1965). A review of sentence completion methods in personality assessment. *Journal of Projective Techniques and Personality Assessment, 29,* 12–45.

Goldstein, B. L., & Patterson, P. O. (1988). Turning back the Title VII clock: The resegregation of the American work force through validity generalization. *Journal of Vocational Behavior, 33,* 452–462.

Goodenough, F. L. (1949). *Mental testing: Its history, principles, and applications.* New York: Rinehart.

Gordon, R. A. (1988). Thunder from the left. Review of "Storm over biology: Essays on science, sentiment, and public policy." *Academic Questions, 1,* 74–92.

Gottfredson, L. S. (1986). Societal consequences of the g factor in employment. *Journal of Vocational Behavior, 29,* 379–410.

Gottfredson, L. S. (1988). Reconsidering fairness: A matter of social and ethical priorities. *Journal of Vocational Behavior, 33,* 293–319.

Gottfredson, L. S., & Crouse, J. (1986). Validity versus utility of mental tests: Example of the SAT. *Journal of Vocational Behavior, 29,* 363–378.

Gough, H. G. (1987). *California Psychological Inventory administrator's guide.* Palo Alto, CA: Consulting Psychologists Press.

Gould, S. J. (1981). *The mismeasure of man.* New York: Norton.

Graham, J. R. (1977). *The MMPI: A practical guide.* New York: Oxford University Press.

Graham, J. R. (1990). *MMPI-2: Assessing personality and psychopathology.* New York: Oxford University Press.

Gray, C. W. (1959). *Detection of faking in vocational interest measurement.* Unpublished doctoral dissertation, Minneapolis, University of Minnesota.

Green, B. F. (1988). Construct validity of computer-based tests. In H. Wainer & H. Brown (Eds.), *Test validity.* Hillsdale, NJ: Erlbaum.

Greenberg, J. (1987). A taxonomy of organizational justice theories. *Academy of Management Review, 12,* 9–22.

Greene, R. L. (1991). *The MMPI-2/MMPI: An interpretative manual.* Boston: Allyn & Bacon.

Greenwood, J. M., & McNamara, W. J. (1967). Interrater reliability of situational tests. *Journal of Applied Psychology, 31,* 101–106.

Gross, A. L., & Su, W. (1975). Defining a "fair" or "unbiased" selection model: A question of utility. *Journal of Applied Psychology, 60,* 345–351.

Gross, M. (1963). *The brain watchers.* New York: New American Library.

Guastello, S. J., Guastello, D. D., & Craft, L. L. (1989). Assessment of the Barnum effect in computer-based test interpretations. *Journal of Psychology, 123,* 477–484.

Guastello, S. J., & Rieke, M. L. (1990). The Barnum effect and the validity of computer-based test interpretations. The Human Resource Development Report. *Psychological Assessment, 2,* 186–190.

Guidelines and ethical considerations for assessment center operations. (1989). Pittsburgh, PA: Task Force on Assessment Center Guidelines.

Guidelines for computer-based tests and interpretation. (1986). Washington, DC: American Psychological Association.

Guilford, J. P. (1967). *The nature of human intelligence.* New York: McGraw-Hill.

Guilford, J. P. (1980). Fluid and crystallized intelligences: Two fanciful concepts. *Psychological Bulletin, 88,* 406–412.

Guilford, J. P. (1988). Some changes in the Structure-of-Intellect model. *Educational and Psychological Measurement, 48,* 1–4.

Guilford, J. P., & Guilford, R. B. (1934). An analysis of the factors in a typical test of introversion-extraversion. *Journal of Abnormal and Social Psychology, 28,* 377–399.

Guilford, J. P., & Guilford, R. B. (1939). Personality factors D, R, T and A. *Journal of Abnormal and Social Psychology, 34,* 21–26.

Guilford, J. P., & Hoepfner, R. (1971). *The analysis of intelligence.* New York: McGraw-Hill.

Guion, R. M. (1965a). *Personnel testing.* New York: McGraw-Hill.

Guion, R. M. (1965b). Synthetic validity in a small company: A demonstration. *Personnel Psychology, 18,* 49–63.

Guion, R. M. (1977). Content validity—The source of my discontent. *Applied Psychological Measurement, 1,* 1–10.

Guion, R. M. (1991). Personnel Assessment, selection, and placement. In M. Dunnette & L. Hough (Eds.), *Handbook of industrial and organizational psychology* (2nd ed., Vol. 2), pp. 327–398. Palo Alto, CA: Consulting Psychologists Press.

Guion, R.M., & Cranny, C. J. (1982). A note on concurrent and predictive validity designs. *Journal of Applied Psychology, 67,* 239–244.

Guion, R. M., & Gottier, R. F. (1965). Validity of personality measures in personnel selection. *Personnel Psychology, 18,* 135–164.

Gulliksen, H. (1950). *Theory of mental tests.* New York: Wiley.

Guttman, L., & Levy, S. (1991). Two structural laws for intelligence tests. *Intelligence, 15,* 79–103.

Hakel, M. (1974). Normative personality factors uncovered from readings or personality descriptions: The beholder's eye. *Personnel Psychology, 27,* 409–421.

Hale, M. (1982). History of employment testing. In A. Wigdor, & W. Garner (Eds.), *Ability testing: Uses, consequences, and controversies, Part II: Documentation section.* Washington, DC: National Academy Press.

Hall, V. C., & Mery, M. (1969). The Concept Assessment Kit—Conservation. *Journal of Educational Statistics, 6,* 263–266.

Hambleton, R. K., & Novick, M. R. (1973). Toward an integration of theory and method for criterion-referenced tests. *Journal of Educational Measurement, 10,* 159–170.

Hamilton, J. L. (1983). Measuring response to instruction as an assessment paradigm. *Advances in Learning and Behavioral Disabilities, 2,* 111–133.

Hammer, T. H., & Landau, J. (1981). Methodological issues in the use of absence data. *Journal of Applied Psychology, 66,* 574–581.

Hammond, K. R. (1955). Probabilistic functioning in the clinical method. *Psychological Review, 62,* 255–262.

Hammond, K. R. (1966). *The psychology of Egon Brunswick.* New York: Holt, Rinehart & Winston.

Haney, W. (1981). Validity, vaudeville, and values: A short history of social concerns over standardized testing. *American Psychologist, 36,* 1021–1034.

Hansen, J. C. (1992). A note of thanks to the women's movement. *Journal of Counseling and Development, 70,* 520–521.

Hansen, J. C., & Campbell, D. P. (1985). *Manual for the SVIB-SCII Fourth Edition.* Stanford, CA: Stanford University Press.

Hansen, J. D., & Campbell, D. P. (1985). *Manual for the SVIB-SCII* (4th ed.). Palo Alto, CA: Consulting Psychologists Press.

Harnqvist, K. (1968). Relative changes in intelligence from 13 to 18, II. *Scandinavian Journal of Psychology, 9,* 65–82.

Harris, C. W. (1963). *Problems in measuring change.* Madison, WI: University of Wisconsin Press.

Harris, M. M., & Schaubroeck, J. (1988). A meta-analysis of self-supervisory, self-peer, and peer-supervisory ratings. *Personnel Psychology, 41,* 43–62.

Hartigan, J. A., & Wigdor, A. K. (1989). *Fairness in employment testing: Validity generalization, minority issues, and the General Aptitude Test Battery.* Washington, DC: National Academy Press.

Hartman, D. E. (1986). Artificial intelligence or artificial psychologist? Conceptual issues in clinical microcomputer use. *Professional Psychology: Research and Practice, 17,* 528–534.

Hartshorne, H., & May, M. A. (1928). *Studies in deceit.* New York: Macmillan.

Hastie, R., et al. (1980). *Person memory: The cognitive basis of social perception.* Hillsdale, NJ: Erlbaum.

Hathaway, S. (1972). Where have we gone wrong? The mystery of the missing progress. In J. Butcher (Ed.), *Objective personal-*

ity assessment: Changing perspectives. New York: Academic Press.

Hayes, S. C., Nelson, R. O., & Jarrett, R. B. (1987). The treatment utility of assessment: A functional approach to evaluating assessment quality. *American Psychologist, 42,* 963–974.

Haywood, H., Filler, J., Shifman, M., & Chatelant, G. (1975). Behavioral assessment in mental retardation. In P. McReynolds (Ed.), *Advances in psychological assessment* (Vol. 3). San Francisco: Jossey-Bass.

Hedges, L. V., & Olkin, I. (1985). *Statistical methods for meta-analysis.* New York: Academic Press.

Heilbrun, A. B., Jr., Daniel, J. L., Goodstein, L. D., Stephenson, R. R., & Crites, J. O. (1962). The validity of two-scale pattern interpretation on the California Psychological Inventory. *Journal of Applied Psychology, 46,* 409–416.

Heilman, M. E., & Saruwatari, L. R. (1979). When beauty is beastly: The effects of appearance and sex on evaluations of job applicants for managerial and non-managerial jobs. *Organizational Behavior and Human Performance, 23,* 360–372.

Henly, S. J., Klebe, K. J., McBride, J. R., & Cudeck, R. (1989). Adaptive and conventional versions of the DAT: The first complete battery comparison. *Applied Psychological Measurement, 13,* 363–372.

Henry, E. (1965). What business can learn from Peace Corps selection and training. *Personnel, 42,* 17–25.

Herrnstein, R. (1971). IQ. *The Atlantic Monthly, 228* (3), 43–64.

Hersen, M., & Greaves, S. T. (1971). Rorschach productivity as related to verbal performance. *Journal of Personality Assessment, 35,* 436–441.

Hilgard, E. R. (1989). The early years of intelligence measurement. In R. Linn (Ed.), *Intelligence: Measurement, theory, and public policy.* Urbana, IL: University of Illinois Press.

Hinrichs, J. R. (1978). An eight-year follow-up of a management assessment center. *Journal of Applied Psychology, 63,* 596–601.

Hobbs, N. (1963). A psychologist in the Peace Corps. *American Psychologist, 18,* 47–55.

Hoffman, B. (1962). *The tyranny of testing.* New York: Crowell-Collier.

Hoffman, P. (1960). The paramorphic representation of clinical judgment. *Psychological Bulletin, 57,* 116–131.

Hofner, P. J., & Green, B. F. (1985). The challenge of competence and creativity in computerized psychological testing. *Journal of Consulting and Clinical Psychology, 53,* 826–838.

Hogan, J., & Quigley, A. M. (1986). Physical standards for employment and the courts. *American Psychologist, 41,* 1193–1217.

Hogan, R. T. (1991). Personality and personality measurement. In M. Dunnette & L. Hough (Eds.), *Handbook of industrial and organizational psychology* (2nd ed., Vol. 2), pp. 874–919. Palo Alto, CA: Consulting Psychologists Press.

Holden, C. (1986). Researchers grapple with problems of updating classic psychological test. *Science, 233,* 1249–1251.

Holden, C. (1989). Court ruling rekindles controversy over SATs. *Science, 243,* 885–886.

Holden, R. R., & Fekken, G. C. (1988). Using reaction time to detect faking on a computerized inventory of psychopathology. Presented as Annual Convention of Canadian Psychological Association: Montreal.

Holden, R. R., Fekken, G. C., & Cotton, D. H. G. (1991). Assessing psychopathology using structured test-item response latencies. *Psychological Assessment, 3,* 111–118.

Holden, R. R., & Kroner, D. G. (1992). Relative efficacy of differential response latencies for detecting faking on a self-report measure of psychopathology. *Psychological Assessment, 4,* 170–173.

Holland, J. L. (1973). *Making vocational choices: A theory of careers.* Englewood Cliffs, NJ: Prentice-Hall.

Holland, P. W., & Thayer, D. T. (1988). Differential item performance and the Mantel-Haenszel procedure. In H. Wainer & H. Brown (Eds.), *Test validity.* Hillsdale, NJ: Erlbaum.

Holt, R. R. (1958). Clinical *and* statistical prediction: Reformulation and some new data. *Journal of Abnormal and Social Psychology, 56,* 1–12.

Holt, R. R. (1969). The evaluation of personality assessment. In I. L. Janis (Ed.),

Personality: Dynamics, development and assessment. New York: Harcourt, Brace & World.

Holtzman, W. H. (1968). Holtzman Inkblot Technique. In A. Rabin (Ed.), *Projective techniques in personality assessment.* New York: Springer.

Holtzman, W. H., Thorpe, J. S., Swartz, J. D., & Herron, E. W. (1961). *Inkblot perception and personality: Holtzman Inkblot Technique.* Austin, TX: University of Texas Press.

Honacker, L. M., Hector, V. S., & Harel, T. H. (1986). Perceived validity of computer-versus clinician-generated MMPI reports. *Computers in Human Behavior, 2,* 77–83.

Hopkins, D. K., & Bracht, G. (1975). Ten-year stability of verbal and nonverbal IQ scores. *American Educational Research Journal, 12,* 469–477.

Hopkins, K. (1978). Review of the Cognitive Abilities Tests. In O. K. Buros (Ed.), *The eighth mental measurement yearbook.* Highland Park, NJ: Gryphon Press.

Horn, J. L. (1985). Remodeling old models of intelligence. In B. Wolman (Ed.), *Handbook of intelligence: Theories, measurements and applications.* New York: Wiley.

Horn, J. L., & Cattell, R. B. (1967). Age differences in fluid and crystallized intelligence. *Acta Psychologica, 26,* 107–129.

Hough, L. M., Eaton, N. K., Dunnete, M. D., Kamp, J. D., & McCloy, R. A. (1990). Criterion-related validities of personality constructs and the effect of response distortion on those validities. *Journal of Applied Psychology, 75,* 581–595.

Howard, A. (1974). An assessment of assessment centers. *Academy of Management Journal, 17,* 115–134.

Huck, J. R. (1973). Assessment centers: A review of the external and internal validities. *Personnel Psychology, 26,* 191–193.

Huck, J. R., & Bray, D. W. (1976). Management assessment center evaluations and subsequent job performance of white and black females. *Personnel Psychology, 29,* 13–30.

Hulin, C. L., Drasgow, F., & Parsons, C. K. (1983). *Item response theory: Application to psychological measurement.* Homewood, IL: Dow Jones-Irwin.

Humphreys, L. G. (1978). Relevance of genotype and its environmental counterpart to the theory, interpretation, and nomenclature of ability measures. *Intelligence, 2,* 181–193.

Humphreys, L. G. (1979). The construct of general intelligence. *Intelligence, 3,* 105–120.

Humphreys, L. G. (1989). Intelligence: Three kinds of instability and their consequences for policy. In R. Linn (Ed.), *Intelligence: Measurement, theory, and public policy.* Urbana, IL: University of Illinois Press.

Hunt, E. B., & Pellegrin, J. W. (1985). Using interactive computing to expand intelligence testing. *Intelligence, 9,* 209–236.

Hunt, J. McV. (1975). Reflections on a decade of early education. *Journal of Abnormal Child Psychology, 3,* 275–330.

Hunter, J. E. (1983a). *The dimensionality of the General Aptitude Test Battery (GATB) and the dominance of general factors over specific factors in the prediction of job performance.* USES Test Research Report No. 44. Washington, DC: U.S. Department of Labor.

Hunter, J. E. (1983b). *Fairness of the General Aptitude Test Battery: Ability differences and their impact on minority hiring rates.* USES Test Research Report No. 45. Washington, DC: U.S. Department of Labor.

Hunter, J. E. (1983c). *Overview of validity generalization for the U.S. Employment Service.* USES Test Research Report No. 43. Washington, DC: U.S. Department of Labor.

Hunter, J. E. (1986). Cognitive ability, cognitive aptitudes, job knowledge, and job performance. *Journal of Vocational Behavior, 29,* 340–362.

Hunter, J. E., Crosson, J. J., & Friedman, D. H. (1985). *The validity of the Armed Services Vocational Aptitude Battery (ASVAB) for civilian and military job performance.* HQUSAF/MPXOA (Contract No. F41689-83-C-0025). Washington, DC: Department of Defense.

Hunter, J. E., & Hunter, R. F. (1984). Validity and utility of alternate predictors of job performance. *Psychological Bulletin, 96,* 72–98.

Hunter, J. E., & Schmidt, F. (1976). A critical analysis of the statistical and ethical implications of various definitions of "test bias." *Psychological Bulletin, 83,* 1053–1071.

Hunter, J. E., & Schmidt, F. L. (1982). Fitting people to jobs: The impact of personnel selection on national productivity. In M. Dunnette & E. Fleishman (Eds.), *Human performance and productivity: Human capability assessment.* Hillsdale, NJ: Erlbaum.

Hunter, J. E., & Schmidt, F. L. (1990). *Methods of meta-analysis.* Newbury Park, CA: Sage.

Hunter, J., Schmidt, F., & Hunter, R. (1979). Differential validity of employment tests by race: A comprehensive review and analysis. *Psychological Bulletin, 86,* 721–735.

Hunter, J. E., Schmidt, F. L., & Jackson, G. B. (1982). *Meta-analysis: Cumulating research findings across studies,* Beverly Hills, CA: Sage.

Hunter, J. E., Schmidt, F. L., & Pearlman, K. (1982). History and accuracy of validity generalization equations: A response to the Callender and Osburn reply. *Journal of Applied Psychology, 67,* 853–856.

Hursch, C., Hammond, K., & Hursch, J. (1964). Some methodological considerations in multiple-cue probability studies. *Psychological Review, 71,* 42–60.

Hutt, M. (1977). *The Hutt adaptation of the Bender-Gestalt test* (3rd ed.). New York: Grune & Stratton.

Hyde, J. S., & Linn, M. C. (1988). Gender differences in verbal ability: A meta-analysis. *Psychological Bulletin, 104,* 53–69.

Ilgen, D. R., & Hollenback, J. (1977). The role of job satisfaction in absence behavior. *Organizational Behavior and Human Performance, 19,* 148–161.

Ironson, G. H., & Subkoviak, M. J. (1979). A comparison of several methods of assessing bias. *Journal of Educational Measurement, 16,* 209–225.

Jackson, D. N. (1967). Acquiescence response styles: Problems of identification and control. In I. A. Barg (Ed.), *Response set in personality assessment.* Chicago: Aldine.

Jackson, D. N. (1977). *Jackson Vocational Interest Survey Manual.* London, Ontario: Research Psychologists Press.

Jackson, D. N. (1984). *Multidimensional Aptitude Battery Manual.* Port Huron, MI: Research Psychologists Press.

Jackson, D. N. (1984). *Personality Research Form Manual.* Port Huron, MI: Research Psychologists Press.

Jackson, D. N., & Guthrie, G. M. (1968). Multitrait-multimethod evaluation of the Personality Research Form. *Proceedings of the 76th Annual Convention of the American Psychological Association, 3,* 177–178.

Jackson, G. D. (1975). On the report of the ad hoc committee on educational uses of tests with disadvantaged students. *American Psychologist, 30,* 88–93.

Jacobs, R., Kafry, D., & Zedeck, S. (1980). Expectations of behaviorally anchored rating scales. *Personnel Psychology, 33,* 595–640.

James, L. R. (1973). Criterion models and construct validity for criteria. *Psychological Bulletin, 80,* 75–83.

James, L. R., Demaree, R. G., & Mulaik, S. A. (1986). A note on validity generalization procedures. *Journal of Applied Psychology, 71,* 440–450.

Janz, T. (1982). Initial comparisons of patterned behavior description interviews versus unstructured interviews. *Journal of Applied Psychology, 67,* 577–582.

Jencks, C. (1972). *Inequality: The reassessment of the effect of family and schooling in America.* New York: Basic Books.

Jensen, A. R. (1969). How much can we boost IQ and scholastic achievement? *Harvard Educational Review, 39,* 1–123.

Jensen, A. R. (1972). *Genetics and education.* London: Methuen.

Jensen, A. R. (1974). How biased are culture-loaded tests? *Genetic Psychology Monographs, 90,* 185–244.

Jensen, A. R. (1975). The meaning of heritability in the behavioral and social sciences. *Educational Psychologist, 11,* 171–183.

Jensen, A. R. (1980). *Bias in mental testing.* New York: Free Press.

Jensen, A. R. (1982). The chronometry of intelligence. In R. J. Sternberg (Ed.), *A componental approach to intellectual development* (Vol. 1). Hillsdale, NJ: Erlbaum.

Jensen, A. R. (1986). g : Artifact or reality? *Journal of Vocational Behavior, 29,* 301–331.

Johansson, C. B. (1976). *Manual for the Career Assessment Inventory.* Minneapolis, MN: National Computer Systems.

Johansson, C. B. (1986). *Career Assessment Inventory, the enhanced version.* Minneapolis, MN: National Computer Systems.

Johansson, C. B. (1984). *Manual for Career Assessment Inventory.* Minneapolis, MN: National Computer Systems.

Johansson, C. B., & Harmon, L. W. (1972). Strong Vocational Interest Blank: One form or two? *Journal of Counseling Psychology, 19,* 404–410.

Johnson, D. F., & Mihal, W. L. (1973). The performance of blacks and whites in manual vs. computerized testing environments. *American Psychologist, 28,* 694–699.

Jones, L. V., & Applebaum, M. I. (1989). Psychometric methods. *Annual Review of Psychology, 40,* 23–43.

Joseph, A. (1977). *Intelligence, IQ, and race— When, how, and why they became associated.* San Francisco: R & E Research Associates.

Judiesch, M. K., Schmidt, F. L., & Mount, M. K. (1992). Estimates of the dollar value of employee output in utility analyses: An empirical test of two theories. *Journal of Applied Psychology, 77,* 234–250.

Kamin, L. (1974). *The science and politics of IQ.* Hillsdale, NJ: Erlbaum.

Kamphaus, R. W., & Reynolds, C. R. (1987). *Clinical and research applications of the K-ABC.* Circle Pines, MN: American Guidance Service.

Kane, R. L. (1986). Comparison of Halstead-Reitan and Luria-Nebraska Neuropsychological Batteries. In T. Incagnoli, C. Goldstein, & C. Golden (Eds.), *Clinical application of neuropsychological test batteries.* New York: Plenum.

Kaplan, M. (1983). A woman's view of DSM-III. *American Psychologist, 38,* 786–792.

Katz, L., & Dalby, J. T. (1981). Computer and manual administration of the Eysenck Personality Inventory. *Journal of Clinical Psychology, 37,* 586–588.

Katz, M. R. (1987). Theory and practice: The rationale for a career guidance workbook. *Career Development Quarterly, 36,* 31–44.

Katzell, R., & Dyer, F. (1977). Differential validity revived. *Journal of Applied Psychology, 62,* 137–145.

Kaufman, A. S. (1975). Factor analysis of the WISC-R at eleven age levels between 6½

and 16½ years. *Journal of Consulting and Clinical Psychology, 43,* 135–147.

Kaufman, A. S. (1979). *Intelligence testing with the WISC-R.* New York: Wiley.

Kaufman, A. S., & Kamphaus, R. W. (1984). Factor analysis of the Kaufman Assessment Battery for Children (K-ABC) for ages 2½ through 12½ years. *Journal of Educational Psychology, 76,* 623–637.

Kaufman, A. S., Kamphaus, R. W., & Kaufman, N. L. (1985). New directions in intelligence testing: The Kaufman Assessment Battery for Children (K-ABC). In B. Wolman (Ed.), *Handbook of Intelligence: Theories, measurements, and applications.* New York: Wiley.

Kaufman, A. S., & Kaufman, N. L. (1983a). *K-ABC administration and scoring manual.* Circle Pines, MN: American Guidance Service.

Kaufman, A. S., & Kaufman, N. L. (1983b). *K-ABC interpretive manual.* Circle Pines, MN: American Guidance Service.

Kavanaugh, M. J. (1971). The content issue in performance appraisal: A review. *Personnel Psychology, 24,* 653–668.

Kavanaugh, M. J., MacKinney, A., & Wolins, L. (1971). Issues in managerial performance: Multitrait-multimethod analysis of ratings. *Psychological Bulletin, 75,* 34–49.

Kemery, E. R., Mossholder, K. W., & Roth, L. (1987). The power of the Schmidt-Hunter additive model of validity generalization. *Journal of Applied Psychology, 72,* 30–37.

Kendell, R. E. (1991). Relationship between DSM-IV and ICD-10. *Journal of Abnormal Psychology, 100,* 297–301.

Keyser, D. J., & Sweetland, R. C. (1984). *Test critiques* (Vol. 1). Kansas City, MO: Test Corporation of America.

King, G. (1978). Review of the MMPI. In O. Buros (Ed.). *The eighth mental measurement yearbook.* Highland Park, NJ: Gryphon Press.

Kingstrom, P. O., & Bass, A. R. (1981). A critical analysis of studies comparing behaviorally anchored rating scales (BARS) and other rating formats. *Personnel Psychology, 34,* 263–289.

Kirchener, W. K. (1961). "Real-life" faking on the Strong Vocational Interest Blank by sales applicants. *Journal of Applied Psychology, 45,* 273–276.

Kleinmuntz, B. (1968). *Formal representation of human judgment.* New York: Wiley.

Kleinmuntz, B. (1970). Clinical information processing by computer. In *New Directions in Psychology* (Vol. 4). New York: Holt, Rinehart & Winston.

Klimoski, R., & Brickner, M. (1987). Why do assessment centers work? The puzzle of assessment center validity. *Personnel Psychology, 40,* 243–260.

Klimoski, R. J., & Strickland, W. J. (1977). Assessment centers—Valid or merely prescient? *Personnel Psychology, 30,* 353–361.

Korchin, S. J., & Schuldberg, D. (1981). The future of clinical assessment. *American Psychologist, 36,* 1147–1158.

Kraiger, K., & Teachout, M. S. (1990). Generalizability theory as construct-related evidence of the validity of job performance ratings. *Human Performance, 3,* 19–36.

Kramer, J. J. (1988). Computer-based test interpretation in psychoeducational assessment: An initial appraisal. *Journal of School Psychology, 26,* 143–154.

Kramer, J. J., Henning-Stout, M., Ullman, D. P., & Schellenberg, R. P. (1987). The viability of scatter analysis on the WISC-R and the SBIS: Examining a vestige. *Journal of Psychoeducational Assessment, 5,* 37–47.

Krantz, D. H., Luce, R. D., Suppes, P., & Tversky, A. (1971). *Foundations of measurement, Vol. 1: Additive and polynomial representations.* New York: Academic Press.

Kuder, G. F. (1970). *Kuder DD Occupational Interest Survey general manual.* Chicago: Science Research Associates.

Kuder, G. F. (1977). *Activity interests and occupational choice.* Chicago: Science Research Associates.

Kuder, G. F., & Diamond, E. E. (1979). *Kuder DD Occupational Interest Survey general manual* (2nd ed.). Chicago: Science Research Associates.

Kuder, G., & Richardson, M. (1937). The theory of the estimation of test reliability. *Psychometrika, 2,* 151–160.

Kusyszyn, I. (1968). Comparison of judgmental methods with endorsements in the assessment of personality traits. *Journal of Applied Psychology, 52,* 227–233.

Labrentz, E., Linkenhoker, F., & Aaron, P. (1976). Recognition and reproduction of Bender-Gestalt figures: A developmental study of the lag between perception and performance. *Psychology in the Schools, 13,* 128–133.

Lacks, P. (1984). *Bender & Gestalt screening for brain dysfunction.* New York: Wiley.

Lambert, N., Windmiller, M., Cole, L., & Figueroa, R. (1975). *Manual for the AAMD Adaptive Behavior Scale, public school version, 1974.* Washington, DC: American Association on Mental Deficiency.

Lance, C. E., Teachout, M. S., & Donnelly, T. M. (1992). Specification of the criterion construct space: An application of hierarchical confirmatory factor analysis. *Journal of Applied Psychology, 77,* 437–452.

Landy, F. J. (1978). Adventures in implied psychology: On the value of true negatives. *American Psychologist, 33,* 756–760.

Landy, F. J. (1985). *The psychology of work behavior* (3rd ed.). Homewood, IL: Dorsey Press.

Landy, F. J. (1987). Stamp collecting versus science: Validation as hypothesis testing. *American Psychologist, 41,* 1183–1192.

Landy, F. J. (1988). *Test validity yearbook: Organizational.* Hillsdale, NJ: Erlbaum.

Landy, F. J., & Farr, J. L. (1980). Performance rating. *Psychological Bulletin, 87,* 72–107.

Landy, F. J., & Farr, J. L. (1983). *The measurement of work performance: Methods, theory, and applications.* New York: Academic Press.

Landy, F. J., & Trumbo, D. A. (1980). *Psychology of work behavior* (revised ed.). Homewood, IL: Dorsey Press.

Lang, R. J. (1978). Multivariate classification of daycare patients: Personality as a dimensional continuum. *Journal of Consulting and Clinical Psychology, 46,* 1212–1226.

Lanning, K. (1989). Detection of invalid response patterns on the California Psychological Inventory. *Applied Psychological Measurement, 13,* 45–56.

Larry, P. v. *Wilson Riles.* (1972). U.S. District Court for the Northern District of California. No. C-71-227ORFP.

Last, C. G., & Hersen, M. (1987). *Issues in diagnostic research.* New York: Plenum.

Latham, G. P., Fay, C. H., & Saari, L. M. (1979). The development of behavioral observation scales for appraising the performance of foremen. *Personnel Psychology, 32,* 299–316.

Latham, G. P., & Pursell, E. D. (1975). Measuring absenteeism from the opposite side of the coin. *Journal of Applied Psychology, 60,* 369–371.

Latham, G., Saari, L., & Fay, C. (1980). BOS, BES, and baloney: Raising Kane with Bernardin. *Personnel Psychology, 33,* 815–821.

Latham, G. P., Saari, L. M., Pursell, E. D., & Campion, M. A. (1980). The situational interview. *Journal of Applied Psychology, 65,* 422–427.

Latham, G., & Wexley, K. (1977). Behavioral observation scales. *Journal of Applied Psychology, 30,* 255–268.

Laughon, P. (1990). The dynamic assessment of intelligence: A review of three approaches. *School Psychology Review, 19,* 459–470.

Laurent, J., Swerdlik, M., & Ryburn, M. (1992). Review of validity research on the Stanford-Binet Intelligence Scale: Fourth Edition. *Psychological Assessment, 4,* 102–112.

Lawshe, C. H. (1975). A quantitative approach to content validity. *Personnel Psychology, 28,* 563–575.

Lawler, E. E. (1967). The multitrait-multimethod approach to measuring managerial job performance. *Journal of Applied Psychology, 51,* 369–381.

Layon, R. (1984). Personality assessment. *Annual Review of Psychology, 35,* 667–701.

Lerner, B. (1983). Reality, utopia, and performance appraisal: Another view. In F. Landy, S. Zedeck, J. Cleveland (Eds.), *Performance measurement and theory.* Hillsdale, NJ: Erlbaum.

Lerner, B. (1989). Intelligence and the laws. In R. Linn (Ed.), *Intelligence: Measurement, theory, and public policy.* Urbana, IL: University of Illinois Press.

Levitt, E. E. (1990). A structural analysis of the impact of MMPI-2 on MMPI-1. *Journal of Personality Assessment, 55,* 562–567.

Lewis, L., & Sinnett, E. R. (1987). An introduction to neuropsychological assessment. *Journal of Counseling and Development, 66,* 126–130.

Lewis, M. (1973). Infant intelligence tests: Their use and misuse. *Human Development, 16,* 108–118.

Li, C. C. (1975). *Path analysis—A primer.* Pacific Grove, CA: Boxwood Press.

Lichtenberg, J. W. (1985). On the distinction between projective and nonprojective assessment. *Journal of Counseling and Development, 64,* 3–4.

Lieblich, I., Ben-Shakar, G., Kugelmass, S., & Cohen, Y. (1978). Decision theory approach to the problem of polygraph interrogation. *Journal of Applied Psychology, 63,* 489–498.

Linn, R. (1982). Ability testing: Individual differences, prediction, and differential prediction. In A. Wigdor & W. Garner (Eds.), *Ability testing: Uses, consequences, and controversies* (Part II). Washington, DC: National Academy Press.

Lipsett, L., & Wilson, J. W. (1954). Do suitable interests and mental ability lead to job satisfaction? *Educational and Psychological Measurement, 11,* 373–380.

Locke, E. A. (1983). Performance appraisal under capitalism, socialism, and the mixed economy. In F. Landy, S. Zedeck, & J. Cleveland (Eds.), *Performance measurement and theory.* Hillsdale, NJ: Erlbaum.

Loehlin, J. C., Lindzey, G., & Spuhler, J. N. (1975). *Race differences in intelligence.* San Francisco: Freeman.

Lohman, D. F. (1992). *Implications of cognitive psychology for selection and classification: Three critical assumptions.* Presented at ARI Conference on Selection and Classification in the Military, Alexandria, VA.

London, M., & Bray, D. W. (1980). Ethical issues in testing and evaluation for personnel decisions. *American Psychologist, 35,* 890–901.

Lopez, F. M. (1966). *Evaluating executive decision making.* Research Study 75. New York: American Management Association.

Lord, F. M. (1952). The relation of the reliability of multiple-choice tests to the distribution of item difficulties. *Psychometrika, 17,* 181–194.

Lord, F. M. (1953). On the statistical treatment of football numbers. *American Psychologist, 8,* 750–751.

Lord, F. M. (1977). Practical applications of item characteristic curve theory. *Journal of Educational Measurement, 14,* 117–138.

Lord, F. M. (1980). *Applications of item response theory to practical testing problems.* Hillsdale, NJ: Erlbaum.

Lord, F. M., & Novick, M. (1968). *Statistical theories of mental test scores.* Reading, MA: Addison-Wesley.

Lord, R. G., & Maher, K. J. (1991). Cognitive theory in industrial and organizational psychology. In M. Dunnette & L. Hough (Eds.), *Handbook of industrial and organizational psychology* (2nd ed., Vol. 2), pp. 1–62. Palo Alto, CA: Consulting Psychologists Press.

Lowman, R. (1989). *Pre-employment screening for psychopathology: A guide to professional practice.* Sarasota, FL: Professional Resource Exchange.

Lubin, B., Larsen, R., & Matarazzo, J. (1984). Patterns of psychological test usage in the United States. *American Psychologist, 39,* 451–454.

Lumsden, J. (1976). Test theory. *Annual Review of Psychology, 27,* 251–280.

Lykken, D. T. (1979). The detection of deception. *Psychological Bulletin, 86,* 47–53.

Machover, K. (1949). *Personality projection in the drawing of the human figure.* Springfield, IL: Thomas.

Maddi, J. (1984). Personology for the 1980's. In R. Zucker, J. Aranoff, & A. Rabin (Eds.), *Personality and the prediction of behavior.* New York: Academic Press.

Mael, F. A. (1991). A conceptual rationale for the domain of attributes of biodata items. *Personnel Psychology, 44,* 763–792.

Magnusson, D., & Backteman, G. (1978). Longitudinal stability of person characteristics: Intelligence and creativity. *Applied Psychological Measurement, 2,* 481–490.

Manning, W. H. (1976). Some current controversies in educational measurement. *Educational Testing Service Reports,* 25–43.

Margenau, H. (1950). *The nature of physical reality.* New York: McGraw-Hill.

Marks, R., & Seeman, W. (1963). *Actuarial description of abnormal personality.* Baltimore, MD: Williams & Wilkins.

Marks, R., Seeman, W., & Haller, P. (1974). *The actuarial use of the MMPI with adolescents and adults.* Baltimore, MD: Williams & Wilkins.

Marley, M. (1982). *Organic brain pathology and the Bender-Gestalt test: A differential diagnostic scoring system.* New York: Grune & Stratton.

Martin, S. L., & Terris, W. (1991). Predicting infrequent behavior: Clarifying the impact on false-positive rates. *Journal of Applied Psychology, 76,* 484–487.

Maser, J. D., Kaebler, C., & Weise, R. E. (1991). International use and attitudes toward DSM-III and DSM-III-R: Growing consensus in psychiatric classification. *Journal of Abnormal Psychology, 100,* 271–279.

Matarazzo, J. D. (1972). *Wechsler's measurement and appraisal of adult intelligence.* Baltimore, MD: Williams & Wilkins.

Matarazzo, J. D. (1983). Computerized psychological testing. *Science, 221,* 323.

Matarazzo, J. D. (1986). Computerized clinical psychological test interpretations: Unvalidated plus all mean and no sigma. *American Psychologist, 41,* 14–24.

Matarazzo, J. D. (1992). Psychological testing and assessment in the 21st century. *American Psychologist, 47,* 1007–1018.

Matarazzo, J. D., & Herman, D. O. (1985). Clinical uses of the WAIS-R: Base rates of differences between VIQ and PIQ in the WAIS-R standardization sample. In B. Wolman (Ed.), *Handbook of intelligence: Theories, measurements, and applications.* New York: Wiley.

Matarazzo, J. D., & Weins, A. N. (1977). Black Intelligence Test of Cultural Homogeneity and Wechsler Adult Intelligence Scale scores of black and white police applicants. *Journal of Applied Psychology, 62,* 57–63.

Maxwell, S. E., & Delaney, H. D. (1990). *Designing experiments and analysing data.* Belmont, CA: Wadsworth.

Mayfield, E. C., Brown, S., & Hamstra, B. W. (1980). Selection interviews in the life insurance industry: An update of research and practice. *Personnel Psychology, 33,* 225–239.

Mazzeo, J., & Harvey, A. L. (1988). *The equivalence of scores from automated and conventional educational tests: A review of the literature.* College Board Report No. 88-8. New York: College Entrance Examination Board.

McArthur, C. (1954). Long term validity of the Strong Interest Test in two subcultures. *Journal of Applied Psychology, 38*, 346–354.

McArthur, C. (1968). Comment on studies of clinical versus statistical prediction. *Journal of Counseling Psychology, 15*, 172–173.

McArthur, C. (1992). Rumblings of a distant drum. *Journal of Counseling and Development, 70*, 517–519.

McCormick, E. J. (1979). *Job analysis: Methods and applications.* New York: Amacom.

McCormick, E. J., & Ilgen, D. (1980). *Industrial and organizational psychology* (7th ed.). Englewood Cliffs, NJ: Prentice-Hall.

McCrae, R. R., & Costa, P. T., Jr. (1985). Updating Norman's "adequate taxonomy": Intelligence and personality dimensions in natural language and questionnaires. *Journal of Personality and Social Psychology, 49*, 710–721.

McCrae, R. R., & Costa, P. T., Jr. (1986). Clinical assessment can benefit from recent advances in personality psychology. *American Psychologist, 51*, 1001–1002.

McCrae, R. R., & Costa, P. T., Jr. (1987). Validation of the five-factor model of personality across instruments and observers. *Journal of Personality and Social Psychology, 52*, 81–90.

McCrae, R. R., & Costa, P. T., Jr. (1989). The structure of interpersonal traits: Wiggin's circumplex and the five-factor model. *Journal of Personality and Social Psychology, 56*, 586–595.

McDaniel, M. A., & Jones, J. W. (1988). Predicting employee theft: A quantitative review of the validity of a standardized measure of dishonesty. *Journal of Business and Psychology, 2*, 327–345.

McFie, J. (1960). Psychological testing in clinical neurology. *Journal of Nervous and Mental Disease, 131*, 383–393.

McGurk, F. C. (1975). Race differences— Twenty years later. *Homo, 26*, 219–239.

McLemore, C. W., & Benjamin, L. S. (1979). Whatever happened to interpersonal diagnosis: A psychosocial alternative to DSM-III. *American Psychologist, 34*, 17–34.

McNemar, Q. (1942). *The revision of the Stanford-Binet Scale: An analysis of the standardization data.* Boston: Houghton-Mifflin.

McRae, G. G. (1959). *The relationships of job satisfaction and earlier measured interests.* Unpublished doctoral dissertation, Gainesville, University of Florida.

McReynolds, P. (1968). An introduction to psychological assessment. In P. McReynolds (Ed.), *Advances in psychological assessment* (Vol. 1). Palo Alto, CA: Science and Behavior Books.

McReynolds, P. (1989). Diagnosis and clinical assessment: Current status and major issues. *Annual Review of Psychology, 40*, 83–108.

McReynolds, W. T. (1979). DSM-III and the future of applied social science. *Professional Psychology, 10*, 123–132.

McShane, D., & Cook, U. (1985). Transcultural intellectual assessment: Performance by Hispanics on the Wechsler Scales. In B. Wolman (Ed.), *Handbook of intelligence: Theories, measurements, and applications.* New York: Wiley.

Mead, A. D., & Drasgow, F. (1992). Effects of administration: A meta-analysis. Unpublished manuscript. University of Illinois, Champaign, Illinois.

Meehl, P. E. (1954). *Clinical versus statistical prediction: A theoretical analysis and a review of the evidence.* Minneapolis: University of Minnesota Press.

Meehl, P. E. (1957). When shall we use our heads instead of formula? *Journal of Counseling Psychology, 4*, 268–273.

Meehl, P. E. (1965). Seer over sign: The first good example. *Journal of Experimental Research in Personality, 1*, 27–32.

Meehl, P. E. (1972). Reactions, reflections, projections. In J. Butcher (Ed.), *Objective personality assessment: Changing perspectives.* New York: Academic Press.

Megargee, E. I. (1972). *The California Psychological Inventory handbook.* San Francisco: Jossey-Bass.

Meier, M. J. (1985). Review of Halstead-Reitan Neuropsychological Test Battery. *The ninth mental measurements yearbook.* Lincoln, NE: Buros Institute of Mental Measurements.

Menninger, W., & English, J. (1965). Psychiatric casualties from overseas Peace Corps service. *Bulletin of the Menninger Clinic, 29*, 148–158.

Mercer, J. R. (1973). *Labelling the mentally retarded.* Los Angeles: University of California Press.

Mercer, J. R. (1979). Theoretical constructs of adaptive behavior: Movement from a medical to a socioeconomic perspective. In W. A. Coulter & H. W. Morrow (Eds.), *Adaptive behavior: Concepts and measurement.* New York: Grune & Stratton.

Mercer, J. R., & Lewis, J. F. (1978). *System of multicultural pluralistic assessment (SOMPA).* New York: Psychological Corporation.

Merz, W. R. (1984). Kaufman Assessment Battery for Children. *Test critiques* (Vol. 1). Kansas City: Test Corporation of America.

Messick, S. (1988). The once and future issues of validity: Assessing the meaning and consequences of measurement. In H. Wainer & H. Brown (Eds.), *Test validity.* Hillsdale, NJ: Erlbaum.

Messick, S. (1989). Meaning and values in test validation: The science and ethics of assessment. *Educational Researcher, 18*(2), 5–11.

Meyer, V., & Jones, H. G. (1957). Patterns of cognitive test performance as functions of lateral localization of cerebral abnormalities in the temporal lobe. *Journal of Mental Science, 103,* 758–772.

Micceri, T. (1989). The unicorn, the normal curve, and other improbable creatures. *Psychological Bulletin, 105,* 156–166.

Miles, T. R. (1957). Contributions to intelligence testing and the theory of intelligence. I. On defining intelligence. *British Journal of Educational Psychology, 27,* 153–165.

Milkovich, G. T., & Wigdor, A. K. (1991). *Pay for performance: Evaluating performance appraisal and merit pay.* Washington, DC: National Academy Press.

Miller, K. M. (1975). *Psychological testing in personnel assessment.* New York: Wiley.

Miller, L. S., Bergstrom, D. A., Cross, H. J., & Grube, J. W. (1981). Opinions and use of the DSM system by practicing psychologists. *Professional Psychology, 12,* 385–390.

Miller, R. C., & Berman, J. S. (1983). The efficacy of cognitive behavior therapies: A quantitative review of the research evidence. *Psychological Bulletin, 94,* 39–53.

Millon, T., & Klerman, G. L. (1987). *Contemporary directions in psychopathology: Toward DSM-IV.* New York: Guilford Press.

Miner, M. G., & Miner, J. B. (1978). *Employee selection within the law.* Washington, DC: Bureau of National Affairs.

Mischel, W., & Peake, P. K. (1982). Beyond déjà vu in the search for cross-situational consistency. *Psychological Review, 89,* 730–755.

Mitchell, J. V. (1983). *Tests in print III.* Lincoln, NE: University of Nebraska Press.

Mitchell, J. V. (1985). *The ninth mental measurements yearbook.* Lincoln, NE: Buros Institute of Mental Measurements.

Mitchell, J. V., & Pierce-Jones, J. (1960). A factor analysis of Gough's California Psychological Inventory. *Journal of Consulting Psychology, 24,* 453–456.

Mitchell, T. R., & Klimoski, R. J. (1986). Estimating the validity of cross-validity estimation. *Journal of Applied Psychology, 71,* 311–317.

Mohrman, A. M., & Lawler, E. E. (1983). Motivation and performance-appraisal behavior. In F. Landy, S. Zedeck, & J. Cleveland (Eds.), *Performance measurement and theory.* Hillsdale, NJ: Erlbaum.

Moreland, K. L. (1990). Some observations on computer-assisted psychological testing, *Journal of Personality Assessment, 55,* 820–823.

Moreno, K. E., Wetzel, C. D., McBride, J. R., & Weiss, D. J. (1984). Relationship between corresponding Armed Services Vocational Aptitude Battery and computerized adaptive testing-subtesting? *Applied Psychological Measurement, 8,* 155–163.

Morey, L., & Ochoa, E. (1989). An investigation of adherence to diagnostic criteria: Clinical diagnosis of the DSM-III personality disorders. *Journal of Personality Disorders, 3,* 180–192.

Motowidlo, S. J., Dunnette, M. D., Carter, G. W., Tippins, N., Werner, S., Griffiths, J. R., & Vaughan, M. J. (1992). Studies of the behavioral interview. *Journal of Applied Psychology.*

Mumford, M. D., Uhlman, C. E., & Kilcullen, R. N. (1992). The structure of life history: Implications for the construct validity of background data scales. *Human Performance, 5,* 109–137.

Mumford, M. D., Weeks, J. L., Harding, F. D., & Fleishman, E. A. (1988). Relations between student characteristics, course content, and training outcomes: An integrated modeling effort. *Journal of Applied Psychology, 73,* 443–456.

Munley, P. H., & Zarantonello, M. M. (1990). A comparison of MMPI profile types with corresponding estimated MMPI-2 profiles. *Journal of Clinical Psychology, 46,* 803–811.

Murphy, K. R. (1979). Convergent and discriminant validity of regression models and subjectivity weighted models of decision-making processes. Unpublished Doctoral dissertation, Pennsylvania State University.

Murphy, K. R. (1982). Difficulties in the statistical control of halo. *Journal of Applied Psychology, 67,* 161–164.

Murphy, K. R. (1983). Fooling yourself with cross-validation. Single-sample designs. *Personnel Psychology, 36,* 111–118.

Murphy, K. R. (1984a). Review of Armed Services Vocational Aptitude Battery. In D. Keyser & R. Sweetland (Eds.), *Test critiques* (Vol. 1). Kansas City, MO: Test Corporation of America.

Murphy, K. R. (1984b). Review of Wonderlic Personnel Test. In D. Keyser & R. Sweetland (Eds.), *Test critiques* (Vol. 1). Kansas City, MO: Test Corporation of America.

Murphy, K. R. (1986). When your top choice turns you down: Effects of rejected offers on selection test utility. *Psychological Bulletin, 99,* 133–138.

Murphy, K. R. (1987a). Accuracy of clinical vs. computerized test interpretations. *American Psychologist, 42,* 192–193.

Murphy, K. R. (1987b). Detecting infrequent deception. *Journal of Applied Psychology, 72,* 611–614.

Murphy, K. R. (1988). Psychological measurement: Abilities and skills. In C. Cooper & I. Robertson (Eds.), *International review of industrial and organizational psychology* (Vol. 3). New York: Wiley.

Murphy, K. R. (1989a). Dimensions of job performance. In R. Dillon & J. Pelligrino (Eds.), *Testing: Applied and theoretical perspectives.* New York: Praeger.

Murphy, K. R. (1989b). Is the relationship between cognitive ability and job performance stable over time? *Human Performance, 2,* 183–200.

Murphy, K. R. (1993). *Honesty in the workplace.* Pacific Grove, CA: Brooks/Cole.

Murphy, K. R., & Balzer, W. K. (1981). *Rater errors and rating accuracy.* Presented at annual conference of American Psychological Association, Los Angeles.

Murphy, K. R., & Balzer, W. K. (1986). Systematic distortions in memory-based behavior ratings and performance evaluations: Consequences for rating accuracy. *Journal of Applied Psychology, 71,* 39–44.

Murphy, K. R., & Balzer, W. K. (1989). Rater errors and rating accuracy. *Journal of Applied Psychology, 74,* 619–624.

Murphy, K. R., Balzer, W. K., Kellam, K., & Armstrong, J. (1984). Effects of the purpose of rating on accuracy in observing teacher behavior and evaluating teacher performance. *Journal of Educational Psychology, 76,* 45–54.

Murphy, K. R., Balzer, W. K., Lockhart, M., & Eisenman, E. (1985). Effects of previous performance on evaluations of present performance. *Journal of Applied Psychology, 70,* 72–84.

Murphy, K. R., & Cleveland, J. N. (1991). *Performance appraisal: An organizational perspective.* Boston: Allyn & Bacon.

Murphy, K. R., & Constans, J. I. (1987). Behavioral anchors as a source of bias in rating. *Journal of Applied Psychology, 72,* 573–579.

Murphy, K. R., & Constans, J. I. (1988). Psychological issues in scale format research: Behavioral anchors as a source of bias in rating. In R. Cardy, S. Puffer, & J. Newman (Eds.), *Advances in information processing in organizations* (Vol. 3). Greenwich, CT: JAI Press.

Murphy, K. R., Garcia, M., Kerkar, S., Martin, C., & Balzer, W. (1982). Relationship between observational accuracy and accuracy in evaluating performance. *Journal of Applied Psychology, 67,* 320–325.

Murphy, K. R., Martin, C., & Garcia, M. (1982). Do behavioral observation scales measure observation? *Journal of Applied Psychology, 67,* 562–567.

Murphy, K. R., Philbin, T. A., & Adams, S. R. (1989). Effect of purpose of observation on accuracy of immediate and delayed performance ratings. *Organizational Behavior and Human Decision Processes, 43,* 336–354.

Murray, H. A. (1938). *Explorations in personality.* Cambridge, MA: Harvard University Press.

Naglieri, J. A. (1988). *Draw-a-Person: A quantitative scoring system.* New York: Psychological Corporation.

Nairn, A., et al. (1980). *The reign of ETS: The corporation that makes up minds.* The Ralph Nader Report on the Educational Testing Service, New York.

Narens, L., & Luce, R. D. (1986). Measurement: A theory of numerical assignments. *Psychological Bulletin, 99,* 166–180.

Nay, W. (1979). *Multimethod clinical assessment.* New York: Gardner Press.

Neisser, U. (1979). The concept of intelligence. *Intelligence, 3,* 217–227.

Nesselroade, J. R., & Reese, H. W. (1973). *Life-span developmental psychology: Methodological issues.* New York: Academic Press.

Newmark, C. (1979). *MMPI: Clinical and research trends.* New York: Praeger.

Nicholson, R. A., & Hogan, R. (1990). The construct validity of social desirability. *American Psychologist, 45,* 290–292.

Nicholson, R. A., & Kugler, K. E. (1991). Competent and incompetent criminal defendants: A quantitative review. *Psychological Bulletin, 109,* 355–370.

Nicholson, R. A., Robertson, H. C., Johnson, W. G., & Jensen, G. (1988). A comparison of instruments for assessing competency to stand trial. *Law and Human Behavior, 12,* 313–321.

Nisbett, R., & Ross, L. (1980). *Human inference: Strategies and shortcomings in social judgment.* Englewood Cliffs, NJ: Prentice-Hall.

Nisbett, R., & Wilson, T. D. (1977). Telling more than you can know: Verbal reports on mental processes. *Psychological Review, 84,* 231–259.

Nunnally, J. C. (1982). *Psychometric Theory* (2nd ed.). New York: McGraw-Hill.

Nystedt, L., & Murphy, K. (1979). Some conditions affecting the utility of subjectively weighted models in decision making. *Perceptual and Motor Skills, 49,* 583–590.

Oakland, T., & Parmelee, R. (1985). Mental measurement of minority group children. In B. Wolman (Ed.), *Handbook of intelligence: Theories, measurements, and applications.* New York: Wiley.

O'Bannon, R. M., Goldinger, L. A., & Appleby, J. D. (1989). *Honesty and integrity testing: A practical guide.* Atlanta: Applied Information Resources.

Office of Strategic Services (OSS) Assessment Staff. (1948). *Assessment of men: Selection of personnel for the Office of Strategic Services.* New York: Rinehart.

Office of Technology Assessment (1990). *The use of integrity tests for preemployment screening.* Washington, DC: U.S. Congress Office of Technology Assessment.

Olkin, I. (1992). Reconcilable differences: Gleaning insight from conflicting scientific studies. *Sciences, 32* (4), 30–36.

Ones, D. S., Viswesvaran, C., & Schmidt, F. L. (In press). Meta-analysis of integrity test validities. *Journal of Applied Psychology.*

Orpen, C. (1985). Patterned behavior description interviews versus unstructured interviews: A comparative validity study. *Journal of Applied Psychology, 70,* 774–776.

Osburn, H. G., Callender, J. C., Greener, J. M., & Ashworth, S. (1983). Statistical power of tests of the situational specificity hypothesis in validity generalization studies: A cautionary note. *Journal of Applied Psychology, 68,* 115–122.

Ostendorf, F., Angleitner, A., & Ruch, W. (1983). *Convergent and discriminant validation of the German Personality Research Form.* West Germany: University of Bielefeld.

Owen, D. (1985). *None of the above: Behind the myth of scholastic aptitude.* Boston: Houghton-Mifflin.

Owens, W. A. (1971). A quasi-actuarial basis for individual assessment. *American Psychologist, 26,* 992–999.

Owens, W. A. (1976). Background data. In M. Dunnette (Ed.), *Handbook of industrial and organization psychology.* Chicago: Rand McNally.

Owens, W. A., & Schoenfeldt, L. F. (1979). Toward a classification of persons. *Journal of Applied Psychology, 65,* 569–607.

Page, E. B. (1985). Review of Kaufman Assessment Battery for Children. *The ninth mental measurements yearbook.* Lincoln, NE: Buros Institute of Mental Measurements.

Parker, K. C. H., Hanson, R. K., & Hunsley, J. (1988). MMPI, Rorschach, and WAIS: A meta-analytic comparison of reliability, stability, and validity. *Psychological Bulletin, 103,* 367–373.

Parkinson, C. N. (1957). The short list of principles of selection. In C. N. Parkinson, *Parkinson's law.* New York: Houghton-Mifflin.

Parsons, F. (1909). *Choosing a vocation.* Boston: Houghton-Mifflin.

Pascal, G. R., & Suttell, B. J. (1951). *The Bender-Gestalt test: Quantification and validity for adults.* New York: Grune & Stratton.

Payne, J. E., Mercer, C. D., Payne, A., & Davinson, R. G. (1973). *Head Start: A tragicomedy with epilogue.* New York: Behavioral Publications.

Pearlman, K., Schmidt, F. L., & Hunter, J. E. (1980). Validity generalization results for tests used to predict job proficiency and training success in clerical occupations. *Journal of Applied Psychology, 65,* 373–406.

Penn, S., & Bowser, S. (1977). *Assessment of rater bias in performance evaluations.* Presented at American Psychological Association Annual Convention, New York.

Joint Committee for Educational Evaluation. *Personnel evaluation standards.* Newbury Park, CA: Sage.

Pervin, L. A. (1980). *Personality theory and assessment.* New York: Wiley.

Pervin, L. A. (1985). Personality: Current controversies, issues, and directions. *Annual Review of Psychology, 36,* 83–114.

Piotrowski, C., & Keller, J. W. (1984). Psychodiagnostic testing in APA-approved clinical psychology programs. *Professional Psychology: Research and Practice, 15,* 450–456.

Piotrowski, C., & Keller, J. W. (1989a). Psychological testing in outpatient mental health facilities: A national study. *Professional Psychology: Research and Practice, 20,* 423–425.

Piotrowski, C., & Keller, J. W. (1989b). Use of assessment in mental health clinics and services. *Psychological Reports, 64,* 1298.

Podlesny, J. A., & Raskin, D. C. (1977). Physiological measures and the detection of deception. *Psychological Bulletin, 84,* 782–799.

Plomin, R., & Rende, R. (1991). Human behavioral genetics. *Annual Review of Psychology, 42,* 161–190.

Prediger, D. J. (1987). Validity of the new Armed Services Vocational Aptitude Battery cluster scores in career planning. *Career Development Quarterly, 36,* 113–125.

Prince, R. J., & Guastello, S. J. (1990). The Barnum effect in a computerized Rorschach interpretation system. *Journal of Personality, 124,* 217–222.

Pulakos, E. D., Borman, W. C., & Hough, L. M. (1988). Test validation for scientific understanding: Two demonstrations of an approach to studying predictor-criterion linkages. *Personnel Psychology, 41,* 703–716.

Rabin, A. I. (1981). Projective methods: A historical introduction. In A. Rabin (Ed.), *Assessment with projective techniques: A concise introduction.* New York: Springer.

Rahman, M., & Eysenck, S. (1978). Psychoticism and response to treatment in neurotic patients. *Behavioral Research and Therapy, 16,* 183–189.

Rapaport, D., Gill, M. M., & Schafer, R. (1968). *Diagnostic psychological testing* (revised ed.). R. Holt (Ed.). New York: International Universities.

Rasch, G. (1960). *Probabilistic models for some intelligence and attainment tests.* Copenhagen: Danish Institute for Educational Research.

Raven, J. C. (1938). *Progressive Matrices: A perceptual test of intelligence,* Individual Form. London: H. K. Lewis.

Raven, J. C. (1947). *Coloured Progressive Matrices.* London: H. K. Lewis.

Raven, J. C. (1960). *Guide to the Standard Progressive Matrices.* London: H. K. Lewis.

Ree, M. J., & Earles, J. A. (1991). The stability of g across different methods of estimation. *Intelligence, 15,* 271–278.

Rees, A. H., & Palmer, F. H. (1970). Factors related to changes in mental test performance. *Developmental Psychology Monograph, 3,* No. 2, Part 2.

Reilly, R. R., & Chao, G. T. (1982). Validity and fairness of some alternate employee selection procedures. *Personnel Psychology,* *35,* 1–67.

Reise, S. P., & Due, A. M. (1991). The influences of test characteristics on the detection of aberrant response patterns. *Applied Psychological Measurement, 15,* 217–226.

Reynolds, C., & Brown, R. (1984). *Perspectives on bias in mental testing.* New York: Plenum.

Reynolds, S. B. (1988). Review of the Multidimensional Aptitude Battery. In K. Conoley, J. Kramer, & J. Mitchell (Eds.), *Supplement to the ninth mental measurements yearbook.* Lincoln, NE: University of Nebraska Press.

Roback, H. B. (1968). Human figure drawings: Their utility in the clinical psychologist's armentarium for personality assessment. *Psychological Bulletin, 70,* 1–19.

Robb, G. B., Bernardoni, L. C., & Johnson, R. W. (1972). *Assessment of individual mental ability.* Scranton, PA: Intex Educational Publishers.

Robins, L. N., & Helzer, J. E. (1986). Diagnosis and clinical assessment: The current state of psychiatric diagnosis. *Annual Review of Psychology, 47,* 409–432.

Robinson, A. L. (1983). Using time to measure length. *Science, 220,* 1367.

Rogers, R., Thatcher, A., & Cavanaugh, J. L. (1984). Use of the SADS Diagnostic Interview in evaluating legal insanity. *Journal of Clinical Psychology, 40,* 1537–1541.

Ronning, R. R., Glover, J. A., Conoley, J. C., & Witt, J. C. (1987). *The influence of cognitive psychology on testing.* Hillsdale, NJ: Erlbaum.

Rorer, L. G. (1965). The great response-style myth. *Psychological Bulletin, 63,* 129–156.

Rorer, L. G., & Widigor, T. A. (1983). Personality structure and assessment. *Annual Review of Psychology, 34,* 431–463.

Rorschach, H. (1921). *Psychodiagnostik.* Berne: Birchen.

Ross, P. (1966). Reference groups in man-to-man job performance rating. *Personnel Psychology, 19,* 115–142.

Rotter, J. B., & Rafferty, J. E. (1950). *Manual: The Rotter Incomplete Sentences Blank.* New York: Psychological Corporation.

Rotter, J. B., Rafferty, J. E., & Lotsof, A. B. (1954). The validity of the Rotter

Incomplete Sentences Blank: High school form. *Journal of Consulting Psychology, 18,* 105–111.

Rotter, J. B., Rafferty, J. E., & Schachtitz, E. (1949). Validation of the Rotter Incomplete Sentences Blank for college screening. *Journal of Consulting Psychology, 13,* 348–356.

Rotter, J. B., & Willerman, B. (1947). The incomplete sentence test. *Journal of Consulting Psychology, 11,* 43–48.

Rulon, P. J. (1939). A simplified procedure for determining the reliability of a test by split-halves. *Harvard Educational Review, 9,* 99–103.

Ryan, C. (1979). *The testing maze.* Chicago: National Parent Teachers Association.

Ryan, J. J., Paolo, A. M., & Smith, A. J. (1992). Wechsler Adult Intelligence Scale–Revised scatter in brain-damaged patients: A comparison with the standardization sample. *Psychological Assessment, 4,* 63–66.

Rynes, S. C., Heneman, H. G. III, & Schwab, D. P. (1980). Individual reactions to organizational recruitment: A review. *Personnel Psychology, 33,* 529–542.

Saal, F. E. (1979). Mixed standard rating scale: A consistent system for numerically coding inconsistent response combinations. *Journal of Applied Psychology, 64,* 422–428.

Saal, F. E., Downey, R. G., & Lahey, M. A. (1980). Rating the ratings: Assessing the psychometric quality of rating data. *Psychological Bulletin, 88,* 413–428.

Sackett, P. R. (1987). Assessment centers and content validity: Some neglected issues. *Personnel Psychology, 40,* 13–25.

Sackett, P. R., Burris, L. R., & Callahan, C. (1989). Integrity testing for personnel selection: An update. *Personnel Psychology, 42,* 491–529.

Sackett, P. R., & Decker, P. J. (1979). Detection of deception in the employment context: A review and critique. *Personnel Psychology, 32,* 487–506.

Sackett, P. R., & Dreher, G. F. (1982). Constructs and assessment center dimensions: Some troubling empirical findings. *Journal of Applied Psychology, 67,* 401–410.

Sackett, P. R., & Hakel, M. D. (1979). Temporal stability and individual differences in using assessment information to form overall ratings. *Organizational Behavior and Human Performance, 23,* 120–137.

Sackett, P. R., & Harris, M. M. (1984). Honesty testing for personnel selection: A review and critique. *Personnel Psychology, 37,* 221–245.

Sackett, P. R., & Harris, M. M. (1985). Honesty testing for personnel selection: A review and critique. In H. J. Bernardin and D. A. Bownas (Eds.), *Personality assessment in organizations.* New York: Praeger.

Sackett, P. R., & Wilson, M. A. (1982). Factors affecting the consensus judgment process in managerial assessment centers. *Journal of Applied Psychology, 67,* 10–17.

Sackett, P. R., Zedeck, S., & Fogli, L. (1988). Relationship between measures of typical and maximal job performance. *Journal of Applied Psychology, 73,* 482–486.

Sawyer, J. (1966). Measurement *and* prediction, clinical *and* statistical. *Psychological Bulletin, 66,* 178–200.

Sax, G. (1984). The Lorge-Thorndike Intelligence Tests/Cognitive Abilities Test. In D. Keyser & R. Sweetland (Eds.), *Test critiques* (Vol. 1). Kansas City, MO: Test Corporation of America.

Saxe, L. (1990). The social significance of lying. Invited address, Annual Convention of the American Psychological Association, Boston.

Scarr, S. (1981). *Race, social class, and individual differences in I.Q.* Hillsdale, NJ: Erlbaum.

Scarr, S. (1988). Race and gender as psychological variables: Social and ethical issues. *American Psychologist, 43,* 56–59.

Scarr, S. (1989). Protecting general intelligence: Constructs and consequences for interventions. In R. Linn (Ed.), *Intelligence: Measurement, theory, and public policy.* Urbana, IL: University of Illinois Press.

Schacht, T. E. (1985a). DSM-III and the politics of truth. *American Psychologist, 40,* 513–521.

Schacht, T. E. (1985b). Reply to Spitzer's "Politics-science dichotomy syndrome." *American Psychologist, 40,* 562–563.

Schacht, T., & Nathan, P. (1977). But is it good for psychologists? Appraisal and status of DSM-III. *American Psychologist, 32,* 1017–1025.

Schafer, C. (1989, May). Curriculum alignment behind nation's above-average scores. *Guidepost, 31,* 29.

Schaie, K. W. (1974). Translations in gerontology: From lab to life. Intellectual functioning. *American Psychologist, 29,* 802–807.

Schaie, K. W., & LaBouvie-Vief, G. (1974). Generational versus ontogenetic components of change in adult cognitive behavior. A fourteen-year cross-sequential study. *Developmental Psychology, 10,* 305–320.

Schaie, K. W., & Strother, C. S. (1968). A cross-sequential study of age changes in cognitive behavior. *Psychological Bulletin, 70,* 671–680.

Schippman, J. S., Prien, E., & Katz, J. A. (1990). Reliability and validity of in-basket performance measures. *Personnel Psychology, 43,* 837–859.

Schmidt, F., Berner, J., & Hunter, J. (1973). Racial differences in validity of employment tests: Reality or illusion? *Journal of Applied Psychology, 58,* 5–9.

Schmidt, F. L., Gast-Rosenberg, I., & Hunter, J. E. (1980). Validity generalization results for computer programmers. *Journal of Applied Psychology, 65,* 643–661.

Schmidt, F. L., & Hunter, J. E. (1977). Development and a general solution to the problem of validity generalization. *Journal of Applied Psychology, 62,* 529–540.

Schmidt, F. L., & Hunter, J. E. (1981). Employment testing: Old theories and new research findings. *American Psychologist, 36,* 1128–1137.

Schmidt, F. L., & Hunter, J. E. (1983). Individual differences in productivity: An empirical test of estimates derived from studies of selection procedure utility. *Journal of Applied Psychology, 68,* 407–414.

Schmidt, F. L., Hunter, J. E., & Caplan, J. R. (1981). Validity generalization results for two jobs in the petroleum industry. *Journal of Applied Psychology, 66,* 261–273.

Schmidt, F. L., Hunter, J. E., McKenzie, R. C., & Muldrow, T. W. (1979). Impact and valid selection procedures on work force productivity. *Journal of Applied Psychology, 64,* 609–626.

Schmidt, F. L., Hunter, J. E., & Pearlman, K. (1981). Task differences as moderators of aptitude test validity in selection: A red herring. *Journal of Applied Psychology, 66,* 166–185.

Schmidt, F. L., Hunter, J. E., & Pearlman, K. (1982a). Assessing the economic impact of personnel programs on work force productivity. *Personnel Psychology, 35,* 333–347.

Schmidt, F. L., Hunter, J. E., & Pearlman, K. (1982b). Progress in validity generalization: Comments on Callender and Osburn and further developments. *Journal of Applied Psychology, 67,* 835–845.

Schmidt, F. L., Hunter, J. E., Pearlman, K., Hirsch, H. R., Sackett, P. R., Schmitt, N., Tenopyr, M. L., Kehoe, J., & Zedeck, S. (1985). Forty questions about validity generalizations and meta-analysis with commentaries. *Personnel Psychology, 37,* 407–422.

Schmidt, F. L., Hunter, J. E., Pearlman, K., & Shane, G. S. (1979). Further tests of the Schmidt-Hunter Bayesian validity generalization procedure. *Personnel Psychology, 32,* 257–281.

Schmitt, N. (1976). Social and situational determinants of interviewer decisions: Implications for the employment interview. *Personnel Psychology, 29,* 79–101.

Schmitt, N. (1977). Interrater agreement in dimensionality and confirmation of assessment center judgments. *Journal of Applied Psychology, 62,* 171–176.

Schmitt, N., & Coyle, B. W. (1976). Applicant decisions in the employment interview. *Journal of Applied Psychology, 61,* 184–192.

Schmitt, N., Gooding, R. Z., Noe, R. A., & Kirsch, M. (1984). Metaanalysis of validity studies published between 1964 and 1982 and the investigation of study characteristics. *Personnel Psychology, 37,* 407–422.

Schmitt, N., Mellon, P., & Bylenga, C. (1978). Sex differences in validity for academic and employment criteria and different types of predictors. *Journal of Applied Psychology, 63,* 145–150.

Schmitt, N., & Stults, D. M. (1986). Methodology review: Analysis of multitrait-multimethod matrices. *Applied Psychological Measurement, 10,* 1–22.

Schockley, W. (1972). Dysgenics, geneticity, and raceology: A challenge to the intellectual responsibility of educators. *Phi Delta Kappan, 53,* 297–307.

Schoonman, W. (1989). *An applied study of computerized adaptive testing.* Amsterdam: Swete & Zeitlinger.

Schwab, D. P., & Heneman, H. G. (1969). Relationship between interview structure and inter-interviewer reliability in an employment situation. *Journal of Applied Psychology, 53,* 214–217.

Schwab, D. P., Heneman, H., & DeCotiis, T. (1975). Behaviorally anchored rating scales: A review of the literature. *Personnel Psychology, 28,* 549–562.

Schwab, D. P., & Oliver, R. L. (1974). Predicting tenure with biographical data: Exhuming buried evidence. *Personnel Psychology, 27,* 125–128.

Senna, C. (1973). *The fallacy of IQ.* New York: Third Press.

Seymour, R. T. (1988). Why plaintiff's counsel challenge tests, and how they can successfully challenge the theory of validity generalization. *Journal of Vocational Behavior, 33,* 331–364.

Shanker, A. (1988, April 24). Time for truth in testing. *New York Times,* p. 4.

Shannon, C., & Weaver, W. (1949). *The mathematical theory of communication.* Urbana, IL: University of Illinois Press.

Sharf, J. C. (1988). Litigating personnel measurement policy. *Journal of Vocational Behavior, 33,* 235–271.

Shavelson, R. J., & Webb, N. M. (1981). Generalizability theory—1973–1980. *British Journal of Mathematical and Statistical Psychology, 34,* 133–166.

Shavelson, R. J., Webb, N. M., & Rowley, G. L. (1989). Generalizability theory. *American Psychologist, 44,* 922–932.

Shepard, L. A. (1982). Definitions of bias. In R. Berk (Ed.), *Handbook for detecting test bias.* Baltimore: Johns Hopkins University Press.

Shweder, R. A., & D'Andrade, R. G. (1980). The systematic distortion hypothesis. In R. A. Schweder (Ed.), *Fallible judgment in behavioral research: New directions for methodology of social and behavioral science* (Vol. 4). San Francisco: Jossey-Bass.

Siegel, S. (1956). *Nonparametric statistics for the behavioral sciences.* New York: McGraw-Hill.

Silverstein, A. B. (1968). Validity of a new approach to the design of WAIS, WISC, and WPPSI short forms. *Journal of Consulting and Clinical Psychology, 32,* 478–479.

Silverstein, A. B. (1970). Reappraisal of the validity of WAIS, WISC and WPPSI short forms. *Journal of Consulting and Clinical Psychology, 34,* 12–14.

Silverstein, A. R. (1988). Review of the Multidimensional Aptitude Battery. In K. Conoley, J. Kramre, & J. Mitchell (Eds.), *Supplement to the ninth mental measurements yearbook.* Lincoln, NE: University of Nebraska Press.

Skager, R. (1982). On the use and importance of tests of ability in admission to postsecondary education. In A. Wigdor & W. Garner (Eds.), *Ability testing: Uses, consequences, and controversies.* Washington, DC: National Academy Press.

Skinner, H. A., & Pakula, A. (1986). Challenge of computers in psychological assessment. *Professional Psychology: Research and Practice, 17,* 44–50.

Slaney, R. B., & Russell, J. E. (1981). An investigation of different levels of agreement between expressed and inventoried interests among college women. *Journal of Counseling Psychology, 28,* 221–228.

Slovic, P., & Lichtenstein, S. (1971). Comparison of Bayesian and regression approaches to the study of information processing in judgment. *Organizational Behavior and Human Performance, 6,* 649–744.

Smith, D., & Kraft, W. A. (1983). DSM-III: Do psychologists really want an alternative? *American Psychologist, 38,* 777–785.

Smith, F. D. (1991). Work samples as measures of performance. In A. Wigdor and B. Green (Eds.), *Performance assessment for the workplace* (Vol. 2). Washington, DC: National Academy Press.

Smith, M., & Glass, G. V. (1977). Meta-analysis of psychotherapy outcome studies. *American Psychologist, 32,* 752–760.

Smith, P., & Kendall, L. (1963). Retranslation & Expectations: An approach to the construction and unambiguous anchors for rating scales. *Journal of Applied Psychology, 47,* 149–155.

Smock, C. D. (1970). Goldschmid-Bentler Concept Assessment Kit—Conservation. *Professional Psychology, 1,* 491–493.

Snyder, D. K., Widiger, T. A., & Hoover, D. W. (1990). Methodological considerations in validating computer-based test interpretations: Controlling for response bias. *Psychological Assessment, 2,* 470–477.

Snyderman, M., & Rothman, S. (1987). Survey of expert opinion on intelligence and aptitude testing. *American Psychologist, 42,* 137–144.

Society for Industrial and Organizational Psychology, Inc. (1987). *Principles for the validation and use of personnel selection procedures* (3rd ed.). College Park, MD: Author.

Sokal, M. (1987). *Psychological testing and American society, 1890–1930.* New Brunswick, NJ: Rutgers University Press.

Spearman, C. (1904). The proof and measurement of association between two things. *American Journal of Psychology, 15,* 72–101.

Spearman, C. (1923). *The nature of "intelligence" and principles of cognition.* London: Macmillan.

Spearman, C. (1927). *The abilities of man.* New York: Macmillan.

Spitzer, R. L. (1985). DSM-III and the politics-science dichotomy syndrome: A response to Thomas E. Schacht's "DSM-III and the politics of truth." *American Psychologist, 40,* 522–526.

Spitzer, R. L., Williams, B. W., & Skodol, A. E. (1980). DSM-III: The major achievements and an overview. *American Journal of Psychiatry, 137,* 151–164.

Spitzer, R. L., Williams, J. B., Gibbon, M. G., & Furst, M. B. (1990). *SCID-II.* Washington, DC: American Psychiatric Press.

Spokane, A. R. (1979). Occupational preference and the validity of the Strong-Campbell Interest Inventory for college women and men. *Journal of Counseling Psychology, 26,* 312–318.

Spool, M. D. (1978). Training programs for observers of behavior: A review. *Personnel Psychology, 31,* 853–888.

Spraings, V. (1966). *The Spraings multiple choice Bender Gestalt test.* Olympia, WA: Sherwood Press.

Spreen, O., & Strauss, E. (1991). *A compendium of neuropsychological tests: Administration, norms, and commentary.* New York: Oxford University Press.

Standards for educational and psychological testing. (1985). Washington, DC: American Psychological Association.

Stanley, J. C. (1961). Analysis of an unreplicated three-way classification with applications to rater bias and trait independence. *Psychometrika, 26,* 205–219.

Stanley, J. (1971). Reliability. In R. Thorndike (Ed.), *Educational measurement* (2nd ed.). Washington, DC: American Council on Education.

Stead, W. H., & Shartle, C. L. (1940). *Occupational counseling techniques.* New York: American Book.

Steers, R. M., & Rhodes, S. R. (1978). Major influences on employee attendance: A process model. *Journal of Applied Psychology, 63,* 391–407.

Steinmetz, H. C. (1932). Measuring ability to fake occupational interest. *Journal of Applied Psychology, 16,* 123–130.

Stephenson, R. R. (1965). A comparison of responses to a vocational interest test taken under standard conditions at recruiting stations and responses to the same test taken as a self-administered test at home. Paper presented at the annual convention of the American Personnel and Guidance Association, Minneapolis, MN.

Sternberg, R. J. (1977). *Intelligence, information processing, and analogical reasoning: The componential analysis of human abilities.* Hillsdale, NJ: Erlbaum.

Sternberg, R. J. (1980). Sketch of a componential subtheory of human intelligence. *Behavioral and Brain Sciences, 3,* 573–584.

Sternberg, R. J. (1981a). Toward a unified componential theory of human intelligence, I. Fluid abilities. In M. Friedman, J. Das, & N. O'Connor (Eds.), *Intelligence and learning.* New York: Plenum.

Sternberg, R. J. (1981b). Testing and cognitive psychology. *American Psychologist, 36,* 1181–1189.

Sternberg, R. J. (1982). A componential approach to intellectual development. In R. J. Sternberg (Ed.), *Advances in the psychol-ogy of human intelligence* (Vol. 1). Hillsdale, NJ: Erlbaum.

Sternberg, R. J. (1984). What should intelligence tests test? Implications of a triarchic theory of intelligence for intelligence testing. *Educational Research, 13,* 5–15.

Sternberg, R. J. (1985). *Beyond IQ: A triarchic theory of human intelligence.* New York: Cambridge University Press.

Sternberg, R. J. (1991). Death, taxes, and bad intelligence tests. *Intelligence, 15,* 257–269.

Stevens, S. S. (1946). On the theory of scales of measurement. *Science, 103,* 677–680.

Stevens, S. S. (1951). Mathematics, measurement, and psychophysics. In S. S. Stevens (Ed.), *Handbook of experimental psychology.* New York: Wiley.

Stevens, S. S. (1961). The psychophysics of sensory function. In W. A. Rosenblith (Ed.), *Sensory communication.* New York: Wiley.

Steward, V. (1947, January). The problem of detecting fudging on vocational interest tests. *Personnel reports for sales executives.* Los Angeles.

Strommer, E. (1988). Confirmatory factor analysis of the Kaufman Assessment Battery for Children: A reevaluation. *Journal of School Psychology, 26,* 13–23.

Strong, E. K. (1927). *Vocational Interest Blank.* Stanford, CA: Stanford University Press.

Strong, E. K. (1943). *Vocational interests of men and women.* Stanford, CA: Stanford University Press.

Strong, E. K. (1955). *Vocational interests 18 years after college.* Minneapolis, MN: University of Minnesota Press.

Sundberg, N. D. (1977). *Assessment of persons.* Englewood Cliffs, NJ: Prentice-Hall.

Super, D. E. (1973). The Work Values Inventory. In D. Zytowski (Ed.), *Contemporary approaches to interest measurement.* Minneapolis: University of Minnesota Press.

Sussmann, M., & Robertson, D. U. (1986). The validity of validity: An analysis of validation study designs. *Journal of Applied Psychology, 71,* 461–468.

Swensen, C. H. (1957). Empirical evaluations of human figure drawings. *Psychological Bulletin, 54,* 431–466.

Swensen, C. H. (1968). Empirical evaluations of human figure drawings. *Psychological Bulletin, 70,* 20–44.

Swensen, W., Pearson, J., & Osborne, D. (1973). *An MMPI sourcebook: Basic item, scale, and pattern data on 50,000 medical patients.* Minneapolis: University of Minnesota Press.

Tagiuri, R., & Petrillo, L. (1958). *Person perception and interpersonal behavior.* Stanford, CA: Stanford University Press.

Tarvis, C. (1992). *The mismeasure of woman.* New York: Simon & Schuster.

Taylor, H. C., & Russell, J. T. (1939). The relationship of validity coefficients to the practical effectiveness of tests in selection. *Journal of Applied Psychology, 23,* 565–578.

Technical recommendations for psychological tests and diagnostic techniques. (1954). Washington, DC: American Psychological Association.

Tellegen, A., Lykken, D. T., Bouchard, T. J., Wilcox, K. J., et al. (1988). Personality similarity in twins reared apart and together. *Journal of Personality and Social Psychology, 54,* 1031–1039.

Tenopyr, M. L. (1981). The realities of employment testing. *American Psychologist, 36,* 1120–1127.

Tenopyr, M. L., & Oeltjen, P. D. (1982). Personnel selection and classification. *Annual Review of Psychology, 33,* 581–618.

Terman, L. M. (1916). *The measurement of intelligence.* Boston: Houghton-Mifflin.

Terman, L. M., & Merrill, M. A. (1937). *Measuring intelligence.* Boston: Houghton-Mifflin.

Terman, L. M., & Merrill, M. A. (1960). *Stanford-Binet Intelligence Scale: Manual for the third revision, Form L–M.* Boston: Houghton-Mifflin.

Terman, L. M., & Merrill, M. A. (1973). *Stanford-Binet Intelligence Scale: 1972 norms edition.* Boston: Houghton-Mifflin.

Tett, R. P., Jackson, D. N., & Rothstein, M. (1991). Personality measures as predictors of job performance: A meta-analytic review. *Personnel Psychology, 44,* 703–742.

Thetford, W. N. (1965). Review of the Holtzman Inkblot Test. In O. K. Buros (Ed.), *The sixth mental measurements yearbook.* Highland Park, NJ: Gryphon Press.

Thissen, D., & Steinberg, L. (1988). Data analysis using item response theory. *Psychological Bulletin, 104,* 385–395.

Thissen, D., Steinberg, L., & Gerrard, M. (1986). Beyond group-mean differences: The concept of item bias. *Psychological Bulletin, 99,* 118–128.

Thomas, H. (1988). What is the interpretation of the validity generalization estimate $S^2_p = S^2_r - S^2_e$? *Journal of Applied Psychology, 73,* 679–682.

Thorndike, E. L. (1912). The permanence of interests and their relation to abilities. *Popular Science Monthly, 81,* 449–456.

Thorndike, E. L. (1920). A constant error in psychological ratings. *Journal of Applied Psychology, 4,* 25–29.

Thorndike, R. L. (1949). *Personnel selection.* New York: Wiley.

Thorndike, R. L. (1951). Reliability. In E. Lindquist (Ed.), *Educational measurement.* Washington, DC: American Council on Education.

Thorndike, R. L. (1985). The central role of general ability in prediction. *Multivariate Behavioral Research, 20,* 241–254.

Thorndike, R. L., Hagen, E. P., & Sattler, J. M. (1986). *The Stanford-Binet Intelligence Scale, fourth edition: Technical Manual.* Chicago: Riverside.

Thornton, G. C., III (1992). *Assessment centers in human resource management.* Reading, MA: Addison-Wesley.

Thornton, G. C., III, & Byham, W. C. (1982). *Assessment centers and managerial performance.* New York: Academic Press.

Thurstone, L. L. (1927). A law of comparative judgment. *Psychological Review, 34,* 273–286.

Thurstone, L. L. (1935). *Vectors of the mind: Multiple-factor analysis for the isolation of primary traits.* Chicago: University of Chicago Press.

Thurstone, L. L. (1938). *Primary mental abilities.* Psychometric Monographs, No. 1. Chicago: University of Chicago Press.

Tolor, A., & Brannigan, G. (1980). *Research and clinical applications of the Bender-Gestalt test.* Springfield, IL: Thomas.

Torgerson, W. (1958). *Theory and methods of scaling.* New York: Wiley.

Tucker, D. H., & Rowe, P. M. (1977). Consulting the application form prior to the interview: An essential step in the selection process. *Journal of Applied Psychology, 62,* 283–287.

Turban, D. B., Sanders, P. A., Francis, D. J., & Osburn, H. G. (1989). Construct equivalence as an approach to replacing validated cognitive ability selection tests. *Journal of Applied Psychology, 74,* 62–71.

Ulosevich, S. N., Michael, W. B., & Bachelor, P. (1991). Higher-order factors in structure-of-intellect (SOI) aptitude tests hypothesized to portray constructs of military leadership: A re-analysis of an SOI data base. *Educational and Psychological Measurement, 51,* 15–37.

Ulrich, L. D., & Trumbo, D. A. (1965). The selection interview since 1949. *Psychological Bulletin, 63,* 100–116.

Uniform guidelines on employee selection procedures. (1978). *Federal Register, 43* (166), 38296–38309.

Urry, V. W. (1977). Tailored testing: Successful application of latent trait theory. *Journal of Educational Measurement, 14,* 181–196.

Urry, V. W., & Dorans, N. J. (1981). *Tailored testing: Its theory or practice, Part I. The basic model, the normal ogive submodel, and the tailoring algorithms.* San Diego, CA: Navy Personnel Research Development Center.

U.S. Congress Office of Technology Assessment. (1987). *The electronic supervisor: New Technology, new tensions* (OTA-CIT-333). Washington, DC: U.S. Government Printing Office.

Vale, C. D., Keller, L. S., & Bentz, V. J. (1986). Development and validation of a computerized interpretation system for personnel tests. *Personnel Psychology, 39,* 525–542.

Vandenberg, S. G., & Vogler, G. P. (1985). Genetic determinants of intelligence. In B. Wolman (Ed.), *Handbook of intelligence. Theories, measurements and applications,* p. 3–57. New York: Wiley.

Vernon, P. A. (1985). Review of Multidimensional Aptitude Battery. In D. Keyser & R. Sweetland (Eds.), *Test critiques* (Vol. 2). Kansas City, MO: Test Corporation of America.

Vernon, P. E. (1960). *The structure of human abilities* (revised ed.). London: Methuen.

Vernon, P. E. (1965). Ability factors and environmental influences. *American Psychologist, 20,* 723–733.

Veroff, J., McClelland, L., & Marquis, K. (1971). *Measuring intelligence and achievement motivations in surveys.* Ann Arbor, MI: Survey Research Center. Institute for Social Research, University of Michigan.

Vinberg, R., & Joyner, J. N. (1982). Performance measurement in the military services. In F. Landy, S. Zedeck, & J. Cleveland (Eds.), *Performance measurement and theory.* Hillsdale, NJ: Erlbaum.

Wade, T. C., & Baker, T. B. (1977). Opinions and use of psychological tests. *American Psychologist, 32,* 874–882.

Wagner, R. F. (1949). The employment interview: A critical summary. *Personnel Psychology, 2,* 17–46.

Wainer, H. (1976). Estimating coefficients in linear models: It don't make no never mind. *Psychological Bulletin, 83,* 213–217.

Wainer, H. (1988). How accurately can we assess changes in minority performance on the SAT? *American Psychologist, 43,* 774–778.

Wainer, H., & Braun, H. I. (1988). *Test validity.* Hillsdale, NJ: Erlbaum.

Wallace, W. L. (1950). The relationship of certain variables to discrepancy between expressed and inventoried vocational interest. *American Psychologist, 5,* 354.

Wallbrown, F. H., Blaha, J., & Wherry, R. J. (1973). The hierarchical factor structure of the Wechsler Preschool and Primary Scale of Intelligence. *Journal of Consulting and Clinical Psychology, 41,* 356–362.

Waller, M. I. (1989). Modeling guessing behavior: A comparison of two IRT models. *Applied Psychological Measurement, 13,* 233–243.

Webb, J., & McNamara, K. (1979). Configural interpretation of the MMPI. In C. Newmark (Ed.), *MMPI: Clinical and research trends.* New York: Praeger.

Webster, E. C. (1964). *Decision making in the employment interview.* Montreal: Industrial Relations Centre, McGill University Press.

Webster, E. C. (1982). *The employment interview: A social judgment process.* Schomberg, Ont.: Canada: S.I.P.

Wechsler, D. (1939). *The measurement of adult intelligence*. Baltimore: Williams & Wilkins.

Wechsler, D. (1955). *Manual for the Wechsler Adult Intelligence Scale*. New York: The Psychological Corporation.

Wechsler, D. (1958). *The measurement and appraisal of adult intelligence* (4th ed.). Baltimore: Williams & Wilkins.

Wechsler, D. (1987). *Wechsler memory scale—revised*. New York: Psychological Corporation.

Weiss, D. J. (1978). Review of Armed Services Vocational Aptitude Battery. In O. K. Buros (Ed.), *The eighth mental measurements yearbook*. Highland Park, NJ: Gryphon Press.

Weiss, D. J. (1983). *New horizons in testing: Latent trait testing and computerized adaptive testing*. New York: Academic Press.

Weiss, D. J., & Davinson, N. L. (1981). Test theory and methods. *Annual Review of Psychology, 32*, 629–658.

Welsh, J. R., Kucinkas, S. K., & Curran, L. T. (1990). *Armed Services Vocational Aptitude Battery (ASVAB): Integrative review of validity studies*. Brooks Air Force Base.

Wernimont, P. F. (1962). Re-evaluation of a weighted application blank for office personnel. *Journal of Applied Psychology, 46*, 417–419.

Wernimont, P. F., & Campbell, J. P. (1968). Signs, samples, and criteria. *Journal of Applied Psychology, 52*, 372–376.

Wherry, R. J., & Bartlett, C. J. (1982). The control of bias in ratings: A theory of rating. *Personnel Psychology, 35*, 521–551.

Whimbey, A. (1980). Students can learn to be better problem solvers. *Educational Leadership, 37*, 560–565.

Widiger, T. A., & Trull, T. J. (1991). Diagnosis and clinical assessment. *Annual Review of Psychology, 42*, 109–133.

Wiesner, W. H., & Cronshaw, S. F. (1988). A meta-analytic investigation of the impact of interview format and degree of structure on the validity of the interview. *Journal of Occupational Psychology, 61*, 275–290.

Wigdor, A. (1982). Psychological testing and the law of employment discrimination. In A. Wigdor & W. Garner, *Ability testing: Uses, consequences and controversies, Part II: Documentation section*. Washington, DC: National Academy Press.

Wigdor, A. K., & Garner, W. R. (1982a). *Ability testing: Uses, consequences, and controversies, Part I: Report of the committee*. Washington, DC: National Academy Press.

Wigdor, A. K., & Garner, W. R. (1982b). *Ability testing: Uses, consequences, and controversies, Part II: Documentation section*. Washington, DC: National Academy Press.

Wigdor, A. K., & Green, B. F. (1991). *Performance assessment in the workplace*. Washington, DC: National Academy Press.

Wiggins, J. (1973). *Personality and prediction: Principles of personality assessment*. Reading, MA: Addison-Wesley.

Wiggins, N., & Kohen, E. (1971). Man versus model of man revisited: The forecasting of graduate success. *Journal of Personality and Social Psychology, 19*, 100–106.

Wilcox, R. (1992). Why can methods for comparing means have relatively low power and what can you do to correct the problem? *Current Directions in Psychological Science, 1*, 101–105.

Williams, R. L. (1971). Abuses and misuses in testing black children. *Counseling Psychologist, 2*, 62–77.

Williams, R. L. (1972). The BITCH-100: A culture-specific test. Paper presented at the annual convention of the American Psychological Association, Honolulu, HI.

Williams, R. L. (1974). Scientific racism and IQ: The silent mugging of the black community. *Psychology Today, 7*(12), 32–41.

Wilson, K. M. (1989, Spring). A study of the long-term stability of GRE test scores. Report No. 86-18R. In J. Pfleiderer, *GRE Board Newsletter, 5*. Princeton, NJ: Graduate Record Examinations Board.

Wing, H. (1992). Review of the Bennett Mechanical Comprehension Test. In J. Kramer and J. Conoley (Eds.), *Eleventh mental measurements yearbook*. Lincoln, NE: Buros Institute of Mental Measurements.

Wise, P. S. (1989). *The use of assessment techniques by applied psychologists*. Belmont, CA: Wadsworth.

Wissler, C. (1901). The correlation of mental and physical traits. *Psychological Monographs, 3*(6, Whole No. 16).

Wolfe, J. (1976). The effects and effectiveness of simulations in business policy teaching applications. *Academy of Management Review, 1,* 47–56.

Wollowick, H. B., & McNamara, W. J. (1969). Relationship of the components of an assessment center to management success. *Journal of Applied Psychology, 53,* 348–352.

Yntema, D., & Torgerson, W. (1961). Man-computer cooperation in decisions requiring common sense. *IEE Transactions on Human Factors in Electronics, 2,* 20–26.

Zeidner, J., & Johnson, C. (1992). *Is personnel classification a concept whose time has passed?* Presented at ARI Conference on Selection and Classification in the Military, Alexandria, VA.

Zigler, E., & Valentine, J. (1980). *Project Head Start: A legacy of the war on poverty.* New York: Free Press.

Zimmerman, I. L., & Woo-Sam, J. M. (1972). Research with the Wechsler Intelligence Scale for Children, 1960–1970. *Psychology in the Schools, 9,* 232–271.

Zimmerman, I. L., & Woo-Sam, J. M. (1985). Clinical applications. In B. Wolman (Ed.), *Handbook of intelligence: Theories, measurements, and applications.* New York: Wiley.

Zimmerman, M. (1990). Is DSM-IV needed at all? *Archives of General Psychiatry, 47,* 974–976.

Zimmerman, M., Jampala, V. C., Sierles, F. S., & Taylor, M. A. (1991). DSM-IV: A nosology before its time? *American Journal of Psychiatry, 148,* 463–467.

Zonana, H. V. (1984). The first presidential assassination attempt. *Bulletin of the American Academy of Psychiatry and Law, 12,* 309–322.

Zubin, J., Eron, L. D., & Schumer, F. (1965). *An experimental approach to projective techniques.* New York: Wiley.

Zucker, R. A., Aranoff, J., & Rabin, A. I. (1984). *Personality and the prediction of behavior.* New York: Academic Press.

Zytowski, D. G. (1976). Predictive validity of the Kuder Occupational Interest Survey: A 12- to 19-year follow-up. *Journal of Counseling Psychology, 3,* 221–233.

Zytowski, D. G. (1985). *Kuder DD manual supplement.* Chicago: Science Research Associates.

Zytowski, D. G., & Borgan, F. H. (1983). Assessment. In W. Walsh & S. Osipaw (Eds.), *Handbook of vocational psychology* (Vol. 2). Hillsdale, NJ: Erlbaum.

Zytowski, D. G., & Laing, J. (1978). Validity of other-gender-normed scales on the Kuder Occupational Interest Survey. *Journal of Counseling Psychology, 3,* 205–209.

Zytowski, D. G., & Warman, R. W. (1982). The changing use of tests in counseling. *Measurement and Evaluation in Guidance, 15,* 147–152.

Author Index

Aaron, P., 435
Abrahams, N. M., 346
Ackerman, P. L., 270, 293
Adair, J. G., 378
Adams, K. M., 195
Adams, S. R., 398
Adorno, T. W., 180
Ahlburg, D. A., 360, 367
Albright, L. E., 373
Alexander, R. A., 70, 132, 134, 148, 371
Allinger, G. M., 205, 207, 386
Allport, G. W., 413
Allran, K. D., 190
Alveres, K. M., 396
American Psychological Association, 15, 107
Anastasi, A., 214, 260
Andrews, L. W., 198
Angoff, W. H., 114, 138, 214, 296
APA Task Force, 370
Applebaum, M., 192, 263–64
Appleby, J. D., 369–70, 372
Aranoff, J., 224
Armstrong, J., 367, 398
Arvey, R. D., 276, 278, 281, 360, 375–76, 378, 361, 452, 472
Ash, R. A., 361
Asher, J. J., 362–63
Ashton, S. G., 342
Ashworth, S., 374
Ayers, J. D., 249

Bachelor, B. A., 207
Backteman, G., 297
Baehr, M., 359
Baker, T. B., 190, 419, 449–50
Balzer, W. K., 29, 394, 397–98, 467

Banks, C. G., 395
Bar-Hillel, M., 368
Barrett, G. V., 70, 132–34, 138, 371
Barrick, M. R., 222, 355
Bartlett, C. J., 280, 396, 398
Bass, A. R., 392, 395
Bass, B. M., 364
Beach, L., 454
Beatty, R. W., 399
Bechtoldt, H. P., 409
Becker, B. E., 400
Begelman, D. A., 443
Bem, D. J., 220
Ben-Abba, E., 368
Bender, L., 434, 436
Benjamin, L. S., 443
Ben-Porath, Y. S., 433
Ben-Shakar, G., 368
Bentson, B., 366
Bentz, V. J., 196–97
Bergstrom, D. A., 443
Berk, R. A., 27, 170, 277, 284
Berman, J. S., 445
Bernardin, H. J., 392, 396, 398, 399
Bernardoni, L. C., 248, 439
Berner, J., 279
Bigley, S. E., 217, 329
Binet, A., 210
Binning, J. F., 138
Birren, J. E., 298
Blaha, J., 242
Blanz, F., 390
Bloom, B. S., 299
Blum, Y., 368
Bobko, P., 400
Boehm, A. E., 300
Boehm, V., 279
Borgan, F. H., 217, 329
Borman, W. C., 119, 366, 383, 393, 398, 470
Bouchard, T. J., 296, 300
Boudreau, J., 148, 401

Bowser, S., 398
Bracht, G., 297
Brandt, J. E., 329
Brannigan, G., 436
Brass, D. J., 366
Braun, H. I., 59, 279
Bray, D. W., 365, 366, 378
Brickner, M., 471
Brown, B. K., 361
Brown, C. A., 384
Brown, G. C., 195
Brown, R., 22, 284
Brown, S. H., 114, 374
Brunswick, E., 453
Brush, D. H., 359
Bryan, J. D., 470
Buckley, J. P., 372
Buckley, M. R., 104
Buckner, D. N., 396
Burke, H. R., 290
Burke, M. J., 401
Buros, O. K., 12
Burris, L. R., 21, 25, 369–70
Butcher, J. N., 196, 427, 433
Butler, M., 438
Byham, W. C., 205–6, 386
Bylenga, C., 279

Callahan, C., 21, 25, 369–70
Callender, J. C., 374
Campbell, D. P., 185, 320, 324, 325, 328, 329, 346
Campbell, D. T., 121, 433
Campbell, J. P., 362
Campbell, R. J., 365
Campion, J. E., 360–61, 452
Campion, M. A., 124, 361

Caplan, J. R., 374
Carrier, M. R., 114
Carroll, J. B., 294
Carson, R. C., 220
Carter, G. W., 361
Carvajal, H., 237
Cascio, W. F., 70, 356, 363, 366, 371, 401
Castellan, N. J., 454
Cattell, J., 209
Cattell, R. B., 207, 224, 232, 286
Cavanaugh, J. L., 472
Chadwick-Jones, J. K., 384
Chao, G. T., 353–60
Chapman, J. P., 221
Chapman, L. J., 221
Chatelant, G., 468
Christal, R., 454, 459
Chiu, K., 386
Cleary, T., 279, 281–82, 289
Cleveland, J., 395, 398–99
Clopton, J., 428
Cocking, R., 459
Cohen, I. S., 416
Cohen, J. A., 102, 242
Cohen, P., 102
Cole, L., 291
Coleman, J. S., 288
Colligan, R. C., 432
Collins, L. M., 102
Combs, C. H., 35, 38
Committee on Ethical Guidelines for Forensic Psychologists, 472
Committee on Psychological Tests and Assessment, 284
Comstock, S. M., 104
Cogner, A. C., 439
Conger, J. C., 439
Conoley, C. W., 196–97
Conoley, J. C., 192

Constans, J., 395
Cook, U., 249
Cooper, A., 443
Cooper, D., 242
Cooper, W., 395, 397–98
Corah, N. L., 416
Corrigan, B., 46, 455, 457–58
Cortina, J. M., 83
Costa, P. T., 222
Cote, J. A., 104
Cotton, D. H. G., 199
Cowles, M., 191
Coyle, B. W., 380
Craft, L. L., 200
Cranny, C. J., 132–33, 396
Crites, J. O., 409, 424
Cronbach, L. J., 2, 6, 7, 21, 28, 77, 83, 85–87, 92, 105, 112, 113, 115, 117, 123, 125, 138, 148, 258, 266, 273, 285, 288, 295, 296, 398, 445, 462
Cronshaw, S. F., 148, 360–61
Cross, H. J., 443
Crosson, J. J., 267
Crouse, J., 19, 262, 271
Crow, J. F., 296
Cudeck, R., 194
Cureton, E. E., 157
Curran, L. T., 267

Dahlstrom, L., 427–28, 431
Dahlstrom, W., 427–28, 431
Dana, J., 459
Dana, R., 459
D'Andrade, R. G., 221, 398
Daniel, J. L., 424
Dankin, S., 367
Darley, J., 451
Darlington, R. B., 359
Davinson, N. L., 193
Davinson, R. G., 300
Davis, C., 191
Davis, W. W., 444
Dawes, R., 35, 38, 46, 440, 455, 457–58, 469–70, 472
Dawes, R. M., 360, 468
Decker, P. J., 370
DeCotiis, T., 392
DeFries, J. C., 294
Delahuntz, R. J., 268
Delaney, H. D., 86

Delessio, A. T., 114
Demaree, R. G., 374
De Nisi, A. S., 395, 399
De Pontbriand, R., 393
De Vries, R., 240
Dickson, D. H., 200
Digman, J. M., 222
Dipboye, R., 393, 452
Dodrill, C. B., 351
Doll, E. E., 291
Dolliver, R. H., 217, 329
Donnelly, T. M., 396
Dorans, N. J., 59, 193
Downey, R. G., 396–97
Drasgow, F., 163, 165, 170, 194, 199, 279, 284
Dreher, G. F., 361, 471
Droege, R. C., 267
Druker, J., 431
Dubois, P. H., 9, 224
Due, A. M., 199
Dunnette, M. D., 223, 355–56, 361
Dyer, F., 299

Eaton, N. K., 223, 355, 470
Eckberg, D. L., 274
Edwards, A. J., 174, 176, 177, 180, 237, 242, 416
Edwards, W., 29
Einhorn, H. J., 361, 458
Eisenman, E., 467
Elwood, D. L., 191
Embertson, S. E., 192
Engelhart, M. D., 158
Epstein, S., 220–21
Eron, L. D., 419, 421
Exner, J. E., 419
Eysenck, H. J., 204, 223, 225, 443, 445
Eysenck, S. B., 223

Fairbanks, B.A., 59
Faley, R. H., 372
Farr, J. L., 383–85, 388, 392–95, 397–99
Faschingbauer, T., 428, 432
Faust, D., 360, 468, 472
Fay, C. H., 393, 394
Fazio, R., 451
Fekken, G. C., 199
Feldman, J., 416
Ferguson, R. L., 314
Feuerstein, R., 468

Figueroa, R., 291
Filler, J., 468
Finkle, R. B., 365, 366
First, M. B., 444
Fiske, D. W., 121, 124
Flanagan, J. C., 83
Fleishman, E. A., 119
Flug, A., 368
Flynn, J. R., 121, 126, 274, 298–300
Fogli, L., 112, 362
Folger, R., 285
Forer, B. R., 419
Fowler, R., 431
Fraboni, M., 242
Frances, A. J., 443, 444
Francis, D. J., 123
Frank, L. K., 220, 224
Frederick, J. T., 401
Fredericksen, N., 124, 363
Freeberg, N. E., 396
Frenkel-Brunswik, E., 180
Friedman, A., 443, 445
Friedman, D. H., 267
Friedman, T., 27, 350–51
Funder, D. C., 220
Furnham, A., 200
Furst, M. B., 195

Gaito, J., 49
Gallucci, N. T., 25
Galton, F., 294
Garb, H. N., 461
Garcia, M., 394, 398
Gardner, H., 270, 293
Garner, W. R., 2, 27, 129, 229, 271, 305, 306, 351, 367, 378, 385
Gast-Rosenberg, I., 374
Gaudet, F. J., 384
Gaugler, B. B., 366
Geary, D. C., 242
George, M. S., 199
Gerber, J., 237
Gerrard, M., 170, 279
Gesell, A. L., 291
Ghiselli, E. E., 354–55, 373, 390
Gibbon, M. G., 195
Gilberstadt, H., 431
Gill, M. M., 247–48, 439
Githens, W. H., 346
Glass, G. V., 445
Glennon, J. R., 373
Gleser, G. C., 28, 77, 85–87, 92, 105, 113, 419, 462

Glover, J., 192
Glutting, J. J., 469
Goldberg, L. R., 342, 454–55, 459
Goldberg, P. A., 423
Golden, C. J., 440
Goldinger, L. A., 369–70, 372
Goldstein, B. L., 21, 23–24
Goodenough, F. L., 211
Gooding, R. Z., 132, 134, 384
Goodstein, L. D., 409, 424
Gordon, R. A., 21, 23, 283
Gottfredson, L. S., 19, 21–23, 271, 284
Gottier, R. F., 355
Gough, H., 406, 409
Gould, S. J., 213
Graham, J. R., 430–32, 433
Grant, D. L., 365
Gray, C. W., 347
Greaves, S. T., 419
Green, B. F., 191, 192
Greenberg, J., 26, 285
Greene, R. L., 433
Greener, J. M., 374
Greenwood, J. M., 365
Griffiths, J. R., 361
Gross, M., 271
Grube, J. B., 443
Gruen, W., 416
Guastello, D. D., 200
Guastello, S. J., 200
Guertler, E., 199
Guilford, J. P., 207, 224, 247, 263
Guilford, R. B., 224
Guion, R. M., 108–11, 131–32, 132–33, 135, 278, 355, 373, 383
Gulliksen, H., 78
Guthrie, G., 413
Gutkin, T. B., 198
Guttman, L., 201

Hagen, E. P., 235–37
Hakel, M. D., 221, 366
Hale, M., 376
Hambleton, R. K., 314
Hammer, T., 384
Hammond, K. R., 453, 459
Hamstra, B. W., 361
Hancock, P., 361

Haney, W., 2
Hansen, J. C., 185, 319, 320, 324, 328
Hanson, R. K., 420
Harding, F. D., 119
Hardy, K., 237
Harel, T. H., 198
Harmon, L. W., 323
Harnqvist, K., 297
Harris, C., 102
Harris, M. M., 370, 395
Hartigan, J. A., 21, 94, 148, 268, 279, 281, 284, 367, 374, 401
Hartman, D. E., 189
Hartshorne, 371
Harvey, A. L., 191
Hastie, R., 398
Hathaway, W., 433
Hayes, S C., 443, 445
Haywood, H., 468
Hector, V. S., 198
Hedges, L. V., 139, 420
Heilburn, A. B., Jr., 409, 424
Heilman, M. E., 360
Helzer, J. E., 453
Heneman, H. G., 361, 380, 392
Henly, S. J., 194
Henning-Stout, M., 440
Henri, V., 210
Henry, E., 464
Herman, D. O., 439
Herrnstein, R., 274
Hersen, M., 419, 443
Hewes, P., 237
Hilgard, E. R., 21
Hinrichs, J. R., 364, 366
Hirsch, H. R., 374
Hobbs, N., 464–65, 468
Hoepfner, R., 207
Hofner, P. J., 192
Hoffman, B., 254, 271, 378
Hoffman, P., 453, 459
Hogan, J., 27
Hogan, R., 180
Hogarth, R. M., 361, 458
Holden, C., 262, 433
Holden, R. R., 199
Holland, J. L., 218–19, 320
Holland, P. W., 59, 170
Hollenback, J., 384
Holt, R. R., 452, 455
Holtzman, W. H., 419
Honacker, L. M., 198
Hood, A. B., 329

Hoover, D. W., 197
Hopkins, D. K., 297
Hopkins, K., 258
Horn, J. L., 102
Hough, L. M., 119, 223, 355–56
Howard, A., 366
Huck, J. R., 366
Hulin, C. L., 163, 165, 170, 194, 279, 284
Humphreys, L. G., 23, 204–5, 219, 270, 279, 281–82, 289, 299
Hunsley, J., 420
Hunt, J. McV., 208, 299
Hunter, J. E., 23–24, 80, 94, 139, 140, 267, 268, 279, 360, 367, 373, 374, 400, 401, 420
Hunter, R. F., 23–24, 140, 279, 360, 367, 401
Hursch, C., 459
Hursch, J., 459
Huselid, M. A., 400
Hutt, M., 436
Hyde, J. S., 22

Ilgen, D. R., 362, 384
Ironson, G. H., 284
Irvin, J. A., 217, 329

Jackson, D. N., 178, 180, 223, 254–56, 271, 344, 346, 355, 411, 413
Jackson, G. D., 274, 420
Jacobs, R., 396
James, L. R., 374, 396
Jampala, V. C., 444
Janz, T., 361
Jarrett, R. B., 443, 445
Jencks, C., 23
Jensen, A. R., 22–23, 27, 104, 126, 148, 204–5, 208, 219, 229, 237, 254, 271, 274, 279, 281–82, 284–88, 291, 294–96, 300, 354, 472
Johansson, C. B., 323, 337, 341
Johnson, C., 267
Johnson, D. F., 191
Johnson, R. W., 248, 439
Johnson, W. G., 472

Jones, H. G., 439
Jones, L. V., 192, 263–64
Joseph, A., 274, 276
Joyner, J. N., 351
Judiesch, M. K., 147, 400

Kaebler, C., 443–44
Kafry, D., 392, 396
Kamin, L., 274
Kamp, J. D., 223, 355–56
Kamphaus, R. W., 245–47, 440
Kane, R. L., 437
Kanfer, R., 279
Kaplan, M., 443
Karren, R., 400
Katz, J. A., 297
Katz, M. R., 266
Katzell, R., 299
Kaufman, A. S., 245–47, 291–92, 439
Kaufman, N. L., 245–47
Kavanaugh, M. J., 123, 395, 396
Kehoe, J., 374
Kellam, K., 398
Keller, J. W., 411, 45
Keller, L. S., 196–97
Kelly, I. W., 200
Kemery, E. R., 374
Kemmerer, B. E., 196–97
Kendall, L., 392, 444
Kendrick, S., 279, 281–82, 289
Kerkar, S., 398
Kerner, W. K., 347
Kilcullen, R. N., 356, 359
King, G., 427
Kingstrom, P. O., 392
Kirchener, W. K., 347
Kirsch, M., 132, 134, 384
Klebe, K. J., 194
Klerman, G. L., 443
Klimoski, R. J., 359, 366, 470, 471
Klinmuntz, B., 453
Kohen, E., 459
Kohlberg, L., 249
Korchin, S. J., 449–50, 452
Kraft, W. A., 443
Kraiger, K., 396
Kramer, J. J., 195, 440
Krantz, D. H., 30
Kroner, D. G., 199
Kucinkas, S. K., 267

Kuder, G. F., 83, 335
Kugler, K. E., 472–73
Kusyszyn, I., 413

LaBouvie-Vief, G., 297–98
Labrentz, E., 435
Lacks, P., 435
Lahey, M. A., 396–97
Laing, J., 336
Lambert, N., 291
Lance, C. E., 396
Landau, J., 384
Landy, F. J., 107, 123–25, 137–38, 360, 372, 375, 383–85, 388, 392–95, 397–99
Lanning, K., 19
Larsen, R., 424, 450
Last, C. G., 443
Latham, G. P., 124, 361, 384, 393, 394
Laurent, J., 237
Lawler, E. E., 398–99
Lawshe, C. H., 112
Layon, R., 431
Lerner, B., 21, 22, 398
Levinson, D. J., 180
Levitt, E. E., 433
Levy, S., 201
Lewis, J. F., 292, 293
Li, C. C., 294–96
Lichtenburg, J. W., 406
Lichtenstein, S., 454
Lindzey, G., 295
Linkenhoker, F., 435
Linn, M. C., 22
Linn, R., 274, 279, 281–82
Lipsett, L., 336
Locke, R. A., 398
Lockhart, M., 467
Loehlin, J. C., 295
Lohman, D. F., 270
London, M., 378
Lopez, F. M., 363
Lord, F. M., 49, 51, 78, 79, 92, 156, 162, 165, 269
Lotsof, A. B., 422
Lowman, R., 371
Lubin, B., 424, 450
Luce, R. D., 30, 35
Lumsden, J., 85, 94
Lykken, D. T., 296

Machover, K., 423
MacKinney, A., 123, 396

Maddi, J., 220–21, 223, 225
Mael, F. A., 359
Magnusson, D., 297
Maher, K. J., 269
Manning, W. H., 305
Marks, R., 431
Marley, M., 436
Marquis, K., 291
Martin, C., 21, 394, 398
Maser, J. D., 443–44
Matarazzo, J. D., 198, 209–11, 238, 241, 288, 297, 424, 431, 439, 450
Maxwell, S. E., 86, 294
May, M. A., 371
Mayfield, E. C., 361
Mazzeo, J., 191
McArthur, C., 316, 329, 455
McBride, J. R., 194
McClelland, L., 291
McCloy, R. A., 223, 355–56
McCormick, E. J., 362
McCrae, R. R., 222
McDermott, P. A., 469
McFie, J., 439
McGurk, F. C., 288
McKenzie, R. C., 400
McLemore, C. W., 443
McNamara, K., 363–64, 430
McNamara, W. J., 365
McRae, G. G., 336
McReynolds, P., 442–43, 446, 449–50, 453
McReynolds, W. T., 443
McShane, D., 249
Mead, A. D., 194
Meadow, A., 416
Meehl, P. E., 117, 360, 431, 455, 468
Megargee, E. I., 409
Mellon, P., 279
Mercer, C. D., 300
Mercer, J. R., 208, 291, 292–93
Merrill, M. A., 232
Merz, W. R., 297
Messick, S., 149
Meyer, V., 439
Micceri, T., 53
Michael, W. B., 207
Miele, G. M., 444
Mihal, W. L., 191
Miles, T. R., 204
Milkovich, G. T., 403

Miller, K. M., 350
Miller, L. S., 443
Miller, R. C., 445
Millon, T., 443
Miner, J. B., 360
Miner, M. G., 360
Mischel, W., 220
Mitchell, J. V., 12, 409
Mitchell, T. R., 359
Mohrman, A. M., 398–99
Moreland, K. L., 195–97
Morey, L., 443
Mossholder, K. W., 374
Motowidlo, S. J., 361
Mount, M. K., 147, 222, 355, 400
Mulaik, S. A., 374
Muldrow, T. W., 400
Mumford, M., 119, 356, 359
Munley, P. H., 443
Murphy, K. R., 25, 27, 103, 143, 148, 200–201, 266–67, 270–71, 293, 351–52, 359, 368–69, 385, 394, 395, 396–97, 398–99, 401, 440, 455, 458, 460, 467, 471
Murray, H. A., 174, 411, 415, 420, 421

Naglieri, J. A., 423
Nairn, A., 140, 271
Nanda, H., 77, 85–87, 92, 113
Narens, L., 35
Nathan, P., 442
Nay, W., 451
Neisser, U., 204
Nelson, R. O., 443, 445
Nesselroade, J. R., 297, 298
Neumann, I., 346
Newman, J. R., 29
Newmark, C., 427
Nicholson, N., 384
Nicholson, R. A., 472–73
Nisbett, R. A., 402, 452
Noe, R.A., 132, 134, 384
Novick, N. R., 78, 79, 92, 162, 314
Nunnally, J. C., 79, 101, 159
Nystedt, L., 440, 455

Oakland, T., 249
O'Bannon, R. M., 369–70, 372
Ochoa, E., 443
Odbert, H. S., 413
Oeltjen, P. D., 361
Office of Strategic Services, 364, 463–64, 467
Office of Technology Assessment, 370
Offord, K. P., 432
Oldham, G. R., 363
O'Leary, B., 280
Oliver, R. L., 359
Olkin, I., 139, 420
Ones, D. S., 139, 370
Orpen, C., 361
Osborne, D., 432
Osburn, H. G., 123, 374
Ostendorf, F., 413
Owen, D., 306
Owens, W. A., 356, 359

Page, E. B., 247
Pakula, A., 198
Palmer, F. H., 297
Paolo, A. M., 440
Parker, K. C. H., 420
Parkington, J., 400
Parmelee, R., 249
Parsons, F., 165, 218, 279, 284
Pascal, G. R., 435
Patterson, P. O., 21, 23–24
Payne, J. E., 300
Peake, P. K., 220
Pearlman, K., 140, 374, 400
Pearson, J., 432
Penn, S., 398
Pervin, L. A., 220–21
Petrillo, L., 230
Philbin, T. A., 398
Phillips, J. S., 132, 134
Pierce-Jones, J., 409
Pincus, H. A., 444
Piotrowski, C., 411, 450
Plake, B. S., 196–97
Plomin, R., 23, 294, 295–96
Prediger, D. J., 267
Prien, E., 297
Prince, R. J., 200
Pulakos, E. D., 119
Pursell, E. D., 124, 361, 384

Quigley, A. M., 27

Rabin, A. I., 224, 450
Rafferty, J. E., 422
Rahman, M., 445
Rajaratnam, N., 77, 85–87, 92, 113
Ramos, R. A., 401
Rapaport, D., 247–48, 439
Rasch, G., 162
Rees, A. H., 297
Reese, H. W., 297–98
Reike, M. L., 200
Reilly, R. R., 356, 360, 362, 366
Reise, S. P., 199
Rende, R., 23, 295–96
Retzlaff, P., 438
Reynolds, C. R., 22, 284, 440
Reynolds, S. B., 256
Rhodes, S. R., 384
Richardson, M., 83
Ringwall, E. A., 416
Roback, H. B., 423
Robb, G. B., 248, 439
Robertson, D. U., 134
Robertson, H. C., 472
Robins, L. N., 453
Robinson, A. L., 2
Rogers, R., 472
Ronning, R. R., 192
Rorer, L. G., 180, 220
Rorschach, H., 224, 417, 418
Rosenthal, D. B., 366
Ross, L., 452
Ross, P., 395
Rosse, R. L., 470
Roth, L., 374
Rothman, S., 22, 28
Rothstein, M., 223, 355
Rotter, J. B., 422
Rowe, P. M., 361
Rowley, G. L., 87
Ruch, W., 413
Rulon, P. J., 83
Russell, J. E., 217
Russell, J. T., 144
Ryan, C., 254, 271
Ryan, J. J., 440
Ryburn, M., 237
Rynes, S. C., 380

Saal, F. E., 391, 396–97
Saari, L. M., 124, 361, 393, 394

Sackett, P. R., 21, 25, 112, 362, 366, 369–70, 374, 470–71
Sanders, P. A., 123
Sanford, R. N., 180
Saruwatari, L. R., 360
Sattler, J. M., 235–37
Sawyer, J., 455, 470
Sax, G., 257–58
Saxe, L., 371
Scarr, S., 2, 3, 21, 274, 283
Schacht, T., 442, 446
Schachtitz, E., 422
Schafer, R., 247–48, 439
Schaie, K. W., 297–98
Schaubroeck, J., 395
Schellenberg, R. P., 440
Schmidt, F. L., 23, 80, 94, 139, 140, 147, 279, 373, 374, 380, 400, 420
Schmitt, N., 123, 132, 134, 279, 360, 366, 370, 374, 380, 384
Schockley, W., 274
Schoenfeldt, L. F., 359
Schofield, S., 200
Schoonman, W., 194
Schuldberg, D., 449–50, 452
Schumer, F., 419, 421
Schwab, D. P., 359, 361, 380, 392
Sciarrino, J. A., 362–63
Seeman, W., 431
Segal, N. L., 300
Seymour, R. T., 27–28, 149
Shane, G. S., 374
Shanker, A., 308
Shannon, C., 105
Sharf, J. C., 149
Shartle, C. L., 356
Shavelson, R. J., 87
Shepard, L. A., 21, 275, 284
Sheppard, C., 384
Shifman, M., 468
Shippman, J. S., 297
Siegel, S., 49
Sierles, F. S., 444
Silverstein, A. B., 244
Silverstein, A. R., 256
Simon, T., 210
Skager, R., 19
Skinner, H. A., 198, 199
Skodol, A. E., 441
Slaney, R. B., 217
Slovic, P., 342, 454

Smith, A. J., 440
Smith, D., 443
Smith, F. D., 385
Smith, K., 237
Smith, M., 445
Smith, P. C., 392
Smith, W. J., 373
Smock, C. D., 249
Snow, R. E., 445
Snyder, D. K., 197
Snyderman, M., 22, 28
Spearman, C., 93, 205, 215
Spitzer, R. L., 195, 441, 446
Spokane, A. R., 323
Spool, M. D., 397
Spraings, V., 437
Spuhler, J. N., 295
Standards for Educational and Psychological Testing, 14, 107, 138
Stanley, J. C., 77, 123
Stead, W. H., 356
Steers, R. M., 384
Steinberg, L., 165
Steinmetz, H. C., 346
Stephenson, R. R., 346, 424
Sternberg, R. J., 192, 204, 208, 270, 293
Stevens, S. S., 35
Steward, V., 346
Strauss, E., 437
Strickland, W. J., 366, 470
Strommer, E., 247
Strong, E. K., 216–17, 328, 346
Strother, C. S., 297
Stults, D. M., 123
Subkoviak, M. J., 284
Sulsky, L. M., 29, 397–98
Sundberg, N. D., 451
Super, D. E., 216
Suppes, P., 30
Sussmann, M., 134
Suttell, B. J., 435
Sweetland, R. C., 12
Swensen, C. H., 423
Swenson, W., 432
Swerdlik, M., 237

Tagiuri, R., 230
Taylor, H. C., 144
Taylor, M. A., 444
Teachout, M. S., 396

Tellegen, A., 296
Tenopyr, M. L., 350, 361, 374
Terman, L. M., 211, 232
Terris, W., 21
Tett, R. P., 223, 355
Thatcher, A., 472
Thayer, D. T., 170
Thetford, W. N., 419
Thissen, D., 165, 170, 279
Thomas, H., 374
Thorndike, E. L., 217, 397
Thorndike, R. L., 74–75, 235–37
Thornton, G. C., 205–6, 366, 386
Thurstone, L. L., 206
Tilly, S. M., 444
Tippins, N., 361
Tolor, A., 436
Torgerson, W., 46, 386
Trull, T. J., 444
Trumbo, D. A., 360
Trusheim, D., 262
Tucker, D. H., 361
Turban, D. B., 123
Turner, J., 395
Tversky, A., 30, 35, 38

Ullman, D. P., 356, 359, 440
Ulosevich, S. N., 207
Ulrich, L. D., 360
Urry, V. W., 168, 193

Vale, C. D., 196–97
Valentine, J., 300
Vallon, W. R., 393
Vandenberg, S. G., 295
Vanderploeg, R., 438
Vaughan, M. J., 361
Veroff, J., 291
Vernon, P. E., 206–7, 214, 232, 255
Veroff, J., 291
Vinberg, R., 351
Viswesvaran, C., 139, 370
Vogler, G. P., 295

Wade, T. C., 190, 419, 449–50
Wagner, R., 360
Wainer, H., 279, 283, 458
Wakefield, J., 443, 445
Wallace, W. L., 346

Wallbrown, F. H., 242
Waller, M. I., 199
Walter, C. S., 398
Warmon, R. W., 417
Warner, M. H., 351
Weaver, K., 237
Weaver, W., 105
Webb, J., 430
Webb, N. M., 87
Webster, E. C., 360
Wechsler, D., 238, 297, 430
Weeks, J. L., 119
Weins, A. N., 288
Weise, R. E., 443–44
Weiss, D. J., 165, 193, 194, 266
Welsh, G., 267, 427–28, 431
Werner, S., 361
Wernimont, P. F., 359, 362
Wesman, A., 279, 281–82, 289
Wherry, R. J., 242, 396–98
Whimbey, A., 299
Whitworth, R. H., 242
Widiger, T. A., 197, 444
Widigor, T. A., 220
Wiesner, W. H., 360–61
Wigdor, A. K., 2, 21, 27, 94, 129, 148, 229, 268, 271, 279, 281, 284, 305, 306, 351, 367, 374, 378, 385, 401, 403
Wiggins, J., 143, 398, 449, 463, 465–69
Wiggins, N., 459
Wilcox, K. J., 296
Wilcox, R., 53
Williams, B. W., 441
Williams, C. L., 433
Williams, E. B., 27, 350–51
Williams, G. B., 359
Williams, J. B., 195
Williams, K. J., 395–99
Williams, R. L., 274, 276, 28
Willerman, B., 422
Wilson, J. W., 336
Wilson, K. M., 304
Wilson, M. A., 470
Wilson, T D., 402
Windmiller, M., 291
Wing, H., 355
Wise, P. S., 11
Wissler, C., 209

Witt, J. C., 192
Wolins, L., 123, 396
Wollowick, H. B., 363–64
Woo-Sam, J. M., 439

Yntema, D., 46

Zarantells, M. M., 443
Zedeck, S., 112, 362, 374, 392, 396

Zeidner, J., 267
Zigler, E., 300
Zimmerman, I. L., 439
Zimmerman, M., 444
Ziskin, J., 472

Zonana, H. Y., 471
Zubin, J., 419, 421
Zucker, R. A., 224
Zytowski, D., 217, 331, 336, 417

SUBJECT INDEX

Ability testing
    controversies, 21–24
    fairness, 23, 26–29
Absenteeism, 384
Achievement vs. aptitude testing,
    263–64
Acquiescence (see Response
    styles)
Adaptive Behavior, 291–93
Adaptive Behavior Scale, 291
Adaptive testing, 192–95 (see also
    Test administration)
Affirmative action, 23–24
American College Testing Pro-
    gram, 260, 303–4, 306
Americans with Disabilities Act,
    28
Analysis of variance, 86
Anchor test, 58–59
Application blanks, 356–60
Armed Services Vocational Apti-
    tude Battery, 131, 265–67
Army Alpha/Army Beta, 9
Assessment centers, 364–66, 470–
    71
Attenuation, correction for, 93–95
Authoritarianism (see Response
    styles)

Bandwidth vs. fidelity, 104–5,
    225, 440
Barnum effect, 200
Basal vs. ceiling level, 234
Base rate
    and decisions, 141, 143–46
    definition, 143
Bender Visual-Motor Gestalt
    Test, 434–37
Bennett Mechanical Comprehen-
    sion Test, 354–55
Bias
    cultural, 277, 285
    definition, 275–76
    intercepts, 279–82
    measurement, 278–79

in prediction, 279–82
    effects on minorities, 281–82
    slopes, 279–82
Biodata, 356–60 (see also Applica-
    tion blanks)
Black Intelligence Test of Cultural
    Homogeneity, 287–88
Bootstrapping, 455

California Achievement Test, 64,
    307
California Psychological Inven-
    tory, 406–11
Career Assessment Inventory,
    337–42, 348
Carry-over effects, 80
Certification, 10 (see also Licens-
    ing)
Civil Rights Act, 15
Clinical Analysis Questionnaire
    (see Sixteen Personality Fac-
    tors Test)
Clinical assessment, 449–61
Clinical judgment, 453–61
Clinical vs. statistical prediction,
    454–61
Coefficient alpha, 83
Cognitive Abilities Test, 256–58
Cognititve psychology and test-
    ing, 269–70
College Entrance Examination
    Board, 9 (see also Scholastic
    Aptitude Test)
Computer-based test interpreta-
    tion
    applications, 195–97
    controversies, 197–98
    MMPI, 431
Computerized adaptive testing
    (see Adaptive testing)
Computerized testing, 189–90
Concept Assessment Kit, 249
Conditions of measurement
    effects on scores, 4–5
    and generalizability, 85–88

Confidence intervals (see Stan-
    dard error)
Configural interpretation, 430–
    31, 438–41, 458–61
Consistency, in behavior, 220, 221
Constructs
    characteristics, 114–15
    explication, 115–17
    psychological, 115–17
Content domain
    boundaries, 109–10
    content validity, 107, 110
    structure, 109, 110
Content validity ratio, 112–13
Correlation coefficient, 43–45
    (see also Validity)
Criterion, 131
Criterion-keyed test, 356–59, 428,
    437
Criterion measures
    characteristics of, 131
    validity of, 131, 395–99
Criterion-referenced testing, 313–
    14
Cross-validation, 357–59
Culture Fair Intelligence Test, 286
Culture-reduced testing, 285–87,
    289–91
Curriculum alignment, 313–14
Cutoff scores, 70

Decisions
    absolute, 20–21
    comparative, 20–21
    impact of test on, 141–48
    individual, 19–21
    institutional, 19–21
    outcomes, 141–43
    random, 143, 145–46
Developmental integrative model,
    359
Deviation score, 42
Diagnosis
    clinical, 441–46
    neurological, 437–38

Diagnostic and Statistical Manual of Mental Disorders, 441–46
Differential Aptitude Test, 61
Differential validity (*see* Validity)
Difficulty (*see* Item analysis)
Discrimination (*see* Item analysis)
Distractor (*see* Item analysis)
Draw-a-Person Test, 423–24

Educational testing
    in career planning, 311–12
    in educational planning, 309–11
    in evaluating student performance, 307–9
Edwards Personal Preference Schedule, 415–17
Empirical scoring (*see* Criterion-keyed test)
Equal Employment Opportunity Commission, 15
Equating, 56–59
Error (*see* Measurement)
Ethical principles, 14–15, 476–92
Ethical standards (*see* Standards)
Exner scoring system, 412–20 (*see also* Rorschach Inkblot Test)
Expectancy tables, 67–70

Factor analysis, 46–48, 120–21
Fairness, 23–24, 26–29
Faking, 199–200

General Aptitude Test Battery, 267–69
General mental ability (*see* Intelligence)
Generalizability theory, 85–88
Gesell Developmental Scales, 274
Golden Rule agreement, 284
Graduate Record Examination, 260–63, 304
Graphology, 368
Group factors (*see* Primary mental abilities)
Group X item interaction, 277–78

Halo (*see* Rater errors)
Halstead-Reitan Neuropsychiatric Battery, 437
Heritability, 273–74, 293–96
    twin studies, 295–96
Holland's vocational types, 218–19, 321
Holtzman Inkblot Test, 419–20 (*see also* Rorschach Inkblot Test)
Honesty testing (*see* Integrity)

Horizontal percentage method, 356–59
Hutt adaptation (*see* Bender Visual Motor Gestalt Test)
Hypothesis confirmation bias, 451–52

In-basket test, 363
Indifference of indicator, 215
Individual testing
    examiner effects, 230–31
    standardization, 4–5
Informed consent, 25–26
Insanity, 471–73
Integrity
    interviews, 372
    testing, 26, 369–72
Intelligence
    componential theories, 208
    decline with age, 297–98
    definition, 203–5
    environmental factors, 295–96
    fluid vs. crystallized, 207–8, 232–34
    hereditary factors, 273–74, 293–96
    hierarchical models, 206
    quotient, 211–12
    stability, 296–300
Intelligence testing
    controversies, 21–24
    group, 212–13
    individual, 210–11
    minorities, 249–50
    nonverbal, 245–46, 288–89
Interests
    expressed vs. inventoried, 217
    measurement
        actuarial approach, 218–19
        history, 217–18
        trait and factor approach, 219–20
    personnel selection, 346–47, 349–51
Interview
    clinical, 451–53
    employment, 360–62
Invasion of privacy, 24–26
Iowa Tests of Basic Skills, 307
Iowa Tests of Educational Development, 307
Ipsative scoring, 226–27
Item analysis
    difficulty, 154–56
        p value, 155
    discrimination, 156–60
        D statistic, 157–58
        inter-item correlation, 159–60
        item-total correlation, 158–59
    distractors, 152–54

interaction among item characteristics, 160–62
Item characteristic curve
    difficulty, 162–65
    discrimination, 163–64
    distractors, 166–67
Item content, 173–74
Item response alternatives, 175
Item response theory, 59, 162–71
    item bias, 170–71
    tailored testing, 167–68 (*see also* Adaptive tests)
    test equating, 59
Item writing, 172–75

Jackson Vocational Interest Survey, 342–46, 348

Kaufman Assessment Battery for Children, 245–47
Kuder Occupational Interest Survey, 329–46, 348

Lake Wobegon phenomenon, 308
Law School Admissions Test, 305
Leaderless group discussion, 364
Learning Potential Assessment Device, 468
Leniency (*see* Rater errors)
Lens model, 454–55
Licensing, 351
Lie detector (*see* Polygraph)
Luria-Nebraska Neuropsychological Battery, 437

Maximal vs. typical performance, 6, 362
Mean, 41–42, 500
Measurement
    definition, 33–34
    error, 74–78, 84–85
        as function of test score, 77–78
        sources of, 73–75
    scales, 35–38
        comparison of, 34
        and statistics, 48–49
Mechanical comprehension, 354–55
Median, 449, 500
Mental age, 211–12
Mentally retarded, classification of, 209–10
Mental Measurements Yearbook, 12–13
Meta-analysis, 139–40
Method bias, 123
Minnesota Clerical Test, 353–54

Minnesota Multiphasic Personality Inventory, 9–25, 223–24, 420, 427–33
Minnesota Paper Form Board, 184
Mode, 499–500
Multidimensional Aptitude Battery, 254–66
Multiple choice items
  construction, 152–53
  response processes, 253–54, 262
Multitrait-multimethod matrix, 121–23

National Academy of Sciences, 2
National Assessment of Educational Progress (*see* Program evaluation)
Neuropsychological assessment, 437–38 (*see also* Diagnosis)
Normal distribution
  normalization, 54–55
  percentiles, 53–56
Norming tests, 181–82, 185–86
Norms
  interpretation, 65–67
  and IQ, 70–71
  types
    age, 61–63
    grade, 63–65
    percentile ranks, 60–61
    profiles, 65

Office of Strategic Services, 224, 364, 462–64, 467–68

Pair comparison (*see* Ranking techniques)
Peace Corps, 464–68
Performance measures
  judgmental, 383, 386–95
  objective, 383–85
  value, 399–401
Performance tests
  bias, 288–89
  intelligence testing, 237–47, 285–93
Personal Data Sheet, 223
Personality measurement
  history, 223–24, 405–6
  methods, 224
  nature of, 220–23
Personality Research Form, 178, 411–13
Personality taxonomies, 222–23
Personal Outlook Inventory, 379
Personnel testing
  extent of, 349–51
  in military, 350–51
  validity, 366–68, 373–76

Piaget's theories and ability tests, 249
Polygraph, 25
Prediction (*see also* Regression)
  clinical vs. statistical, 454–58
Primary mental abilities, 205–6
Project Head Start, 299–300
Projective tests
  history of, 224, 417
  reliability and validity of, 420
Psychological Screening Inventory, 179
Psychological test, 3
Psychometrics, 14

Range restriction
  correction, 135–37
  definition, 135
Ranking techniques, 386–88
Rater errors, 396–98
Rating accuracy, 398–99
Rating scales
  behaviorally anchored, 390–93
  behavioral observation, 393–94
  graphic, 388–90
  judgment processes, 394–95, 399
  mixed-standard, 391
Raven's Progressive Matrices, 289–91
raw score, 51
Reactivity, 79–80
Regression
  linear, 45–46
  toward the mean, 92
Reliability
  coefficient, 78
  composite scores, 102–3
  consistency, 73–76
  difference scores, 101–2
  estimation
    alternate forms methods, 81–83
    internal-consistency methods, 83–84
    split-half methods, 83–84, 101
    true-retest methods, 79–81
  generalizability theory, 85–88
  speed tests, 100–101
  temporal stability, 80
  test length, 82–83
  test-score model, 75–78
  typical levels, 104
  and validity, 93–95
Response sets
  dissimulation, 179–80
  random responding, 178
  social desirability, 177

Response style
  acquiescence, 180
  criticalness, 180
Rorschach Inkblot Test
  description of, 417–19
  modifications of, 419–20 (*see also* Holtzman Inkblot Test and Exner scoring system)
Rotter Incomplete Sentences Blank, 421–23

Sampling, behavior, 3–4
Scale blending, 424–25
Scale construction
  empirical scales, 176
  factor-analytic scales, 176
  rational scales, 176
Scales of measurement (*see* Measurement)
Scatter analysis, 248
Scatter plots, 44, 69
Schedule of Affective Disorders and Schizophrenia, 453, 472
Scholastic Aptitude Test, 4, 9–10, 59, 303, 306
Scholastic aptitude testing
  coaching effects, 306
  identification of exceptionality, 306–7
  prediction efficiency of, 305–6
  retesting effects, 304
  use with educationally disadvantaged, 304
Scoring rules (*see* Test scoring)
Selection ratio
  and decisions, 144–47
  definition, 144
Self-fulfilling prophecy, 428
Sex bias in interest testing, 173, 323–24
Situational test, 363–65
Sixteen Personality Factors Test, 413–15
Skew, 500–501
Social Desirability, 415–16 (*see also* Response sets)
Spearman-Brown formula, 97
Stability (*see* Reliability)
Stakeholders, 30
Standard Age Score, 232–36
Standard deviation
  definition, 42
  of performance, 147–48
Standard error of measurement, 91, 96
Standardization, 182–83 (*see also* Norming tests)
Standards
  ethical, 14–15
  testing, 14–15

Standards for Educational and Psychological Testing, 14, 29, 107, 210–12, 231–37
Stanford-Binet Intelligence Scale, 61, 191, 192, 212, 218, 251, 426
Stanine (*see* Transformations)
Strong-Campbell Interest Inventory (*see* Strong Interest Inventory)
Strong interest inventory, 65, 217–19, 314–27, 348
Structured assessment programs, 461–71
Structure of intellect, 207–8
System of Multicultural Pluralistic Assessment, 292–93

Tailored testing (*see* Item response theory)
Taylor-Russell tables, 144–45
Test administration
  adaptive, 192–95, 234–36
  standardization, 4, 210–11, 212–13, 230–31
  testing minorities, 249–50
Test critiques, 12
Tests
  publication of, 183–84
  revising, 184–85
Test scoring
  computerized, 188–90, 195–98
  rules, 5–6
Test types
  behavior observation, 7–8

performance tests, 6–7
  self-report, 8
  psychomotor, 7
Tests in Print, 12, 14
Thematic Apperception Test, 224, 420–21, 450
Tracking, 290
Traits, 221–22
Transformations
  area, 54–56
    percentiles, 54–56
    stanines, 55, 56
  linear
    T scores, 54
    z scores, 43, 51–53, 502–3
True score
  definition, 76–77
  estimated, 92
T scores (*see* Transformations)
Two-factor theory, 205
Two-point code (*see* Configural interpretations)

Utility, 147–48

Validity
  coefficient, 140–41
    interpretation, 140–41
  criterion-related, 133–37
  for decisions
    concurrent strategies, 133–37
    predictive strategies, 132–33

differential, 281
  four faces, 107
  generalization, 373–77
  of inferences, 40
  of measurement
    construct validity, 107, 117–24
    content validity (*see* Content domain)
    convergent, 121–22
    discriminant, 122–23
    intelligence tests, 126–27
  of predictions, 130–31
Variance, 42
Vineland Social Maturity Scale, 291
Vocational interests (*see* Interests)

Wechsler Adult Intelligence Scale, 237–42
  short forms, 242
Wechsler Intelligence Scale for Children, 242–44
  short forms, 244, 225
Wechsler Preschool and Preschool and Primary Scale of Intelligence, 244–45
Wonderlic Personnel Test, 362–64, 385
Work sample, 362–64, 385

Z score (*see* Transformations)